KATRINA'S GHOST

Darrin Bell

BELLCARTOONS
.COM

Other books by Darrin Bell

Another Stereotype Bites the Dust: a Candorville Collection
Candorville: Thank God for Culture Clash
Peace, Love & Lattes: a Rudy Park Collection
Rudy Park: The People Must Be Wired

Candorville is distributed internationally by the Washington Post Writers Group

ISBN-13: 978-1973810643

ISBN-10: 1973810646

Candorville can be viewed on the Internet at

www.Candorville.com

Join the Candorville Facebook group at

www.facebook.com/candorvillecomics

Follow Candorville on Twitter at

www.twitter.com/candorville

Author's Preface

It's happening again. I've just taken my niece Eve to a college fair in Anaheim, and now we're sitting in the car at Sonic eating chicken wraps and tater tots under the stars (or more accurately for the LA area, "under the star"). "I don't think it's a coincidence," I say, as I tear off and discard a bit of extra tortilla. "A little anonymous man holding shopping bags steps into a street in China, raises his hand, and stops a column of tanks dead in its tracks with only the force of his will." Eve stops chewing her tater tot. I have her attention. Now it's time to spring my theory on her: "Just hours later, Communism died."

As usual, my theory's met with silence. And a puzzled look. She resumes chewing her tator tot.

"But what about Poland?" Eve asks. "Things were happening in Poland at least as far back as Solidarity in the Eighties. Don't you think *that's* what led to this?" A little trepidation. She probably doesn't want to embarrass her uncle by being smarter than him. Good niece. You shall still inherit my comic book collection. But I'm not fazed by this challenge. Nobody ever agrees with me on this. I'm used to it. I was counting on it.

"It started long before then," I parry, "it started with the Berlin Airlift." Now she's confused, right where I want her. "Eastern Europe wanted its freedom as soon as the Soviet Union stole it from them. The people never stopped hoping for it and working to make it real. Every generation that lived behind the Iron Curtain struggled for more and more economic and political liberty. In Hungary, in Czechoslovakia, in Poland... people kept demanding freedom even though they knew their dictators would be brutal in their response."

I pick up a napkin and squish some grease out of a couple tater tots. I sip some ice cold Diet Coke through a straw. I love the taste of Aspartame in the evening. Eve's quiet. The type of quiet that comes over you when you're listening to the recollections of someone who was *there*. "I'm not *that* old," I say. "I didn't see all that first hand." She laughs. "But I grew up in the tail end of it all. In the Eighties, when we all were sure of exactly two things: (1) Anything remotely related to homosexuality was inherently funny, and (2) we were all going to die in a field of mushroom clouds, and the unlucky survivors would roam the deserts on dune buggies competing with face-paint-wearing mutants for the last bottle of water." We were wrong on both counts.

"But I digress." She laughs again.

I flash back to the first time I ever made Eve laugh. 1993. I was wearing parachute pants. I had just shaved two parallel lines in the hair on each side of my head that crossed in an "X" in the back. She was bundled up in a furry white blanket on the couch. I picked her up and made a weird face. Nothing. She just stared. I had to up my game. In my best high-pitched cockney voice I recited a Shakespearean sonnet I'd just memorized for AP English. Something about slings and arrows and outrageous fortune. Still no laugh. But she did smile. I had to capitalize on that. I HAD to fan that ember into a flame, but I didn't know what else to do. To distract her until I figured out my next move, I turned her horizontal as if she were Superman and spun her around and around and around. ...Until she puked on my brand new Reeboks.

"Oh @#$%!" I said.

HUGE laugh. *Huge*.

I can still hear it. I tear up a little at the thought that I just took that puker to a college fair and now I'm sitting in the car with her discussing politics and history, and making her laugh without worrying about my shoes.

"Here's the thing," I say, pulling myself back to *now*. "Two forces move society forward." She stops chewing again. "Gradual pressure and sudden shock." She's following me here. "Think of it as tectonic plates." Ever since she was a baby, I knew I could always keep Eve's attention by seeming random. "They press against each other, slide across each other, get pulled apart, or plunge under and over each other. They do it slowly, gradually. Pressure builds up. Potential energy accumulates." Good. The aspartame hasn't yet corroded my memories of Walter Alvarez's Geology 10 seminars at Berkeley.

"The rock along those fault lines stretches and bends as it's pulled in opposing directions by the two tectonic plates." I bring it home: "Eastern Europe was a rock being pulled in opposing directions by two tectonic plates." Her mouth drops open. Her eyes seem to brighten. We always perk up when we hear an analogy we've never heard before, and realize it fits. Analogies are comforting. The universe seems to make more sense, somehow. I bet the first caveman or cavewoman who grunted an analogy was revered, adored by the opposite sex, and eaten by the other cavemen who thought they'd be able to digest and assume his or her magical powers.

"You know how earthquakes start?" Eve's entranced. "A single rock breaks under the pressure," I say before nibbling on my chicken wrap and leaning back into my chair, "and a fraction of a split second later that burst of kinetic energy ripples through every rock along the faultline and they all break. The plates jump, and they jump far." I prop up my left foot on the driver's side door pocket. I notice the Sonic intercom right beside my window and imagine the Sonic cashier is listening in, just happens to moonlight as a professional geologist and she's barely holding her tongue the whole time. "The Tienanmen Square Massacre wasn't new. It was the exact same pressure the fault line had experienced for the last fifty years. It was the same bending of the rock."

I move in for the kill. "The little man in China was the first rock to break."

"Not the man himself, but the *image* he created. The image that people saw all over the world. The image that people faxed and smuggled into communist countries. The image of a vulnerable, ephemeral human being literally staring down the inhuman machinery of the immortal State itself. That stirred up something primal in everyone who saw it. That moment was the broken rock that started the earthquake."

Hours later, Solidarity crushed the Communist Party in elections in Poland. Months later, Hungary followed Poland's lead, killed its single-party dictatorship and sent the Soviet Army packing. Almost simultaneously, Germany accelerated a long-gestating reunification idea and the Berlin Wall fell, just five decades after the blockade and the airlift. Tienanmen sparked a long-simmering earthquake that freed Poland, then Hungary, then Germany, Czechoslovakia, Bulgaria, Romania, Albania and finally Yugoslavia; before turning eastward and disintegrating the Soviet Union itself.

"When societal pressure gradually builds up," I summarize, "it often takes a single image to bring the earthquake."

Eve settles back into her seat. She hasn't touched her food in minutes. She notices it's there and starts eating again. I realize my drink is empty, so I rest it between my legs, waiting for the ice to melt so I can drink *that*.

We're alone in the parking lot. There's a cool breeze. I turn on the radio. Some guy's singing about one million fireflies. Eve loves the song. I think it's one of those songs you love for a week, after which you want to surrender your eardrums to the authorities every time you hear it.

"There've been earthquakes in this country too," I say as a leaf, or maybe it's a discarded wrapper, skitters over the asphalt in the shadows.

"Hurricane Katrina was our Tienanmen moment." Eve cocks her head quizzically. "Yeah. That changed everything," she concurs. It's as if a shadow falls over her eyes. A veil of memory and frustration and sadness. Or maybe I'm projecting.

I go on: "You know how 'Candorville' has always been a little skeptical of the government?" I ask. She just laughs and sips her drink. "Well," I say, glancing up to the left and remembering, "I used to get a lot of hate mail. Tons. Every time I lampooned the President, or Donald Rumsfeld, or Condoleezza Rice, or anyone in the administration, people would come unglued."

It was true. No matter how innocuous the satire, the simple fact that I was depicting our leaders as having feet of clay (as most leaders do) was enough to earn me the enmity of the masses. It's easy to forget, now, what it was like to live in post-9/11 America. It's easy to forget what happened to the Dixie Chix, or Bill Maher, or most editorial cartoonists. Whoever publicly suggested that our leaders didn't know best or that our leaders were often disingenuous, was seen as delusional, crazy, dangerous, Marxist, or, worst of all, "*liberal*." It's easy to forget that there was a four year-long period of time when people would say "why do you hate America," and they didn't mean it as a punchline.

They conflated the President with the country, they had such faith in the man. Of course they did. He was a leader. He was resolute. He seemed to possess so much certainty and so little doubt. That sort of thing is as captivating and infectious as it is dangerous.

I finish my last tater tot. "Letter after letter, email after email would angrily assert to me that the President had an ace up his sleeve, that there's no way his administration could be as incompetent, reckless or corrupt as we satirists portrayed it to be."

"...Until Hurricane Katrina."

Until we turned on our TVs to see an American city drowning; to see thousands of poor black people clinging to rooftops, freeway overpasses and trees; to see black bodies floating in the flood waters or lying unburied on the streets once the waters receded; to hear that the National Guard rescue vehicles that should've saved many of these people were instead being used in an unnecessary war in Iraq; to find that the administration's response to the disaster was wholly inadequate, and the man in charge of FEMA was an unqualified crony.

The day before Hurricane Katrina was an average day: I received 14 pieces of hate mail. In the years before Hurricane Katrina I received 1289 pieces of hate mail (and that's only the hate mail I haven't yet deleted). In the four years since Hurricane Katrina, I've received seven pieces of hate mail, and six of them have been in response to my recent critiques of President Obama.

"Those of us who'd been skeptical of the administration were suddenly joined by tens of millions more voices. The country swept the opposition party into power. The country turned on the president's war. The persistence of the critics was a tectonic plate pushing gradually but firmly against the trauma of 9/11. Hurricane Katrina was the rock that broke. The country turned on the President and his party. The indignation generations of decent Americans felt about slavery, Jim Crow, casual bigotry, lynchings and institutionalized discrimination was a tectonic plate pushing gradually but firmly against history. The televised deaths of thousands of poor black and white Americans was the rock that broke. Four years later we swore in our first black President."

"Katrina brought the earthquake." I drop the empty Sonic box on the back seat and turn on the ignition.

-Darrin Bell

For Eve

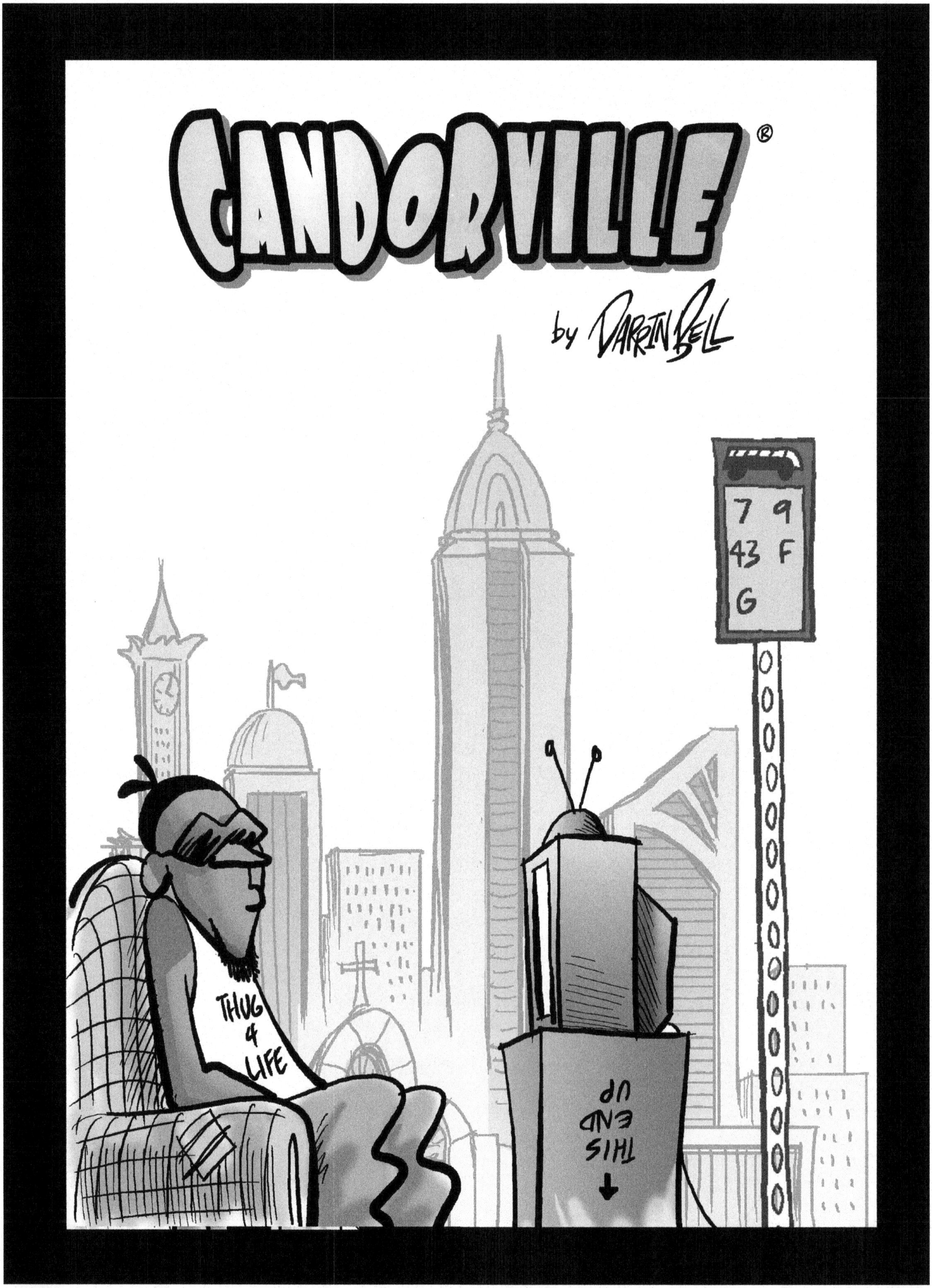
CANDORVILLE®
by DARRIN BELL
7 9
43 F
G
THUG 4 LIFE
THIS END UP

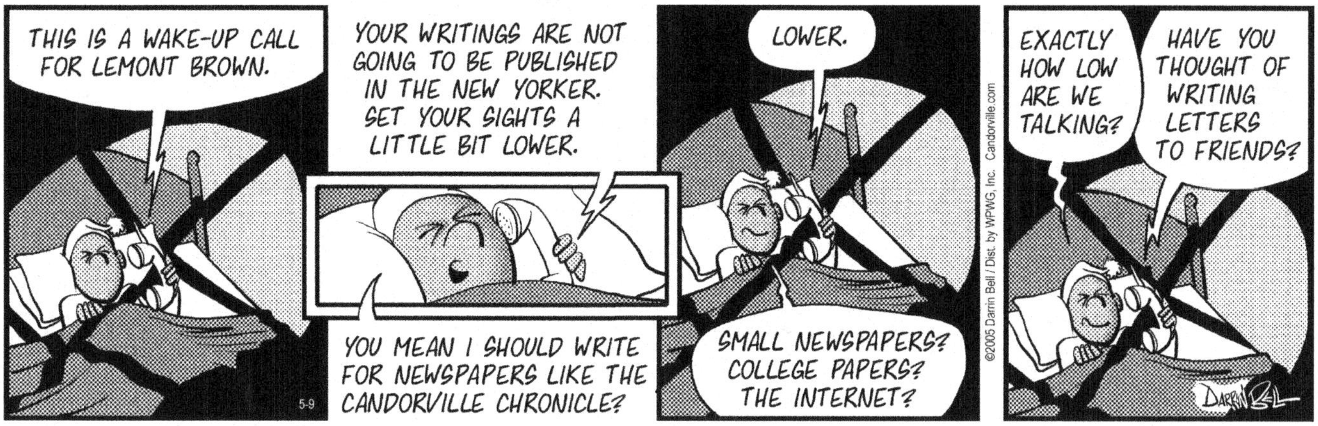
THIS IS A WAKE-UP CALL FOR LEMONT BROWN.
YOUR WRITINGS ARE NOT GOING TO BE PUBLISHED IN THE NEW YORKER. SET YOUR SIGHTS A LITTLE BIT LOWER.
YOU MEAN I SHOULD WRITE FOR NEWSPAPERS LIKE THE CANDORVILLE CHRONICLE?
LOWER.
SMALL NEWSPAPERS? COLLEGE PAPERS? THE INTERNET?
EXACTLY HOW LOW ARE WE TALKING?
HAVE YOU THOUGHT OF WRITING LETTERS TO FRIENDS?
©2005 Darrin Bell / Dist. by WPWG, Inc. Candorville.com
DARRIN BELL
5-9

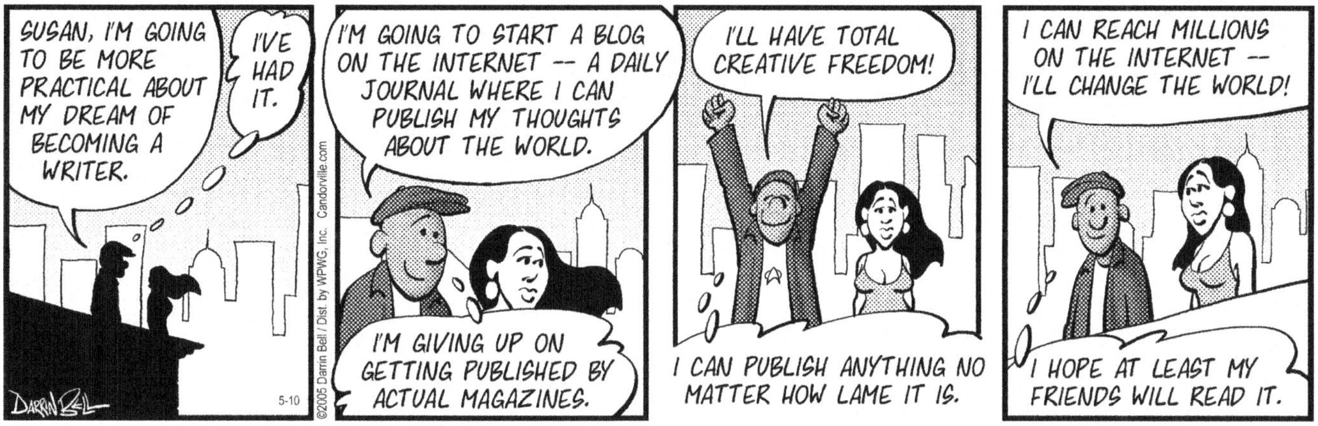
SUSAN, I'M GOING TO BE MORE PRACTICAL ABOUT MY DREAM OF BECOMING A WRITER.
I'VE HAD IT.
I'M GOING TO START A BLOG ON THE INTERNET -- A DAILY JOURNAL WHERE I CAN PUBLISH MY THOUGHTS ABOUT THE WORLD.
I'M GIVING UP ON GETTING PUBLISHED BY ACTUAL MAGAZINES.
I'LL HAVE TOTAL CREATIVE FREEDOM!
I CAN PUBLISH ANYTHING NO MATTER HOW LAME IT IS.
I CAN REACH MILLIONS ON THE INTERNET -- I'LL CHANGE THE WORLD!
I HOPE AT LEAST MY FRIENDS WILL READ IT.
DARRIN BELL
5-10
©2005 Darrin Bell / Dist. by WPWG, Inc. Candorville.com

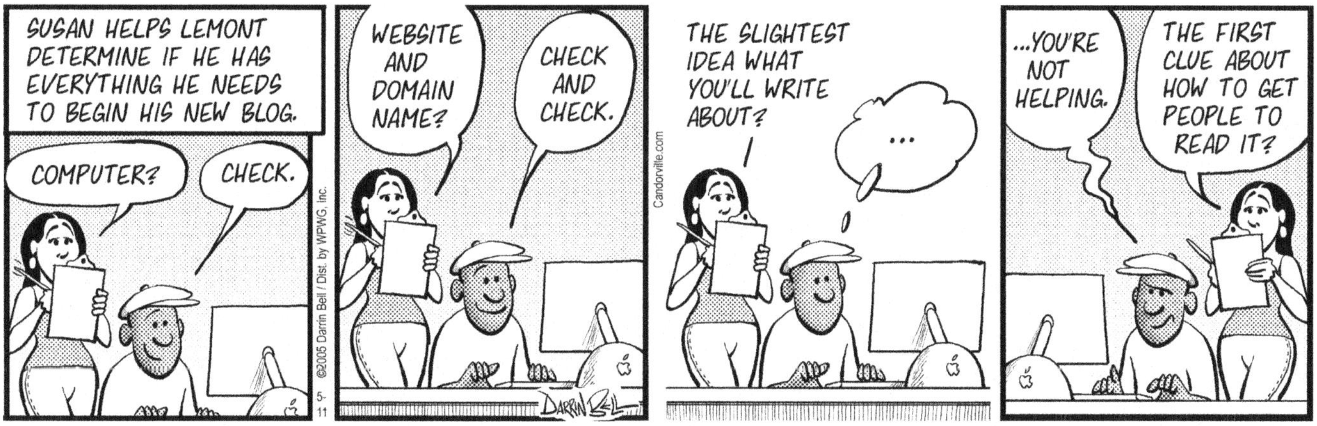
SUSAN HELPS LEMONT DETERMINE IF HE HAS EVERYTHING HE NEEDS TO BEGIN HIS NEW BLOG.
COMPUTER?
CHECK.
WEBSITE AND DOMAIN NAME?
CHECK AND CHECK.
THE SLIGHTEST IDEA WHAT YOU'LL WRITE ABOUT?
...
...YOU'RE NOT HELPING.
THE FIRST CLUE ABOUT HOW TO GET PEOPLE TO READ IT?
©2005 Darrin Bell / Dist. by WPWG, Inc.
Candorville.com
5-11
DARRIN BELL

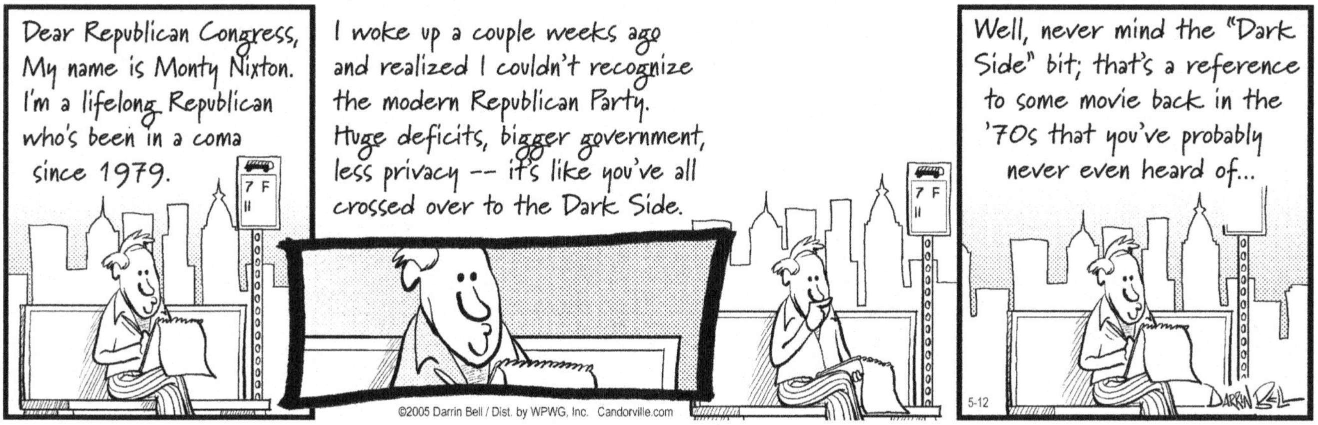
Dear Republican Congress,
My name is Monty Nixton. I'm a lifelong Republican who's been in a coma since 1979.
I woke up a couple weeks ago and realized I couldn't recognize the modern Republican Party. Huge deficits, bigger government, less privacy -- it's like you've all crossed over to the Dark Side.
Well, never mind the "Dark Side" bit; that's a reference to some movie back in the '70s that you've probably never even heard of...
7 F
5-12
DARRIN BELL

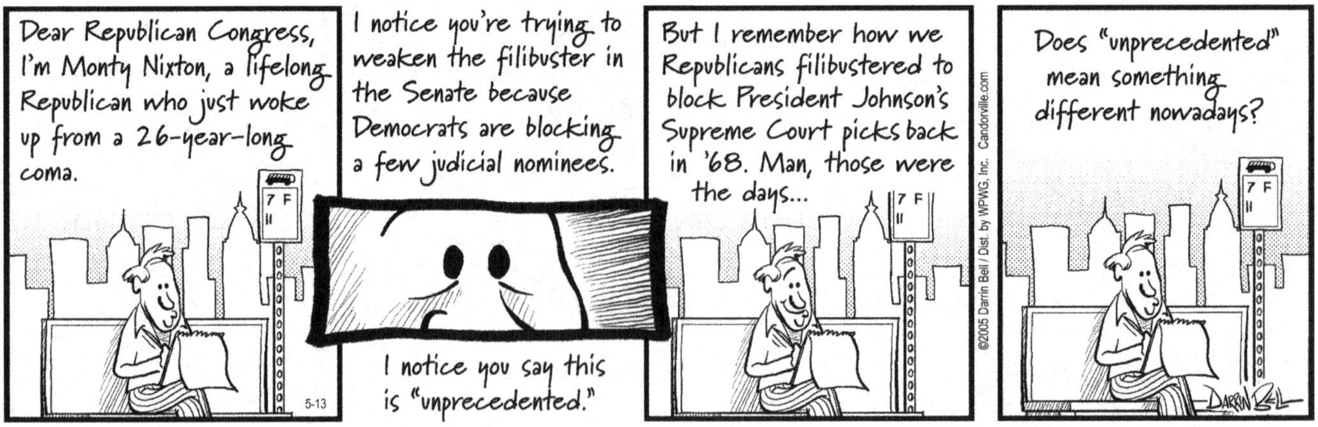
Dear Republican Congress, I'm Monty Nixton, a lifelong Republican who just woke up from a 26-year-long coma.
I notice you're trying to weaken the filibuster in the Senate because Democrats are blocking a few judicial nominees.
I notice you say this is "unprecedented."
But I remember how we Republicans filibustered to block President Johnson's Supreme Court picks back in '68. Man, those were the days...
Does "unprecedented" mean something different nowadays?
5-13
©2005 Darrin Bell / Dist. by WPWG, Inc. Candorville.com
DARRIN BELL

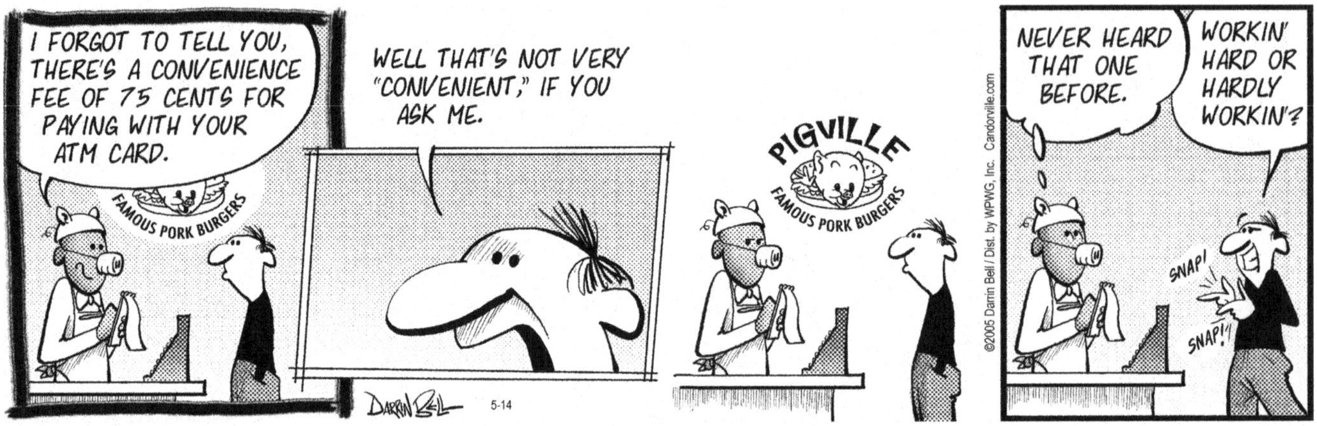
I FORGOT TO TELL YOU, THERE'S A CONVENIENCE FEE OF 75 CENTS FOR PAYING WITH YOUR ATM CARD.
FAMOUS PORK BURGERS
WELL THAT'S NOT VERY "CONVENIENT," IF YOU ASK ME.
PIGVILLE
FAMOUS PORK BURGERS
NEVER HEARD THAT ONE BEFORE.
WORKIN' HARD OR HARDLY WORKIN'?
SNAP!
SNAP!
DARRIN BELL
5-14
©2005 Darrin Bell / Dist. by WPWG, Inc. Candorville.com

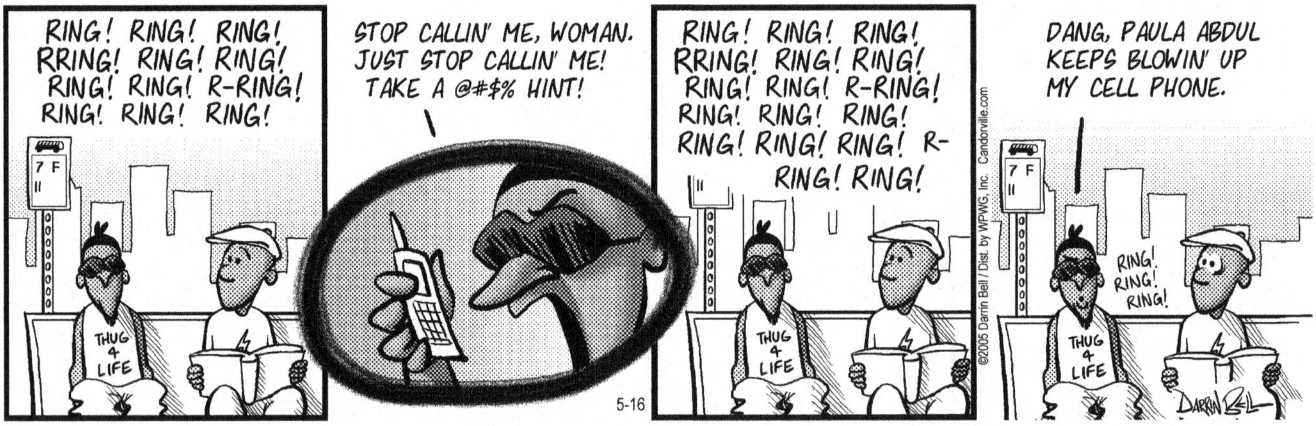
RING! RING! RING! RRING! RING! RING! RING! RING! R-RING! RING! RING! RING!
THUG 4 LIFE
STOP CALLIN' ME, WOMAN. JUST STOP CALLIN' ME! TAKE A @#$% HINT!
5-16
RING! RING! RING! RRING! RING! RING! RING! RING! R-RING! RING! RING! RING! RING! RING! RING! R-RING! RING!
THUG 4 LIFE
DANG, PAULA ABDUL KEEPS BLOWIN' UP MY CELL PHONE.
RING! RING! RING!
THUG 4 LIFE
DARRIN BELL
©2005 Darrin Bell / Dist. by WPWG, Inc. Candorville.com

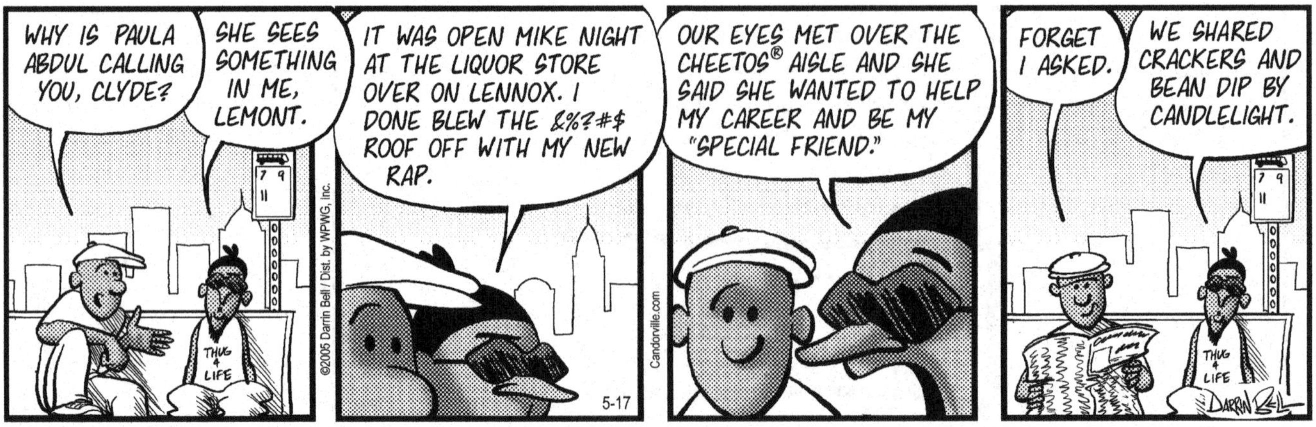
WHY IS PAULA ABDUL CALLING YOU, CLYDE?
SHE SEES SOMETHING IN ME, LEMONT.
THUG 4 LIFE
©2005 Darrin Bell / Dist. by WPWG, Inc.
IT WAS OPEN MIKE NIGHT AT THE LIQUOR STORE OVER ON LENNOX. I DONE BLEW THE &%?#$ ROOF OFF WITH MY NEW RAP.
5-17
Candorville.com
OUR EYES MET OVER THE CHEETOS® AISLE AND SHE SAID SHE WANTED TO HELP MY CAREER AND BE MY "SPECIAL FRIEND."
FORGET I ASKED.
WE SHARED CRACKERS AND BEAN DIP BY CANDLELIGHT.
THUG 4 LIFE
DARRIN BELL

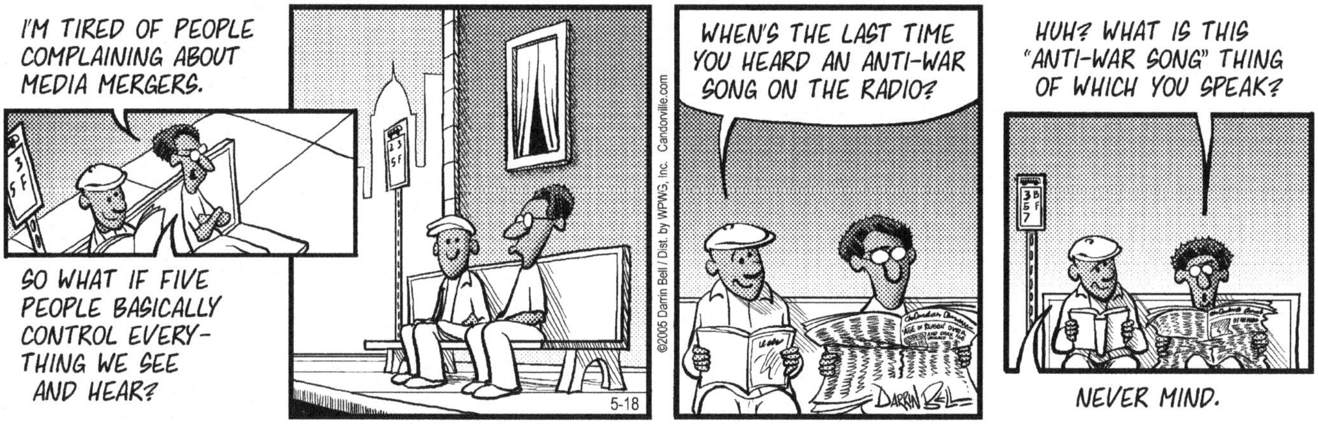
I'M TIRED OF PEOPLE COMPLAINING ABOUT MEDIA MERGERS.
SO WHAT IF FIVE PEOPLE BASICALLY CONTROL EVERY-THING WE SEE AND HEAR?
©2005 Darrin Bell / Dist. by WPWG, Inc. Candorville.com
5-18
WHEN'S THE LAST TIME YOU HEARD AN ANTI-WAR SONG ON THE RADIO?
DARRIN BELL
HUH? WHAT IS THIS "ANTI-WAR SONG" THING OF WHICH YOU SPEAK?
NEVER MIND.

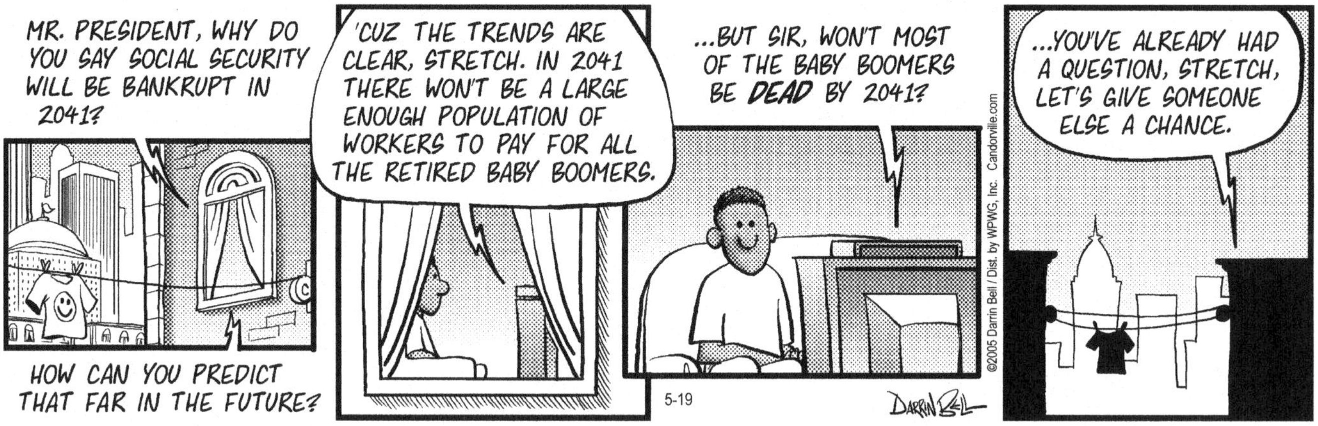
MR. PRESIDENT, WHY DO YOU SAY SOCIAL SECURITY WILL BE BANKRUPT IN 2041?
HOW CAN YOU PREDICT THAT FAR IN THE FUTURE?
'CUZ THE TRENDS ARE CLEAR, STRETCH. IN 2041 THERE WON'T BE A LARGE ENOUGH POPULATION OF WORKERS TO PAY FOR ALL THE RETIRED BABY BOOMERS.
...BUT SIR, WON'T MOST OF THE BABY BOOMERS BE *DEAD* BY 2041?
5-19
DARRIN BELL
©2005 Darrin Bell / Dist. by WPWG, Inc. Candorville.com
...YOU'VE ALREADY HAD A QUESTION, STRETCH, LET'S GIVE SOMEONE ELSE A CHANCE.

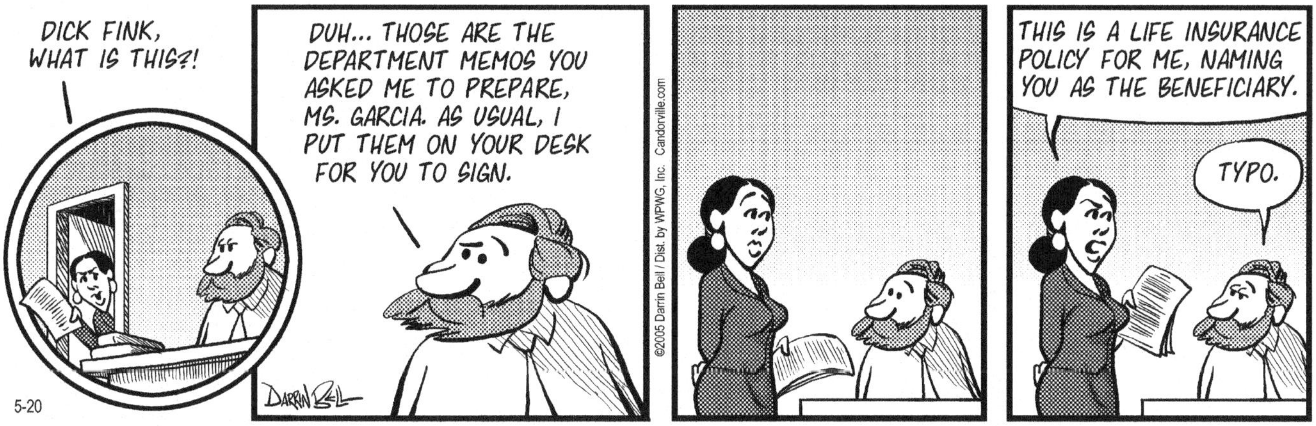
DICK FINK, WHAT IS THIS?!
5-20
DARRIN BELL
DUH... THOSE ARE THE DEPARTMENT MEMOS YOU ASKED ME TO PREPARE, MS. GARCIA. AS USUAL, I PUT THEM ON YOUR DESK FOR YOU TO SIGN.
©2005 Darrin Bell / Dist. by WPWG, Inc. Candorville.com
THIS IS A LIFE INSURANCE POLICY FOR ME, NAMING YOU AS THE BENEFICIARY.
TYPO.

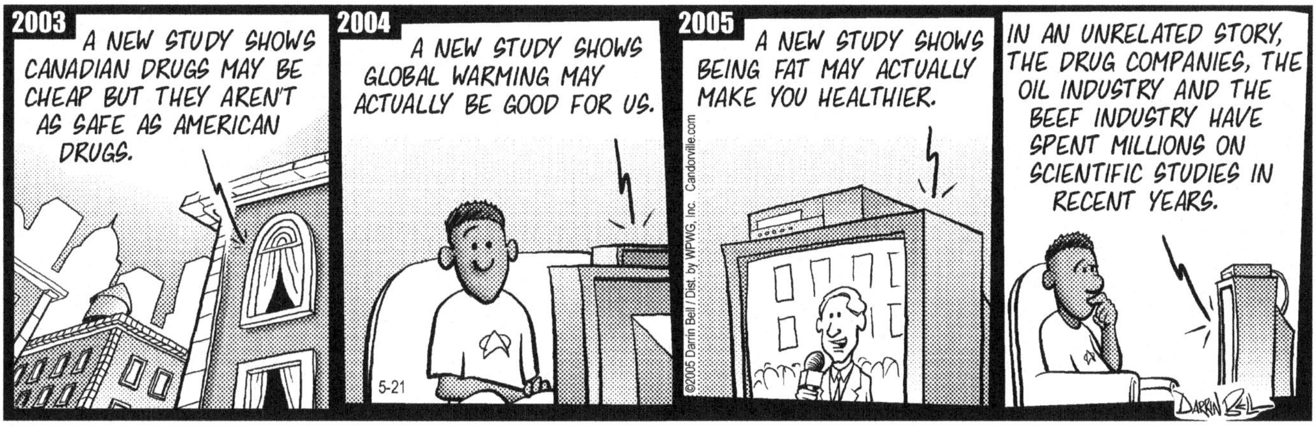
2003
A NEW STUDY SHOWS CANADIAN DRUGS MAY BE CHEAP BUT THEY AREN'T AS SAFE AS AMERICAN DRUGS.
2004
A NEW STUDY SHOWS GLOBAL WARMING MAY ACTUALLY BE GOOD FOR US.
5-21
2005
A NEW STUDY SHOWS BEING FAT MAY ACTUALLY MAKE YOU HEALTHIER.
©2005 Darrin Bell / Dist. by WPWG, Inc. Candorville.com
IN AN UNRELATED STORY, THE DRUG COMPANIES, THE OIL INDUSTRY AND THE BEEF INDUSTRY HAVE SPENT MILLIONS ON SCIENTIFIC STUDIES IN RECENT YEARS.
DARRIN BELL

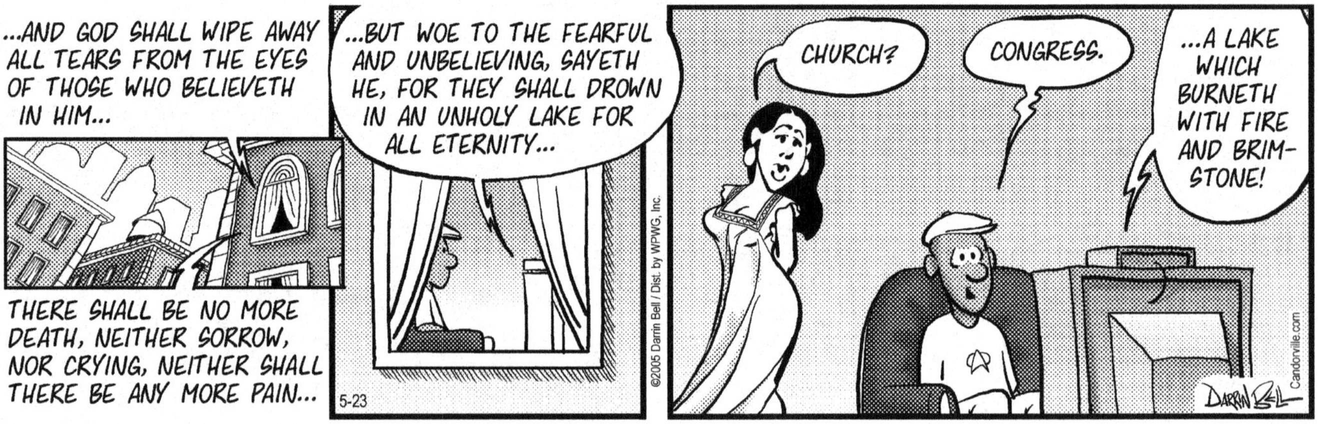
...AND GOD SHALL WIPE AWAY ALL TEARS FROM THE EYES OF THOSE WHO BELIEVETH IN HIM...
THERE SHALL BE NO MORE DEATH, NEITHER SORROW, NOR CRYING, NEITHER SHALL THERE BE ANY MORE PAIN...
5-23
...BUT WOE TO THE FEARFUL AND UNBELIEVING, SAYETH HE, FOR THEY SHALL DROWN IN AN UNHOLY LAKE FOR ALL ETERNITY...
©2005 Darrin Bell / Dist. by WPWG, Inc.
CHURCH?
CONGRESS.
...A LAKE WHICH BURNETH WITH FIRE AND BRIMSTONE!
DARRIN BELL
Candorville.com

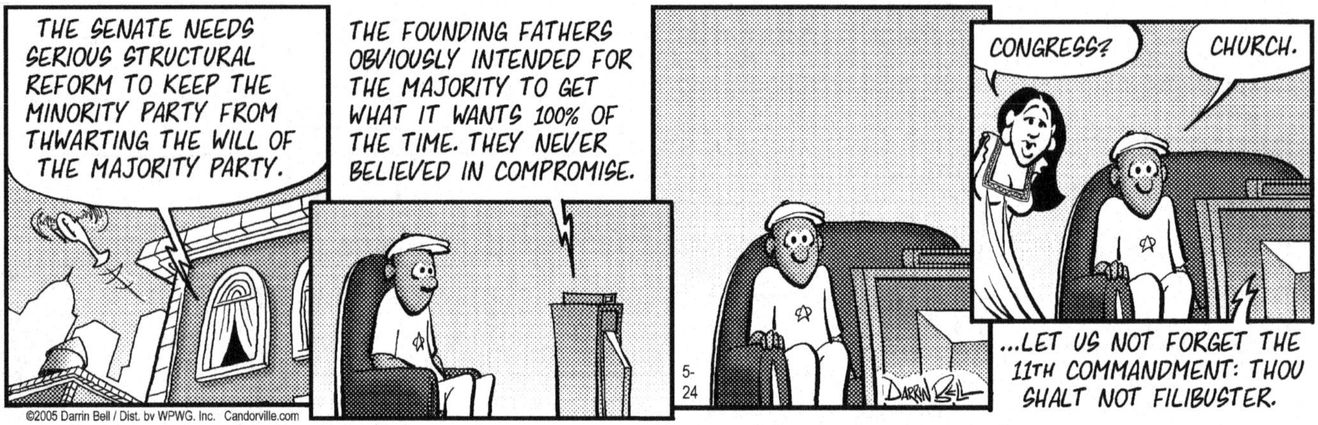
THE SENATE NEEDS SERIOUS STRUCTURAL REFORM TO KEEP THE MINORITY PARTY FROM THWARTING THE WILL OF THE MAJORITY PARTY.
©2005 Darrin Bell / Dist. by WPWG, Inc. Candorville.com
THE FOUNDING FATHERS OBVIOUSLY INTENDED FOR THE MAJORITY TO GET WHAT IT WANTS 100% OF THE TIME. THEY NEVER BELIEVED IN COMPROMISE.
5-24
DARRIN BELL
CONGRESS?
CHURCH.
...LET US NOT FORGET THE 11TH COMMANDMENT: THOU SHALT NOT FILIBUSTER.

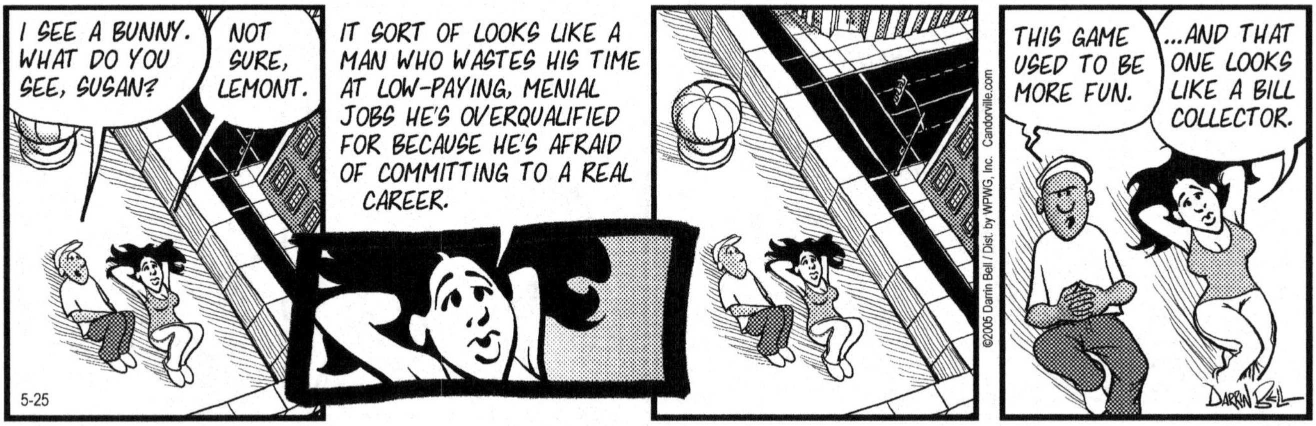
I SEE A BUNNY. WHAT DO YOU SEE, SUSAN?
NOT SURE, LEMONT.
5-25
IT SORT OF LOOKS LIKE A MAN WHO WASTES HIS TIME AT LOW-PAYING, MENIAL JOBS HE'S OVERQUALIFIED FOR BECAUSE HE'S AFRAID OF COMMITTING TO A REAL CAREER.
©2005 Darrin Bell / Dist. by WPWG, Inc. Candorville.com
THIS GAME USED TO BE MORE FUN.
...AND THAT ONE LOOKS LIKE A BILL COLLECTOR.
DARRIN BELL

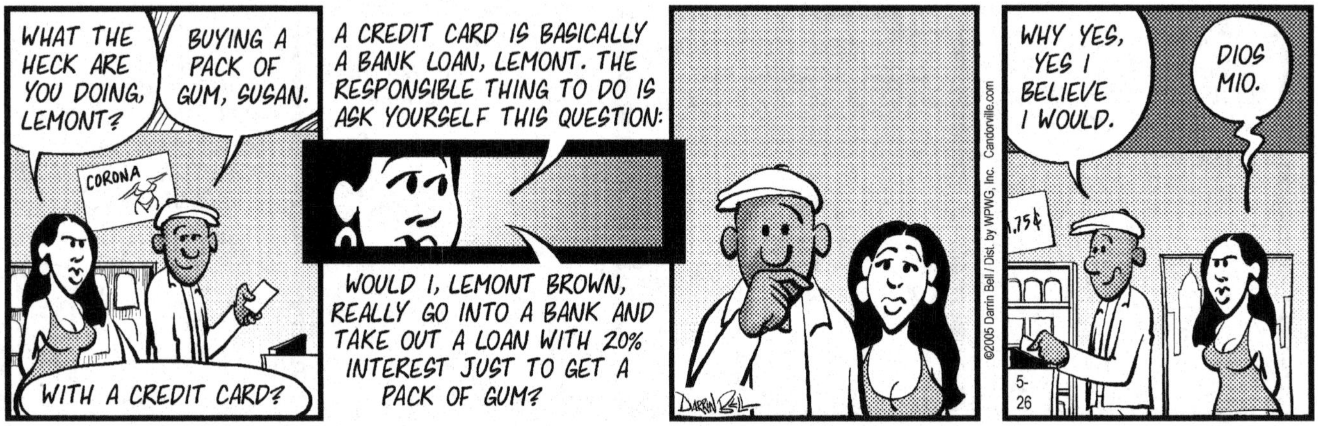
WHAT THE HECK ARE YOU DOING, LEMONT?
BUYING A PACK OF GUM, SUSAN.
CORONA
WITH A CREDIT CARD?
A CREDIT CARD IS BASICALLY A BANK LOAN, LEMONT. THE RESPONSIBLE THING TO DO IS ASK YOURSELF THIS QUESTION:
WOULD I, LEMONT BROWN, REALLY GO INTO A BANK AND TAKE OUT A LOAN WITH 20% INTEREST JUST TO GET A PACK OF GUM?
DARRIN BELL
©2005 Darrin Bell / Dist. by WPWG, Inc. Candorville.com
WHY YES, YES I BELIEVE I WOULD.
DIOS MIO.
1.75¢
5-26

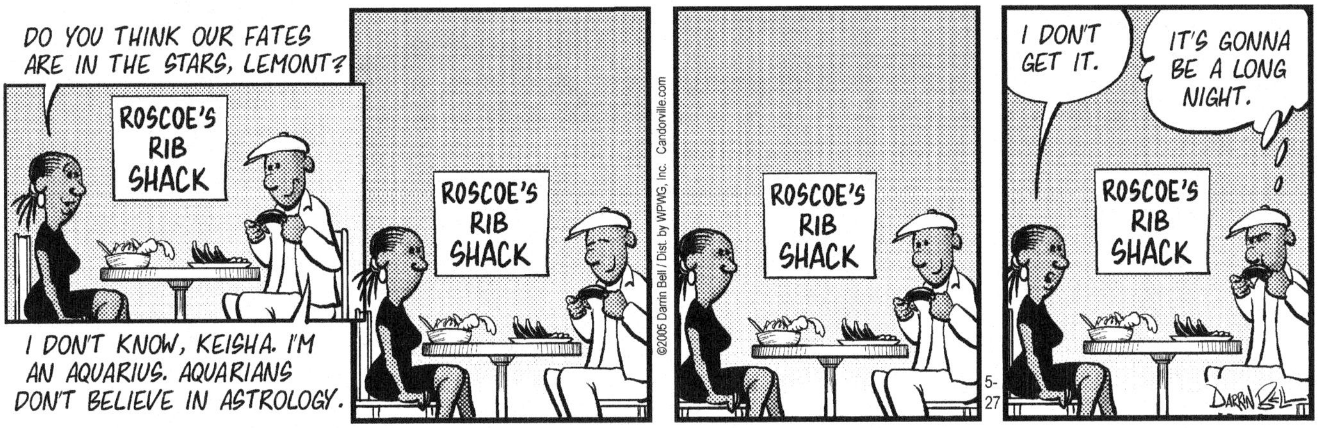
DO YOU THINK OUR FATES ARE IN THE STARS, LEMONT?
ROSCOE'S RIB SHACK
I DON'T KNOW, KEISHA. I'M AN AQUARIUS. AQUARIANS DON'T BELIEVE IN ASTROLOGY.
©2005 Darrin Bell / Dist. by WPWG, Inc. Candorville.com
5-27
I DON'T GET IT.
IT'S GONNA BE A LONG NIGHT.
DARRIN BELL

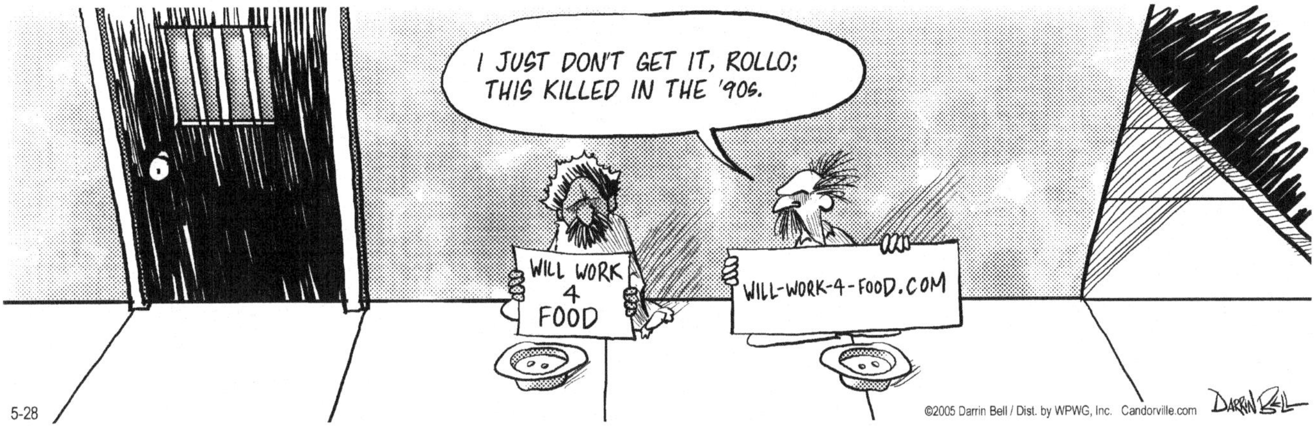
I JUST DON'T GET IT, ROLLO; THIS KILLED IN THE '90s.
WILL WORK 4 FOOD
WILL-WORK-4-FOOD.COM
5-28
©2005 Darrin Bell / Dist. by WPWG, Inc. Candorville.com
DARRIN BELL

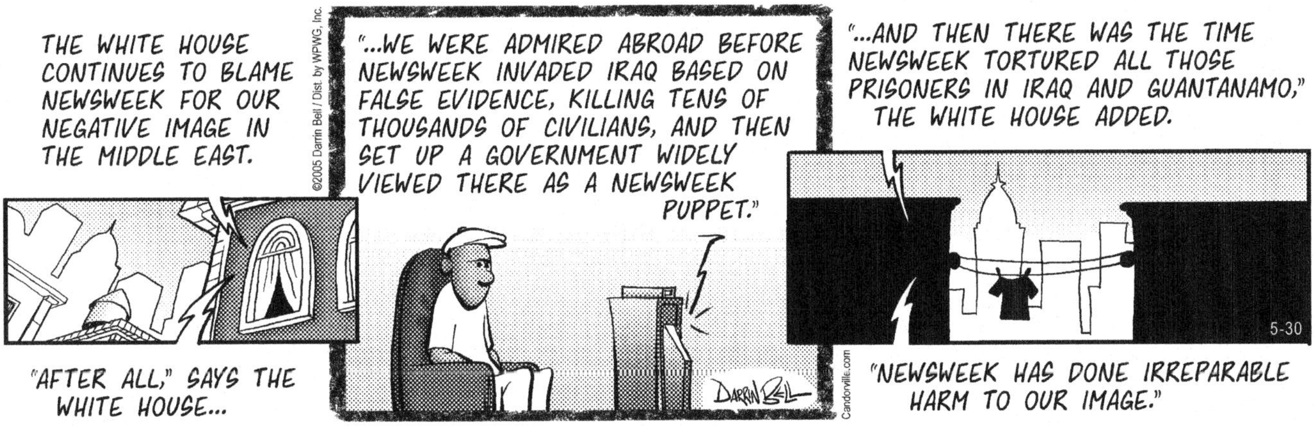
THE WHITE HOUSE CONTINUES TO BLAME NEWSWEEK FOR OUR NEGATIVE IMAGE IN THE MIDDLE EAST.
"AFTER ALL," SAYS THE WHITE HOUSE...
©2005 Darrin Bell / Dist. by WPWG, Inc.
"...WE WERE ADMIRED ABROAD BEFORE NEWSWEEK INVADED IRAQ BASED ON FALSE EVIDENCE, KILLING TENS OF THOUSANDS OF CIVILIANS, AND THEN SET UP A GOVERNMENT WIDELY VIEWED THERE AS A NEWSWEEK PUPPET."
DARRIN BELL
Candorville.com
"...AND THEN THERE WAS THE TIME NEWSWEEK TORTURED ALL THOSE PRISONERS IN IRAQ AND GUANTANAMO," THE WHITE HOUSE ADDED.
5-30
"NEWSWEEK HAS DONE IRREPARABLE HARM TO OUR IMAGE."

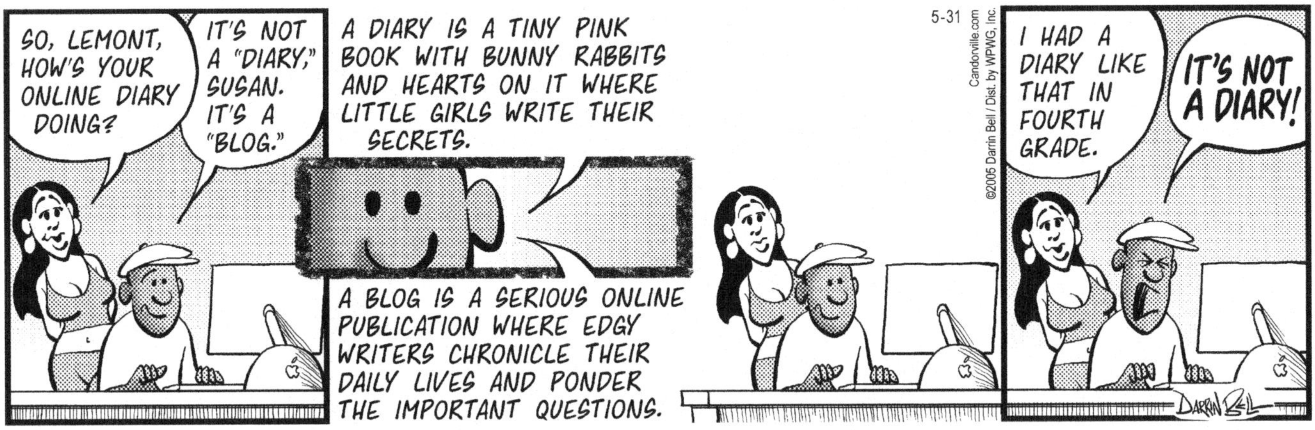
SO, LEMONT, HOW'S YOUR ONLINE DIARY DOING?
IT'S NOT A "DIARY," SUSAN. IT'S A "BLOG."
A DIARY IS A TINY PINK BOOK WITH BUNNY RABBITS AND HEARTS ON IT WHERE LITTLE GIRLS WRITE THEIR SECRETS.
A BLOG IS A SERIOUS ONLINE PUBLICATION WHERE EDGY WRITERS CHRONICLE THEIR DAILY LIVES AND PONDER THE IMPORTANT QUESTIONS.
5-31
©2005 Darrin Bell / Dist. by WPWG, Inc. Candorville.com
I HAD A DIARY LIKE THAT IN FOURTH GRADE.
IT'S NOT A DIARY!
DARRIN BELL

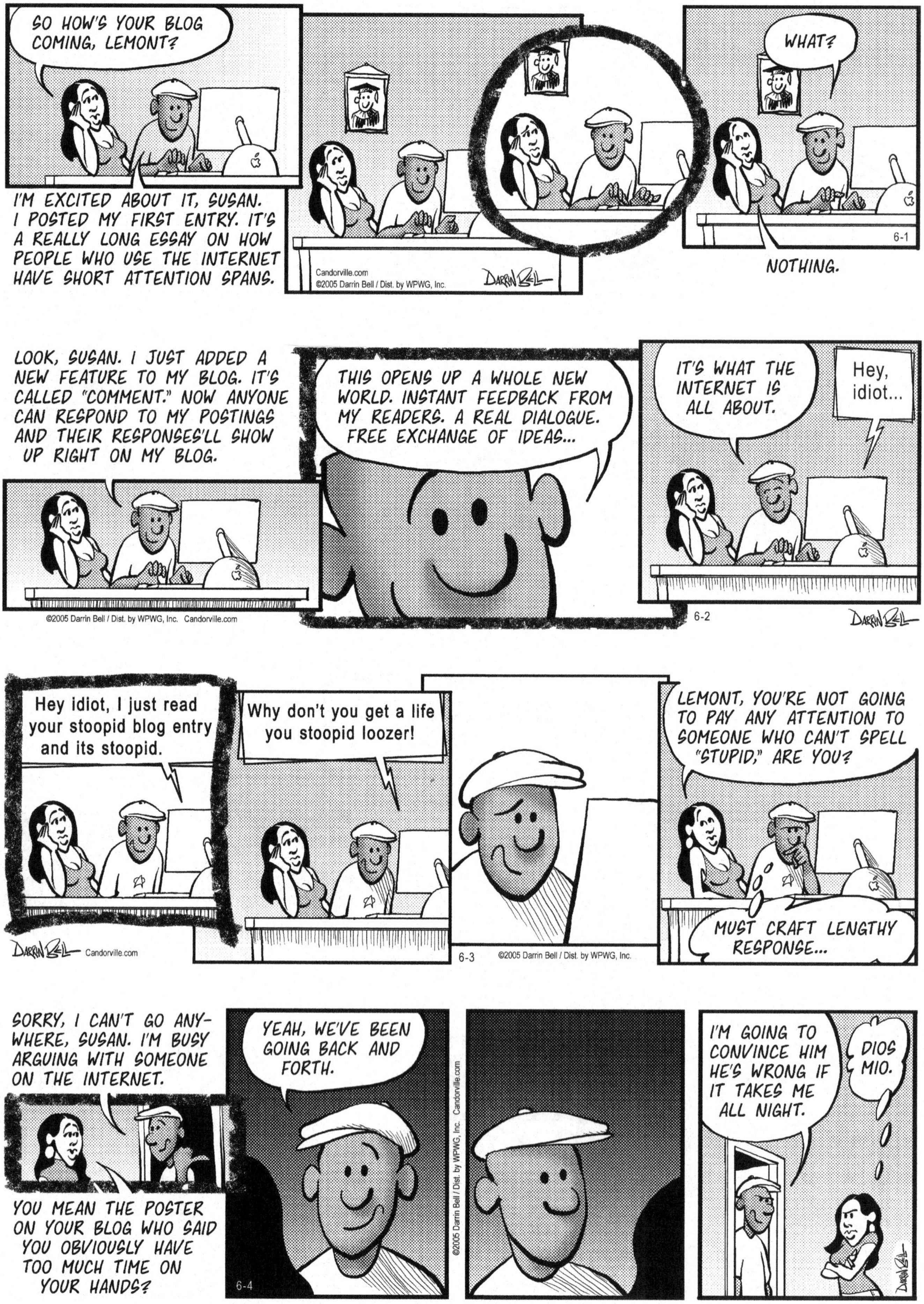
SO HOW'S YOUR BLOG COMING, LEMONT?
I'M EXCITED ABOUT IT, SUSAN. I POSTED MY FIRST ENTRY. IT'S A REALLY LONG ESSAY ON HOW PEOPLE WHO USE THE INTERNET HAVE SHORT ATTENTION SPANS.
Candorville.com
©2005 Darrin Bell / Dist. by WPWG, Inc.
DARRIN BELL
WHAT?
NOTHING.
6-1
LOOK, SUSAN. I JUST ADDED A NEW FEATURE TO MY BLOG. IT'S CALLED "COMMENT." NOW ANYONE CAN RESPOND TO MY POSTINGS AND THEIR RESPONSES'LL SHOW UP RIGHT ON MY BLOG.
THIS OPENS UP A WHOLE NEW WORLD. INSTANT FEEDBACK FROM MY READERS. A REAL DIALOGUE. FREE EXCHANGE OF IDEAS...
IT'S WHAT THE INTERNET IS ALL ABOUT.
Hey, idiot...
©2005 Darrin Bell / Dist. by WPWG, Inc. Candorville.com
6-2
DARRIN BELL
Hey idiot, I just read your stoopid blog entry and its stoopid.
Why don't you get a life you stoopid loozer!
LEMONT, YOU'RE NOT GOING TO PAY ANY ATTENTION TO SOMEONE WHO CAN'T SPELL "STUPID," ARE YOU?
MUST CRAFT LENGTHY RESPONSE...
DARRIN BELL Candorville.com
6-3
©2005 Darrin Bell / Dist. by WPWG, Inc.
SORRY, I CAN'T GO ANYWHERE, SUSAN. I'M BUSY ARGUING WITH SOMEONE ON THE INTERNET.
YOU MEAN THE POSTER ON YOUR BLOG WHO SAID YOU OBVIOUSLY HAVE TOO MUCH TIME ON YOUR HANDS?
YEAH, WE'VE BEEN GOING BACK AND FORTH.
6-4
©2005 Darrin Bell / Dist. by WPWG, Inc. Candorville.com
I'M GOING TO CONVINCE HIM HE'S WRONG IF IT TAKES ME ALL NIGHT.
DIOS MIO.
DARRIN BELL

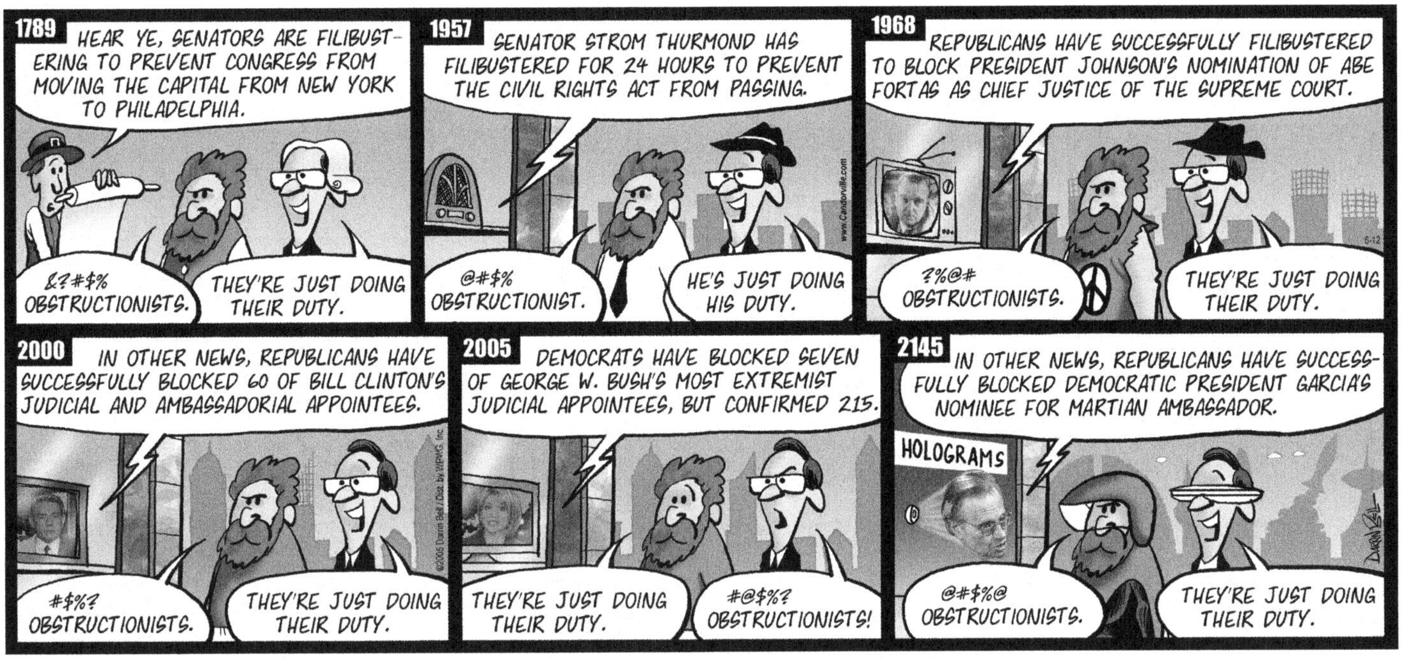
1789
HEAR YE, SENATORS ARE FILIBUSTERING TO PREVENT CONGRESS FROM MOVING THE CAPITAL FROM NEW YORK TO PHILADELPHIA.
&?#$% OBSTRUCTIONISTS.
THEY'RE JUST DOING THEIR DUTY.
1957
SENATOR STROM THURMOND HAS FILIBUSTERED FOR 24 HOURS TO PREVENT THE CIVIL RIGHTS ACT FROM PASSING.
@#$% OBSTRUCTIONIST.
HE'S JUST DOING HIS DUTY.
1968
REPUBLICANS HAVE SUCCESSFULLY FILIBUSTERED TO BLOCK PRESIDENT JOHNSON'S NOMINATION OF ABE FORTAS AS CHIEF JUSTICE OF THE SUPREME COURT.
?%@# OBSTRUCTIONISTS.
THEY'RE JUST DOING THEIR DUTY.
2000
IN OTHER NEWS, REPUBLICANS HAVE SUCCESSFULLY BLOCKED 60 OF BILL CLINTON'S JUDICIAL AND AMBASSADORIAL APPOINTEES.
#$%? OBSTRUCTIONISTS.
THEY'RE JUST DOING THEIR DUTY.
2005
DEMOCRATS HAVE BLOCKED SEVEN OF GEORGE W. BUSH'S MOST EXTREMIST JUDICIAL APPOINTEES, BUT CONFIRMED 215.
THEY'RE JUST DOING THEIR DUTY.
#@$%? OBSTRUCTIONISTS!
2145
IN OTHER NEWS, REPUBLICANS HAVE SUCCESSFULLY BLOCKED DEMOCRATIC PRESIDENT GARCIA'S NOMINEE FOR MARTIAN AMBASSADOR.
HOLOGRAMS
@#$%@ OBSTRUCTIONISTS.
THEY'RE JUST DOING THEIR DUTY.

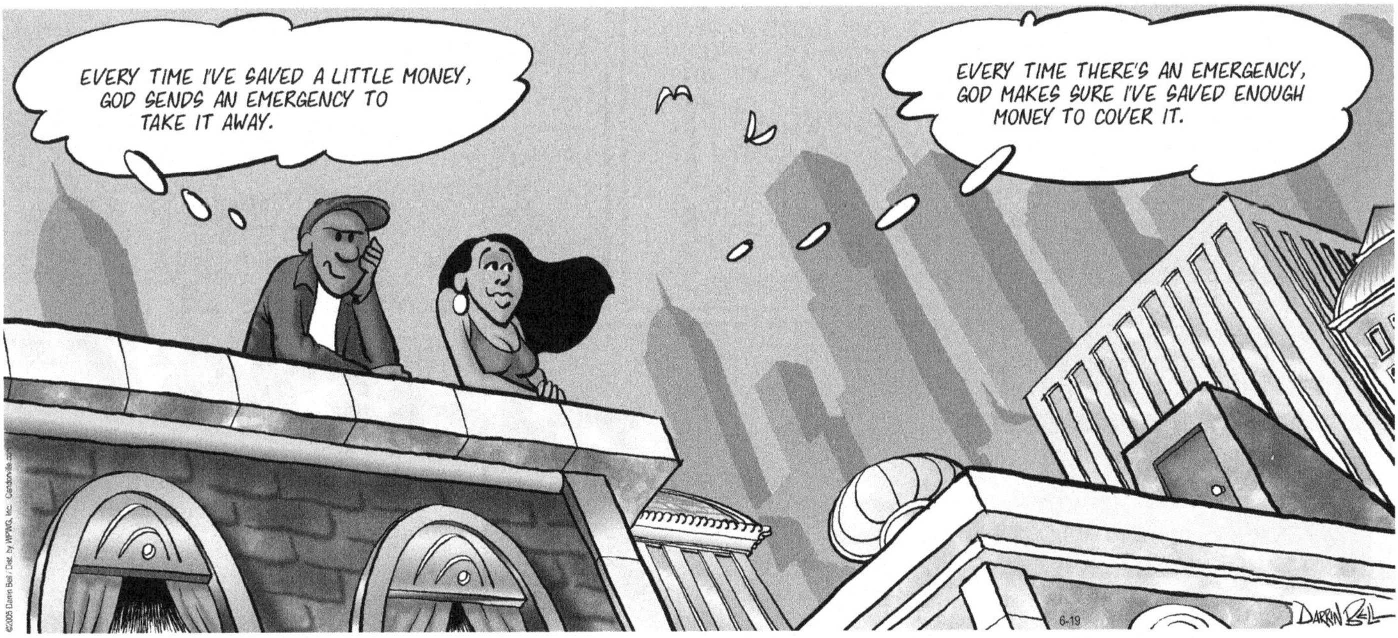
EVERY TIME I'VE SAVED A LITTLE MONEY, GOD SENDS AN EMERGENCY TO TAKE IT AWAY.
EVERY TIME THERE'S AN EMERGENCY, GOD MAKES SURE I'VE SAVED ENOUGH MONEY TO COVER IT.

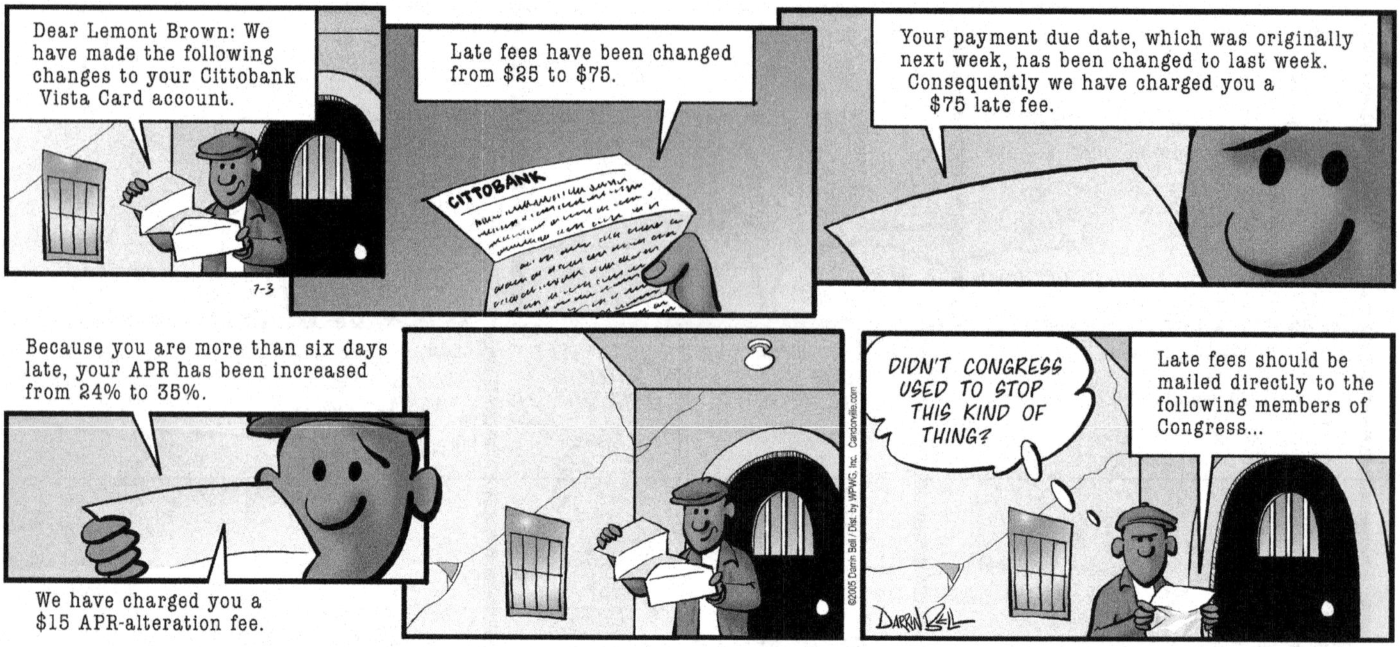
Dear Lemont Brown: We have made the following changes to your Cittobank Vista Card account.
Late fees have been changed from $25 to $75.
CITTOBANK
Your payment due date, which was originally next week, has been changed to last week. Consequently we have charged you a $75 late fee.
7-3
Because you are more than six days late, your APR has been increased from 24% to 35%.
We have charged you a $15 APR-alteration fee.
©2005 Darrin Bell / Dist. by WPWG, Inc. Candorville.com
DIDN'T CONGRESS USED TO STOP THIS KIND OF THING?
Late fees should be mailed directly to the following members of Congress...
DARRIN BELL

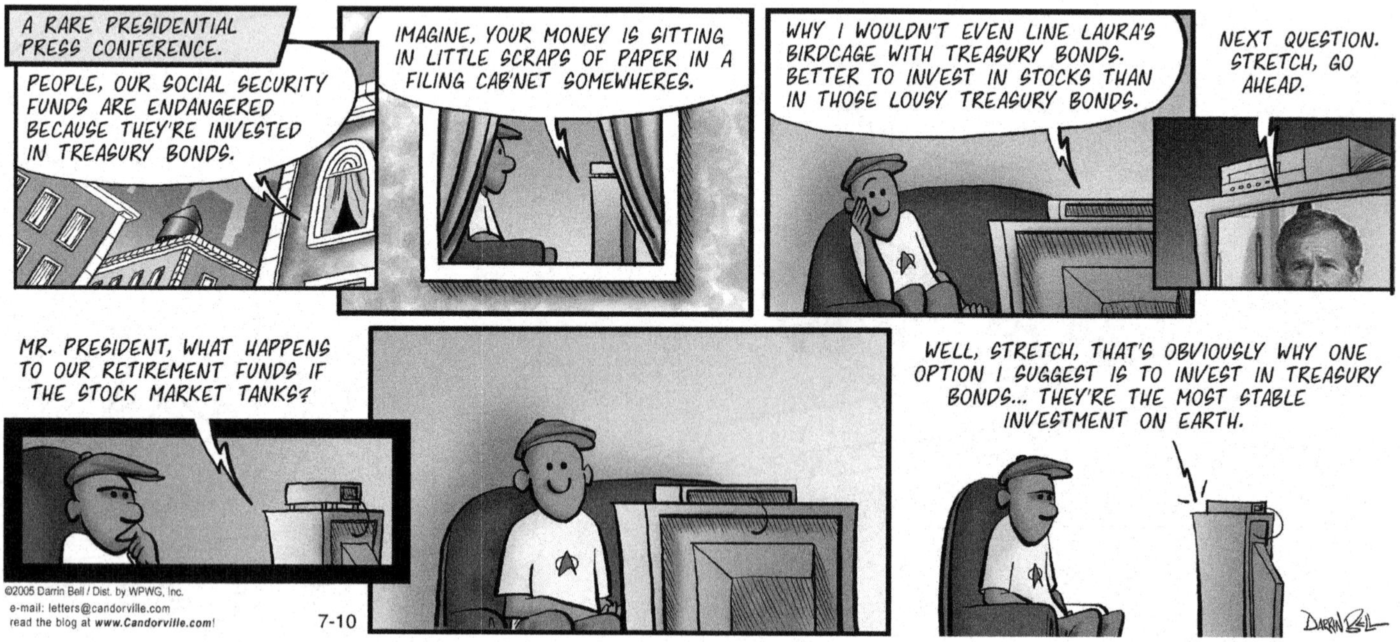
A RARE PRESIDENTIAL PRESS CONFERENCE.
PEOPLE, OUR SOCIAL SECURITY FUNDS ARE ENDANGERED BECAUSE THEY'RE INVESTED IN TREASURY BONDS.
IMAGINE, YOUR MONEY IS SITTING IN LITTLE SCRAPS OF PAPER IN A FILING CAB'NET SOMEWHERES.
WHY I WOULDN'T EVEN LINE LAURA'S BIRDCAGE WITH TREASURY BONDS. BETTER TO INVEST IN STOCKS THAN IN THOSE LOUSY TREASURY BONDS.
NEXT QUESTION. STRETCH, GO AHEAD.
MR. PRESIDENT, WHAT HAPPENS TO OUR RETIREMENT FUNDS IF THE STOCK MARKET TANKS?
©2005 Darrin Bell / Dist. by WPWG, Inc.
e-mail: letters@candorville.com
read the blog at www.Candorville.com!
7-10
WELL, STRETCH, THAT'S OBVIOUSLY WHY ONE OPTION I SUGGEST IS TO INVEST IN TREASURY BONDS... THEY'RE THE MOST STABLE INVESTMENT ON EARTH.
DARRIN BELL

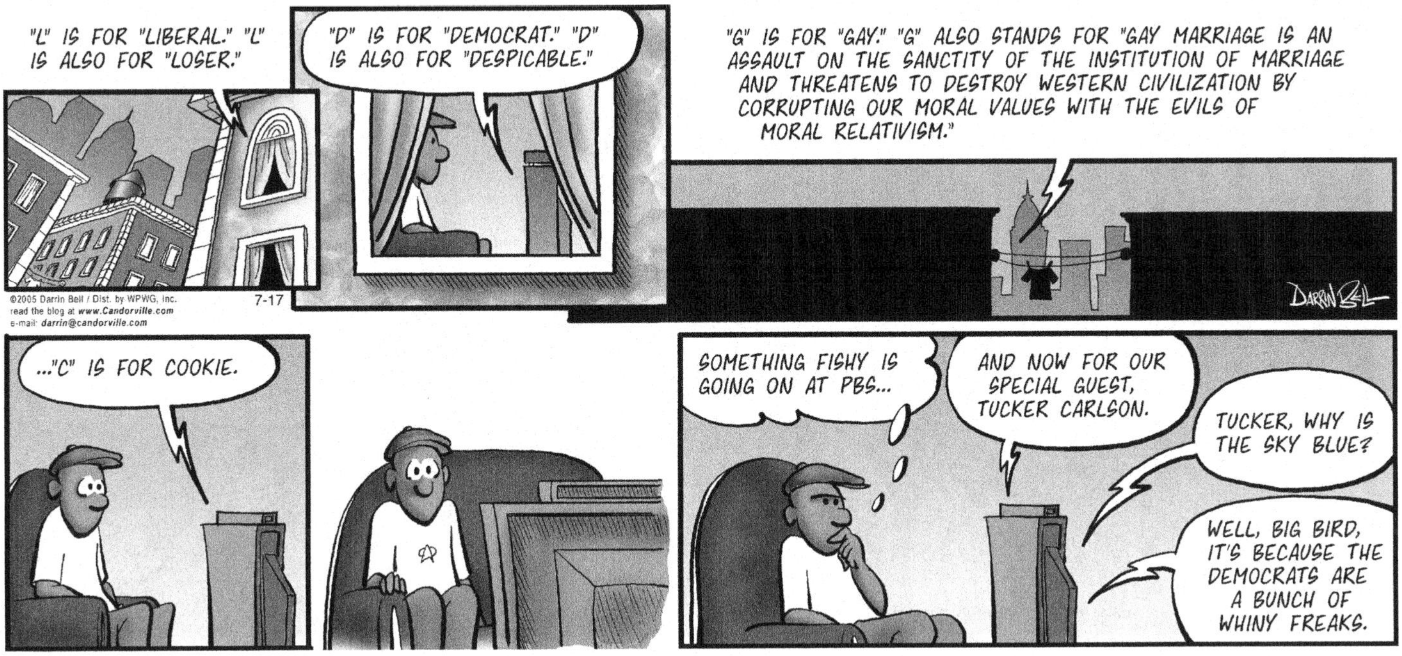
"L" IS FOR "LIBERAL." "L" IS ALSO FOR "LOSER."
"D" IS FOR "DEMOCRAT." "D" IS ALSO FOR "DESPICABLE."
"G" IS FOR "GAY." "G" ALSO STANDS FOR "GAY MARRIAGE IS AN ASSAULT ON THE SANCTITY OF THE INSTITUTION OF MARRIAGE AND THREATENS TO DESTROY WESTERN CIVILIZATION BY CORRUPTING OUR MORAL VALUES WITH THE EVILS OF MORAL RELATIVISM."
©2005 Darrin Bell / Dist. by WPWG, Inc.
read the blog at www.Candorville.com
e-mail: darrin@candorville.com
7-17
DARRIN BELL
..."C" IS FOR COOKIE.
SOMETHING FISHY IS GOING ON AT PBS...
AND NOW FOR OUR SPECIAL GUEST, TUCKER CARLSON.
TUCKER, WHY IS THE SKY BLUE?
WELL, BIG BIRD, IT'S BECAUSE THE DEMOCRATS ARE A BUNCH OF WHINY FREAKS.

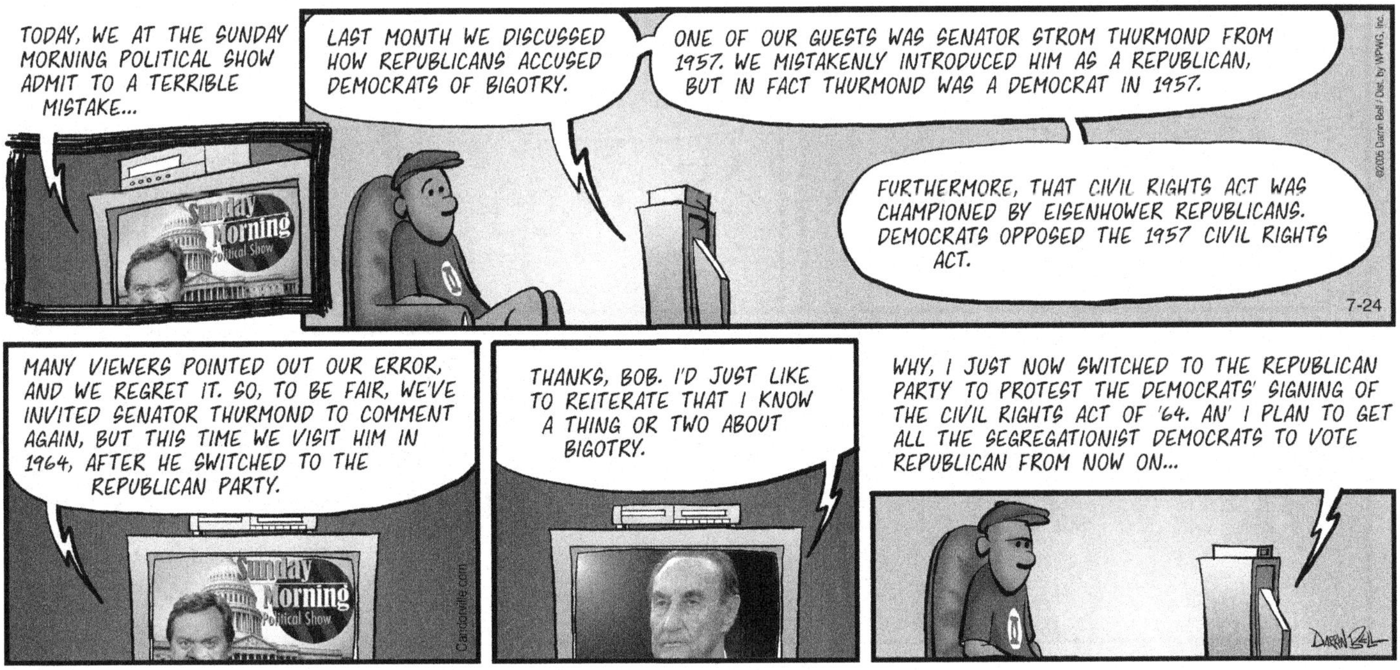
TODAY, WE AT THE SUNDAY MORNING POLITICAL SHOW ADMIT TO A TERRIBLE MISTAKE...
Sunday Morning Political Show
LAST MONTH WE DISCUSSED HOW REPUBLICANS ACCUSED DEMOCRATS OF BIGOTRY.
ONE OF OUR GUESTS WAS SENATOR STROM THURMOND FROM 1957. WE MISTAKENLY INTRODUCED HIM AS A REPUBLICAN, BUT IN FACT THURMOND WAS A DEMOCRAT IN 1957.
FURTHERMORE, THAT CIVIL RIGHTS ACT WAS CHAMPIONED BY EISENHOWER REPUBLICANS. DEMOCRATS OPPOSED THE 1957 CIVIL RIGHTS ACT.
©2005 Darrin Bell / Dist. by WPWG, Inc.
7-24
MANY VIEWERS POINTED OUT OUR ERROR, AND WE REGRET IT. SO, TO BE FAIR, WE'VE INVITED SENATOR THURMOND TO COMMENT AGAIN, BUT THIS TIME WE VISIT HIM IN 1964, AFTER HE SWITCHED TO THE REPUBLICAN PARTY.
Sunday Morning Political Show
Candorville.com
THANKS, BOB. I'D JUST LIKE TO REITERATE THAT I KNOW A THING OR TWO ABOUT BIGOTRY.
WHY, I JUST NOW SWITCHED TO THE REPUBLICAN PARTY TO PROTEST THE DEMOCRATS' SIGNING OF THE CIVIL RIGHTS ACT OF '64. AN' I PLAN TO GET ALL THE SEGREGATIONIST DEMOCRATS TO VOTE REPUBLICAN FROM NOW ON...
DARRIN BELL

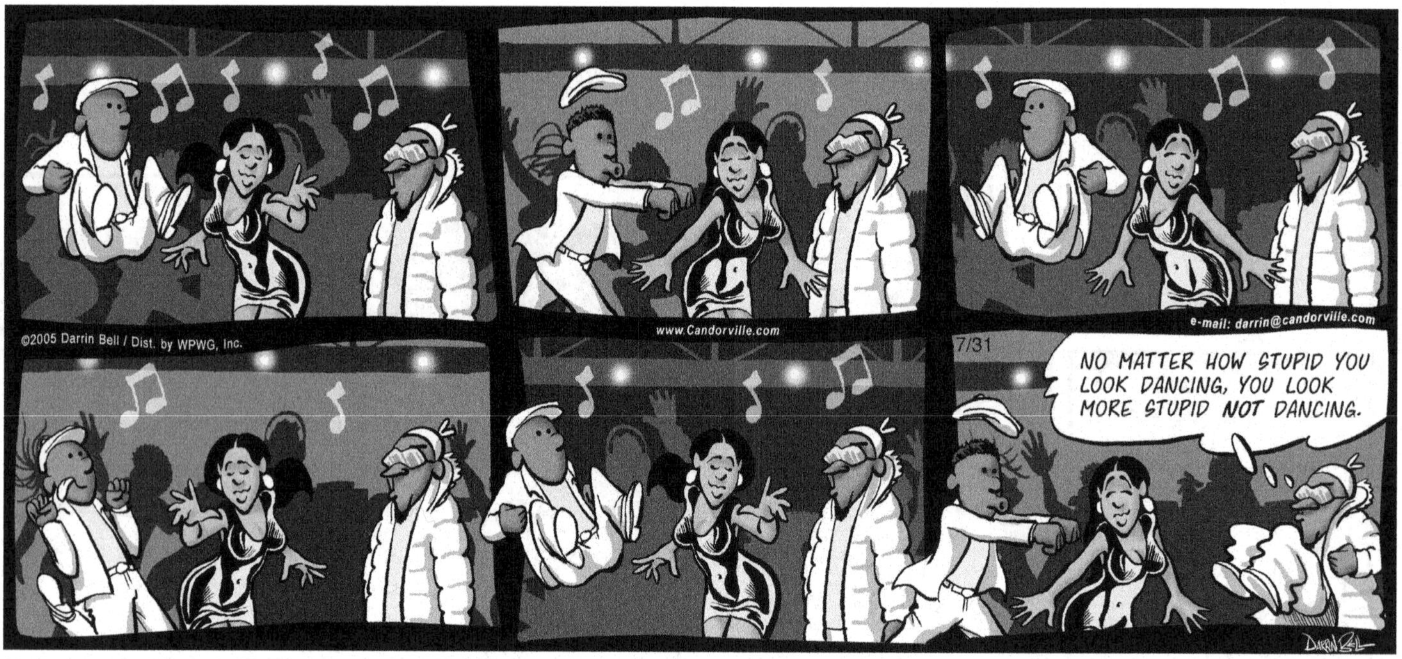
©2005 Darrin Bell / Dist. by WPWG, Inc.
www.Candorville.com
e-mail: darrin@candorville.com
7/31
NO MATTER HOW STUPID YOU LOOK DANCING, YOU LOOK MORE STUPID **NOT** DANCING.
DARRIN BELL

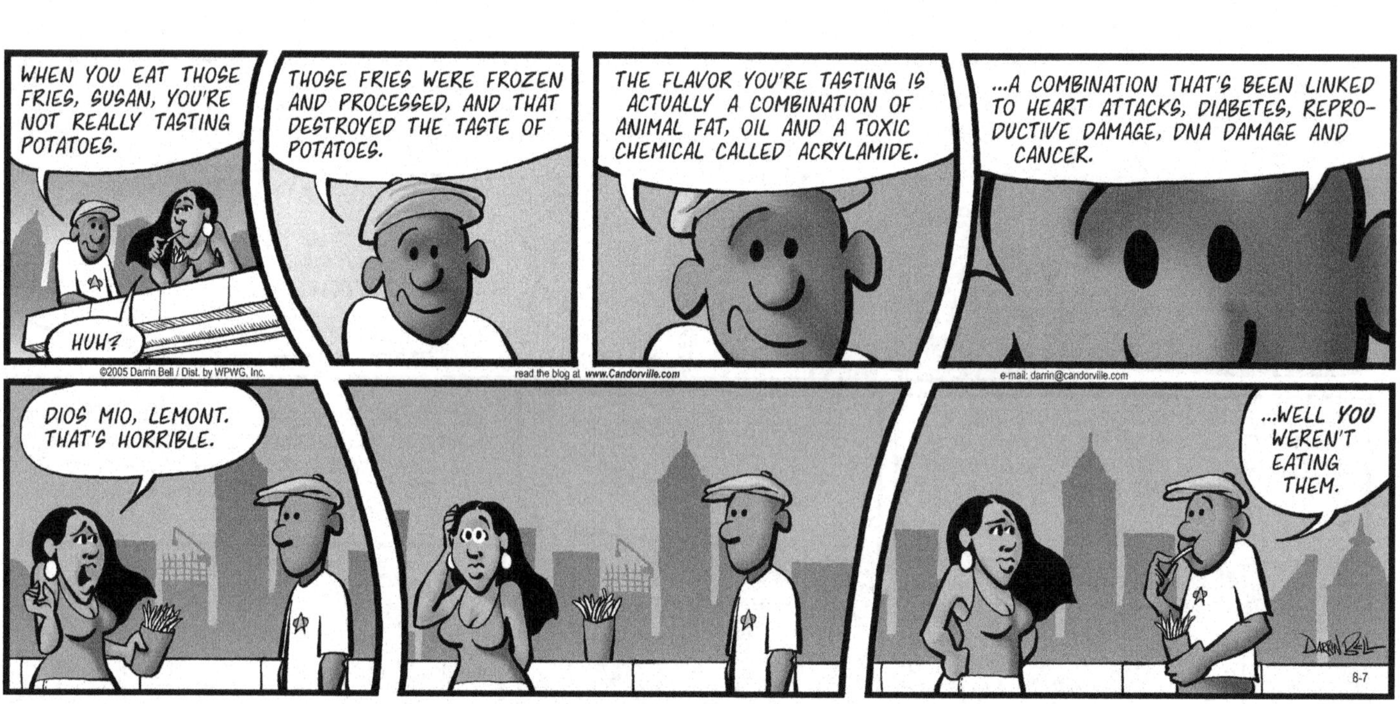
WHEN YOU EAT THOSE FRIES, SUSAN, YOU'RE NOT REALLY TASTING POTATOES.
HUH?
THOSE FRIES WERE FROZEN AND PROCESSED, AND THAT DESTROYED THE TASTE OF POTATOES.
THE FLAVOR YOU'RE TASTING IS ACTUALLY A COMBINATION OF ANIMAL FAT, OIL AND A TOXIC CHEMICAL CALLED ACRYLAMIDE.
...A COMBINATION THAT'S BEEN LINKED TO HEART ATTACKS, DIABETES, REPRODUCTIVE DAMAGE, DNA DAMAGE AND CANCER.
©2005 Darrin Bell / Dist. by WPWG, Inc.
read the blog at www.Candorville.com
e-mail: darrin@candorville.com
DIOS MIO, LEMONT. THAT'S HORRIBLE.
...WELL *YOU* WEREN'T EATING THEM.
DARRIN BELL
8-7

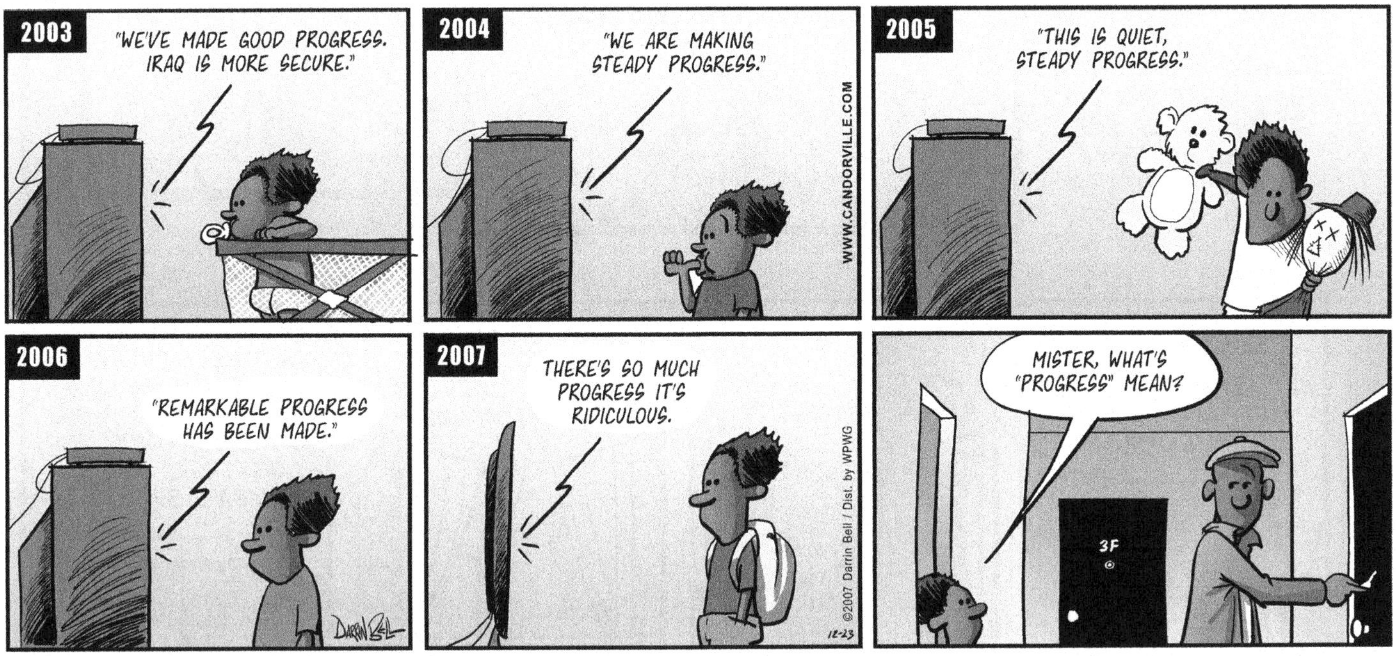
2003
"WE'VE MADE GOOD PROGRESS. IRAQ IS MORE SECURE."
2004
"WE ARE MAKING STEADY PROGRESS."
WWW.CANDORVILLE.COM
2005
"THIS IS QUIET, STEADY PROGRESS."
2006
"REMARKABLE PROGRESS HAS BEEN MADE."
DARRIN BELL
2007
THERE'S SO MUCH PROGRESS IT'S RIDICULOUS.
©2007 Darrin Bell / Dist. by WPWG
12-23
MISTER, WHAT'S "PROGRESS" MEAN?
3F

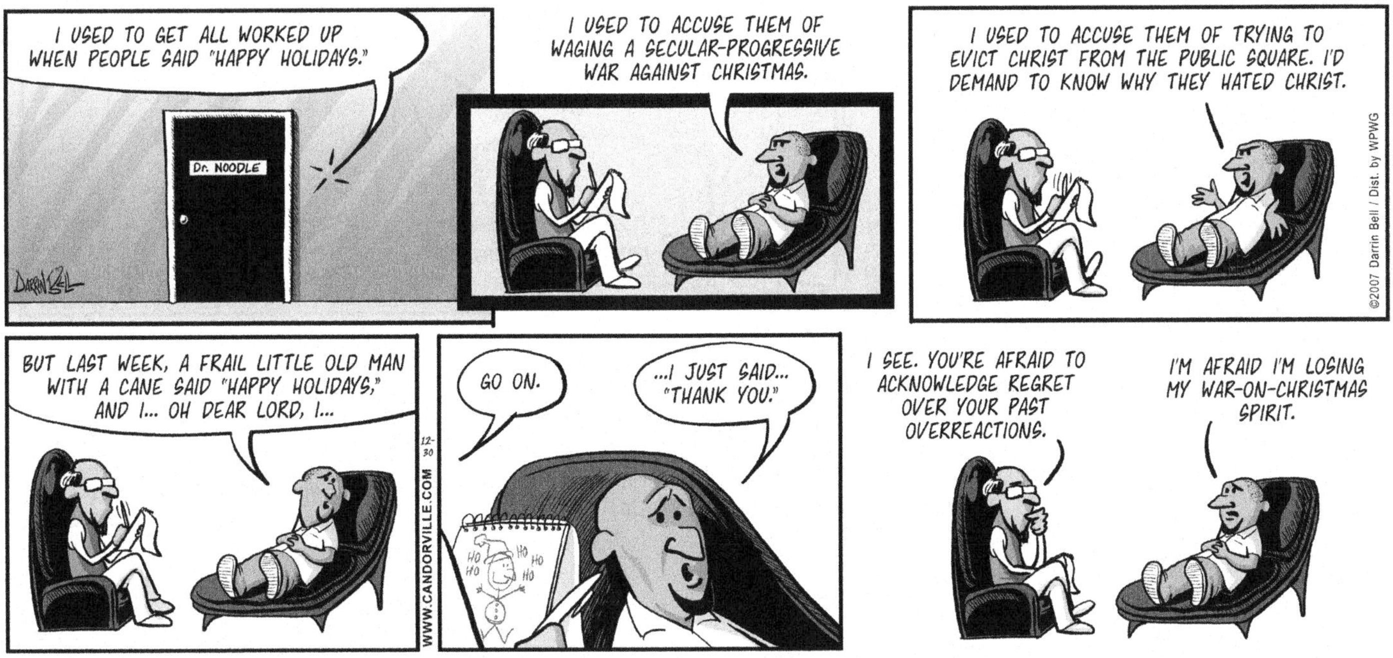
I USED TO GET ALL WORKED UP WHEN PEOPLE SAID "HAPPY HOLIDAYS."
Dr. NOODLE
DARRIN BELL
I USED TO ACCUSE THEM OF WAGING A SECULAR-PROGRESSIVE WAR AGAINST CHRISTMAS.
I USED TO ACCUSE THEM OF TRYING TO EVICT CHRIST FROM THE PUBLIC SQUARE. I'D DEMAND TO KNOW WHY THEY HATED CHRIST.
©2007 Darrin Bell / Dist. by WPWG
BUT LAST WEEK, A FRAIL LITTLE OLD MAN WITH A CANE SAID "HAPPY HOLIDAYS," AND I... OH DEAR LORD, I...
12-30
WWW.CANDORVILLE.COM
GO ON.
...I JUST SAID... "THANK YOU."
HO HO HO HO HO
I SEE. YOU'RE AFRAID TO ACKNOWLEDGE REGRET OVER YOUR PAST OVERREACTIONS.
I'M AFRAID I'M LOSING MY WAR-ON-CHRISTMAS SPIRIT.

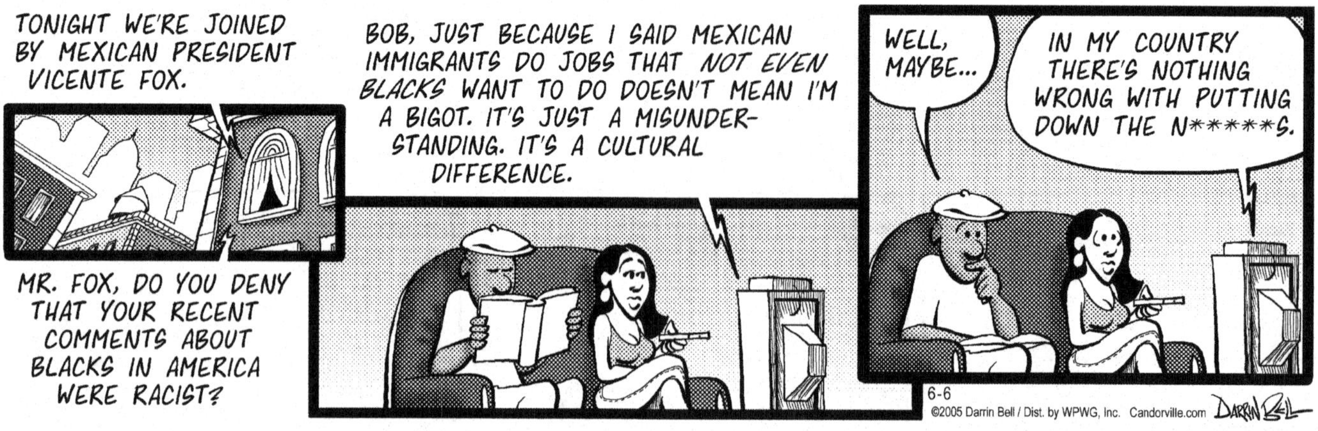
TONIGHT WE'RE JOINED BY MEXICAN PRESIDENT VICENTE FOX.
MR. FOX, DO YOU DENY THAT YOUR RECENT COMMENTS ABOUT BLACKS IN AMERICA WERE RACIST?
BOB, JUST BECAUSE I SAID MEXICAN IMMIGRANTS DO JOBS THAT *NOT EVEN BLACKS* WANT TO DO DOESN'T MEAN I'M A BIGOT. IT'S JUST A MISUNDERSTANDING. IT'S A CULTURAL DIFFERENCE.
WELL, MAYBE...
IN MY COUNTRY THERE'S NOTHING WRONG WITH PUTTING DOWN THE N*****S.
6-6
©2005 Darrin Bell / Dist. by WPWG, Inc. Candorville.com DARRIN BELL

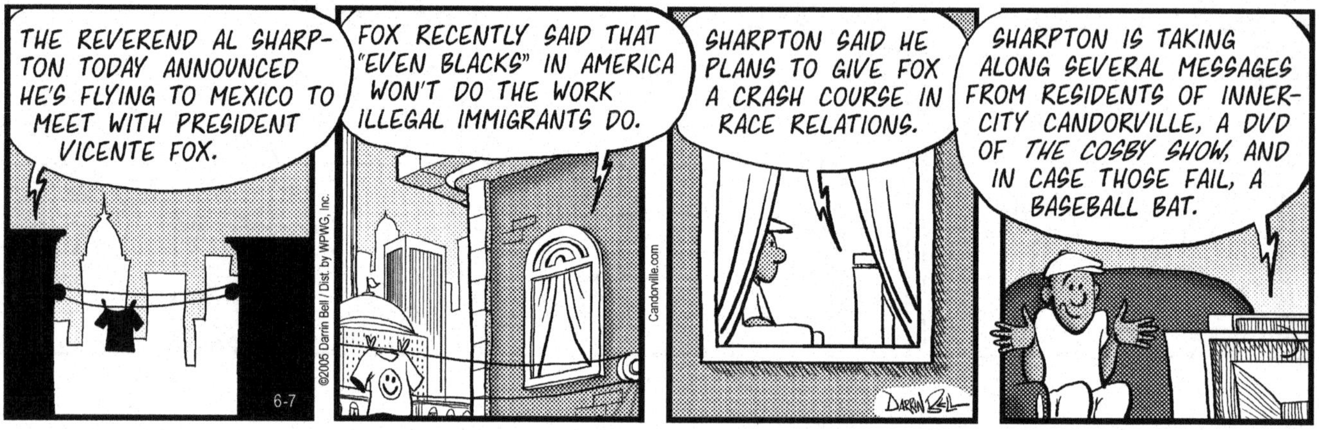
THE REVEREND AL SHARPTON TODAY ANNOUNCED HE'S FLYING TO MEXICO TO MEET WITH PRESIDENT VICENTE FOX.
6-7
©2005 Darrin Bell / Dist. by WPWG, Inc.
FOX RECENTLY SAID THAT "EVEN BLACKS" IN AMERICA WON'T DO THE WORK ILLEGAL IMMIGRANTS DO.
Candorville.com
SHARPTON SAID HE PLANS TO GIVE FOX A CRASH COURSE IN RACE RELATIONS.
DARRIN BELL
SHARPTON IS TAKING ALONG SEVERAL MESSAGES FROM RESIDENTS OF INNER-CITY CANDORVILLE, A DVD OF *THE COSBY SHOW,* AND IN CASE THOSE FAIL, A BASEBALL BAT.

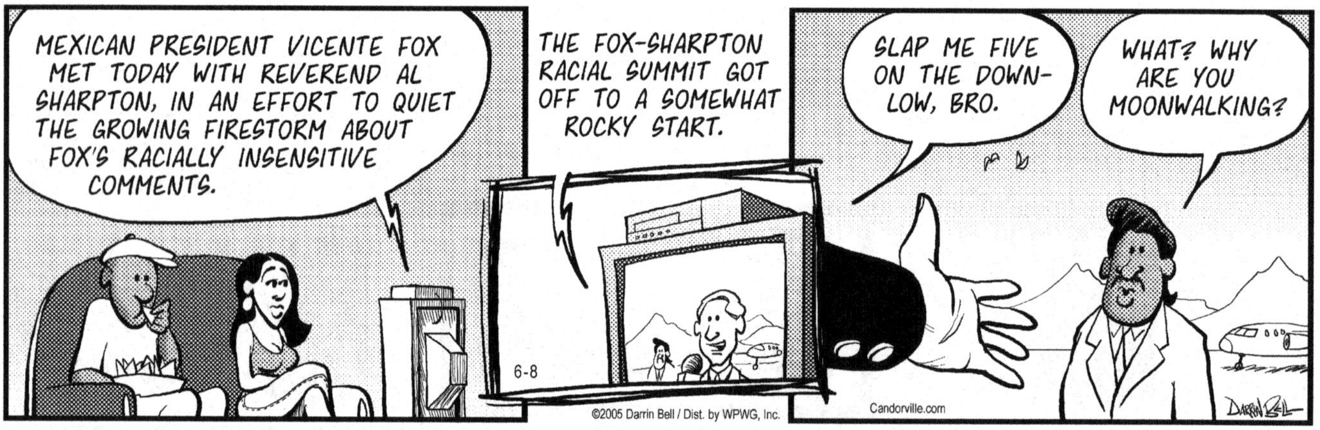
MEXICAN PRESIDENT VICENTE FOX MET TODAY WITH REVEREND AL SHARPTON, IN AN EFFORT TO QUIET THE GROWING FIRESTORM ABOUT FOX'S RACIALLY INSENSITIVE COMMENTS.
THE FOX-SHARPTON RACIAL SUMMIT GOT OFF TO A SOMEWHAT ROCKY START.
6-8
©2005 Darrin Bell / Dist. by WPWG, Inc.
SLAP ME FIVE ON THE DOWN-LOW, BRO.
WHAT? WHY ARE YOU MOONWALKING?
Candorville.com
DARRIN BELL

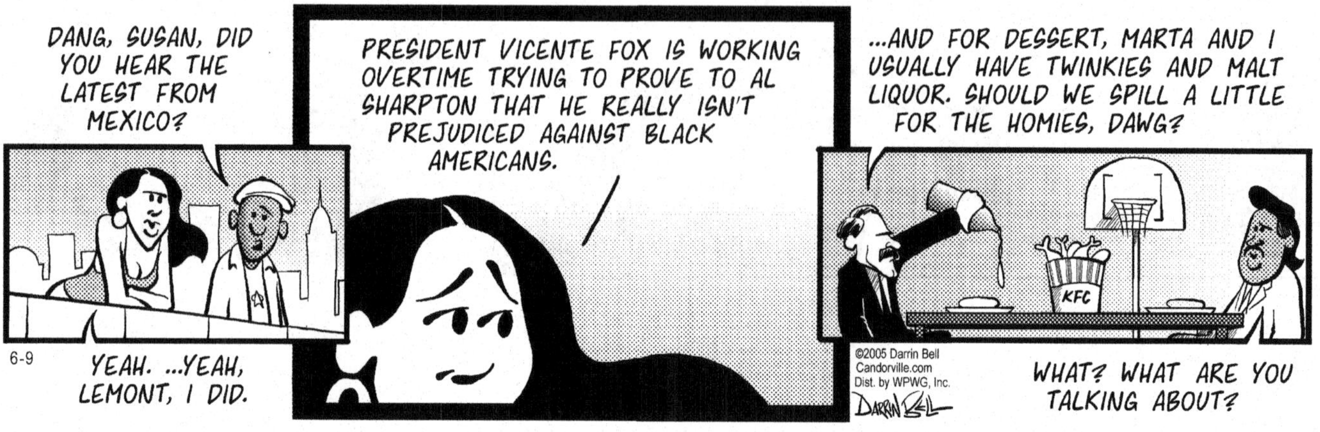
DANG, SUSAN, DID YOU HEAR THE LATEST FROM MEXICO?
YEAH. ...YEAH, LEMONT, I DID.
6-9
PRESIDENT VICENTE FOX IS WORKING OVERTIME TRYING TO PROVE TO AL SHARPTON THAT HE REALLY ISN'T PREJUDICED AGAINST BLACK AMERICANS.
...AND FOR DESSERT, MARTA AND I USUALLY HAVE TWINKIES AND MALT LIQUOR. SHOULD WE SPILL A LITTLE FOR THE HOMIES, DAWG?
KFC
WHAT? WHAT ARE YOU TALKING ABOUT?
©2005 Darrin Bell
Candorville.com
Dist. by WPWG, Inc.
DARRIN BELL

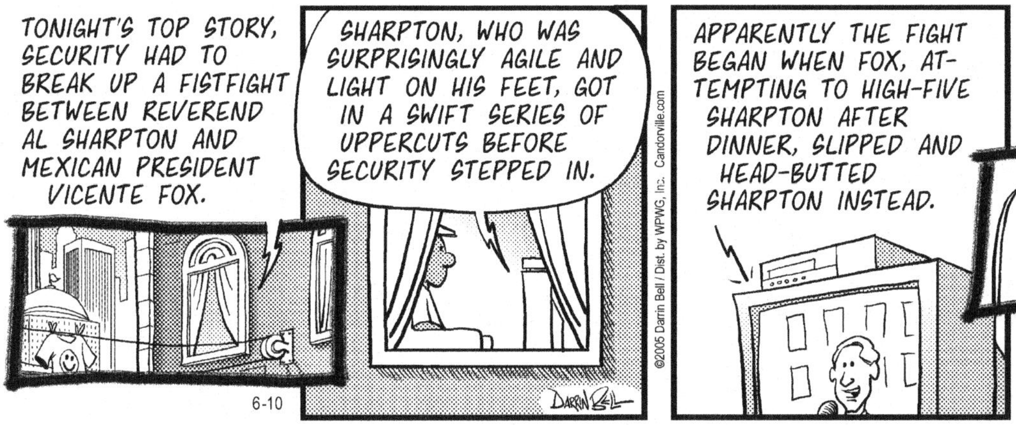
TONIGHT'S TOP STORY, SECURITY HAD TO BREAK UP A FISTFIGHT BETWEEN REVEREND AL SHARPTON AND MEXICAN PRESIDENT VICENTE FOX.
SHARPTON, WHO WAS SURPRISINGLY AGILE AND LIGHT ON HIS FEET, GOT IN A SWIFT SERIES OF UPPERCUTS BEFORE SECURITY STEPPED IN.
APPARENTLY THE FIGHT BEGAN WHEN FOX, ATTEMPTING TO HIGH-FIVE SHARPTON AFTER DINNER, SLIPPED AND HEAD-BUTTED SHARPTON INSTEAD.
DON'T YOU PEOPLE HAVE A WAR IN THE MIDDLE EAST TO COVER?
...IN OTHER NEWS, MICHAEL JACKSON IS STILL WEIRD.
6-10
©2005 Darrin Bell / Dist. by WPWG, Inc. Candorville.com
DARRIN BELL

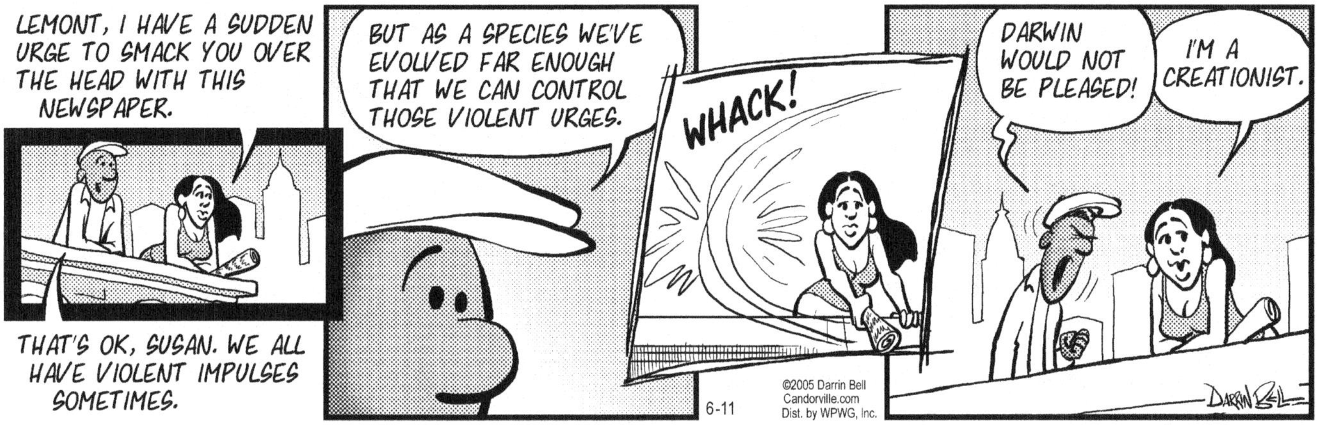
LEMONT, I HAVE A SUDDEN URGE TO SMACK YOU OVER THE HEAD WITH THIS NEWSPAPER.
THAT'S OK, SUSAN. WE ALL HAVE VIOLENT IMPULSES SOMETIMES.
BUT AS A SPECIES WE'VE EVOLVED FAR ENOUGH THAT WE CAN CONTROL THOSE VIOLENT URGES.
WHACK!
DARWIN WOULD NOT BE PLEASED!
I'M A CREATIONIST.
6-11
©2005 Darrin Bell Candorville.com Dist. by WPWG, Inc.
DARRIN BELL

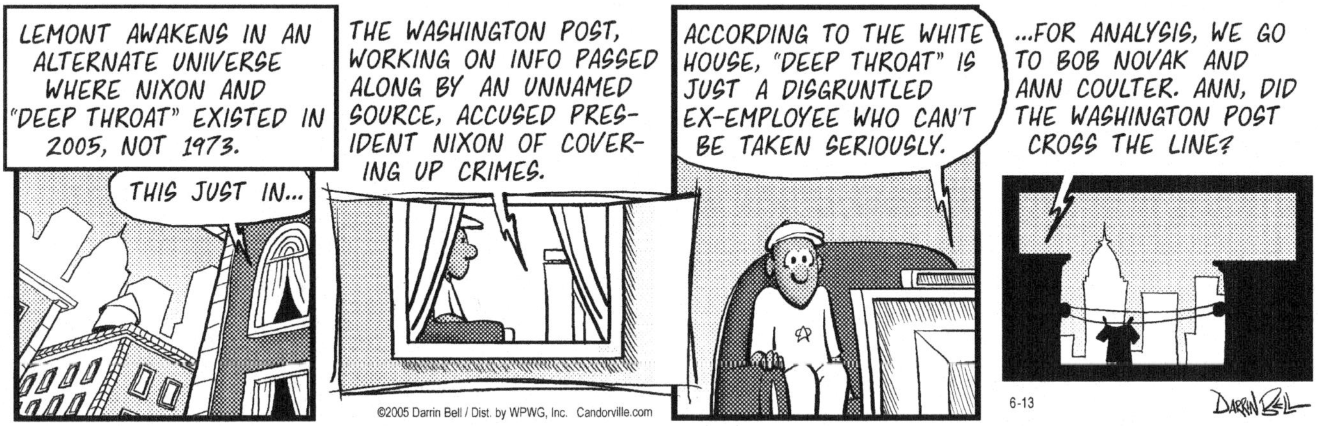
LEMONT AWAKENS IN AN ALTERNATE UNIVERSE WHERE NIXON AND "DEEP THROAT" EXISTED IN 2005, NOT 1973.
THIS JUST IN...
THE WASHINGTON POST, WORKING ON INFO PASSED ALONG BY AN UNNAMED SOURCE, ACCUSED PRESIDENT NIXON OF COVERING UP CRIMES.
ACCORDING TO THE WHITE HOUSE, "DEEP THROAT" IS JUST A DISGRUNTLED EX-EMPLOYEE WHO CAN'T BE TAKEN SERIOUSLY.
...FOR ANALYSIS, WE GO TO BOB NOVAK AND ANN COULTER. ANN, DID THE WASHINGTON POST CROSS THE LINE?
©2005 Darrin Bell / Dist. by WPWG, Inc. Candorville.com
6-13
DARRIN BELL

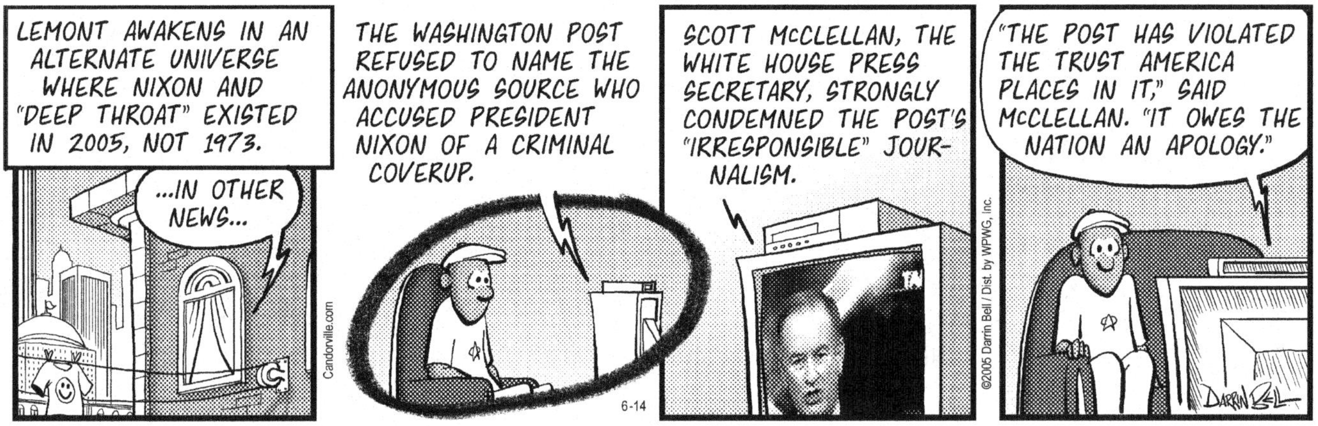
LEMONT AWAKENS IN AN ALTERNATE UNIVERSE WHERE NIXON AND "DEEP THROAT" EXISTED IN 2005, NOT 1973.
...IN OTHER NEWS...
THE WASHINGTON POST REFUSED TO NAME THE ANONYMOUS SOURCE WHO ACCUSED PRESIDENT NIXON OF A CRIMINAL COVERUP.
SCOTT McCLELLAN, THE WHITE HOUSE PRESS SECRETARY, STRONGLY CONDEMNED THE POST'S "IRRESPONSIBLE" JOURNALISM.
"THE POST HAS VIOLATED THE TRUST AMERICA PLACES IN IT," SAID McCLELLAN. "IT OWES THE NATION AN APOLOGY."
Candorville.com
6-14
©2005 Darrin Bell / Dist. by WPWG, Inc.
DARRIN BELL

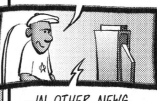

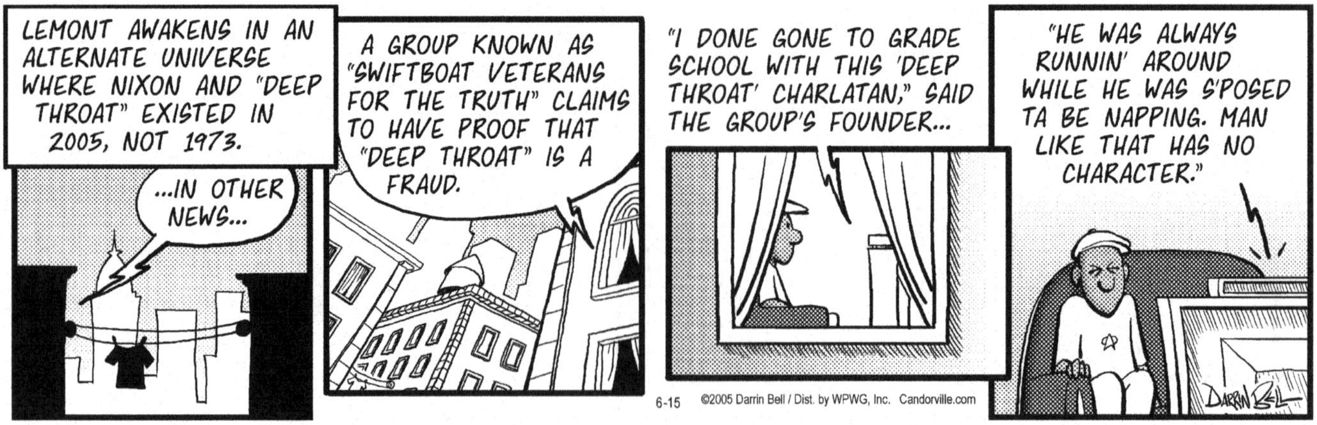
LEMONT AWAKENS IN AN ALTERNATE UNIVERSE WHERE NIXON AND "DEEP THROAT" EXISTED IN 2005, NOT 1973.
...IN OTHER NEWS...
A GROUP KNOWN AS "SWIFTBOAT VETERANS FOR THE TRUTH" CLAIMS TO HAVE PROOF THAT "DEEP THROAT" IS A FRAUD.
"I DONE GONE TO GRADE SCHOOL WITH THIS 'DEEP THROAT' CHARLATAN," SAID THE GROUP'S FOUNDER...
"HE WAS ALWAYS RUNNIN' AROUND WHILE HE WAS S'POSED TA BE NAPPING. MAN LIKE THAT HAS NO CHARACTER."
6-15 ©2005 Darrin Bell / Dist. by WPWG, Inc. Candorville.com
DARRIN BELL

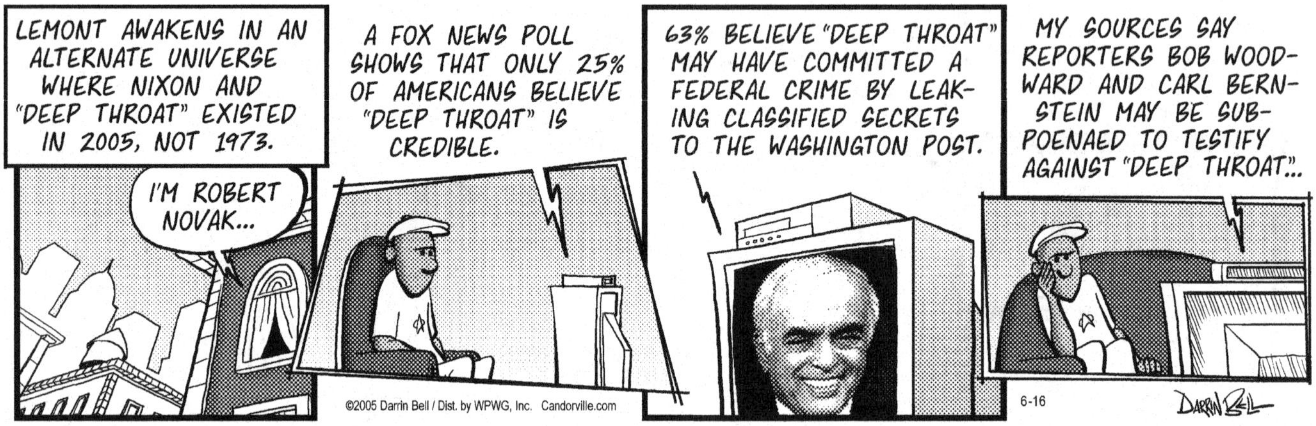
LEMONT AWAKENS IN AN ALTERNATE UNIVERSE WHERE NIXON AND "DEEP THROAT" EXISTED IN 2005, NOT 1973.
I'M ROBERT NOVAK...
A FOX NEWS POLL SHOWS THAT ONLY 25% OF AMERICANS BELIEVE "DEEP THROAT" IS CREDIBLE.
©2005 Darrin Bell / Dist. by WPWG, Inc. Candorville.com
63% BELIEVE "DEEP THROAT" MAY HAVE COMMITTED A FEDERAL CRIME BY LEAKING CLASSIFIED SECRETS TO THE WASHINGTON POST.
MY SOURCES SAY REPORTERS BOB WOODWARD AND CARL BERNSTEIN MAY BE SUBPOENAED TO TESTIFY AGAINST "DEEP THROAT"...
6-16
DARRIN BELL

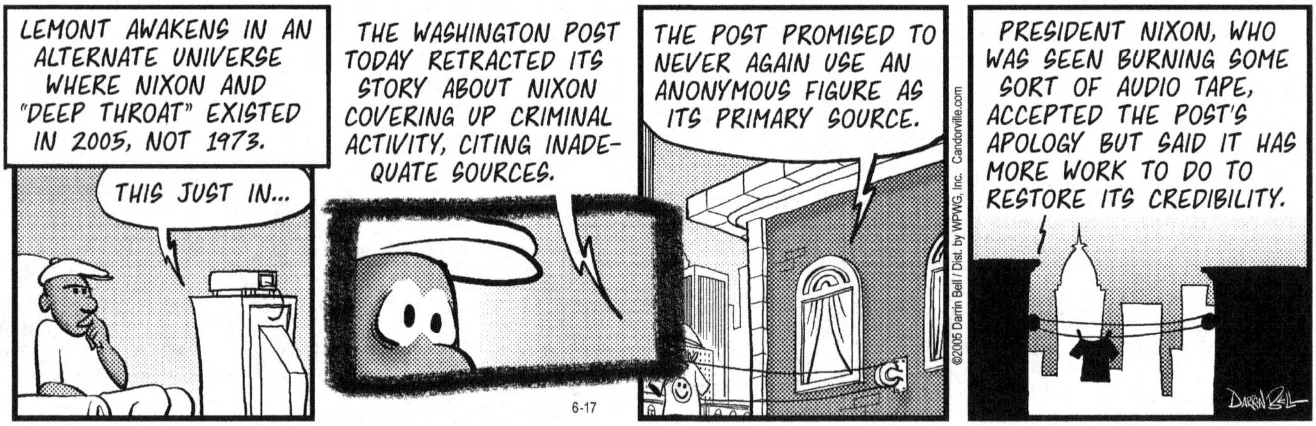
LEMONT AWAKENS IN AN ALTERNATE UNIVERSE WHERE NIXON AND "DEEP THROAT" EXISTED IN 2005, NOT 1973.
THIS JUST IN...
THE WASHINGTON POST TODAY RETRACTED ITS STORY ABOUT NIXON COVERING UP CRIMINAL ACTIVITY, CITING INADEQUATE SOURCES.
6-17
THE POST PROMISED TO NEVER AGAIN USE AN ANONYMOUS FIGURE AS ITS PRIMARY SOURCE.
©2005 Darrin Bell / Dist. by WPWG, Inc. Candorville.com
PRESIDENT NIXON, WHO WAS SEEN BURNING SOME SORT OF AUDIO TAPE, ACCEPTED THE POST'S APOLOGY BUT SAID IT HAS MORE WORK TO DO TO RESTORE ITS CREDIBILITY.
DARRIN BELL

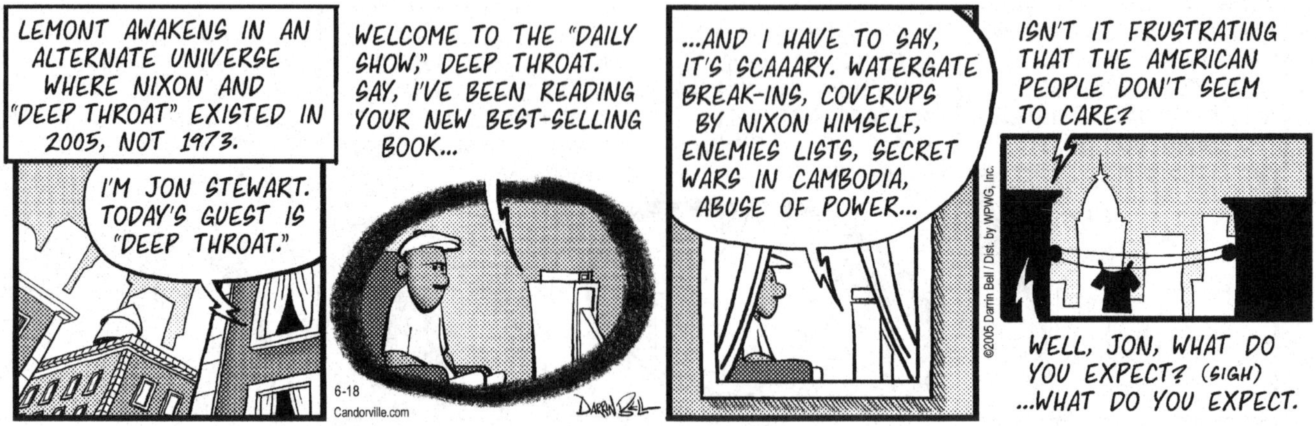
LEMONT AWAKENS IN AN ALTERNATE UNIVERSE WHERE NIXON AND "DEEP THROAT" EXISTED IN 2005, NOT 1973.
I'M JON STEWART. TODAY'S GUEST IS "DEEP THROAT."
WELCOME TO THE "DAILY SHOW," DEEP THROAT. SAY, I'VE BEEN READING YOUR NEW BEST-SELLING BOOK...
6-18
Candorville.com
DARRIN BELL
...AND I HAVE TO SAY, IT'S SCAAARY. WATERGATE BREAK-INS, COVERUPS BY NIXON HIMSELF, ENEMIES LISTS, SECRET WARS IN CAMBODIA, ABUSE OF POWER...
©2005 Darrin Bell / Dist. by WPWG, Inc.
ISN'T IT FRUSTRATING THAT THE AMERICAN PEOPLE DON'T SEEM TO CARE?
WELL, JON, WHAT DO YOU EXPECT? (SIGH) ...WHAT DO YOU EXPECT.

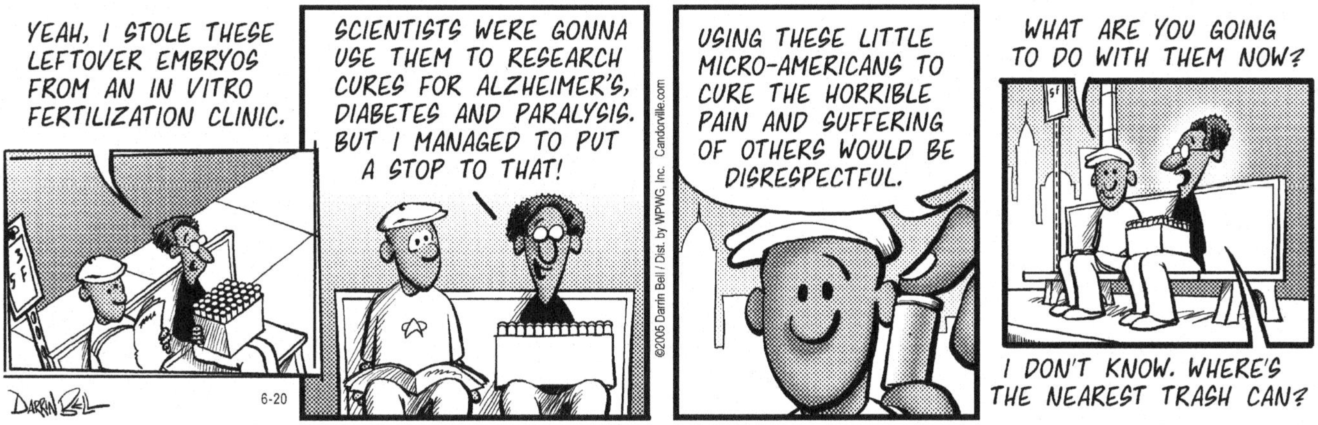
YEAH, I STOLE THESE LEFTOVER EMBRYOS FROM AN IN VITRO FERTILIZATION CLINIC.
SCIENTISTS WERE GONNA USE THEM TO RESEARCH CURES FOR ALZHEIMER'S, DIABETES AND PARALYSIS. BUT I MANAGED TO PUT A STOP TO THAT!
USING THESE LITTLE MICRO-AMERICANS TO CURE THE HORRIBLE PAIN AND SUFFERING OF OTHERS WOULD BE DISRESPECTFUL.
WHAT ARE YOU GOING TO DO WITH THEM NOW?
I DON'T KNOW. WHERE'S THE NEAREST TRASH CAN?
DARRIN BELL
6-20
©2005 Darrin Bell / Dist. by WPWG, Inc. Candorville.com

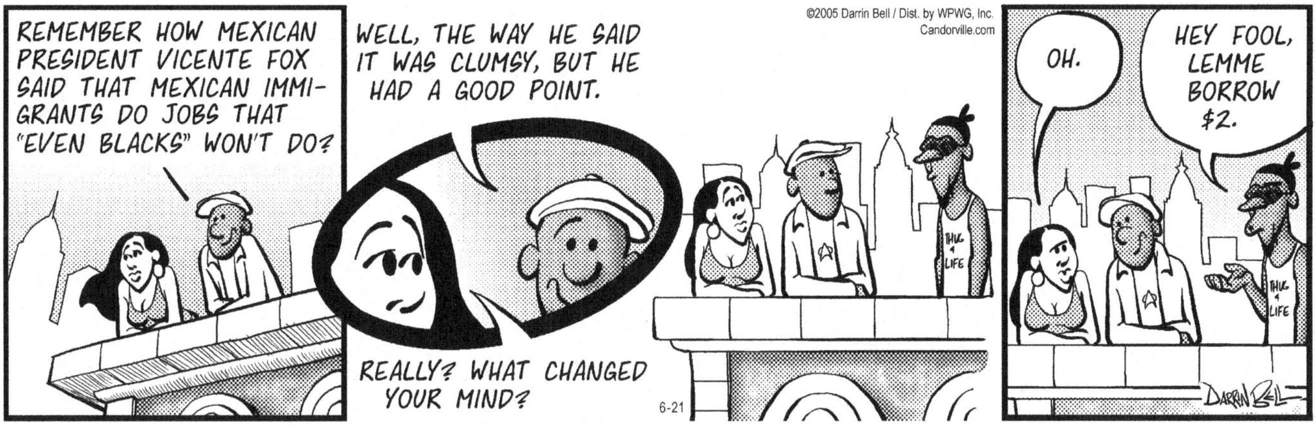
REMEMBER HOW MEXICAN PRESIDENT VICENTE FOX SAID THAT MEXICAN IMMIGRANTS DO JOBS THAT "EVEN BLACKS" WON'T DO?
WELL, THE WAY HE SAID IT WAS CLUMSY, BUT HE HAD A GOOD POINT.
REALLY? WHAT CHANGED YOUR MIND?
OH.
HEY FOOL, LEMME BORROW $2.
©2005 Darrin Bell / Dist. by WPWG, Inc. Candorville.com
6-21
DARRIN BELL

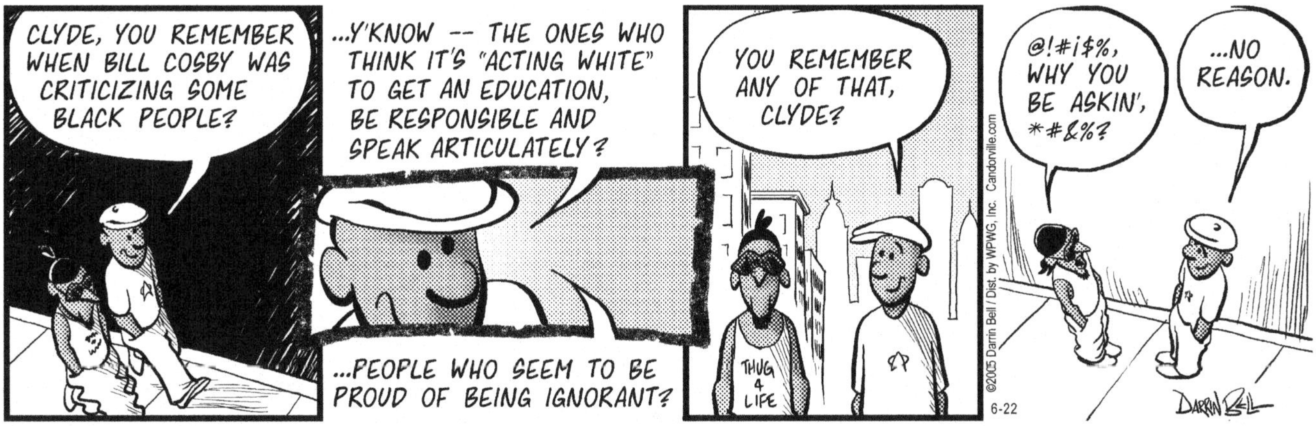
CLYDE, YOU REMEMBER WHEN BILL COSBY WAS CRITICIZING SOME BLACK PEOPLE?
...Y'KNOW -- THE ONES WHO THINK IT'S "ACTING WHITE" TO GET AN EDUCATION, BE RESPONSIBLE AND SPEAK ARTICULATELY?
...PEOPLE WHO SEEM TO BE PROUD OF BEING IGNORANT?
YOU REMEMBER ANY OF THAT, CLYDE?
@!#i$%, WHY YOU BE ASKIN', *#&%?
...NO REASON.
©2005 Darrin Bell / Dist. by WPWG, Inc. Candorville.com
6-22
DARRIN BELL

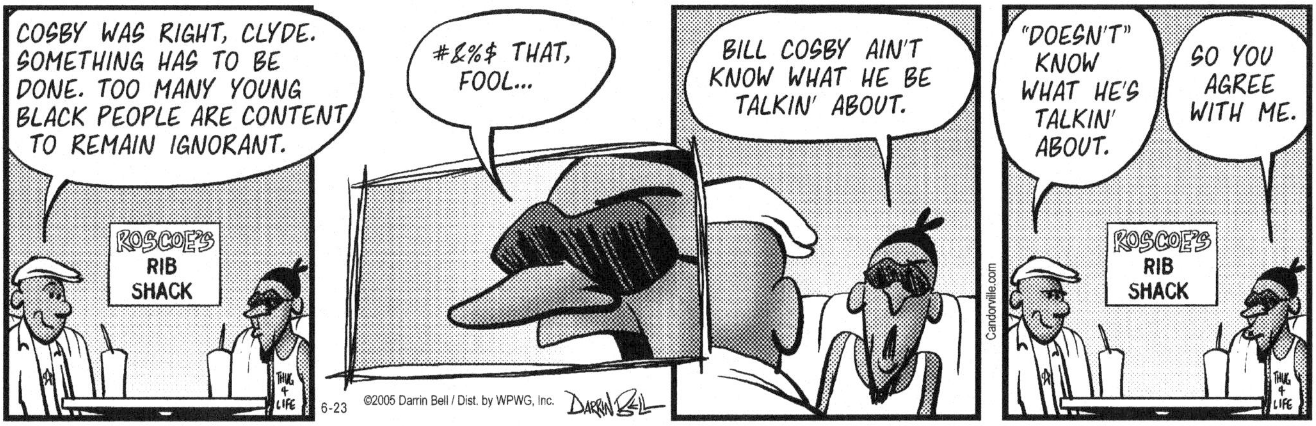
COSBY WAS RIGHT, CLYDE. SOMETHING HAS TO BE DONE. TOO MANY YOUNG BLACK PEOPLE ARE CONTENT TO REMAIN IGNORANT.
ROSCOE'S RIB SHACK
#&%$ THAT, FOOL...
BILL COSBY AIN'T KNOW WHAT HE BE TALKIN' ABOUT.
"DOESN'T" KNOW WHAT HE'S TALKIN' ABOUT.
SO YOU AGREE WITH ME.
ROSCOE'S RIB SHACK
6-23
©2005 Darrin Bell / Dist. by WPWG, Inc.
DARRIN BELL
Candorville.com

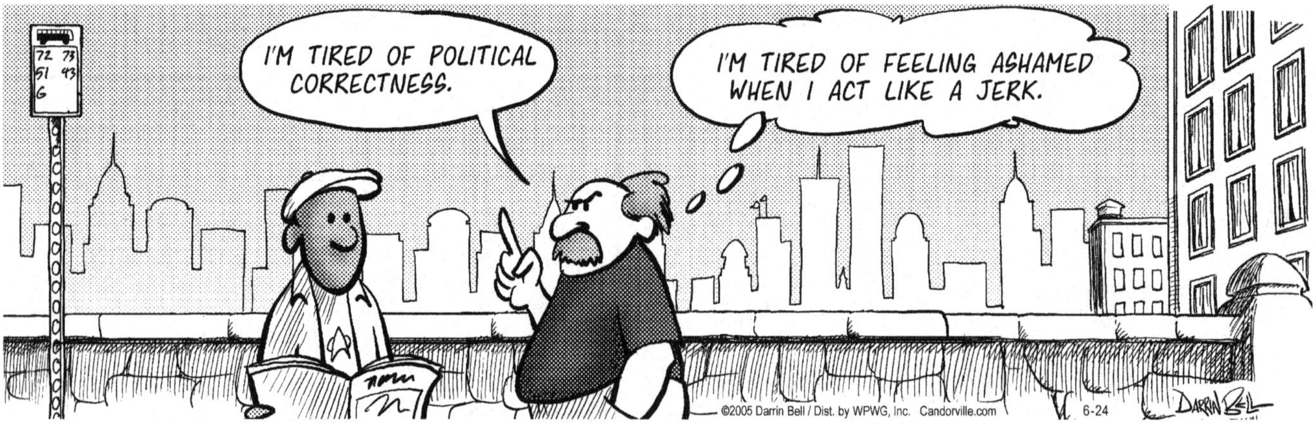
72 73 51 93 G
I'M TIRED OF POLITICAL CORRECTNESS.
I'M TIRED OF FEELING ASHAMED WHEN I ACT LIKE A JERK.
©2005 Darrin Bell / Dist. by WPWG, Inc. Candorville.com
6-24
DARRIN BELL

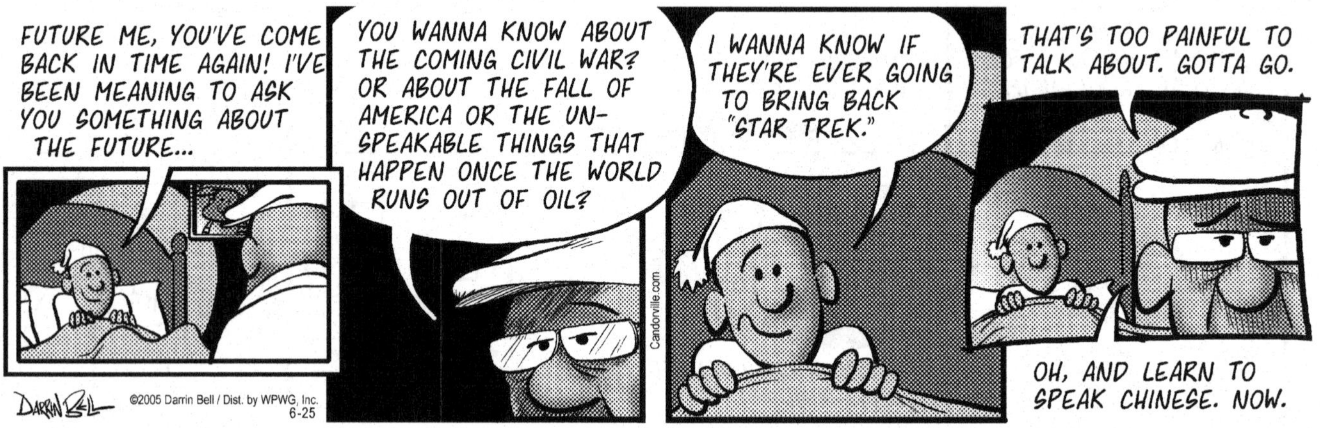
FUTURE ME, YOU'VE COME BACK IN TIME AGAIN! I'VE BEEN MEANING TO ASK YOU SOMETHING ABOUT THE FUTURE...
YOU WANNA KNOW ABOUT THE COMING CIVIL WAR? OR ABOUT THE FALL OF AMERICA OR THE UNSPEAKABLE THINGS THAT HAPPEN ONCE THE WORLD RUNS OUT OF OIL?
I WANNA KNOW IF THEY'RE EVER GOING TO BRING BACK "STAR TREK."
THAT'S TOO PAINFUL TO TALK ABOUT. GOTTA GO.
OH, AND LEARN TO SPEAK CHINESE. NOW.
DARRIN BELL
©2005 Darrin Bell / Dist. by WPWG, Inc.
6-25
Candorville.com

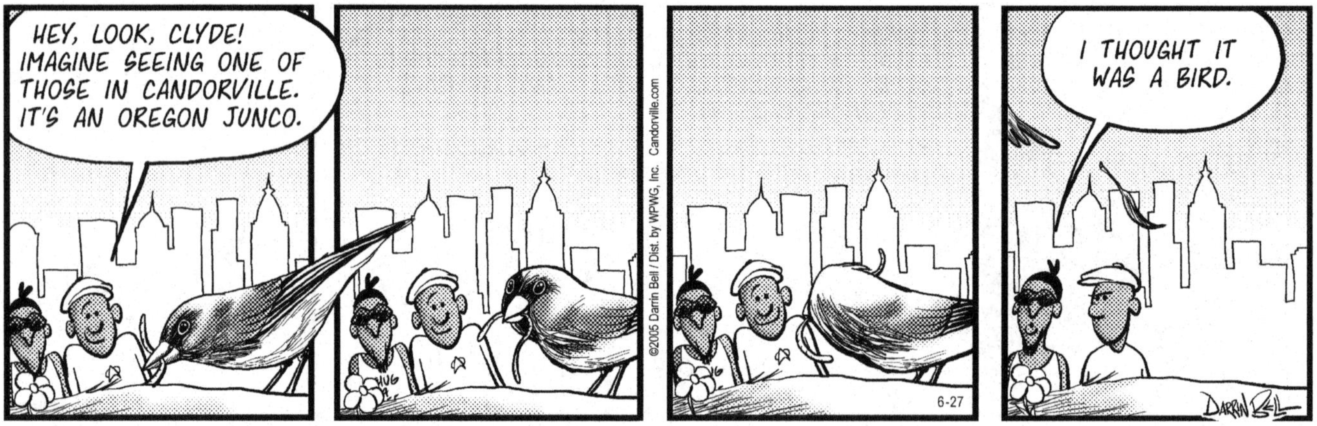
HEY, LOOK, CLYDE! IMAGINE SEEING ONE OF THOSE IN CANDORVILLE. IT'S AN OREGON JUNCO.
©2005 Darrin Bell / Dist. by WPWG, Inc. Candorville.com
6-27
I THOUGHT IT WAS A BIRD.
DARRIN BELL

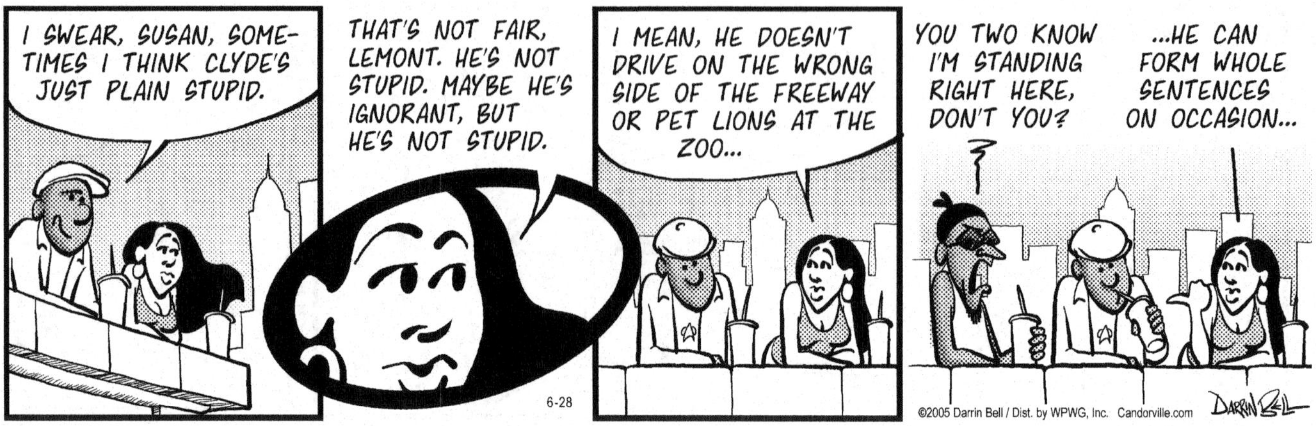
I SWEAR, SUSAN, SOMETIMES I THINK CLYDE'S JUST PLAIN STUPID.
THAT'S NOT FAIR, LEMONT. HE'S NOT STUPID. MAYBE HE'S IGNORANT, BUT HE'S NOT STUPID.
6-28
I MEAN, HE DOESN'T DRIVE ON THE WRONG SIDE OF THE FREEWAY OR PET LIONS AT THE ZOO...
YOU TWO KNOW I'M STANDING RIGHT HERE, DON'T YOU?
...HE CAN FORM WHOLE SENTENCES ON OCCASION...
©2005 Darrin Bell / Dist. by WPWG, Inc. Candorville.com
DARRIN BELL

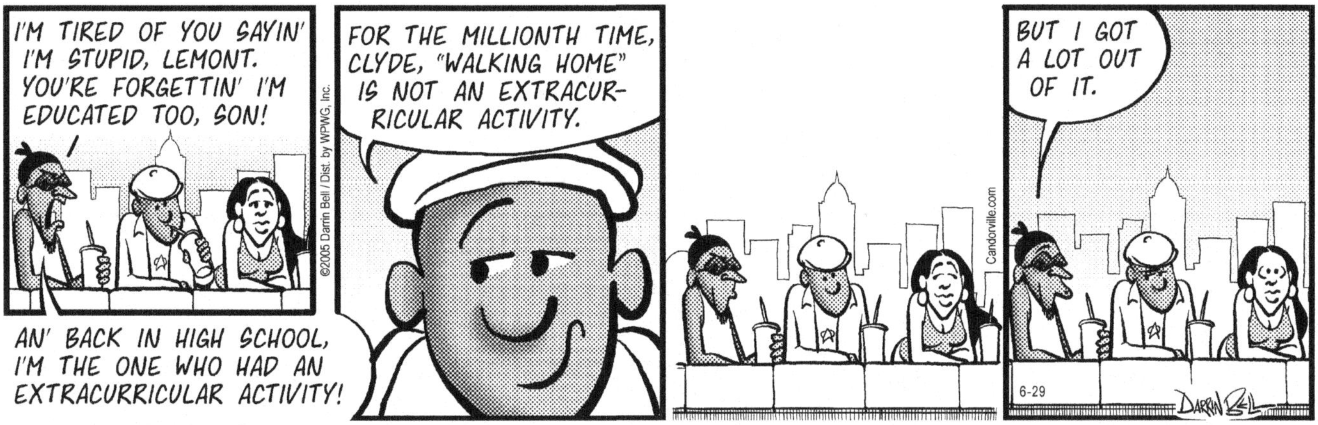
I'M TIRED OF YOU SAYIN' I'M STUPID, LEMONT. YOU'RE FORGETTIN' I'M EDUCATED TOO, SON!
AN' BACK IN HIGH SCHOOL, I'M THE ONE WHO HAD AN EXTRACURRICULAR ACTIVITY!
FOR THE MILLIONTH TIME, CLYDE, "WALKING HOME" IS NOT AN EXTRACURRICULAR ACTIVITY.
BUT I GOT A LOT OUT OF IT.
©2005 Darrin Bell / Dist. by WPWG, Inc.
Candorville.com
6-29
DARRIN BELL

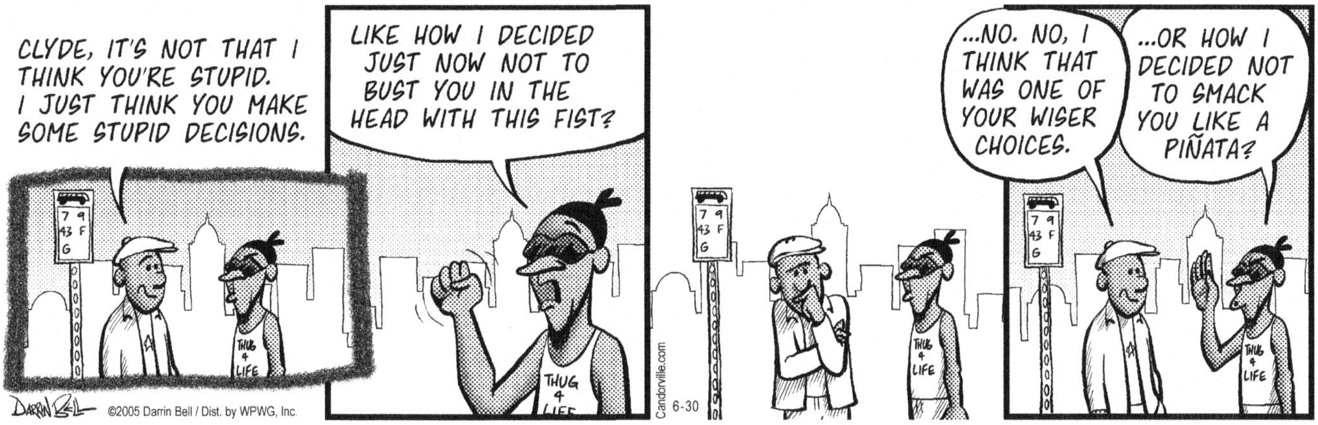
CLYDE, IT'S NOT THAT I THINK YOU'RE STUPID. I JUST THINK YOU MAKE SOME STUPID DECISIONS.
LIKE HOW I DECIDED JUST NOW NOT TO BUST YOU IN THE HEAD WITH THIS FIST?
...NO. NO, I THINK THAT WAS ONE OF YOUR WISER CHOICES.
...OR HOW I DECIDED NOT TO SMACK YOU LIKE A PIÑATA?
DARRIN BELL ©2005 Darrin Bell / Dist. by WPWG, Inc.
Candorville.com
6-30

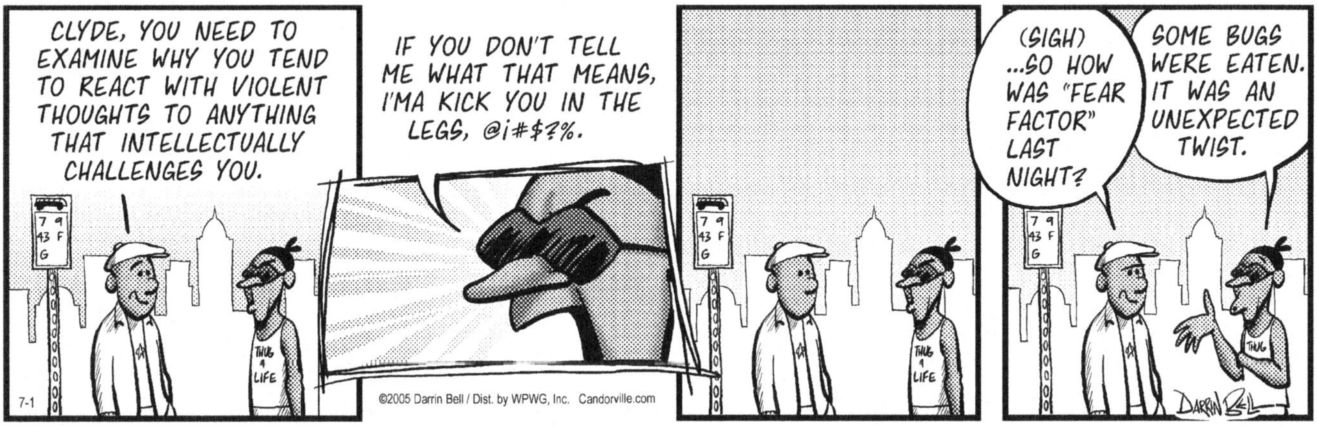
CLYDE, YOU NEED TO EXAMINE WHY YOU TEND TO REACT WITH VIOLENT THOUGHTS TO ANYTHING THAT INTELLECTUALLY CHALLENGES YOU.
IF YOU DON'T TELL ME WHAT THAT MEANS, I'MA KICK YOU IN THE LEGS, @i#$?%.
(SIGH) ...SO HOW WAS "FEAR FACTOR" LAST NIGHT?
SOME BUGS WERE EATEN. IT WAS AN UNEXPECTED TWIST.
7-1
©2005 Darrin Bell / Dist. by WPWG, Inc. Candorville.com
DARRIN BELL

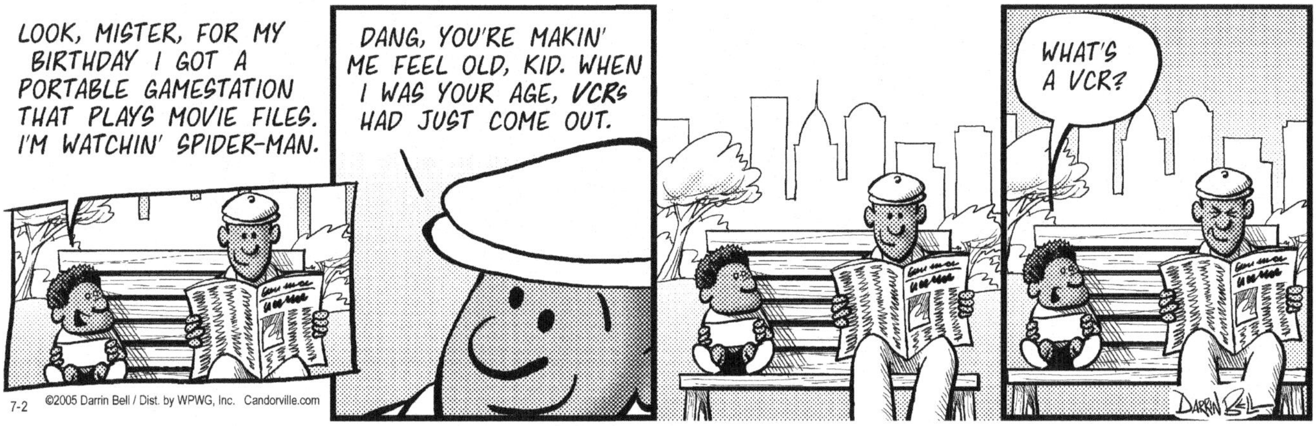
LOOK, MISTER, FOR MY BIRTHDAY I GOT A PORTABLE GAMESTATION THAT PLAYS MOVIE FILES. I'M WATCHIN' SPIDER-MAN.
DANG, YOU'RE MAKIN' ME FEEL OLD, KID. WHEN I WAS YOUR AGE, ***VCRs*** HAD JUST COME OUT.
WHAT'S A VCR?
7-2 ©2005 Darrin Bell / Dist. by WPWG, Inc. Candorville.com
DARRIN BELL

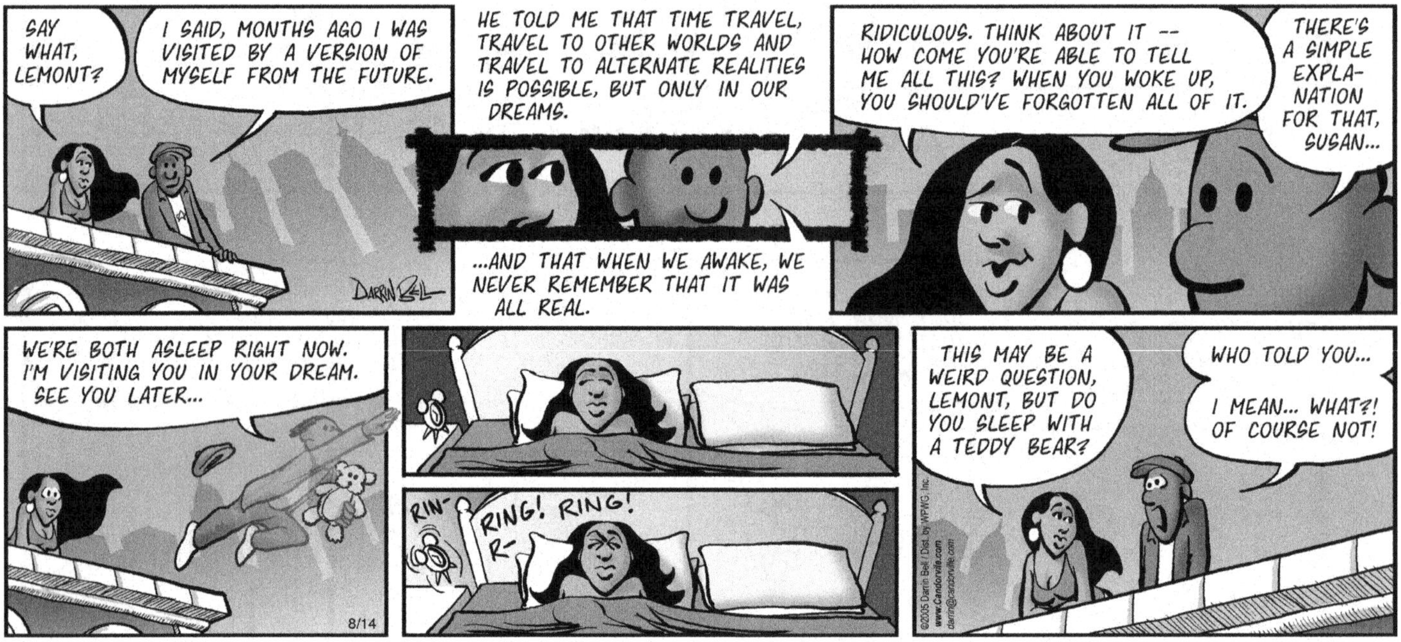
SAY WHAT, LEMONT?
I SAID, MONTHS AGO I WAS VISITED BY A VERSION OF MYSELF FROM THE FUTURE.
DARRIN BELL
HE TOLD ME THAT TIME TRAVEL, TRAVEL TO OTHER WORLDS AND TRAVEL TO ALTERNATE REALITIES IS POSSIBLE, BUT ONLY IN OUR DREAMS.
...AND THAT WHEN WE AWAKE, WE NEVER REMEMBER THAT IT WAS ALL REAL.
RIDICULOUS. THINK ABOUT IT -- HOW COME YOU'RE ABLE TO TELL ME ALL THIS? WHEN YOU WOKE UP, YOU SHOULD'VE FORGOTTEN ALL OF IT.
THERE'S A SIMPLE EXPLANATION FOR THAT, SUSAN...
WE'RE BOTH ASLEEP RIGHT NOW. I'M VISITING YOU IN YOUR DREAM. SEE YOU LATER...
8/14
RIN-
RING! RING! R-
©2005 Darrin Bell / Dist. by WPWG, Inc. www.Candorville.com darrin@candorville.com
THIS MAY BE A WEIRD QUESTION, LEMONT, BUT DO YOU SLEEP WITH A TEDDY BEAR?
WHO TOLD YOU...
I MEAN... WHAT?! OF COURSE NOT!

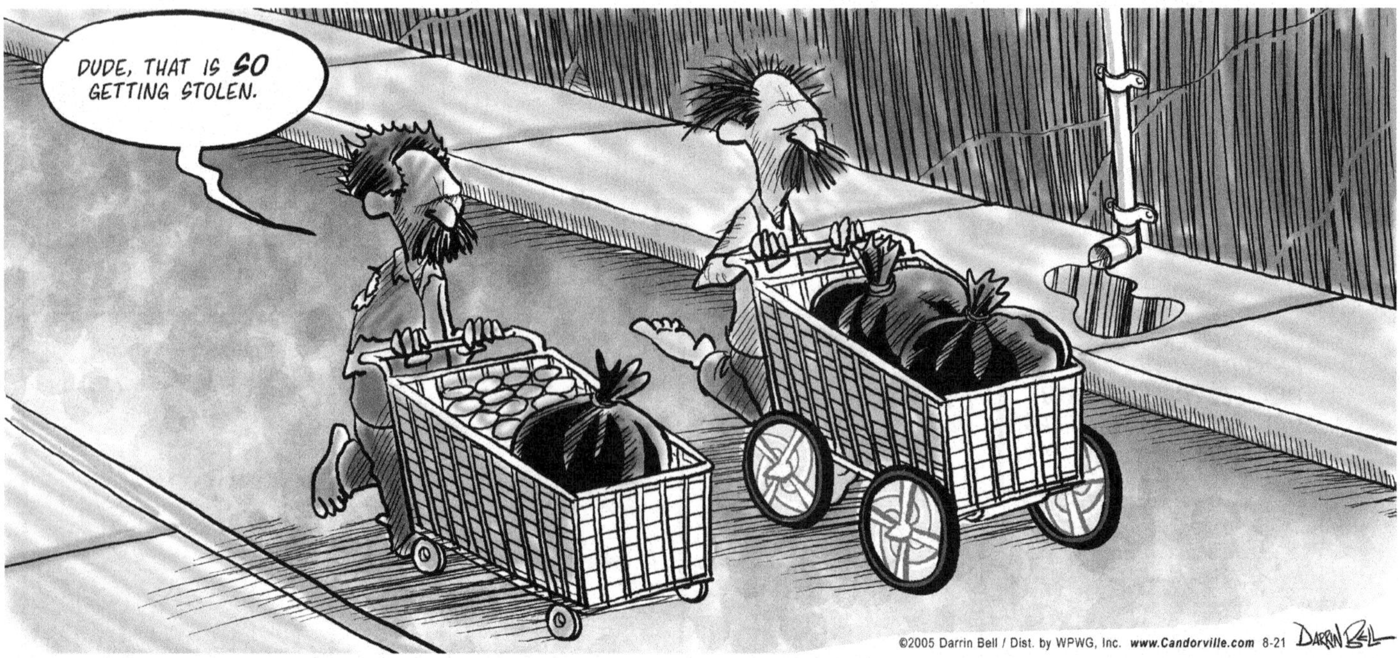
DUDE, THAT IS SO GETTING STOLEN.
©2005 Darrin Bell / Dist. by WPWG, Inc. www.Candorville.com 8-21
DARRIN BELL

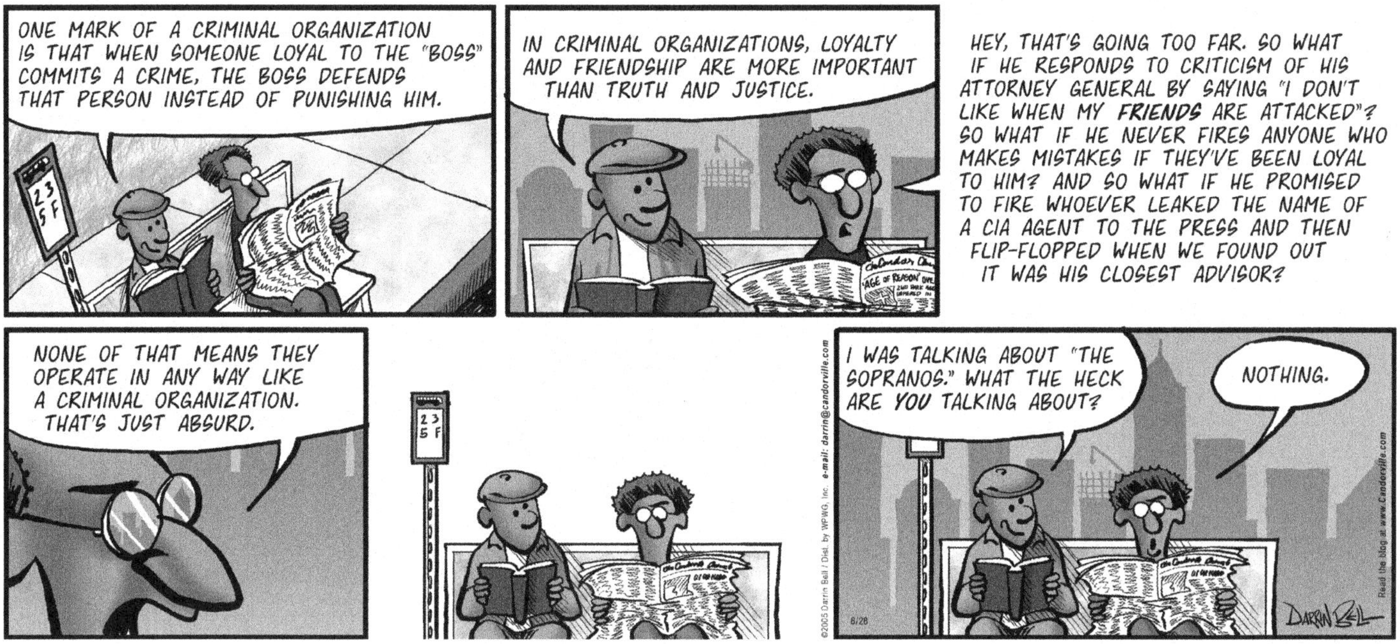
ONE MARK OF A CRIMINAL ORGANIZATION IS THAT WHEN SOMEONE LOYAL TO THE "BOSS" COMMITS A CRIME, THE BOSS DEFENDS THAT PERSON INSTEAD OF PUNISHING HIM.
23 5 F
IN CRIMINAL ORGANIZATIONS, LOYALTY AND FRIENDSHIP ARE MORE IMPORTANT THAN TRUTH AND JUSTICE.
HEY, THAT'S GOING TOO FAR. SO WHAT IF HE RESPONDS TO CRITICISM OF HIS ATTORNEY GENERAL BY SAYING "I DON'T LIKE WHEN MY **FRIENDS** ARE ATTACKED"? SO WHAT IF HE NEVER FIRES ANYONE WHO MAKES MISTAKES IF THEY'VE BEEN LOYAL TO HIM? AND SO WHAT IF HE PROMISED TO FIRE WHOEVER LEAKED THE NAME OF A CIA AGENT TO THE PRESS AND THEN FLIP-FLOPPED WHEN WE FOUND OUT IT WAS HIS CLOSEST ADVISOR?
NONE OF THAT MEANS THEY OPERATE IN ANY WAY LIKE A CRIMINAL ORGANIZATION. THAT'S JUST ABSURD.
23 5 F
©2005 Darrin Bell / Dist. by WPWG, Inc. e-mail: darrin@candorville.com
I WAS TALKING ABOUT "THE SOPRANOS." WHAT THE HECK ARE **YOU** TALKING ABOUT?
NOTHING.
Read the blog at www.Candorville.com
DARRIN BELL

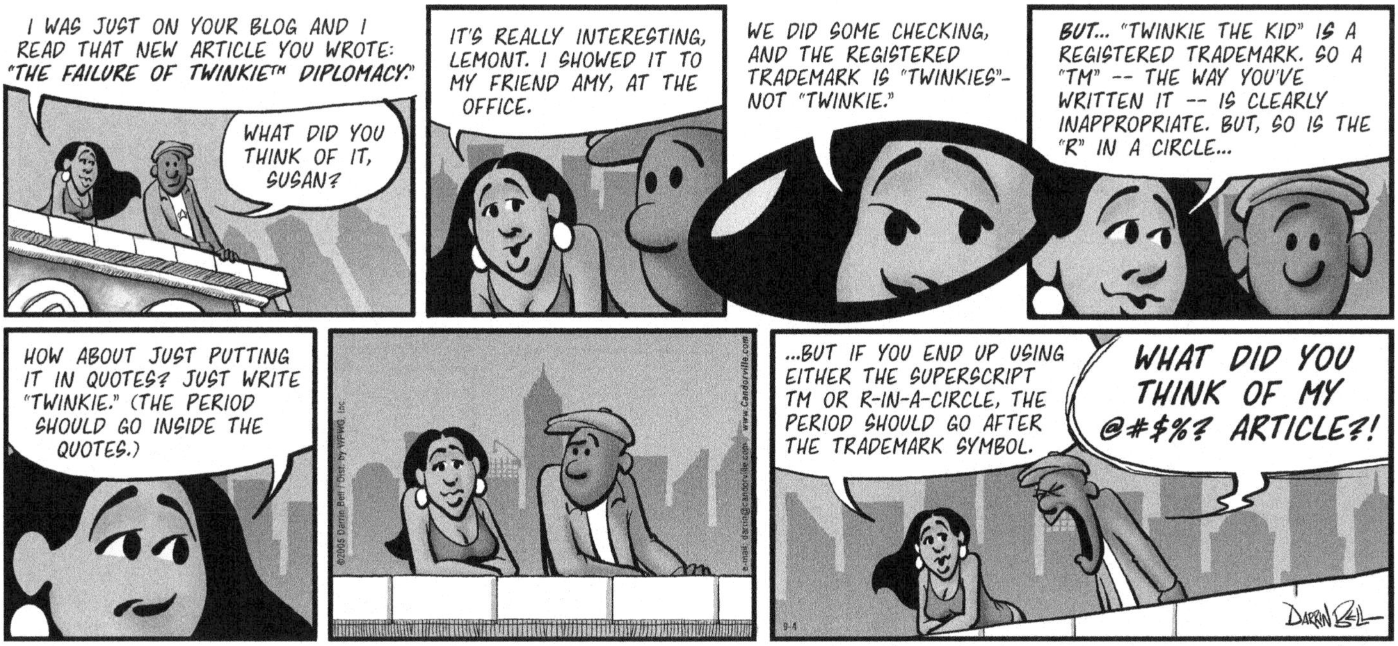
I WAS JUST ON YOUR BLOG AND I READ THAT NEW ARTICLE YOU WROTE: **"THE FAILURE OF TWINKIE™ DIPLOMACY."**
WHAT DID YOU THINK OF IT, SUSAN?
IT'S REALLY INTERESTING, LEMONT. I SHOWED IT TO MY FRIEND AMY, AT THE OFFICE.
WE DID SOME CHECKING, AND THE REGISTERED TRADEMARK IS "TWINKIES"- NOT "TWINKIE."
BUT... "TWINKIE THE KID" **IS** A REGISTERED TRADEMARK. SO A "TM" -- THE WAY YOU'VE WRITTEN IT -- IS CLEARLY INAPPROPRIATE. BUT, SO IS THE "R" IN A CIRCLE...
HOW ABOUT JUST PUTTING IT IN QUOTES? JUST WRITE "TWINKIE." (THE PERIOD SHOULD GO INSIDE THE QUOTES.)
©2005 Darrin Bell / Dist. by WPWG, Inc. e-mail: darrin@candorville.com www.Candorville.com
...BUT IF YOU END UP USING EITHER THE SUPERSCRIPT TM OR R-IN-A-CIRCLE, THE PERIOD SHOULD GO AFTER THE TRADEMARK SYMBOL.
WHAT DID YOU THINK OF MY @#$%? ARTICLE?!
DARRIN BELL

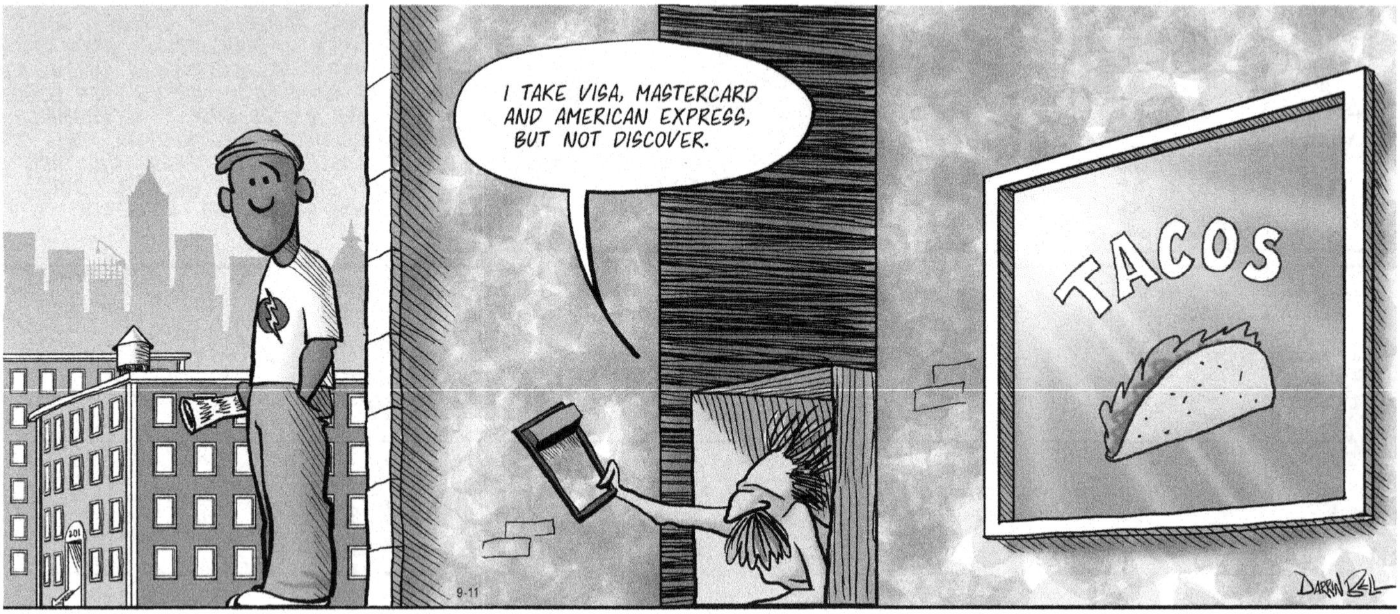
I TAKE VISA, MASTERCARD AND AMERICAN EXPRESS, BUT NOT DISCOVER.
TACOS
9-11
DARRIN BELL

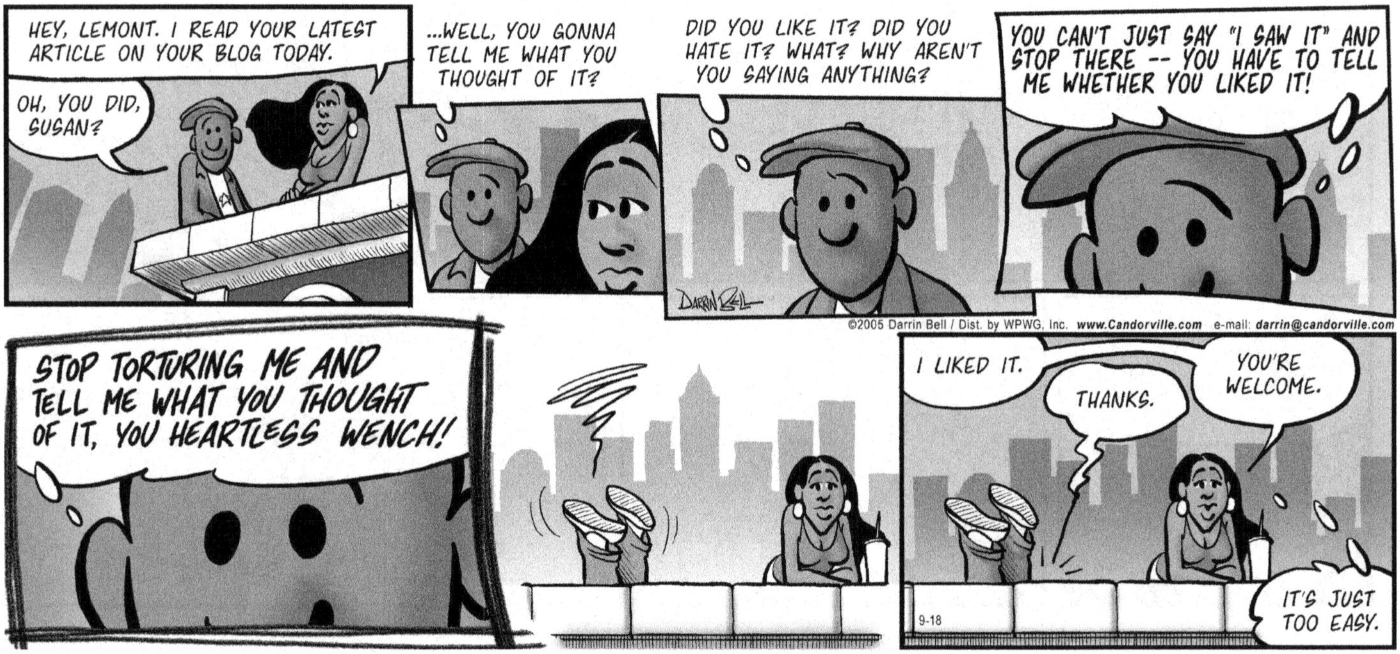
HEY, LEMONT. I READ YOUR LATEST ARTICLE ON YOUR BLOG TODAY.
OH, YOU DID, SUSAN?
...WELL, YOU GONNA TELL ME WHAT YOU THOUGHT OF IT?
DID YOU LIKE IT? DID YOU HATE IT? WHAT? WHY AREN'T YOU SAYING ANYTHING?
DARRIN BELL
YOU CAN'T JUST SAY "I SAW IT" AND STOP THERE -- YOU HAVE TO TELL ME WHETHER YOU LIKED IT!
STOP TORTURING ME AND TELL ME WHAT YOU THOUGHT OF IT, YOU HEARTLESS WENCH!
I LIKED IT.
THANKS.
YOU'RE WELCOME.
IT'S JUST TOO EASY.
9-18

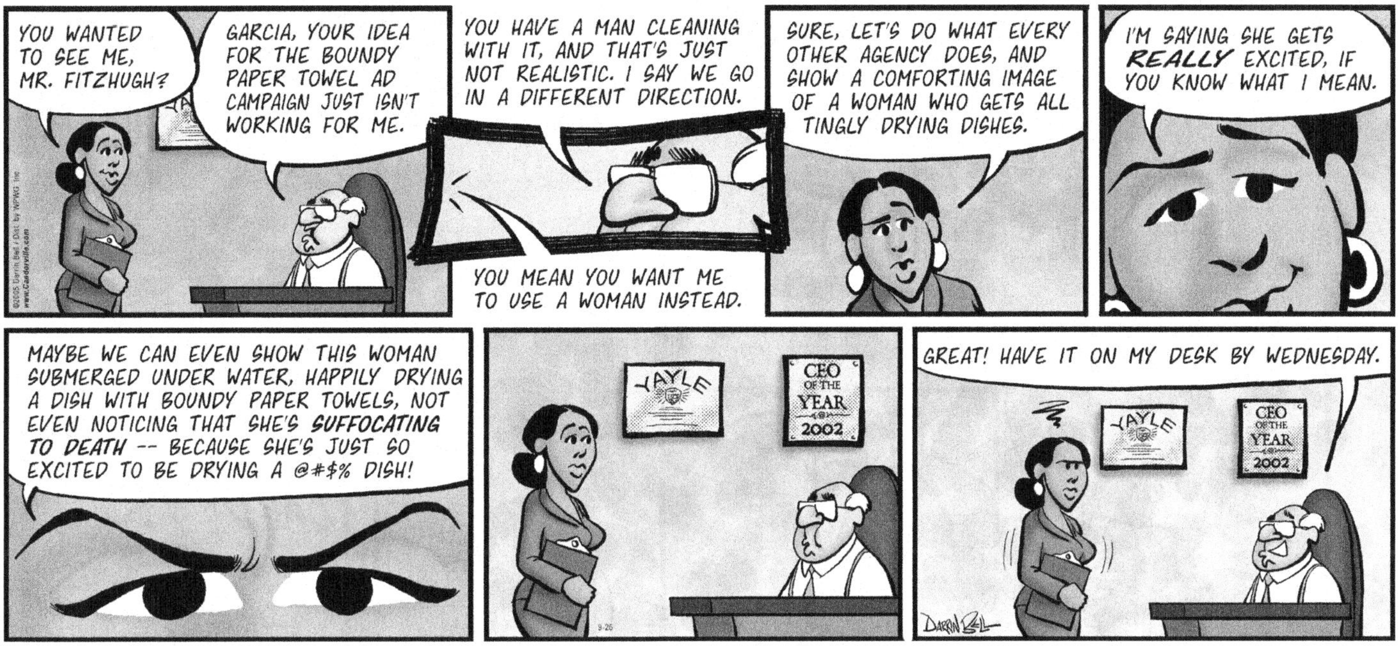
YOU WANTED TO SEE ME, MR. FITZHUGH?
GARCIA, YOUR IDEA FOR THE BOUNDY PAPER TOWEL AD CAMPAIGN JUST ISN'T WORKING FOR ME.
YOU HAVE A MAN CLEANING WITH IT, AND THAT'S JUST NOT REALISTIC. I SAY WE GO IN A DIFFERENT DIRECTION.
YOU MEAN YOU WANT ME TO USE A WOMAN INSTEAD.
SURE, LET'S DO WHAT EVERY OTHER AGENCY DOES, AND SHOW A COMFORTING IMAGE OF A WOMAN WHO GETS ALL TINGLY DRYING DISHES.
I'M SAYING SHE GETS REALLY EXCITED, IF YOU KNOW WHAT I MEAN.
MAYBE WE CAN EVEN SHOW THIS WOMAN SUBMERGED UNDER WATER, HAPPILY DRYING A DISH WITH BOUNDY PAPER TOWELS, NOT EVEN NOTICING THAT SHE'S SUFFOCATING TO DEATH -- BECAUSE SHE'S JUST SO EXCITED TO BE DRYING A @#$% DISH!
YAYLE
CEO OF THE YEAR 2002
GREAT! HAVE IT ON MY DESK BY WEDNESDAY.
DARRIN BELL

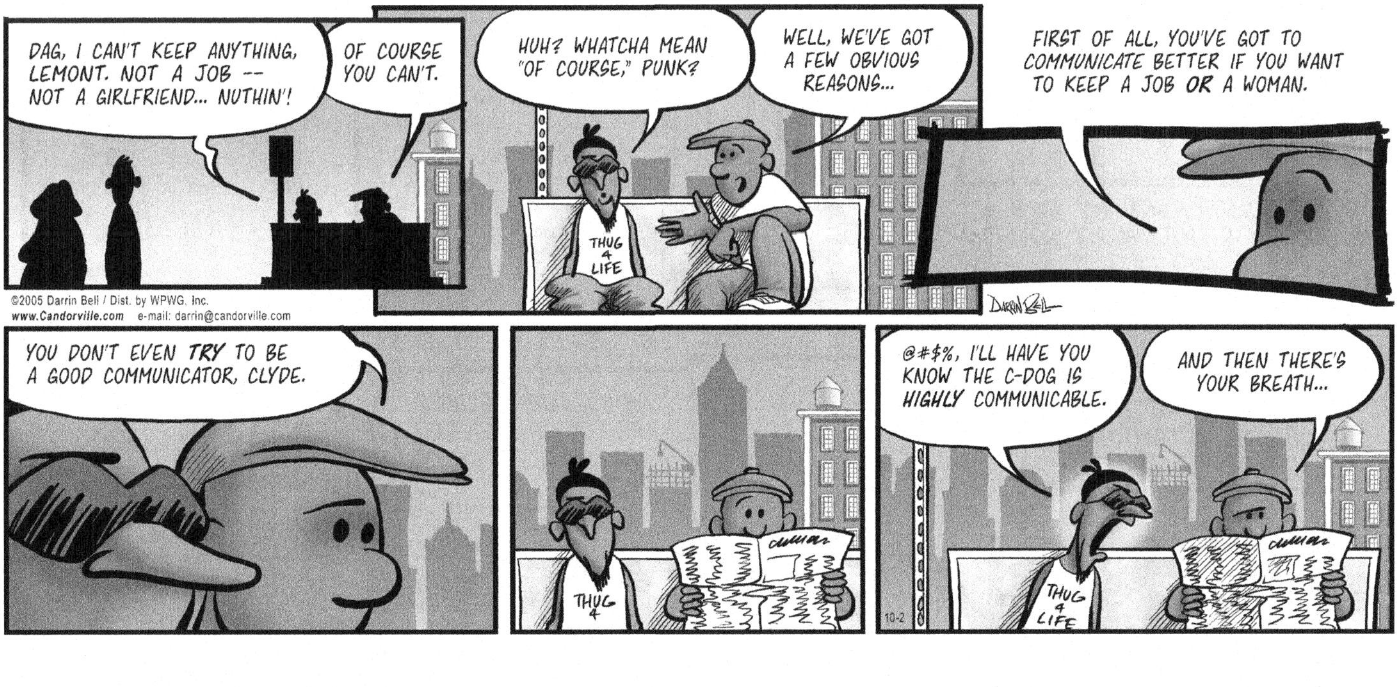
DAG, I CAN'T KEEP ANYTHING, LEMONT. NOT A JOB -- NOT A GIRLFRIEND... NUTHIN'!
OF COURSE YOU CAN'T.
HUH? WHATCHA MEAN "OF COURSE," PUNK?
WELL, WE'VE GOT A FEW OBVIOUS REASONS...
THUG 4 LIFE
FIRST OF ALL, YOU'VE GOT TO COMMUNICATE BETTER IF YOU WANT TO KEEP A JOB OR A WOMAN.
©2005 Darrin Bell / Dist. by WPWG, Inc.
www.Candorville.com e-mail: darrin@candorville.com
DARRIN BELL
YOU DON'T EVEN TRY TO BE A GOOD COMMUNICATOR, CLYDE.
@#$%, I'LL HAVE YOU KNOW THE C-DOG IS HIGHLY COMMUNICABLE.
AND THEN THERE'S YOUR BREATH...

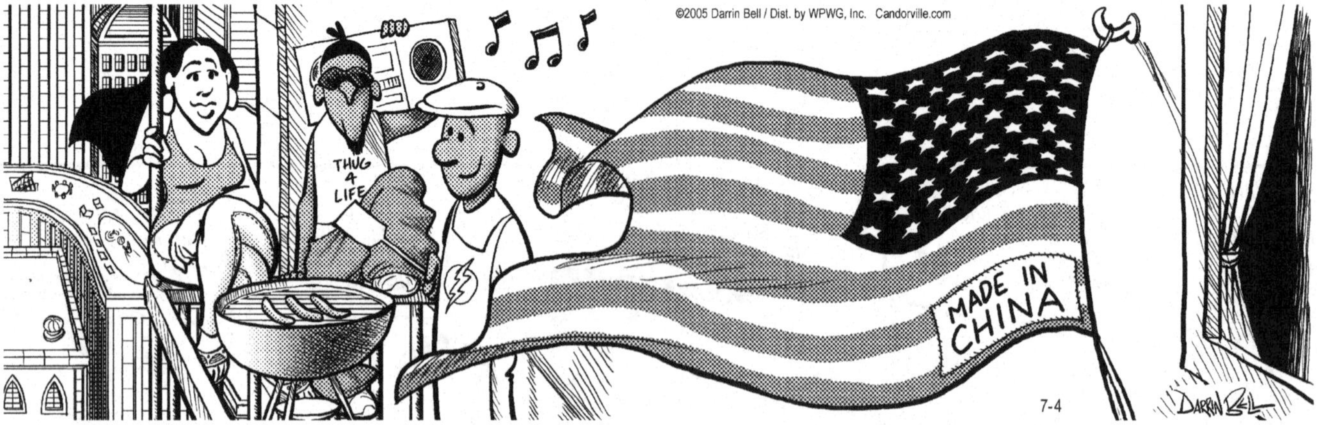
©2005 Darrin Bell / Dist. by WPWG, Inc. Candorville.com
THUG 4 LIFE
MADE IN CHINA
7-4
DARRIN BELL

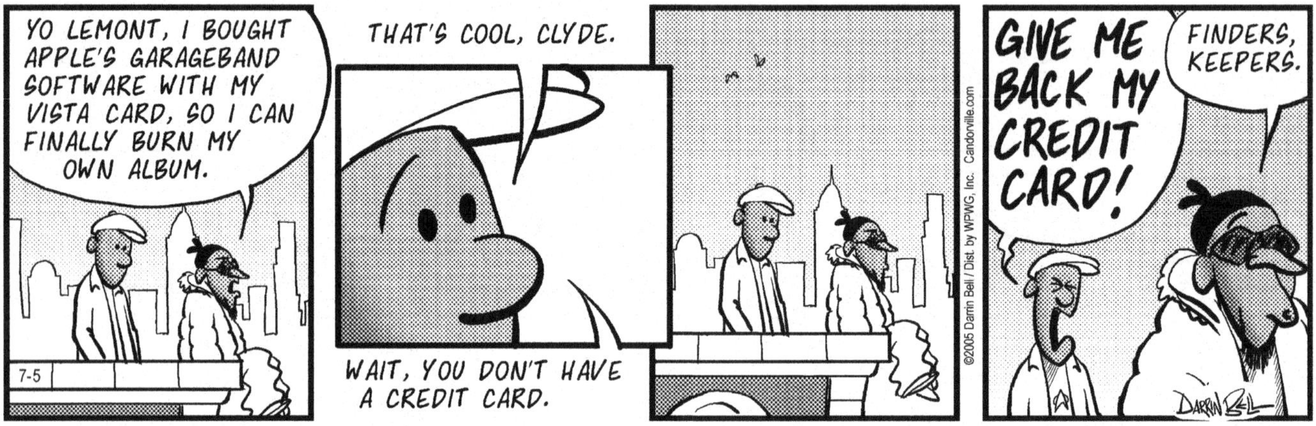
YO LEMONT, I BOUGHT APPLE'S GARAGEBAND SOFTWARE WITH MY VISTA CARD, SO I CAN FINALLY BURN MY OWN ALBUM.
7-5
THAT'S COOL, CLYDE.
WAIT, YOU DON'T HAVE A CREDIT CARD.
©2005 Darrin Bell / Dist. by WPWG, Inc. Candorville.com
GIVE ME BACK MY CREDIT CARD!
FINDERS, KEEPERS.
DARRIN BELL

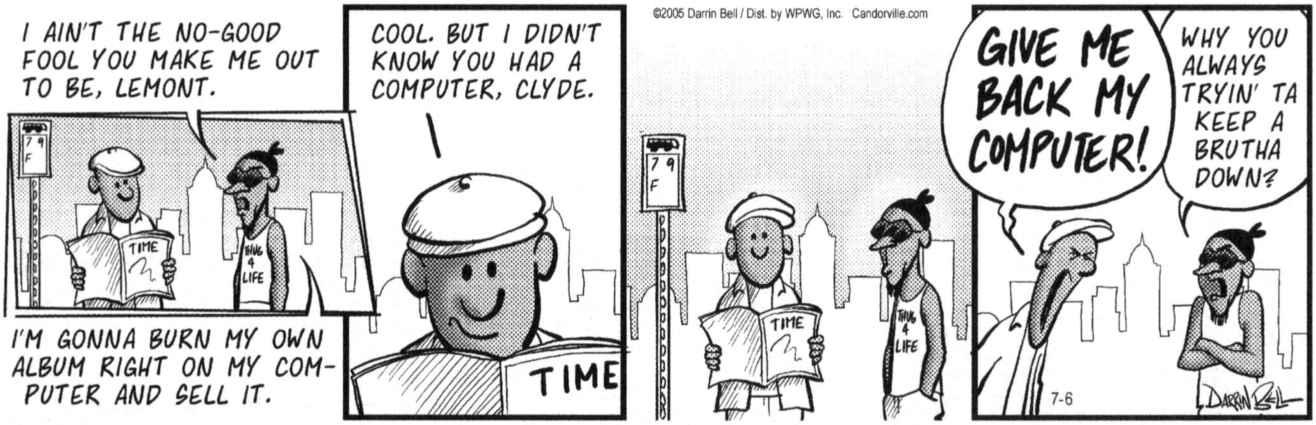
I AIN'T THE NO-GOOD FOOL YOU MAKE ME OUT TO BE, LEMONT.
TIME
THUG 4 LIFE
I'M GONNA BURN MY OWN ALBUM RIGHT ON MY COMPUTER AND SELL IT.
COOL. BUT I DIDN'T KNOW YOU HAD A COMPUTER, CLYDE.
TIME
©2005 Darrin Bell / Dist. by WPWG, Inc. Candorville.com
GIVE ME BACK MY COMPUTER!
WHY YOU ALWAYS TRYIN' TA KEEP A BRUTHA DOWN?
7-6
DARRIN BELL

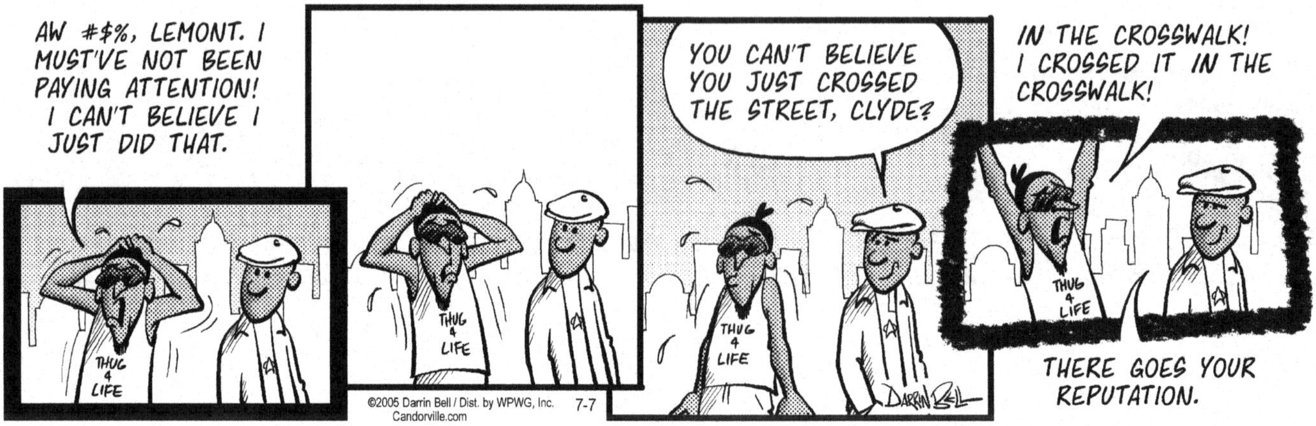
AW #$%, LEMONT. I MUST'VE NOT BEEN PAYING ATTENTION! I CAN'T BELIEVE I JUST DID THAT.
THUG 4 LIFE
©2005 Darrin Bell / Dist. by WPWG, Inc. Candorville.com
7-7
YOU CAN'T BELIEVE YOU JUST CROSSED THE STREET, CLYDE?
DARRIN BELL
IN THE CROSSWALK! I CROSSED IT IN THE CROSSWALK!
THERE GOES YOUR REPUTATION.

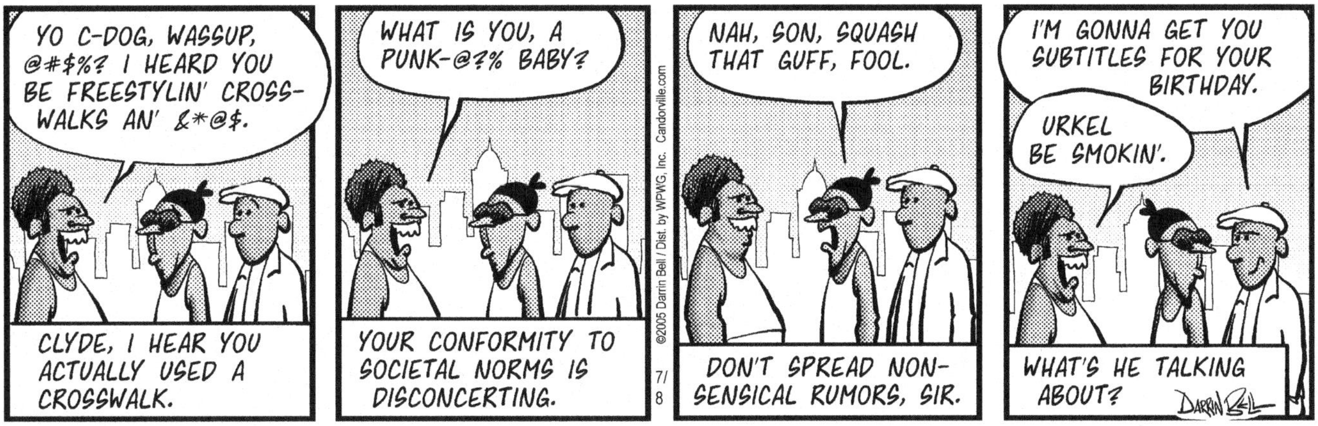
YO C-DOG, WASSUP, @#$%? I HEARD YOU BE FREESTYLIN' CROSS-WALKS AN' &*@$.
CLYDE, I HEAR YOU ACTUALLY USED A CROSSWALK.
WHAT IS YOU, A PUNK-@?% BABY?
YOUR CONFORMITY TO SOCIETAL NORMS IS DISCONCERTING.
©2005 Darrin Bell / Dist. by WPWG, Inc. Candorville.com
7/8
NAH, SON, SQUASH THAT GUFF, FOOL.
DON'T SPREAD NON-SENSICAL RUMORS, SIR.
I'M GONNA GET YOU SUBTITLES FOR YOUR BIRTHDAY.
URKEL BE SMOKIN'.
WHAT'S HE TALKING ABOUT?
DARRIN BELL

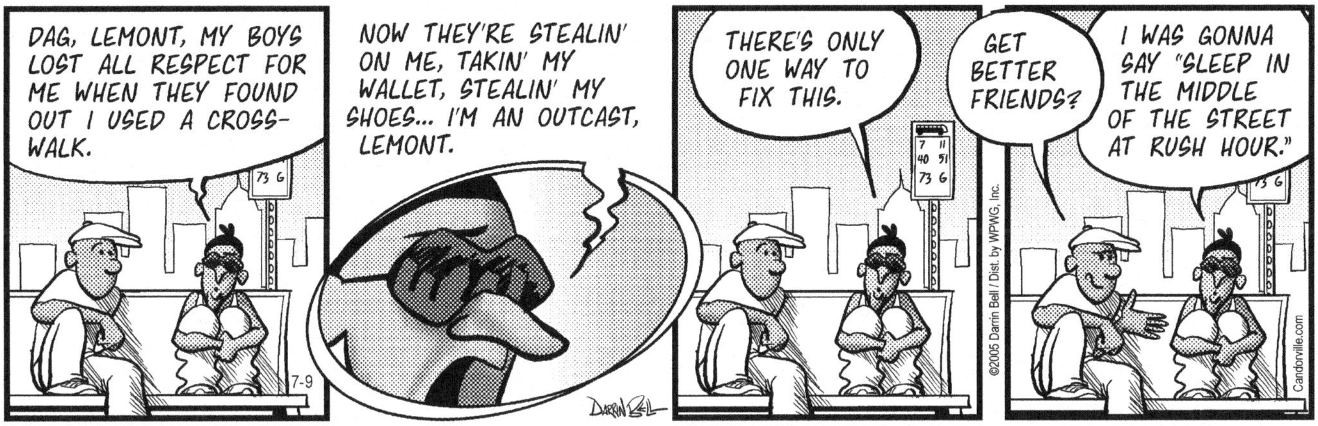
DAG, LEMONT, MY BOYS LOST ALL RESPECT FOR ME WHEN THEY FOUND OUT I USED A CROSS-WALK.
73 G
7-9
NOW THEY'RE STEALIN' ON ME, TAKIN' MY WALLET, STEALIN' MY SHOES... I'M AN OUTCAST, LEMONT.
DARRIN BELL
THERE'S ONLY ONE WAY TO FIX THIS.
7 11
40 51
73 G
©2005 Darrin Bell / Dist. by WPWG, Inc.
GET BETTER FRIENDS?
I WAS GONNA SAY "SLEEP IN THE MIDDLE OF THE STREET AT RUSH HOUR."
Candorville.com

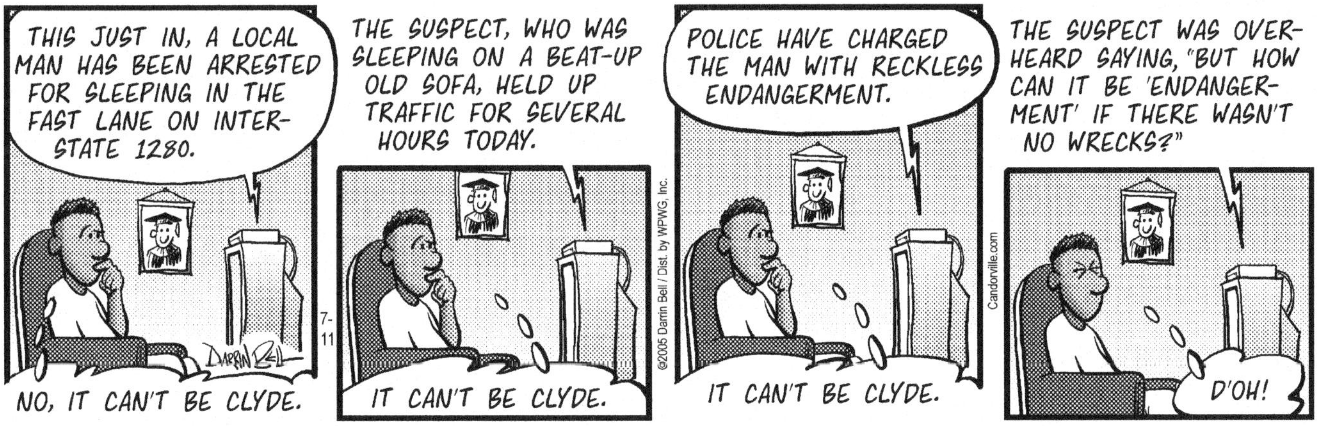
THIS JUST IN, A LOCAL MAN HAS BEEN ARRESTED FOR SLEEPING IN THE FAST LANE ON INTER-STATE 1280.
DARRIN BELL
7-11
NO, IT CAN'T BE CLYDE.
THE SUSPECT, WHO WAS SLEEPING ON A BEAT-UP OLD SOFA, HELD UP TRAFFIC FOR SEVERAL HOURS TODAY.
©2005 Darrin Bell / Dist. by WPWG, Inc.
IT CAN'T BE CLYDE.
POLICE HAVE CHARGED THE MAN WITH RECKLESS ENDANGERMENT.
IT CAN'T BE CLYDE.
Candorville.com
THE SUSPECT WAS OVER-HEARD SAYING, "BUT HOW CAN IT BE 'ENDANGER-MENT' IF THERE WASN'T NO WRECKS?"
D'OH!

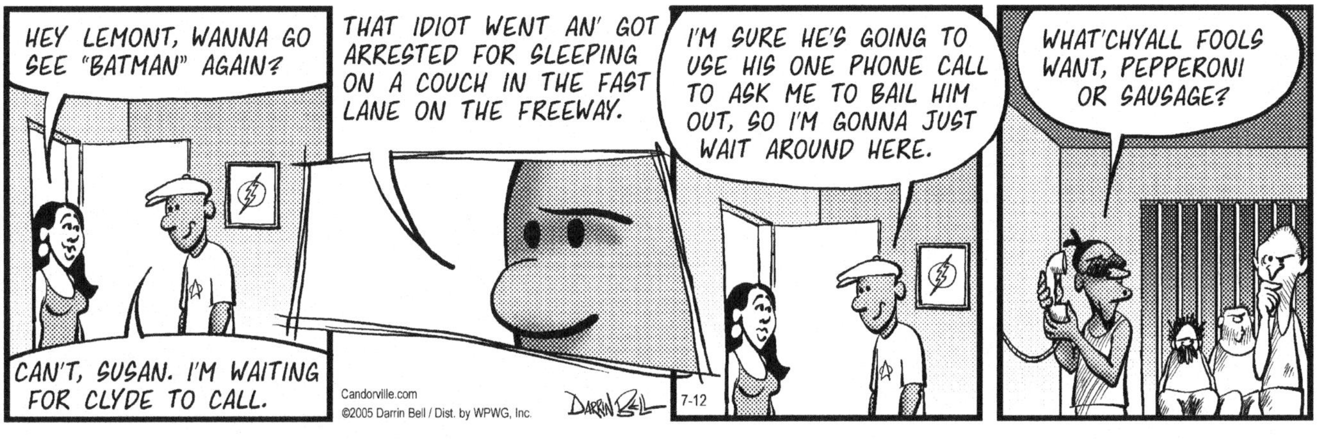
HEY LEMONT, WANNA GO SEE "BATMAN" AGAIN?
CAN'T, SUSAN. I'M WAITING FOR CLYDE TO CALL.
THAT IDIOT WENT AN' GOT ARRESTED FOR SLEEPING ON A COUCH IN THE FAST LANE ON THE FREEWAY.
Candorville.com
©2005 Darrin Bell / Dist. by WPWG, Inc.
DARRIN BELL
I'M SURE HE'S GOING TO USE HIS ONE PHONE CALL TO ASK ME TO BAIL HIM OUT, SO I'M GONNA JUST WAIT AROUND HERE.
7-12
WHAT'CHYALL FOOLS WANT, PEPPERONI OR SAUSAGE?

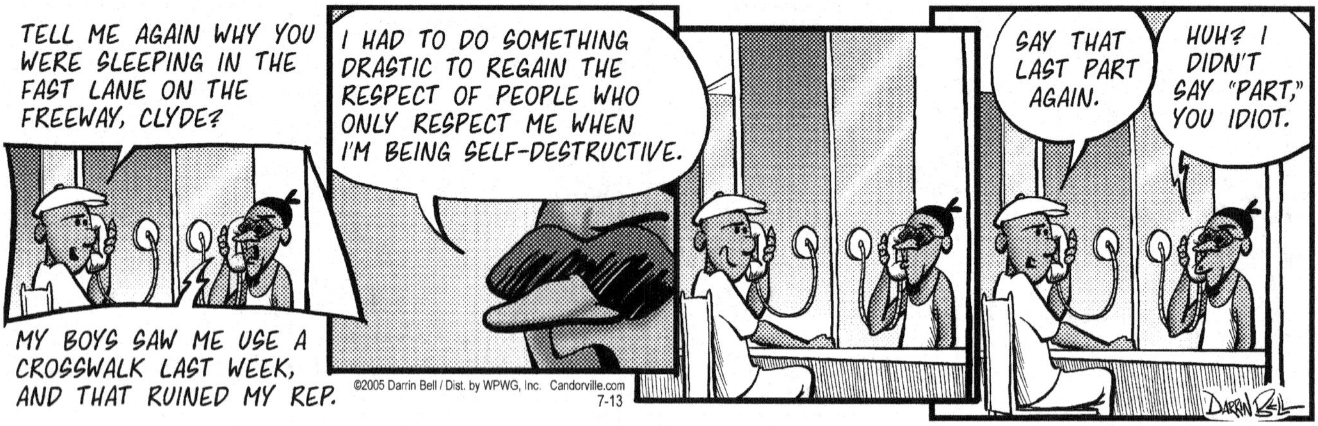
TELL ME AGAIN WHY YOU WERE SLEEPING IN THE FAST LANE ON THE FREEWAY, CLYDE?
MY BOYS SAW ME USE A CROSSWALK LAST WEEK, AND THAT RUINED MY REP.
I HAD TO DO SOMETHING DRASTIC TO REGAIN THE RESPECT OF PEOPLE WHO ONLY RESPECT ME WHEN I'M BEING SELF-DESTRUCTIVE.
©2005 Darrin Bell / Dist. by WPWG, Inc. Candorville.com
7-13
SAY THAT LAST PART AGAIN.
HUH? I DIDN'T SAY "PART," YOU IDIOT.
DARRIN BELL

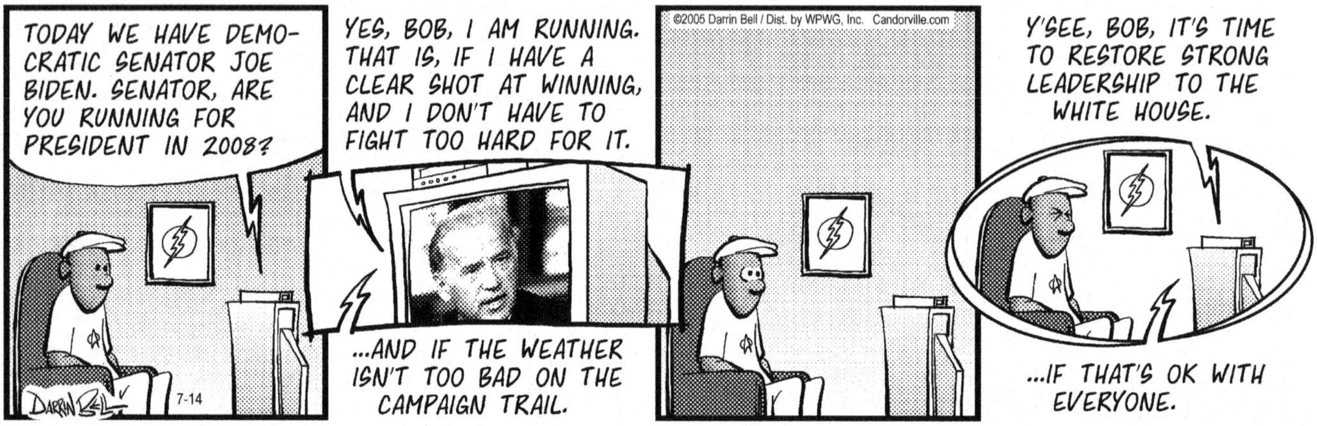
TODAY WE HAVE DEMOCRATIC SENATOR JOE BIDEN. SENATOR, ARE YOU RUNNING FOR PRESIDENT IN 2008?
DARRIN BELL
7-14
YES, BOB, I AM RUNNING. THAT IS, IF I HAVE A CLEAR SHOT AT WINNING, AND I DON'T HAVE TO FIGHT TOO HARD FOR IT.
...AND IF THE WEATHER ISN'T TOO BAD ON THE CAMPAIGN TRAIL.
©2005 Darrin Bell / Dist. by WPWG, Inc. Candorville.com
Y'SEE, BOB, IT'S TIME TO RESTORE STRONG LEADERSHIP TO THE WHITE HOUSE.
...IF THAT'S OK WITH EVERYONE.

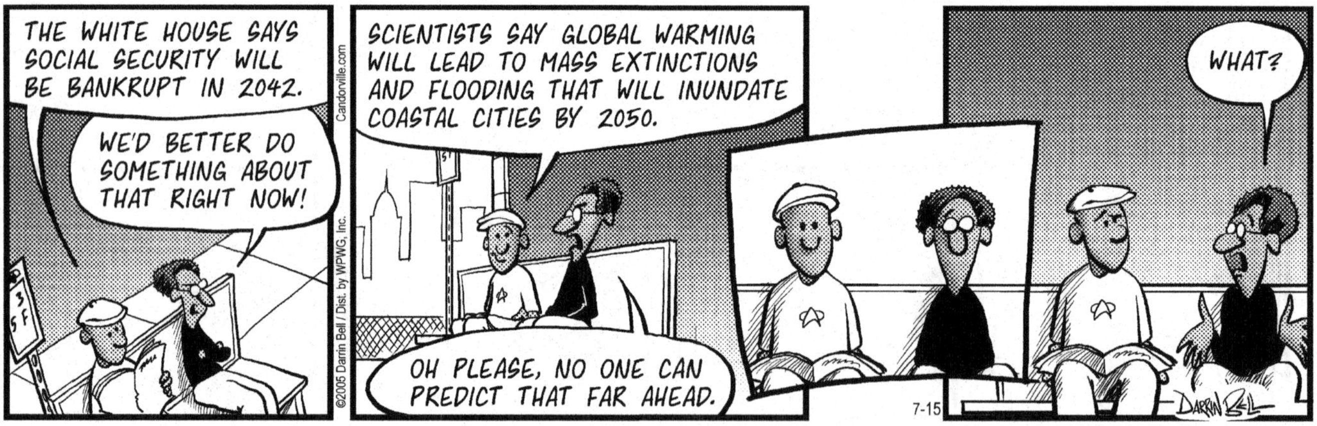
THE WHITE HOUSE SAYS SOCIAL SECURITY WILL BE BANKRUPT IN 2042.
WE'D BETTER DO SOMETHING ABOUT THAT RIGHT NOW!
©2005 Darrin Bell / Dist. by WPWG, Inc. Candorville.com
SCIENTISTS SAY GLOBAL WARMING WILL LEAD TO MASS EXTINCTIONS AND FLOODING THAT WILL INUNDATE COASTAL CITIES BY 2050.
OH PLEASE, NO ONE CAN PREDICT THAT FAR AHEAD.
7-15
WHAT?
DARRIN BELL

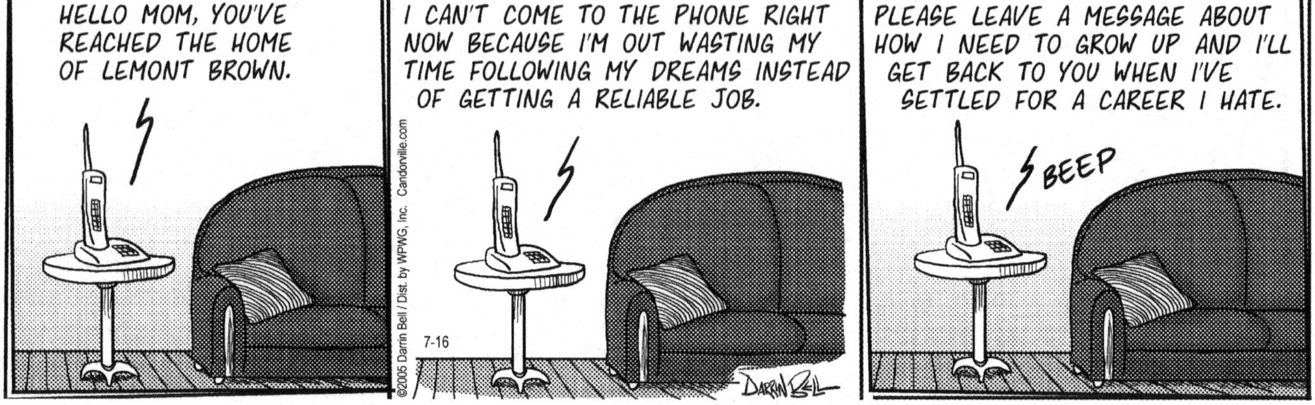
HELLO MOM, YOU'VE REACHED THE HOME OF LEMONT BROWN.
©2005 Darrin Bell / Dist. by WPWG, Inc. Candorville.com
7-16
I CAN'T COME TO THE PHONE RIGHT NOW BECAUSE I'M OUT WASTING MY TIME FOLLOWING MY DREAMS INSTEAD OF GETTING A RELIABLE JOB.
DARRIN BELL
PLEASE LEAVE A MESSAGE ABOUT HOW I NEED TO GROW UP AND I'LL GET BACK TO YOU WHEN I'VE SETTLED FOR A CAREER I HATE.
BEEP

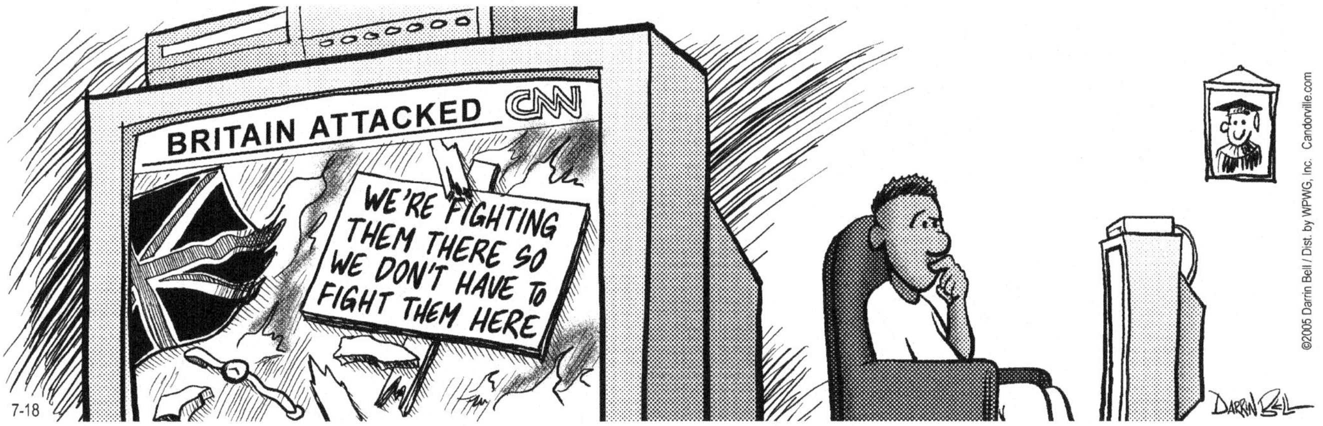
BRITAIN ATTACKED
CNN
WE'RE FIGHTING THEM THERE SO WE DON'T HAVE TO FIGHT THEM HERE
7-18
DARRIN BELL
©2005 Darrin Bell / Dist. by WPWG, Inc. Candorville.com

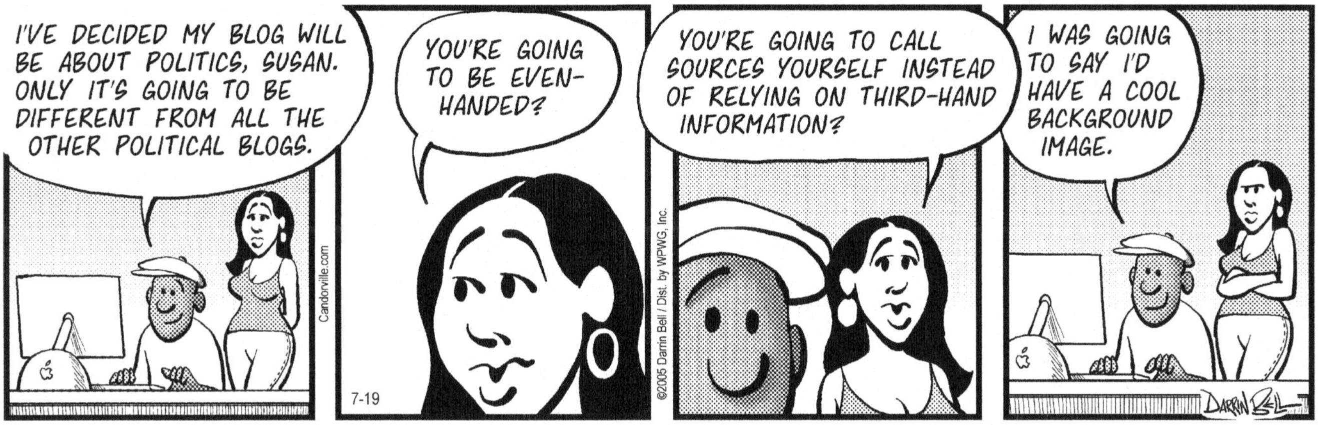
I'VE DECIDED MY BLOG WILL BE ABOUT POLITICS, SUSAN. ONLY IT'S GOING TO BE DIFFERENT FROM ALL THE OTHER POLITICAL BLOGS.
Candorville.com
YOU'RE GOING TO BE EVEN-HANDED?
7-19
©2005 Darrin Bell / Dist. by WPWG, Inc.
YOU'RE GOING TO CALL SOURCES YOURSELF INSTEAD OF RELYING ON THIRD-HAND INFORMATION?
I WAS GOING TO SAY I'D HAVE A COOL BACKGROUND IMAGE.
DARRIN BELL

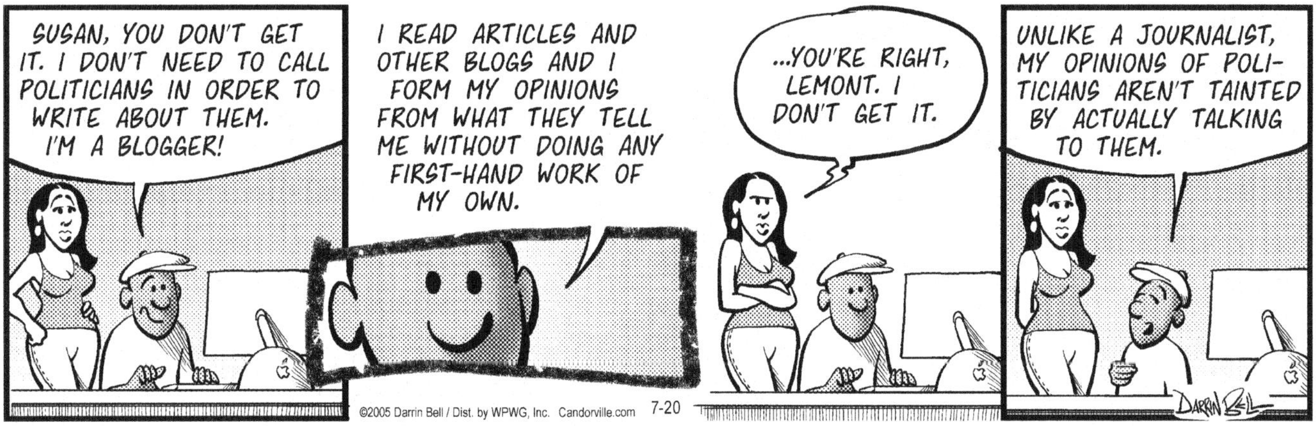
SUSAN, YOU DON'T GET IT. I DON'T NEED TO CALL POLITICIANS IN ORDER TO WRITE ABOUT THEM. I'M A BLOGGER!
I READ ARTICLES AND OTHER BLOGS AND I FORM MY OPINIONS FROM WHAT THEY TELL ME WITHOUT DOING ANY FIRST-HAND WORK OF MY OWN.
...YOU'RE RIGHT, LEMONT. I DON'T GET IT.
UNLIKE A JOURNALIST, MY OPINIONS OF POLITICIANS AREN'T TAINTED BY ACTUALLY TALKING TO THEM.
©2005 Darrin Bell / Dist. by WPWG, Inc. Candorville.com
7-20
DARRIN BELL

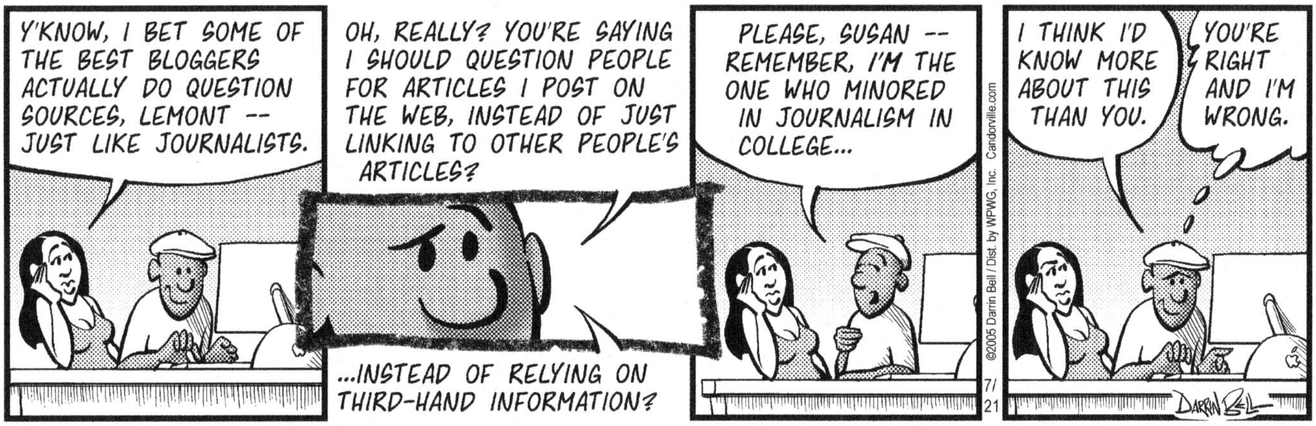
Y'KNOW, I BET SOME OF THE BEST BLOGGERS ACTUALLY DO QUESTION SOURCES, LEMONT -- JUST LIKE JOURNALISTS.
OH, REALLY? YOU'RE SAYING I SHOULD QUESTION PEOPLE FOR ARTICLES I POST ON THE WEB, INSTEAD OF JUST LINKING TO OTHER PEOPLE'S ARTICLES?
...INSTEAD OF RELYING ON THIRD-HAND INFORMATION?
PLEASE, SUSAN -- REMEMBER, I'M THE ONE WHO MINORED IN JOURNALISM IN COLLEGE...
©2005 Darrin Bell / Dist. by WPWG, Inc. Candorville.com
7/21
I THINK I'D KNOW MORE ABOUT THIS THAN YOU.
YOU'RE RIGHT AND I'M WRONG.
DARRIN BELL

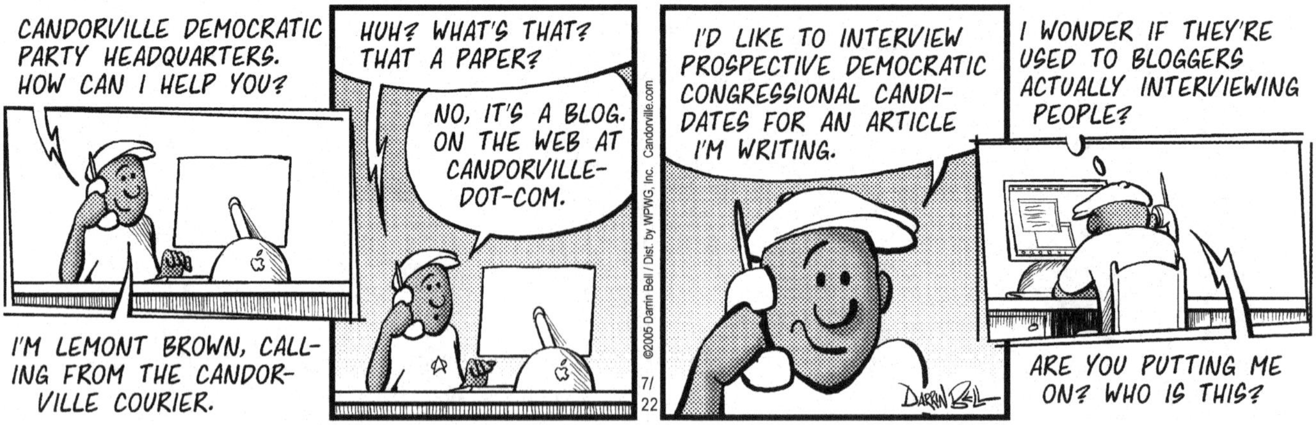
CANDORVILLE DEMOCRATIC PARTY HEADQUARTERS. HOW CAN I HELP YOU?
I'M LEMONT BROWN, CALLING FROM THE CANDORVILLE COURIER.
HUH? WHAT'S THAT? THAT A PAPER?
NO, IT'S A BLOG. ON THE WEB AT CANDORVILLE-DOT-COM.
7/22
©2005 Darrin Bell / Dist. by WPWG, Inc. Candorville.com
I'D LIKE TO INTERVIEW PROSPECTIVE DEMOCRATIC CONGRESSIONAL CANDIDATES FOR AN ARTICLE I'M WRITING.
I WONDER IF THEY'RE USED TO BLOGGERS ACTUALLY INTERVIEWING PEOPLE?
ARE YOU PUTTING ME ON? WHO IS THIS?
DARRIN BELL

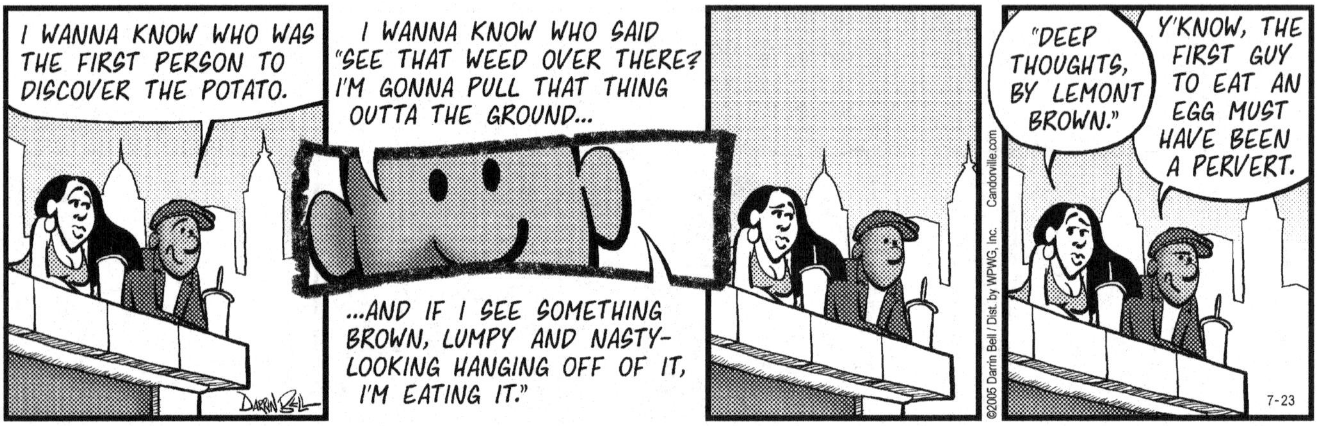
I WANNA KNOW WHO WAS THE FIRST PERSON TO DISCOVER THE POTATO.
I WANNA KNOW WHO SAID "SEE THAT WEED OVER THERE? I'M GONNA PULL THAT THING OUTTA THE GROUND...
...AND IF I SEE SOMETHING BROWN, LUMPY AND NASTY-LOOKING HANGING OFF OF IT, I'M EATING IT."
DARRIN BELL
©2005 Darrin Bell / Dist. by WPWG, Inc. Candorville.com
"DEEP THOUGHTS, BY LEMONT BROWN."
Y'KNOW, THE FIRST GUY TO EAT AN EGG MUST HAVE BEEN A PERVERT.
7-23

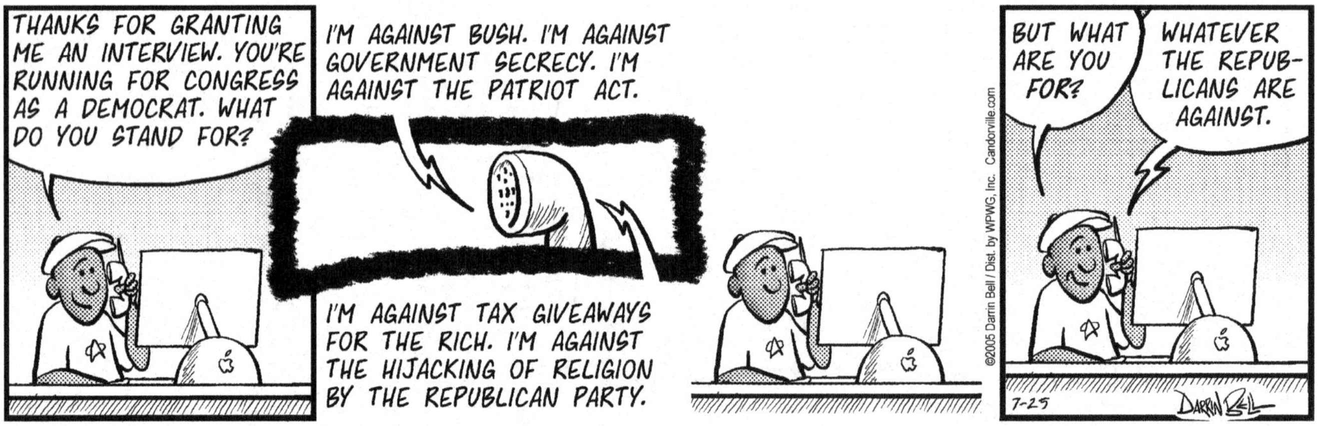
THANKS FOR GRANTING ME AN INTERVIEW. YOU'RE RUNNING FOR CONGRESS AS A DEMOCRAT. WHAT DO YOU STAND FOR?
I'M AGAINST BUSH. I'M AGAINST GOVERNMENT SECRECY. I'M AGAINST THE PATRIOT ACT.
I'M AGAINST TAX GIVEAWAYS FOR THE RICH. I'M AGAINST THE HIJACKING OF RELIGION BY THE REPUBLICAN PARTY.
©2005 Darrin Bell / Dist. by WPWG, Inc. Candorville.com
BUT WHAT ARE YOU FOR?
WHATEVER THE REPUBLICANS ARE AGAINST.
7-25
DARRIN BELL

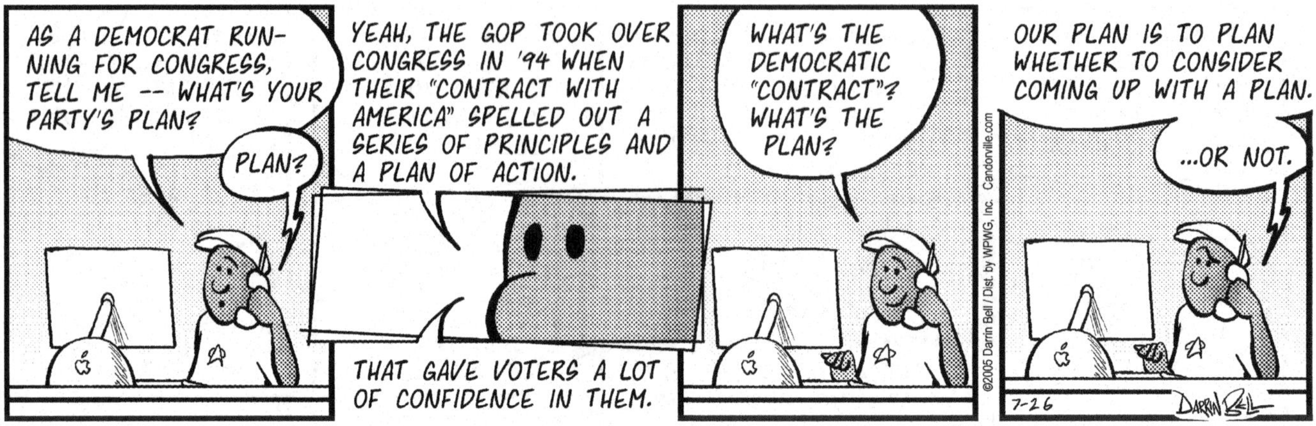
AS A DEMOCRAT RUNNING FOR CONGRESS, TELL ME -- WHAT'S YOUR PARTY'S PLAN?
PLAN?
YEAH, THE GOP TOOK OVER CONGRESS IN '94 WHEN THEIR "CONTRACT WITH AMERICA" SPELLED OUT A SERIES OF PRINCIPLES AND A PLAN OF ACTION.
THAT GAVE VOTERS A LOT OF CONFIDENCE IN THEM.
WHAT'S THE DEMOCRATIC "CONTRACT"? WHAT'S THE PLAN?
©2005 Darrin Bell / Dist. by WPWG, Inc. Candorville.com
OUR PLAN IS TO PLAN WHETHER TO CONSIDER COMING UP WITH A PLAN.
...OR NOT.
7-26
DARRIN BELL

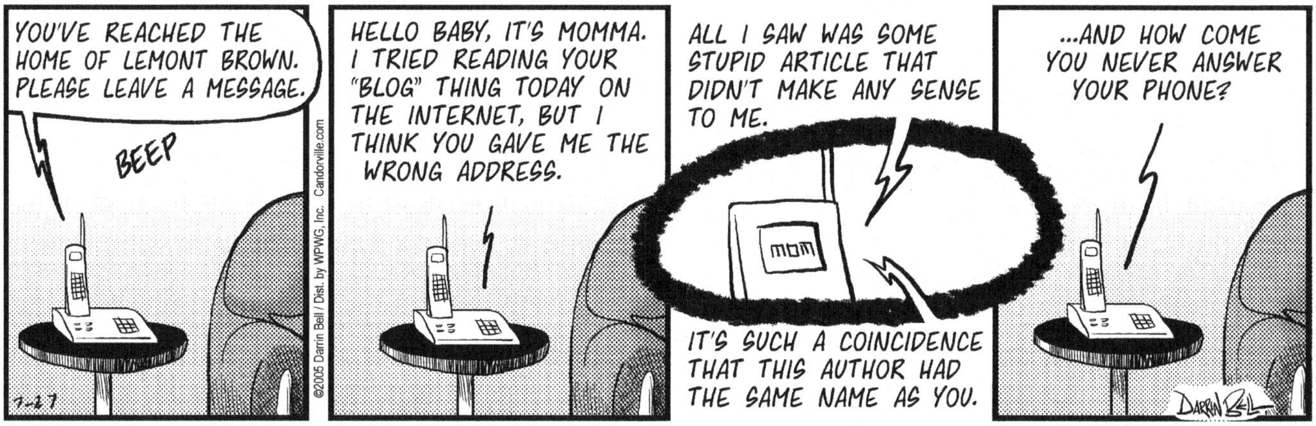
YOU'VE REACHED THE HOME OF LEMONT BROWN. PLEASE LEAVE A MESSAGE.
BEEP
HELLO BABY, IT'S MOMMA. I TRIED READING YOUR "BLOG" THING TODAY ON THE INTERNET, BUT I THINK YOU GAVE ME THE WRONG ADDRESS.
ALL I SAW WAS SOME STUPID ARTICLE THAT DIDN'T MAKE ANY SENSE TO ME.
MOM
IT'S SUCH A COINCIDENCE THAT THIS AUTHOR HAD THE SAME NAME AS YOU.
...AND HOW COME YOU NEVER ANSWER YOUR PHONE?
©2005 Darrin Bell / Dist. by WPWG, Inc. Candorville.com
DARRIN BELL

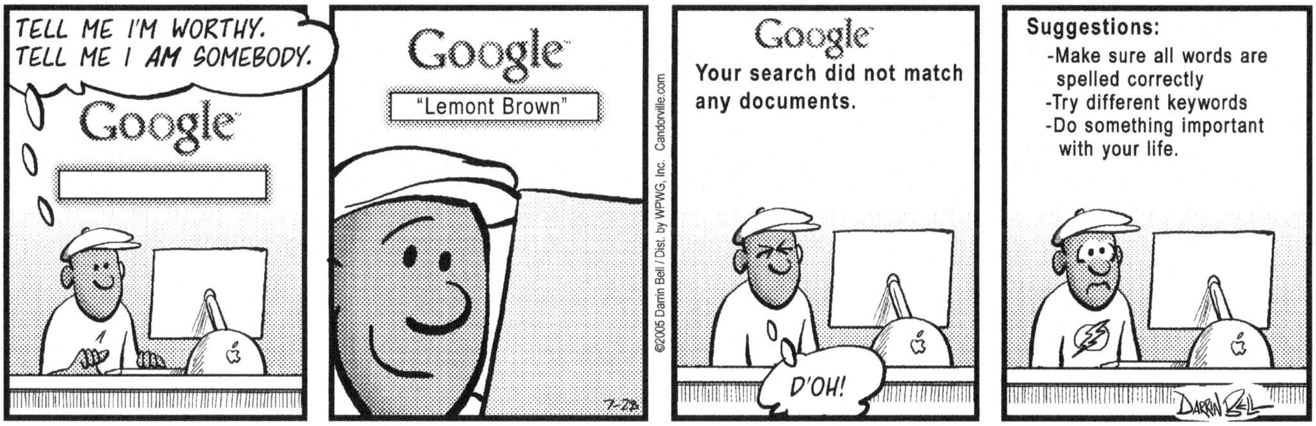
TELL ME I'M WORTHY. TELL ME I *AM* SOMEBODY.
Google
Google
"Lemont Brown"
Google
Your search did not match any documents.
D'OH!
Suggestions:
-Make sure all words are spelled correctly
-Try different keywords
-Do something important with your life.
©2005 Darrin Bell / Dist. by WPWG, Inc. Candorville.com
DARRIN BELL

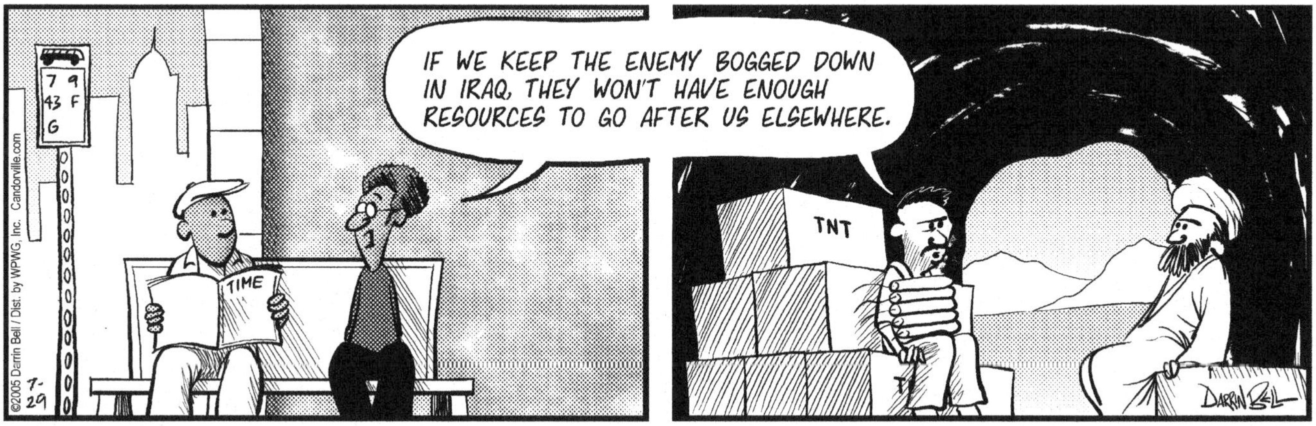
7 9
43 F
G
TIME
IF WE KEEP THE ENEMY BOGGED DOWN IN IRAQ, THEY WON'T HAVE ENOUGH RESOURCES TO GO AFTER US ELSEWHERE.
TNT
©2005 Darrin Bell / Dist. by WPWG, Inc. Candorville.com
DARRIN BELL

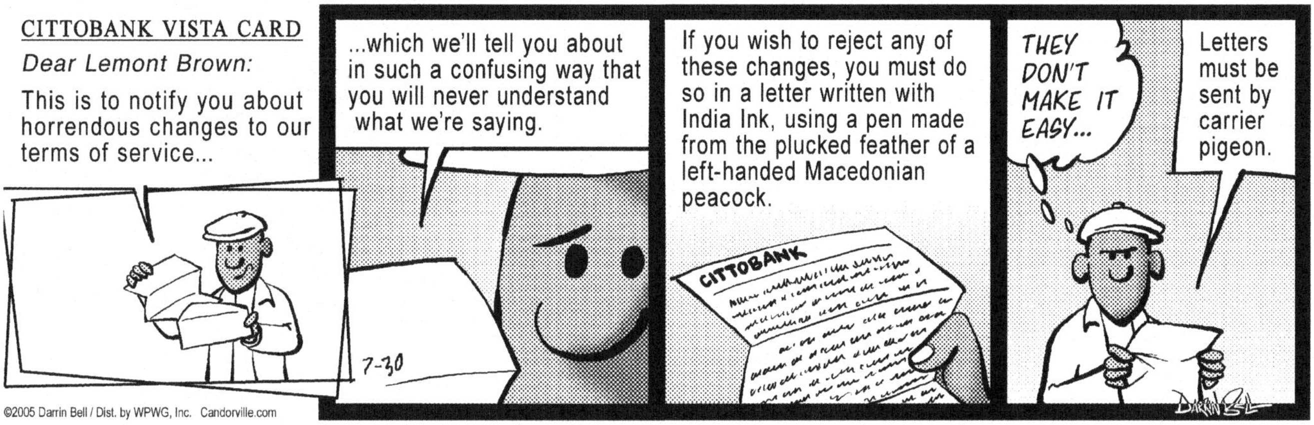
CITTOBANK VISTA CARD
Dear Lemont Brown:
This is to notify you about horrendous changes to our terms of service...
...which we'll tell you about in such a confusing way that you will never understand what we're saying.
If you wish to reject any of these changes, you must do so in a letter written with India Ink, using a pen made from the plucked feather of a left-handed Macedonian peacock.
CITTOBANK
THEY DON'T MAKE IT EASY...
Letters must be sent by carrier pigeon.
©2005 Darrin Bell / Dist. by WPWG, Inc. Candorville.com
DARRIN BELL

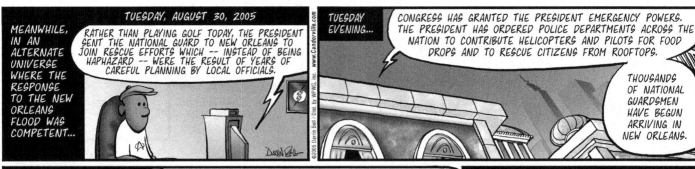

TUESDAY, AUGUST 30, 2005
MEANWHILE, IN AN ALTERNATE UNIVERSE WHERE THE RESPONSE TO THE NEW ORLEANS FLOOD WAS COMPETENT...
RATHER THAN PLAYING GOLF TODAY, THE PRESIDENT SENT THE NATIONAL GUARD TO NEW ORLEANS TO JOIN RESCUE EFFORTS WHICH -- INSTEAD OF BEING HAPHAZARD -- WERE THE RESULT OF YEARS OF CAREFUL PLANNING BY LOCAL OFFICIALS.
©2005 Darrin Bell / Dist. by WPWG, Inc. www.Candorville.com
TUESDAY EVENING...
CONGRESS HAS GRANTED THE PRESIDENT EMERGENCY POWERS. THE PRESIDENT HAS ORDERED POLICE DEPARTMENTS ACROSS THE NATION TO CONTRIBUTE HELICOPTERS AND PILOTS FOR FOOD DROPS AND TO RESCUE CITIZENS FROM ROOFTOPS.
THOUSANDS OF NATIONAL GUARDSMEN HAVE BEGUN ARRIVING IN NEW ORLEANS.
WEDNESDAY, AUGUST 31, 2005
THE SKY IS FILLED WITH HELICOPTERS. THE PRESIDENT HAS ORDERED GREYHOUND TO SEND ALL AREA BUSES TO NEW ORLEANS, AND CALLS ON TRUCK OWNERS IN THE REGION TO VOLUNTEER TO EVACUATE THE DESPERATE CITIZENS.
INSTEAD OF CONDEMNING PEOPLE FOR TAKING WHAT THEY NEED TO SURVIVE, THE WHITE HOUSE HAS ORDERED NATIONAL GUARD TROOPS TO CRACK DOWN ONLY ON THOSE LOOTING NON-ESSENTIALS.
INSTEAD OF BLAMING THE VICTIMS, THE HEAD OF FEMA HAS NOTED THAT THE POOR DIDN'T HAVE THE RESOURCES TO EVACUATE THE CITY.
10-9
THURSDAY, SEPTEMBER 1, 2005...
NEW ORLEANS HAS BEEN DEVASTATED, BUT QUICK ACTION BY AUTHORITIES GAVE PEOPLE ENOUGH HOPE THAT FEW RESORTED TO VIOLENCE. IT COULD HAVE BEEN MUCH WORSE...
...AND INSTEAD OF SPENDING THOUSANDS OF DOLLARS ON SHOES IN NEW YORK, CONDOLEEZZA RICE IS DOING HER JOB.

LEMONT, WHERE WAS DICK CHENEY WHILE PEOPLE WERE DYING IN THE NEW ORLEANS FLOOD?
WELL... WAY I SEE IT, THERE ARE THREE POSSIBILITIES, SUSAN.
"OPTION ONE: HE WAS BASS FISHING IN THE ONE PART OF WYOMING WHERE THERE'S NO CELL PHONE SERVICE, NO TV AND NO TIN CANS ON STRINGS.
"OPTION TWO: AFTER CHENEY #7 DIED OF A HEART ATTACK, CHENEY #8 WAS BUSY BEING CLONED IN THE WHITE HOUSE BASEMENT'S SECRET LABORATORY. HE COULDN'T BE REACHED BY PHONE BECAUSE HE WAS STILL GESTATING IN HIS VAT."
OPTION THREE: CHENEY HAD MORE IMPORTANT THINGS TO DO.
10-16
I THINK NUMBER TWO SOUNDS MOST REALISTIC.
ME TOO.
©2005 Darrin Bell / Dist. by WPWG, Inc. Candorville.com

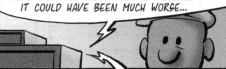

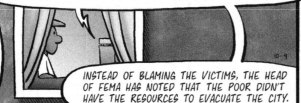

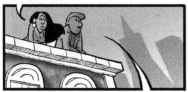

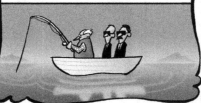

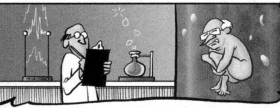

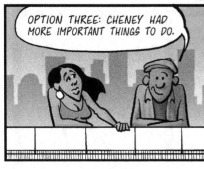

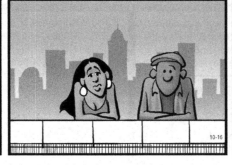

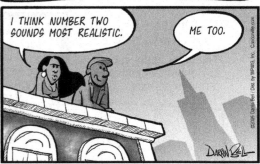

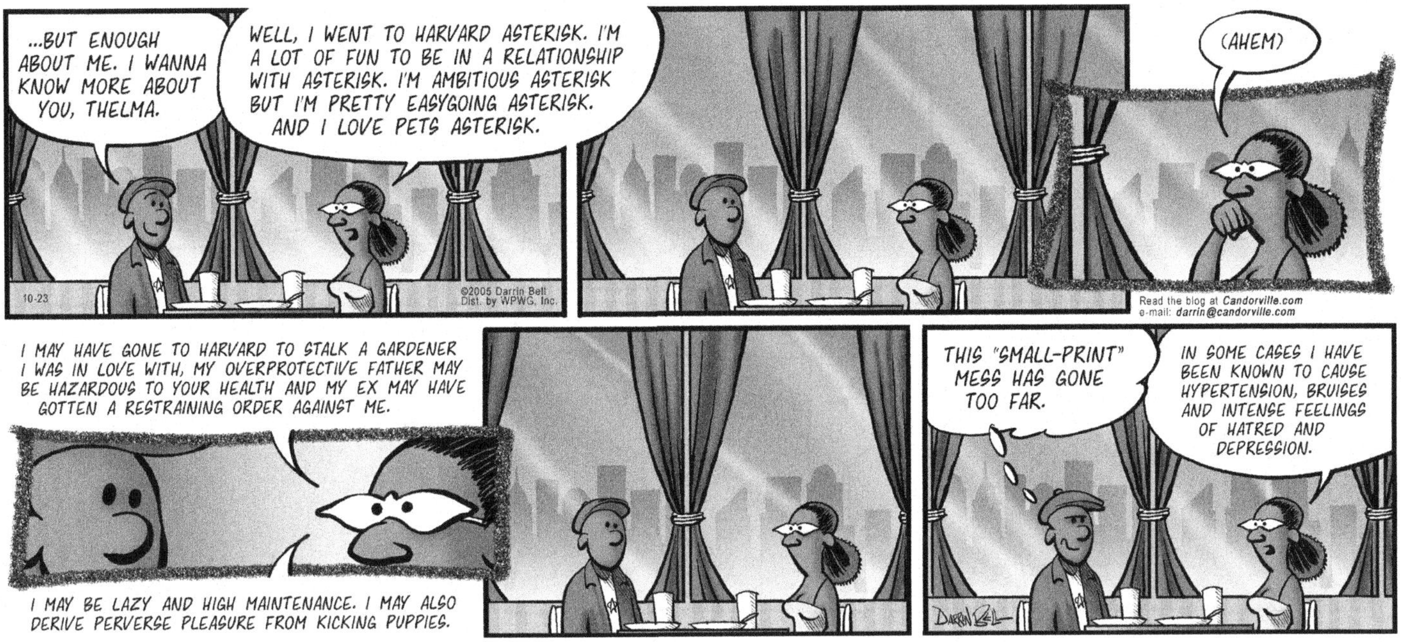
...BUT ENOUGH ABOUT ME. I WANNA KNOW MORE ABOUT YOU, THELMA.
WELL, I WENT TO HARVARD ASTERISK. I'M A LOT OF FUN TO BE IN A RELATIONSHIP WITH ASTERISK. I'M AMBITIOUS ASTERISK BUT I'M PRETTY EASYGOING ASTERISK. AND I LOVE PETS ASTERISK.
10-23
©2005 Darrin Bell Dist. by WPWG, Inc.
(AHEM)
Read the blog at Candorville.com
e-mail: darrin@candorville.com
I MAY HAVE GONE TO HARVARD TO STALK A GARDENER I WAS IN LOVE WITH, MY OVERPROTECTIVE FATHER MAY BE HAZARDOUS TO YOUR HEALTH AND MY EX MAY HAVE GOTTEN A RESTRAINING ORDER AGAINST ME.
I MAY BE LAZY AND HIGH MAINTENANCE. I MAY ALSO DERIVE PERVERSE PLEASURE FROM KICKING PUPPIES.
THIS "SMALL-PRINT" MESS HAS GONE TOO FAR.
IN SOME CASES I HAVE BEEN KNOWN TO CAUSE HYPERTENSION, BRUISES AND INTENSE FEELINGS OF HATRED AND DEPRESSION.
DARRIN BELL

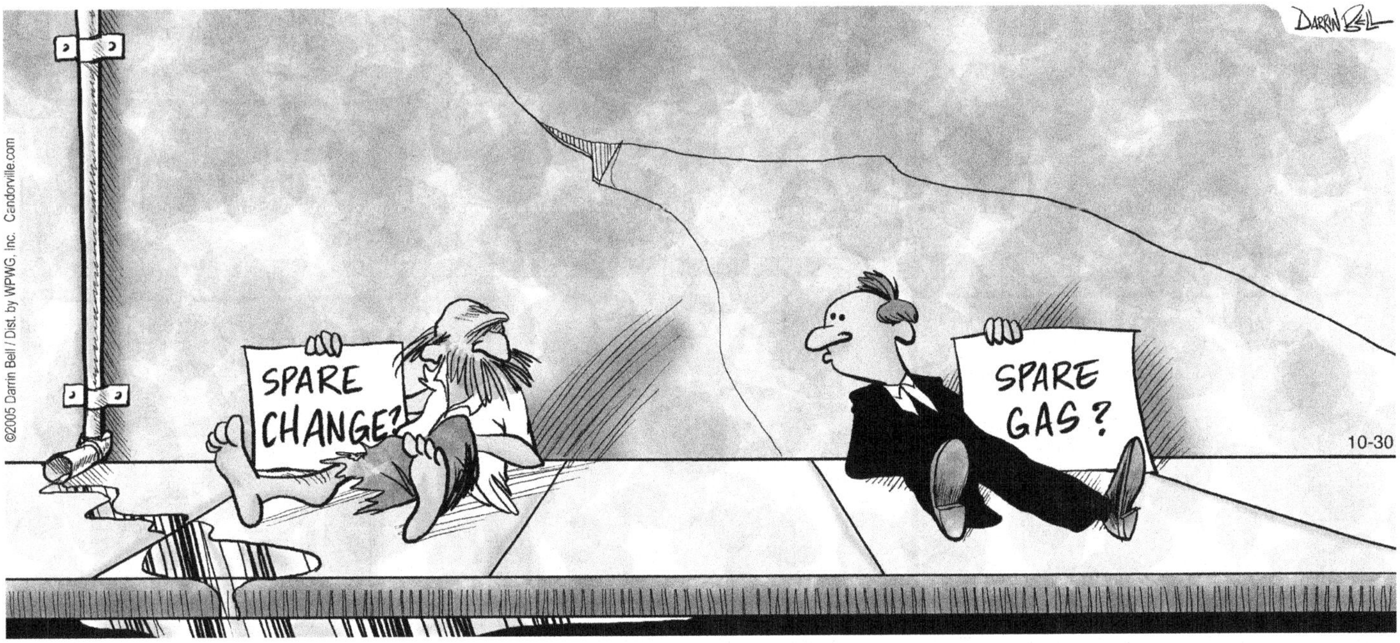
DARRIN BELL
©2005 Darrin Bell / Dist. by WPWG, Inc. Candorville.com
SPARE CHANGE?
SPARE GAS ?
10-30

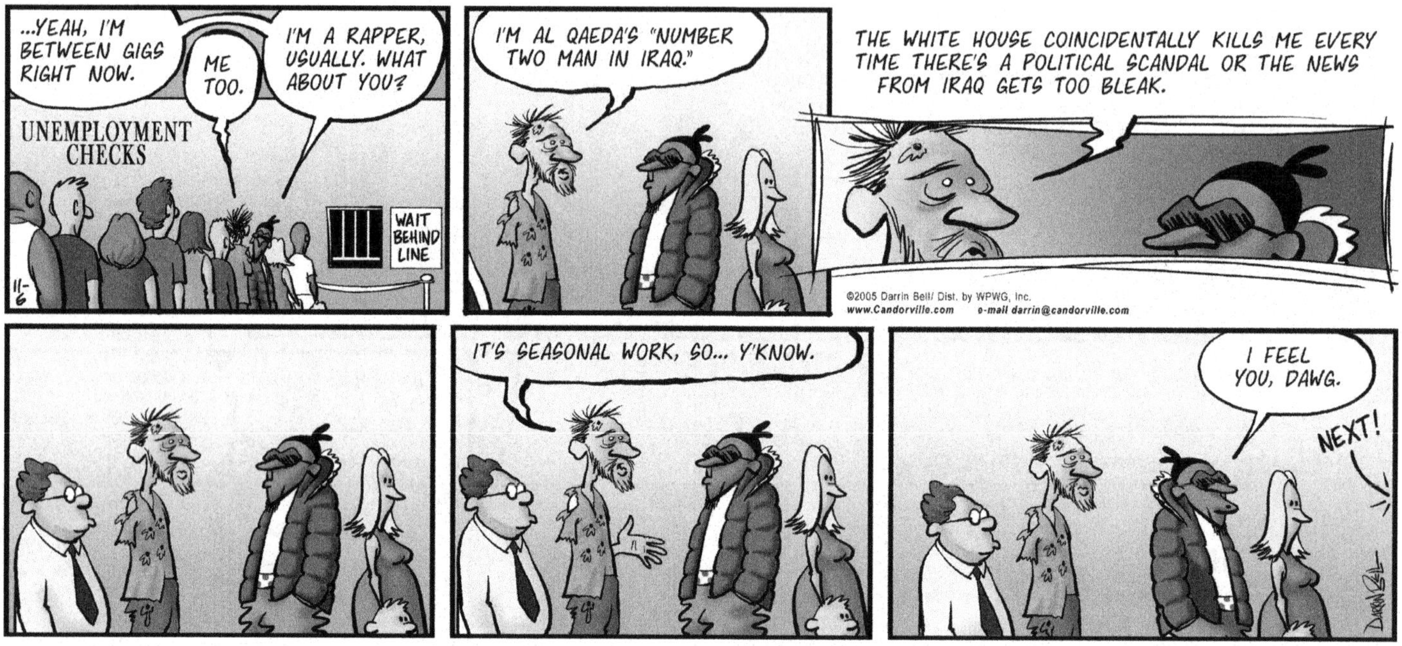
...YEAH, I'M BETWEEN GIGS RIGHT NOW.
ME TOO.
I'M A RAPPER, USUALLY. WHAT ABOUT YOU?
UNEMPLOYMENT CHECKS
WAIT BEHIND LINE
11-6
I'M AL QAEDA'S "NUMBER TWO MAN IN IRAQ."
THE WHITE HOUSE COINCIDENTALLY KILLS ME EVERY TIME THERE'S A POLITICAL SCANDAL OR THE NEWS FROM IRAQ GETS TOO BLEAK.
©2005 Darrin Bell/ Dist. by WPWG, Inc.
www.Candorville.com e-mail darrin@candorville.com
IT'S SEASONAL WORK, SO... Y'KNOW.
I FEEL YOU, DAWG.
NEXT!
DARRIN BELL

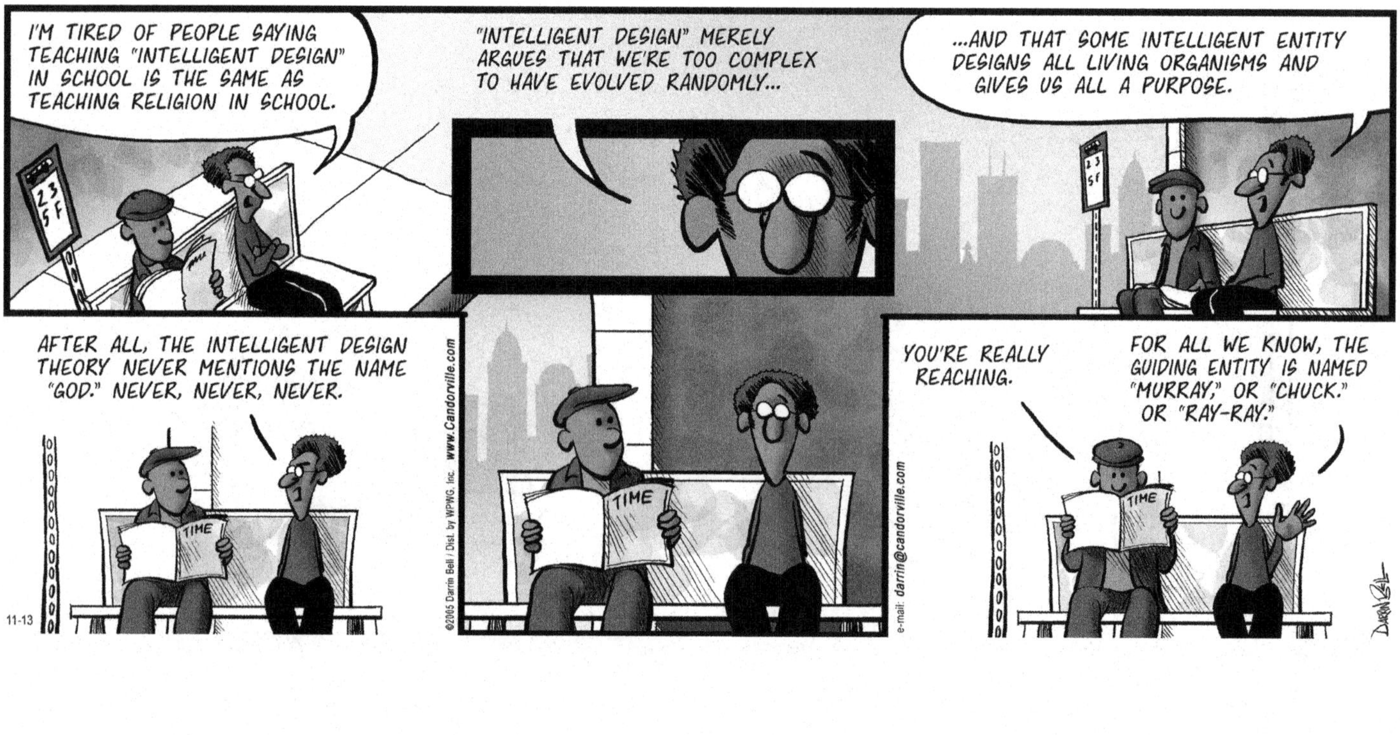
I'M TIRED OF PEOPLE SAYING TEACHING "INTELLIGENT DESIGN" IN SCHOOL IS THE SAME AS TEACHING RELIGION IN SCHOOL.
"INTELLIGENT DESIGN" MERELY ARGUES THAT WE'RE TOO COMPLEX TO HAVE EVOLVED RANDOMLY...
...AND THAT SOME INTELLIGENT ENTITY DESIGNS ALL LIVING ORGANISMS AND GIVES US ALL A PURPOSE.
AFTER ALL, THE INTELLIGENT DESIGN THEORY NEVER MENTIONS THE NAME "GOD." NEVER, NEVER, NEVER.
TIME
11-13
©2005 Darrin Bell / Dist. by WPWG, Inc. www.Candorville.com
e-mail: darrin@candorville.com
YOU'RE REALLY REACHING.
FOR ALL WE KNOW, THE GUIDING ENTITY IS NAMED "MURRAY," OR "CHUCK." OR "RAY-RAY."
DARRIN BELL

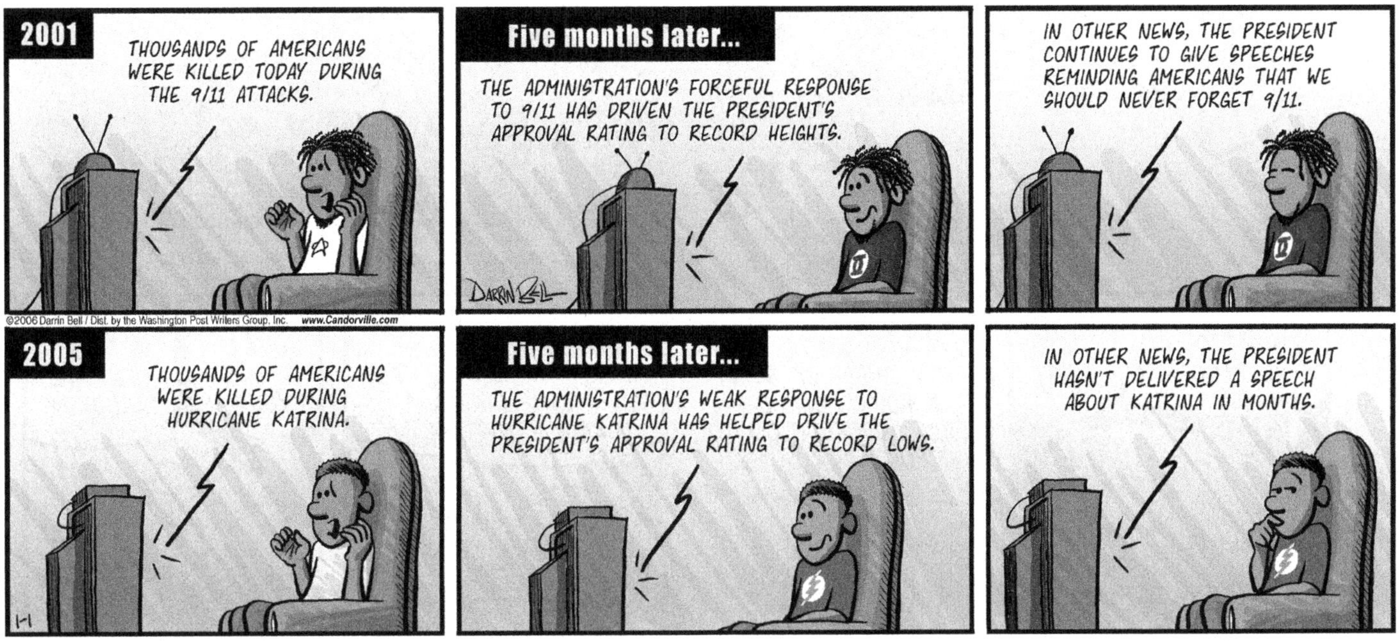
2001
THOUSANDS OF AMERICANS WERE KILLED TODAY DURING THE 9/11 ATTACKS.
Five months later...
THE ADMINISTRATION'S FORCEFUL RESPONSE TO 9/11 HAS DRIVEN THE PRESIDENT'S APPROVAL RATING TO RECORD HEIGHTS.
DARRIN BELL
IN OTHER NEWS, THE PRESIDENT CONTINUES TO GIVE SPEECHES REMINDING AMERICANS THAT WE SHOULD NEVER FORGET 9/11.
©2006 Darrin Bell / Dist. by the Washington Post Writers Group, Inc. www.Candorville.com
2005
THOUSANDS OF AMERICANS WERE KILLED DURING HURRICANE KATRINA.
1-1
Five months later...
THE ADMINISTRATION'S WEAK RESPONSE TO HURRICANE KATRINA HAS HELPED DRIVE THE PRESIDENT'S APPROVAL RATING TO RECORD LOWS.
IN OTHER NEWS, THE PRESIDENT HASN'T DELIVERED A SPEECH ABOUT KATRINA IN MONTHS.

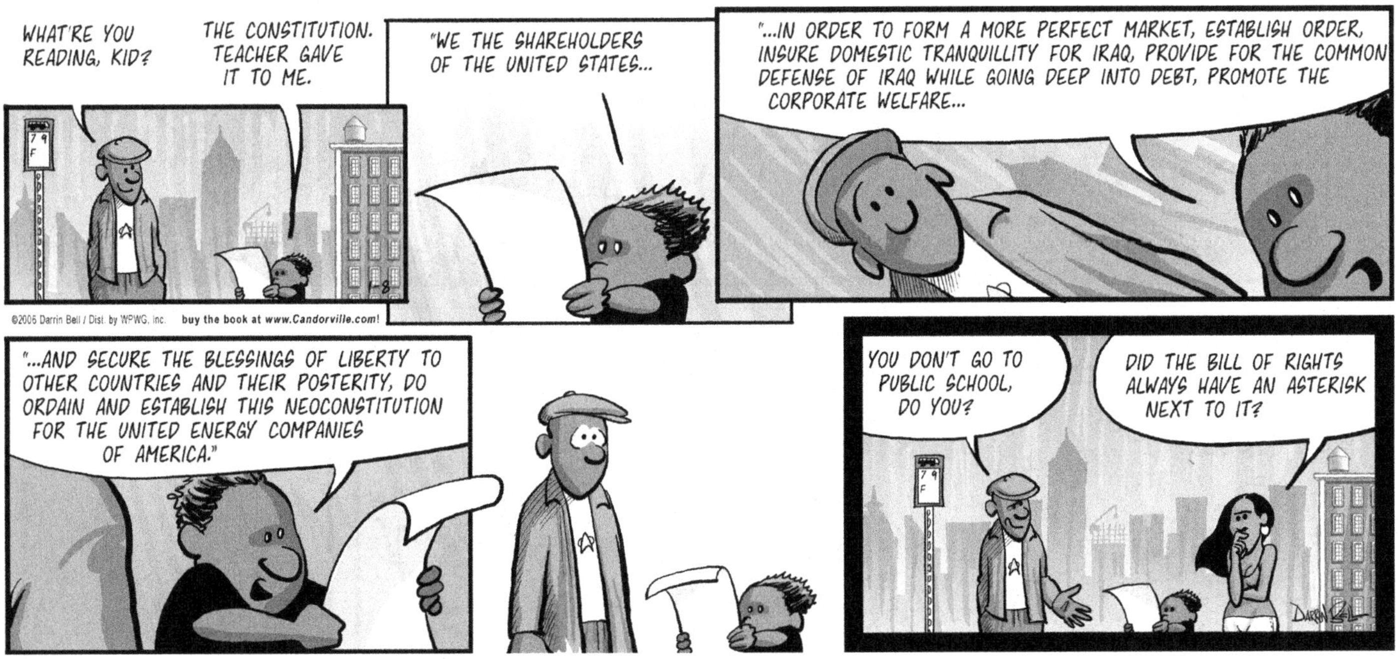
WHAT'RE YOU READING, KID?
THE CONSTITUTION. TEACHER GAVE IT TO ME.
1-8
©2006 Darrin Bell / Dist. by WPWG, Inc. buy the book at www.Candorville.com!
"WE THE SHAREHOLDERS OF THE UNITED STATES...
"...IN ORDER TO FORM A MORE PERFECT MARKET, ESTABLISH ORDER, INSURE DOMESTIC TRANQUILLITY FOR IRAQ, PROVIDE FOR THE COMMON DEFENSE OF IRAQ WHILE GOING DEEP INTO DEBT, PROMOTE THE CORPORATE WELFARE...
"...AND SECURE THE BLESSINGS OF LIBERTY TO OTHER COUNTRIES AND THEIR POSTERITY, DO ORDAIN AND ESTABLISH THIS NEOCONSTITUTION FOR THE UNITED ENERGY COMPANIES OF AMERICA."
YOU DON'T GO TO PUBLIC SCHOOL, DO YOU?
DID THE BILL OF RIGHTS ALWAYS HAVE AN ASTERISK NEXT TO IT?
DARRIN BELL

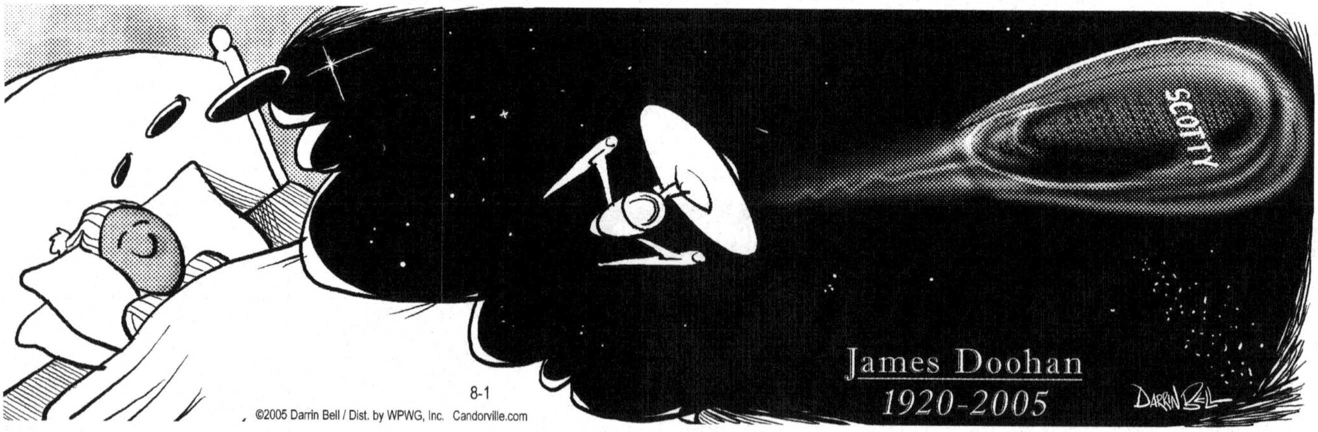
SCOTTY
James Doohan
1920-2005
8-1
©2005 Darrin Bell / Dist. by WPWG, Inc. Candorville.com
DARRIN BELL

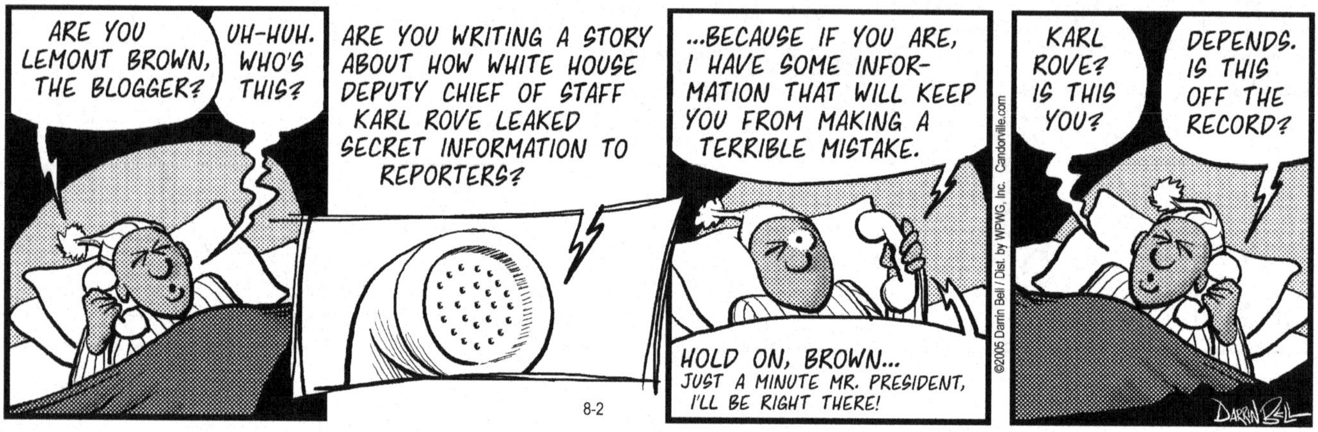
ARE YOU LEMONT BROWN, THE BLOGGER?
UH-HUH. WHO'S THIS?
ARE YOU WRITING A STORY ABOUT HOW WHITE HOUSE DEPUTY CHIEF OF STAFF KARL ROVE LEAKED SECRET INFORMATION TO REPORTERS?
...BECAUSE IF YOU ARE, I HAVE SOME INFORMATION THAT WILL KEEP YOU FROM MAKING A TERRIBLE MISTAKE.
HOLD ON, BROWN... JUST A MINUTE MR. PRESIDENT, I'LL BE RIGHT THERE!
KARL ROVE? IS THIS YOU?
DEPENDS. IS THIS OFF THE RECORD?
8-2
©2005 Darrin Bell / Dist. by WPWG, Inc. Candorville.com
DARRIN BELL

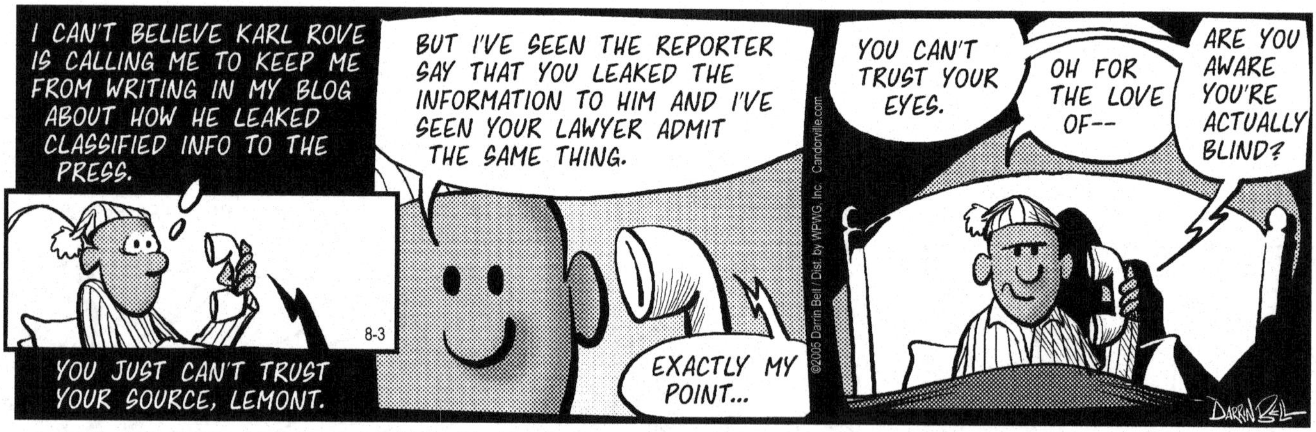
I CAN'T BELIEVE KARL ROVE IS CALLING ME TO KEEP ME FROM WRITING IN MY BLOG ABOUT HOW HE LEAKED CLASSIFIED INFO TO THE PRESS.
YOU JUST CAN'T TRUST YOUR SOURCE, LEMONT.
BUT I'VE SEEN THE REPORTER SAY THAT YOU LEAKED THE INFORMATION TO HIM AND I'VE SEEN YOUR LAWYER ADMIT THE SAME THING.
EXACTLY MY POINT...
YOU CAN'T TRUST YOUR EYES.
OH FOR THE LOVE OF--
ARE YOU AWARE YOU'RE ACTUALLY BLIND?
8-3
©2005 Darrin Bell / Dist. by WPWG, Inc. Candorville.com
DARRIN BELL

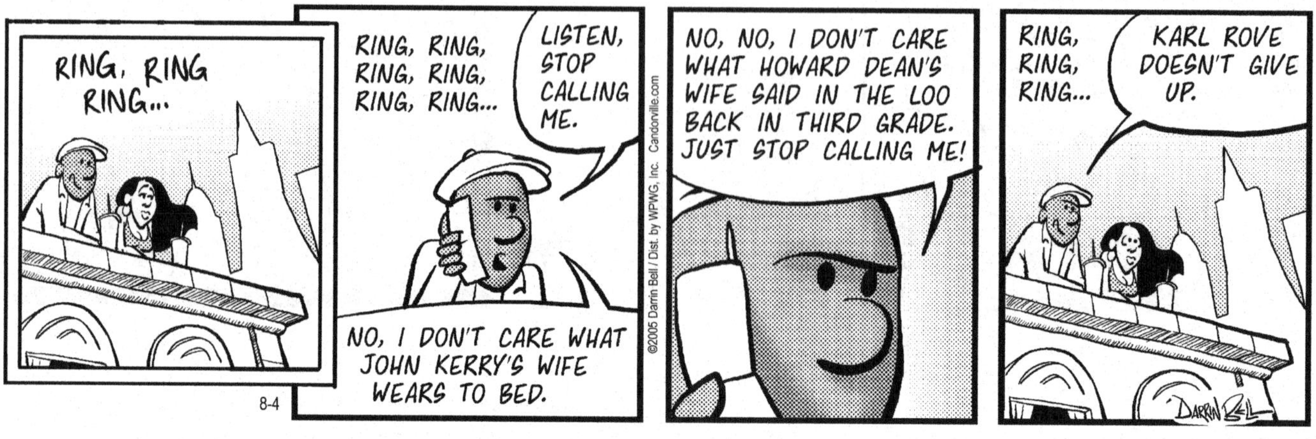
RING, RING RING...
RING, RING, RING, RING, RING, RING...
LISTEN, STOP CALLING ME.
NO, I DON'T CARE WHAT JOHN KERRY'S WIFE WEARS TO BED.
NO, NO, I DON'T CARE WHAT HOWARD DEAN'S WIFE SAID IN THE LOO BACK IN THIRD GRADE. JUST STOP CALLING ME!
RING, RING, RING...
KARL ROVE DOESN'T GIVE UP.
8-4
©2005 Darrin Bell / Dist. by WPWG, Inc. Candorville.com
DARRIN BELL

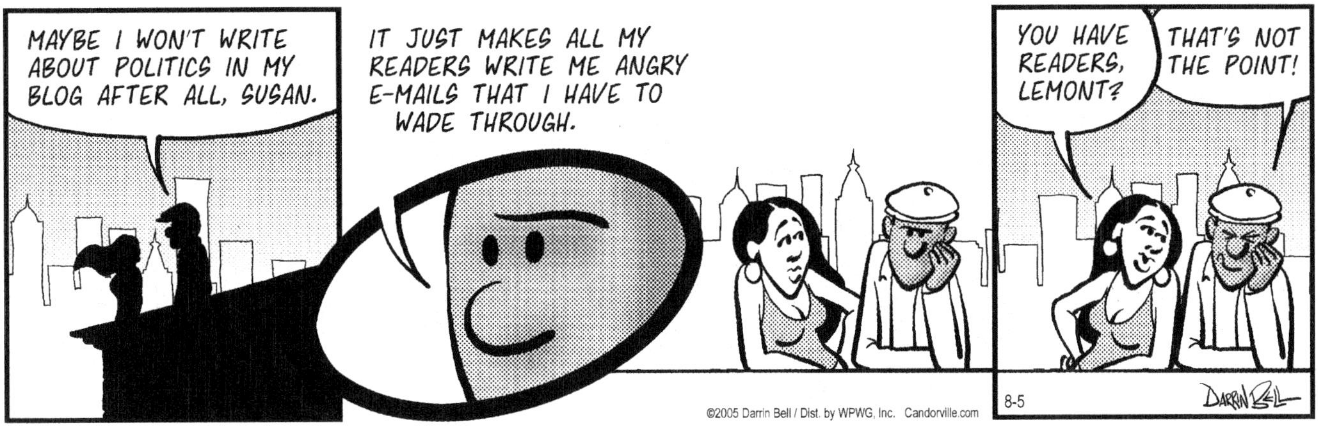
MAYBE I WON'T WRITE ABOUT POLITICS IN MY BLOG AFTER ALL, SUSAN.
IT JUST MAKES ALL MY READERS WRITE ME ANGRY E-MAILS THAT I HAVE TO WADE THROUGH.
YOU HAVE READERS, LEMONT?
THAT'S NOT THE POINT!
©2005 Darrin Bell / Dist. by WPWG, Inc. Candorville.com
8-5
DARRIN BELL

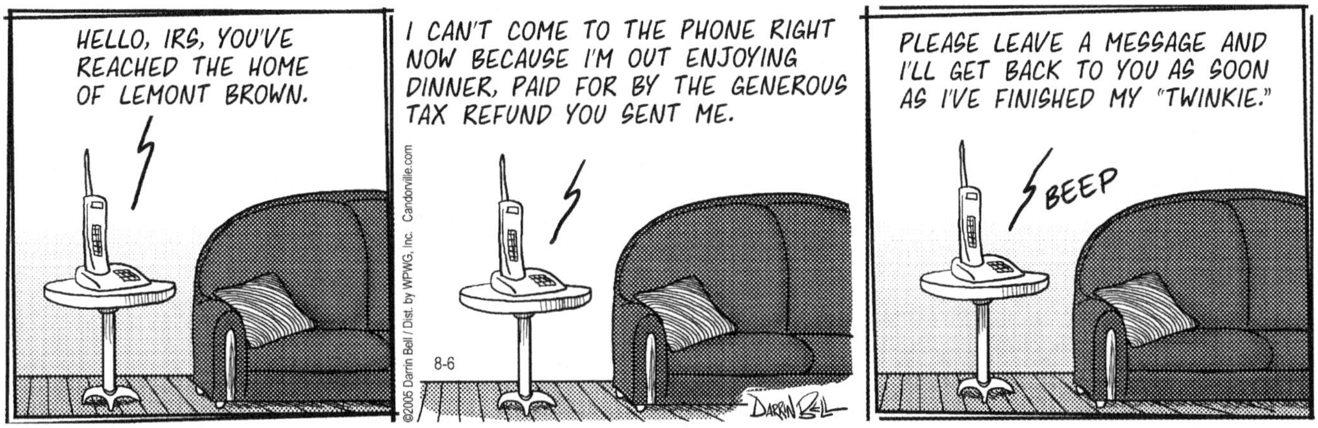
HELLO, IRS, YOU'VE REACHED THE HOME OF LEMONT BROWN.
I CAN'T COME TO THE PHONE RIGHT NOW BECAUSE I'M OUT ENJOYING DINNER, PAID FOR BY THE GENEROUS TAX REFUND YOU SENT ME.
PLEASE LEAVE A MESSAGE AND I'LL GET BACK TO YOU AS SOON AS I'VE FINISHED MY "TWINKIE."
BEEP
©2005 Darrin Bell / Dist. by WPWG, Inc. Candorville.com
8-6
DARRIN BELL

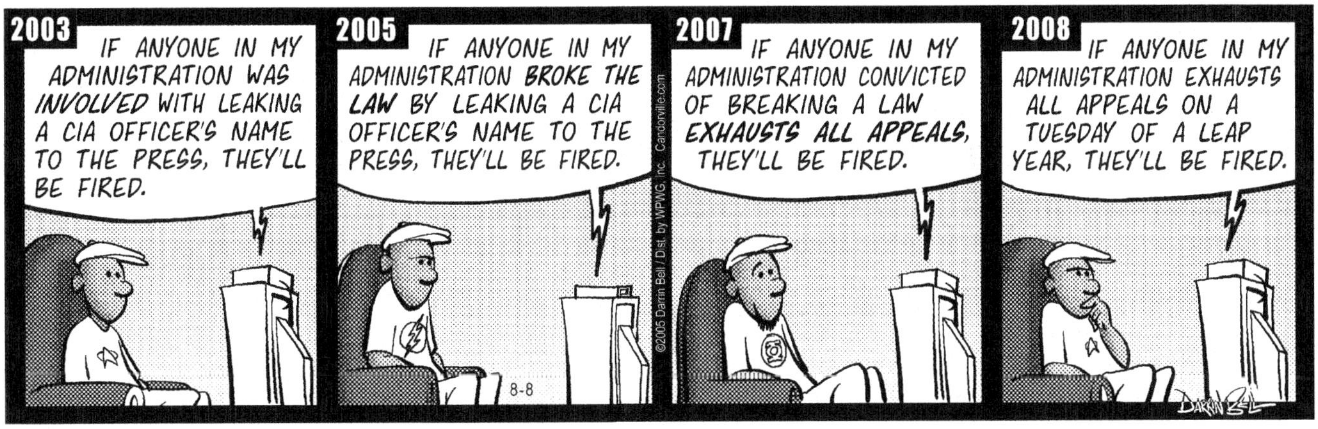
2003
IF ANYONE IN MY ADMINISTRATION WAS INVOLVED WITH LEAKING A CIA OFFICER'S NAME TO THE PRESS, THEY'LL BE FIRED.
2005
IF ANYONE IN MY ADMINISTRATION BROKE THE LAW BY LEAKING A CIA OFFICER'S NAME TO THE PRESS, THEY'LL BE FIRED.
2007
IF ANYONE IN MY ADMINISTRATION CONVICTED OF BREAKING A LAW EXHAUSTS ALL APPEALS, THEY'LL BE FIRED.
2008
IF ANYONE IN MY ADMINISTRATION EXHAUSTS ALL APPEALS ON A TUESDAY OF A LEAP YEAR, THEY'LL BE FIRED.
©2005 Darrin Bell / Dist. by WPWG, Inc. Candorville.com
8-8
DARRIN BELL

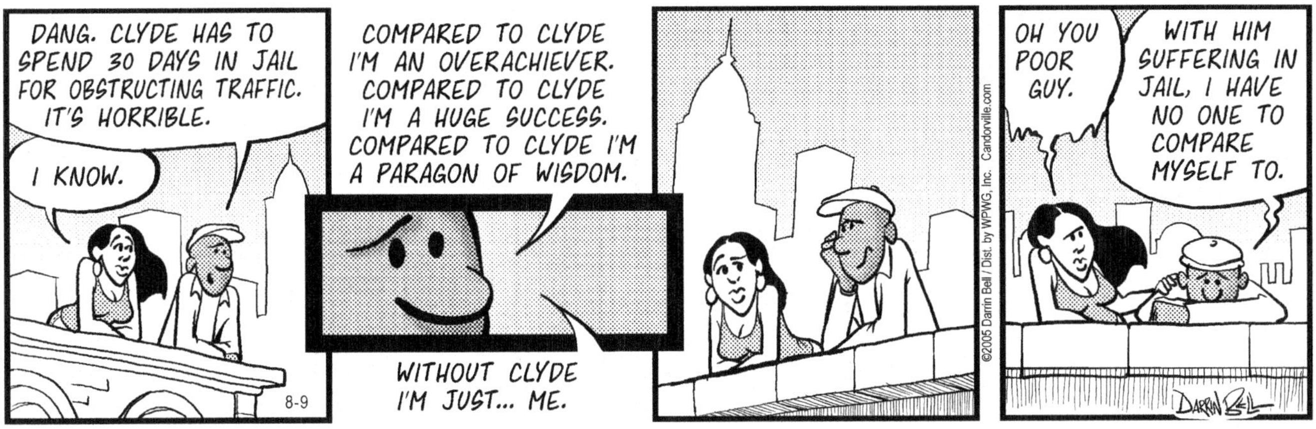
DANG. CLYDE HAS TO SPEND 30 DAYS IN JAIL FOR OBSTRUCTING TRAFFIC. IT'S HORRIBLE.
I KNOW.
COMPARED TO CLYDE I'M AN OVERACHIEVER. COMPARED TO CLYDE I'M A HUGE SUCCESS. COMPARED TO CLYDE I'M A PARAGON OF WISDOM.
WITHOUT CLYDE I'M JUST... ME.
OH YOU POOR GUY.
WITH HIM SUFFERING IN JAIL, I HAVE NO ONE TO COMPARE MYSELF TO.
©2005 Darrin Bell / Dist. by WPWG, Inc. Candorville.com
8-9
DARRIN BELL

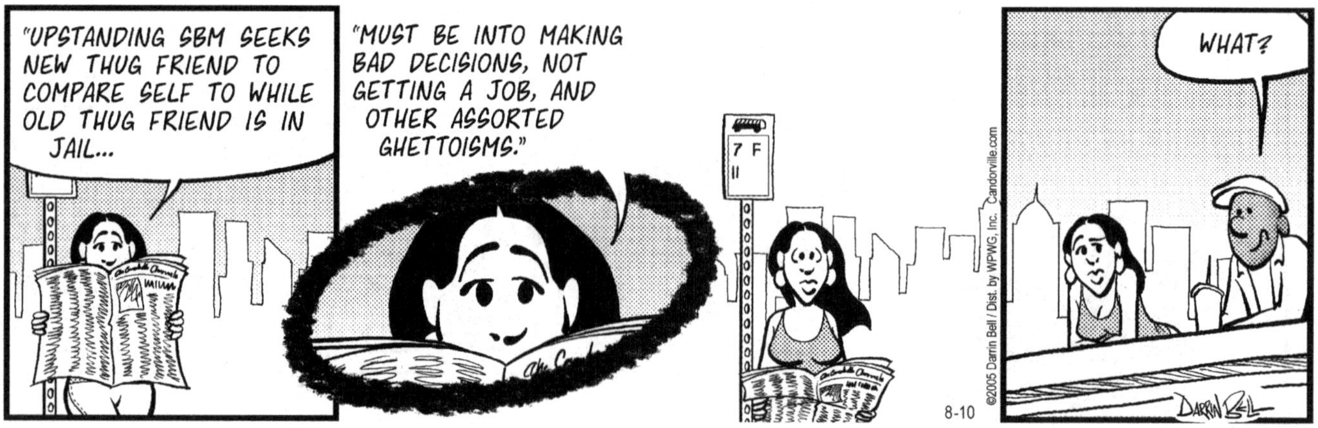

"UPSTANDING SBM SEEKS NEW THUG FRIEND TO COMPARE SELF TO WHILE OLD THUG FRIEND IS IN JAIL...
"MUST BE INTO MAKING BAD DECISIONS, NOT GETTING A JOB, AND OTHER ASSORTED GHETTOISMS."
WHAT?
8-10
©2005 Darrin Bell / Dist. by WPWG, Inc. Candorville.com
DARRIN BELL

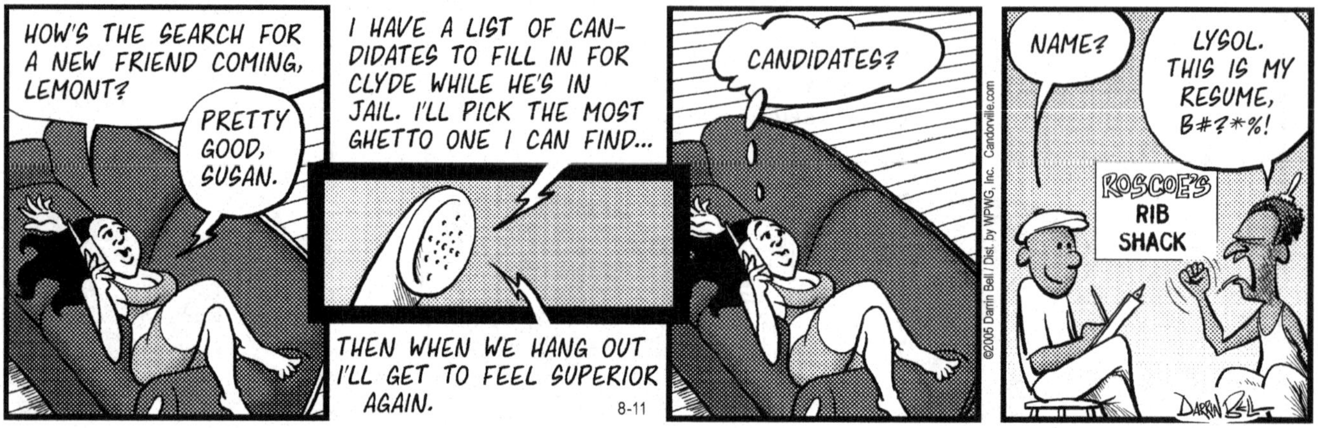

HOW'S THE SEARCH FOR A NEW FRIEND COMING, LEMONT?
PRETTY GOOD, SUSAN.
I HAVE A LIST OF CANDIDATES TO FILL IN FOR CLYDE WHILE HE'S IN JAIL. I'LL PICK THE MOST GHETTO ONE I CAN FIND...
THEN WHEN WE HANG OUT I'LL GET TO FEEL SUPERIOR AGAIN.
8-11
CANDIDATES?
NAME?
LYSOL. THIS IS MY RESUME, B#?*%!
ROSCOE'S RIB SHACK
©2005 Darrin Bell / Dist. by WPWG, Inc. Candorville.com
DARRIN BELL

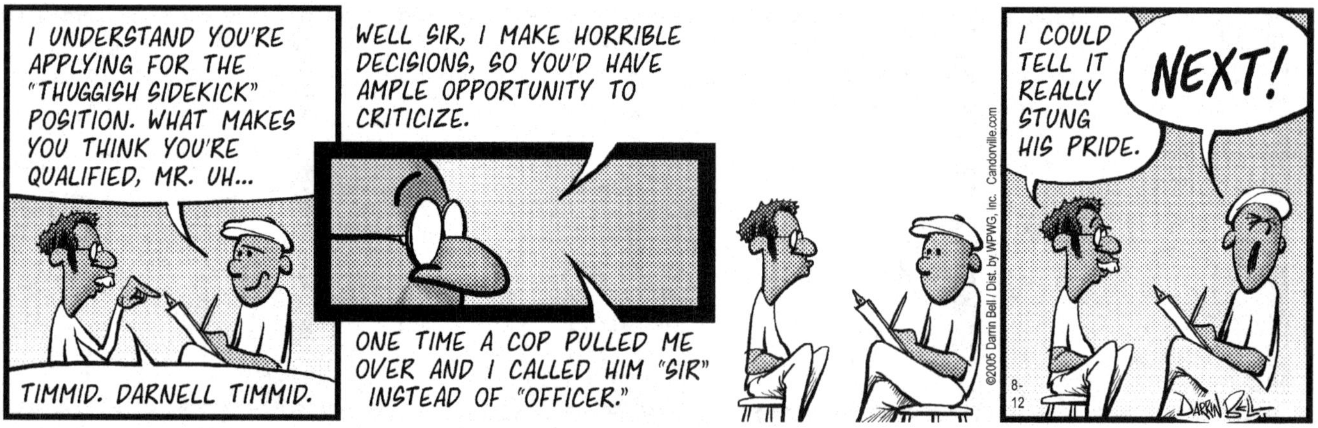

I UNDERSTAND YOU'RE APPLYING FOR THE "THUGGISH SIDEKICK" POSITION. WHAT MAKES YOU THINK YOU'RE QUALIFIED, MR. UH...
TIMMID. DARNELL TIMMID.
WELL SIR, I MAKE HORRIBLE DECISIONS, SO YOU'D HAVE AMPLE OPPORTUNITY TO CRITICIZE.
ONE TIME A COP PULLED ME OVER AND I CALLED HIM "SIR" INSTEAD OF "OFFICER."
©2005 Darrin Bell / Dist. by WPWG, Inc. Candorville.com
I COULD TELL IT REALLY STUNG HIS PRIDE.
NEXT!
8-12
DARRIN BELL

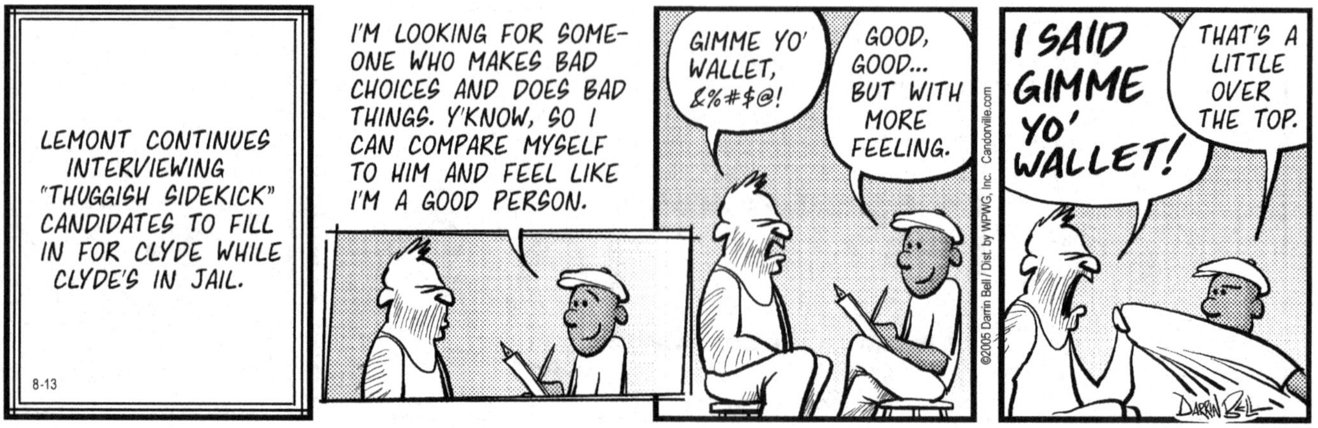

LEMONT CONTINUES INTERVIEWING "THUGGISH SIDEKICK" CANDIDATES TO FILL IN FOR CLYDE WHILE CLYDE'S IN JAIL.
8-13
I'M LOOKING FOR SOMEONE WHO MAKES BAD CHOICES AND DOES BAD THINGS. Y'KNOW, SO I CAN COMPARE MYSELF TO HIM AND FEEL LIKE I'M A GOOD PERSON.
GIMME YO' WALLET, &%#$@!
GOOD, GOOD... BUT WITH MORE FEELING.
©2005 Darrin Bell / Dist. by WPWG, Inc. Candorville.com
I SAID GIMME YO' WALLET!
THAT'S A LITTLE OVER THE TOP.
DARRIN BELL

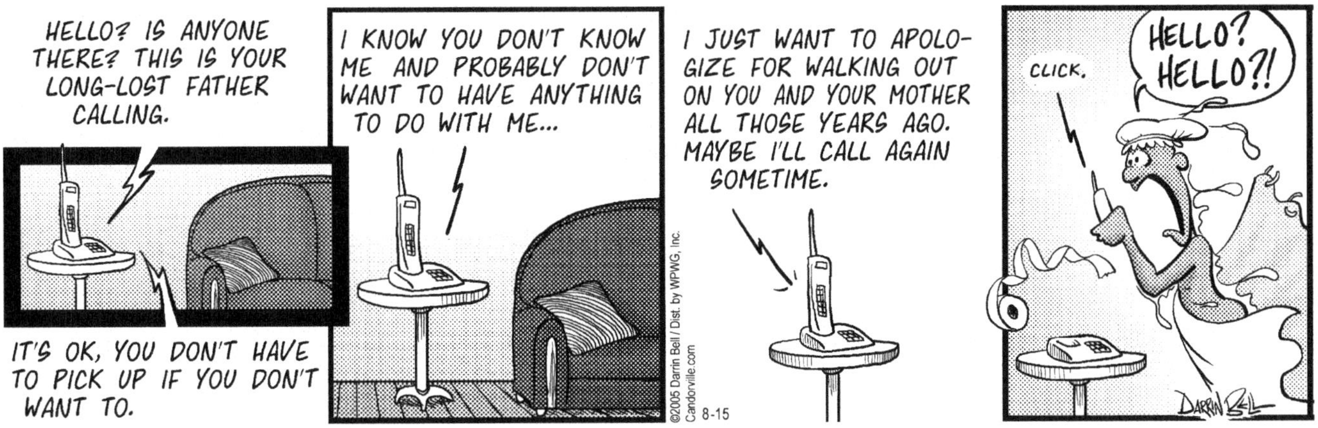
HELLO? IS ANYONE THERE? THIS IS YOUR LONG-LOST FATHER CALLING.
IT'S OK, YOU DON'T HAVE TO PICK UP IF YOU DON'T WANT TO.
I KNOW YOU DON'T KNOW ME AND PROBABLY DON'T WANT TO HAVE ANYTHING TO DO WITH ME...
©2005 Darrin Bell / Dist. by WPWG, Inc. Candorville.com
8-15
I JUST WANT TO APOLOGIZE FOR WALKING OUT ON YOU AND YOUR MOTHER ALL THOSE YEARS AGO. MAYBE I'LL CALL AGAIN SOMETIME.
CLICK.
HELLO? HELLO?!
DARRIN BELL

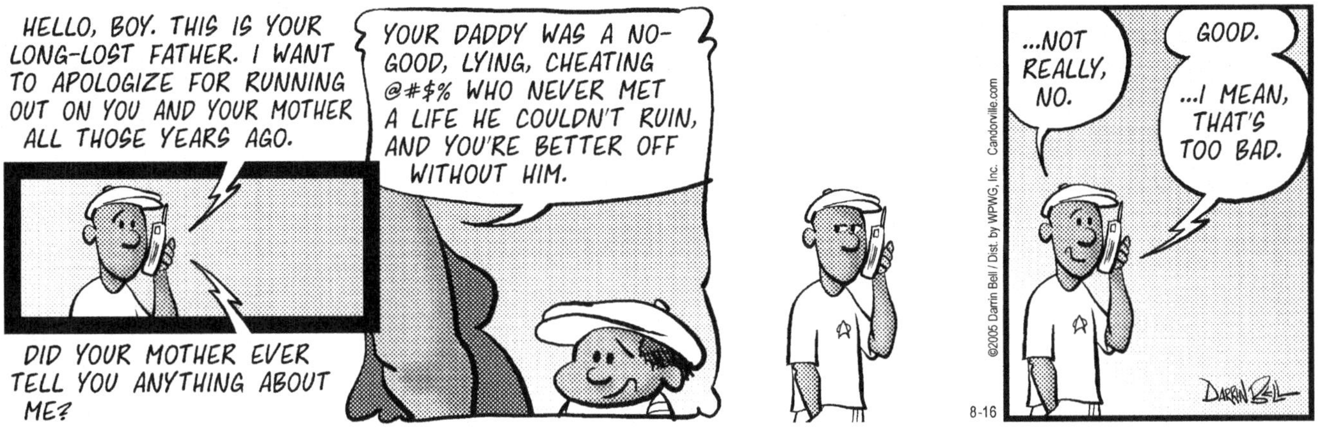
HELLO, BOY. THIS IS YOUR LONG-LOST FATHER. I WANT TO APOLOGIZE FOR RUNNING OUT ON YOU AND YOUR MOTHER ALL THOSE YEARS AGO.
DID YOUR MOTHER EVER TELL YOU ANYTHING ABOUT ME?
YOUR DADDY WAS A NO-GOOD, LYING, CHEATING @#$% WHO NEVER MET A LIFE HE COULDN'T RUIN, AND YOU'RE BETTER OFF WITHOUT HIM.
...NOT REALLY, NO.
GOOD.
...I MEAN, THAT'S TOO BAD.
©2005 Darrin Bell / Dist. by WPWG, Inc. Candorville.com
8-16
DARRIN BELL

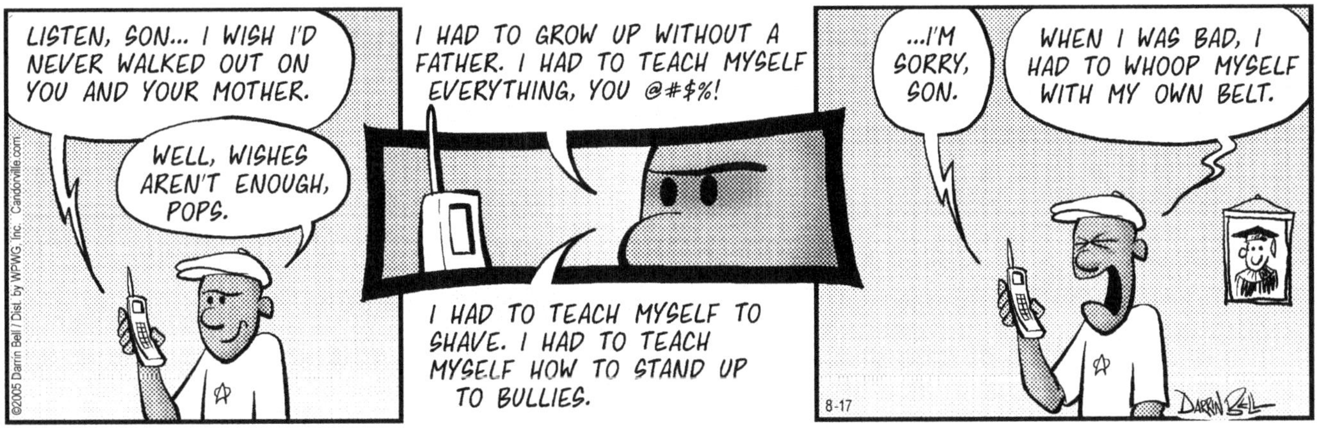
LISTEN, SON... I WISH I'D NEVER WALKED OUT ON YOU AND YOUR MOTHER.
WELL, WISHES AREN'T ENOUGH, POPS.
©2005 Darrin Bell / Dist. by WPWG, Inc. Candorville.com
I HAD TO GROW UP WITHOUT A FATHER. I HAD TO TEACH MYSELF EVERYTHING, YOU @#$%!
I HAD TO TEACH MYSELF TO SHAVE. I HAD TO TEACH MYSELF HOW TO STAND UP TO BULLIES.
...I'M SORRY, SON.
WHEN I WAS BAD, I HAD TO WHOOP MYSELF WITH MY OWN BELT.
8-17
DARRIN BELL

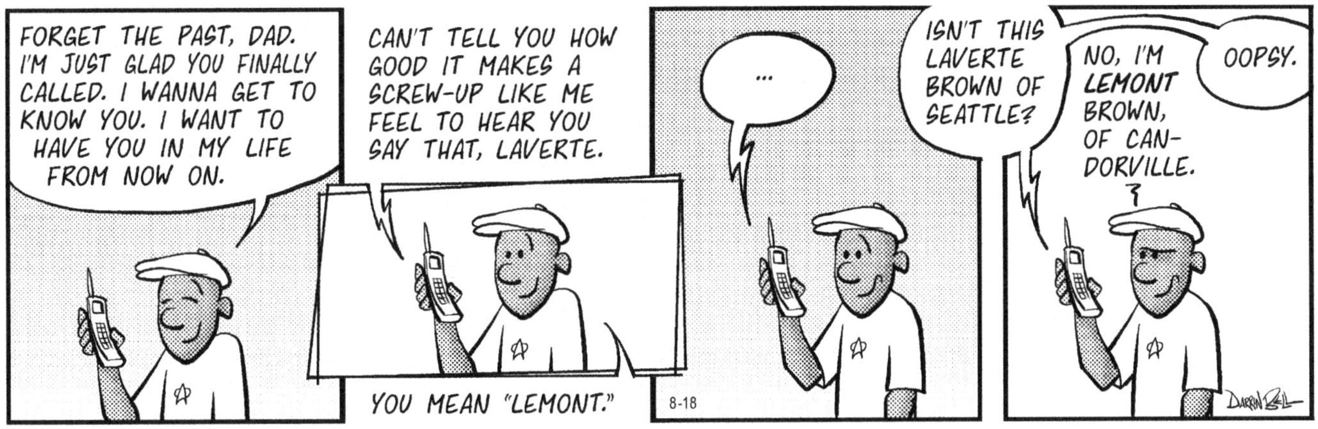
FORGET THE PAST, DAD. I'M JUST GLAD YOU FINALLY CALLED. I WANNA GET TO KNOW YOU. I WANT TO HAVE YOU IN MY LIFE FROM NOW ON.
CAN'T TELL YOU HOW GOOD IT MAKES A SCREW-UP LIKE ME FEEL TO HEAR YOU SAY THAT, LAVERTE.
YOU MEAN "LEMONT."
...
8-18
ISN'T THIS LAVERTE BROWN OF SEATTLE?
NO, I'M **LEMONT** BROWN, OF CANDORVILLE.
OOPSY.
DARRIN BELL

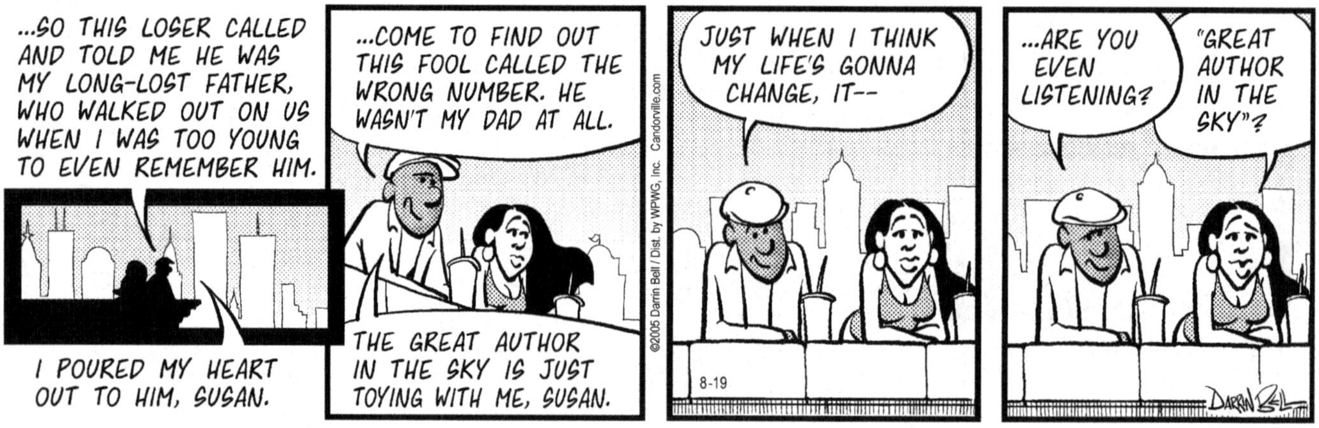
...SO THIS LOSER CALLED AND TOLD ME HE WAS MY LONG-LOST FATHER, WHO WALKED OUT ON US WHEN I WAS TOO YOUNG TO EVEN REMEMBER HIM.
I POURED MY HEART OUT TO HIM, SUSAN.
...COME TO FIND OUT THIS FOOL CALLED THE WRONG NUMBER. HE WASN'T MY DAD AT ALL.
THE GREAT AUTHOR IN THE SKY IS JUST TOYING WITH ME, SUSAN.
©2005 Darrin Bell / Dist. by WPWG, Inc. Candorville.com
JUST WHEN I THINK MY LIFE'S GONNA CHANGE, IT--
8-19
...ARE YOU EVEN LISTENING?
"GREAT AUTHOR IN THE SKY"?
DARRIN BELL

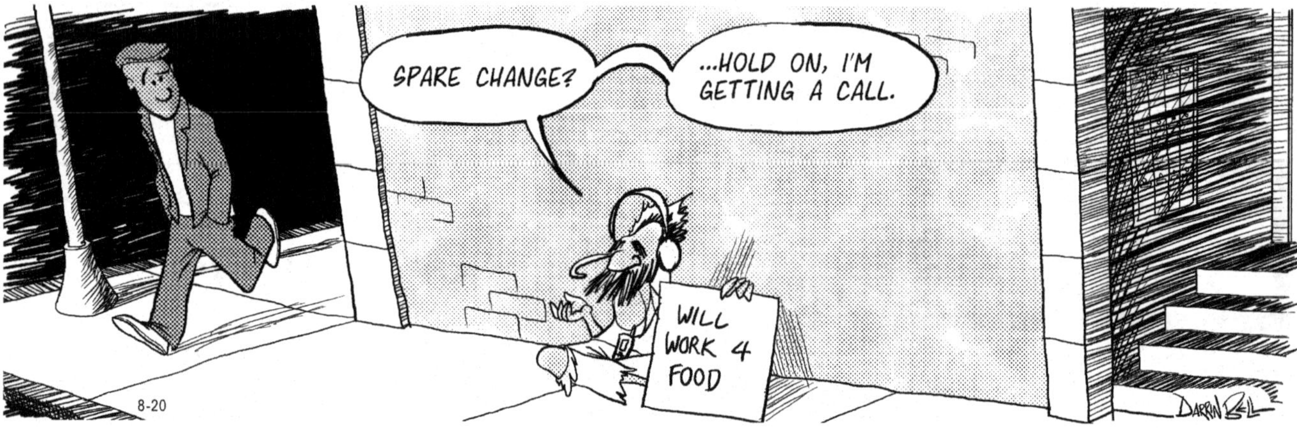
SPARE CHANGE?
...HOLD ON, I'M GETTING A CALL.
WILL WORK 4 FOOD
8-20
©2005 Darrin Bell / Dist. by WPWG, Inc. Candorville.com
DARRIN BELL

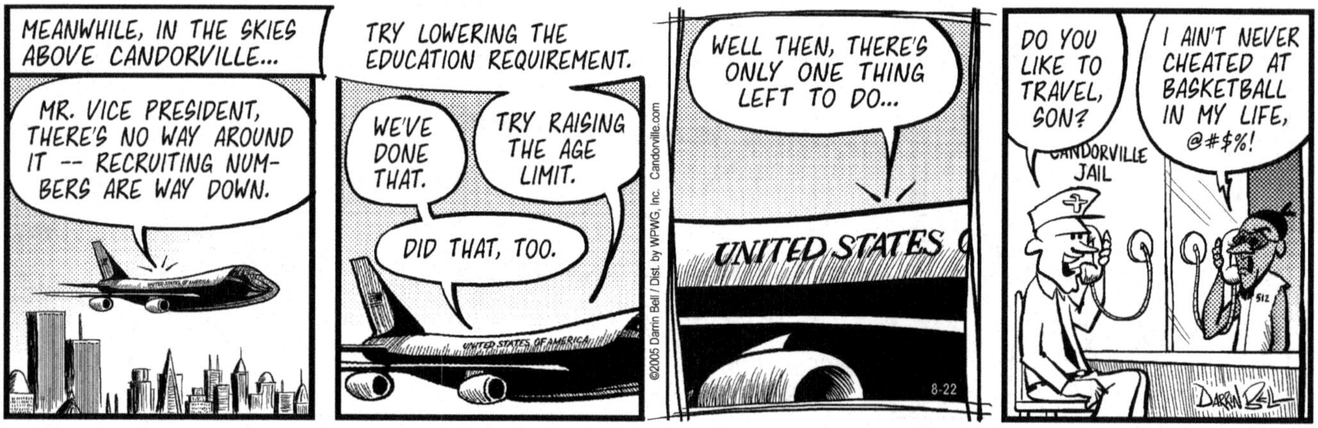
MEANWHILE, IN THE SKIES ABOVE CANDORVILLE...
MR. VICE PRESIDENT, THERE'S NO WAY AROUND IT -- RECRUITING NUMBERS ARE WAY DOWN.
TRY LOWERING THE EDUCATION REQUIREMENT.
WE'VE DONE THAT.
TRY RAISING THE AGE LIMIT.
DID THAT, TOO.
©2005 Darrin Bell / Dist. by WPWG, Inc. Candorville.com
WELL THEN, THERE'S ONLY ONE THING LEFT TO DO...
UNITED STATES
8-22
DO YOU LIKE TO TRAVEL, SON?
I AIN'T NEVER CHEATED AT BASKETBALL IN MY LIFE, @#$%!
CANDORVILLE JAIL
DARRIN BELL

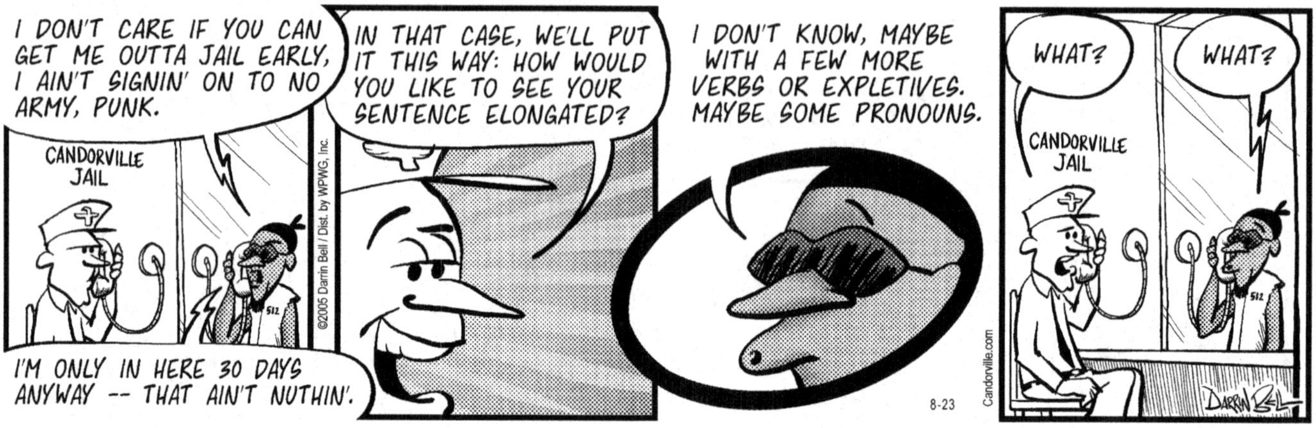
I DON'T CARE IF YOU CAN GET ME OUTTA JAIL EARLY, I AIN'T SIGNIN' ON TO NO ARMY, PUNK.
CANDORVILLE JAIL
I'M ONLY IN HERE 30 DAYS ANYWAY -- THAT AIN'T NUTHIN'.
©2005 Darrin Bell / Dist. by WPWG, Inc.
IN THAT CASE, WE'LL PUT IT THIS WAY: HOW WOULD YOU LIKE TO SEE YOUR SENTENCE ELONGATED?
I DON'T KNOW, MAYBE WITH A FEW MORE VERBS OR EXPLETIVES. MAYBE SOME PRONOUNS.
8-23
Candorville.com
WHAT?
WHAT?
CANDORVILLE JAIL
DARRIN BELL

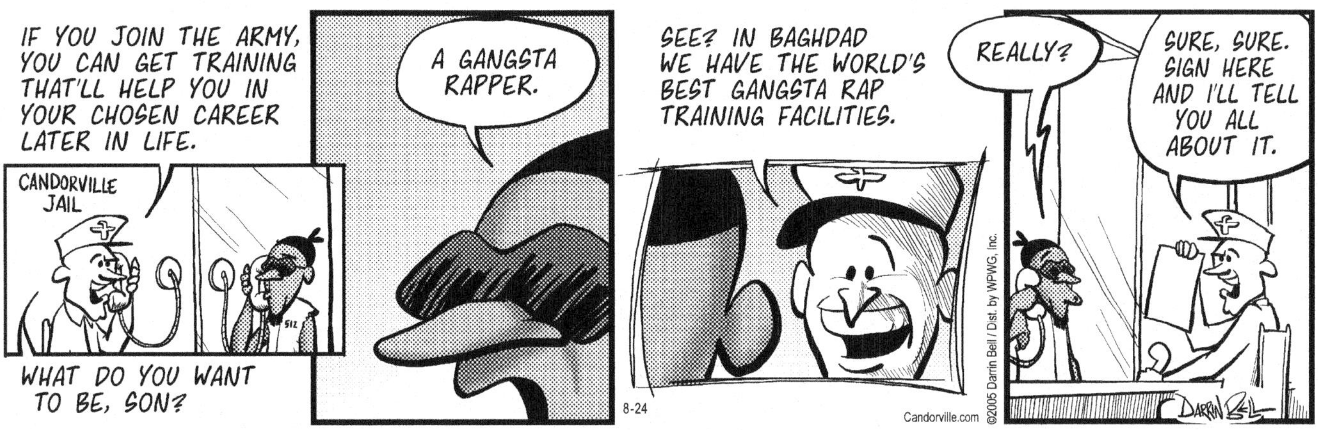
IF YOU JOIN THE ARMY, YOU CAN GET TRAINING THAT'LL HELP YOU IN YOUR CHOSEN CAREER LATER IN LIFE.
CANDORVILLE JAIL
WHAT DO YOU WANT TO BE, SON?
A GANGSTA RAPPER.
SEE? IN BAGHDAD WE HAVE THE WORLD'S BEST GANGSTA RAP TRAINING FACILITIES.
REALLY?
SURE, SURE. SIGN HERE AND I'LL TELL YOU ALL ABOUT IT.
8-24
Candorville.com
©2005 Darrin Bell / Dist. by WPWG, Inc.
DARRIN BELL

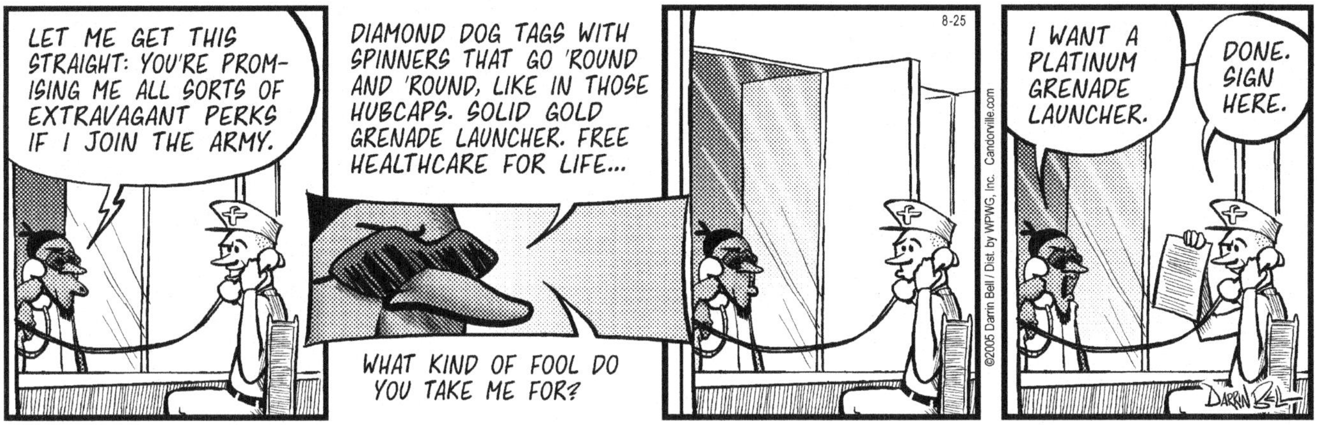
LET ME GET THIS STRAIGHT: YOU'RE PROMISING ME ALL SORTS OF EXTRAVAGANT PERKS IF I JOIN THE ARMY.
DIAMOND DOG TAGS WITH SPINNERS THAT GO 'ROUND AND 'ROUND, LIKE IN THOSE HUBCAPS. SOLID GOLD GRENADE LAUNCHER. FREE HEALTHCARE FOR LIFE...
WHAT KIND OF FOOL DO YOU TAKE ME FOR?
8-25
©2005 Darrin Bell / Dist. by WPWG, Inc. Candorville.com
I WANT A PLATINUM GRENADE LAUNCHER.
DONE. SIGN HERE.
DARRIN BELL

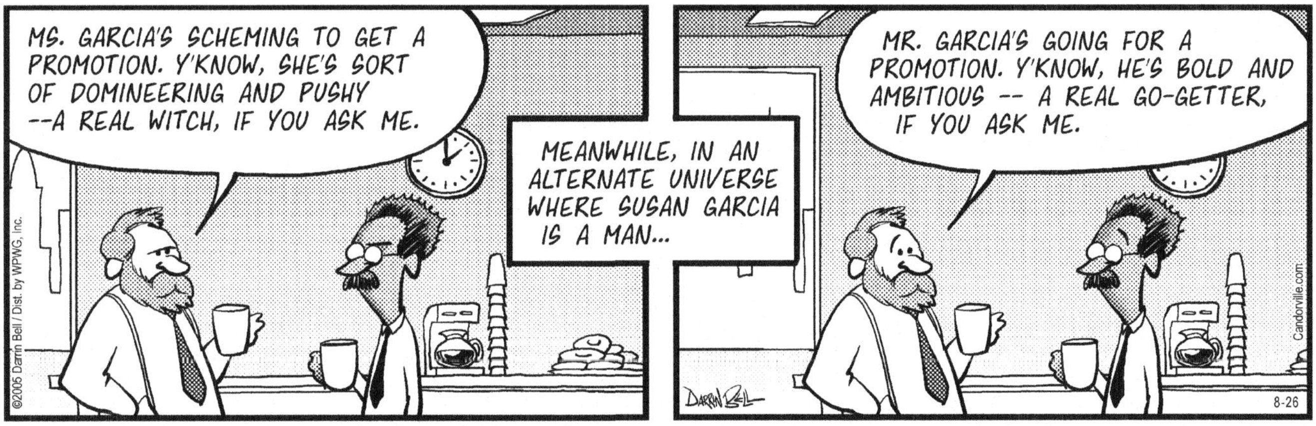
MS. GARCIA'S SCHEMING TO GET A PROMOTION. Y'KNOW, SHE'S SORT OF DOMINEERING AND PUSHY --A REAL WITCH, IF YOU ASK ME.
©2005 Darrin Bell / Dist. by WPWG, Inc.
DARRIN BELL
MEANWHILE, IN AN ALTERNATE UNIVERSE WHERE SUSAN GARCIA IS A MAN...
MR. GARCIA'S GOING FOR A PROMOTION. Y'KNOW, HE'S BOLD AND AMBITIOUS -- A REAL GO-GETTER, IF YOU ASK ME.
Candorville.com
8-26

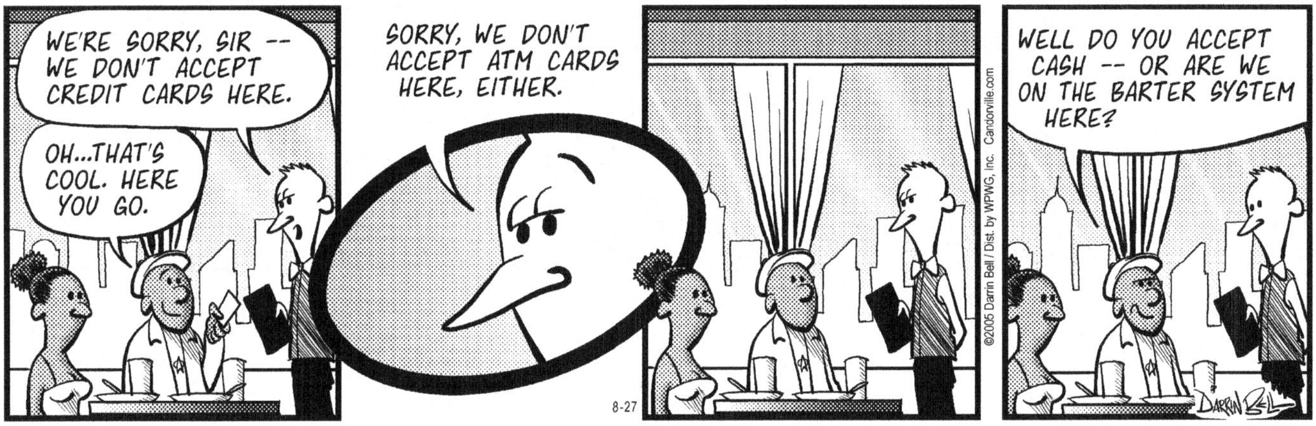
WE'RE SORRY, SIR -- WE DON'T ACCEPT CREDIT CARDS HERE.
OH...THAT'S COOL. HERE YOU GO.
SORRY, WE DON'T ACCEPT ATM CARDS HERE, EITHER.
8-27
©2005 Darrin Bell / Dist. by WPWG, Inc. Candorville.com
WELL DO YOU ACCEPT CASH -- OR ARE WE ON THE BARTER SYSTEM HERE?
DARRIN BELL

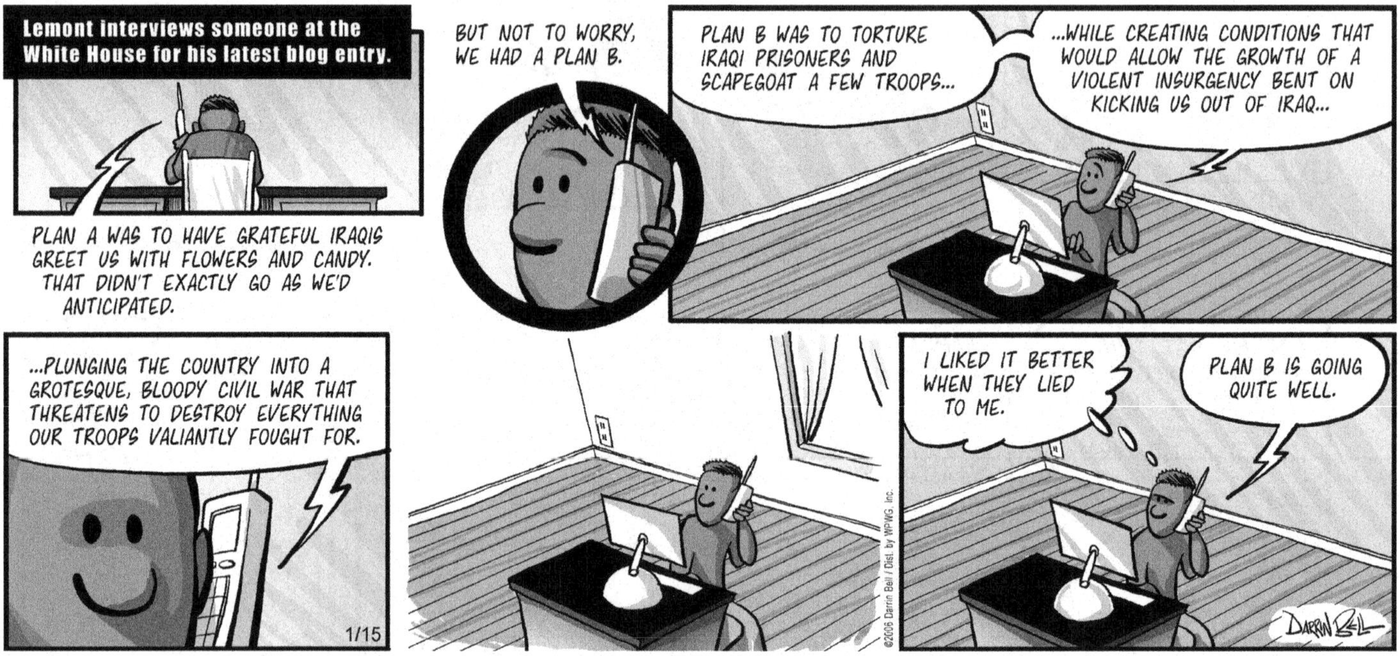
Lemont interviews someone at the White House for his latest blog entry.
PLAN A WAS TO HAVE GRATEFUL IRAQIS GREET US WITH FLOWERS AND CANDY. THAT DIDN'T EXACTLY GO AS WE'D ANTICIPATED.
BUT NOT TO WORRY, WE HAD A PLAN B.
PLAN B WAS TO TORTURE IRAQI PRISONERS AND SCAPEGOAT A FEW TROOPS...
...WHILE CREATING CONDITIONS THAT WOULD ALLOW THE GROWTH OF A VIOLENT INSURGENCY BENT ON KICKING US OUT OF IRAQ...
...PLUNGING THE COUNTRY INTO A GROTESQUE, BLOODY CIVIL WAR THAT THREATENS TO DESTROY EVERYTHING OUR TROOPS VALIANTLY FOUGHT FOR.
1/15
©2006 Darrin Bell / Dist. by WPWG, Inc.
I LIKED IT BETTER WHEN THEY LIED TO ME.
PLAN B IS GOING QUITE WELL.
DARRIN BELL

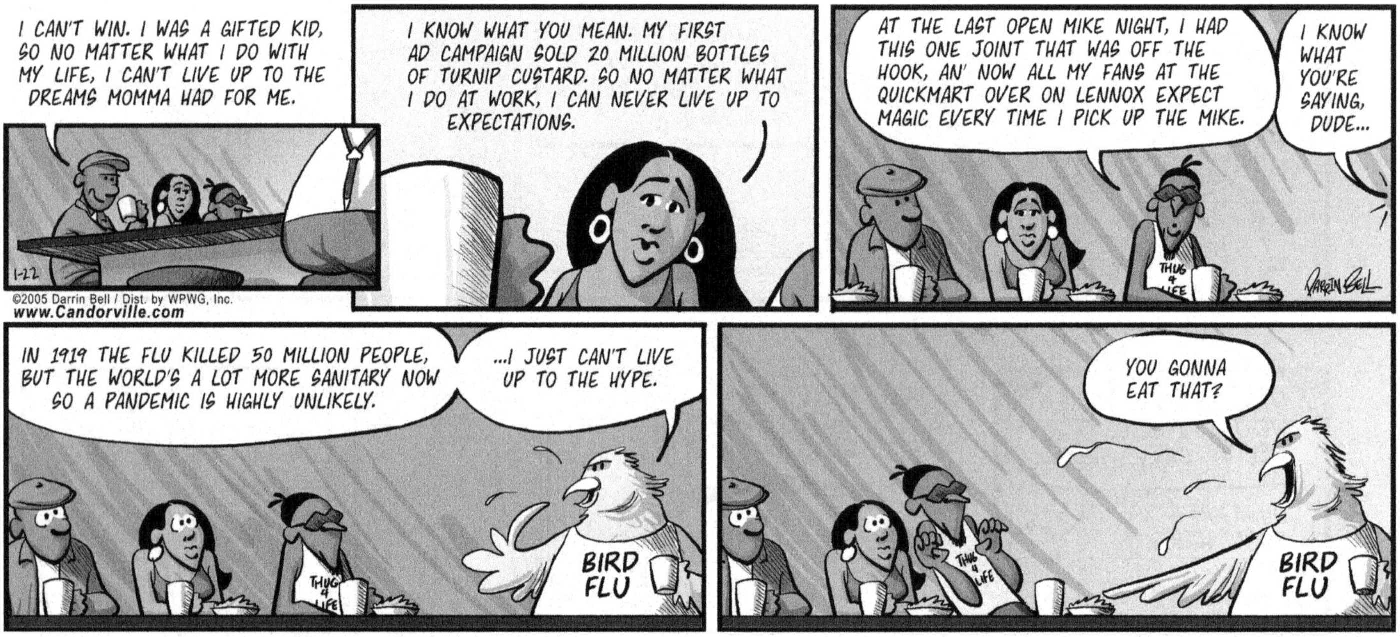
I CAN'T WIN. I WAS A GIFTED KID, SO NO MATTER WHAT I DO WITH MY LIFE, I CAN'T LIVE UP TO THE DREAMS MOMMA HAD FOR ME.
1-22
©2005 Darrin Bell / Dist. by WPWG, Inc.
www.Candorville.com
I KNOW WHAT YOU MEAN. MY FIRST AD CAMPAIGN SOLD 20 MILLION BOTTLES OF TURNIP CUSTARD. SO NO MATTER WHAT I DO AT WORK, I CAN NEVER LIVE UP TO EXPECTATIONS.
AT THE LAST OPEN MIKE NIGHT, I HAD THIS ONE JOINT THAT WAS OFF THE HOOK, AN' NOW ALL MY FANS AT THE QUICKMART OVER ON LENNOX EXPECT MAGIC EVERY TIME I PICK UP THE MIKE.
I KNOW WHAT YOU'RE SAYING, DUDE...
THUG 4 LIFE
DARRIN BELL
IN 1919 THE FLU KILLED 50 MILLION PEOPLE, BUT THE WORLD'S A LOT MORE SANITARY NOW SO A PANDEMIC IS HIGHLY UNLIKELY.
...I JUST CAN'T LIVE UP TO THE HYPE.
BIRD FLU
YOU GONNA EAT THAT?
BIRD FLU

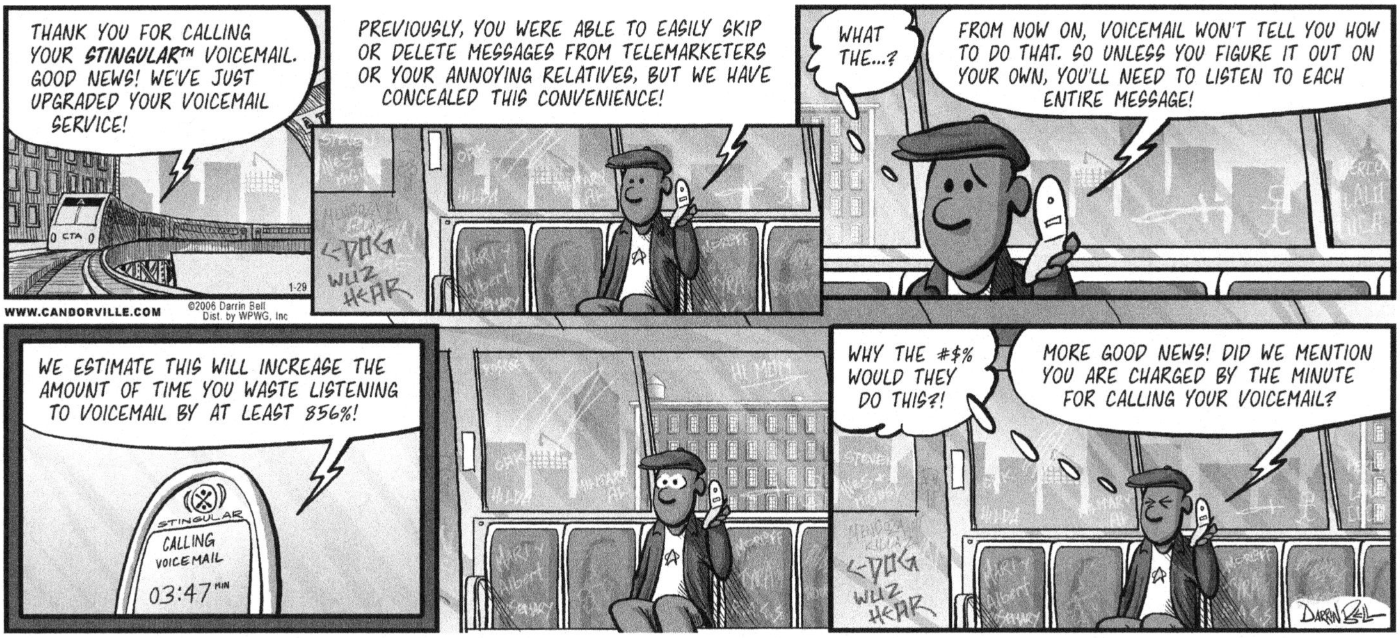
THANK YOU FOR CALLING YOUR STINGULAR™ VOICEMAIL. GOOD NEWS! WE'VE JUST UPGRADED YOUR VOICEMAIL SERVICE!
PREVIOUSLY, YOU WERE ABLE TO EASILY SKIP OR DELETE MESSAGES FROM TELEMARKETERS OR YOUR ANNOYING RELATIVES, BUT WE HAVE CONCEALED THIS CONVENIENCE!
WHAT THE...?
FROM NOW ON, VOICEMAIL WON'T TELL YOU HOW TO DO THAT. SO UNLESS YOU FIGURE IT OUT ON YOUR OWN, YOU'LL NEED TO LISTEN TO EACH ENTIRE MESSAGE!
WE ESTIMATE THIS WILL INCREASE THE AMOUNT OF TIME YOU WASTE LISTENING TO VOICEMAIL BY AT LEAST 856%!
STINGULAR
CALLING VOICEMAIL
03:47 MIN
WHY THE #$% WOULD THEY DO THIS?!
MORE GOOD NEWS! DID WE MENTION YOU ARE CHARGED BY THE MINUTE FOR CALLING YOUR VOICEMAIL?
C-DOG WUZ HEAR
WWW.CANDORVILLE.COM
©2006 Darrin Bell Dist. by WPWG, Inc
1-29
DARRIN BELL

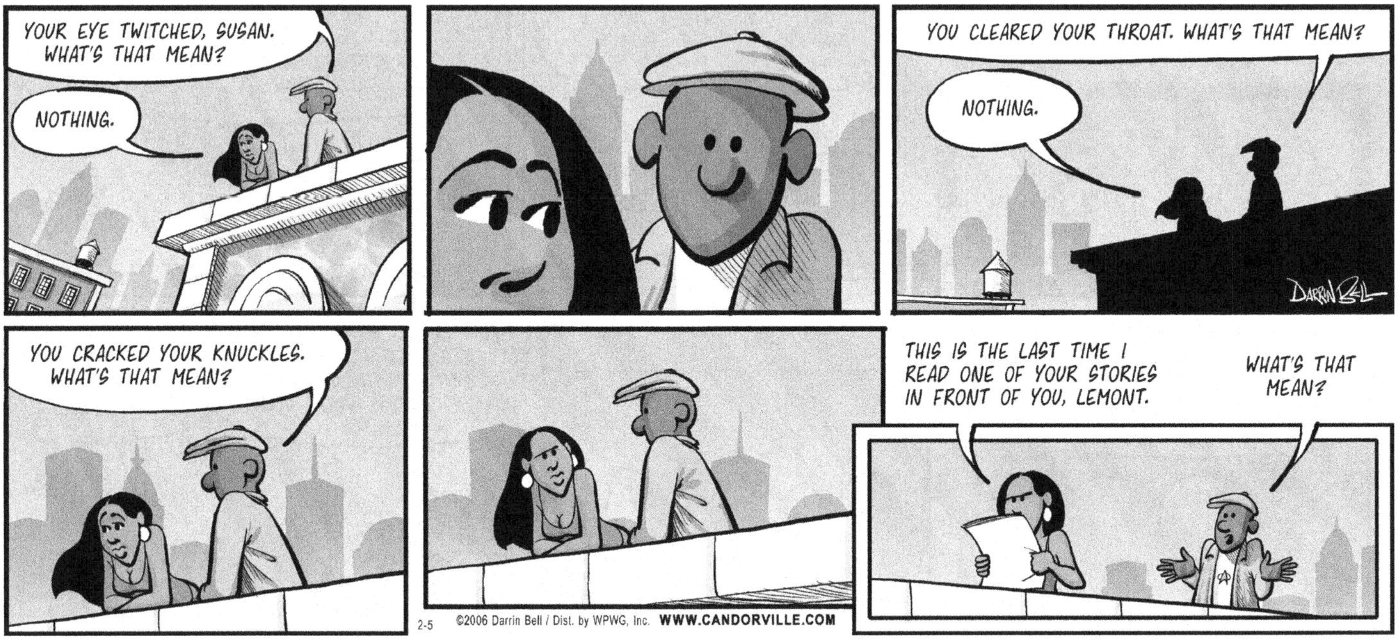
YOUR EYE TWITCHED, SUSAN. WHAT'S THAT MEAN?
NOTHING.
YOU CLEARED YOUR THROAT. WHAT'S THAT MEAN?
NOTHING.
DARRIN BELL
YOU CRACKED YOUR KNUCKLES. WHAT'S THAT MEAN?
THIS IS THE LAST TIME I READ ONE OF YOUR STORIES IN FRONT OF YOU, LEMONT.
WHAT'S THAT MEAN?
2-5
©2006 Darrin Bell / Dist. by WPWG, Inc. WWW.CANDORVILLE.COM

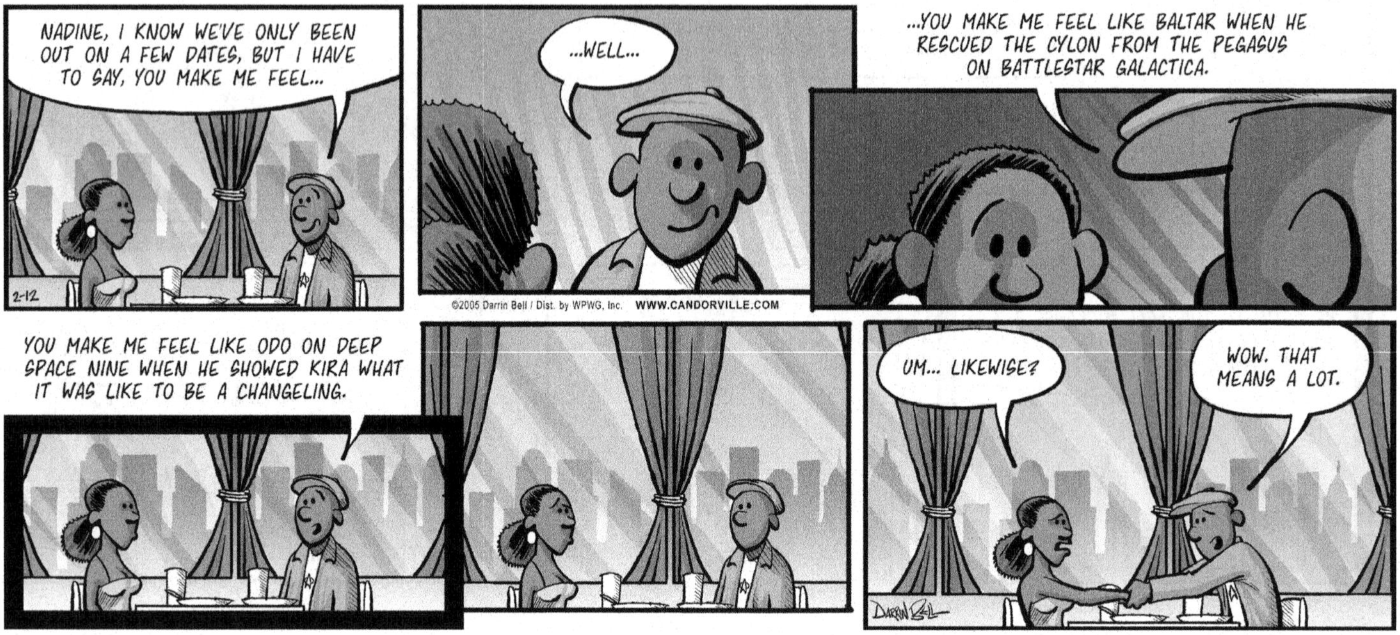
NADINE, I KNOW WE'VE ONLY BEEN OUT ON A FEW DATES, BUT I HAVE TO SAY, YOU MAKE ME FEEL...
2-12
...WELL...
©2005 Darrin Bell / Dist. by WPWG, Inc. WWW.CANDORVILLE.COM
...YOU MAKE ME FEEL LIKE BALTAR WHEN HE RESCUED THE CYLON FROM THE PEGASUS ON BATTLESTAR GALACTICA.
YOU MAKE ME FEEL LIKE ODO ON DEEP SPACE NINE WHEN HE SHOWED KIRA WHAT IT WAS LIKE TO BE A CHANGELING.
UM... LIKEWISE?
WOW. THAT MEANS A LOT.
DARRIN BELL

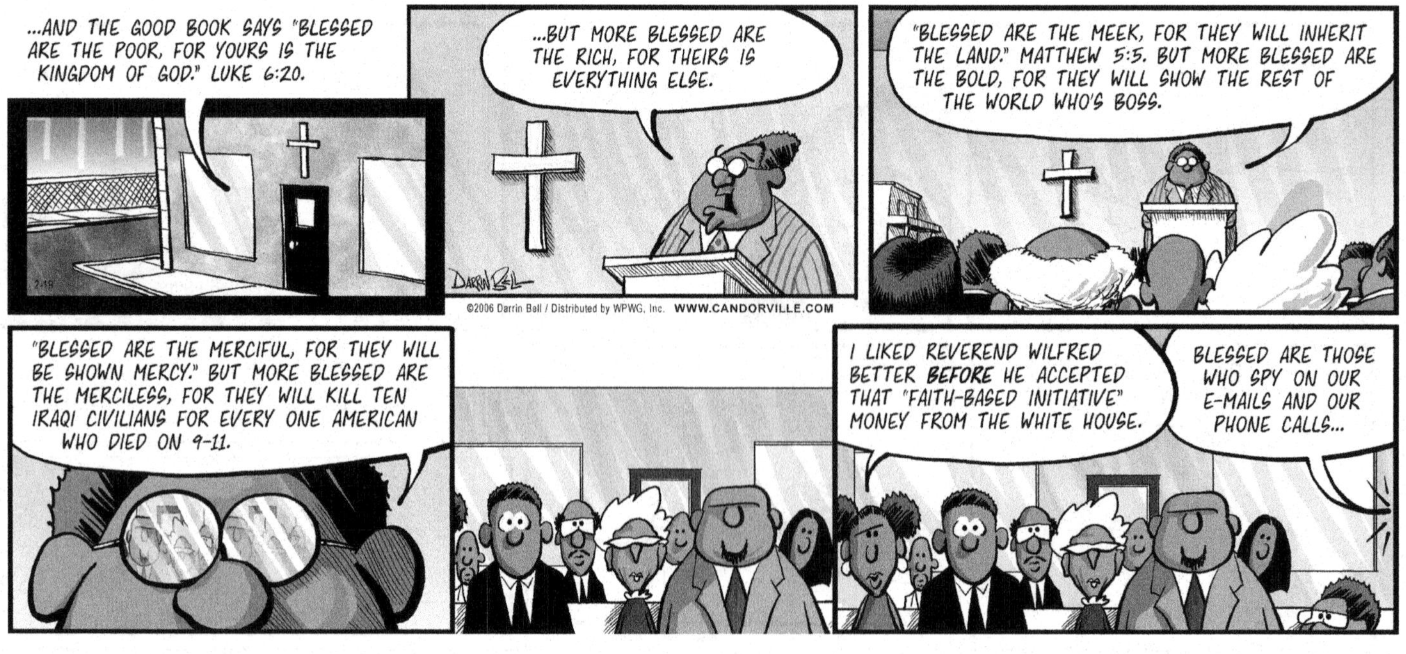
...AND THE GOOD BOOK SAYS "BLESSED ARE THE POOR, FOR YOURS IS THE KINGDOM OF GOD." LUKE 6:20.
...BUT MORE BLESSED ARE THE RICH, FOR THEIRS IS EVERYTHING ELSE.
DARRIN BELL
©2006 Darrin Bell / Distributed by WPWG, Inc. WWW.CANDORVILLE.COM
"BLESSED ARE THE MEEK, FOR THEY WILL INHERIT THE LAND." MATTHEW 5:5. BUT MORE BLESSED ARE THE BOLD, FOR THEY WILL SHOW THE REST OF THE WORLD WHO'S BOSS.
"BLESSED ARE THE MERCIFUL, FOR THEY WILL BE SHOWN MERCY." BUT MORE BLESSED ARE THE MERCILESS, FOR THEY WILL KILL TEN IRAQI CIVILIANS FOR EVERY ONE AMERICAN WHO DIED ON 9-11.
I LIKED REVEREND WILFRED BETTER BEFORE HE ACCEPTED THAT "FAITH-BASED INITIATIVE" MONEY FROM THE WHITE HOUSE.
BLESSED ARE THOSE WHO SPY ON OUR E-MAILS AND OUR PHONE CALLS...

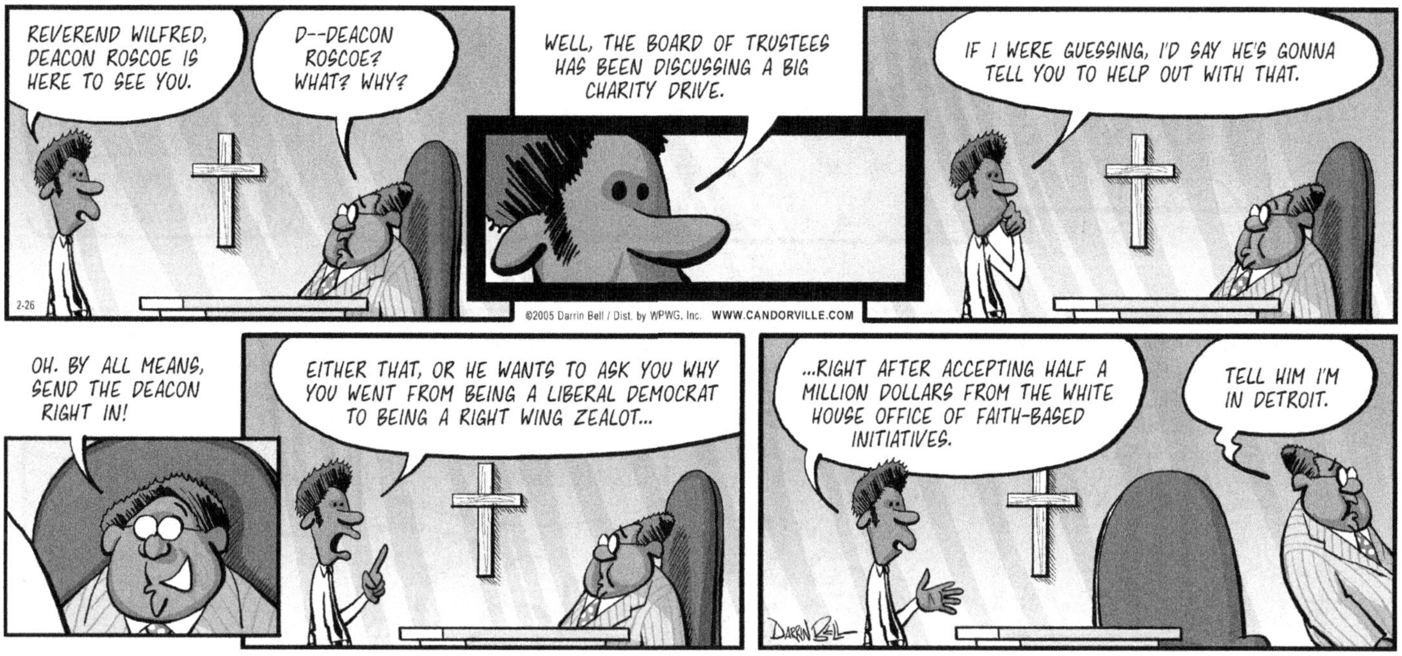
REVEREND WILFRED, DEACON ROSCOE IS HERE TO SEE YOU.
D--DEACON ROSCOE? WHAT? WHY?
WELL, THE BOARD OF TRUSTEES HAS BEEN DISCUSSING A BIG CHARITY DRIVE.
IF I WERE GUESSING, I'D SAY HE'S GONNA TELL YOU TO HELP OUT WITH THAT.
2-26
©2005 Darrin Bell / Dist. by WPWG, Inc. WWW.CANDORVILLE.COM
OH. BY ALL MEANS, SEND THE DEACON RIGHT IN!
EITHER THAT, OR HE WANTS TO ASK YOU WHY YOU WENT FROM BEING A LIBERAL DEMOCRAT TO BEING A RIGHT WING ZEALOT...
...RIGHT AFTER ACCEPTING HALF A MILLION DOLLARS FROM THE WHITE HOUSE OFFICE OF FAITH-BASED INITIATIVES.
TELL HIM I'M IN DETROIT.
DARRIN BELL

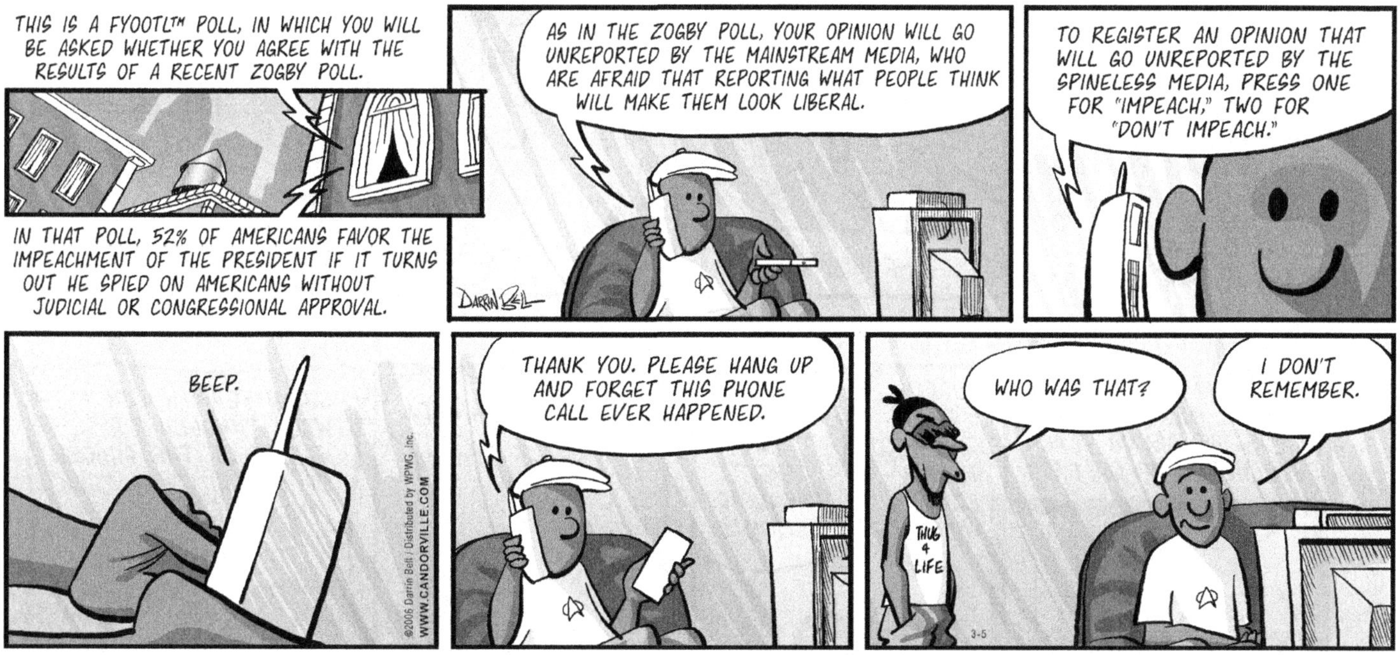
THIS IS A FYOOTL™ POLL, IN WHICH YOU WILL BE ASKED WHETHER YOU AGREE WITH THE RESULTS OF A RECENT ZOGBY POLL.
IN THAT POLL, 52% OF AMERICANS FAVOR THE IMPEACHMENT OF THE PRESIDENT IF IT TURNS OUT HE SPIED ON AMERICANS WITHOUT JUDICIAL OR CONGRESSIONAL APPROVAL.
AS IN THE ZOGBY POLL, YOUR OPINION WILL GO UNREPORTED BY THE MAINSTREAM MEDIA, WHO ARE AFRAID THAT REPORTING WHAT PEOPLE THINK WILL MAKE THEM LOOK LIBERAL.
DARRIN BELL
TO REGISTER AN OPINION THAT WILL GO UNREPORTED BY THE SPINELESS MEDIA, PRESS ONE FOR "IMPEACH," TWO FOR "DON'T IMPEACH."
BEEP.
©2006 Darrin Bell / Distributed by WPWG, Inc.
WWW.CANDORVILLE.COM
THANK YOU. PLEASE HANG UP AND FORGET THIS PHONE CALL EVER HAPPENED.
WHO WAS THAT?
I DON'T REMEMBER.
THUG 4 LIFE
3-5

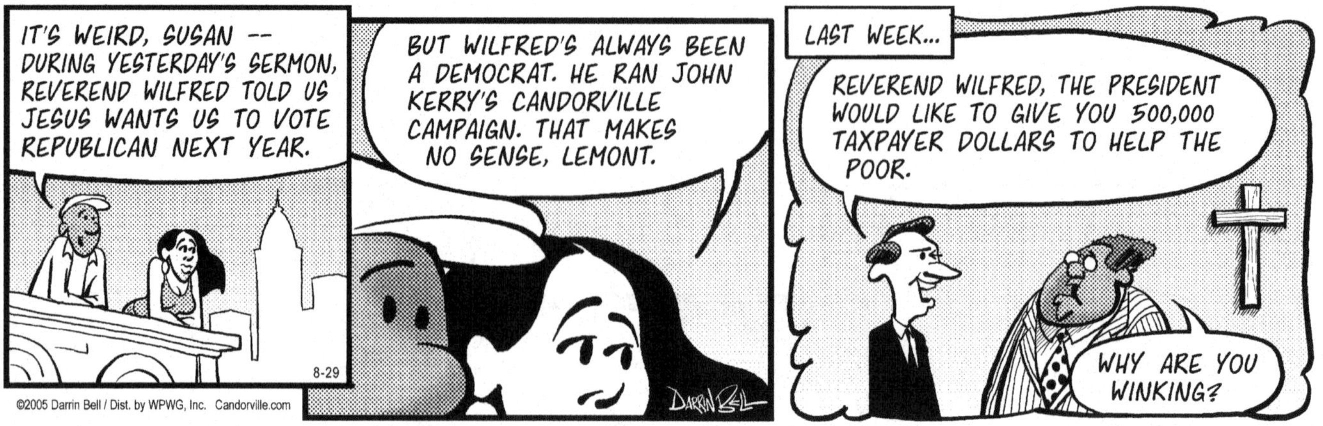
IT'S WEIRD, SUSAN -- DURING YESTERDAY'S SERMON, REVEREND WILFRED TOLD US JESUS WANTS US TO VOTE REPUBLICAN NEXT YEAR.
BUT WILFRED'S ALWAYS BEEN A DEMOCRAT. HE RAN JOHN KERRY'S CANDORVILLE CAMPAIGN. THAT MAKES NO SENSE, LEMONT.
LAST WEEK...
REVEREND WILFRED, THE PRESIDENT WOULD LIKE TO GIVE YOU 500,000 TAXPAYER DOLLARS TO HELP THE POOR.
WHY ARE YOU WINKING?
8-29
©2005 Darrin Bell / Dist. by WPWG, Inc. Candorville.com
DARRIN BELL

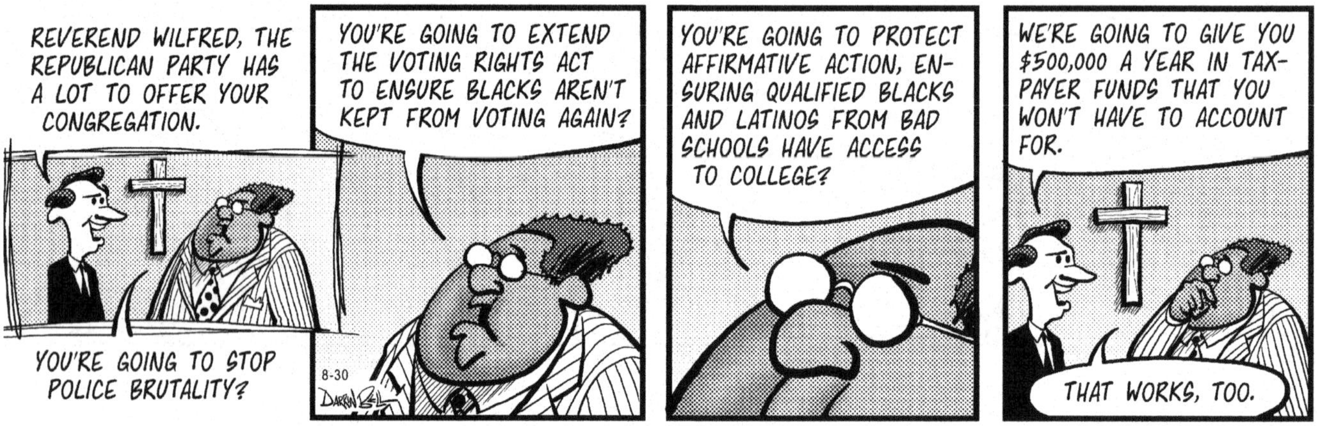
REVEREND WILFRED, THE REPUBLICAN PARTY HAS A LOT TO OFFER YOUR CONGREGATION.
YOU'RE GOING TO STOP POLICE BRUTALITY?
YOU'RE GOING TO EXTEND THE VOTING RIGHTS ACT TO ENSURE BLACKS AREN'T KEPT FROM VOTING AGAIN?
YOU'RE GOING TO PROTECT AFFIRMATIVE ACTION, ENSURING QUALIFIED BLACKS AND LATINOS FROM BAD SCHOOLS HAVE ACCESS TO COLLEGE?
WE'RE GOING TO GIVE YOU $500,000 A YEAR IN TAXPAYER FUNDS THAT YOU WON'T HAVE TO ACCOUNT FOR.
THAT WORKS, TOO.
8-30
DARRIN BELL

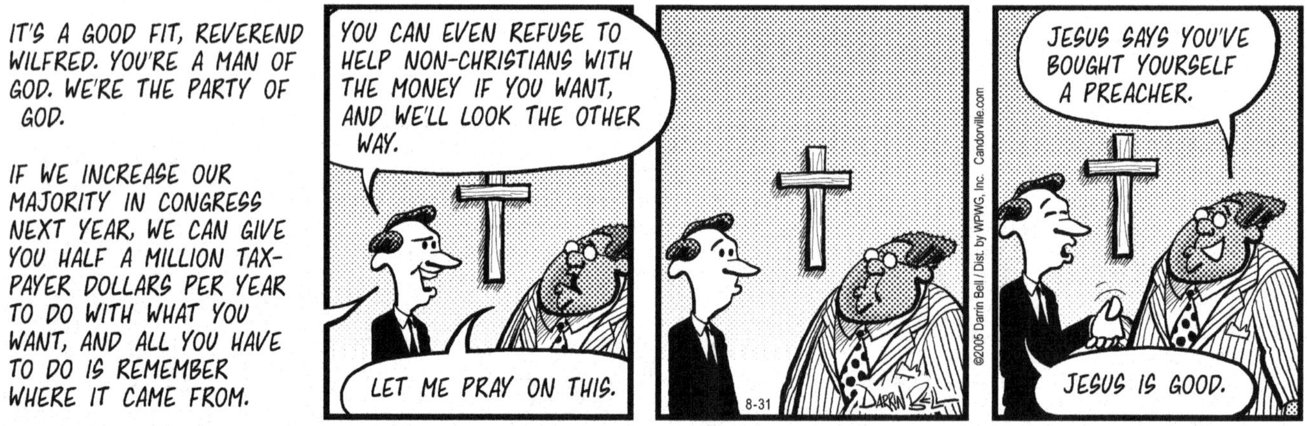
IT'S A GOOD FIT, REVEREND WILFRED. YOU'RE A MAN OF GOD. WE'RE THE PARTY OF GOD.
IF WE INCREASE OUR MAJORITY IN CONGRESS NEXT YEAR, WE CAN GIVE YOU HALF A MILLION TAXPAYER DOLLARS PER YEAR TO DO WITH WHAT YOU WANT, AND ALL YOU HAVE TO DO IS REMEMBER WHERE IT CAME FROM.
YOU CAN EVEN REFUSE TO HELP NON-CHRISTIANS WITH THE MONEY IF YOU WANT, AND WE'LL LOOK THE OTHER WAY.
LET ME PRAY ON THIS.
JESUS SAYS YOU'VE BOUGHT YOURSELF A PREACHER.
JESUS IS GOOD.
8-31
DARRIN BELL
©2005 Darrin Bell / Dist. by WPWG, Inc. Candorville.com

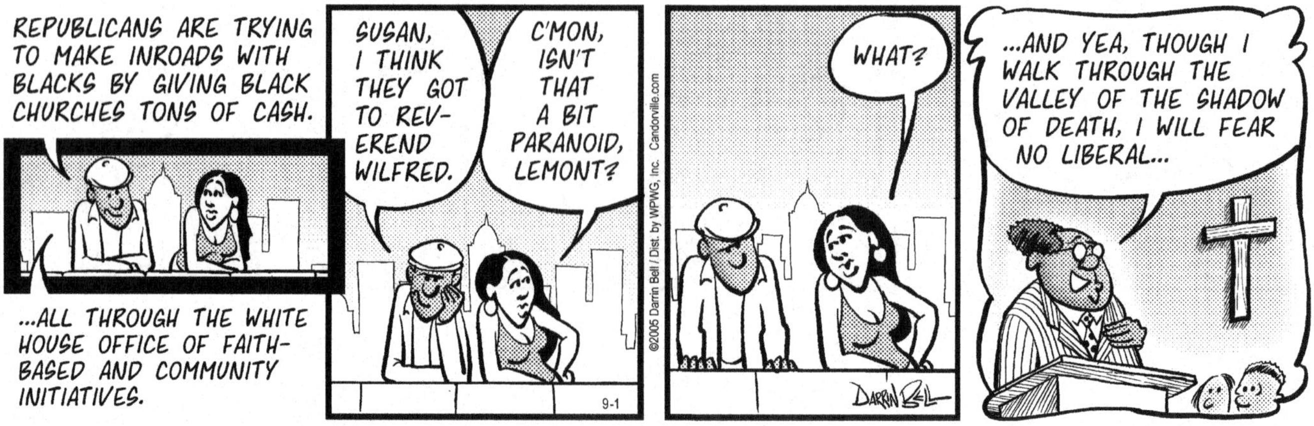
REPUBLICANS ARE TRYING TO MAKE INROADS WITH BLACKS BY GIVING BLACK CHURCHES TONS OF CASH.
...ALL THROUGH THE WHITE HOUSE OFFICE OF FAITH-BASED AND COMMUNITY INITIATIVES.
SUSAN, I THINK THEY GOT TO REVEREND WILFRED.
C'MON, ISN'T THAT A BIT PARANOID, LEMONT?
WHAT?
...AND YEA, THOUGH I WALK THROUGH THE VALLEY OF THE SHADOW OF DEATH, I WILL FEAR NO LIBERAL...
9-1
©2005 Darrin Bell / Dist. by WPWG, Inc. Candorville.com
DARRIN BELL

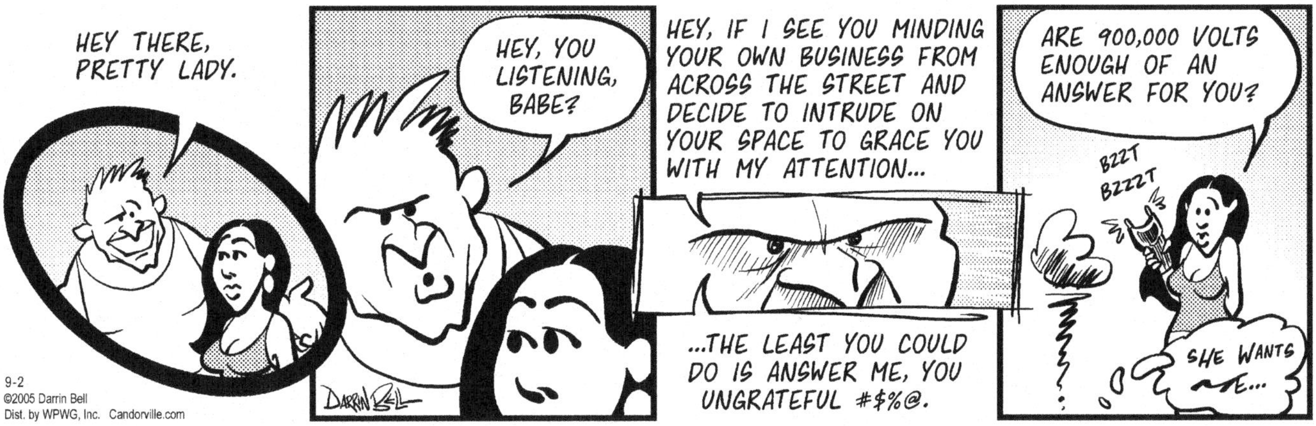
HEY THERE, PRETTY LADY.
HEY, YOU LISTENING, BABE?
HEY, IF I SEE YOU MINDING YOUR OWN BUSINESS FROM ACROSS THE STREET AND DECIDE TO INTRUDE ON YOUR SPACE TO GRACE YOU WITH MY ATTENTION...
...THE LEAST YOU COULD DO IS ANSWER ME, YOU UNGRATEFUL #$%@.
ARE 900,000 VOLTS ENOUGH OF AN ANSWER FOR YOU?
BZZT
BZZZT
SHE WANTS
9-2
©2005 Darrin Bell
Dist. by WPWG, Inc. Candorville.com
DARRIN BELL

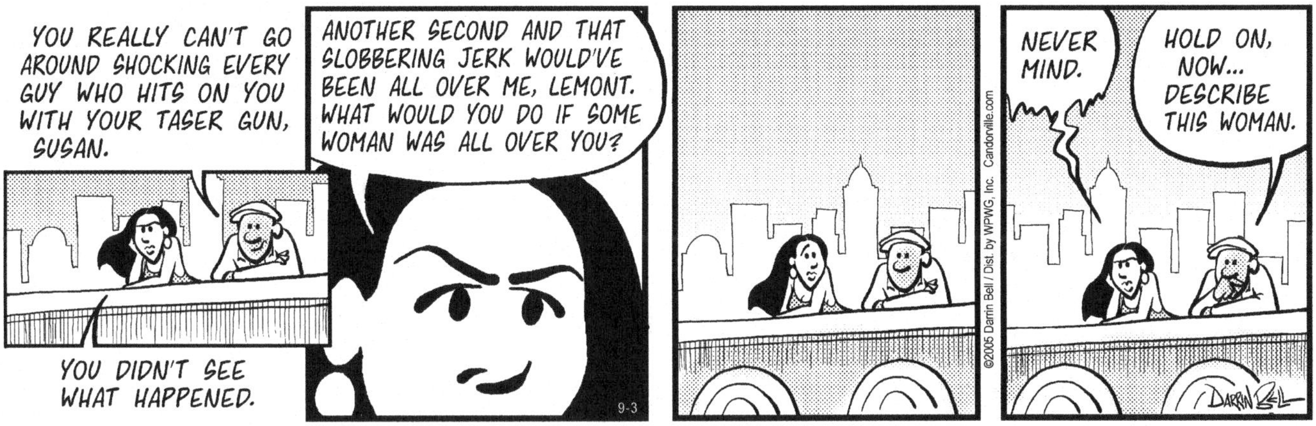
YOU REALLY CAN'T GO AROUND SHOCKING EVERY GUY WHO HITS ON YOU WITH YOUR TASER GUN, SUSAN.
YOU DIDN'T SEE WHAT HAPPENED.
ANOTHER SECOND AND THAT SLOBBERING JERK WOULD'VE BEEN ALL OVER ME, LEMONT. WHAT WOULD YOU DO IF SOME WOMAN WAS ALL OVER YOU?
9-3
©2005 Darrin Bell / Dist. by WPWG, Inc. Candorville.com
NEVER MIND.
HOLD ON, NOW... DESCRIBE THIS WOMAN.
DARRIN BELL

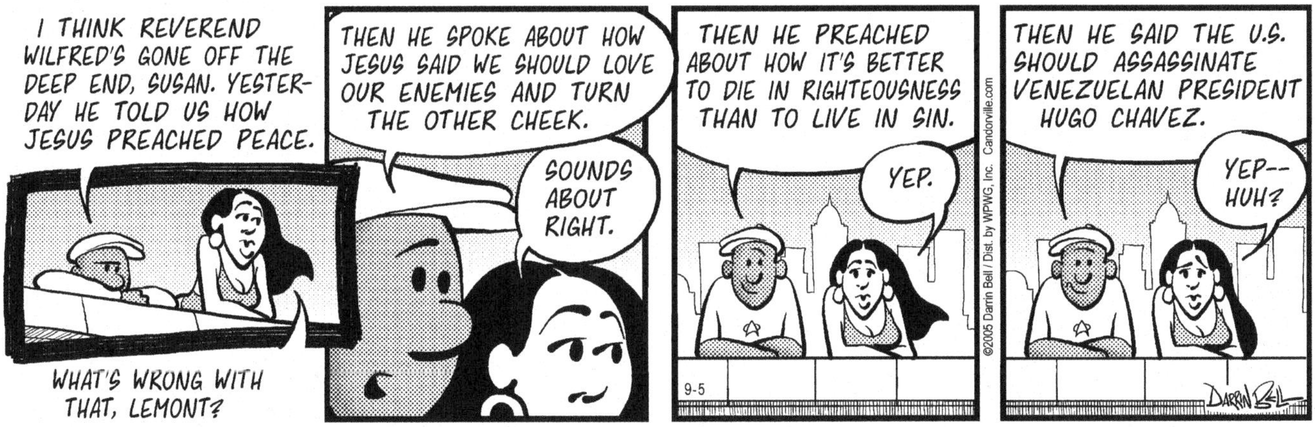
I THINK REVEREND WILFRED'S GONE OFF THE DEEP END, SUSAN. YESTERDAY HE TOLD US HOW JESUS PREACHED PEACE.
WHAT'S WRONG WITH THAT, LEMONT?
THEN HE SPOKE ABOUT HOW JESUS SAID WE SHOULD LOVE OUR ENEMIES AND TURN THE OTHER CHEEK.
SOUNDS ABOUT RIGHT.
THEN HE PREACHED ABOUT HOW IT'S BETTER TO DIE IN RIGHTEOUSNESS THAN TO LIVE IN SIN.
YEP.
9-5
©2005 Darrin Bell / Dist. by WPWG, Inc. Candorville.com
THEN HE SAID THE U.S. SHOULD ASSASSINATE VENEZUELAN PRESIDENT HUGO CHAVEZ.
YEP-- HUH?
DARRIN BELL

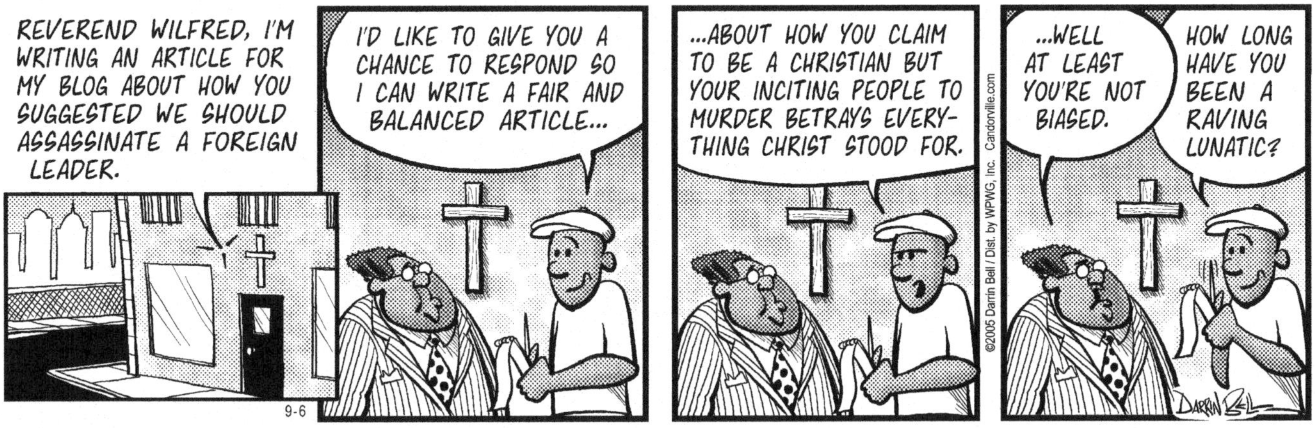
REVEREND WILFRED, I'M WRITING AN ARTICLE FOR MY BLOG ABOUT HOW YOU SUGGESTED WE SHOULD ASSASSINATE A FOREIGN LEADER.
9-6
I'D LIKE TO GIVE YOU A CHANCE TO RESPOND SO I CAN WRITE A FAIR AND BALANCED ARTICLE...
...ABOUT HOW YOU CLAIM TO BE A CHRISTIAN BUT YOUR INCITING PEOPLE TO MURDER BETRAYS EVERYTHING CHRIST STOOD FOR.
©2005 Darrin Bell / Dist. by WPWG, Inc. Candorville.com
...WELL AT LEAST YOU'RE NOT BIASED.
HOW LONG HAVE YOU BEEN A RAVING LUNATIC?
DARRIN BELL

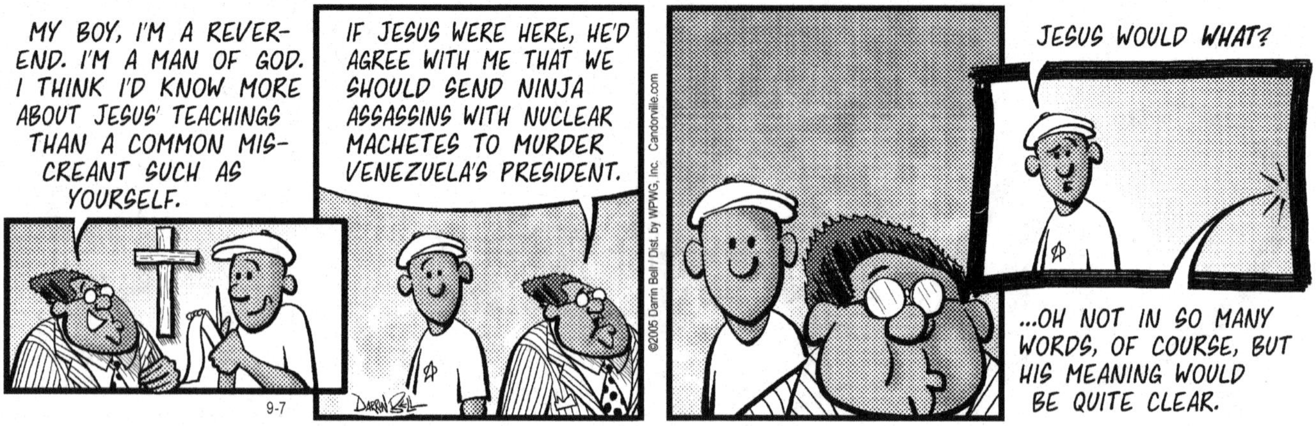
MY BOY, I'M A REVEREND. I'M A MAN OF GOD. I THINK I'D KNOW MORE ABOUT JESUS' TEACHINGS THAN A COMMON MISCREANT SUCH AS YOURSELF.
9-7
IF JESUS WERE HERE, HE'D AGREE WITH ME THAT WE SHOULD SEND NINJA ASSASSINS WITH NUCLEAR MACHETES TO MURDER VENEZUELA'S PRESIDENT.
DARRIN BELL
©2005 Darrin Bell / Dist. by WPWG, Inc. Candorville.com
JESUS WOULD WHAT?
...OH NOT IN SO MANY WORDS, OF COURSE, BUT HIS MEANING WOULD BE QUITE CLEAR.

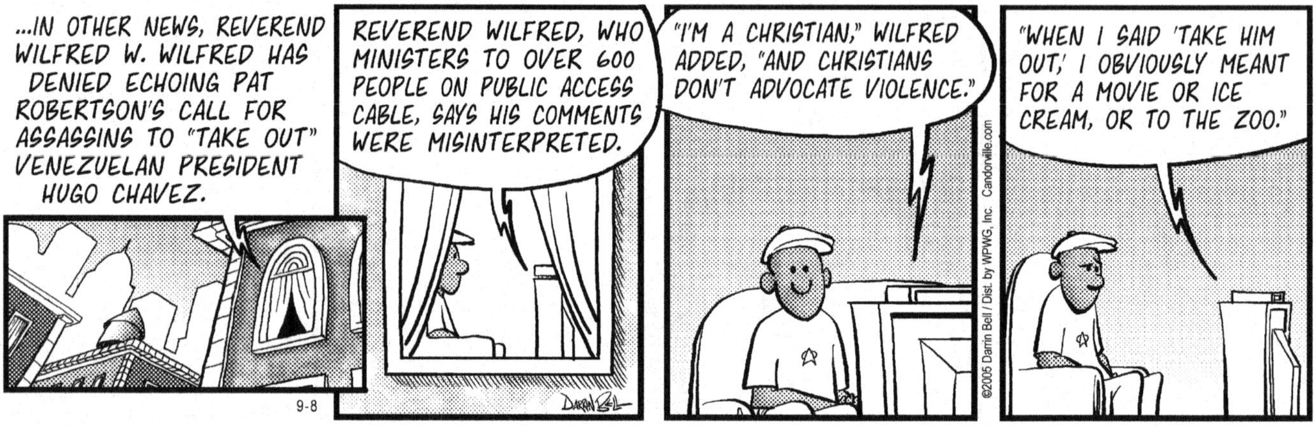
...IN OTHER NEWS, REVEREND WILFRED W. WILFRED HAS DENIED ECHOING PAT ROBERTSON'S CALL FOR ASSASSINS TO "TAKE OUT" VENEZUELAN PRESIDENT HUGO CHAVEZ.
9-8
REVEREND WILFRED, WHO MINISTERS TO OVER 600 PEOPLE ON PUBLIC ACCESS CABLE, SAYS HIS COMMENTS WERE MISINTERPRETED.
DARRIN BELL
"I'M A CHRISTIAN," WILFRED ADDED, "AND CHRISTIANS DON'T ADVOCATE VIOLENCE."
©2005 Darrin Bell / Dist. by WPWG, Inc. Candorville.com
"WHEN I SAID 'TAKE HIM OUT,' I OBVIOUSLY MEANT FOR A MOVIE OR ICE CREAM, OR TO THE ZOO."

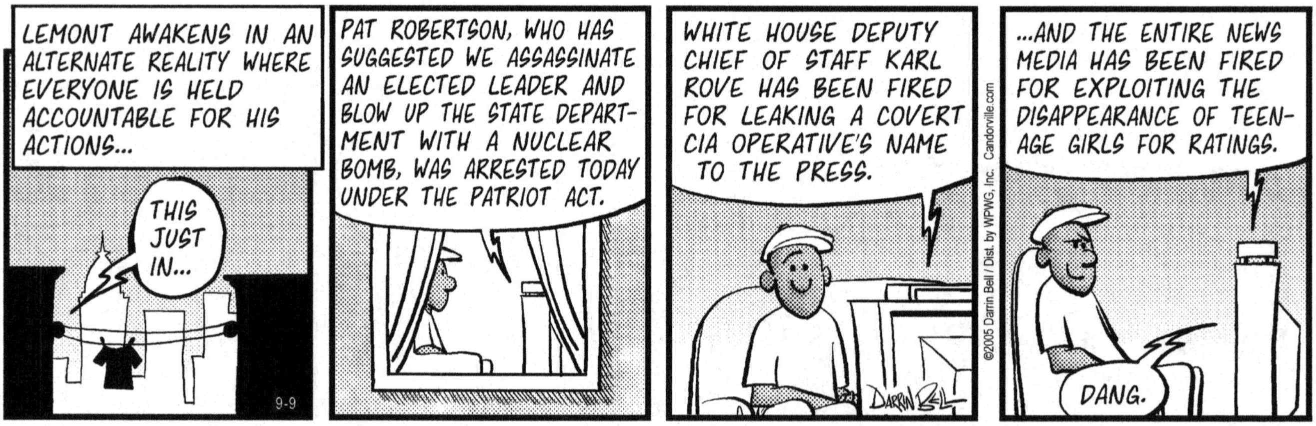
LEMONT AWAKENS IN AN ALTERNATE REALITY WHERE EVERYONE IS HELD ACCOUNTABLE FOR HIS ACTIONS...
THIS JUST IN...
9-9
PAT ROBERTSON, WHO HAS SUGGESTED WE ASSASSINATE AN ELECTED LEADER AND BLOW UP THE STATE DEPARTMENT WITH A NUCLEAR BOMB, WAS ARRESTED TODAY UNDER THE PATRIOT ACT.
WHITE HOUSE DEPUTY CHIEF OF STAFF KARL ROVE HAS BEEN FIRED FOR LEAKING A COVERT CIA OPERATIVE'S NAME TO THE PRESS.
DARRIN BELL
©2005 Darrin Bell / Dist. by WPWG, Inc. Candorville.com
...AND THE ENTIRE NEWS MEDIA HAS BEEN FIRED FOR EXPLOITING THE DISAPPEARANCE OF TEENAGE GIRLS FOR RATINGS.
DANG.

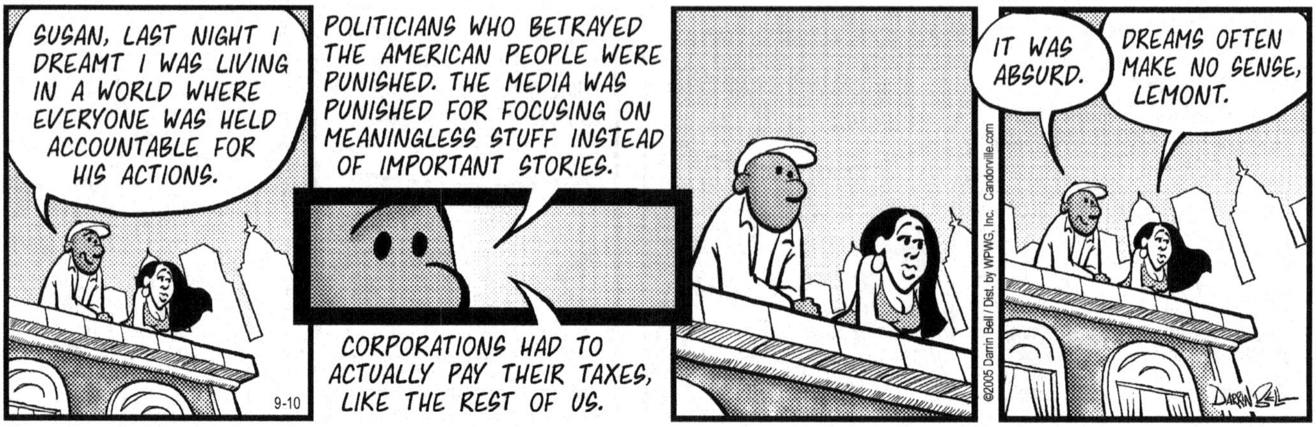
SUSAN, LAST NIGHT I DREAMT I WAS LIVING IN A WORLD WHERE EVERYONE WAS HELD ACCOUNTABLE FOR HIS ACTIONS.
9-10
POLITICIANS WHO BETRAYED THE AMERICAN PEOPLE WERE PUNISHED. THE MEDIA WAS PUNISHED FOR FOCUSING ON MEANINGLESS STUFF INSTEAD OF IMPORTANT STORIES.
CORPORATIONS HAD TO ACTUALLY PAY THEIR TAXES, LIKE THE REST OF US.
©2005 Darrin Bell / Dist. by WPWG, Inc. Candorville.com
IT WAS ABSURD.
DREAMS OFTEN MAKE NO SENSE, LEMONT.
DARRIN BELL

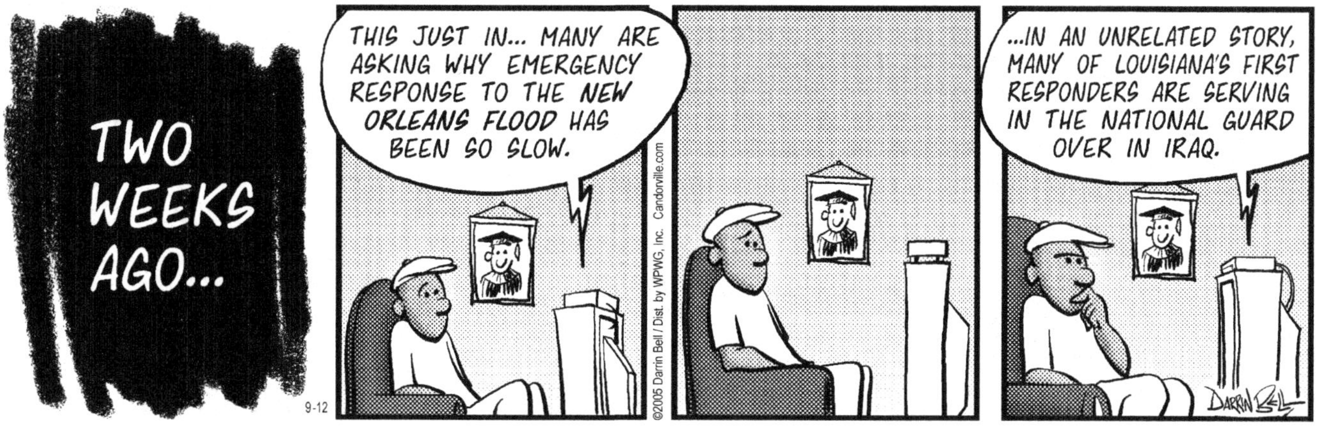
TWO WEEKS AGO...
THIS JUST IN... MANY ARE ASKING WHY EMERGENCY RESPONSE TO THE NEW ORLEANS FLOOD HAS BEEN SO SLOW.
...IN AN UNRELATED STORY, MANY OF LOUISIANA'S FIRST RESPONDERS ARE SERVING IN THE NATIONAL GUARD OVER IN IRAQ.
9-12
©2005 Darrin Bell / Dist. by WPWG, Inc. Candorville.com
DARRIN BELL

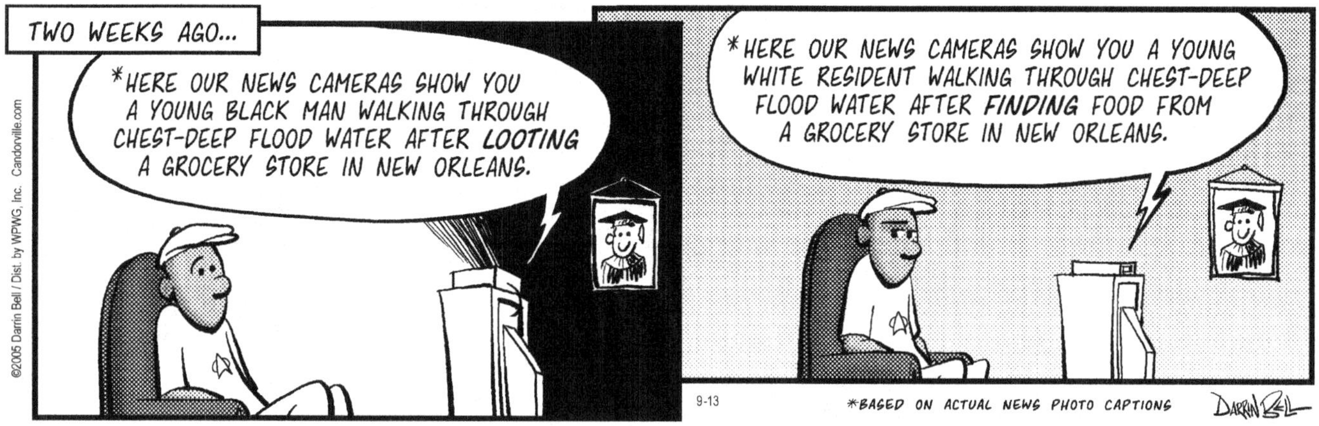
TWO WEEKS AGO...
*HERE OUR NEWS CAMERAS SHOW YOU A YOUNG BLACK MAN WALKING THROUGH CHEST-DEEP FLOOD WATER AFTER LOOTING A GROCERY STORE IN NEW ORLEANS.
*HERE OUR NEWS CAMERAS SHOW YOU A YOUNG WHITE RESIDENT WALKING THROUGH CHEST-DEEP FLOOD WATER AFTER FINDING FOOD FROM A GROCERY STORE IN NEW ORLEANS.
©2005 Darrin Bell / Dist. by WPWG, Inc. Candorville.com
9-13
*BASED ON ACTUAL NEWS PHOTO CAPTIONS
DARRIN BELL

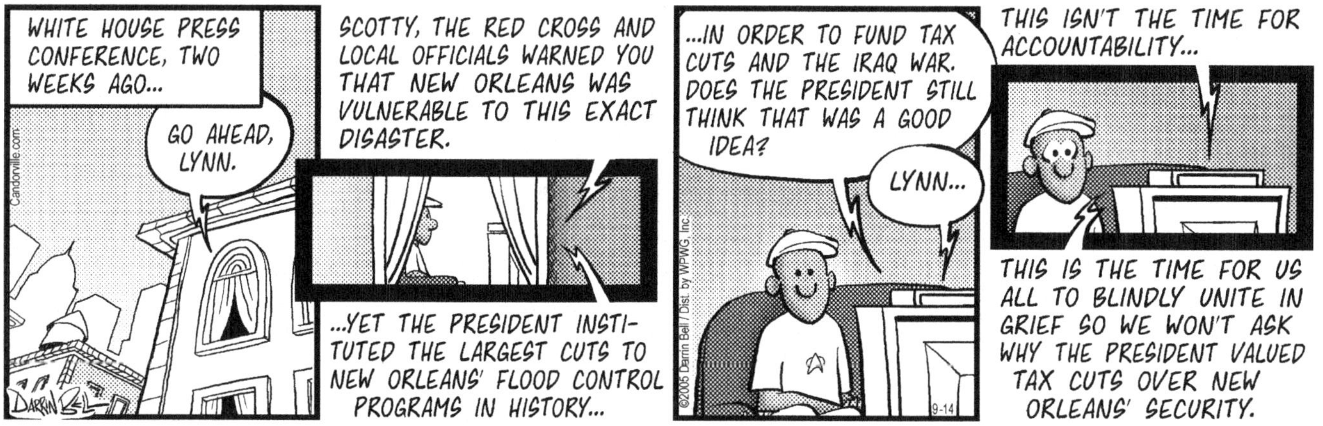
WHITE HOUSE PRESS CONFERENCE, TWO WEEKS AGO...
GO AHEAD, LYNN.
SCOTTY, THE RED CROSS AND LOCAL OFFICIALS WARNED YOU THAT NEW ORLEANS WAS VULNERABLE TO THIS EXACT DISASTER.
...YET THE PRESIDENT INSTITUTED THE LARGEST CUTS TO NEW ORLEANS' FLOOD CONTROL PROGRAMS IN HISTORY...
...IN ORDER TO FUND TAX CUTS AND THE IRAQ WAR. DOES THE PRESIDENT STILL THINK THAT WAS A GOOD IDEA?
LYNN...
THIS ISN'T THE TIME FOR ACCOUNTABILITY...
THIS IS THE TIME FOR US ALL TO BLINDLY UNITE IN GRIEF SO WE WON'T ASK WHY THE PRESIDENT VALUED TAX CUTS OVER NEW ORLEANS' SECURITY.
Candorville.com
©2005 Darrin Bell / Dist. by WPWG, Inc.
9-14
DARRIN BELL

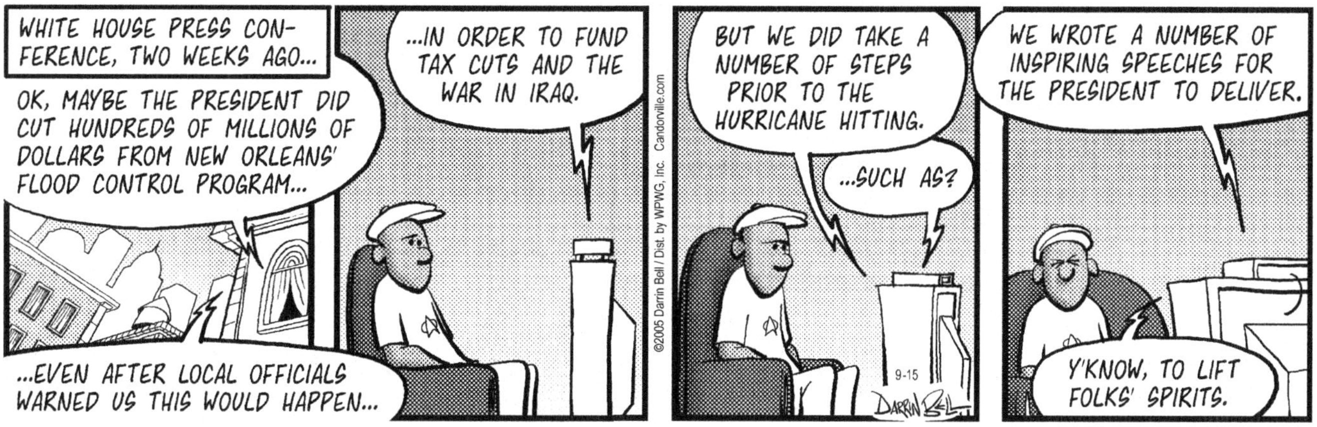
WHITE HOUSE PRESS CONFERENCE, TWO WEEKS AGO...
OK, MAYBE THE PRESIDENT DID CUT HUNDREDS OF MILLIONS OF DOLLARS FROM NEW ORLEANS' FLOOD CONTROL PROGRAM...
...EVEN AFTER LOCAL OFFICIALS WARNED US THIS WOULD HAPPEN...
...IN ORDER TO FUND TAX CUTS AND THE WAR IN IRAQ.
BUT WE DID TAKE A NUMBER OF STEPS PRIOR TO THE HURRICANE HITTING.
...SUCH AS?
WE WROTE A NUMBER OF INSPIRING SPEECHES FOR THE PRESIDENT TO DELIVER.
Y'KNOW, TO LIFT FOLKS' SPIRITS.
©2005 Darrin Bell / Dist. by WPWG, Inc. Candorville.com
9-15
DARRIN BELL

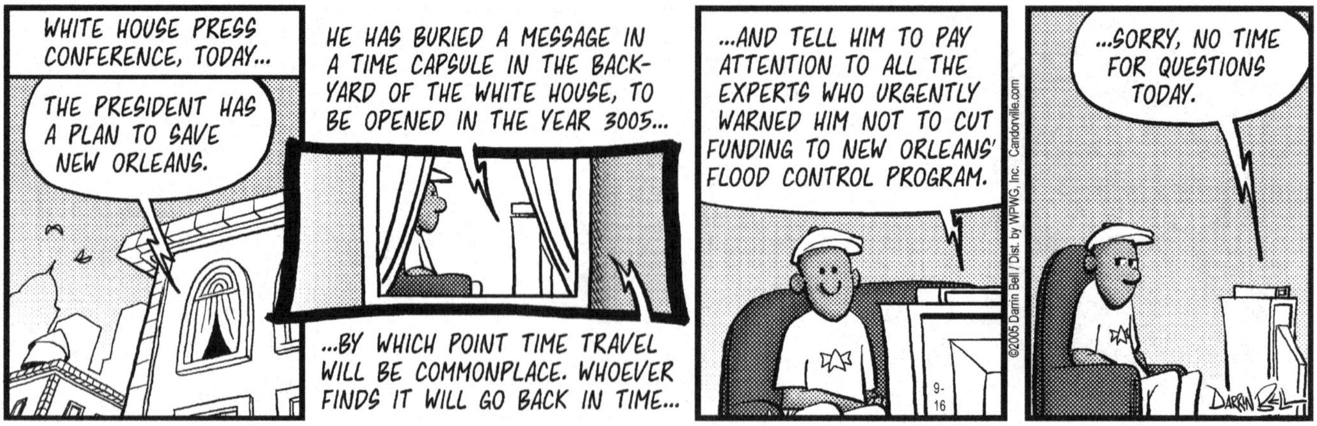
WHITE HOUSE PRESS CONFERENCE, TODAY...
THE PRESIDENT HAS A PLAN TO SAVE NEW ORLEANS.
HE HAS BURIED A MESSAGE IN A TIME CAPSULE IN THE BACKYARD OF THE WHITE HOUSE, TO BE OPENED IN THE YEAR 3005...
...BY WHICH POINT TIME TRAVEL WILL BE COMMONPLACE. WHOEVER FINDS IT WILL GO BACK IN TIME...
...AND TELL HIM TO PAY ATTENTION TO ALL THE EXPERTS WHO URGENTLY WARNED HIM NOT TO CUT FUNDING TO NEW ORLEANS' FLOOD CONTROL PROGRAM.
9-16
©2005 Darrin Bell / Dist. by WPWG, Inc. Candorville.com
...SORRY, NO TIME FOR QUESTIONS TODAY.
DARRIN BELL

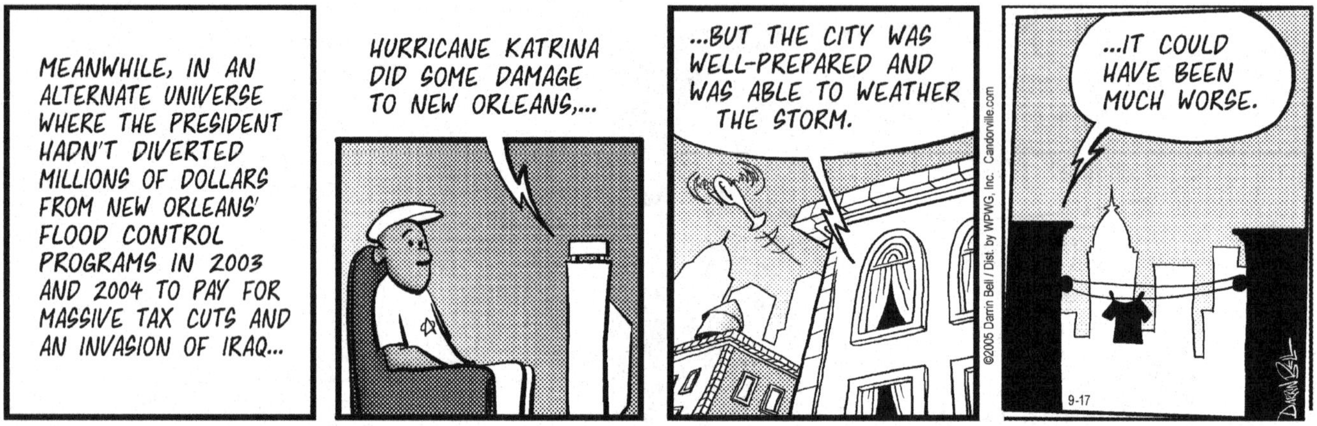
MEANWHILE, IN AN ALTERNATE UNIVERSE WHERE THE PRESIDENT HADN'T DIVERTED MILLIONS OF DOLLARS FROM NEW ORLEANS' FLOOD CONTROL PROGRAMS IN 2003 AND 2004 TO PAY FOR MASSIVE TAX CUTS AND AN INVASION OF IRAQ...
HURRICANE KATRINA DID SOME DAMAGE TO NEW ORLEANS,...
...BUT THE CITY WAS WELL-PREPARED AND WAS ABLE TO WEATHER THE STORM.
©2005 Darrin Bell / Dist. by WPWG, Inc. Candorville.com
...IT COULD HAVE BEEN MUCH WORSE.
9-17
DARRIN BELL

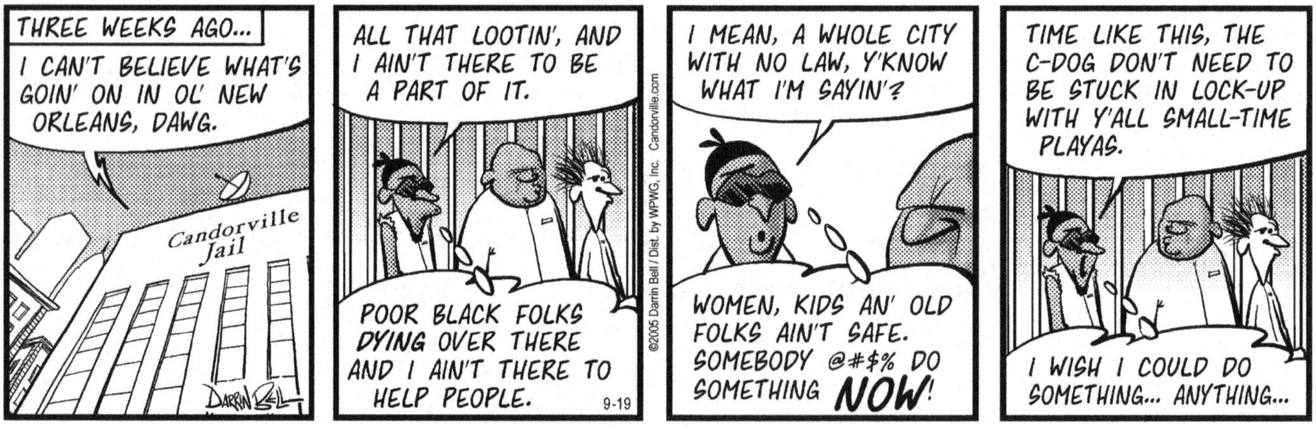
THREE WEEKS AGO...
I CAN'T BELIEVE WHAT'S GOIN' ON IN OL' NEW ORLEANS, DAWG.
Candorville Jail
DARRIN BELL
ALL THAT LOOTIN', AND I AIN'T THERE TO BE A PART OF IT.
POOR BLACK FOLKS DYING OVER THERE AND I AIN'T THERE TO HELP PEOPLE.
9-19
©2005 Darrin Bell / Dist. by WPWG, Inc. Candorville.com
I MEAN, A WHOLE CITY WITH NO LAW, Y'KNOW WHAT I'M SAYIN'?
WOMEN, KIDS AN' OLD FOLKS AIN'T SAFE. SOMEBODY @#$% DO SOMETHING NOW!
TIME LIKE THIS, THE C-DOG DON'T NEED TO BE STUCK IN LOCK-UP WITH Y'ALL SMALL-TIME PLAYAS.
I WISH I COULD DO SOMETHING... ANYTHING...

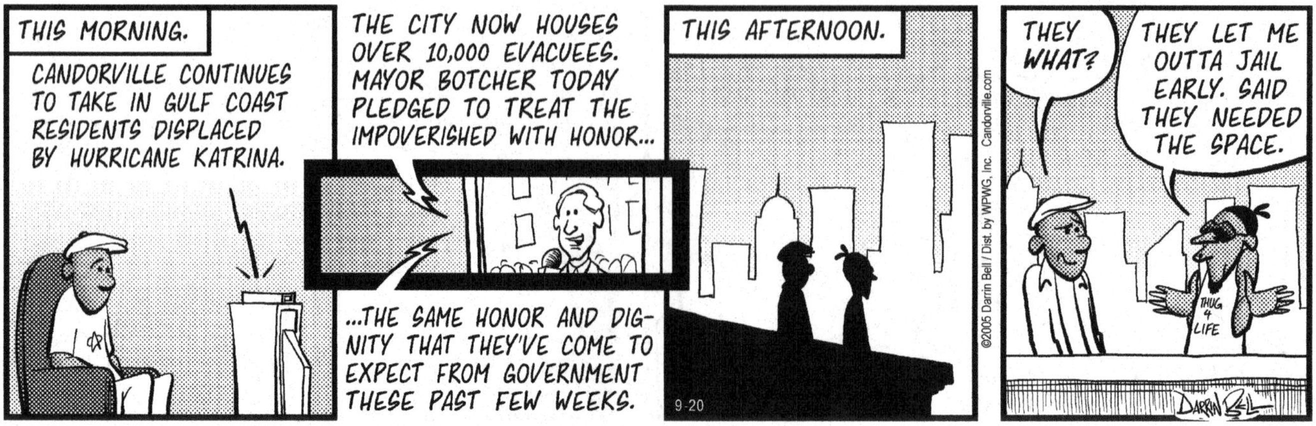
THIS MORNING.
CANDORVILLE CONTINUES TO TAKE IN GULF COAST RESIDENTS DISPLACED BY HURRICANE KATRINA.
THE CITY NOW HOUSES OVER 10,000 EVACUEES. MAYOR BOTCHER TODAY PLEDGED TO TREAT THE IMPOVERISHED WITH HONOR...
...THE SAME HONOR AND DIGNITY THAT THEY'VE COME TO EXPECT FROM GOVERNMENT THESE PAST FEW WEEKS.
THIS AFTERNOON.
9-20
©2005 Darrin Bell / Dist. by WPWG, Inc. Candorville.com
THEY WHAT?
THEY LET ME OUTTA JAIL EARLY. SAID THEY NEEDED THE SPACE.
THUG 4 LIFE
DARRIN BELL

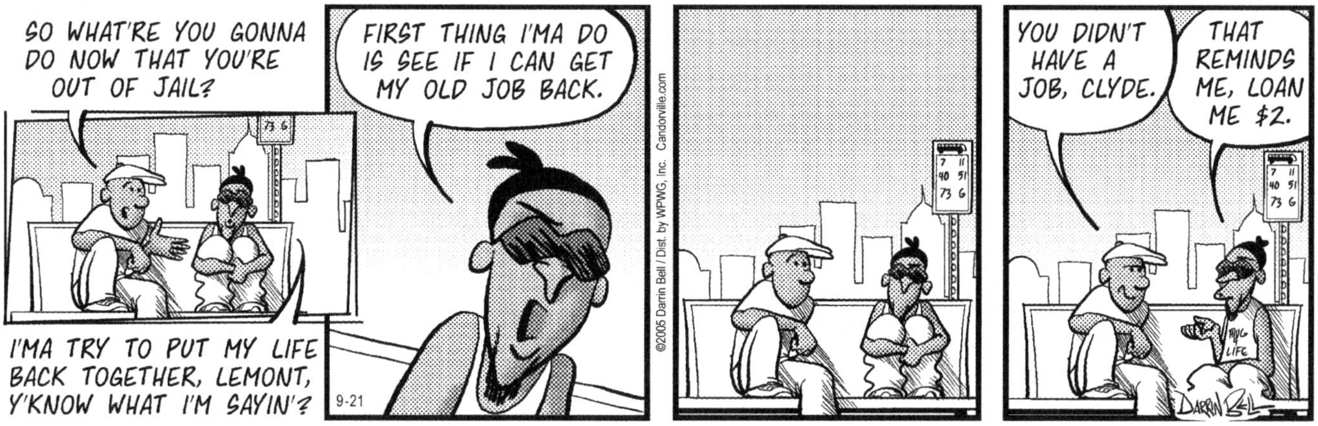
SO WHAT'RE YOU GONNA DO NOW THAT YOU'RE OUT OF JAIL?
I'MA TRY TO PUT MY LIFE BACK TOGETHER, LEMONT, Y'KNOW WHAT I'M SAYIN'?
9-21
FIRST THING I'MA DO IS SEE IF I CAN GET MY OLD JOB BACK.
©2005 Darrin Bell / Dist. by WPWG, Inc. Candorville.com
YOU DIDN'T HAVE A JOB, CLYDE.
THAT REMINDS ME, LOAN ME $2.
THUG 4 LIFE
DARRIN BELL

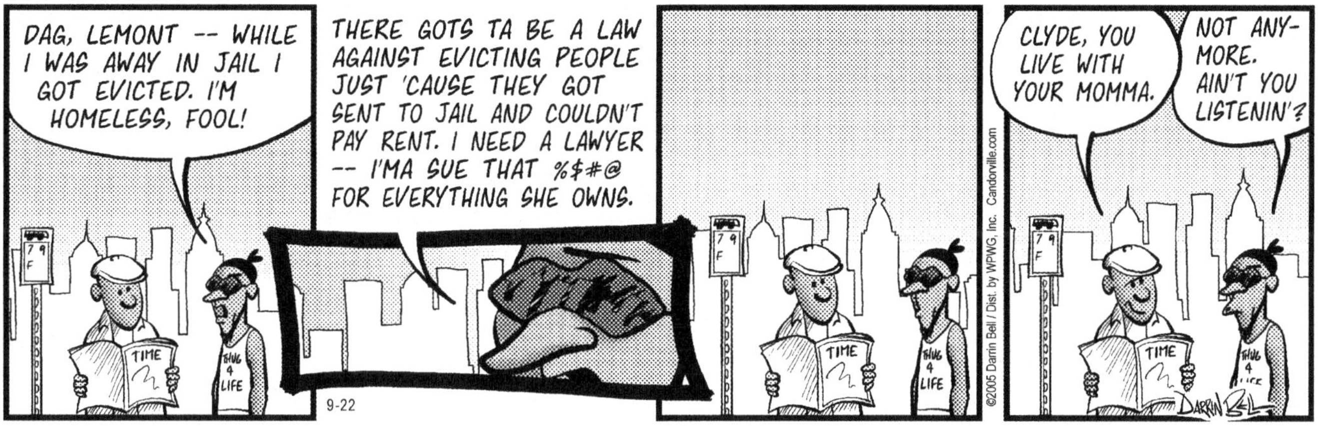
DAG, LEMONT -- WHILE I WAS AWAY IN JAIL I GOT EVICTED. I'M HOMELESS, FOOL!
TIME
THUG 4 LIFE
9-22
THERE GOTS TA BE A LAW AGAINST EVICTING PEOPLE JUST 'CAUSE THEY GOT SENT TO JAIL AND COULDN'T PAY RENT. I NEED A LAWYER -- I'MA SUE THAT %$#@ FOR EVERYTHING SHE OWNS.
©2005 Darrin Bell / Dist. by WPWG, Inc. Candorville.com
CLYDE, YOU LIVE WITH YOUR MOMMA.
NOT ANY-MORE. AIN'T YOU LISTENIN'?
DARRIN BELL

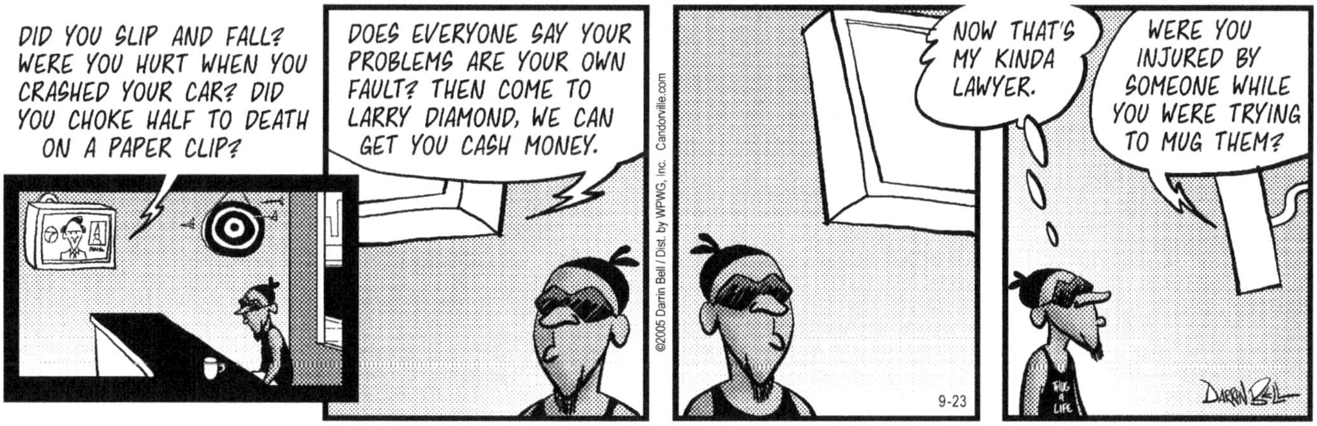
DID YOU SLIP AND FALL? WERE YOU HURT WHEN YOU CRASHED YOUR CAR? DID YOU CHOKE HALF TO DEATH ON A PAPER CLIP?
DOES EVERYONE SAY YOUR PROBLEMS ARE YOUR OWN FAULT? THEN COME TO LARRY DIAMOND, WE CAN GET YOU CASH MONEY.
©2005 Darrin Bell / Dist. by WPWG, Inc. Candorville.com
9-23
NOW THAT'S MY KINDA LAWYER.
WERE YOU INJURED BY SOMEONE WHILE YOU WERE TRYING TO MUG THEM?
THUG 4 LIFE
DARRIN BELL

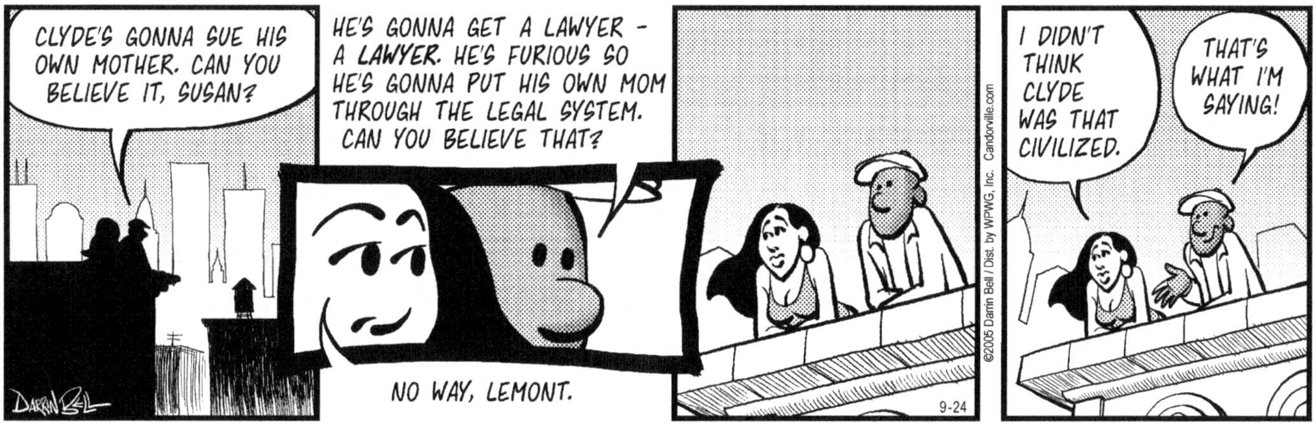
CLYDE'S GONNA SUE HIS OWN MOTHER. CAN YOU BELIEVE IT, SUSAN?
DARRIN BELL
HE'S GONNA GET A LAWYER - A LAWYER. HE'S FURIOUS SO HE'S GONNA PUT HIS OWN MOM THROUGH THE LEGAL SYSTEM. CAN YOU BELIEVE THAT?
NO WAY, LEMONT.
9-24
©2005 Darrin Bell / Dist. by WPWG, Inc. Candorville.com
I DIDN'T THINK CLYDE WAS THAT CIVILIZED.
THAT'S WHAT I'M SAYING!

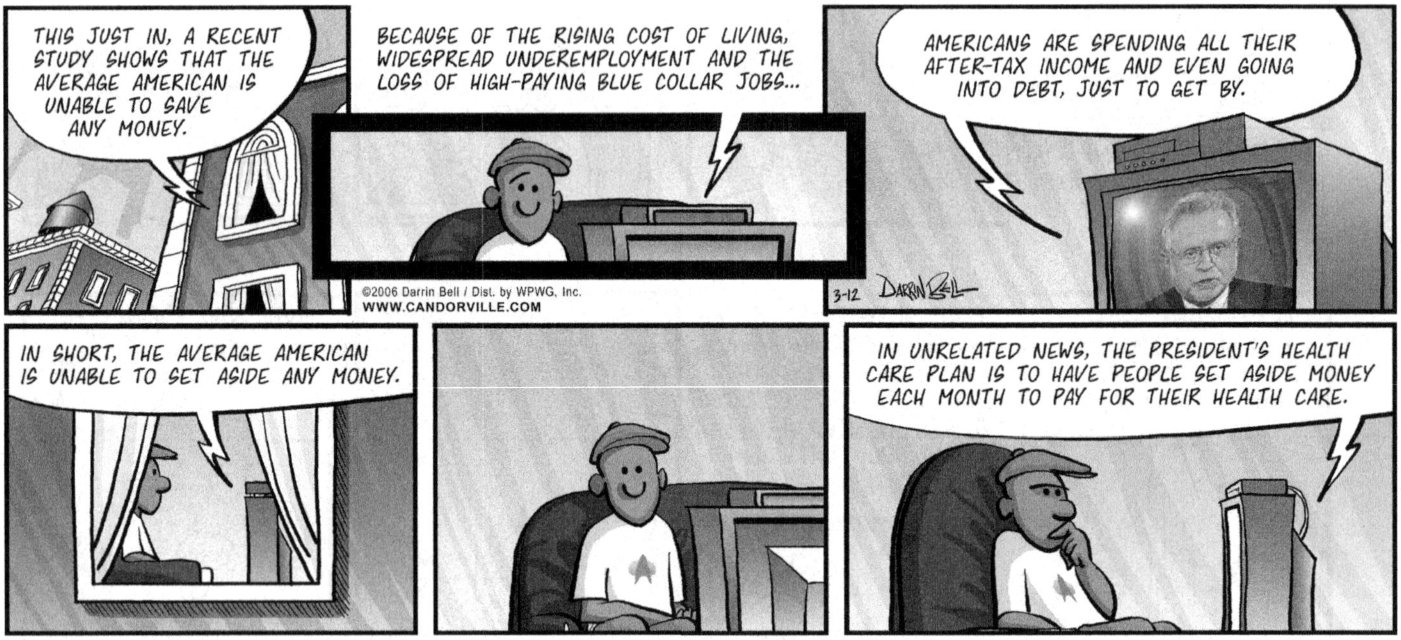
THIS JUST IN, A RECENT STUDY SHOWS THAT THE AVERAGE AMERICAN IS UNABLE TO SAVE ANY MONEY.
BECAUSE OF THE RISING COST OF LIVING, WIDESPREAD UNDEREMPLOYMENT AND THE LOSS OF HIGH-PAYING BLUE COLLAR JOBS...
AMERICANS ARE SPENDING ALL THEIR AFTER-TAX INCOME AND EVEN GOING INTO DEBT, JUST TO GET BY.
©2006 Darrin Bell / Dist. by WPWG, Inc.
WWW.CANDORVILLE.COM
3-12
DARRIN BELL
IN SHORT, THE AVERAGE AMERICAN IS UNABLE TO SET ASIDE ANY MONEY.
IN UNRELATED NEWS, THE PRESIDENT'S HEALTH CARE PLAN IS TO HAVE PEOPLE SET ASIDE MONEY EACH MONTH TO PAY FOR THEIR HEALTH CARE.

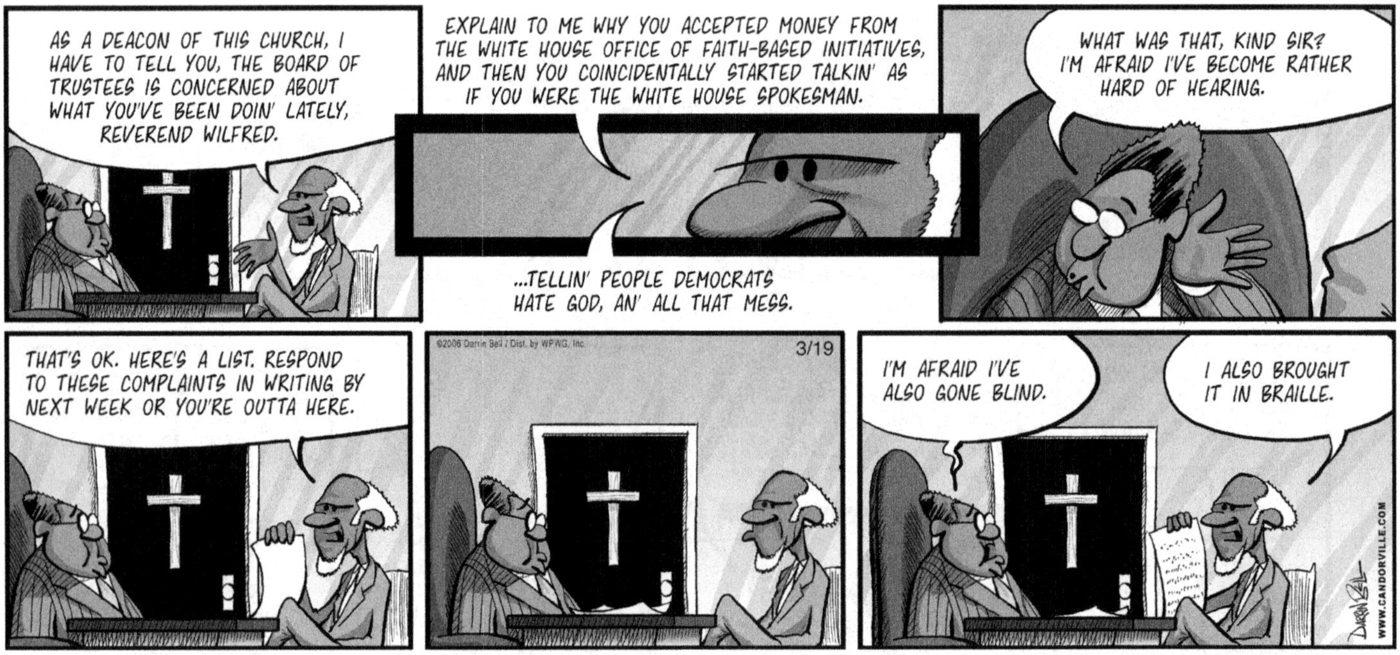
AS A DEACON OF THIS CHURCH, I HAVE TO TELL YOU, THE BOARD OF TRUSTEES IS CONCERNED ABOUT WHAT YOU'VE BEEN DOIN' LATELY, REVEREND WILFRED.
EXPLAIN TO ME WHY YOU ACCEPTED MONEY FROM THE WHITE HOUSE OFFICE OF FAITH-BASED INITIATIVES, AND THEN YOU COINCIDENTALLY STARTED TALKIN' AS IF YOU WERE THE WHITE HOUSE SPOKESMAN.
...TELLIN' PEOPLE DEMOCRATS HATE GOD, AN' ALL THAT MESS.
WHAT WAS THAT, KIND SIR? I'M AFRAID I'VE BECOME RATHER HARD OF HEARING.
THAT'S OK. HERE'S A LIST. RESPOND TO THESE COMPLAINTS IN WRITING BY NEXT WEEK OR YOU'RE OUTTA HERE.
©2006 Darrin Bell / Dist. by WPWG, Inc.
3/19
I'M AFRAID I'VE ALSO GONE BLIND.
I ALSO BROUGHT IT IN BRAILLE.
DARRIN BELL
WWW.CANDORVILLE.COM

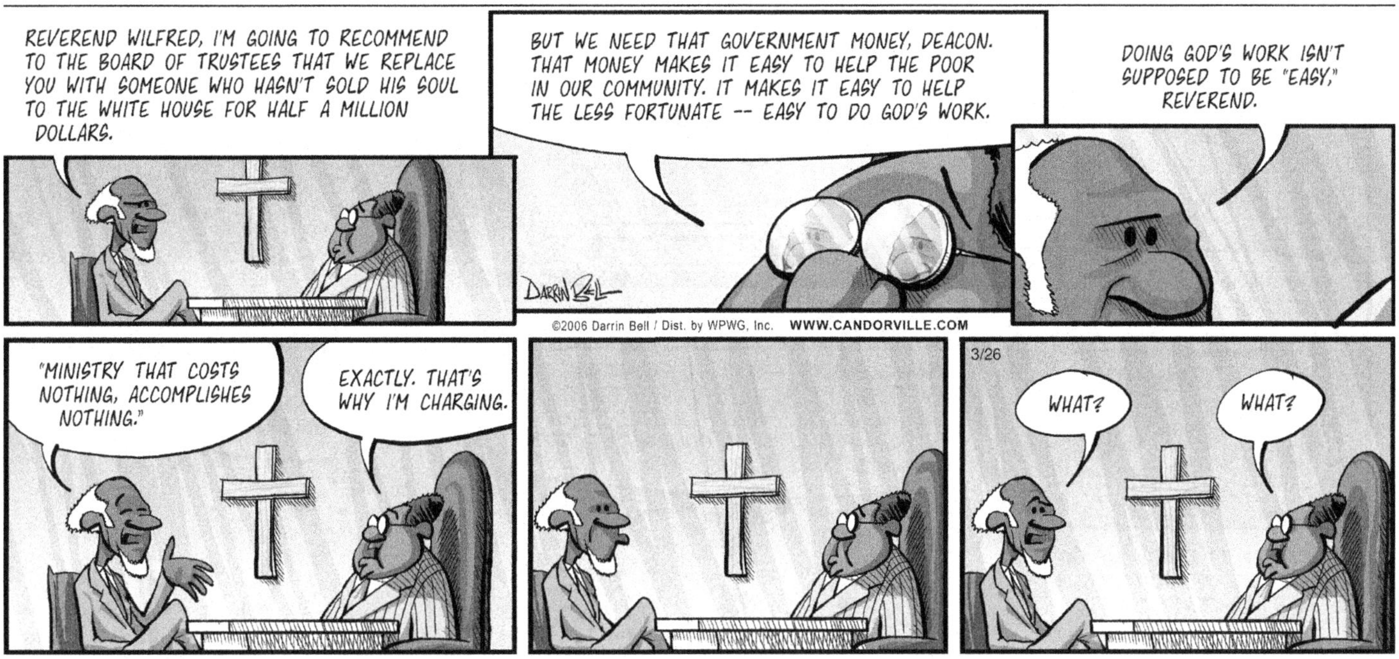
REVEREND WILFRED, I'M GOING TO RECOMMEND TO THE BOARD OF TRUSTEES THAT WE REPLACE YOU WITH SOMEONE WHO HASN'T SOLD HIS SOUL TO THE WHITE HOUSE FOR HALF A MILLION DOLLARS.
BUT WE NEED THAT GOVERNMENT MONEY, DEACON. THAT MONEY MAKES IT EASY TO HELP THE POOR IN OUR COMMUNITY. IT MAKES IT EASY TO HELP THE LESS FORTUNATE -- EASY TO DO GOD'S WORK.
DOING GOD'S WORK ISN'T SUPPOSED TO BE "EASY," REVEREND.
DARRIN BELL
©2006 Darrin Bell / Dist. by WPWG, Inc. WWW.CANDORVILLE.COM
"MINISTRY THAT COSTS NOTHING, ACCOMPLISHES NOTHING."
EXACTLY. THAT'S WHY I'M CHARGING.
3/26
WHAT?
WHAT?

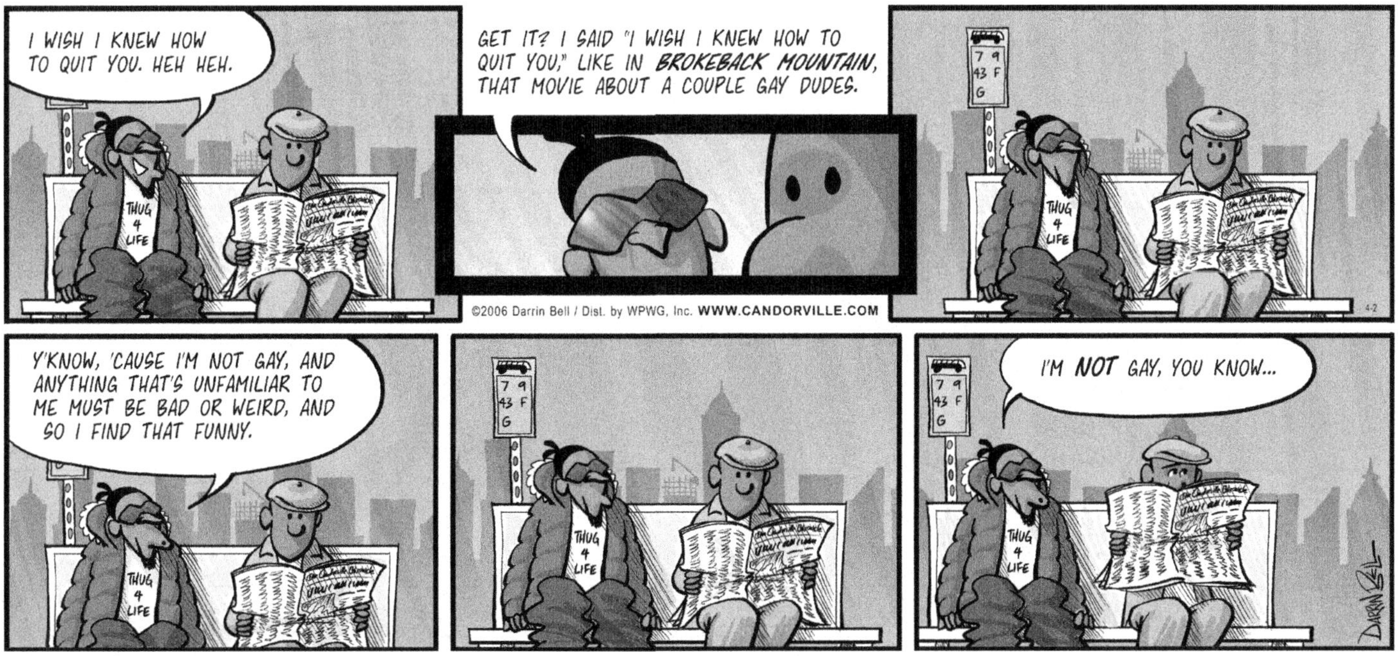
I WISH I KNEW HOW TO QUIT YOU. HEH HEH.
THUG 4 LIFE
GET IT? I SAID "I WISH I KNEW HOW TO QUIT YOU," LIKE IN BROKEBACK MOUNTAIN, THAT MOVIE ABOUT A COUPLE GAY DUDES.
©2006 Darrin Bell / Dist. by WPWG, Inc. WWW.CANDORVILLE.COM
7 9 43 F G
4-2
Y'KNOW, 'CAUSE I'M NOT GAY, AND ANYTHING THAT'S UNFAMILIAR TO ME MUST BE BAD OR WEIRD, AND SO I FIND THAT FUNNY.
I'M NOT GAY, YOU KNOW...
DARRIN BELL

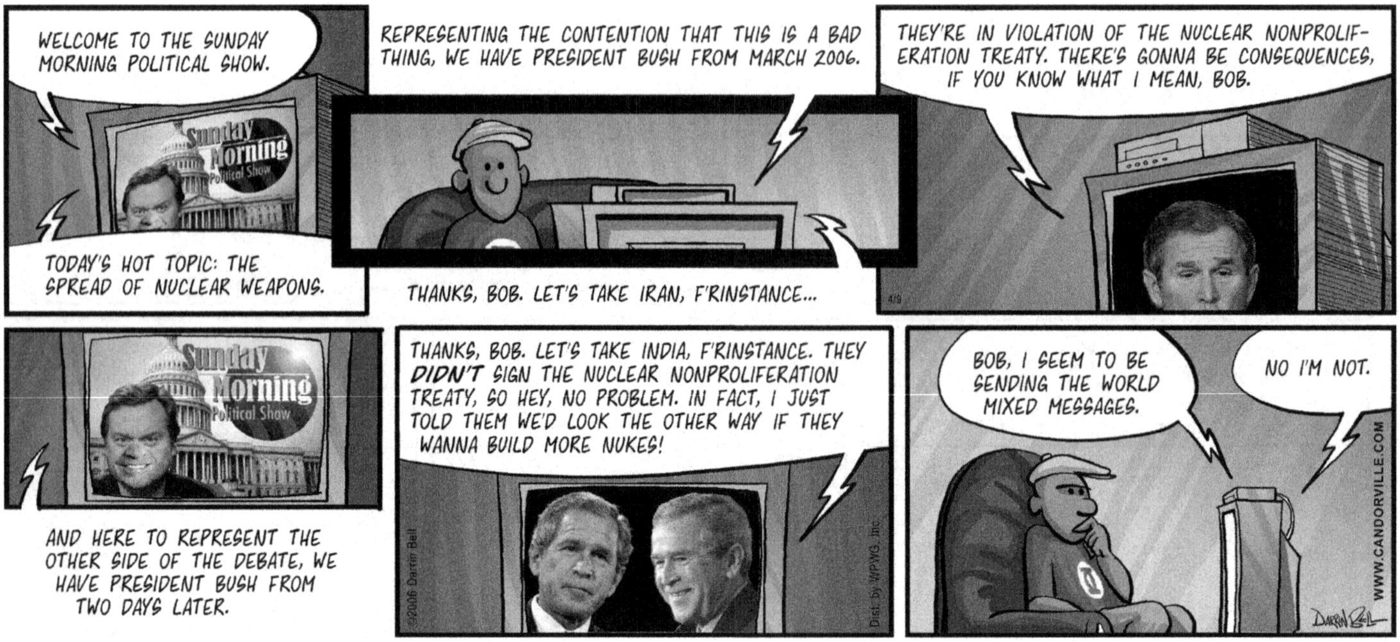
WELCOME TO THE SUNDAY MORNING POLITICAL SHOW.
Sunday Morning Political Show
TODAY'S HOT TOPIC: THE SPREAD OF NUCLEAR WEAPONS.
REPRESENTING THE CONTENTION THAT THIS IS A BAD THING, WE HAVE PRESIDENT BUSH FROM MARCH 2006.
THANKS, BOB. LET'S TAKE IRAN, F'RINSTANCE...
THEY'RE IN VIOLATION OF THE NUCLEAR NONPROLIFERATION TREATY. THERE'S GONNA BE CONSEQUENCES, IF YOU KNOW WHAT I MEAN, BOB.
4/9
Sunday Morning Political Show
AND HERE TO REPRESENT THE OTHER SIDE OF THE DEBATE, WE HAVE PRESIDENT BUSH FROM TWO DAYS LATER.
THANKS, BOB. LET'S TAKE INDIA, F'RINSTANCE. THEY DIDN'T SIGN THE NUCLEAR NONPROLIFERATION TREATY, SO HEY, NO PROBLEM. IN FACT, I JUST TOLD THEM WE'D LOOK THE OTHER WAY IF THEY WANNA BUILD MORE NUKES!
©2006 Darrin Bell
Dist. by WPWG, Inc.
BOB, I SEEM TO BE SENDING THE WORLD MIXED MESSAGES.
NO I'M NOT.
WWW.CANDORVILLE.COM
DARRIN BELL

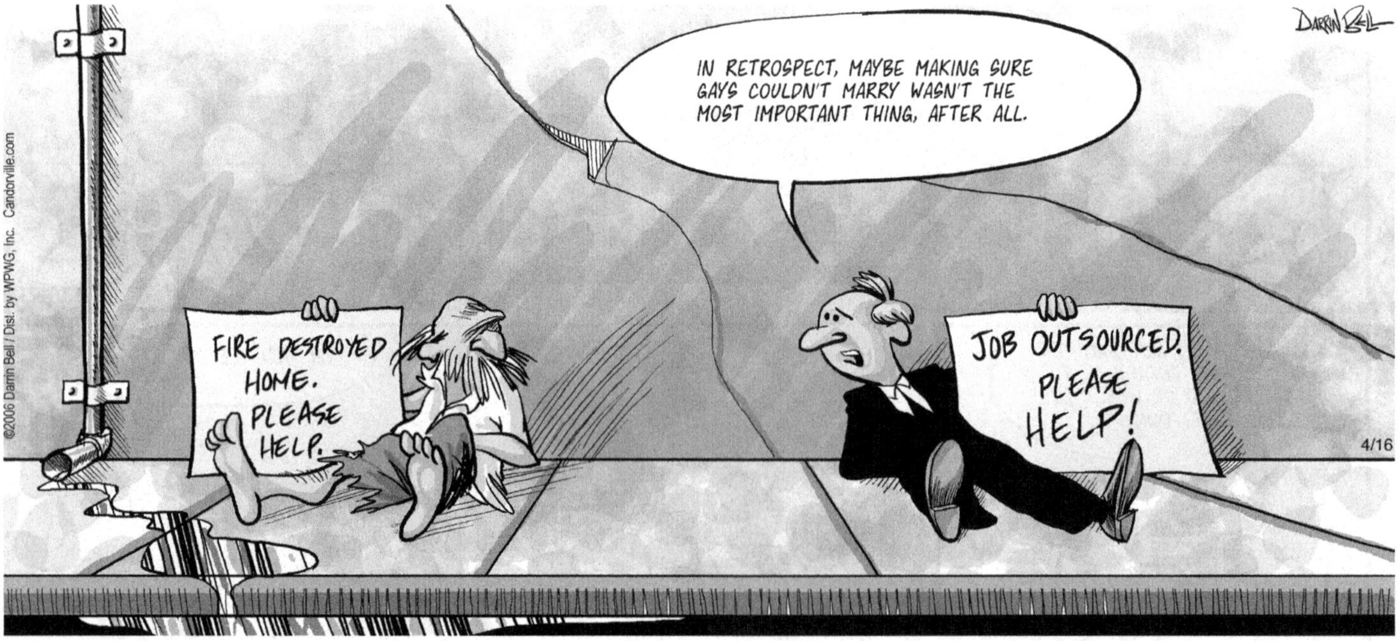
DARRIN BELL
©2006 Darrin Bell / Dist. by WPWG, Inc. Candorville.com
IN RETROSPECT, MAYBE MAKING SURE GAYS COULDN'T MARRY WASN'T THE MOST IMPORTANT THING, AFTER ALL.
FIRE DESTROYED HOME. PLEASE HELP.
JOB OUTSOURCED. PLEASE HELP!
4/16

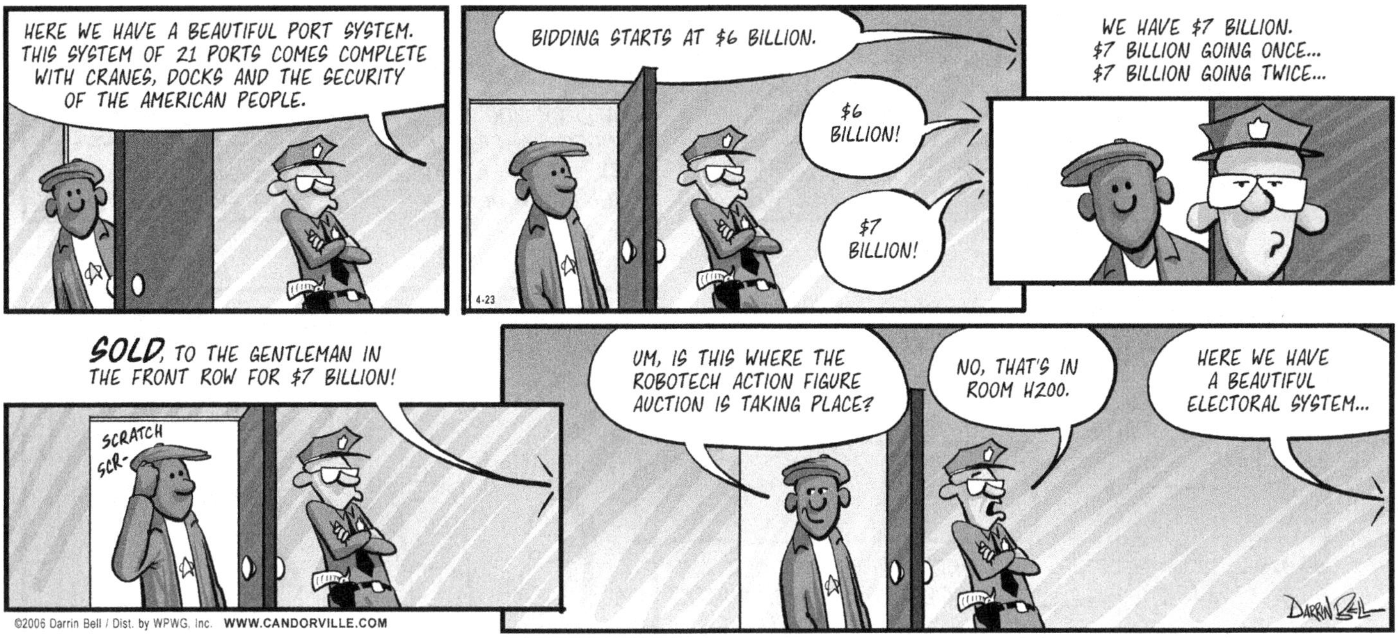
HERE WE HAVE A BEAUTIFUL PORT SYSTEM. THIS SYSTEM OF 21 PORTS COMES COMPLETE WITH CRANES, DOCKS AND THE SECURITY OF THE AMERICAN PEOPLE.
BIDDING STARTS AT $6 BILLION.
$6 BILLION!
$7 BILLION!
4-23
WE HAVE $7 BILLION. $7 BILLION GOING ONCE... $7 BILLION GOING TWICE...
SOLD, TO THE GENTLEMAN IN THE FRONT ROW FOR $7 BILLION!
SCRATCH SCR-
UM, IS THIS WHERE THE ROBOTECH ACTION FIGURE AUCTION IS TAKING PLACE?
NO, THAT'S IN ROOM H200.
HERE WE HAVE A BEAUTIFUL ELECTORAL SYSTEM...
DARRIN BELL
©2006 Darrin Bell / Dist. by WPWG, Inc. WWW.CANDORVILLE.COM

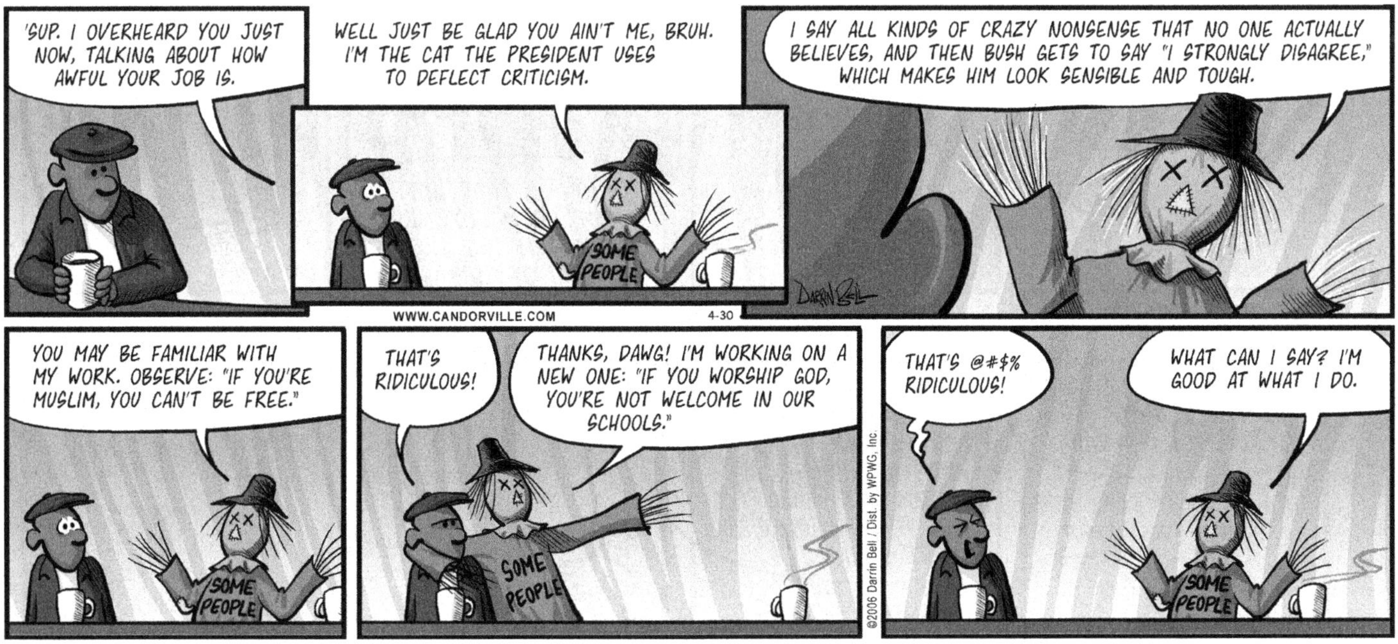
'SUP. I OVERHEARD YOU JUST NOW, TALKING ABOUT HOW AWFUL YOUR JOB IS.
WELL JUST BE GLAD YOU AIN'T ME, BRUH. I'M THE CAT THE PRESIDENT USES TO DEFLECT CRITICISM.
SOME PEOPLE
I SAY ALL KINDS OF CRAZY NONSENSE THAT NO ONE ACTUALLY BELIEVES, AND THEN BUSH GETS TO SAY "I STRONGLY DISAGREE," WHICH MAKES HIM LOOK SENSIBLE AND TOUGH.
DARRIN BELL
WWW.CANDORVILLE.COM 4-30
YOU MAY BE FAMILIAR WITH MY WORK. OBSERVE: "IF YOU'RE MUSLIM, YOU CAN'T BE FREE."
SOME PEOPLE
THAT'S RIDICULOUS!
THANKS, DAWG! I'M WORKING ON A NEW ONE: "IF YOU WORSHIP GOD, YOU'RE NOT WELCOME IN OUR SCHOOLS."
SOME PEOPLE
©2006 Darrin Bell / Dist. by WPWG, Inc.
THAT'S @#$% RIDICULOUS!
WHAT CAN I SAY? I'M GOOD AT WHAT I DO.
SOME PEOPLE

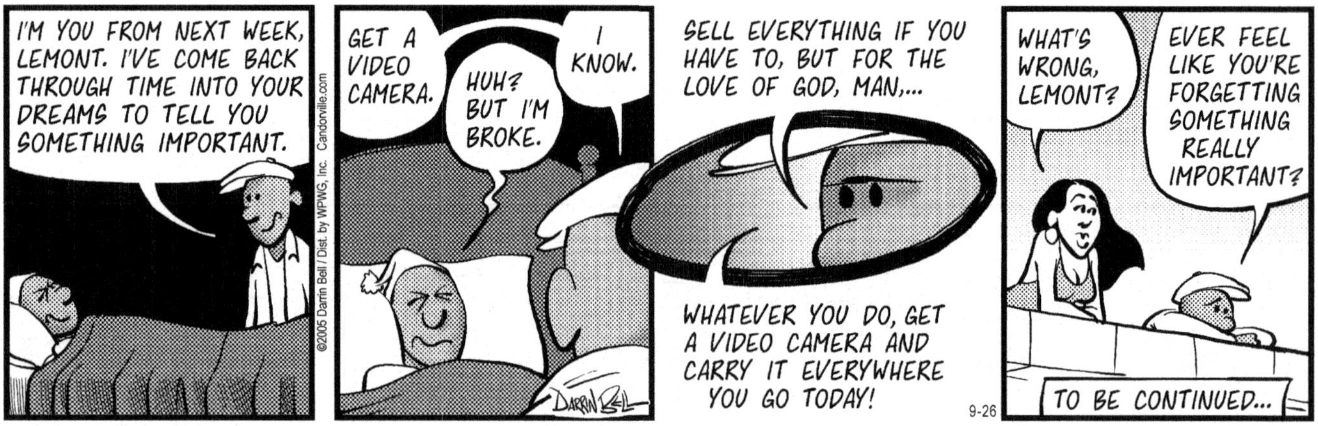
I'M YOU FROM NEXT WEEK, LEMONT. I'VE COME BACK THROUGH TIME INTO YOUR DREAMS TO TELL YOU SOMETHING IMPORTANT.
©2005 Darrin Bell / Dist. by WPWG, Inc. Candorville.com
GET A VIDEO CAMERA.
HUH? BUT I'M BROKE.
I KNOW.
DARRIN BELL
SELL EVERYTHING IF YOU HAVE TO, BUT FOR THE LOVE OF GOD, MAN,...
WHATEVER YOU DO, GET A VIDEO CAMERA AND CARRY IT EVERYWHERE YOU GO TODAY!
9-26
WHAT'S WRONG, LEMONT?
EVER FEEL LIKE YOU'RE FORGETTING SOMETHING REALLY IMPORTANT?
TO BE CONTINUED...

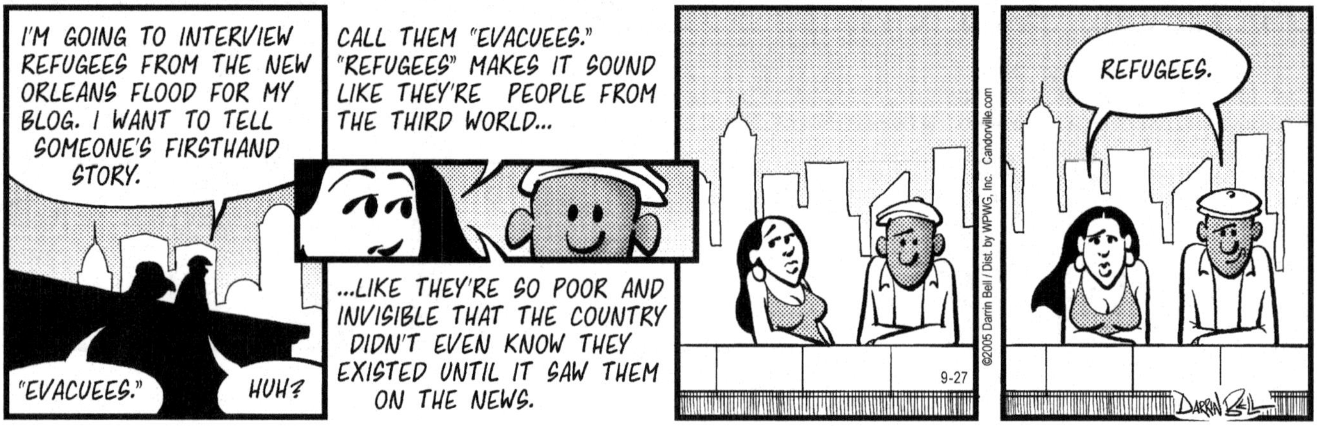
I'M GOING TO INTERVIEW REFUGEES FROM THE NEW ORLEANS FLOOD FOR MY BLOG. I WANT TO TELL SOMEONE'S FIRSTHAND STORY.
"EVACUEES."
HUH?
CALL THEM "EVACUEES." "REFUGEES" MAKES IT SOUND LIKE THEY'RE PEOPLE FROM THE THIRD WORLD...
...LIKE THEY'RE SO POOR AND INVISIBLE THAT THE COUNTRY DIDN'T EVEN KNOW THEY EXISTED UNTIL IT SAW THEM ON THE NEWS.
9-27
©2005 Darrin Bell / Dist. by WPWG, Inc. Candorville.com
REFUGEES.
DARRIN BELL

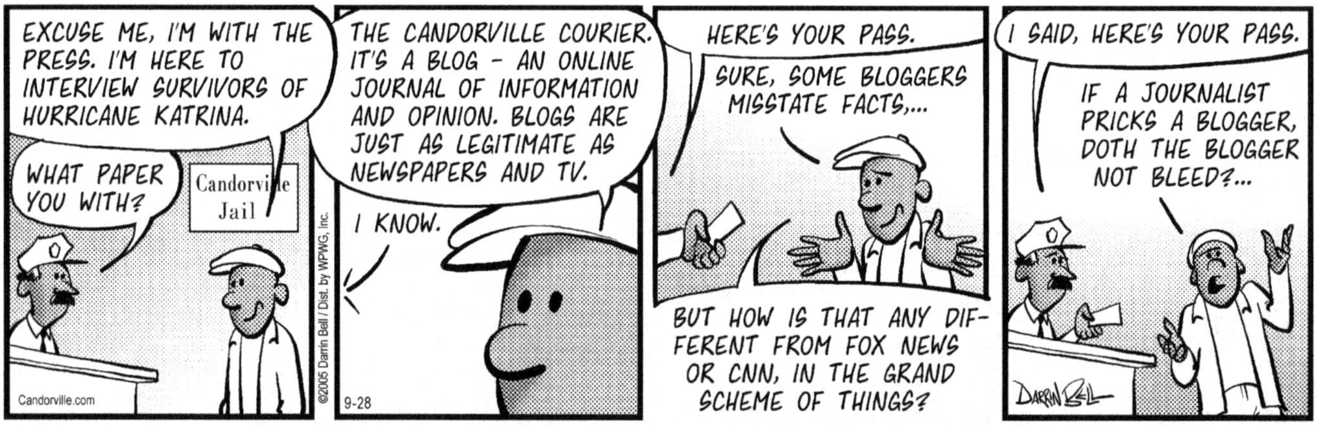
EXCUSE ME, I'M WITH THE PRESS. I'M HERE TO INTERVIEW SURVIVORS OF HURRICANE KATRINA.
WHAT PAPER YOU WITH?
Candorville Jail
Candorville.com
©2005 Darrin Bell / Dist. by WPWG, Inc.
THE CANDORVILLE COURIER. IT'S A BLOG - AN ONLINE JOURNAL OF INFORMATION AND OPINION. BLOGS ARE JUST AS LEGITIMATE AS NEWSPAPERS AND TV.
I KNOW.
9-28
HERE'S YOUR PASS.
SURE, SOME BLOGGERS MISSTATE FACTS,...
BUT HOW IS THAT ANY DIFFERENT FROM FOX NEWS OR CNN, IN THE GRAND SCHEME OF THINGS?
I SAID, HERE'S YOUR PASS.
IF A JOURNALIST PRICKS A BLOGGER, DOTH THE BLOGGER NOT BLEED?...
DARRIN BELL

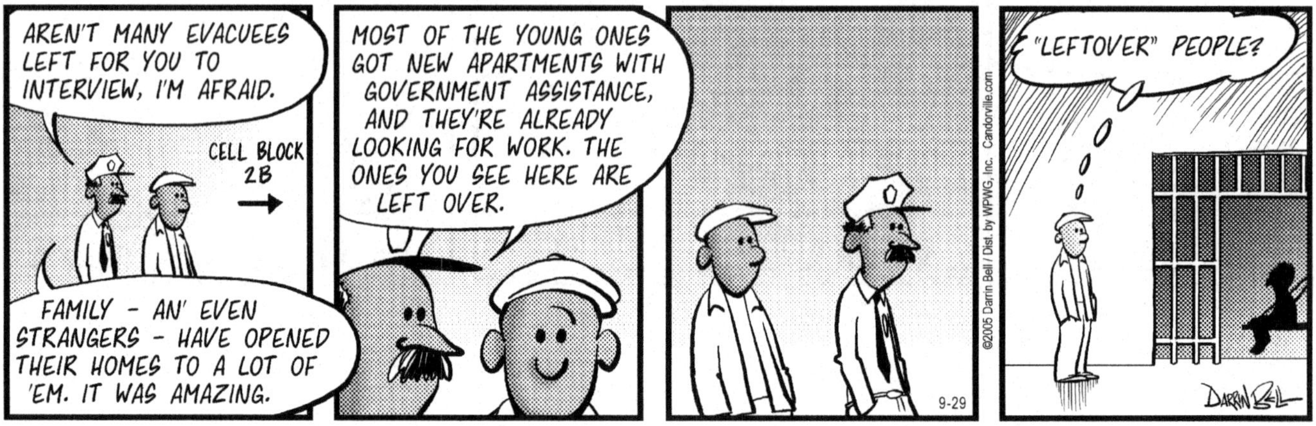
AREN'T MANY EVACUEES LEFT FOR YOU TO INTERVIEW, I'M AFRAID.
CELL BLOCK 2B
FAMILY - AN' EVEN STRANGERS - HAVE OPENED THEIR HOMES TO A LOT OF 'EM. IT WAS AMAZING.
MOST OF THE YOUNG ONES GOT NEW APARTMENTS WITH GOVERNMENT ASSISTANCE, AND THEY'RE ALREADY LOOKING FOR WORK. THE ONES YOU SEE HERE ARE LEFT OVER.
9-29
©2005 Darrin Bell / Dist. by WPWG, Inc. Candorville.com
"LEFTOVER" PEOPLE?
DARRIN BELL

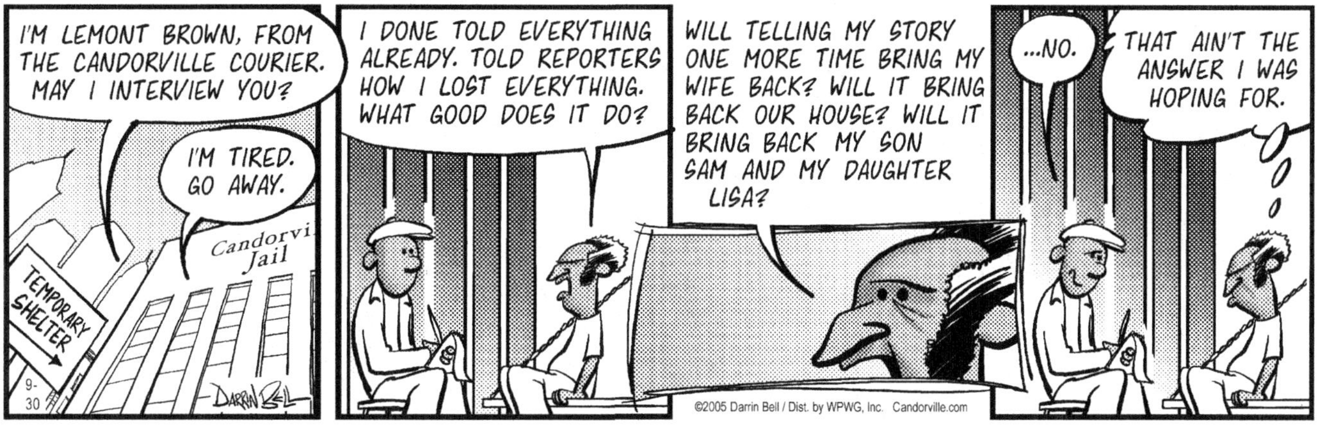
I'M LEMONT BROWN, FROM THE CANDORVILLE COURIER. MAY I INTERVIEW YOU?
I'M TIRED. GO AWAY.
Candorvi Jail
TEMPORARY SHELTER
9-30
DARRIN BELL
I DONE TOLD EVERYTHING ALREADY. TOLD REPORTERS HOW I LOST EVERYTHING. WHAT GOOD DOES IT DO?
WILL TELLING MY STORY ONE MORE TIME BRING MY WIFE BACK? WILL IT BRING BACK OUR HOUSE? WILL IT BRING BACK MY SON SAM AND MY DAUGHTER LISA?
©2005 Darrin Bell / Dist. by WPWG, Inc. Candorville.com
...NO.
THAT AIN'T THE ANSWER I WAS HOPING FOR.

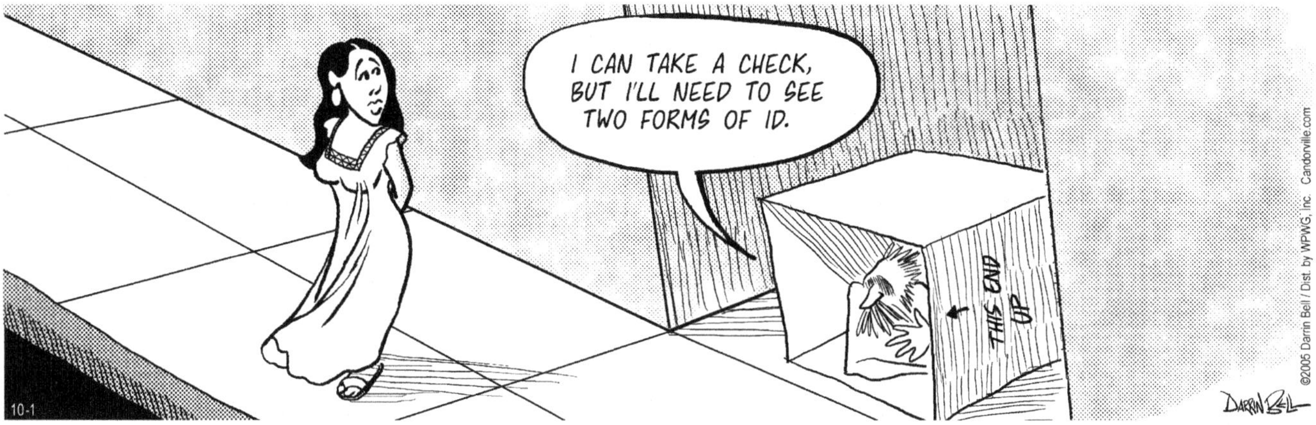
I CAN TAKE A CHECK, BUT I'LL NEED TO SEE TWO FORMS OF ID.
THIS END UP
10-1
©2005 Darrin Bell / Dist. by WPWG, Inc. Candorville.com
DARRIN BELL

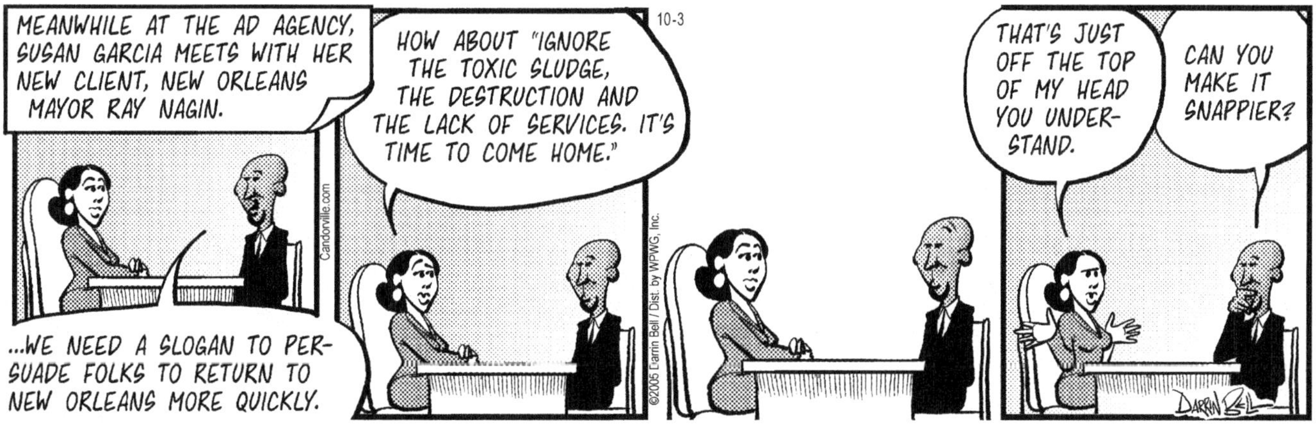
MEANWHILE AT THE AD AGENCY, SUSAN GARCIA MEETS WITH HER NEW CLIENT, NEW ORLEANS MAYOR RAY NAGIN.
Candorville.com
...WE NEED A SLOGAN TO PERSUADE FOLKS TO RETURN TO NEW ORLEANS MORE QUICKLY.
10-3
HOW ABOUT "IGNORE THE TOXIC SLUDGE, THE DESTRUCTION AND THE LACK OF SERVICES. IT'S TIME TO COME HOME."
©2005 Darrin Bell / Dist. by WPWG, Inc.
THAT'S JUST OFF THE TOP OF MY HEAD YOU UNDERSTAND.
CAN YOU MAKE IT SNAPPIER?
DARRIN BELL

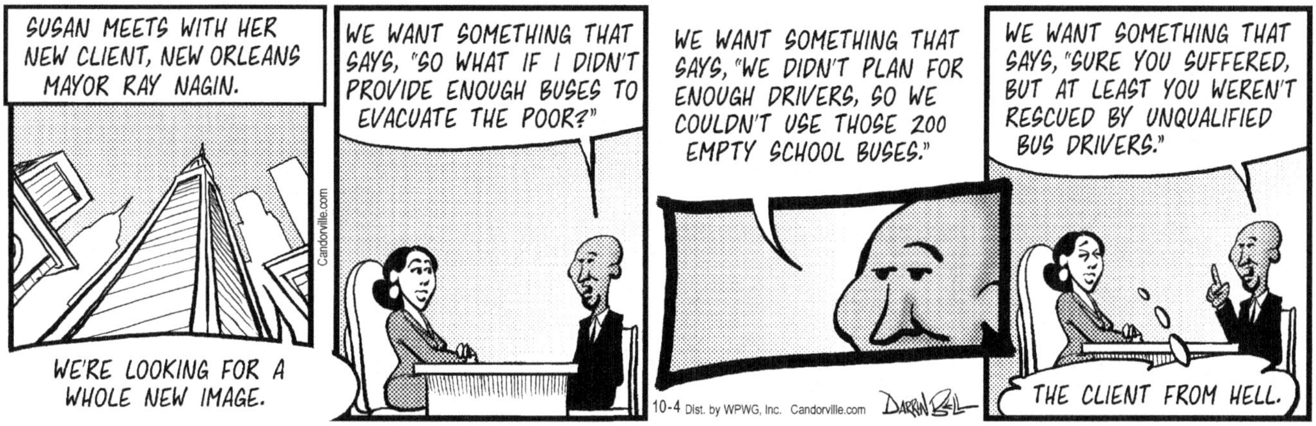
SUSAN MEETS WITH HER NEW CLIENT, NEW ORLEANS MAYOR RAY NAGIN.
Candorville.com
WE'RE LOOKING FOR A WHOLE NEW IMAGE.
WE WANT SOMETHING THAT SAYS, "SO WHAT IF I DIDN'T PROVIDE ENOUGH BUSES TO EVACUATE THE POOR?"
WE WANT SOMETHING THAT SAYS, "WE DIDN'T PLAN FOR ENOUGH DRIVERS, SO WE COULDN'T USE THOSE 200 EMPTY SCHOOL BUSES."
10-4 Dist. by WPWG, Inc. Candorville.com
DARRIN BELL
WE WANT SOMETHING THAT SAYS, "SURE YOU SUFFERED, BUT AT LEAST YOU WEREN'T RESCUED BY UNQUALIFIED BUS DRIVERS."
THE CLIENT FROM HELL.

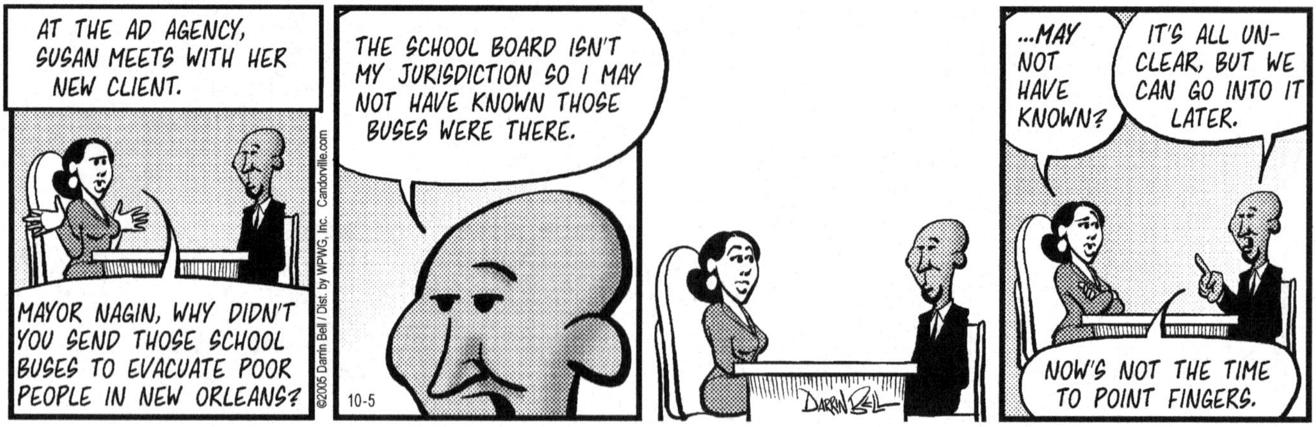
AT THE AD AGENCY, SUSAN MEETS WITH HER NEW CLIENT.
MAYOR NAGIN, WHY DIDN'T YOU SEND THOSE SCHOOL BUSES TO EVACUATE POOR PEOPLE IN NEW ORLEANS?
THE SCHOOL BOARD ISN'T MY JURISDICTION SO I MAY NOT HAVE KNOWN THOSE BUSES WERE THERE.
...MAY NOT HAVE KNOWN?
IT'S ALL UN-CLEAR, BUT WE CAN GO INTO IT LATER.
NOW'S NOT THE TIME TO POINT FINGERS.
10-5
©2005 Darrin Bell / Dist. by WPWG, Inc. Candorville.com

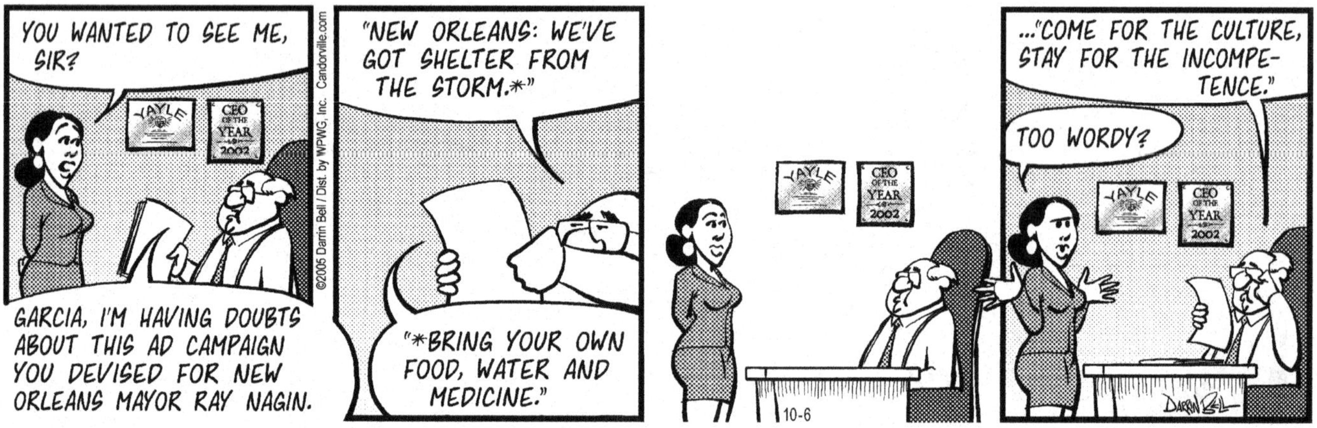
YOU WANTED TO SEE ME, SIR?
GARCIA, I'M HAVING DOUBTS ABOUT THIS AD CAMPAIGN YOU DEVISED FOR NEW ORLEANS MAYOR RAY NAGIN.
"NEW ORLEANS: WE'VE GOT SHELTER FROM THE STORM.*"
"*BRING YOUR OWN FOOD, WATER AND MEDICINE."
YAYLE
CEO OF THE YEAR 2002
..."COME FOR THE CULTURE, STAY FOR THE INCOMPE-TENCE."
TOO WORDY?
10-6
©2005 Darrin Bell / Dist. by WPWG, Inc. Candorville.com

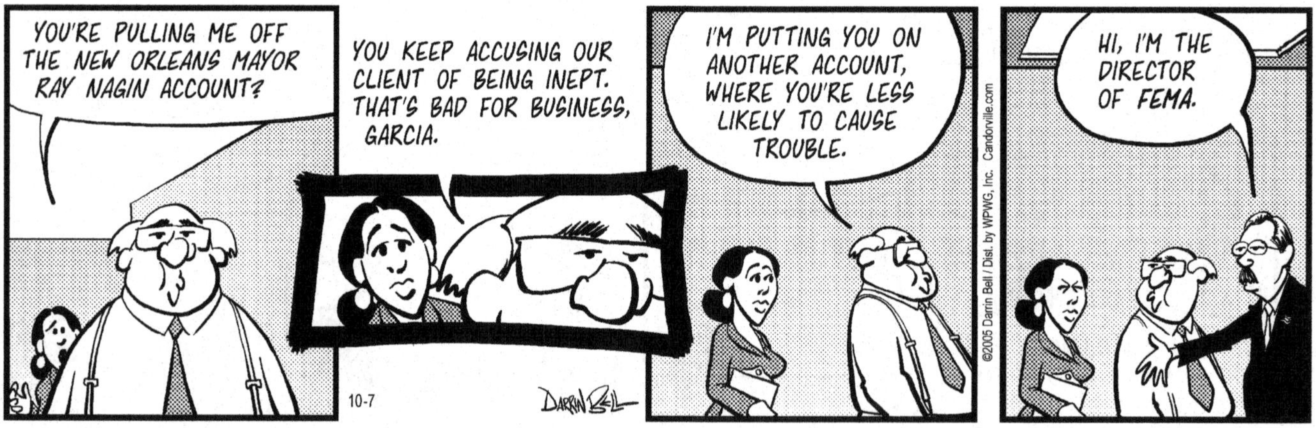
YOU'RE PULLING ME OFF THE NEW ORLEANS MAYOR RAY NAGIN ACCOUNT?
YOU KEEP ACCUSING OUR CLIENT OF BEING INEPT. THAT'S BAD FOR BUSINESS, GARCIA.
I'M PUTTING YOU ON ANOTHER ACCOUNT, WHERE YOU'RE LESS LIKELY TO CAUSE TROUBLE.
HI, I'M THE DIRECTOR OF FEMA.
10-7
©2005 Darrin Bell / Dist. by WPWG, Inc. Candorville.com

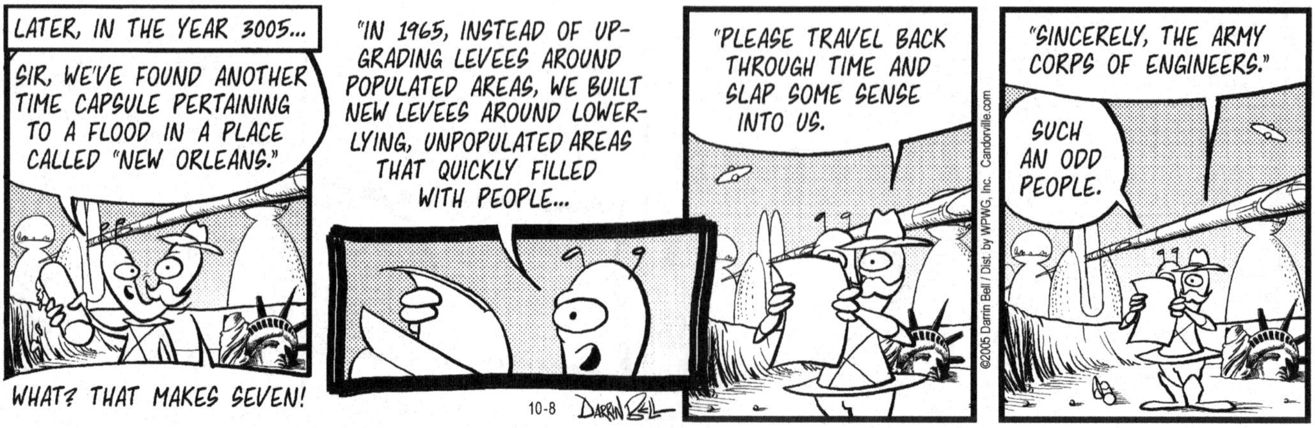
LATER, IN THE YEAR 3005...
SIR, WE'VE FOUND ANOTHER TIME CAPSULE PERTAINING TO A FLOOD IN A PLACE CALLED "NEW ORLEANS."
WHAT? THAT MAKES SEVEN!
"IN 1965, INSTEAD OF UP-GRADING LEVEES AROUND POPULATED AREAS, WE BUILT NEW LEVEES AROUND LOWER-LYING, UNPOPULATED AREAS THAT QUICKLY FILLED WITH PEOPLE...
"PLEASE TRAVEL BACK THROUGH TIME AND SLAP SOME SENSE INTO US.
"SINCERELY, THE ARMY CORPS OF ENGINEERS."
SUCH AN ODD PEOPLE.
10-8
©2005 Darrin Bell / Dist. by WPWG, Inc. Candorville.com

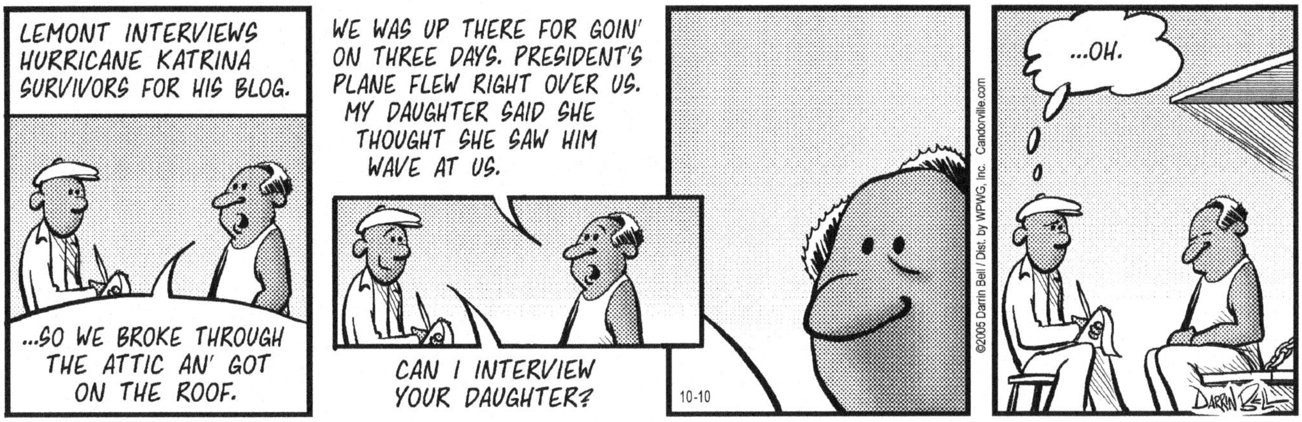
LEMONT INTERVIEWS HURRICANE KATRINA SURVIVORS FOR HIS BLOG.
...SO WE BROKE THROUGH THE ATTIC AN' GOT ON THE ROOF.
WE WAS UP THERE FOR GOIN' ON THREE DAYS. PRESIDENT'S PLANE FLEW RIGHT OVER US. MY DAUGHTER SAID SHE THOUGHT SHE SAW HIM WAVE AT US.
CAN I INTERVIEW YOUR DAUGHTER?
10-10
©2005 Darrin Bell / Dist. by WPWG, Inc. Candorville.com
...OH.
DARRIN BELL

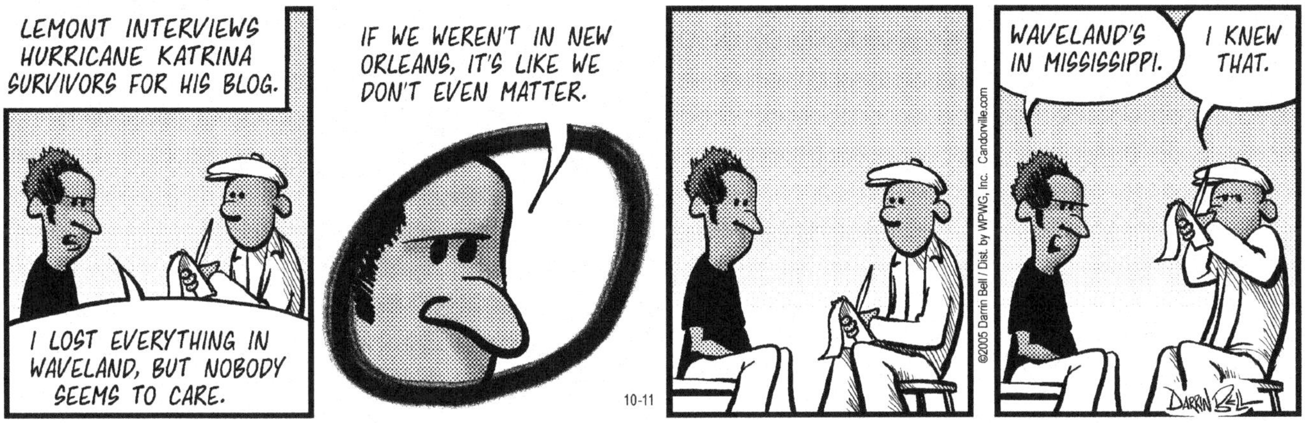
LEMONT INTERVIEWS HURRICANE KATRINA SURVIVORS FOR HIS BLOG.
I LOST EVERYTHING IN WAVELAND, BUT NOBODY SEEMS TO CARE.
IF WE WEREN'T IN NEW ORLEANS, IT'S LIKE WE DON'T EVEN MATTER.
10-11
©2005 Darrin Bell / Dist. by WPWG, Inc. Candorville.com
WAVELAND'S IN MISSISSIPPI.
I KNEW THAT.
DARRIN BELL

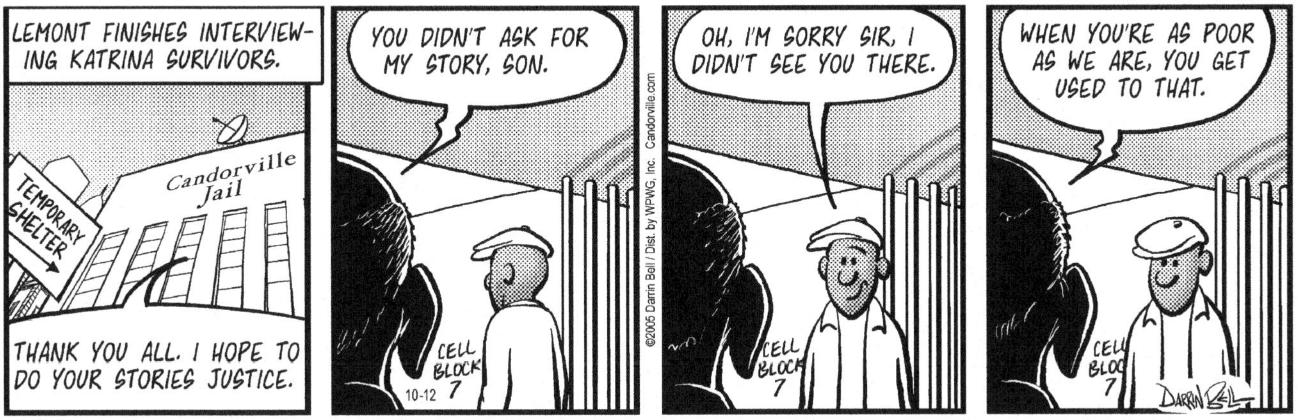
LEMONT FINISHES INTERVIEWING KATRINA SURVIVORS.
TEMPORARY SHELTER
Candorville Jail
THANK YOU ALL. I HOPE TO DO YOUR STORIES JUSTICE.
YOU DIDN'T ASK FOR MY STORY, SON.
CELL BLOCK 7
10-12
©2005 Darrin Bell / Dist. by WPWG, Inc. Candorville.com
OH, I'M SORRY SIR, I DIDN'T SEE YOU THERE.
CELL BLOCK 7
WHEN YOU'RE AS POOR AS WE ARE, YOU GET USED TO THAT.
DARRIN BELL

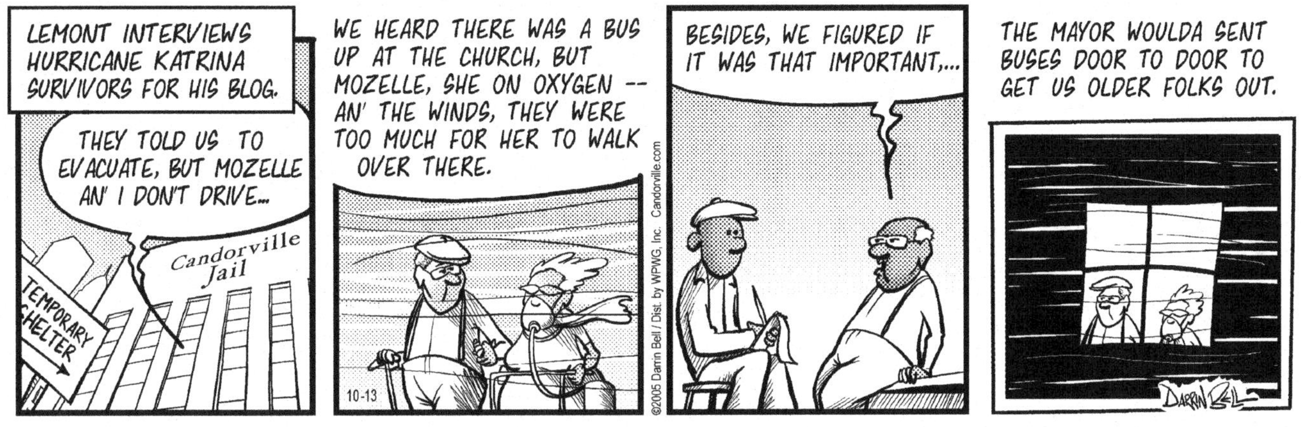
LEMONT INTERVIEWS HURRICANE KATRINA SURVIVORS FOR HIS BLOG.
THEY TOLD US TO EVACUATE, BUT MOZELLE AN' I DON'T DRIVE...
Candorville Jail
TEMPORARY SHELTER
WE HEARD THERE WAS A BUS UP AT THE CHURCH, BUT MOZELLE, SHE ON OXYGEN -- AN' THE WINDS, THEY WERE TOO MUCH FOR HER TO WALK OVER THERE.
10-13
©2005 Darrin Bell / Dist. by WPWG, Inc. Candorville.com
BESIDES, WE FIGURED IF IT WAS THAT IMPORTANT,...
THE MAYOR WOULDA SENT BUSES DOOR TO DOOR TO GET US OLDER FOLKS OUT.
DARRIN BELL

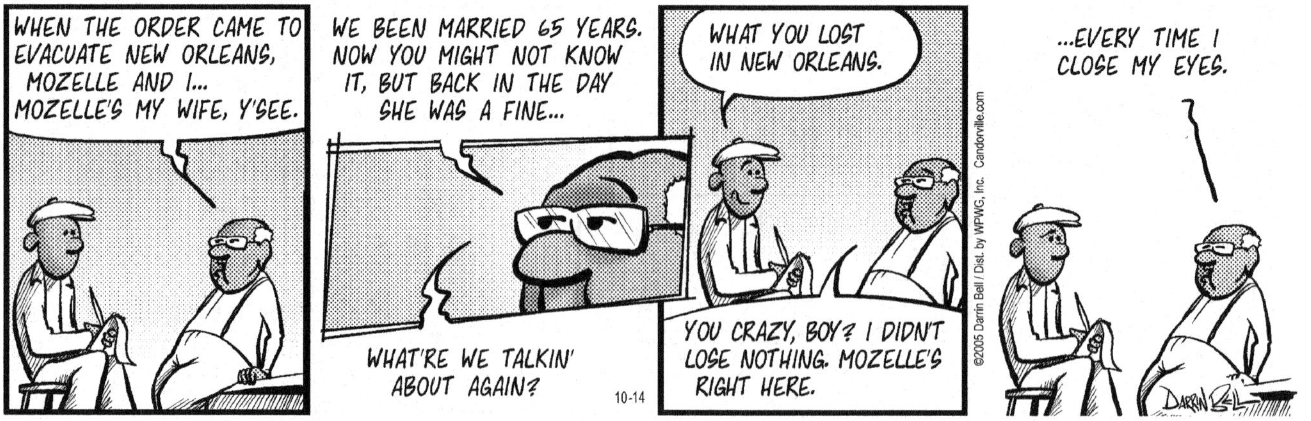
WHEN THE ORDER CAME TO EVACUATE NEW ORLEANS, MOZELLE AND I... MOZELLE'S MY WIFE, Y'SEE.
WE BEEN MARRIED 65 YEARS. NOW YOU MIGHT NOT KNOW IT, BUT BACK IN THE DAY SHE WAS A FINE...
WHAT'RE WE TALKIN' ABOUT AGAIN?
10-14
WHAT YOU LOST IN NEW ORLEANS.
YOU CRAZY, BOY? I DIDN'T LOSE NOTHING. MOZELLE'S RIGHT HERE.
©2005 Darrin Bell / Dist. by WPWG, Inc. Candorville.com
...EVERY TIME I CLOSE MY EYES.
DARRIN BELL

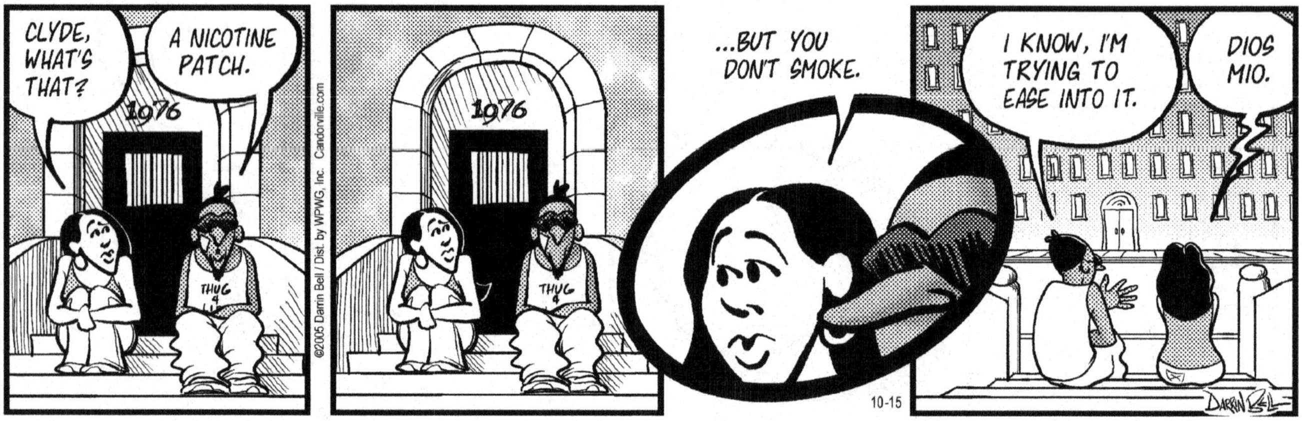
CLYDE, WHAT'S THAT?
A NICOTINE PATCH.
1976
©2005 Darrin Bell / Dist. by WPWG, Inc. Candorville.com
...BUT YOU DON'T SMOKE.
I KNOW, I'M TRYING TO EASE INTO IT.
DIOS MIO.
10-15
DARRIN BELL

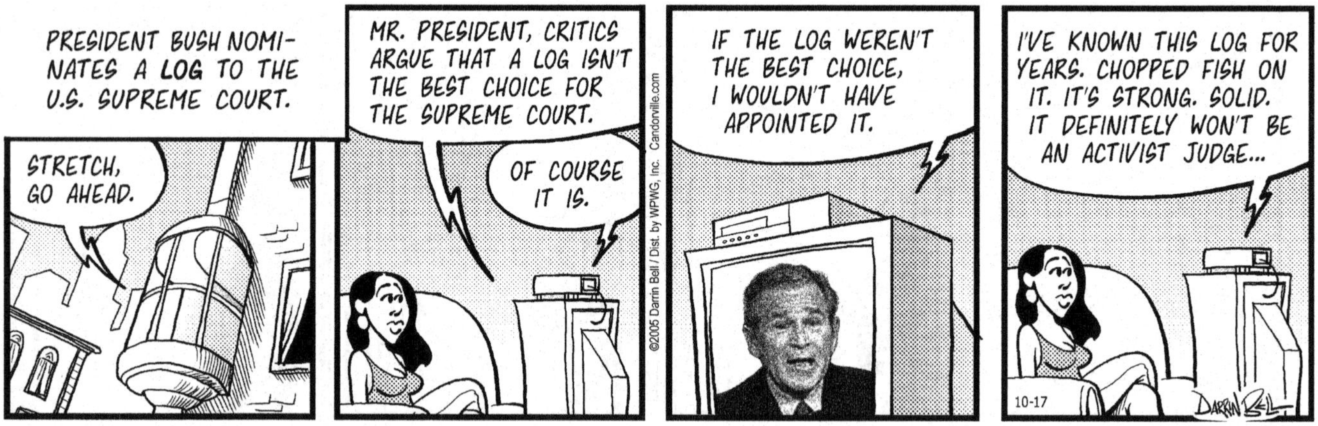
PRESIDENT BUSH NOMINATES A LOG TO THE U.S. SUPREME COURT.
STRETCH, GO AHEAD.
MR. PRESIDENT, CRITICS ARGUE THAT A LOG ISN'T THE BEST CHOICE FOR THE SUPREME COURT.
OF COURSE IT IS.
©2005 Darrin Bell / Dist. by WPWG, Inc. Candorville.com
IF THE LOG WEREN'T THE BEST CHOICE, I WOULDN'T HAVE APPOINTED IT.
I'VE KNOWN THIS LOG FOR YEARS. CHOPPED FISH ON IT. IT'S STRONG. SOLID. IT DEFINITELY WON'T BE AN ACTIVIST JUDGE...
10-17
DARRIN BELL

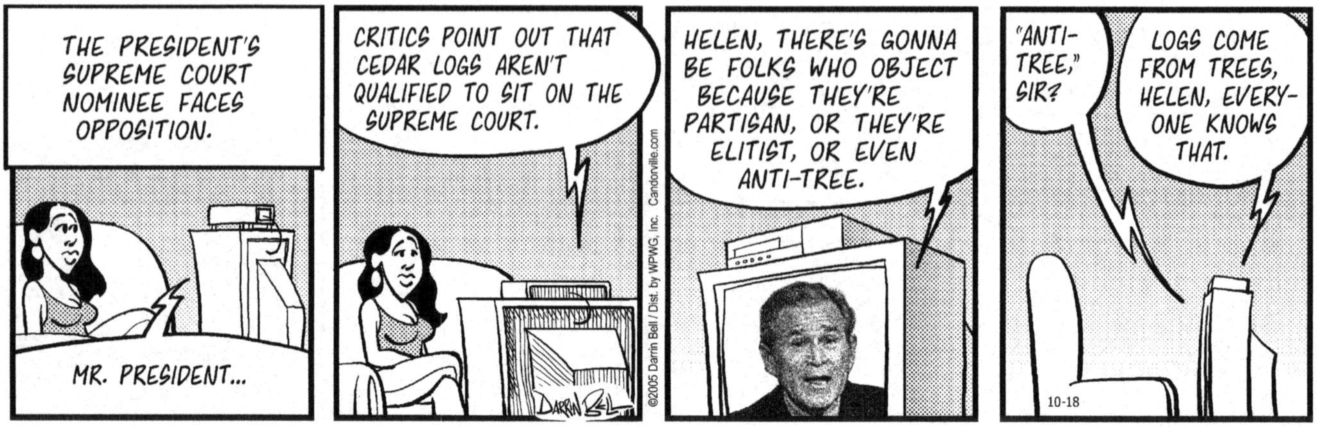
THE PRESIDENT'S SUPREME COURT NOMINEE FACES OPPOSITION.
MR. PRESIDENT...
CRITICS POINT OUT THAT CEDAR LOGS AREN'T QUALIFIED TO SIT ON THE SUPREME COURT.
DARRIN BELL
©2005 Darrin Bell / Dist. by WPWG, Inc. Candorville.com
HELEN, THERE'S GONNA BE FOLKS WHO OBJECT BECAUSE THEY'RE PARTISAN, OR THEY'RE ELITIST, OR EVEN ANTI-TREE.
"ANTI-TREE," SIR?
LOGS COME FROM TREES, HELEN, EVERYONE KNOWS THAT.
10-18

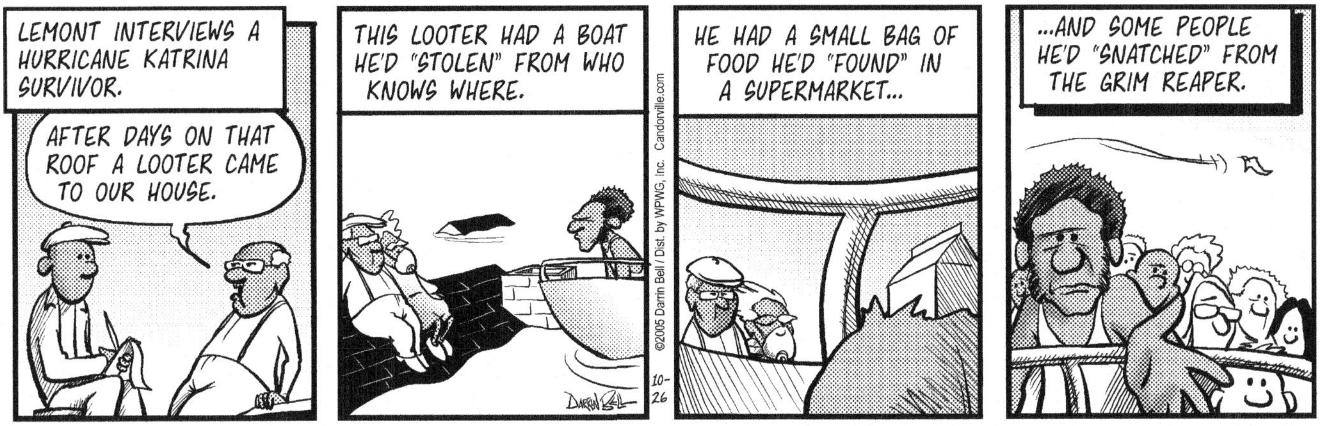
LEMONT INTERVIEWS A HURRICANE KATRINA SURVIVOR.
AFTER DAYS ON THAT ROOF A LOOTER CAME TO OUR HOUSE.
THIS LOOTER HAD A BOAT HE'D "STOLEN" FROM WHO KNOWS WHERE.
HE HAD A SMALL BAG OF FOOD HE'D "FOUND" IN A SUPERMARKET...
...AND SOME PEOPLE HE'D "SNATCHED" FROM THE GRIM REAPER.
©2005 Darrin Bell / Dist. by WPWG, Inc. Candorville.com
10-26
DARRIN BELL

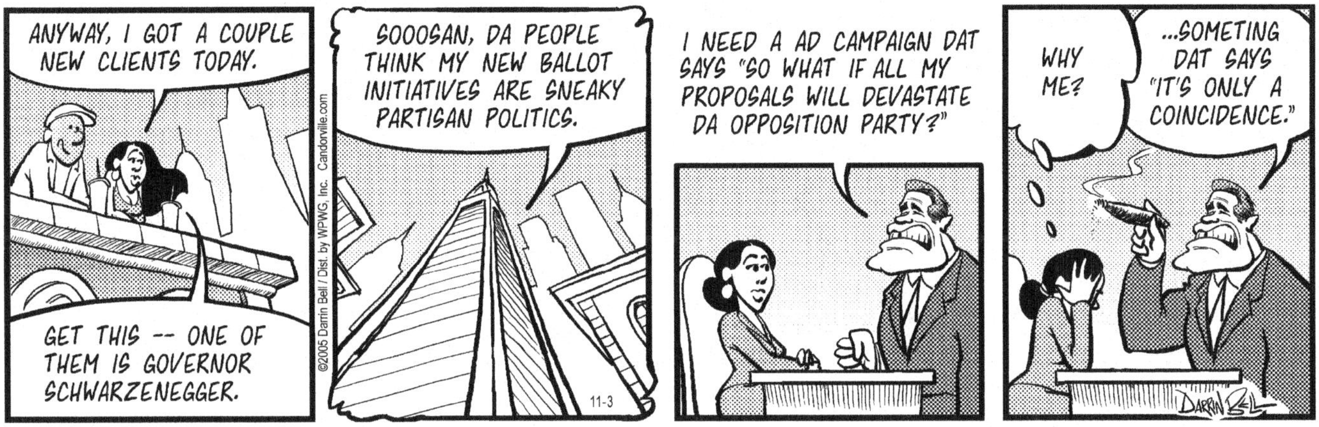
ANYWAY, I GOT A COUPLE NEW CLIENTS TODAY.
GET THIS -- ONE OF THEM IS GOVERNOR SCHWARZENEGGER.
©2005 Darrin Bell / Dist. by WPWG, Inc. Candorville.com
SOOOSAN, DA PEOPLE THINK MY NEW BALLOT INITIATIVES ARE SNEAKY PARTISAN POLITICS.
11-3
I NEED A AD CAMPAIGN DAT SAYS "SO WHAT IF ALL MY PROPOSALS WILL DEVASTATE DA OPPOSITION PARTY?"
WHY ME?
...SOMETING DAT SAYS "IT'S ONLY A COINCIDENCE."
DARRIN BELL

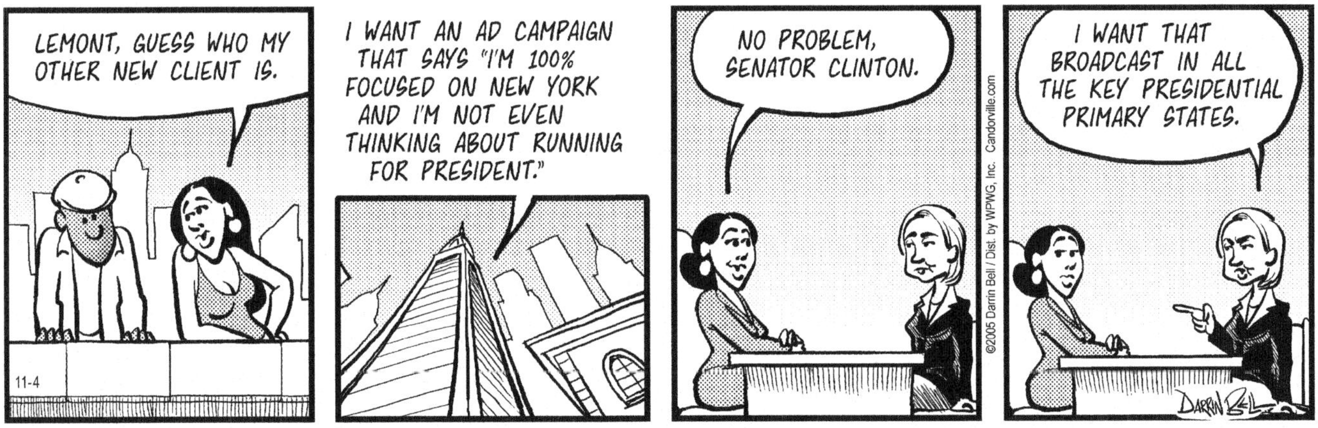
LEMONT, GUESS WHO MY OTHER NEW CLIENT IS.
11-4
I WANT AN AD CAMPAIGN THAT SAYS "I'M 100% FOCUSED ON NEW YORK AND I'M NOT EVEN THINKING ABOUT RUNNING FOR PRESIDENT."
NO PROBLEM, SENATOR CLINTON.
©2005 Darrin Bell / Dist. by WPWG, Inc. Candorville.com
I WANT THAT BROADCAST IN ALL THE KEY PRESIDENTIAL PRIMARY STATES.
DARRIN BELL

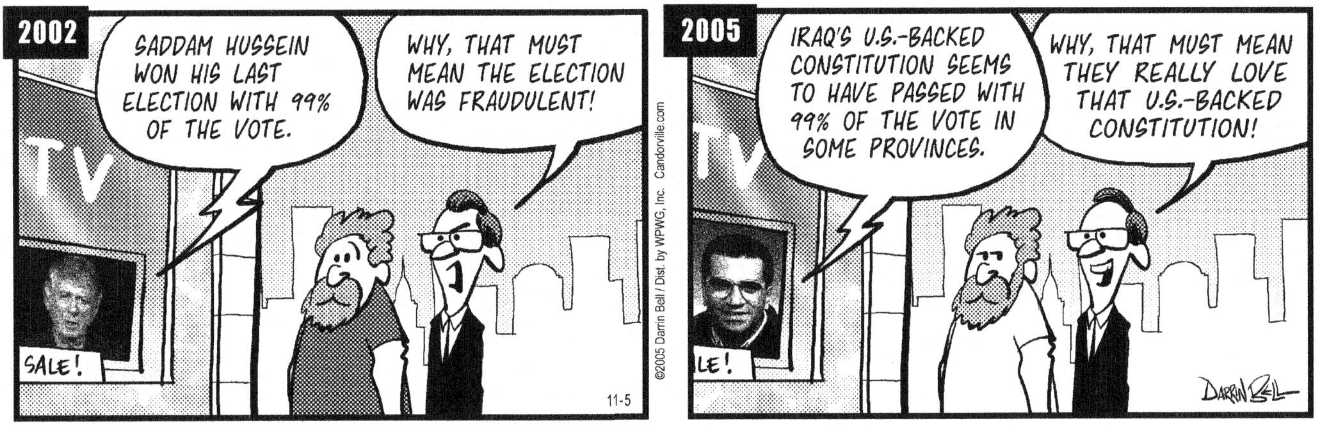
2002
TV
SADDAM HUSSEIN WON HIS LAST ELECTION WITH 99% OF THE VOTE.
WHY, THAT MUST MEAN THE ELECTION WAS FRAUDULENT!
SALE!
11-5
©2005 Darrin Bell / Dist. by WPWG, Inc. Candorville.com
2005
TV
IRAQ'S U.S.-BACKED CONSTITUTION SEEMS TO HAVE PASSED WITH 99% OF THE VOTE IN SOME PROVINCES.
WHY, THAT MUST MEAN THEY REALLY LOVE THAT U.S.-BACKED CONSTITUTION!
LE!
DARRIN BELL

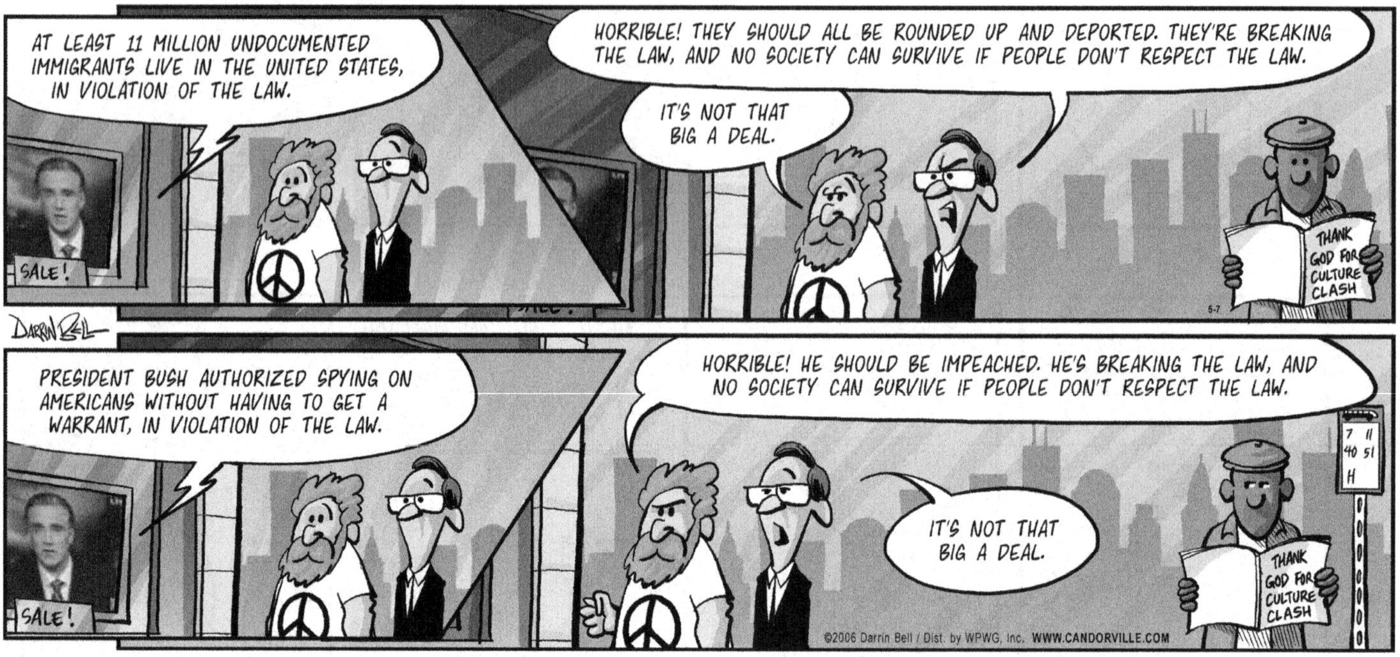
AT LEAST 11 MILLION UNDOCUMENTED IMMIGRANTS LIVE IN THE UNITED STATES, IN VIOLATION OF THE LAW.
SALE!
HORRIBLE! THEY SHOULD ALL BE ROUNDED UP AND DEPORTED. THEY'RE BREAKING THE LAW, AND NO SOCIETY CAN SURVIVE IF PEOPLE DON'T RESPECT THE LAW.
IT'S NOT THAT BIG A DEAL.
THANK GOD FOR CULTURE CLASH
DARRIN BELL
PRESIDENT BUSH AUTHORIZED SPYING ON AMERICANS WITHOUT HAVING TO GET A WARRANT, IN VIOLATION OF THE LAW.
SALE!
HORRIBLE! HE SHOULD BE IMPEACHED. HE'S BREAKING THE LAW, AND NO SOCIETY CAN SURVIVE IF PEOPLE DON'T RESPECT THE LAW.
IT'S NOT THAT BIG A DEAL.
THANK GOD FOR CULTURE CLASH
©2006 Darrin Bell / Dist. by WPWG, Inc. WWW.CANDORVILLE.COM

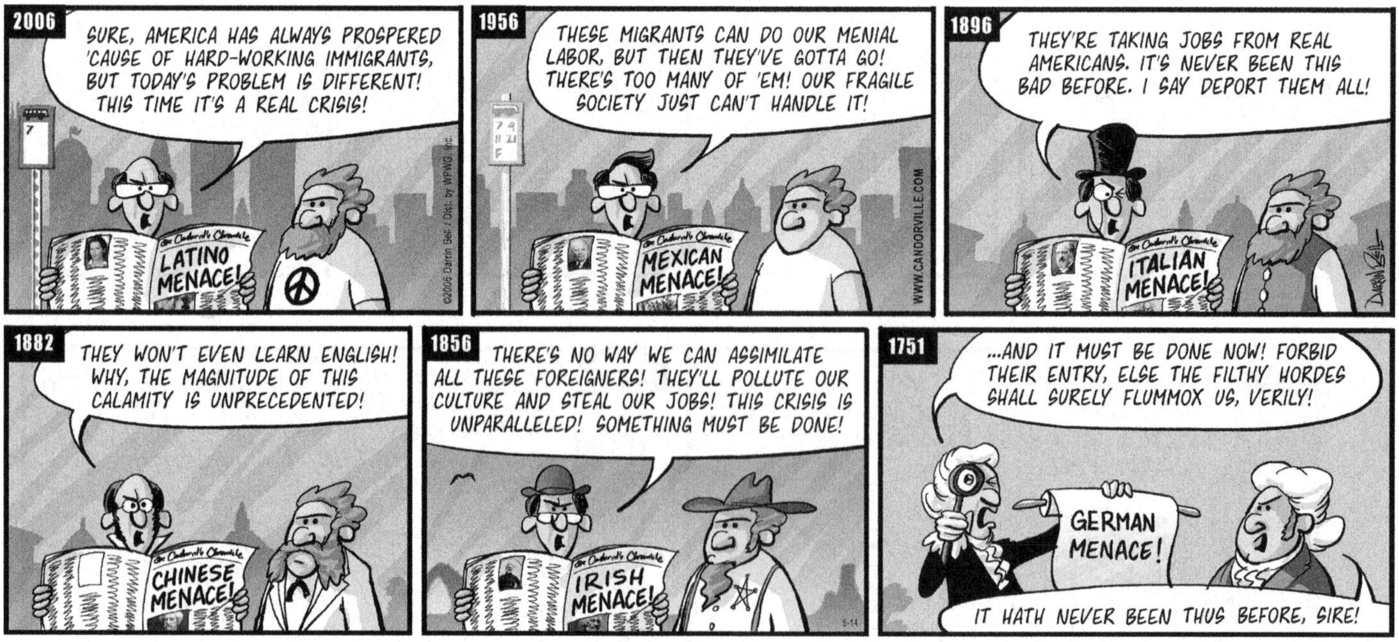
2006
SURE, AMERICA HAS ALWAYS PROSPERED 'CAUSE OF HARD-WORKING IMMIGRANTS, BUT TODAY'S PROBLEM IS DIFFERENT! THIS TIME IT'S A REAL CRISIS!
LATINO MENACE!
©2006 Darrin Bell / Dist. by WPWG Inc.
1956
THESE MIGRANTS CAN DO OUR MENIAL LABOR, BUT THEN THEY'VE GOTTA GO! THERE'S TOO MANY OF 'EM! OUR FRAGILE SOCIETY JUST CAN'T HANDLE IT!
MEXICAN MENACE!
WWW.CANDORVILLE.COM
1896
THEY'RE TAKING JOBS FROM REAL AMERICANS. IT'S NEVER BEEN THIS BAD BEFORE. I SAY DEPORT THEM ALL!
ITALIAN MENACE!
1882
THEY WON'T EVEN LEARN ENGLISH! WHY, THE MAGNITUDE OF THIS CALAMITY IS UNPRECEDENTED!
CHINESE MENACE!
1856
THERE'S NO WAY WE CAN ASSIMILATE ALL THESE FOREIGNERS! THEY'LL POLLUTE OUR CULTURE AND STEAL OUR JOBS! THIS CRISIS IS UNPARALLELED! SOMETHING MUST BE DONE!
IRISH MENACE!
1751
...AND IT MUST BE DONE NOW! FORBID THEIR ENTRY, ELSE THE FILTHY HORDES SHALL SURELY FLUMMOX US, VERILY!
GERMAN MENACE!
IT HATH NEVER BEEN THUS BEFORE, SIRE!

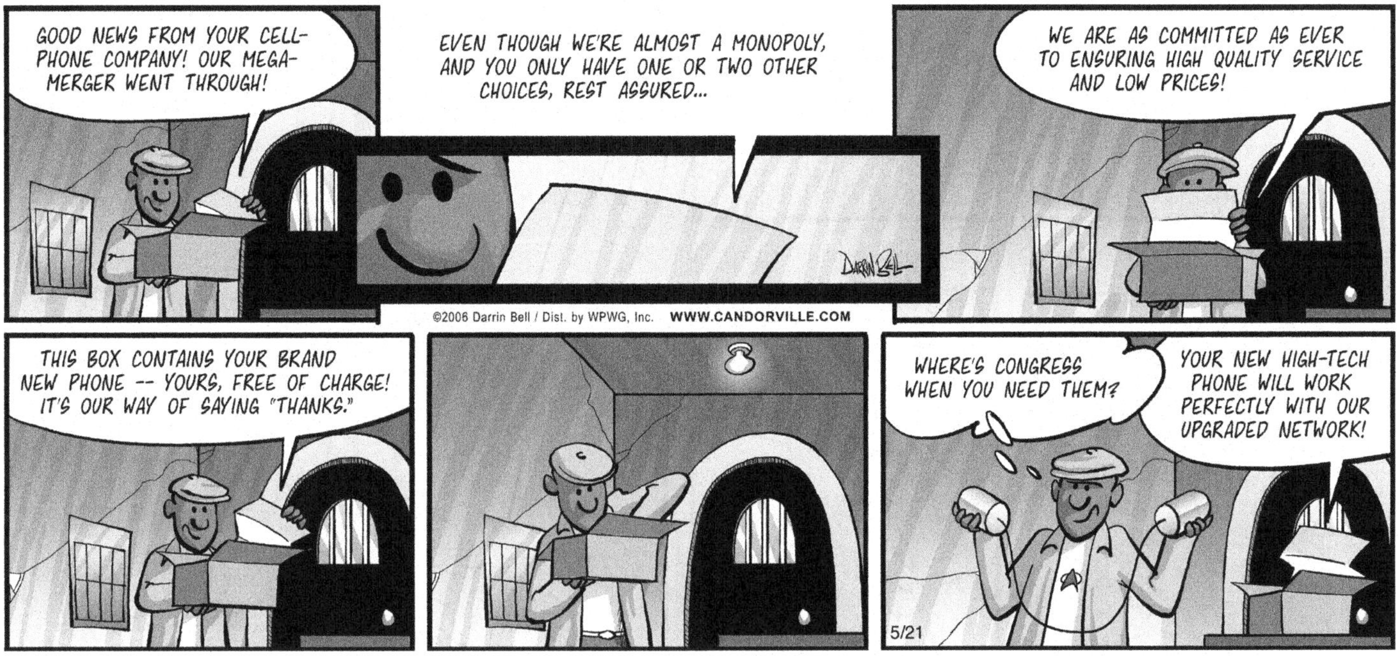
GOOD NEWS FROM YOUR CELL-PHONE COMPANY! OUR MEGA-MERGER WENT THROUGH!
EVEN THOUGH WE'RE ALMOST A MONOPOLY, AND YOU ONLY HAVE ONE OR TWO OTHER CHOICES, REST ASSURED...
WE ARE AS COMMITTED AS EVER TO ENSURING HIGH QUALITY SERVICE AND LOW PRICES!
©2006 Darrin Bell / Dist. by WPWG, Inc. WWW.CANDORVILLE.COM
THIS BOX CONTAINS YOUR BRAND NEW PHONE -- YOURS, FREE OF CHARGE! IT'S OUR WAY OF SAYING "THANKS."
WHERE'S CONGRESS WHEN YOU NEED THEM?
YOUR NEW HIGH-TECH PHONE WILL WORK PERFECTLY WITH OUR UPGRADED NETWORK!
5/21

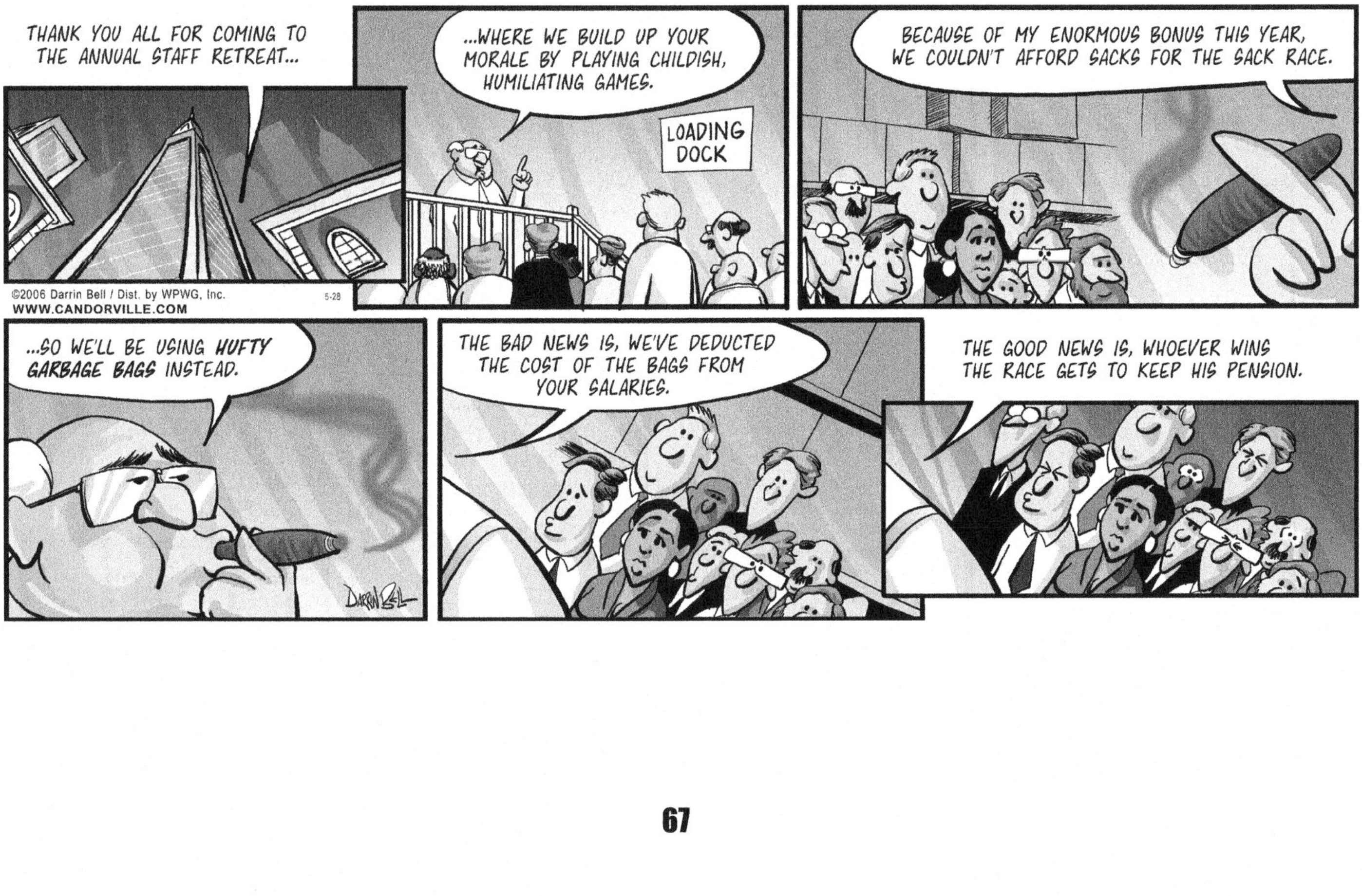
THANK YOU ALL FOR COMING TO THE ANNUAL STAFF RETREAT...
...WHERE WE BUILD UP YOUR MORALE BY PLAYING CHILDISH, HUMILIATING GAMES.
LOADING DOCK
BECAUSE OF MY ENORMOUS BONUS THIS YEAR, WE COULDN'T AFFORD SACKS FOR THE SACK RACE.
©2006 Darrin Bell / Dist. by WPWG, Inc. 5-28
WWW.CANDORVILLE.COM
...SO WE'LL BE USING HUFTY GARBAGE BAGS INSTEAD.
THE BAD NEWS IS, WE'VE DEDUCTED THE COST OF THE BAGS FROM YOUR SALARIES.
THE GOOD NEWS IS, WHOEVER WINS THE RACE GETS TO KEEP HIS PENSION.

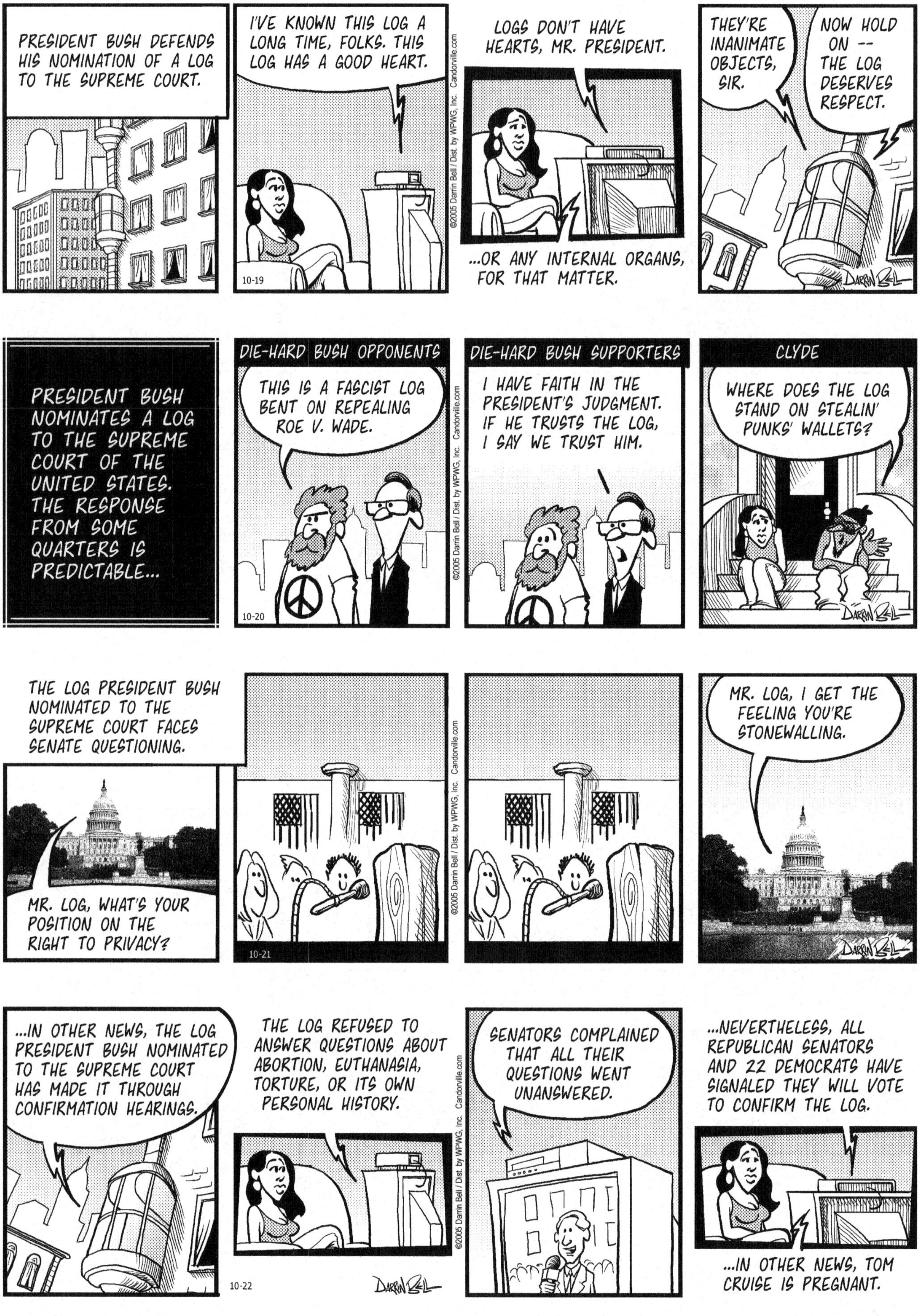
PRESIDENT BUSH DEFENDS HIS NOMINATION OF A LOG TO THE SUPREME COURT.
I'VE KNOWN THIS LOG A LONG TIME, FOLKS. THIS LOG HAS A GOOD HEART.
10-19
©2005 Darrin Bell / Dist. by WPWG, Inc. Candorville.com
LOGS DON'T HAVE HEARTS, MR. PRESIDENT.
...OR ANY INTERNAL ORGANS, FOR THAT MATTER.
THEY'RE INANIMATE OBJECTS, SIR.
NOW HOLD ON -- THE LOG DESERVES RESPECT.
DARRIN BELL
PRESIDENT BUSH NOMINATES A LOG TO THE SUPREME COURT OF THE UNITED STATES. THE RESPONSE FROM SOME QUARTERS IS PREDICTABLE...
DIE-HARD BUSH OPPONENTS
THIS IS A FASCIST LOG BENT ON REPEALING ROE V. WADE.
10-20
©2005 Darrin Bell / Dist. by WPWG, Inc. Candorville.com
DIE-HARD BUSH SUPPORTERS
I HAVE FAITH IN THE PRESIDENT'S JUDGMENT. IF HE TRUSTS THE LOG, I SAY WE TRUST HIM.
CLYDE
WHERE DOES THE LOG STAND ON STEALIN' PUNKS' WALLETS?
DARRIN BELL
THE LOG PRESIDENT BUSH NOMINATED TO THE SUPREME COURT FACES SENATE QUESTIONING.
MR. LOG, WHAT'S YOUR POSITION ON THE RIGHT TO PRIVACY?
10-21
©2005 Darrin Bell / Dist. by WPWG, Inc. Candorville.com
MR. LOG, I GET THE FEELING YOU'RE STONEWALLING.
DARRIN BELL
...IN OTHER NEWS, THE LOG PRESIDENT BUSH NOMINATED TO THE SUPREME COURT HAS MADE IT THROUGH CONFIRMATION HEARINGS.
10-22
THE LOG REFUSED TO ANSWER QUESTIONS ABOUT ABORTION, EUTHANASIA, TORTURE, OR ITS OWN PERSONAL HISTORY.
DARRIN BELL
©2005 Darrin Bell / Dist. by WPWG, Inc. Candorville.com
SENATORS COMPLAINED THAT ALL THEIR QUESTIONS WENT UNANSWERED.
...NEVERTHELESS, ALL REPUBLICAN SENATORS AND 22 DEMOCRATS HAVE SIGNALED THEY WILL VOTE TO CONFIRM THE LOG.
...IN OTHER NEWS, TOM CRUISE IS PREGNANT.

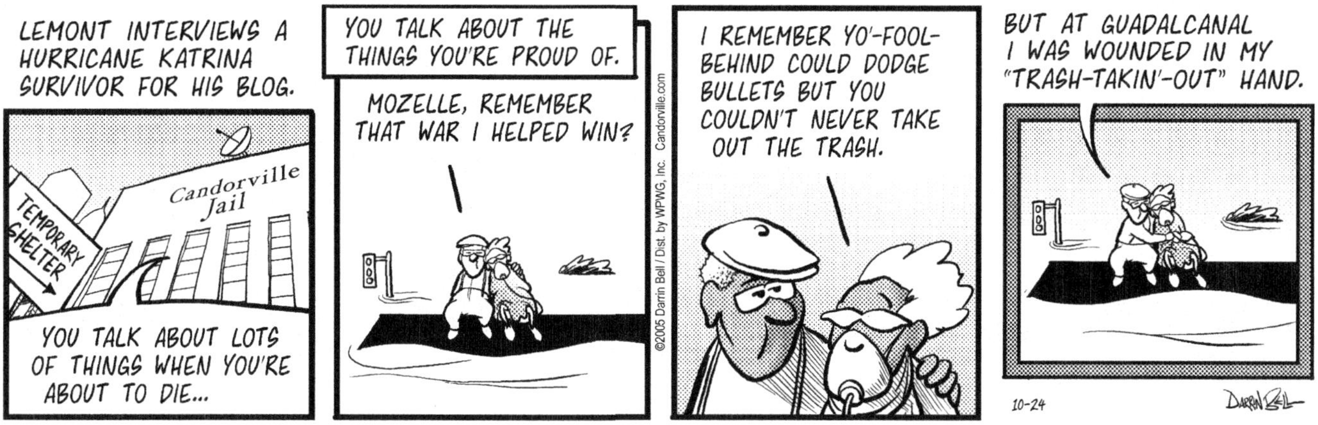
LEMONT INTERVIEWS A HURRICANE KATRINA SURVIVOR FOR HIS BLOG.
TEMPORARY SHELTER
Candorville Jail
YOU TALK ABOUT LOTS OF THINGS WHEN YOU'RE ABOUT TO DIE...
YOU TALK ABOUT THE THINGS YOU'RE PROUD OF.
MOZELLE, REMEMBER THAT WAR I HELPED WIN?
©2005 Darrin Bell / Dist. by WPWG, Inc. Candorville.com
I REMEMBER YO'-FOOL-BEHIND COULD DODGE BULLETS BUT YOU COULDN'T NEVER TAKE OUT THE TRASH.
BUT AT GUADALCANAL I WAS WOUNDED IN MY "TRASH-TAKIN'-OUT" HAND.
10-24
DARRIN BELL

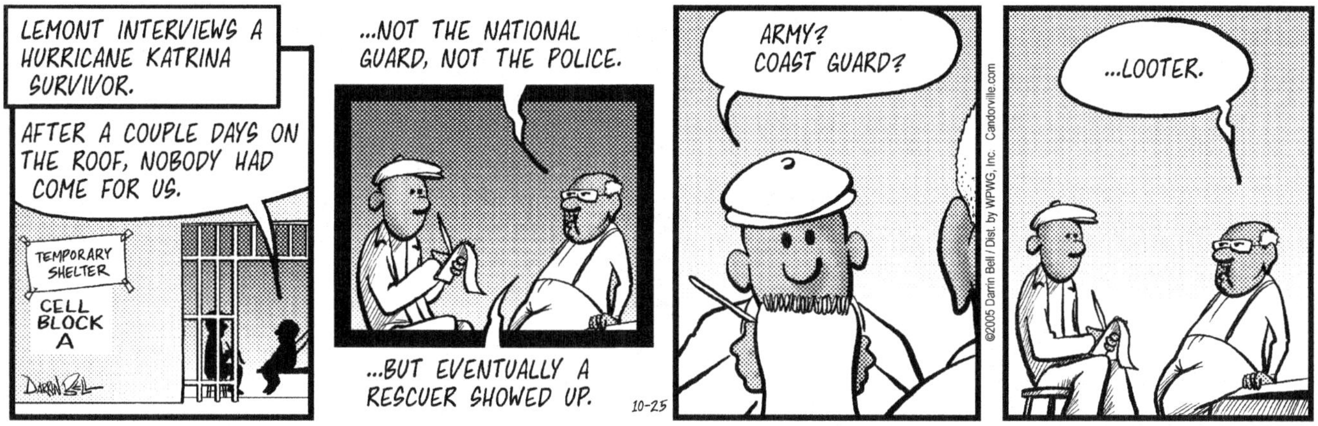
LEMONT INTERVIEWS A HURRICANE KATRINA SURVIVOR.
AFTER A COUPLE DAYS ON THE ROOF, NOBODY HAD COME FOR US.
TEMPORARY SHELTER
CELL BLOCK A
DARRIN BELL
...NOT THE NATIONAL GUARD, NOT THE POLICE.
...BUT EVENTUALLY A RESCUER SHOWED UP.
10-25
ARMY? COAST GUARD?
©2005 Darrin Bell / Dist. by WPWG, Inc. Candorville.com
...LOOTER.

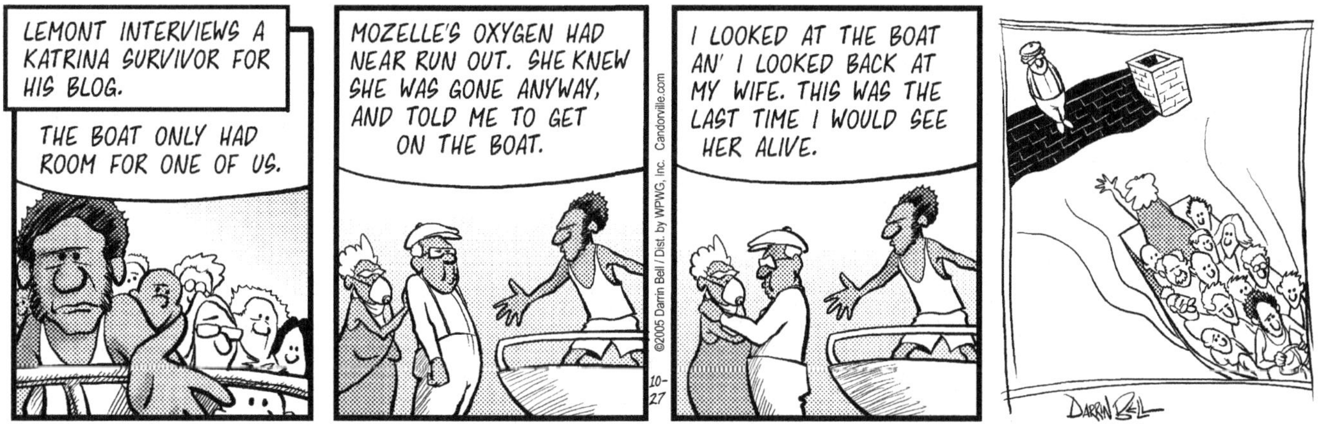
LEMONT INTERVIEWS A KATRINA SURVIVOR FOR HIS BLOG.
THE BOAT ONLY HAD ROOM FOR ONE OF US.
MOZELLE'S OXYGEN HAD NEAR RUN OUT. SHE KNEW SHE WAS GONE ANYWAY, AND TOLD ME TO GET ON THE BOAT.
©2005 Darrin Bell / Dist. by WPWG, Inc. Candorville.com
10-27
I LOOKED AT THE BOAT AN' I LOOKED BACK AT MY WIFE. THIS WAS THE LAST TIME I WOULD SEE HER ALIVE.
DARRIN BELL

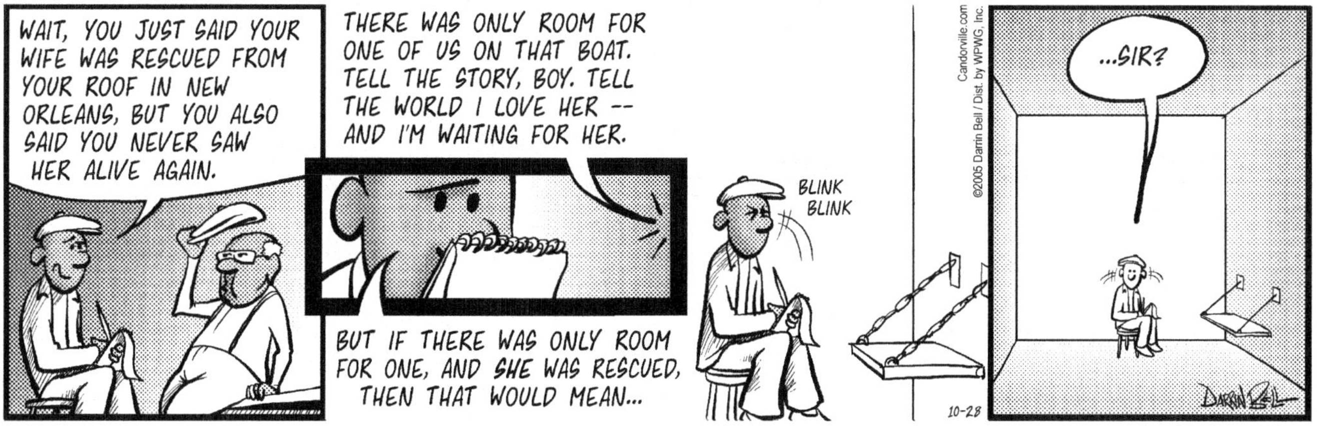
WAIT, YOU JUST SAID YOUR WIFE WAS RESCUED FROM YOUR ROOF IN NEW ORLEANS, BUT YOU ALSO SAID YOU NEVER SAW HER ALIVE AGAIN.
THERE WAS ONLY ROOM FOR ONE OF US ON THAT BOAT. TELL THE STORY, BOY. TELL THE WORLD I LOVE HER -- AND I'M WAITING FOR HER.
BUT IF THERE WAS ONLY ROOM FOR ONE, AND SHE WAS RESCUED, THEN THAT WOULD MEAN...
BLINK BLINK
©2005 Darrin Bell / Dist. by WPWG, Inc. Candorville.com
10-28
...SIR?
DARRIN BELL

Panel 1: SUSAN, CAN YOU BELIEVE PRESIDENT BUSH HAS TAKEN MORE THAN A *YEAR* OF VACATION IN THE PAST FOUR YEARS?

Panel 2: CAN YOU IMAGINE WHAT WOULD HAPPEN TO ME IF I TOOK THAT MUCH TIME OFF FROM WORK?

10-29

Panel 3:

1976

Panel 4: CLYDE, YOU DON'T HAVE A JOB. THAT AIN'T THE POINT.

©2005 Darrin Bell / Dist. by WPWG, Inc. Candorville.com

Panel 5: LEMONT, YOU WOULDN'T BELIEVE THE DAY I HAD AT WORK. TWO BIG-TIME POLITICIANS CAME TO US FOR NEW AD CAMPAIGNS.

10-31

Panel 6: AND OLD MAN FITZHUGH "DOWNSIZED" MY CREATIVE STAFF, LEAVING JUST ME AND DICK FINK.

Panel 7: CAN YOU BELIEVE IT? THE WART ON MY LITTLE TOE HAS MORE CREATIVITY THAN DICK FINK.

Panel 8: SUSAN, I SAID I JUST INTERVIEWED A *GHOST*!

WHY'S IT ALWAYS ABOUT YOU?

©2005 Darrin Bell / Dist. by WPWG, Inc. Candorville.com

Panel 9: DANG. NONE OF MY READERS BELIEVES MY BLOG ENTRY TODAY. YOU'D THINK THEY'D GIVE ME THE BENEFIT OF THE DOUBT.

LET ME EXPLAIN IT TO YOU, LEMONT...

Panel 10: YOU WROTE THAT YOU INTERVIEWED THE *GHOST* OF A MAN WHO DIED DURING HURRICANE KATRINA.

11-1

©2005 Darrin Bell / Dist. by WPWG, Inc. Candorville.com

Panel 11: YOU'RE WEIRD. ET TU, SUSAN?

Panel 12: PEOPLE ARE CALLING ME PATHETIC BECAUSE I WROTE ON MY BLOG THAT I INTERVIEWED A GHOST.

IF ONLY I'D VIDEOTAPED THE INTERVIEW AS PROOF.

Panel 13: THEY'RE SAYING I'M INCOMPETENT AND UNTRUSTWORTHY.

IT'LL BLOW OVER. IT'S NOT SO BAD.

11-2

©2005 Darrin Bell / Dist. by WPWG, Inc. Candorville.com

Panel 14: ONE OF THEM CALLED ME A LOSER, SUSAN. THAT'S NOT TOO BAD.

Panel 15: PRESIDENT BUSH CALLED AND ASKED ME TO BE A SUPREME COURT JUSTICE.

OK, IT'S BAD.

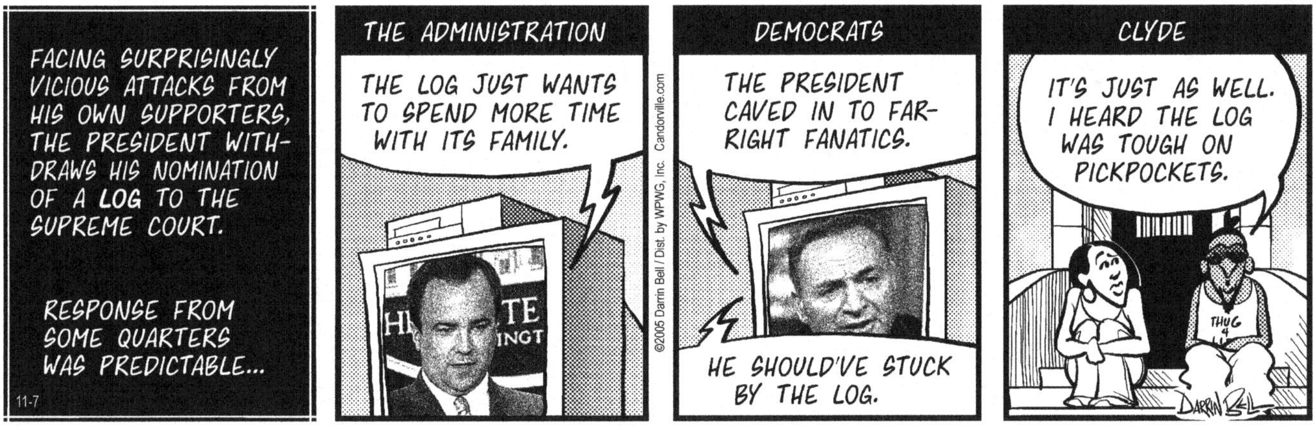
FACING SURPRISINGLY VICIOUS ATTACKS FROM HIS OWN SUPPORTERS, THE PRESIDENT WITHDRAWS HIS NOMINATION OF A LOG TO THE SUPREME COURT.
RESPONSE FROM SOME QUARTERS WAS PREDICTABLE...
11-7
THE ADMINISTRATION
THE LOG JUST WANTS TO SPEND MORE TIME WITH ITS FAMILY.
DEMOCRATS
THE PRESIDENT CAVED IN TO FAR-RIGHT FANATICS.
HE SHOULD'VE STUCK BY THE LOG.
©2005 Darrin Bell / Dist. by WPWG, Inc. Candorville.com
CLYDE
IT'S JUST AS WELL. I HEARD THE LOG WAS TOUGH ON PICKPOCKETS.
THUG 4
DARRIN BELL

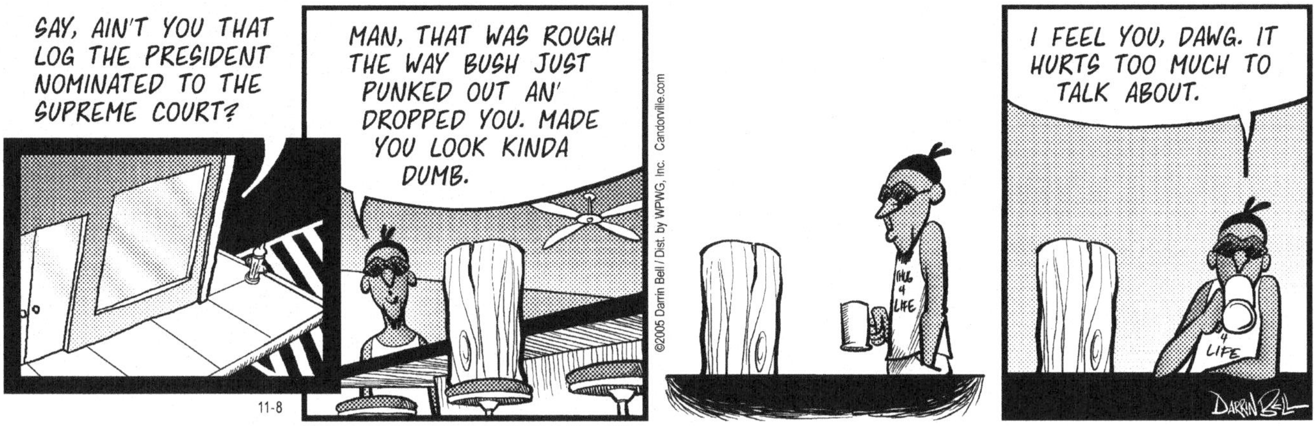
SAY, AIN'T YOU THAT LOG THE PRESIDENT NOMINATED TO THE SUPREME COURT?
11-8
MAN, THAT WAS ROUGH THE WAY BUSH JUST PUNKED OUT AN' DROPPED YOU. MADE YOU LOOK KINDA DUMB.
©2005 Darrin Bell / Dist. by WPWG, Inc. Candorville.com
THUG 4 LIFE
I FEEL YOU, DAWG. IT HURTS TOO MUCH TO TALK ABOUT.
4 LIFE
DARRIN BELL

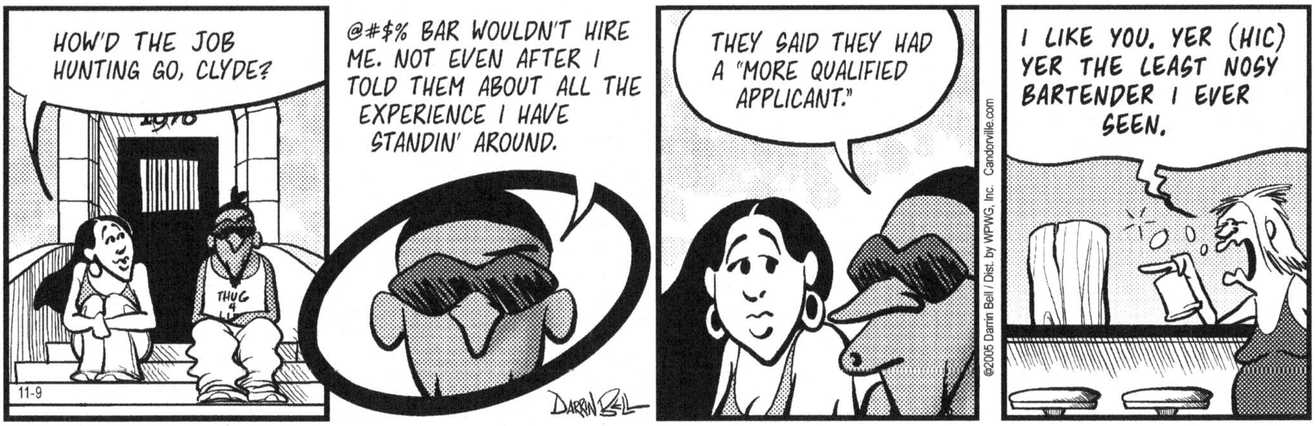
HOW'D THE JOB HUNTING GO, CLYDE?
THUG 4
11-9
@#$% BAR WOULDN'T HIRE ME. NOT EVEN AFTER I TOLD THEM ABOUT ALL THE EXPERIENCE I HAVE STANDIN' AROUND.
DARRIN BELL
THEY SAID THEY HAD A "MORE QUALIFIED APPLICANT."
©2005 Darrin Bell / Dist. by WPWG, Inc. Candorville.com
I LIKE YOU. YER (HIC) YER THE LEAST NOSY BARTENDER I EVER SEEN.

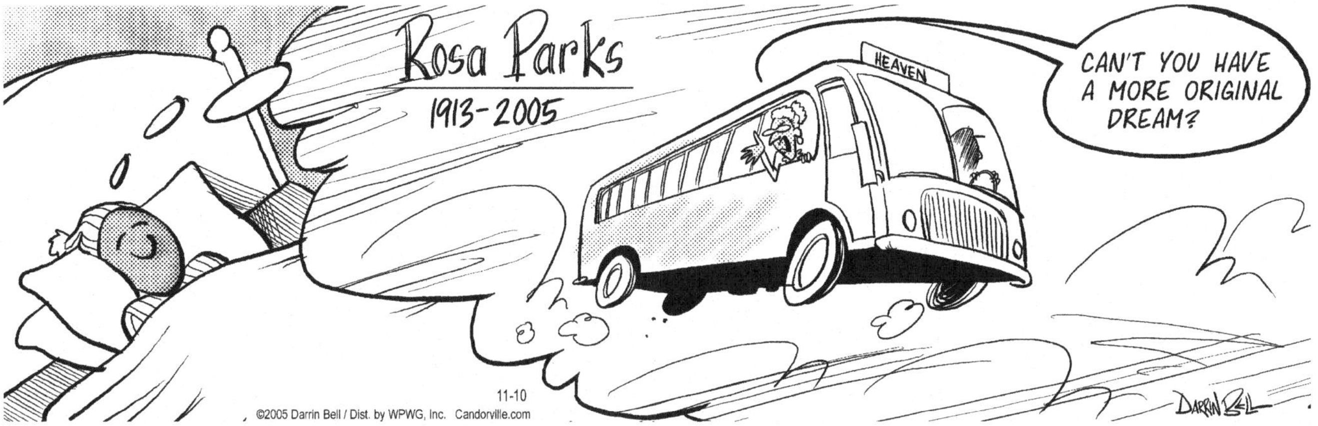
Rosa Parks
1913-2005
HEAVEN
CAN'T YOU HAVE A MORE ORIGINAL DREAM?
11-10
DARRIN BELL

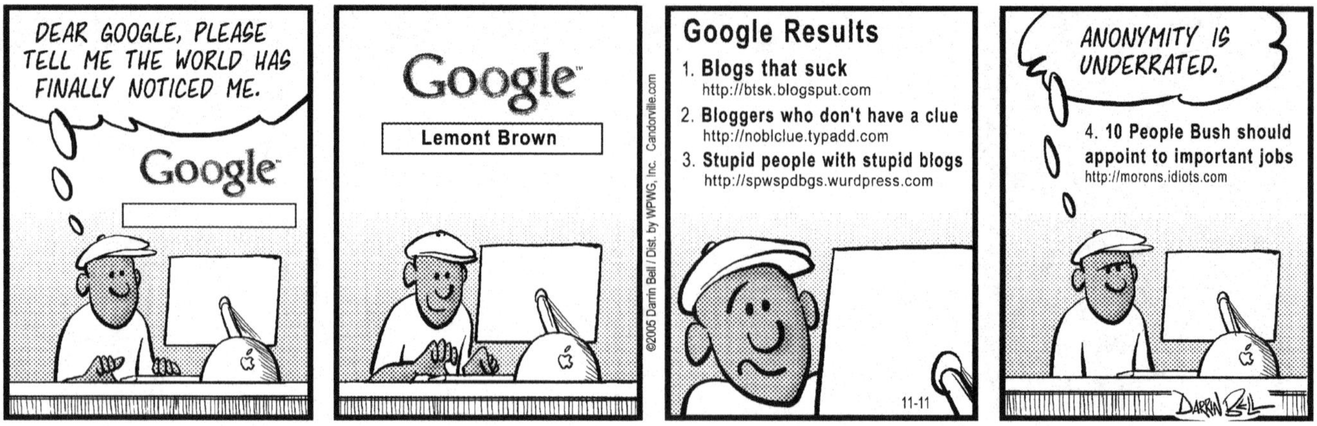
DEAR GOOGLE, PLEASE TELL ME THE WORLD HAS FINALLY NOTICED ME.
Google
Google
Lemont Brown
©2005 Darrin Bell / Dist. by WPWG, Inc. Candorville.com
Google Results
1. Blogs that suck
http://btsk.blogsput.com
2. Bloggers who don't have a clue
http://noblclue.typadd.com
3. Stupid people with stupid blogs
http://spwspdbgs.wurdpress.com
11-11
ANONYMITY IS UNDERRATED.
4. 10 People Bush should appoint to important jobs
http://morons.idiots.com
DARRIN BELL

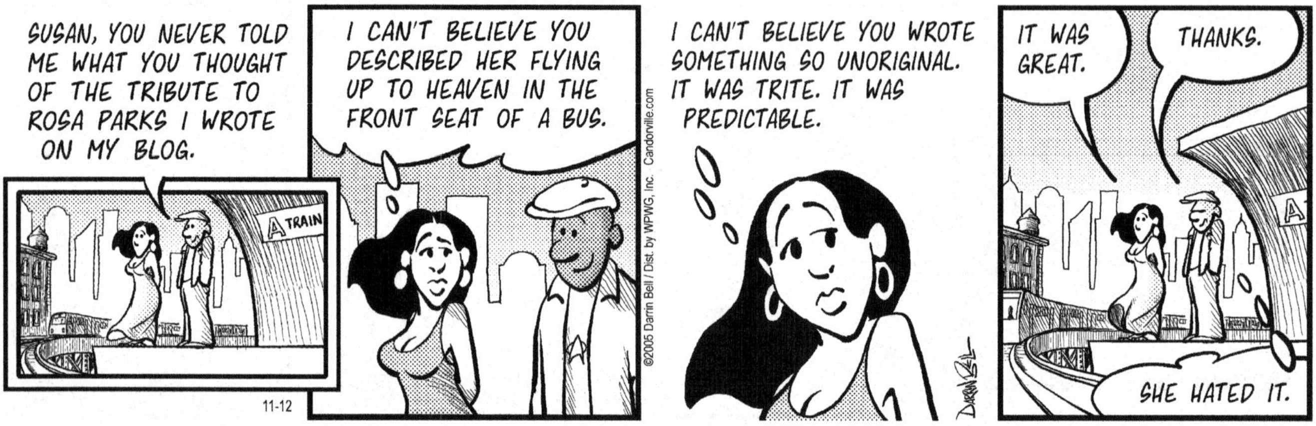
SUSAN, YOU NEVER TOLD ME WHAT YOU THOUGHT OF THE TRIBUTE TO ROSA PARKS I WROTE ON MY BLOG.
A TRAIN
11-12
I CAN'T BELIEVE YOU DESCRIBED HER FLYING UP TO HEAVEN IN THE FRONT SEAT OF A BUS.
©2005 Darrin Bell / Dist. by WPWG, Inc. Candorville.com
I CAN'T BELIEVE YOU WROTE SOMETHING SO UNORIGINAL. IT WAS TRITE. IT WAS PREDICTABLE.
DARRIN BELL
IT WAS GREAT.
THANKS.
SHE HATED IT.

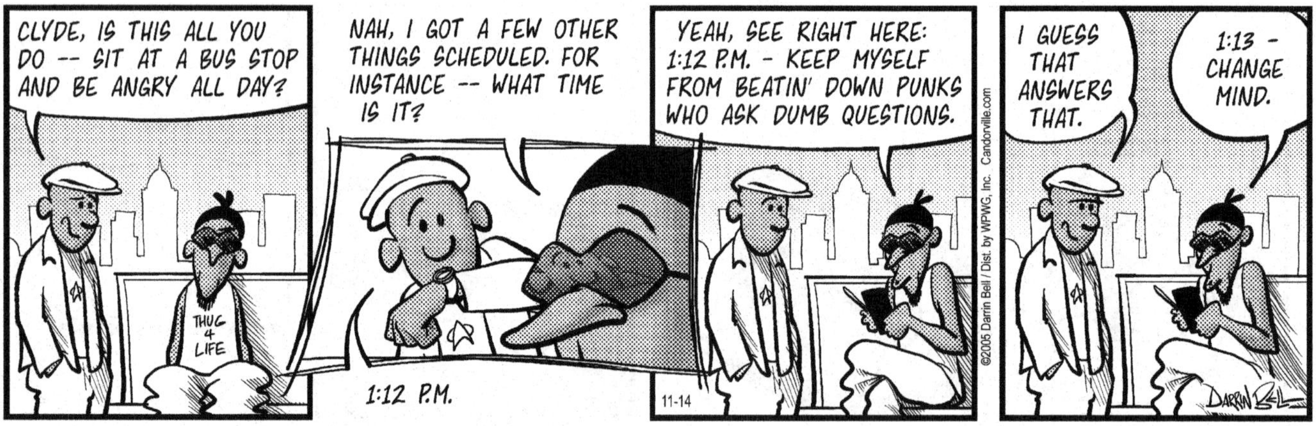
CLYDE, IS THIS ALL YOU DO -- SIT AT A BUS STOP AND BE ANGRY ALL DAY?
THUG 4 LIFE
NAH, I GOT A FEW OTHER THINGS SCHEDULED. FOR INSTANCE -- WHAT TIME IS IT?
1:12 P.M.
YEAH, SEE RIGHT HERE: 1:12 P.M. - KEEP MYSELF FROM BEATIN' DOWN PUNKS WHO ASK DUMB QUESTIONS.
11-14
©2005 Darrin Bell / Dist. by WPWG, Inc. Candorville.com
I GUESS THAT ANSWERS THAT.
1:13 - CHANGE MIND.
DARRIN BELL

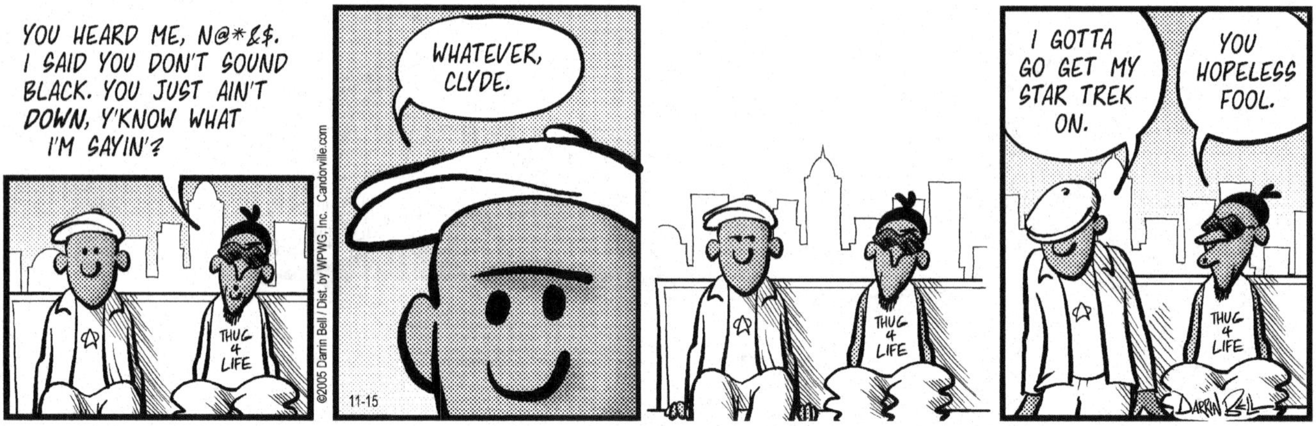
YOU HEARD ME, N@*&$. I SAID YOU DON'T SOUND BLACK. YOU JUST AIN'T DOWN, Y'KNOW WHAT I'M SAYIN'?
THUG 4 LIFE
©2005 Darrin Bell / Dist. by WPWG, Inc. Candorville.com
WHATEVER, CLYDE.
11-15
THUG 4 LIFE
I GOTTA GO GET MY STAR TREK ON.
YOU HOPELESS FOOL.
THUG 4 LIFE
DARRIN BELL

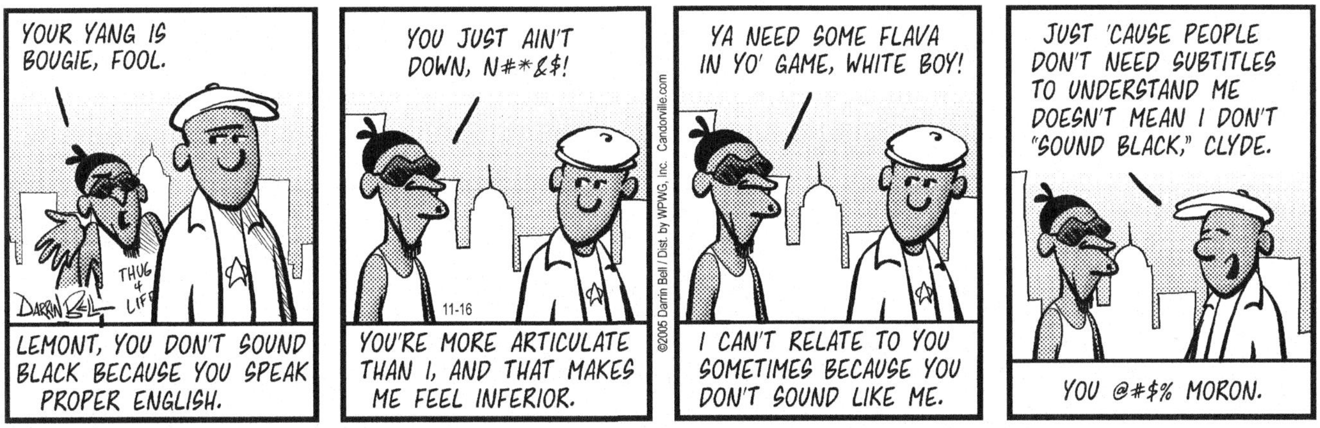
YOUR YANG IS BOUGIE, FOOL.
LEMONT, YOU DON'T SOUND BLACK BECAUSE YOU SPEAK PROPER ENGLISH.
THUG 4 LIFE
YOU JUST AIN'T DOWN, N#*&$!
YOU'RE MORE ARTICULATE THAN I, AND THAT MAKES ME FEEL INFERIOR.
11-16
©2005 Darrin Bell / Dist. by WPWG, Inc. Candorville.com
YA NEED SOME FLAVA IN YO' GAME, WHITE BOY!
I CAN'T RELATE TO YOU SOMETIMES BECAUSE YOU DON'T SOUND LIKE ME.
JUST 'CAUSE PEOPLE DON'T NEED SUBTITLES TO UNDERSTAND ME DOESN'T MEAN I DON'T "SOUND BLACK," CLYDE.
YOU @#$% MORON.

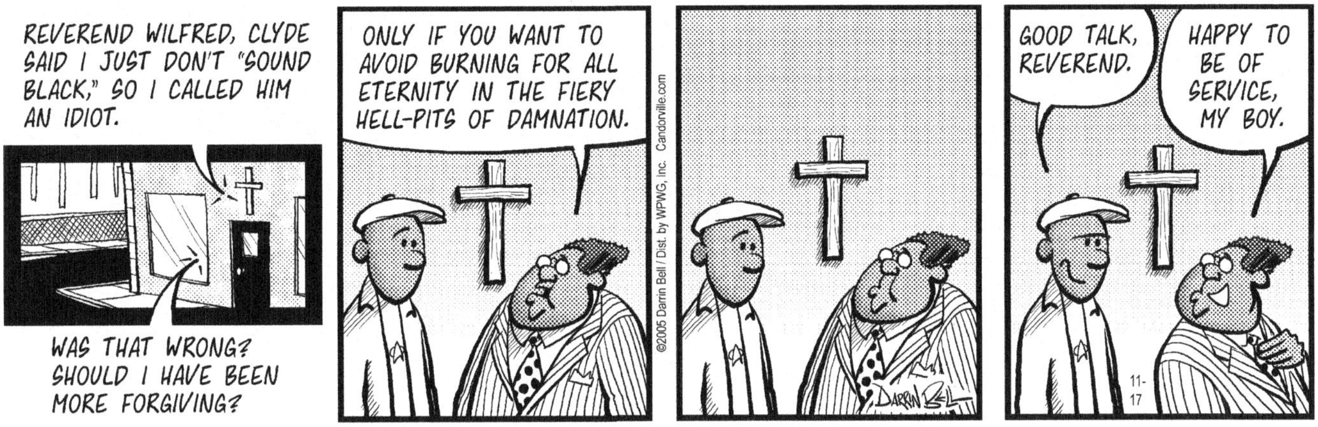
REVEREND WILFRED, CLYDE SAID I JUST DON'T "SOUND BLACK," SO I CALLED HIM AN IDIOT.
WAS THAT WRONG? SHOULD I HAVE BEEN MORE FORGIVING?
ONLY IF YOU WANT TO AVOID BURNING FOR ALL ETERNITY IN THE FIERY HELL-PITS OF DAMNATION.
©2005 Darrin Bell / Dist. by WPWG, Inc. Candorville.com
GOOD TALK, REVEREND.
HAPPY TO BE OF SERVICE, MY BOY.
11-17

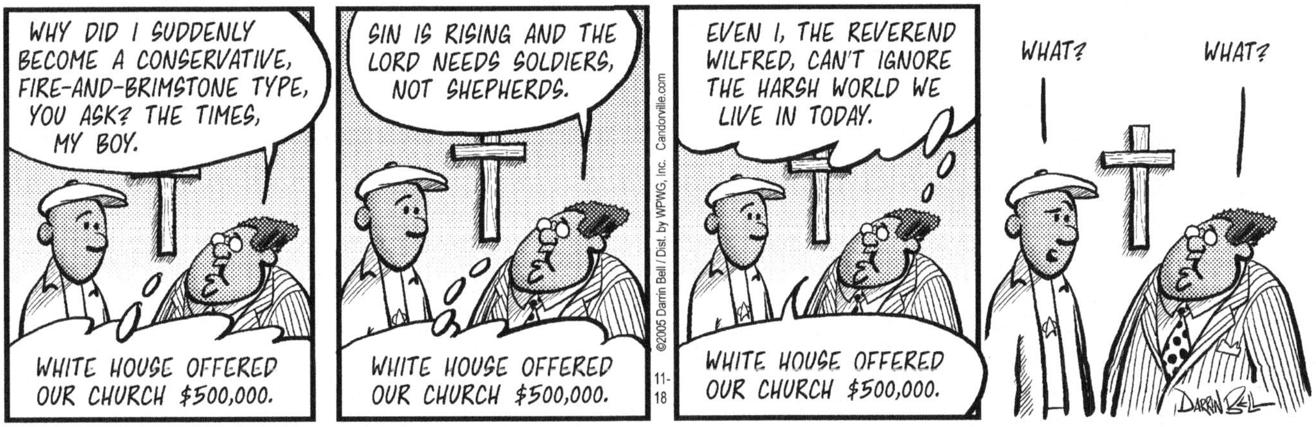
WHY DID I SUDDENLY BECOME A CONSERVATIVE, FIRE-AND-BRIMSTONE TYPE, YOU ASK? THE TIMES, MY BOY.
WHITE HOUSE OFFERED OUR CHURCH $500,000.
SIN IS RISING AND THE LORD NEEDS SOLDIERS, NOT SHEPHERDS.
WHITE HOUSE OFFERED OUR CHURCH $500,000.
©2005 Darrin Bell / Dist. by WPWG, Inc. Candorville.com
11-18
EVEN I, THE REVEREND WILFRED, CAN'T IGNORE THE HARSH WORLD WE LIVE IN TODAY.
WHITE HOUSE OFFERED OUR CHURCH $500,000.
WHAT?
WHAT?

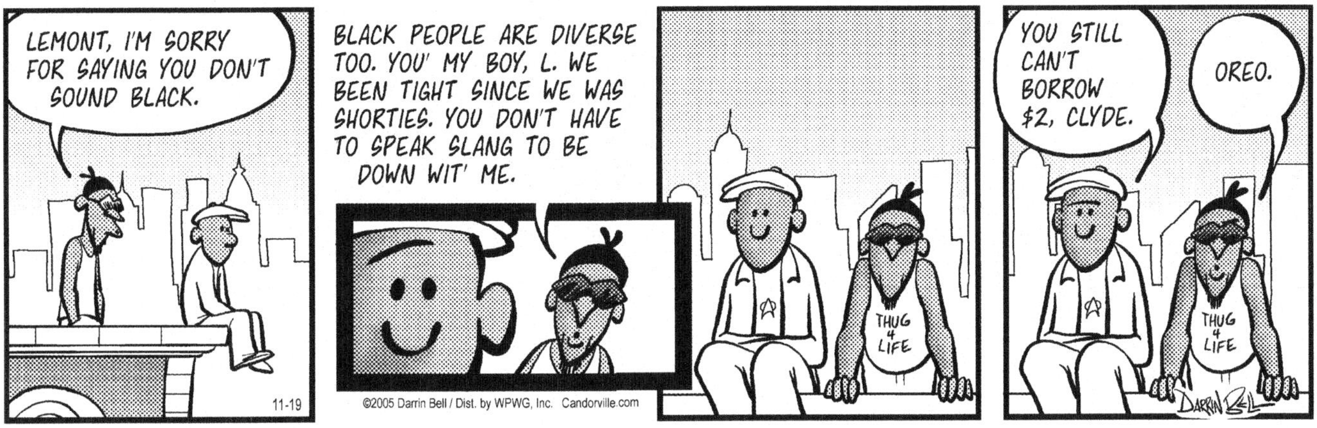
LEMONT, I'M SORRY FOR SAYING YOU DON'T SOUND BLACK.
11-19
BLACK PEOPLE ARE DIVERSE TOO. YOU' MY BOY, L. WE BEEN TIGHT SINCE WE WAS SHORTIES. YOU DON'T HAVE TO SPEAK SLANG TO BE DOWN WIT' ME.
©2005 Darrin Bell / Dist. by WPWG, Inc. Candorville.com
THUG 4 LIFE
YOU STILL CAN'T BORROW $2, CLYDE.
OREO.
THUG 4 LIFE

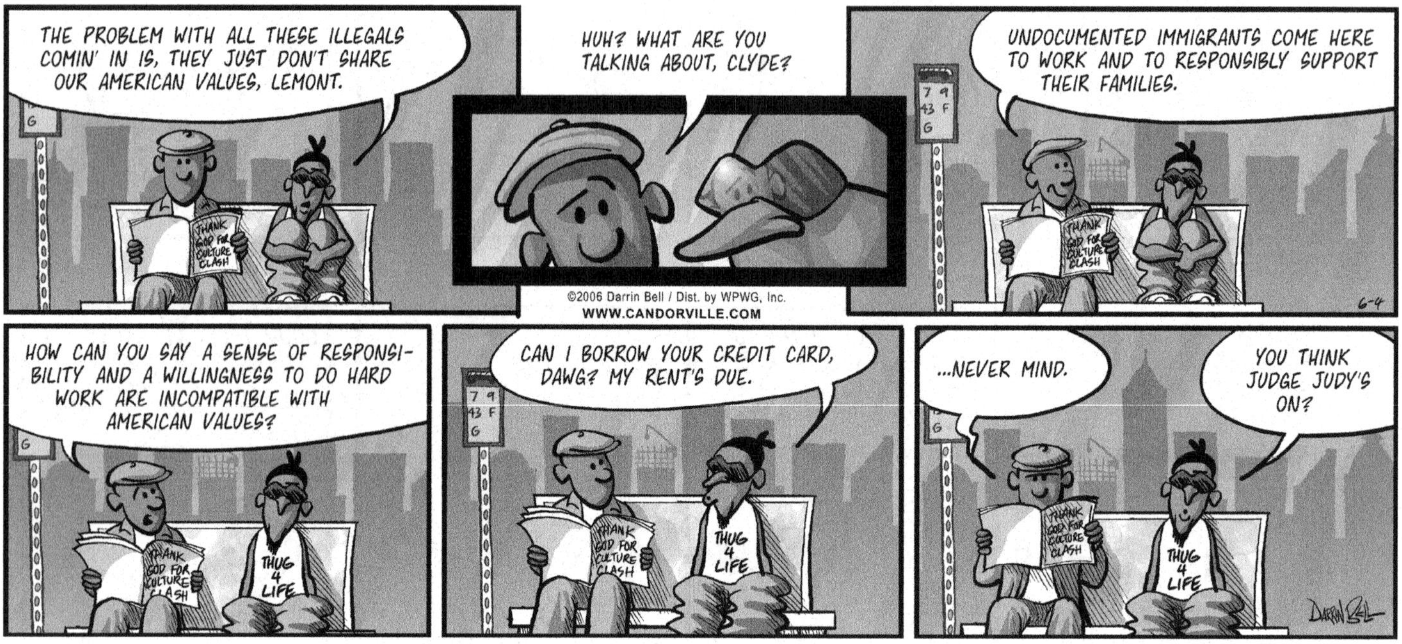
THE PROBLEM WITH ALL THESE ILLEGALS COMIN' IN IS, THEY JUST DON'T SHARE OUR AMERICAN VALUES, LEMONT.
HUH? WHAT ARE YOU TALKING ABOUT, CLYDE?
UNDOCUMENTED IMMIGRANTS COME HERE TO WORK AND TO RESPONSIBLY SUPPORT THEIR FAMILIES.
THANK GOD FOR CULTURE CLASH
©2006 Darrin Bell / Dist. by WPWG, Inc.
WWW.CANDORVILLE.COM
6-4
HOW CAN YOU SAY A SENSE OF RESPONSIBILITY AND A WILLINGNESS TO DO HARD WORK ARE INCOMPATIBLE WITH AMERICAN VALUES?
CAN I BORROW YOUR CREDIT CARD, DAWG? MY RENT'S DUE.
THUG 4 LIFE
...NEVER MIND.
YOU THINK JUDGE JUDY'S ON?
DARRIN BELL

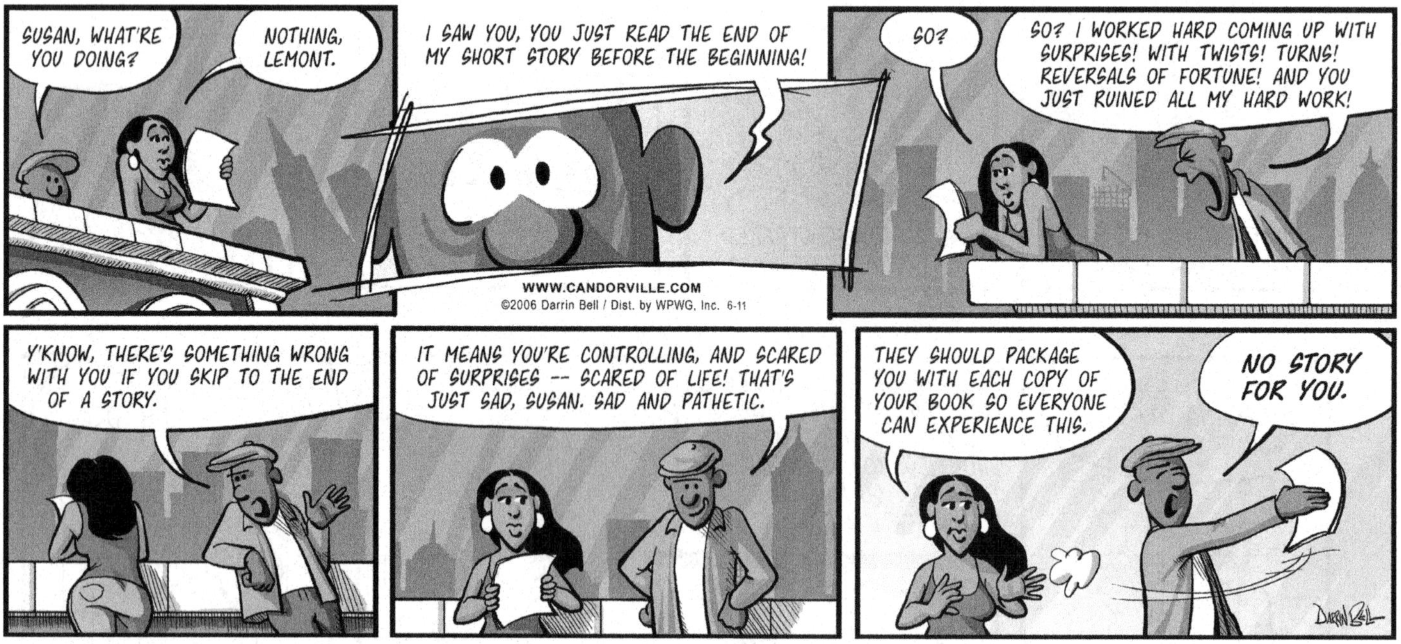
SUSAN, WHAT'RE YOU DOING?
NOTHING, LEMONT.
I SAW YOU, YOU JUST READ THE END OF MY SHORT STORY BEFORE THE BEGINNING!
SO?
SO? I WORKED HARD COMING UP WITH SURPRISES! WITH TWISTS! TURNS! REVERSALS OF FORTUNE! AND YOU JUST RUINED ALL MY HARD WORK!
WWW.CANDORVILLE.COM
©2006 Darrin Bell / Dist. by WPWG, Inc. 6-11
Y'KNOW, THERE'S SOMETHING WRONG WITH YOU IF YOU SKIP TO THE END OF A STORY.
IT MEANS YOU'RE CONTROLLING, AND SCARED OF SURPRISES -- SCARED OF LIFE! THAT'S JUST SAD, SUSAN. SAD AND PATHETIC.
THEY SHOULD PACKAGE YOU WITH EACH COPY OF YOUR BOOK SO EVERYONE CAN EXPERIENCE THIS.
NO STORY FOR YOU.
DARRIN BELL

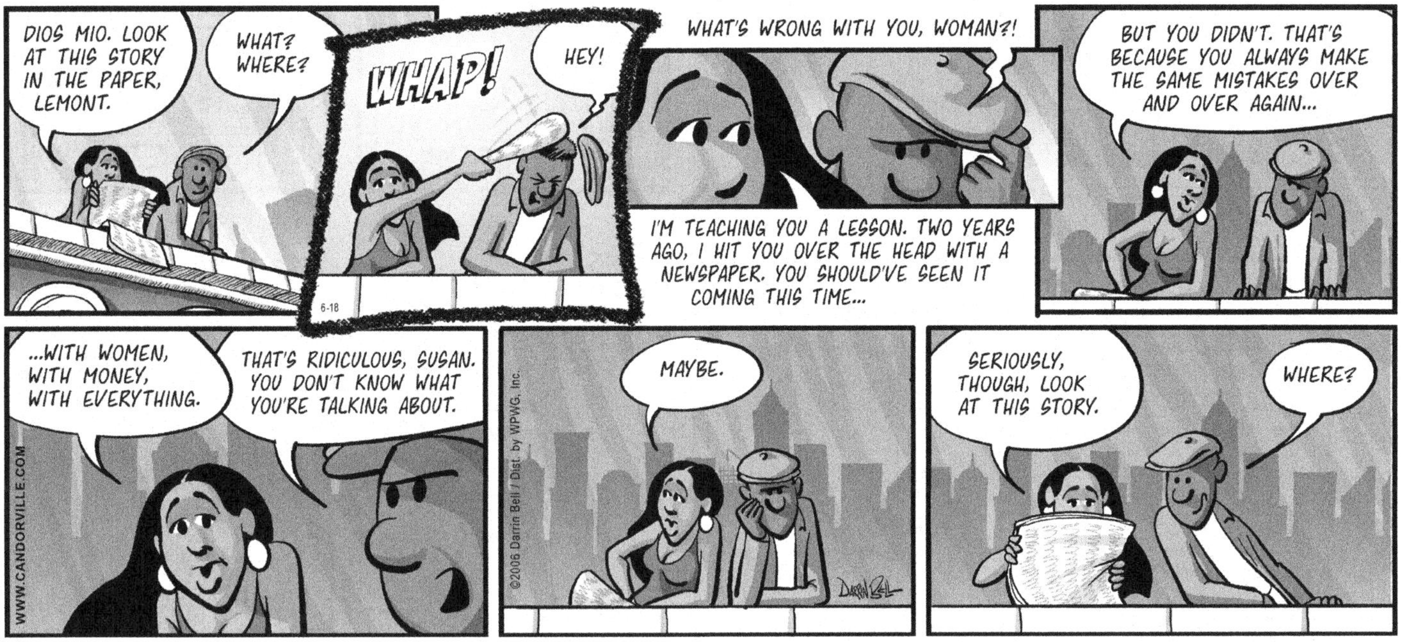
DIOS MIO. LOOK AT THIS STORY IN THE PAPER, LEMONT.
WHAT? WHERE?
WHAP!
HEY!
6-18
WHAT'S WRONG WITH YOU, WOMAN?!
I'M TEACHING YOU A LESSON. TWO YEARS AGO, I HIT YOU OVER THE HEAD WITH A NEWSPAPER. YOU SHOULD'VE SEEN IT COMING THIS TIME...
BUT YOU DIDN'T. THAT'S BECAUSE YOU ALWAYS MAKE THE SAME MISTAKES OVER AND OVER AGAIN...
...WITH WOMEN, WITH MONEY, WITH EVERYTHING.
THAT'S RIDICULOUS, SUSAN. YOU DON'T KNOW WHAT YOU'RE TALKING ABOUT.
WWW.CANDORVILLE.COM
MAYBE.
©2006 Darrin Bell / Dist. by WPWG, Inc.
SERIOUSLY, THOUGH, LOOK AT THIS STORY.
WHERE?

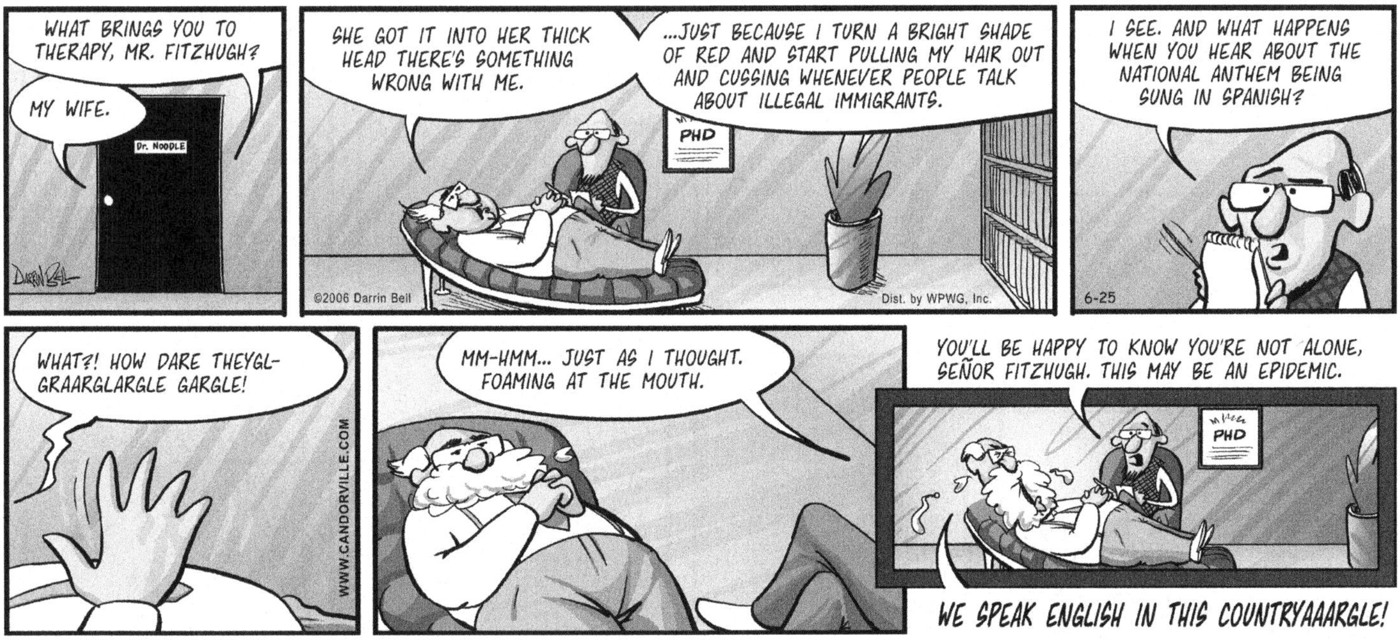
WHAT BRINGS YOU TO THERAPY, MR. FITZHUGH?
MY WIFE.
Dr. NOODLE
SHE GOT IT INTO HER THICK HEAD THERE'S SOMETHING WRONG WITH ME.
...JUST BECAUSE I TURN A BRIGHT SHADE OF RED AND START PULLING MY HAIR OUT AND CUSSING WHENEVER PEOPLE TALK ABOUT ILLEGAL IMMIGRANTS.
PHD
©2006 Darrin Bell
Dist. by WPWG, Inc.
I SEE. AND WHAT HAPPENS WHEN YOU HEAR ABOUT THE NATIONAL ANTHEM BEING SUNG IN SPANISH?
6-25
WHAT?! HOW DARE THEYGL-GRAARGLARGLE GARGLE!
WWW.CANDORVILLE.COM
MM-HMM... JUST AS I THOUGHT. FOAMING AT THE MOUTH.
YOU'LL BE HAPPY TO KNOW YOU'RE NOT ALONE, SEÑOR FITZHUGH. THIS MAY BE AN EPIDEMIC.
PHD
WE SPEAK ENGLISH IN THIS COUNTRYAAARGLE!

Row 1

...SO ANYWAY, WHEN I WAS TEN I DECIDED I WANTED TO BE A WRITER AND BZABZBZBZBABZADABADABZZAZAZBABZ ZBZBABZADABADABZ THE WORLD.

RIB SHACK

WHOAH! WHAT THE HECK JUST HAPPENED?

YOU WERE BORING ME, SO I FAST-FORWARDED YOU WITH THIS NEW REMOTE.

ROSCOE'S RIB SHACK

ROSCOE'S RIB SHACK

WHAT? EVEN IF THAT WERE POSSIBLE, THAT'S UNETHICAL. THAT'S WRONG. THAT'S ZBABZADABADABZADABA...

ROSCOE'S RIB SHACK

11-21

Row 2

I HAD THE WEIRDEST DREAM, SUSAN. MY DATE PULLED OUT A REMOTE CONTROL AND FAST-FORWARDED ME TO SKIP THE BORING PARTS.

11-22

DO YOU THINK I'M BORING?

DIOS MIO, LEMONT. WOULD I, SUSAN GARCIA, HANG OUT WITH SOMEONE WHO'S BORING?

NO. YES.

Row 3

MY LAST FEW DATES TOLD ME I'M BORING. I'VE DECIDED TO DO SOMETHING ABOUT IT.

WHAT -- YOU'RE GONNA TELL MORE JOKES OR SOMETHING?

11-23

I'M GOING TO STAND IN FRONT OF THIS PIECE OF CARDBOARD AND THESE WORDS WILL SEND MY DATE SUBLIMINAL MESSAGES.

FUN FUN EXCITING FUN FUN EXCITING FUN FUN EXCITING FUN FUN EXCITING

FUN FUN FUN FU
NG EXCITING EX
FUN FUN FUN
NG EXCITING EX
FUN FUN
NG EX

YOU'RE NOT ALLOWED TO WATCH ANY MORE PRESIDENTIAL SPEECHES.

HEY, WHAT-EVER WORKS.

EXCITING FUN FUN EXCITING FUN FUN EXCITING FUN FUN

Row 4

LEMONT, I'VE ALWAYS FOUND YOU TO BE A LITTLE BORING. BUT FOR SOME REASON, TONIGHT YOU'VE GOT ME ALL EXCITED.

FUN FUN EXCITING FUN FUN EXCITING FUN FUN EXCIT FUN F EXC FUN EX FUN FUN

HAVE I TOLD YOU ABOUT THE CLIFFHANGER ON "BATTLESTAR GALACTICA"?

OH, PLEEEEASE DO, SUGAR.

ADAMA LAUNCHED VIPERS TO RESCUE CHIEF TYROL FROM THE PEGASUS.

LET'S DISCUSS THIS AT YOUR PLACE.

11-24

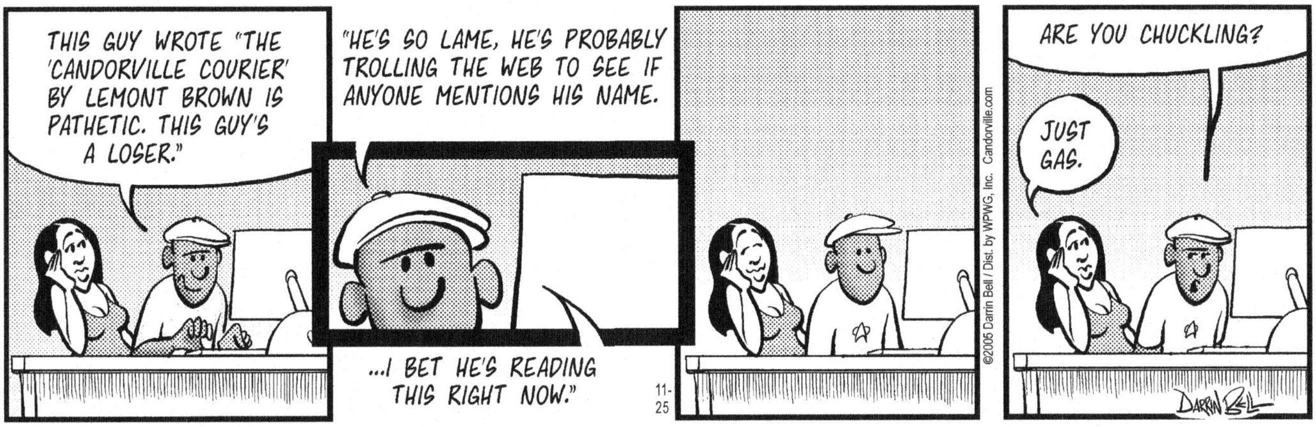
THIS GUY WROTE "THE 'CANDORVILLE COURIER' BY LEMONT BROWN IS PATHETIC. THIS GUY'S A LOSER."
"HE'S SO LAME, HE'S PROBABLY TROLLING THE WEB TO SEE IF ANYONE MENTIONS HIS NAME.
...I BET HE'S READING THIS RIGHT NOW."
11-25
ARE YOU CHUCKLING?
JUST GAS.
©2005 Darrin Bell / Dist. by WPWG, Inc. Candorville.com
DARRIN BELL

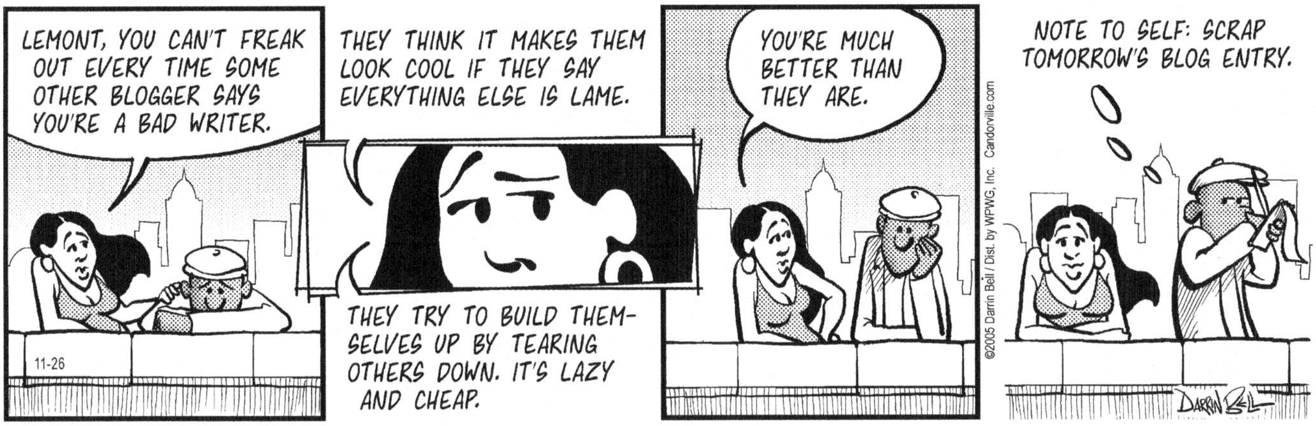
LEMONT, YOU CAN'T FREAK OUT EVERY TIME SOME OTHER BLOGGER SAYS YOU'RE A BAD WRITER.
11-26
THEY THINK IT MAKES THEM LOOK COOL IF THEY SAY EVERYTHING ELSE IS LAME.
THEY TRY TO BUILD THEMSELVES UP BY TEARING OTHERS DOWN. IT'S LAZY AND CHEAP.
YOU'RE MUCH BETTER THAN THEY ARE.
©2005 Darrin Bell / Dist. by WPWG, Inc. Candorville.com
NOTE TO SELF: SCRAP TOMORROW'S BLOG ENTRY.
DARRIN BELL

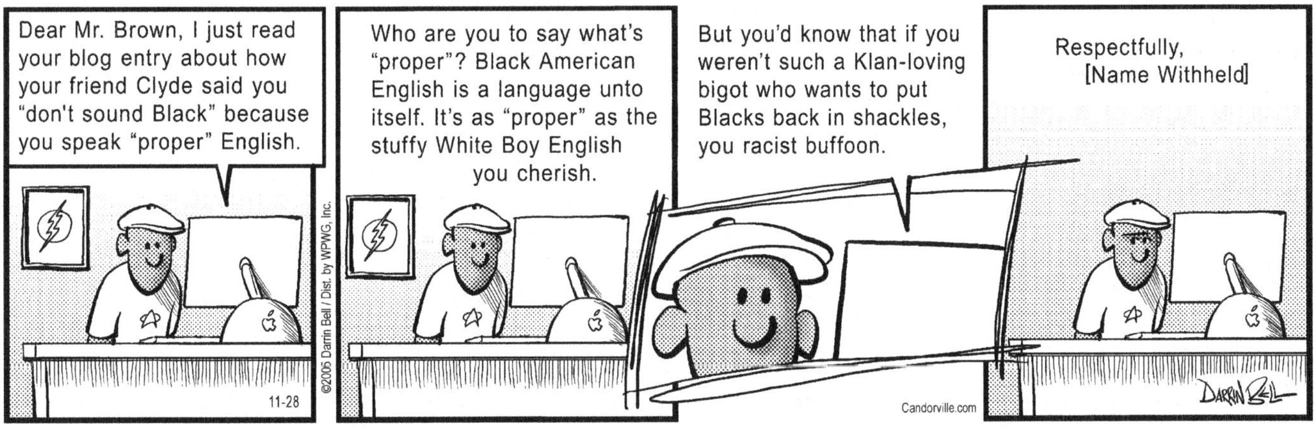
Dear Mr. Brown, I just read your blog entry about how your friend Clyde said you "don't sound Black" because you speak "proper" English.
11-28
©2005 Darrin Bell / Dist. by WPWG, Inc.
Who are you to say what's "proper"? Black American English is a language unto itself. It's as "proper" as the stuffy White Boy English you cherish.
But you'd know that if you weren't such a Klan-loving bigot who wants to put Blacks back in shackles, you racist buffoon.
Candorville.com
Respectfully,
[Name Withheld]
DARRIN BELL

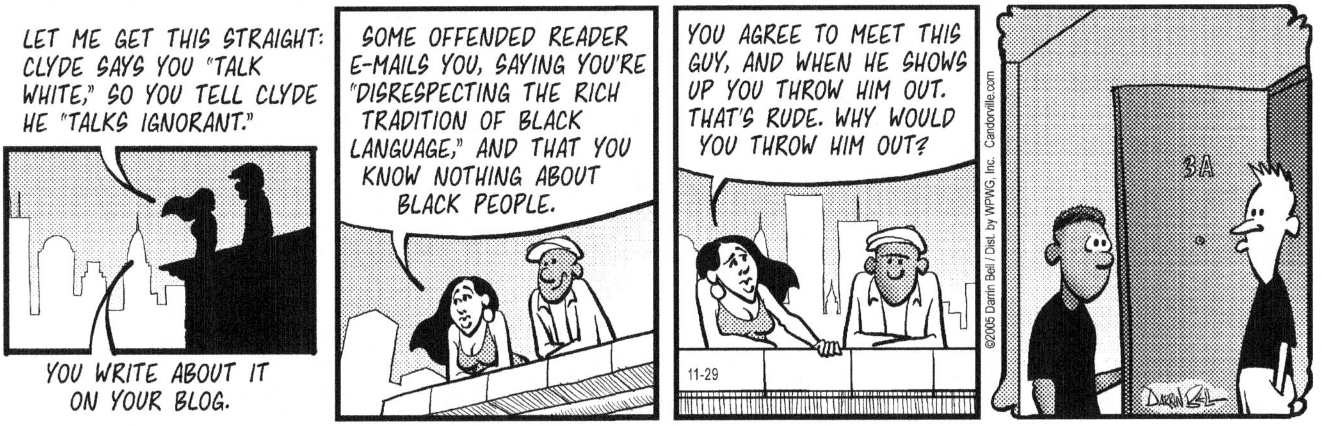
LET ME GET THIS STRAIGHT: CLYDE SAYS YOU "TALK WHITE," SO YOU TELL CLYDE HE "TALKS IGNORANT."
YOU WRITE ABOUT IT ON YOUR BLOG.
SOME OFFENDED READER E-MAILS YOU, SAYING YOU'RE "DISRESPECTING THE RICH TRADITION OF BLACK LANGUAGE," AND THAT YOU KNOW NOTHING ABOUT BLACK PEOPLE.
YOU AGREE TO MEET THIS GUY, AND WHEN HE SHOWS UP YOU THROW HIM OUT. THAT'S RUDE. WHY WOULD YOU THROW HIM OUT?
11-29
©2005 Darrin Bell / Dist. by WPWG, Inc. Candorville.com
3A
DARRIN BELL

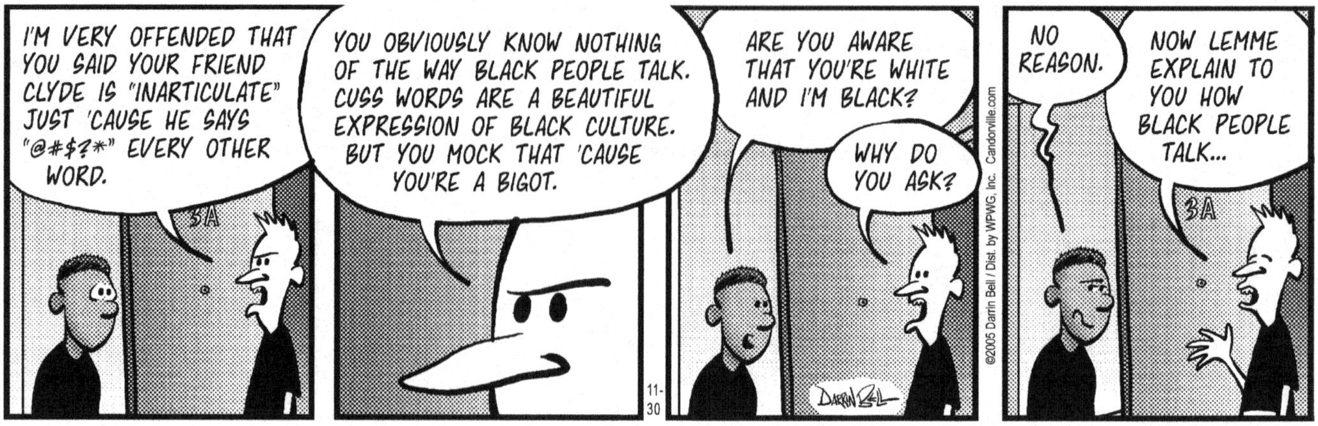
I'M VERY OFFENDED THAT YOU SAID YOUR FRIEND CLYDE IS "INARTICULATE" JUST 'CAUSE HE SAYS "@#$?*" EVERY OTHER WORD.
3A
YOU OBVIOUSLY KNOW NOTHING OF THE WAY BLACK PEOPLE TALK. CUSS WORDS ARE A BEAUTIFUL EXPRESSION OF BLACK CULTURE. BUT YOU MOCK THAT 'CAUSE YOU'RE A BIGOT.
11-30
ARE YOU AWARE THAT YOU'RE WHITE AND I'M BLACK?
WHY DO YOU ASK?
DARRIN BELL
©2005 Darrin Bell / Dist. by WPWG, Inc. Candorville.com
NO REASON.
NOW LEMME EXPLAIN TO YOU HOW BLACK PEOPLE TALK...
3A

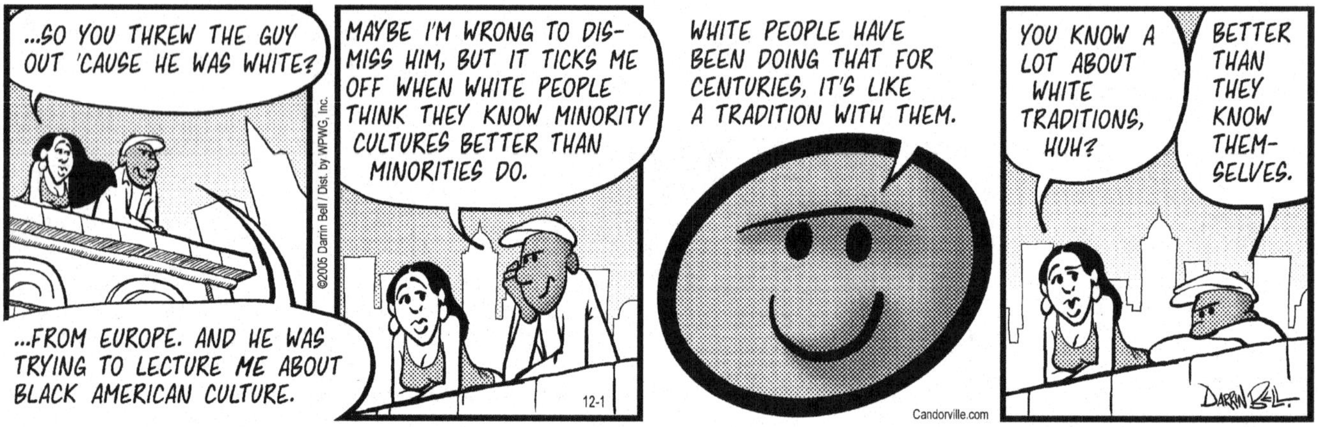
...SO YOU THREW THE GUY OUT 'CAUSE HE WAS WHITE?
...FROM EUROPE. AND HE WAS TRYING TO LECTURE ME ABOUT BLACK AMERICAN CULTURE.
©2005 Darrin Bell / Dist. by WPWG, Inc.
MAYBE I'M WRONG TO DISMISS HIM, BUT IT TICKS ME OFF WHEN WHITE PEOPLE THINK THEY KNOW MINORITY CULTURES BETTER THAN MINORITIES DO.
12-1
WHITE PEOPLE HAVE BEEN DOING THAT FOR CENTURIES, IT'S LIKE A TRADITION WITH THEM.
Candorville.com
YOU KNOW A LOT ABOUT WHITE TRADITIONS, HUH?
BETTER THAN THEY KNOW THEMSELVES.
DARRIN BELL

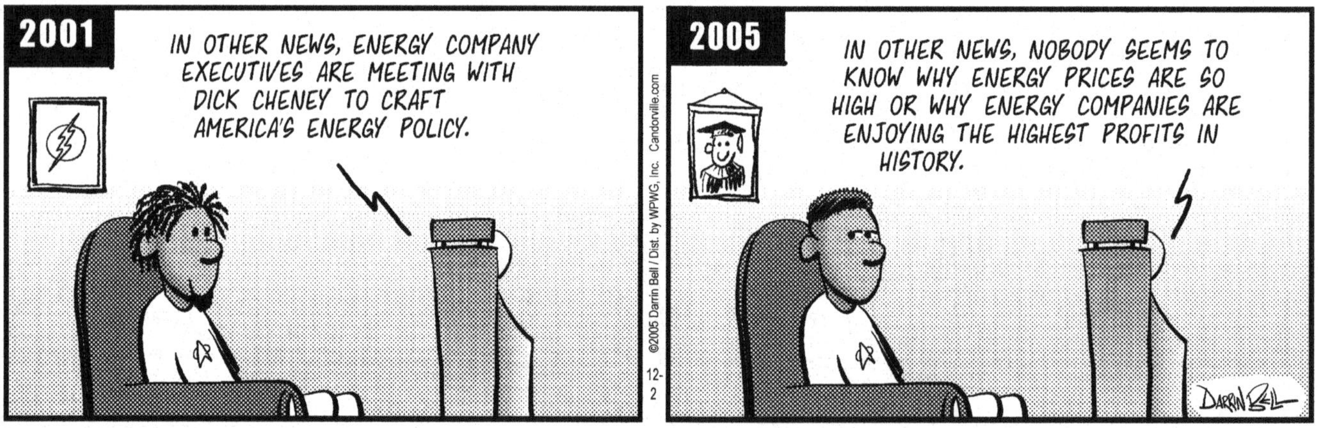
2001
IN OTHER NEWS, ENERGY COMPANY EXECUTIVES ARE MEETING WITH DICK CHENEY TO CRAFT AMERICA'S ENERGY POLICY.
©2005 Darrin Bell / Dist. by WPWG, Inc. Candorville.com
12-2
2005
IN OTHER NEWS, NOBODY SEEMS TO KNOW WHY ENERGY PRICES ARE SO HIGH OR WHY ENERGY COMPANIES ARE ENJOYING THE HIGHEST PROFITS IN HISTORY.
DARRIN BELL

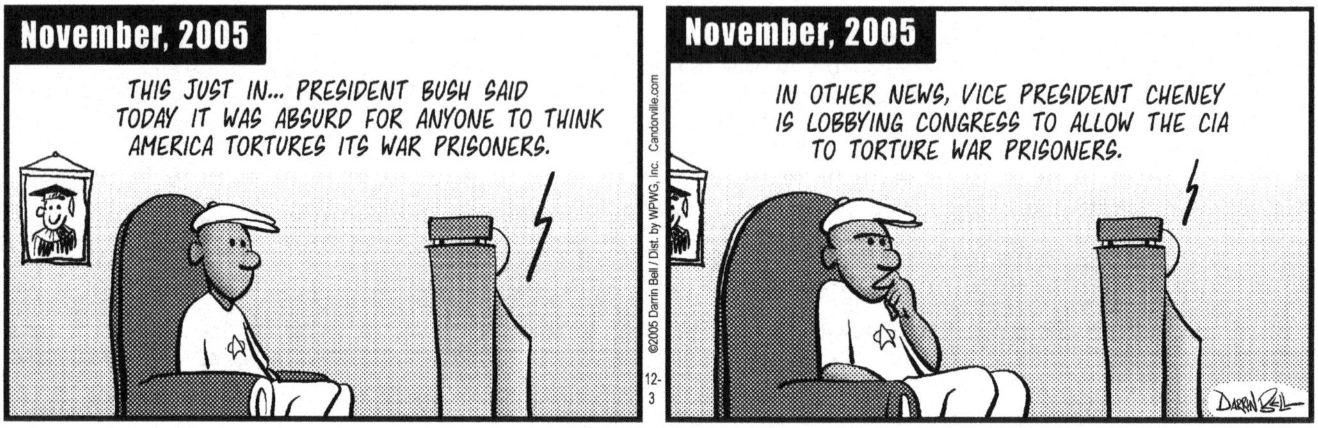
November, 2005
THIS JUST IN... PRESIDENT BUSH SAID TODAY IT WAS ABSURD FOR ANYONE TO THINK AMERICA TORTURES ITS WAR PRISONERS.
©2005 Darrin Bell / Dist. by WPWG, Inc. Candorville.com
12-3
November, 2005
IN OTHER NEWS, VICE PRESIDENT CHENEY IS LOBBYING CONGRESS TO ALLOW THE CIA TO TORTURE WAR PRISONERS.
DARRIN BELL

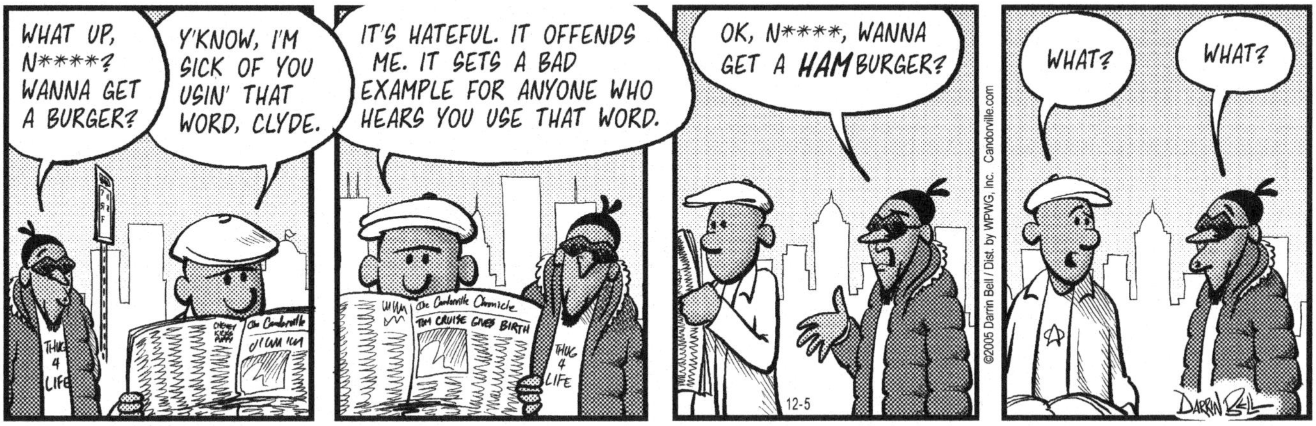
WHAT UP, N****? WANNA GET A BURGER?
Y'KNOW, I'M SICK OF YOU USIN' THAT WORD, CLYDE.
IT'S HATEFUL. IT OFFENDS ME. IT SETS A BAD EXAMPLE FOR ANYONE WHO HEARS YOU USE THAT WORD.
TOM CRUISE GIVES BIRTH
OK, N****, WANNA GET A **HAM**BURGER?
WHAT?
WHAT?
©2005 Darrin Bell / Dist. by WPWG, Inc. Candorville.com
12-5

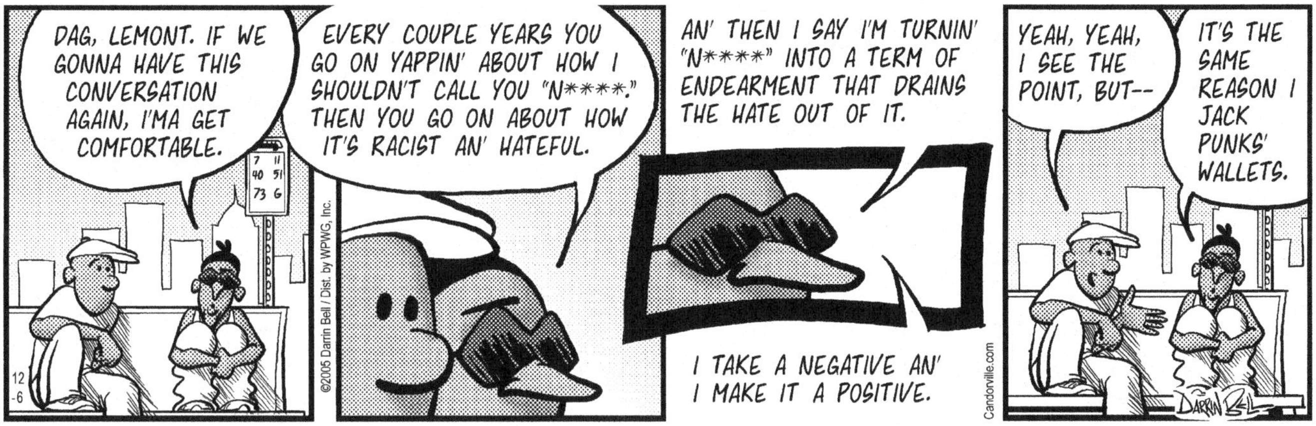
DAG, LEMONT. IF WE GONNA HAVE THIS CONVERSATION AGAIN, I'MA GET COMFORTABLE.
EVERY COUPLE YEARS YOU GO ON YAPPIN' ABOUT HOW I SHOULDN'T CALL YOU "N****." THEN YOU GO ON ABOUT HOW IT'S RACIST AN' HATEFUL.
AN' THEN I SAY I'M TURNIN' "N****" INTO A TERM OF ENDEARMENT THAT DRAINS THE HATE OUT OF IT.
I TAKE A NEGATIVE AN' I MAKE IT A POSITIVE.
YEAH, YEAH, I SEE THE POINT, BUT--
IT'S THE SAME REASON I JACK PUNKS' WALLETS.
©2005 Darrin Bell / Dist. by WPWG, Inc. Candorville.com
12-6

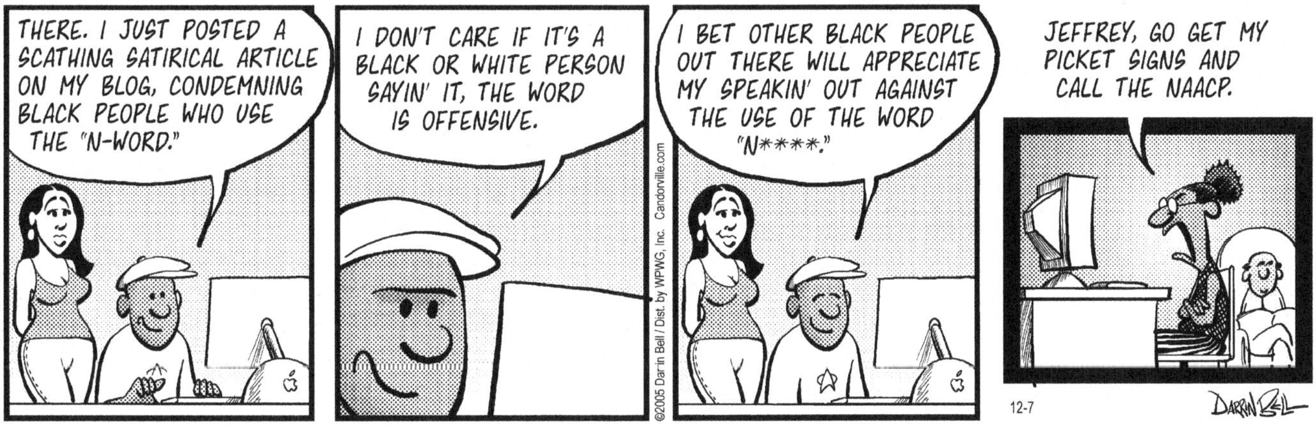
THERE. I JUST POSTED A SCATHING SATIRICAL ARTICLE ON MY BLOG, CONDEMNING BLACK PEOPLE WHO USE THE "N-WORD."
I DON'T CARE IF IT'S A BLACK OR WHITE PERSON SAYIN' IT, THE WORD IS OFFENSIVE.
I BET OTHER BLACK PEOPLE OUT THERE WILL APPRECIATE MY SPEAKIN' OUT AGAINST THE USE OF THE WORD "N****."
JEFFREY, GO GET MY PICKET SIGNS AND CALL THE NAACP.
©2005 Darrin Bell / Dist. by WPWG, Inc. Candorville.com
12-7

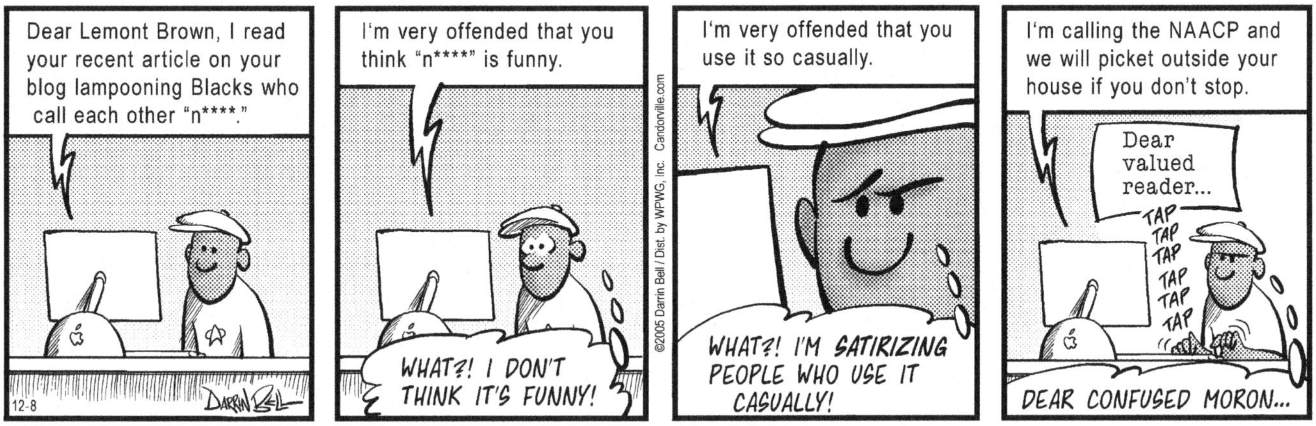
Dear Lemont Brown, I read your recent article on your blog lampooning Blacks who call each other "n****."
I'm very offended that you think "n****" is funny.
WHAT?! I DON'T THINK IT'S FUNNY!
I'm very offended that you use it so casually.
WHAT?! I'M **SATIRIZING** PEOPLE WHO USE IT CASUALLY!
I'm calling the NAACP and we will picket outside your house if you don't stop.
Dear valued reader...
TAP TAP TAP TAP TAP TAP
DEAR CONFUSED MORON...
©2005 Darrin Bell / Dist. by WPWG, Inc. Candorville.com
12-8

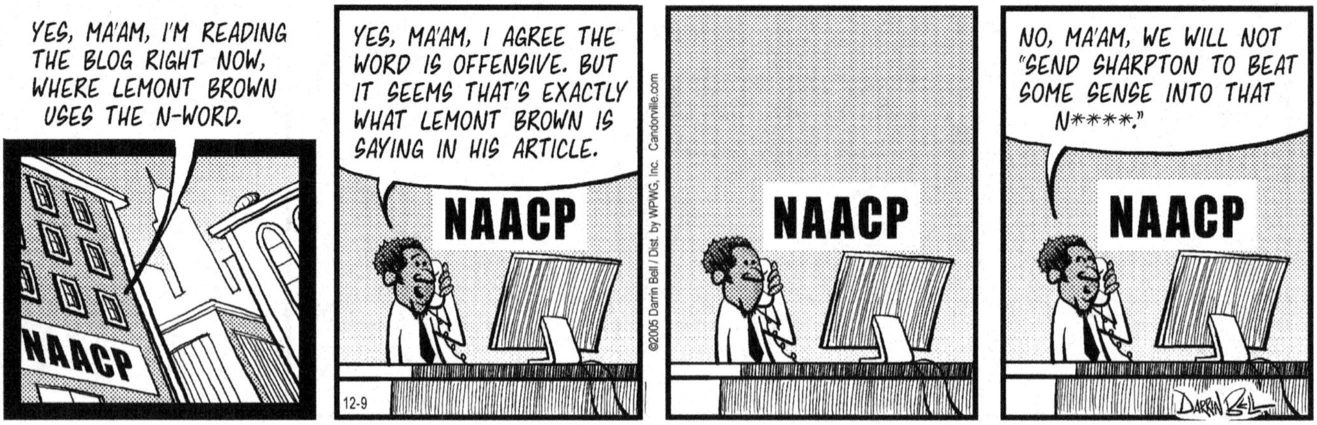
YES, MA'AM, I'M READING THE BLOG RIGHT NOW, WHERE LEMONT BROWN USES THE N-WORD.
NAACP
YES, MA'AM, I AGREE THE WORD IS OFFENSIVE. BUT IT SEEMS THAT'S EXACTLY WHAT LEMONT BROWN IS SAYING IN HIS ARTICLE.
NAACP
12-9
©2005 Darrin Bell / Dist. by WPWG, Inc. Candorville.com
NAACP
NO, MA'AM, WE WILL NOT "SEND SHARPTON TO BEAT SOME SENSE INTO THAT N****."
NAACP
DARRIN BELL

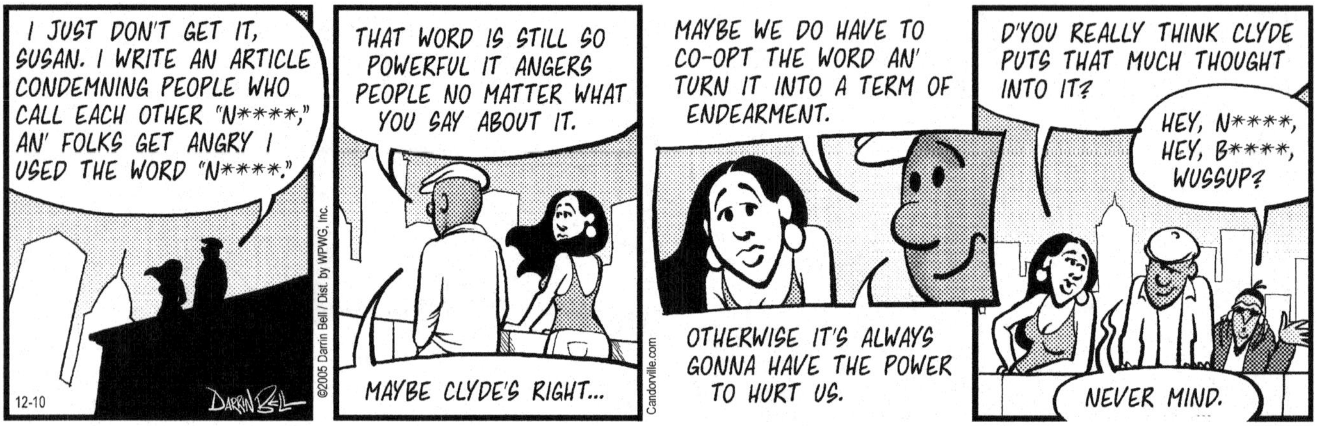
I JUST DON'T GET IT, SUSAN. I WRITE AN ARTICLE CONDEMNING PEOPLE WHO CALL EACH OTHER "N****," AN' FOLKS GET ANGRY I USED THE WORD "N****."
12-10
DARRIN BELL
©2005 Darrin Bell / Dist. by WPWG, Inc.
THAT WORD IS STILL SO POWERFUL IT ANGERS PEOPLE NO MATTER WHAT YOU SAY ABOUT IT.
MAYBE CLYDE'S RIGHT...
Candorville.com
MAYBE WE DO HAVE TO CO-OPT THE WORD AN' TURN IT INTO A TERM OF ENDEARMENT.
OTHERWISE IT'S ALWAYS GONNA HAVE THE POWER TO HURT US.
D'YOU REALLY THINK CLYDE PUTS THAT MUCH THOUGHT INTO IT?
HEY, N****, HEY, B****, WUSSUP?
NEVER MIND.

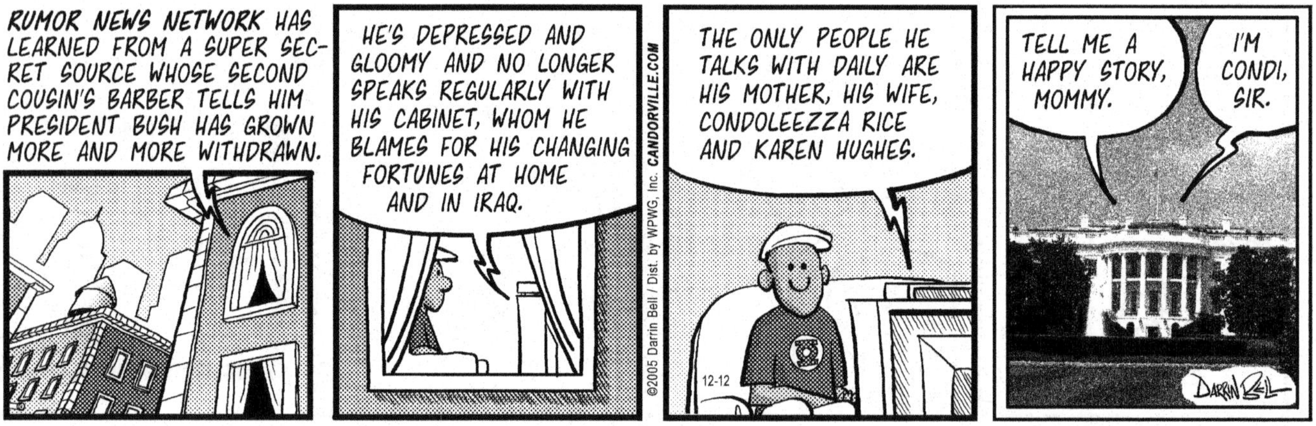
RUMOR NEWS NETWORK HAS LEARNED FROM A SUPER SECRET SOURCE WHOSE SECOND COUSIN'S BARBER TELLS HIM PRESIDENT BUSH HAS GROWN MORE AND MORE WITHDRAWN.
HE'S DEPRESSED AND GLOOMY AND NO LONGER SPEAKS REGULARLY WITH HIS CABINET, WHOM HE BLAMES FOR HIS CHANGING FORTUNES AT HOME AND IN IRAQ.
©2005 Darrin Bell / Dist. by WPWG, Inc. CANDORVILLE.COM
THE ONLY PEOPLE HE TALKS WITH DAILY ARE HIS MOTHER, HIS WIFE, CONDOLEEZZA RICE AND KAREN HUGHES.
12-12
TELL ME A HAPPY STORY, MOMMY.
I'M CONDI, SIR.
DARRIN BELL

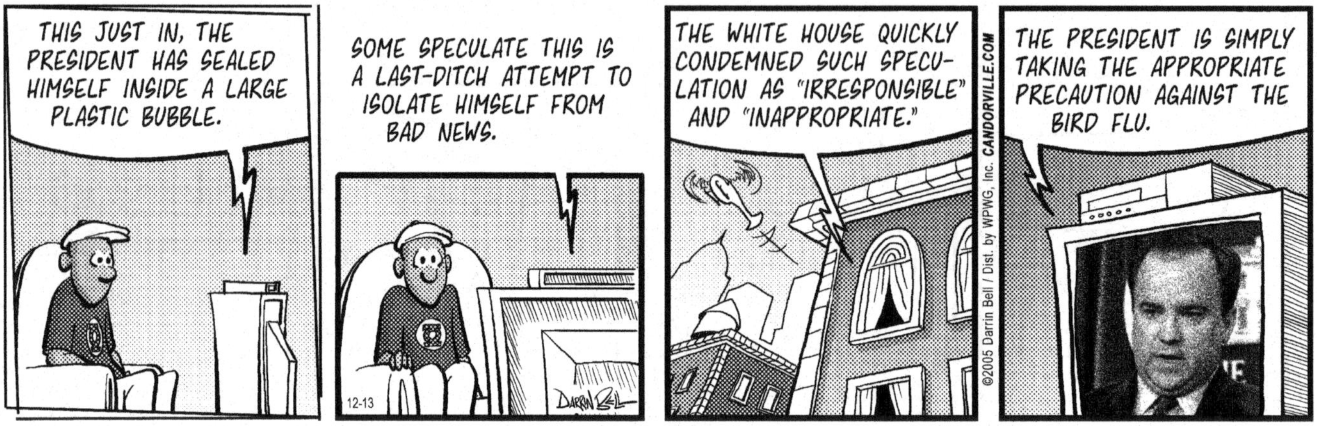
THIS JUST IN, THE PRESIDENT HAS SEALED HIMSELF INSIDE A LARGE PLASTIC BUBBLE.
SOME SPECULATE THIS IS A LAST-DITCH ATTEMPT TO ISOLATE HIMSELF FROM BAD NEWS.
12-13
DARRIN BELL
THE WHITE HOUSE QUICKLY CONDEMNED SUCH SPECULATION AS "IRRESPONSIBLE" AND "INAPPROPRIATE."
©2005 Darrin Bell / Dist. by WPWG, Inc. CANDORVILLE.COM
THE PRESIDENT IS SIMPLY TAKING THE APPROPRIATE PRECAUTION AGAINST THE BIRD FLU.

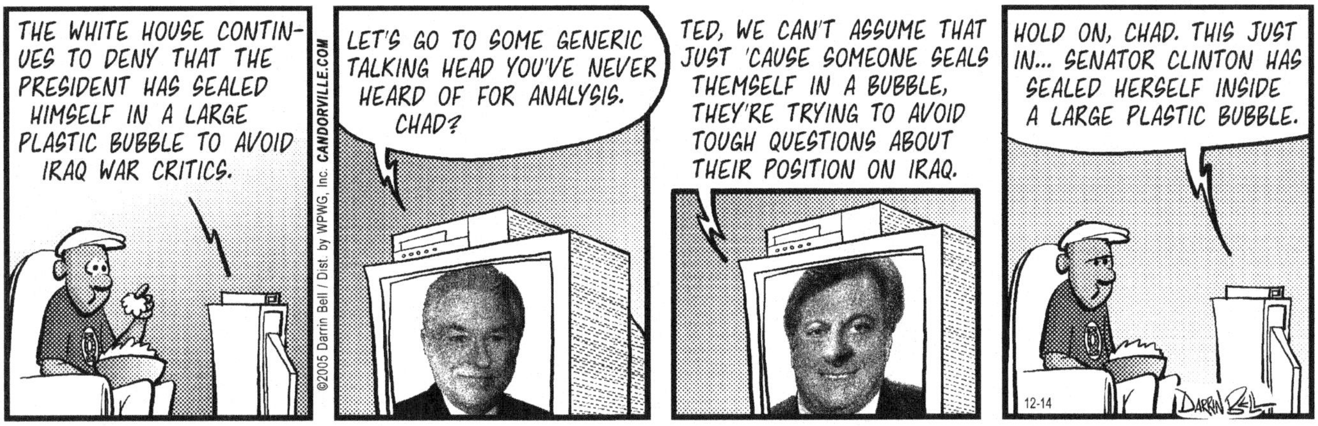
THE WHITE HOUSE CONTINUES TO DENY THAT THE PRESIDENT HAS SEALED HIMSELF IN A LARGE PLASTIC BUBBLE TO AVOID IRAQ WAR CRITICS.
©2005 Darrin Bell / Dist. by WPWG, Inc. CANDORVILLE.COM
LET'S GO TO SOME GENERIC TALKING HEAD YOU'VE NEVER HEARD OF FOR ANALYSIS. CHAD?
TED, WE CAN'T ASSUME THAT JUST 'CAUSE SOMEONE SEALS THEMSELF IN A BUBBLE, THEY'RE TRYING TO AVOID TOUGH QUESTIONS ABOUT THEIR POSITION ON IRAQ.
HOLD ON, CHAD. THIS JUST IN... SENATOR CLINTON HAS SEALED HERSELF INSIDE A LARGE PLASTIC BUBBLE.
12-14
DARRIN BELL

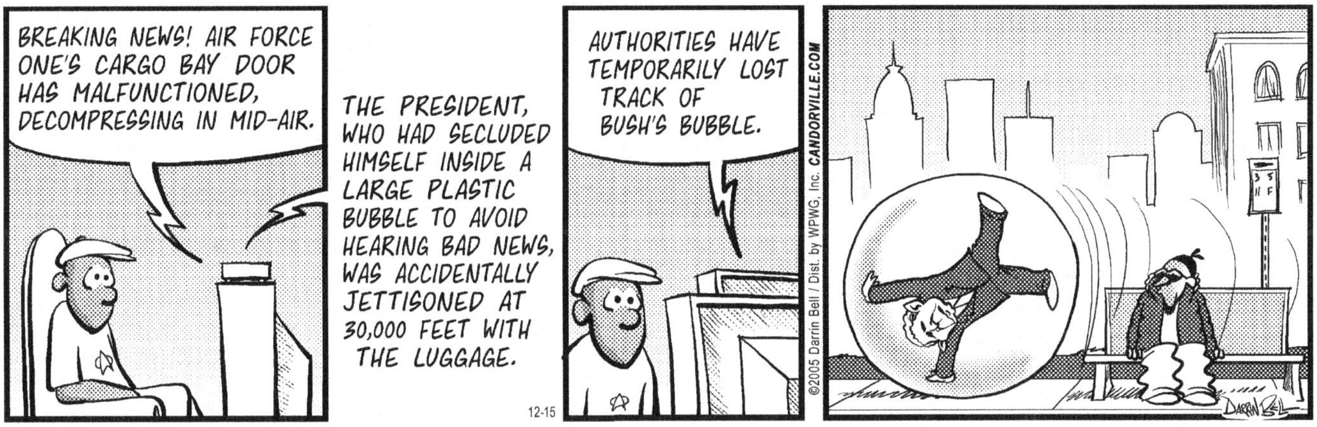
BREAKING NEWS! AIR FORCE ONE'S CARGO BAY DOOR HAS MALFUNCTIONED, DECOMPRESSING IN MID-AIR.
THE PRESIDENT, WHO HAD SECLUDED HIMSELF INSIDE A LARGE PLASTIC BUBBLE TO AVOID HEARING BAD NEWS, WAS ACCIDENTALLY JETTISONED AT 30,000 FEET WITH THE LUGGAGE.
12-15
AUTHORITIES HAVE TEMPORARILY LOST TRACK OF BUSH'S BUBBLE.
©2005 Darrin Bell / Dist. by WPWG, Inc. CANDORVILLE.COM
DARRIN BELL

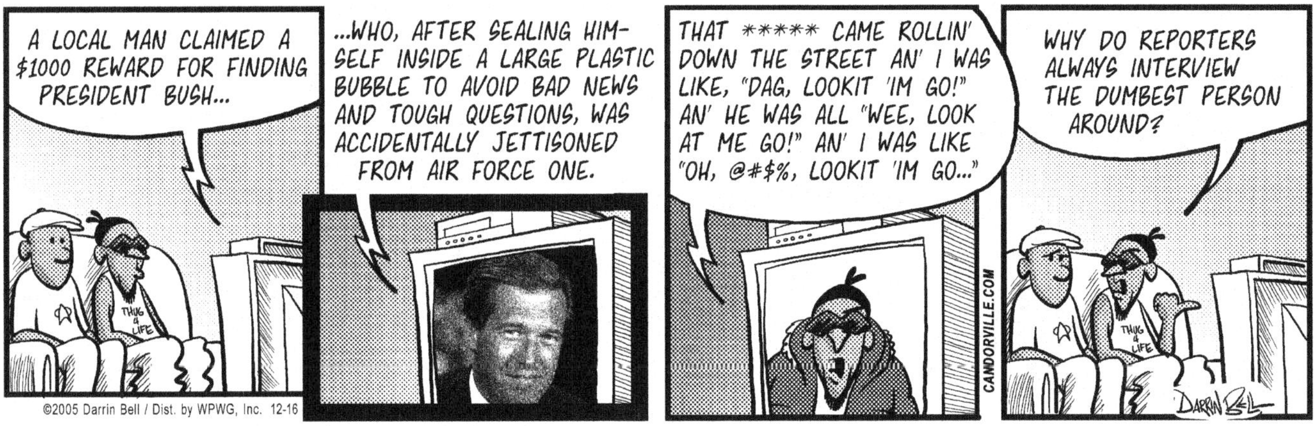
A LOCAL MAN CLAIMED A $1000 REWARD FOR FINDING PRESIDENT BUSH...
©2005 Darrin Bell / Dist. by WPWG, Inc. 12-16
...WHO, AFTER SEALING HIMSELF INSIDE A LARGE PLASTIC BUBBLE TO AVOID BAD NEWS AND TOUGH QUESTIONS, WAS ACCIDENTALLY JETTISONED FROM AIR FORCE ONE.
THAT ***** CAME ROLLIN' DOWN THE STREET AN' I WAS LIKE, "DAG, LOOKIT 'IM GO!" AN' HE WAS ALL "WEE, LOOK AT ME GO!" AN' I WAS LIKE "OH, @#$%, LOOKIT 'IM GO..."
CANDORVILLE.COM
WHY DO REPORTERS ALWAYS INTERVIEW THE DUMBEST PERSON AROUND?
DARRIN BELL

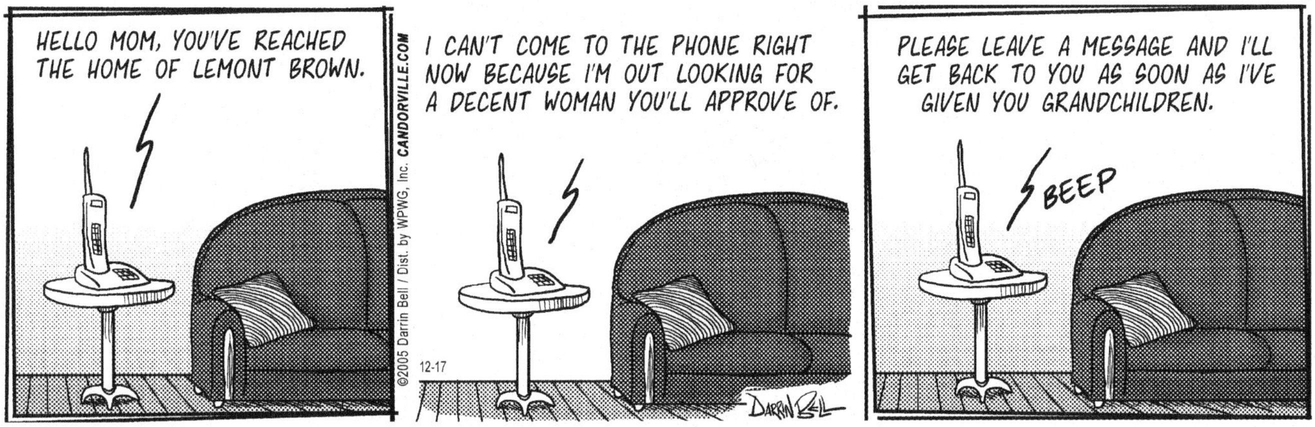
HELLO MOM, YOU'VE REACHED THE HOME OF LEMONT BROWN.
©2005 Darrin Bell / Dist. by WPWG, Inc. CANDORVILLE.COM
I CAN'T COME TO THE PHONE RIGHT NOW BECAUSE I'M OUT LOOKING FOR A DECENT WOMAN YOU'LL APPROVE OF.
12-17
DARRIN BELL
PLEASE LEAVE A MESSAGE AND I'LL GET BACK TO YOU AS SOON AS I'VE GIVEN YOU GRANDCHILDREN.
BEEP

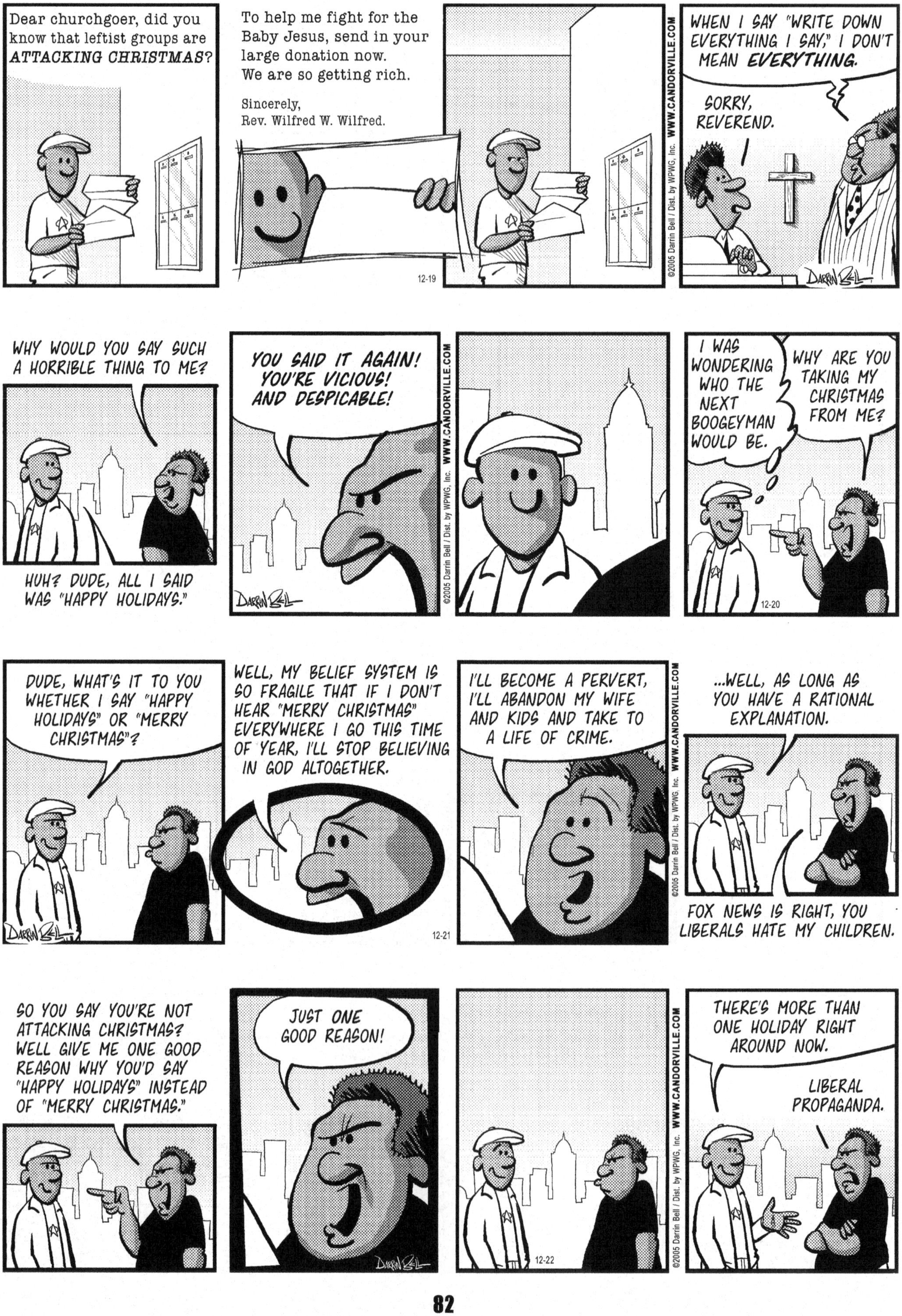
Dear churchgoer, did you know that leftist groups are ATTACKING CHRISTMAS?
To help me fight for the Baby Jesus, send in your large donation now. We are so getting rich.
Sincerely,
Rev. Wilfred W. Wilfred.
12-19
©2005 Darrin Bell / Dist. by WPWG, Inc. WWW.CANDORVILLE.COM
WHEN I SAY "WRITE DOWN EVERYTHING I SAY," I DON'T MEAN EVERYTHING.
SORRY, REVEREND.
DARRIN BELL
WHY WOULD YOU SAY SUCH A HORRIBLE THING TO ME?
HUH? DUDE, ALL I SAID WAS "HAPPY HOLIDAYS."
YOU SAID IT AGAIN! YOU'RE VICIOUS! AND DESPICABLE!
DARRIN BELL
©2005 Darrin Bell / Dist. by WPWG, Inc. WWW.CANDORVILLE.COM
WHY ARE YOU TAKING MY CHRISTMAS FROM ME?
I WAS WONDERING WHO THE NEXT BOOGEYMAN WOULD BE.
12-20
DUDE, WHAT'S IT TO YOU WHETHER I SAY "HAPPY HOLIDAYS" OR "MERRY CHRISTMAS"?
DARRIN BELL
WELL, MY BELIEF SYSTEM IS SO FRAGILE THAT IF I DON'T HEAR "MERRY CHRISTMAS" EVERYWHERE I GO THIS TIME OF YEAR, I'LL STOP BELIEVING IN GOD ALTOGETHER.
12-21
I'LL BECOME A PERVERT, I'LL ABANDON MY WIFE AND KIDS AND TAKE TO A LIFE OF CRIME.
©2005 Darrin Bell / Dist. by WPWG, Inc. WWW.CANDORVILLE.COM
...WELL, AS LONG AS YOU HAVE A RATIONAL EXPLANATION.
FOX NEWS IS RIGHT, YOU LIBERALS HATE MY CHILDREN.
SO YOU SAY YOU'RE NOT ATTACKING CHRISTMAS? WELL GIVE ME ONE GOOD REASON WHY YOU'D SAY "HAPPY HOLIDAYS" INSTEAD OF "MERRY CHRISTMAS."
JUST ONE GOOD REASON!
DARRIN BELL
12-22
©2005 Darrin Bell / Dist. by WPWG, Inc. WWW.CANDORVILLE.COM
THERE'S MORE THAN ONE HOLIDAY RIGHT AROUND NOW.
LIBERAL PROPAGANDA.

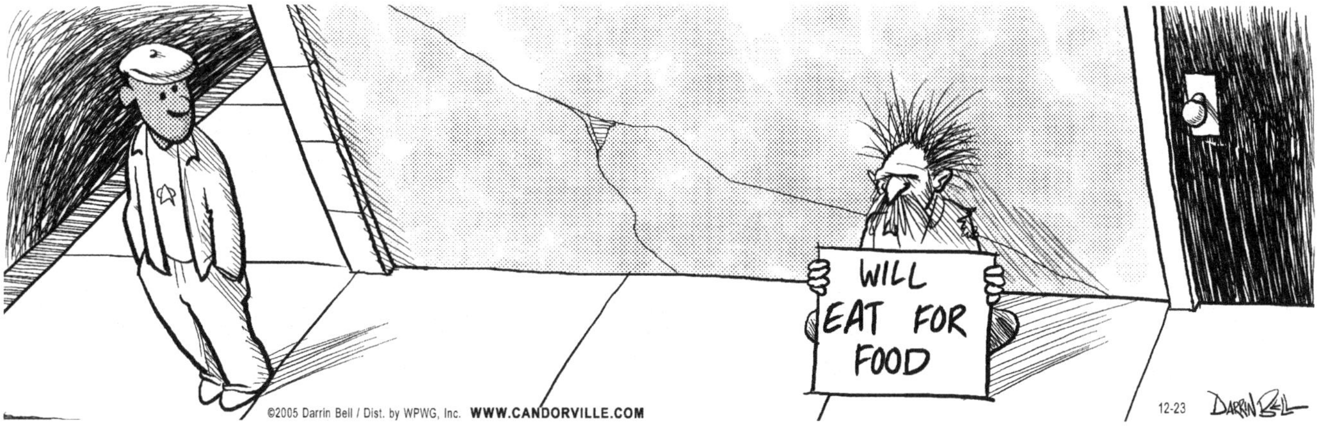
WILL EAT FOR FOOD
©2005 Darrin Bell / Dist. by WPWG, Inc. WWW.CANDORVILLE.COM
12-23
DARRIN BELL

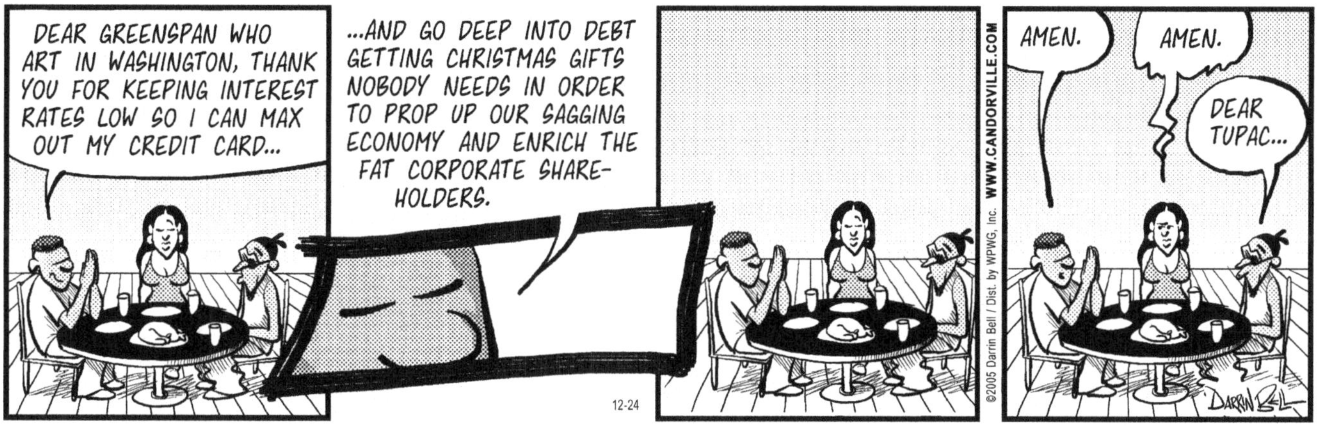
DEAR GREENSPAN WHO ART IN WASHINGTON, THANK YOU FOR KEEPING INTEREST RATES LOW SO I CAN MAX OUT MY CREDIT CARD...
...AND GO DEEP INTO DEBT GETTING CHRISTMAS GIFTS NOBODY NEEDS IN ORDER TO PROP UP OUR SAGGING ECONOMY AND ENRICH THE FAT CORPORATE SHARE-HOLDERS.
12-24
©2005 Darrin Bell / Dist. by WPWG, Inc. WWW.CANDORVILLE.COM
AMEN.
AMEN.
DEAR TUPAC...
DARRIN BELL

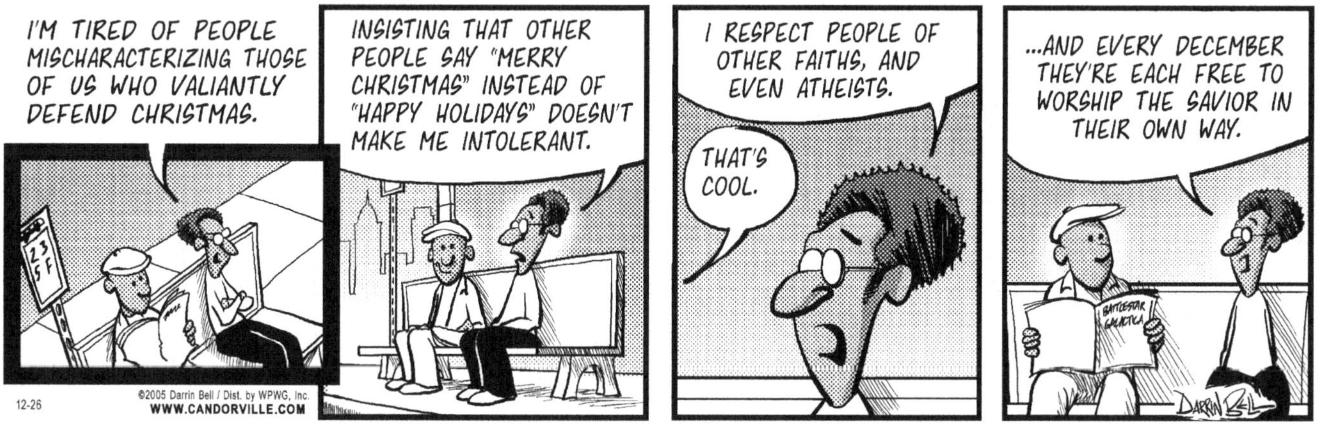
I'M TIRED OF PEOPLE MISCHARACTERIZING THOSE OF US WHO VALIANTLY DEFEND CHRISTMAS.
12-26
©2005 Darrin Bell / Dist. by WPWG, Inc. WWW.CANDORVILLE.COM
INSISTING THAT OTHER PEOPLE SAY "MERRY CHRISTMAS" INSTEAD OF "HAPPY HOLIDAYS" DOESN'T MAKE ME INTOLERANT.
I RESPECT PEOPLE OF OTHER FAITHS, AND EVEN ATHEISTS.
THAT'S COOL.
...AND EVERY DECEMBER THEY'RE EACH FREE TO WORSHIP THE SAVIOR IN THEIR OWN WAY.
DARRIN BELL

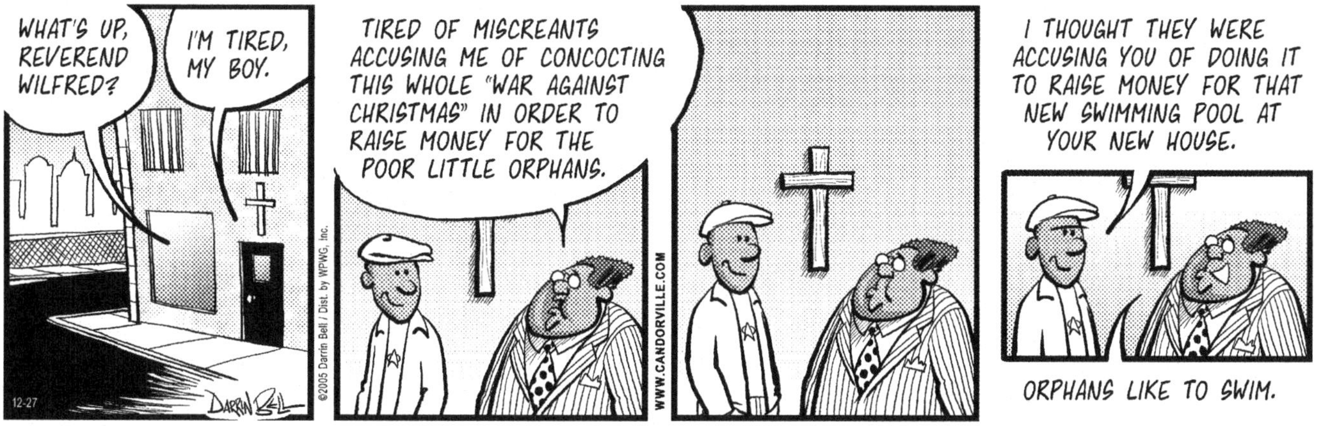
WHAT'S UP, REVEREND WILFRED?
I'M TIRED, MY BOY.
12-27
DARRIN BELL
©2005 Darrin Bell / Dist. by WPWG, Inc.
TIRED OF MISCREANTS ACCUSING ME OF CONCOCTING THIS WHOLE "WAR AGAINST CHRISTMAS" IN ORDER TO RAISE MONEY FOR THE POOR LITTLE ORPHANS.
WWW.CANDORVILLE.COM
I THOUGHT THEY WERE ACCUSING YOU OF DOING IT TO RAISE MONEY FOR THAT NEW SWIMMING POOL AT YOUR NEW HOUSE.
ORPHANS LIKE TO SWIM.

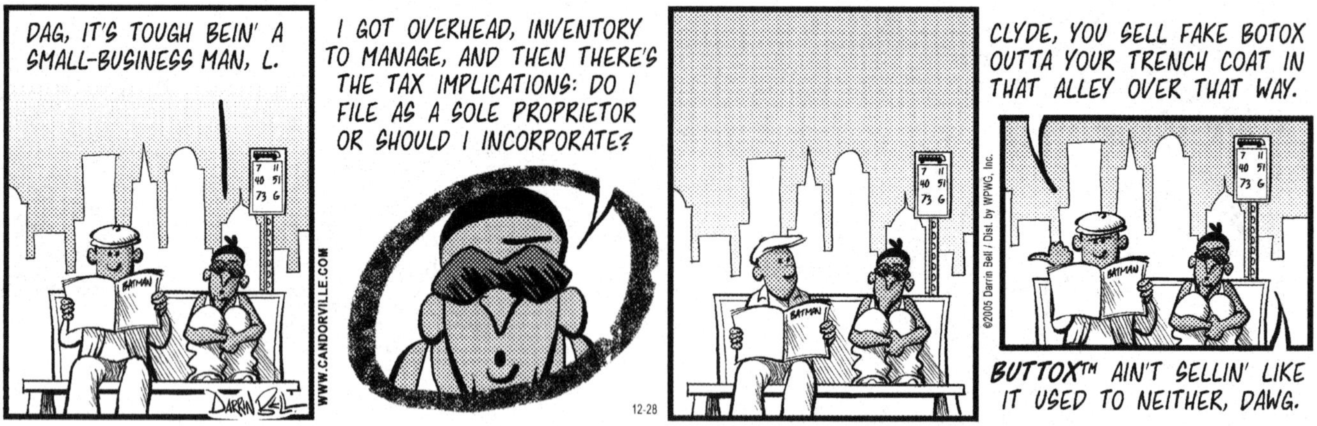
DAG, IT'S TOUGH BEIN' A SMALL-BUSINESS MAN, L.
I GOT OVERHEAD, INVENTORY TO MANAGE, AND THEN THERE'S THE TAX IMPLICATIONS: DO I FILE AS A SOLE PROPRIETOR OR SHOULD I INCORPORATE?
CLYDE, YOU SELL FAKE BOTOX OUTTA YOUR TRENCH COAT IN THAT ALLEY OVER THAT WAY.
BUTTOX™ AIN'T SELLIN' LIKE IT USED TO NEITHER, DAWG.
WWW.CANDORVILLE.COM
©2005 Darrin Bell / Dist. by WPWG, Inc.
12-28

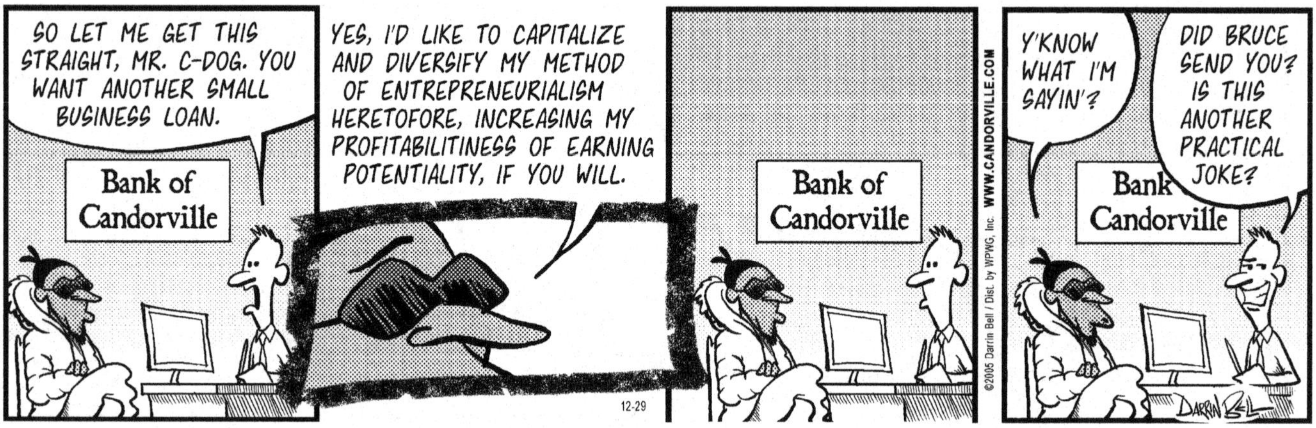
SO LET ME GET THIS STRAIGHT, MR. C-DOG. YOU WANT ANOTHER SMALL BUSINESS LOAN.
Bank of Candorville
YES, I'D LIKE TO CAPITALIZE AND DIVERSIFY MY METHOD OF ENTREPRENEURIALISM HERETOFORE, INCREASING MY PROFITABILITINESS OF EARNING POTENTIALITY, IF YOU WILL.
Y'KNOW WHAT I'M SAYIN'?
DID BRUCE SEND YOU? IS THIS ANOTHER PRACTICAL JOKE?
WWW.CANDORVILLE.COM
©2005 Darrin Bell / Dist. by WPWG, Inc.
12-29

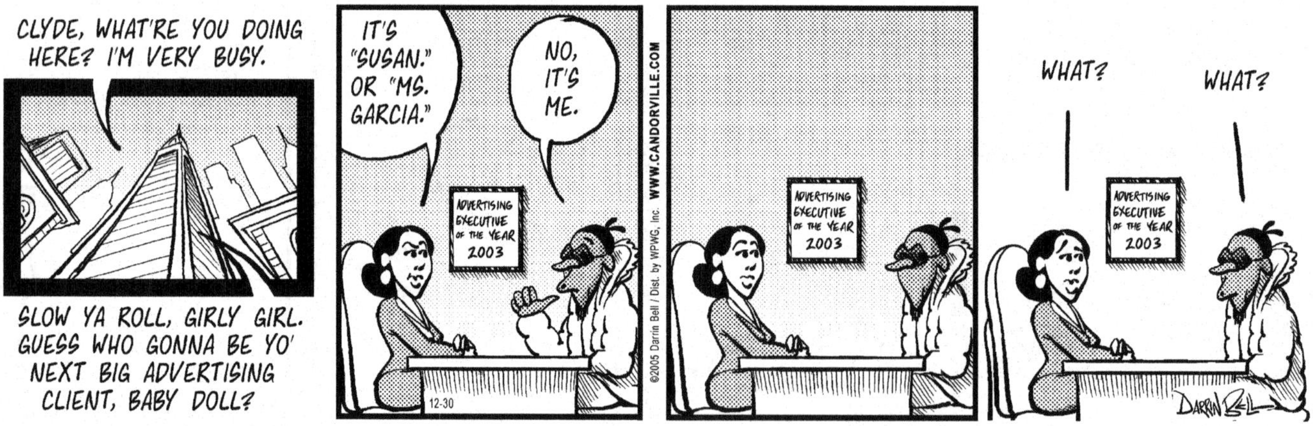
CLYDE, WHAT'RE YOU DOING HERE? I'M VERY BUSY.
SLOW YA ROLL, GIRLY GIRL. GUESS WHO GONNA BE YO' NEXT BIG ADVERTISING CLIENT, BABY DOLL?
IT'S "SUSAN." OR "MS. GARCIA."
NO, IT'S ME.
ADVERTISING EXECUTIVE OF THE YEAR 2003
WHAT?
WHAT?
WWW.CANDORVILLE.COM
©2005 Darrin Bell / Dist. by WPWG, Inc.
12-30

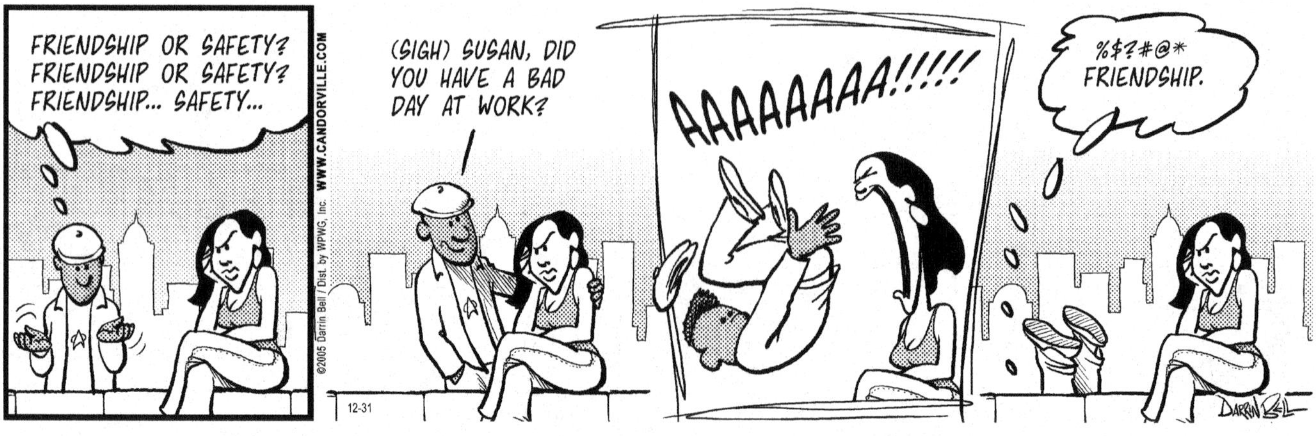
FRIENDSHIP OR SAFETY? FRIENDSHIP OR SAFETY? FRIENDSHIP... SAFETY...
(SIGH) SUSAN, DID YOU HAVE A BAD DAY AT WORK?
AAAAAAAA!!!!!
%$?#@* FRIENDSHIP.
WWW.CANDORVILLE.COM
©2005 Darrin Bell / Dist. by WPWG, Inc.
12-31

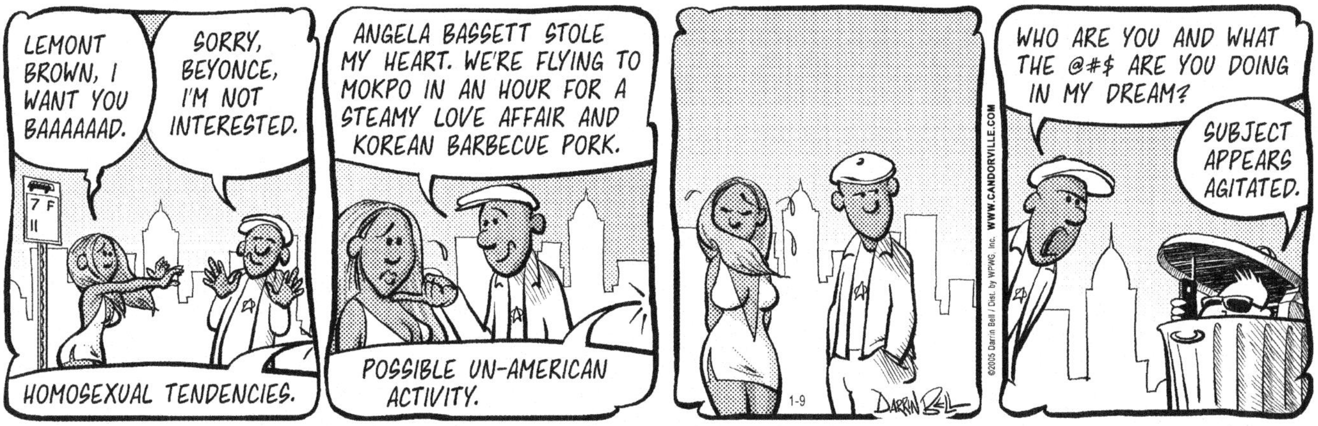
LEMONT BROWN, I WANT YOU BAAAAAAD.
SORRY, BEYONCE, I'M NOT INTERESTED.
HOMOSEXUAL TENDENCIES.
ANGELA BASSETT STOLE MY HEART. WE'RE FLYING TO MOKPO IN AN HOUR FOR A STEAMY LOVE AFFAIR AND KOREAN BARBECUE PORK.
POSSIBLE UN-AMERICAN ACTIVITY.
1-9
©2005 Darrin Bell / Dist. by WPWG, Inc. WWW.CANDORVILLE.COM
DARRIN BELL
WHO ARE YOU AND WHAT THE @#$ ARE YOU DOING IN MY DREAM?
SUBJECT APPEARS AGITATED.

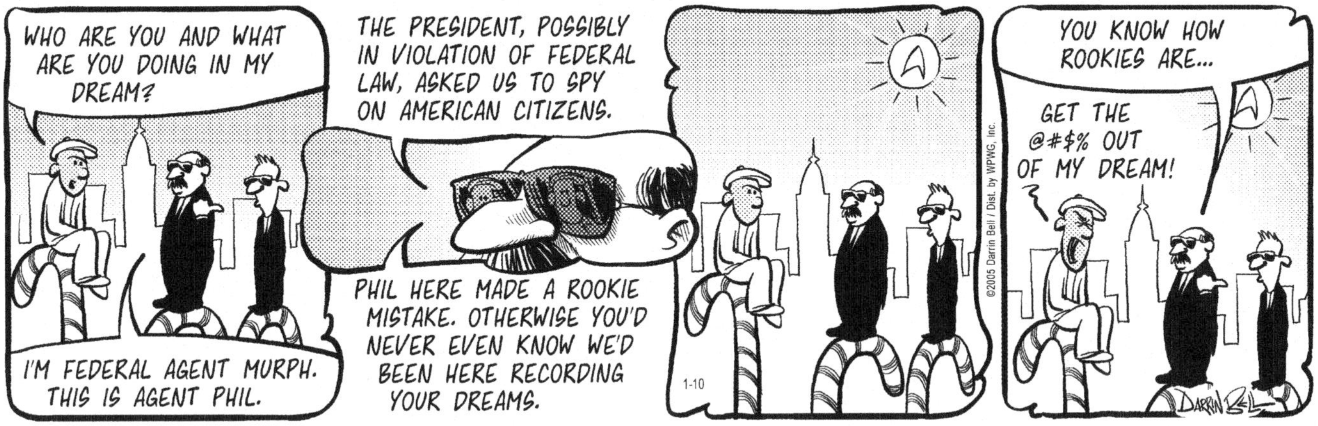
WHO ARE YOU AND WHAT ARE YOU DOING IN MY DREAM?
I'M FEDERAL AGENT MURPH. THIS IS AGENT PHIL.
THE PRESIDENT, POSSIBLY IN VIOLATION OF FEDERAL LAW, ASKED US TO SPY ON AMERICAN CITIZENS.
PHIL HERE MADE A ROOKIE MISTAKE. OTHERWISE YOU'D NEVER EVEN KNOW WE'D BEEN HERE RECORDING YOUR DREAMS.
1-10
©2005 Darrin Bell / Dist. by WPWG, Inc.
YOU KNOW HOW ROOKIES ARE...
GET THE @#$% OUT OF MY DREAM!
DARRIN BELL

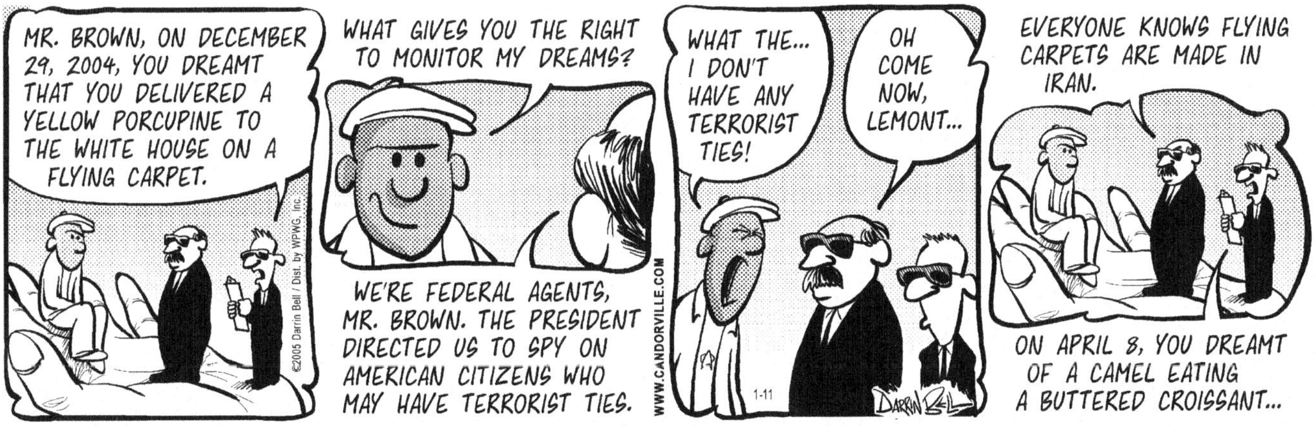
MR. BROWN, ON DECEMBER 29, 2004, YOU DREAMT THAT YOU DELIVERED A YELLOW PORCUPINE TO THE WHITE HOUSE ON A FLYING CARPET.
©2005 Darrin Bell / Dist. by WPWG, Inc.
WHAT GIVES YOU THE RIGHT TO MONITOR MY DREAMS?
WE'RE FEDERAL AGENTS, MR. BROWN. THE PRESIDENT DIRECTED US TO SPY ON AMERICAN CITIZENS WHO MAY HAVE TERRORIST TIES.
WWW.CANDORVILLE.COM
WHAT THE... I DON'T HAVE ANY TERRORIST TIES!
OH COME NOW, LEMONT...
1-11
DARRIN BELL
EVERYONE KNOWS FLYING CARPETS ARE MADE IN IRAN.
ON APRIL 8, YOU DREAMT OF A CAMEL EATING A BUTTERED CROISSANT...

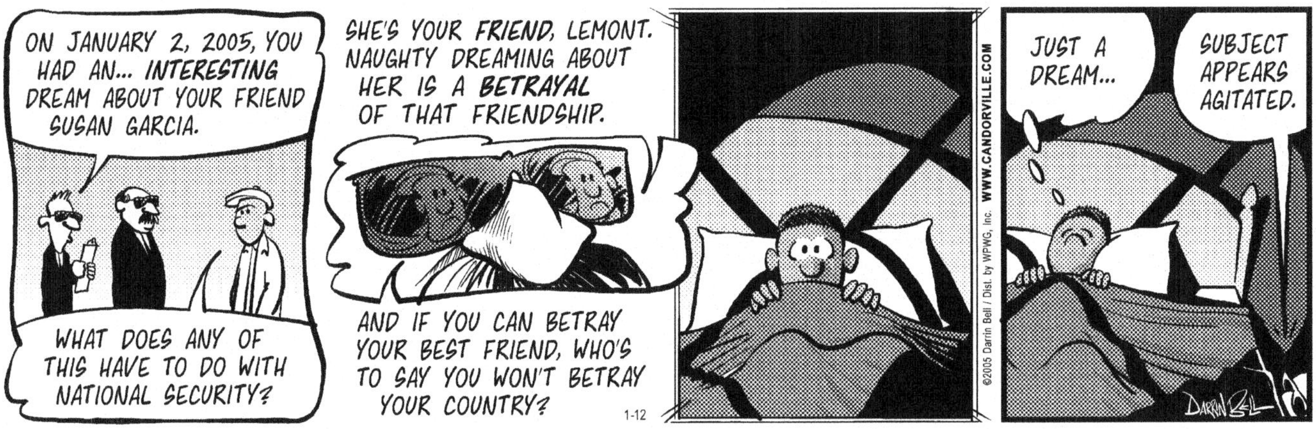
ON JANUARY 2, 2005, YOU HAD AN... **INTERESTING** DREAM ABOUT YOUR FRIEND SUSAN GARCIA.
WHAT DOES ANY OF THIS HAVE TO DO WITH NATIONAL SECURITY?
SHE'S YOUR **FRIEND**, LEMONT. NAUGHTY DREAMING ABOUT HER IS A **BETRAYAL** OF THAT FRIENDSHIP.
AND IF YOU CAN BETRAY YOUR BEST FRIEND, WHO'S TO SAY YOU WON'T BETRAY YOUR COUNTRY?
1-12
©2005 Darrin Bell / Dist. by WPWG, Inc. WWW.CANDORVILLE.COM
JUST A DREAM...
SUBJECT APPEARS AGITATED.
DARRIN BELL

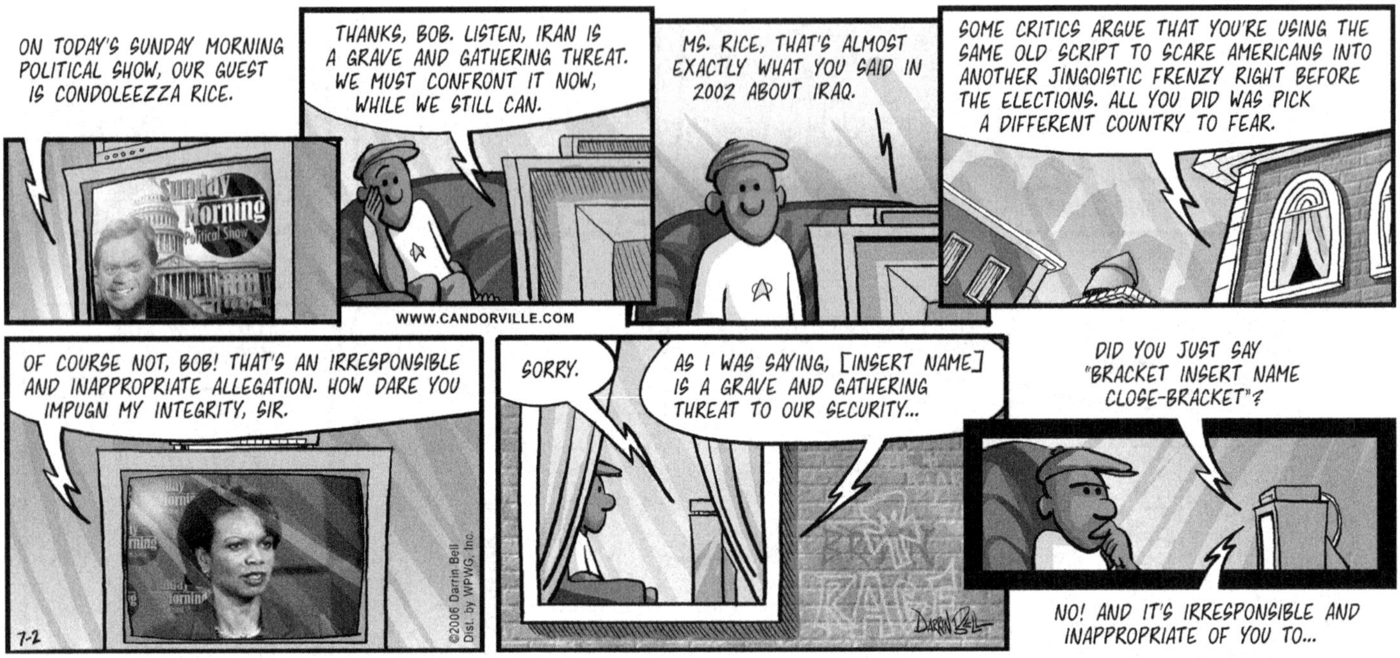
ON TODAY'S SUNDAY MORNING POLITICAL SHOW, OUR GUEST IS CONDOLEEZZA RICE.
Sunday Morning Political Show
THANKS, BOB. LISTEN, IRAN IS A GRAVE AND GATHERING THREAT. WE MUST CONFRONT IT NOW, WHILE WE STILL CAN.
WWW.CANDORVILLE.COM
MS. RICE, THAT'S ALMOST EXACTLY WHAT YOU SAID IN 2002 ABOUT IRAQ.
SOME CRITICS ARGUE THAT YOU'RE USING THE SAME OLD SCRIPT TO SCARE AMERICANS INTO ANOTHER JINGOISTIC FRENZY RIGHT BEFORE THE ELECTIONS. ALL YOU DID WAS PICK A DIFFERENT COUNTRY TO FEAR.
OF COURSE NOT, BOB! THAT'S AN IRRESPONSIBLE AND INAPPROPRIATE ALLEGATION. HOW DARE YOU IMPUGN MY INTEGRITY, SIR.
7-2
©2006 Darrin Bell Dist. by WPWG, Inc.
SORRY.
AS I WAS SAYING, [INSERT NAME] IS A GRAVE AND GATHERING THREAT TO OUR SECURITY...
DARRIN BELL
DID YOU JUST SAY "BRACKET INSERT NAME CLOSE-BRACKET"?
NO! AND IT'S IRRESPONSIBLE AND INAPPROPRIATE OF YOU TO...

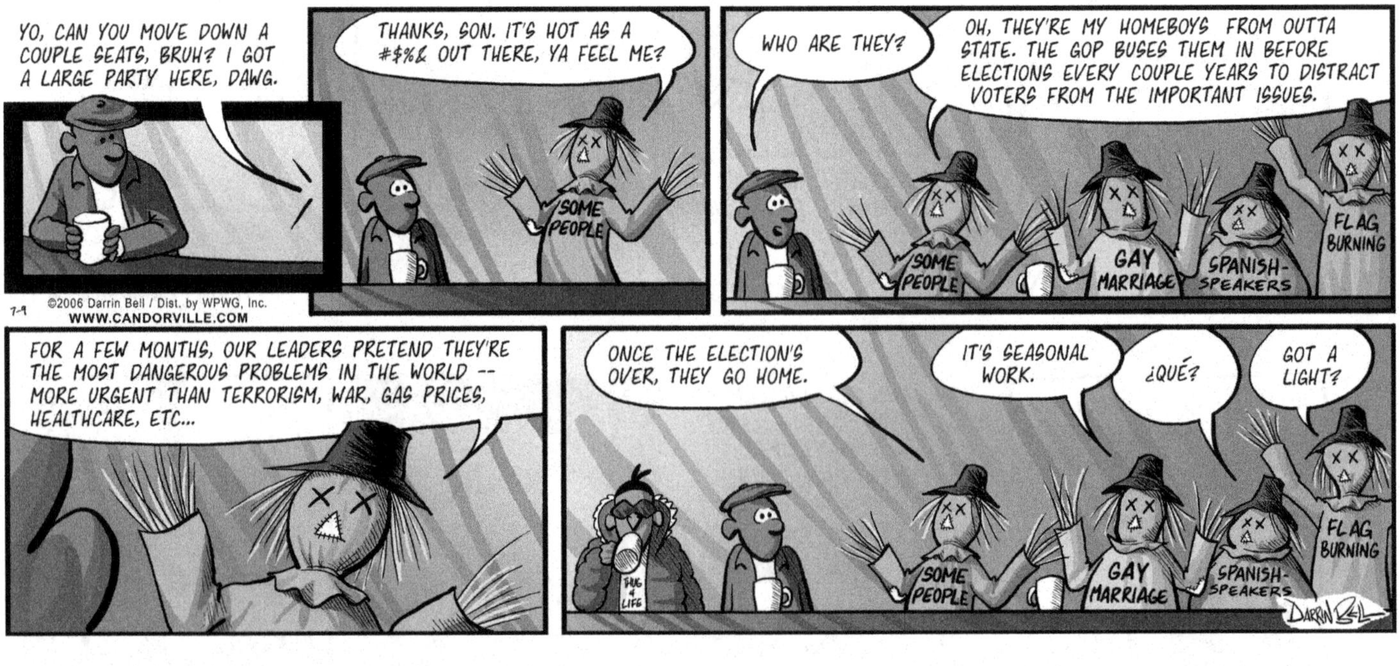
YO, CAN YOU MOVE DOWN A COUPLE SEATS, BRUH? I GOT A LARGE PARTY HERE, DAWG.
THANKS, SON. IT'S HOT AS A #$%& OUT THERE, YA FEEL ME?
SOME PEOPLE
7-9
©2006 Darrin Bell / Dist. by WPWG, Inc.
WWW.CANDORVILLE.COM
WHO ARE THEY?
OH, THEY'RE MY HOMEBOYS FROM OUTTA STATE. THE GOP BUSES THEM IN BEFORE ELECTIONS EVERY COUPLE YEARS TO DISTRACT VOTERS FROM THE IMPORTANT ISSUES.
SOME PEOPLE
GAY MARRIAGE
SPANISH-SPEAKERS
FLAG BURNING
FOR A FEW MONTHS, OUR LEADERS PRETEND THEY'RE THE MOST DANGEROUS PROBLEMS IN THE WORLD -- MORE URGENT THAN TERRORISM, WAR, GAS PRICES, HEALTHCARE, ETC...
ONCE THE ELECTION'S OVER, THEY GO HOME.
IT'S SEASONAL WORK.
¿QUÉ?
GOT A LIGHT?
SOME PEOPLE
GAY MARRIAGE
SPANISH-SPEAKERS
FLAG BURNING
DARRIN BELL

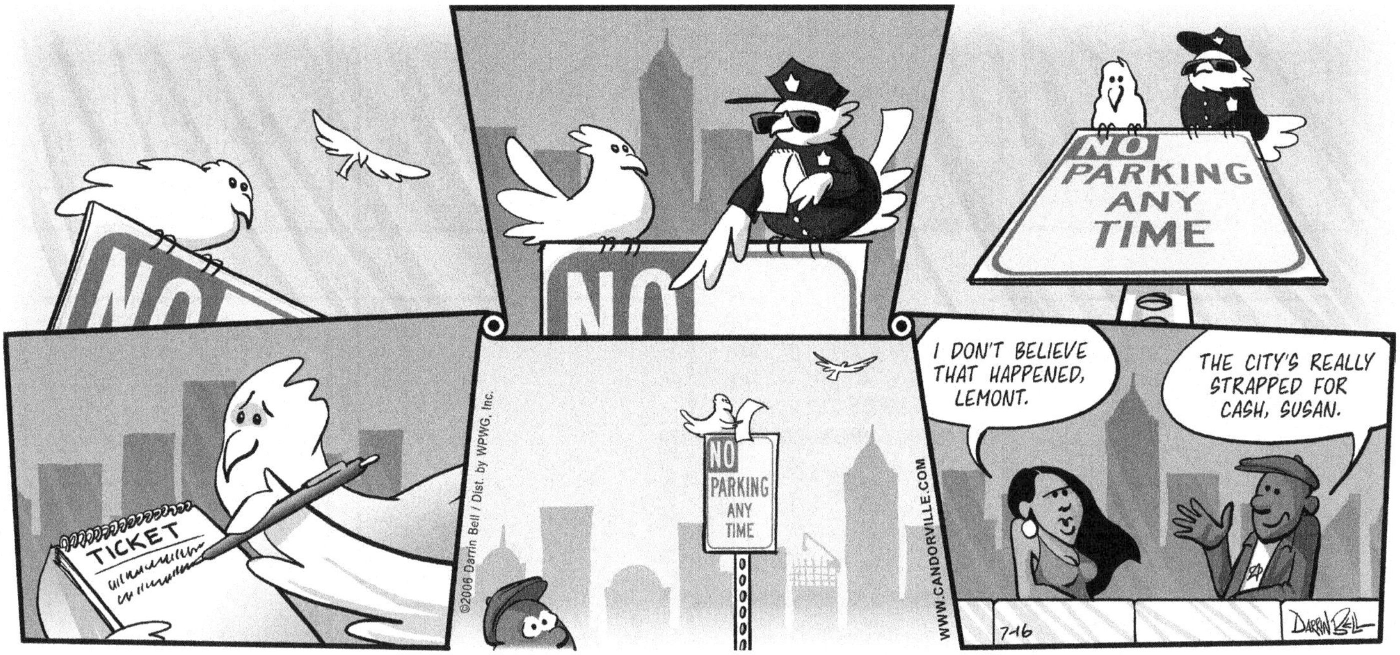

NO
NO
NO PARKING ANY TIME
TICKET
©2006 Darrin Bell / Dist. by WPWG, Inc.
NO PARKING ANY TIME
WWW.CANDORVILLE.COM
I DON'T BELIEVE THAT HAPPENED, LEMONT.
THE CITY'S REALLY STRAPPED FOR CASH, SUSAN.
7-16
DARRIN BELL

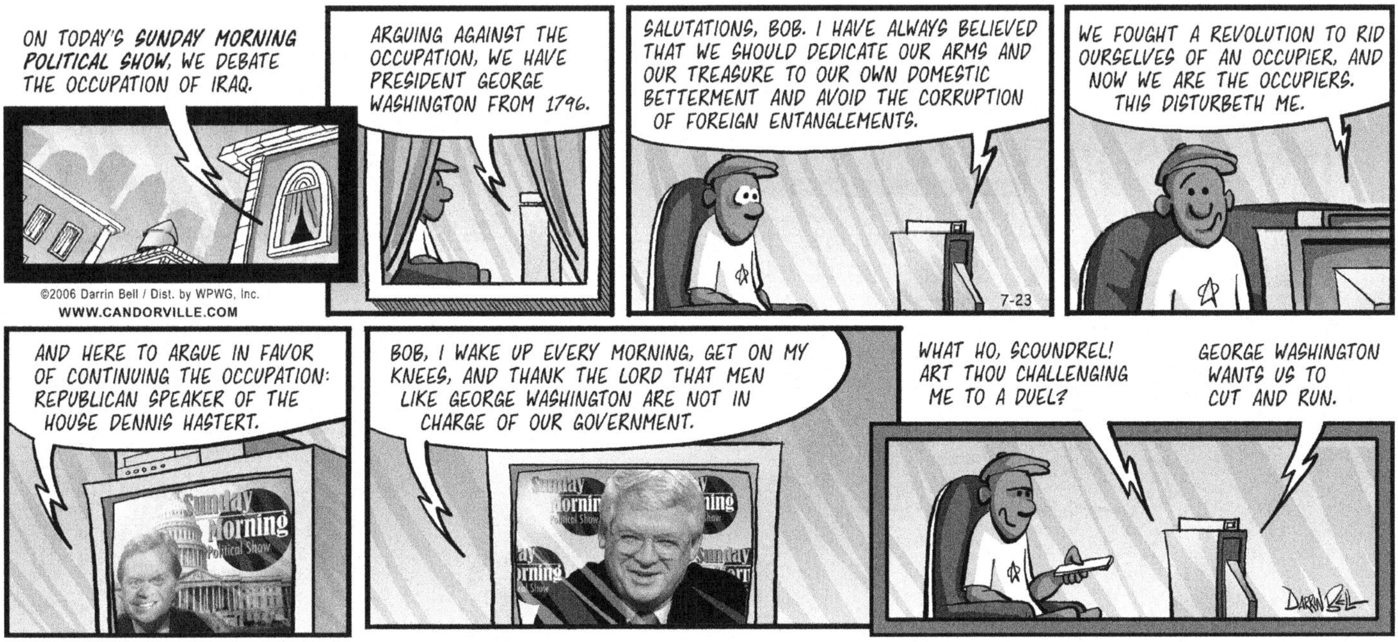

ON TODAY'S SUNDAY MORNING POLITICAL SHOW, WE DEBATE THE OCCUPATION OF IRAQ.
©2006 Darrin Bell / Dist. by WPWG, Inc.
WWW.CANDORVILLE.COM
ARGUING AGAINST THE OCCUPATION, WE HAVE PRESIDENT GEORGE WASHINGTON FROM 1796.
SALUTATIONS, BOB. I HAVE ALWAYS BELIEVED THAT WE SHOULD DEDICATE OUR ARMS AND OUR TREASURE TO OUR OWN DOMESTIC BETTERMENT AND AVOID THE CORRUPTION OF FOREIGN ENTANGLEMENTS.
7-23
WE FOUGHT A REVOLUTION TO RID OURSELVES OF AN OCCUPIER, AND NOW WE ARE THE OCCUPIERS. THIS DISTURBETH ME.
AND HERE TO ARGUE IN FAVOR OF CONTINUING THE OCCUPATION: REPUBLICAN SPEAKER OF THE HOUSE DENNIS HASTERT.
Sunday Morning Political Show
BOB, I WAKE UP EVERY MORNING, GET ON MY KNEES, AND THANK THE LORD THAT MEN LIKE GEORGE WASHINGTON ARE NOT IN CHARGE OF OUR GOVERNMENT.
WHAT HO, SCOUNDREL! ART THOU CHALLENGING ME TO A DUEL?
GEORGE WASHINGTON WANTS US TO CUT AND RUN.
DARRIN BELL

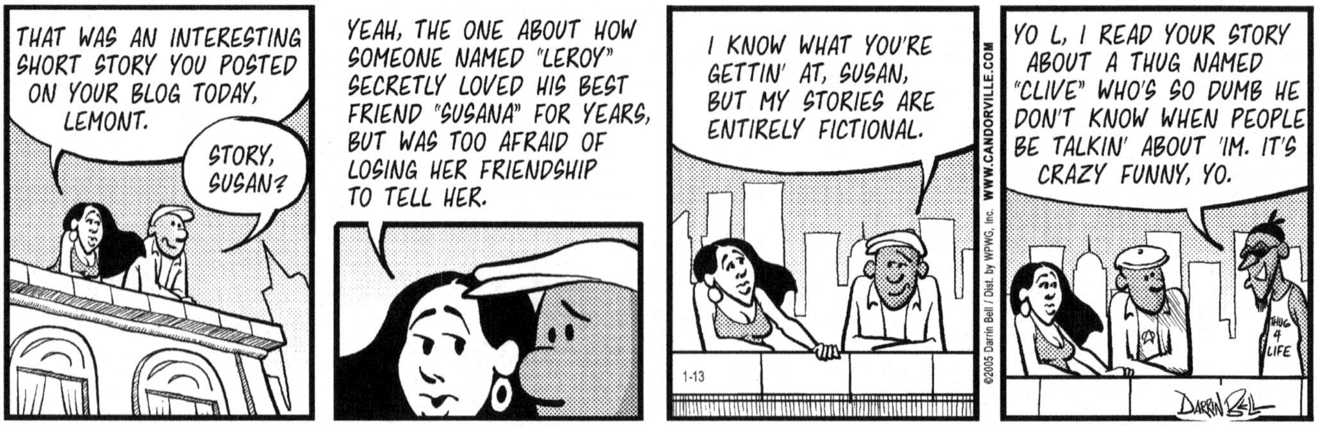
THAT WAS AN INTERESTING SHORT STORY YOU POSTED ON YOUR BLOG TODAY, LEMONT.
STORY, SUSAN?
YEAH, THE ONE ABOUT HOW SOMEONE NAMED "LEROY" SECRETLY LOVED HIS BEST FRIEND "SUSANA" FOR YEARS, BUT WAS TOO AFRAID OF LOSING HER FRIENDSHIP TO TELL HER.
I KNOW WHAT YOU'RE GETTIN' AT, SUSAN, BUT MY STORIES ARE ENTIRELY FICTIONAL.
1-13
©2005 Darrin Bell / Dist. by WPWG, Inc. WWW.CANDORVILLE.COM
YO L, I READ YOUR STORY ABOUT A THUG NAMED "CLIVE" WHO'S SO DUMB HE DON'T KNOW WHEN PEOPLE BE TALKIN' ABOUT 'IM. IT'S CRAZY FUNNY, YO.
THUG 4 LIFE
DARRIN BELL

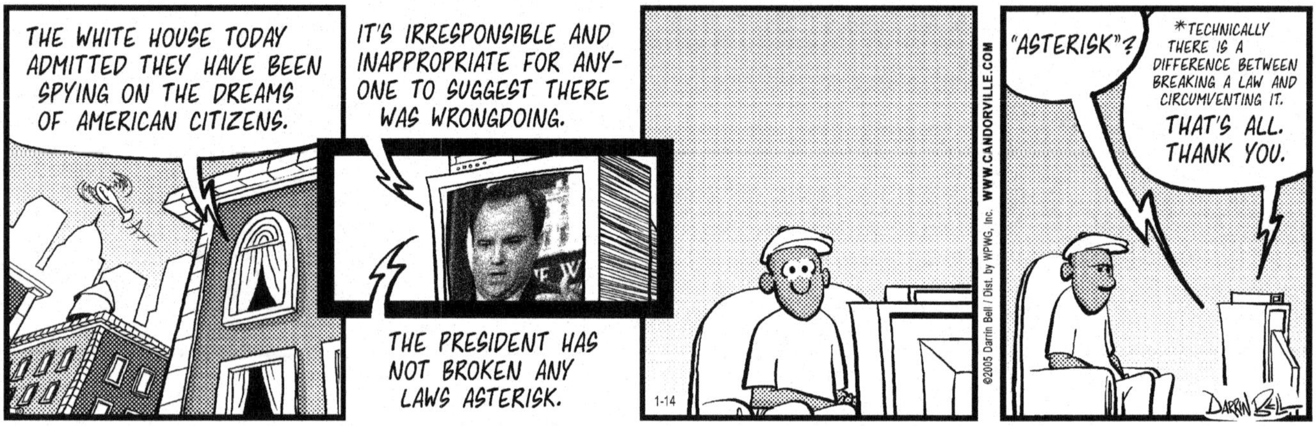
THE WHITE HOUSE TODAY ADMITTED THEY HAVE BEEN SPYING ON THE DREAMS OF AMERICAN CITIZENS.
IT'S IRRESPONSIBLE AND INAPPROPRIATE FOR ANY-ONE TO SUGGEST THERE WAS WRONGDOING.
THE PRESIDENT HAS NOT BROKEN ANY LAWS ASTERISK.
1-14
©2005 Darrin Bell / Dist. by WPWG, Inc. WWW.CANDORVILLE.COM
"ASTERISK"?
*TECHNICALLY THERE IS A DIFFERENCE BETWEEN BREAKING A LAW AND CIRCUMVENTING IT.
THAT'S ALL. THANK YOU.
DARRIN BELL

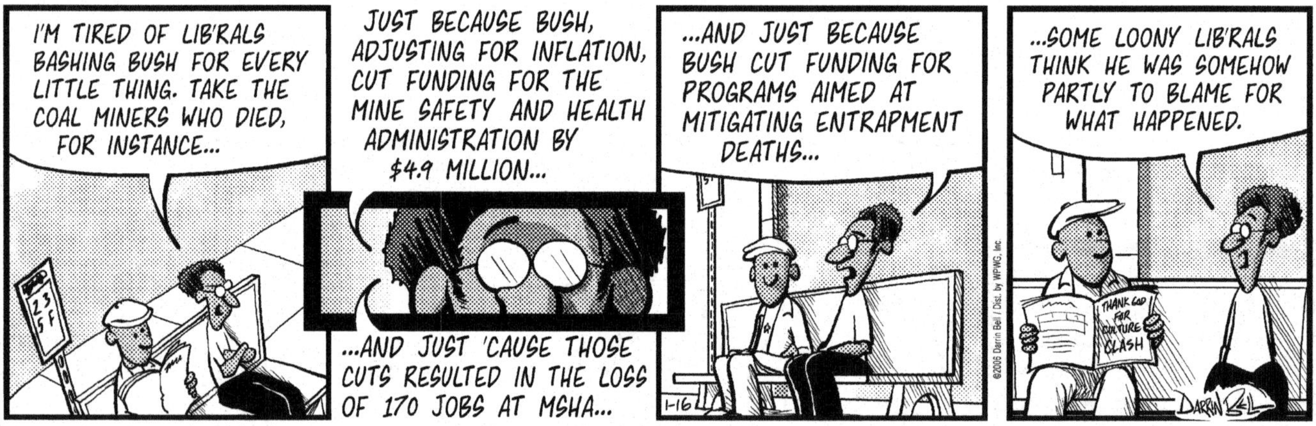
I'M TIRED OF LIB'RALS BASHING BUSH FOR EVERY LITTLE THING. TAKE THE COAL MINERS WHO DIED, FOR INSTANCE...
JUST BECAUSE BUSH, ADJUSTING FOR INFLATION, CUT FUNDING FOR THE MINE SAFETY AND HEALTH ADMINISTRATION BY $4.9 MILLION...
...AND JUST 'CAUSE THOSE CUTS RESULTED IN THE LOSS OF 170 JOBS AT MSHA...
...AND JUST BECAUSE BUSH CUT FUNDING FOR PROGRAMS AIMED AT MITIGATING ENTRAPMENT DEATHS...
1-16
©2006 Darrin Bell / Dist. by WPWG, Inc
...SOME LOONY LIB'RALS THINK HE WAS SOMEHOW PARTLY TO BLAME FOR WHAT HAPPENED.
THANK GOD FOR CULTURE CLASH
DARRIN BELL

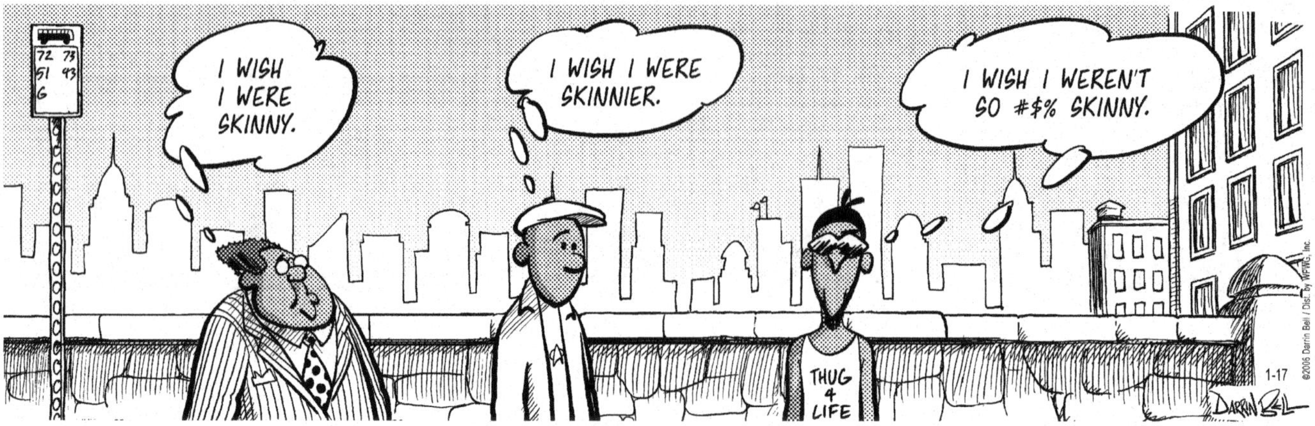
72 73
51 93
G
I WISH I WERE SKINNY.
I WISH I WERE SKINNIER.
I WISH I WEREN'T SO #$% SKINNY.
THUG 4 LIFE
1-17
©2006 Darrin Bell / Dist. by WPWG, Inc.
DARRIN BELL

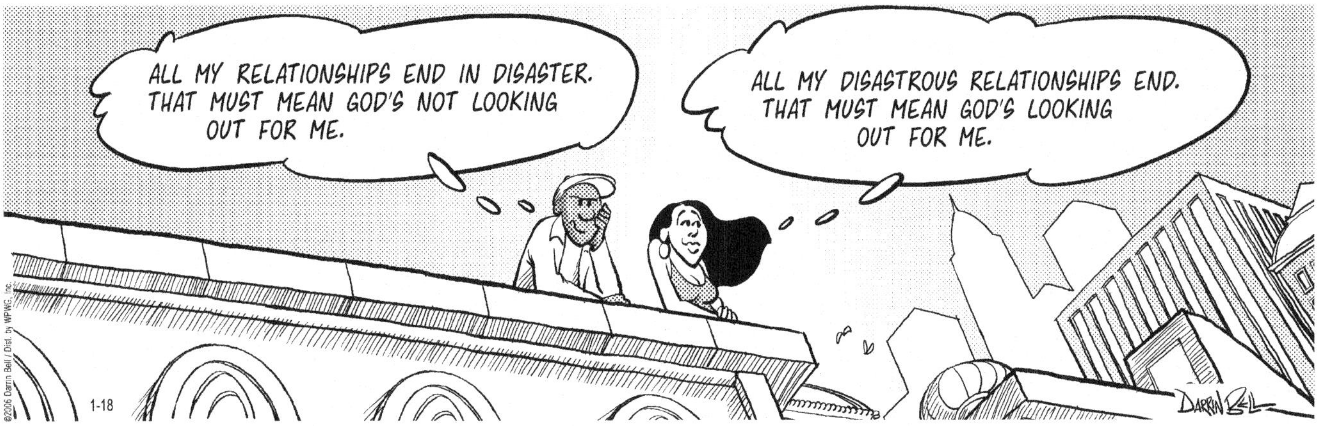
ALL MY RELATIONSHIPS END IN DISASTER. THAT MUST MEAN GOD'S NOT LOOKING OUT FOR ME.
ALL MY DISASTROUS RELATIONSHIPS END. THAT MUST MEAN GOD'S LOOKING OUT FOR ME.
©2006 Darrin Bell / Dist. by WPWG, Inc.
1-18
DARRIN BELL

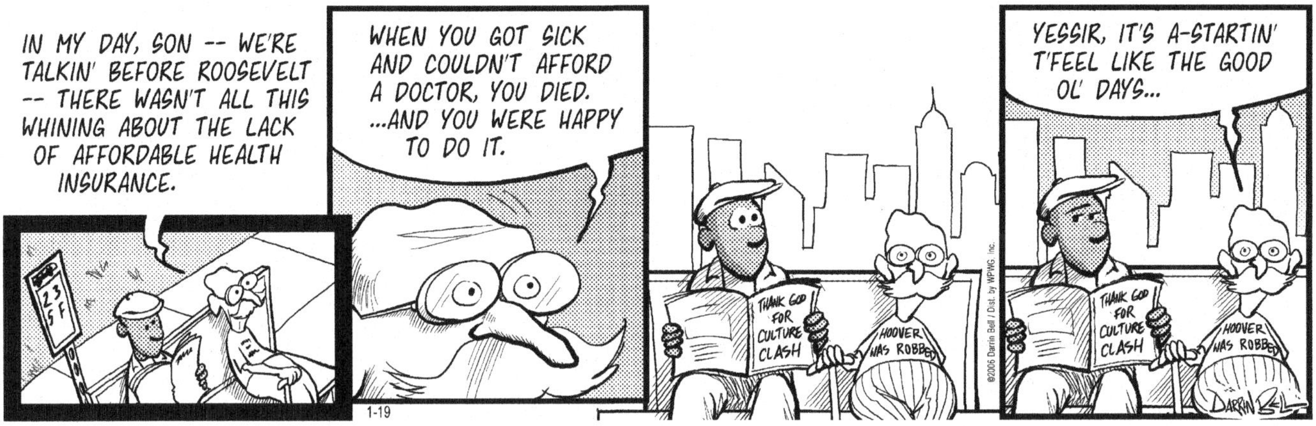
IN MY DAY, SON -- WE'RE TALKIN' BEFORE ROOSEVELT -- THERE WASN'T ALL THIS WHINING ABOUT THE LACK OF AFFORDABLE HEALTH INSURANCE.
WHEN YOU GOT SICK AND COULDN'T AFFORD A DOCTOR, YOU DIED. ...AND YOU WERE HAPPY TO DO IT.
THANK GOD FOR CULTURE CLASH
HOOVER WAS ROBBED
YESSIR, IT'S A-STARTIN' T'FEEL LIKE THE GOOD OL' DAYS...
THANK GOD FOR CULTURE CLASH
HOOVER WAS ROBBED
©2006 Darrin Bell / Dist. by WPWG, Inc.
1-19
DARRIN BELL

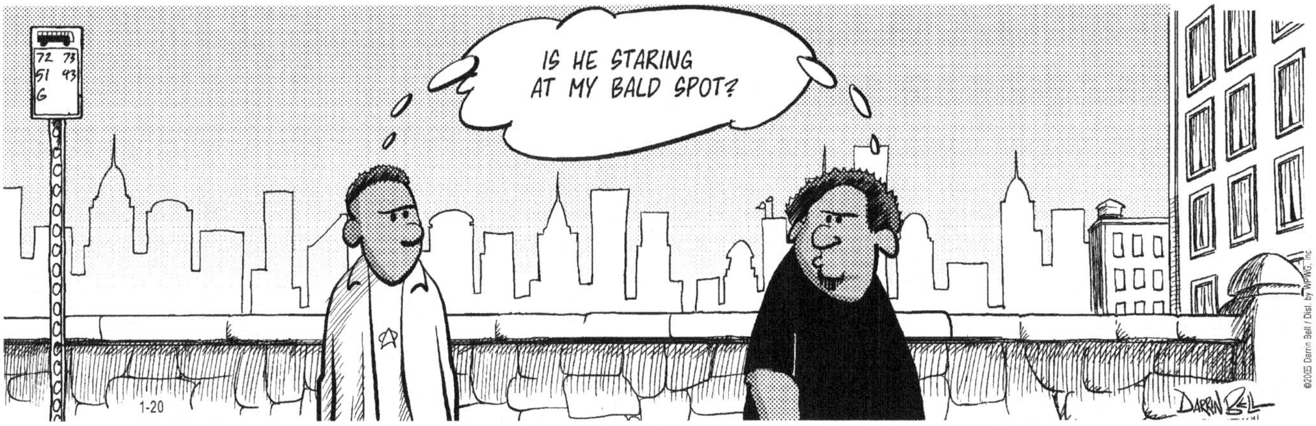
72 73
51 43
G
IS HE STARING AT MY BALD SPOT?
©2005 Darrin Bell / Dist. by WPWG, Inc.
1-20
DARRIN BELL

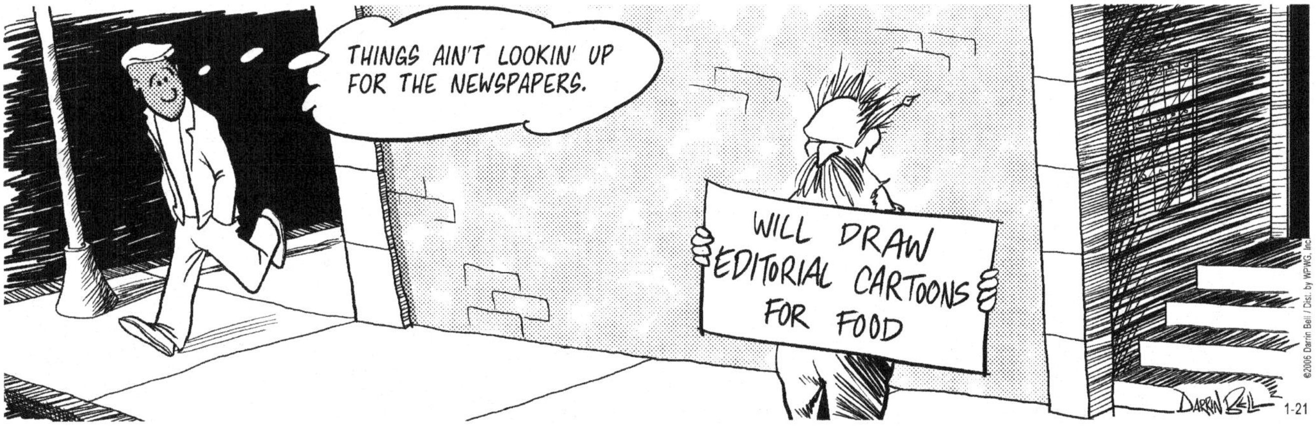
THINGS AIN'T LOOKIN' UP FOR THE NEWSPAPERS.
WILL DRAW EDITORIAL CARTOONS FOR FOOD
©2006 Darrin Bell / Dist. by WPWG, Inc.
DARRIN BELL
1-21

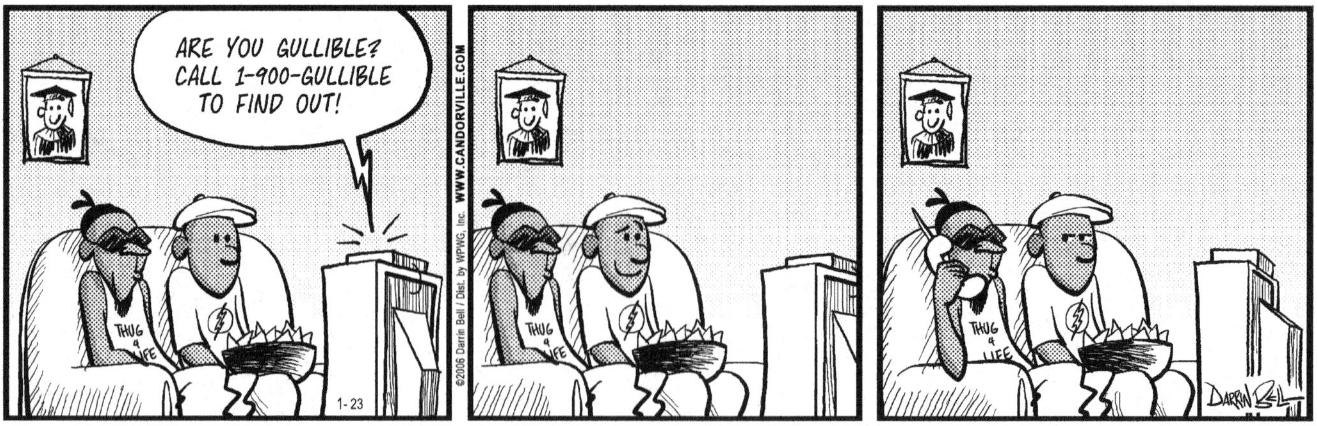
ARE YOU GULLIBLE? CALL 1-900-GULLIBLE TO FIND OUT!
THUG 4 LIFE
1-23
©2006 Darrin Bell / Dist. by WPWG, Inc. WWW.CANDORVILLE.COM
DARRIN BELL

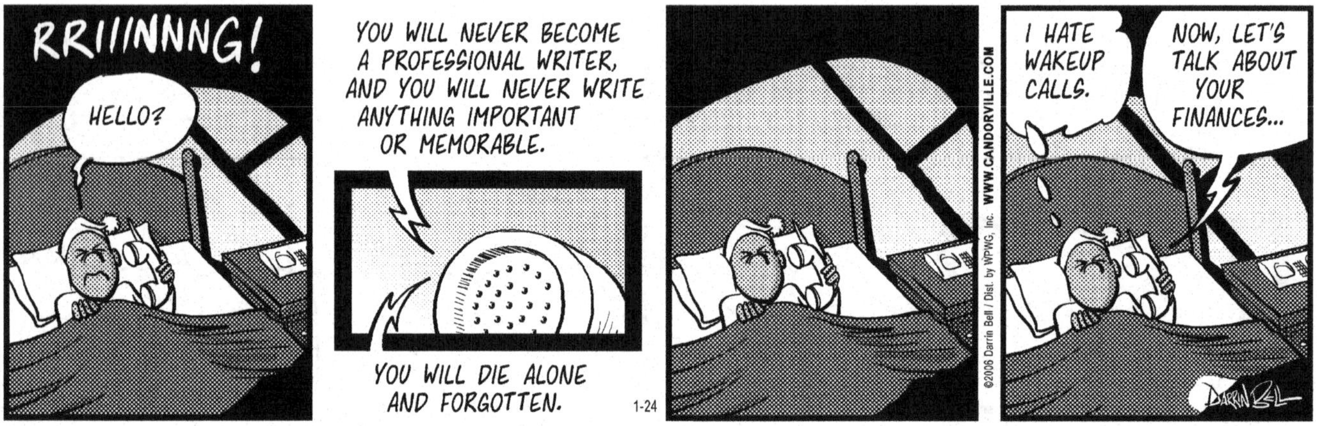
RRIIINNNG!
HELLO?
YOU WILL NEVER BECOME A PROFESSIONAL WRITER, AND YOU WILL NEVER WRITE ANYTHING IMPORTANT OR MEMORABLE.
YOU WILL DIE ALONE AND FORGOTTEN.
1-24
©2006 Darrin Bell / Dist. by WPWG, Inc. WWW.CANDORVILLE.COM
I HATE WAKEUP CALLS.
NOW, LET'S TALK ABOUT YOUR FINANCES...
DARRIN BELL

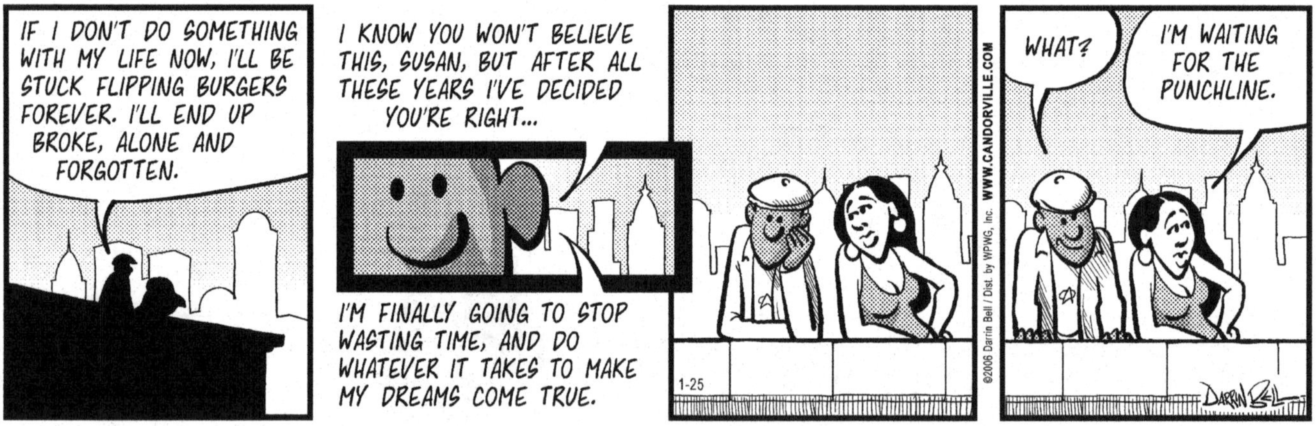
IF I DON'T DO SOMETHING WITH MY LIFE NOW, I'LL BE STUCK FLIPPING BURGERS FOREVER. I'LL END UP BROKE, ALONE AND FORGOTTEN.
I KNOW YOU WON'T BELIEVE THIS, SUSAN, BUT AFTER ALL THESE YEARS I'VE DECIDED YOU'RE RIGHT...
I'M FINALLY GOING TO STOP WASTING TIME, AND DO WHATEVER IT TAKES TO MAKE MY DREAMS COME TRUE.
1-25
©2006 Darrin Bell / Dist. by WPWG, Inc. WWW.CANDORVILLE.COM
WHAT?
I'M WAITING FOR THE PUNCHLINE.
DARRIN BELL

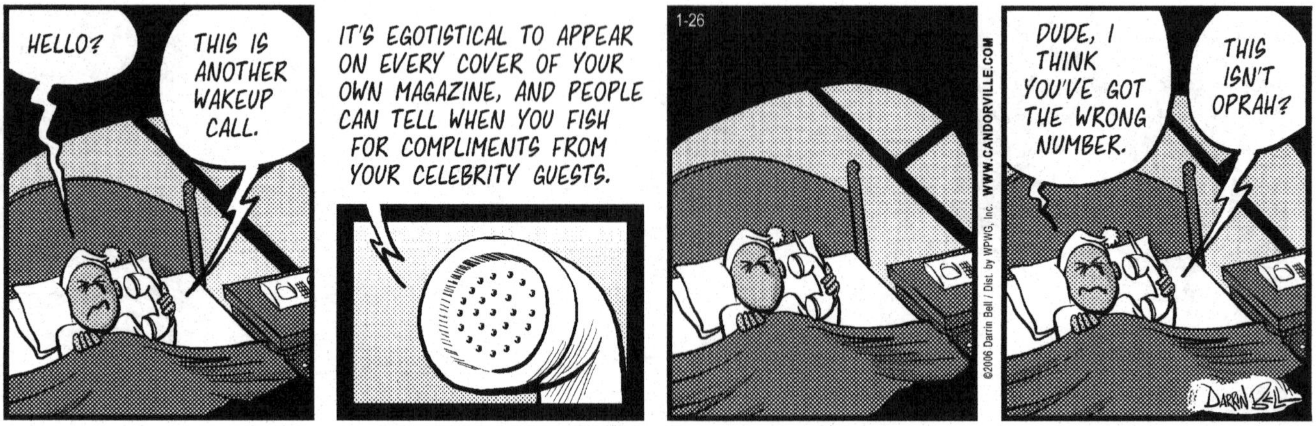
HELLO?
THIS IS ANOTHER WAKEUP CALL.
IT'S EGOTISTICAL TO APPEAR ON EVERY COVER OF YOUR OWN MAGAZINE, AND PEOPLE CAN TELL WHEN YOU FISH FOR COMPLIMENTS FROM YOUR CELEBRITY GUESTS.
1-26
©2006 Darrin Bell / Dist. by WPWG, Inc. WWW.CANDORVILLE.COM
DUDE, I THINK YOU'VE GOT THE WRONG NUMBER.
THIS ISN'T OPRAH?
DARRIN BELL

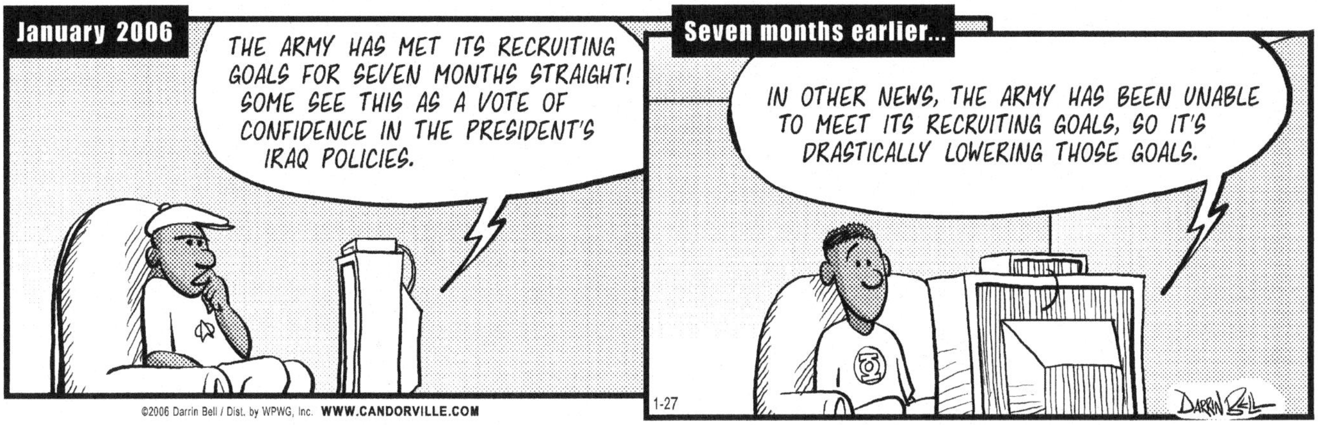
January 2006
THE ARMY HAS MET ITS RECRUITING GOALS FOR SEVEN MONTHS STRAIGHT! SOME SEE THIS AS A VOTE OF CONFIDENCE IN THE PRESIDENT'S IRAQ POLICIES.
Seven months earlier...
IN OTHER NEWS, THE ARMY HAS BEEN UNABLE TO MEET ITS RECRUITING GOALS, SO IT'S DRASTICALLY LOWERING THOSE GOALS.
©2006 Darrin Bell / Dist. by WPWG, Inc. WWW.CANDORVILLE.COM
1-27
DARRIN BELL

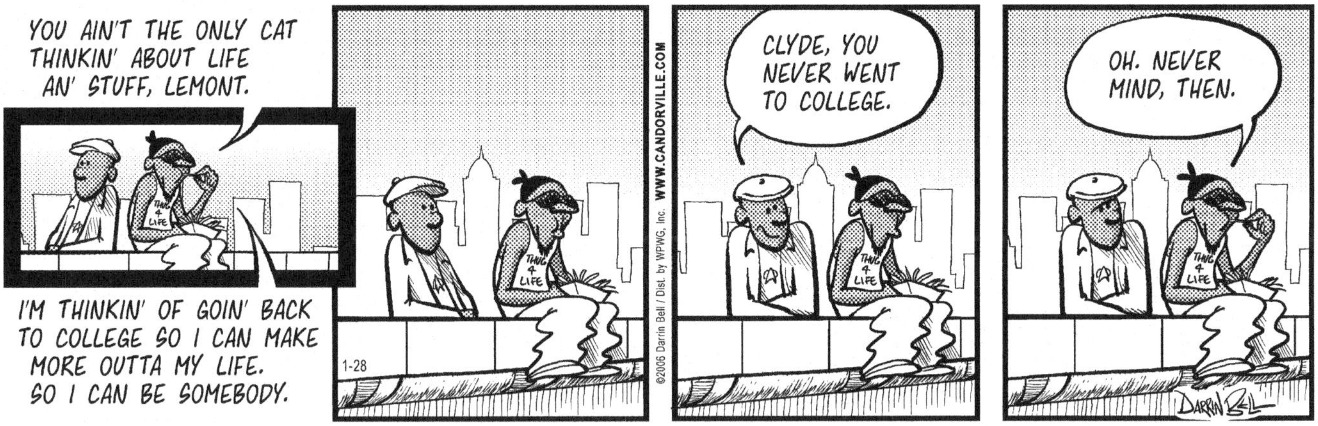
YOU AIN'T THE ONLY CAT THINKIN' ABOUT LIFE AN' STUFF, LEMONT.
I'M THINKIN' OF GOIN' BACK TO COLLEGE SO I CAN MAKE MORE OUTTA MY LIFE. SO I CAN BE SOMEBODY.
1-28
©2006 Darrin Bell / Dist. by WPWG, Inc. WWW.CANDORVILLE.COM
CLYDE, YOU NEVER WENT TO COLLEGE.
OH. NEVER MIND, THEN.
DARRIN BELL

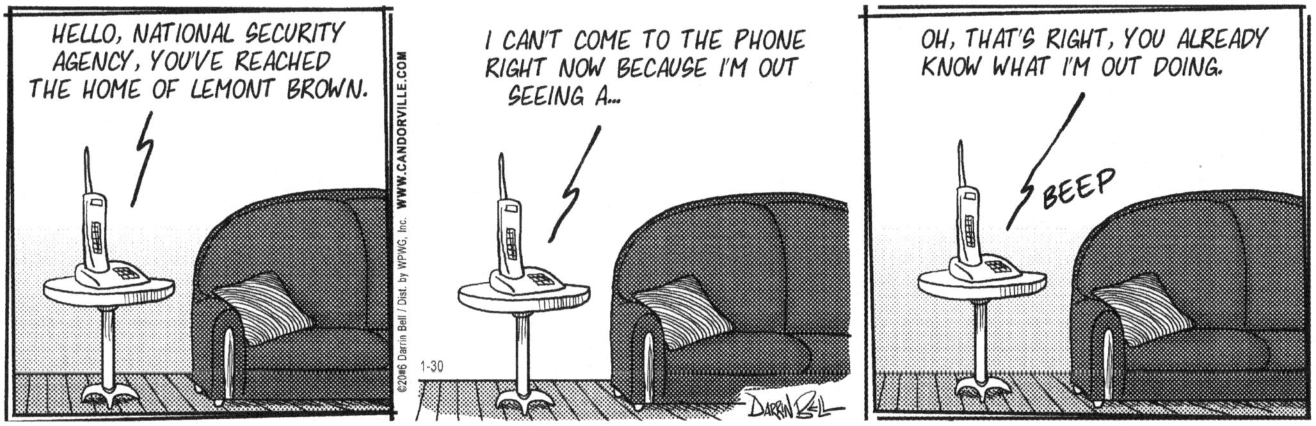
HELLO, NATIONAL SECURITY AGENCY, YOU'VE REACHED THE HOME OF LEMONT BROWN.
©2006 Darrin Bell / Dist. by WPWG, Inc. WWW.CANDORVILLE.COM
I CAN'T COME TO THE PHONE RIGHT NOW BECAUSE I'M OUT SEEING A...
1-30
DARRIN BELL
OH, THAT'S RIGHT, YOU ALREADY KNOW WHAT I'M OUT DOING.
BEEP

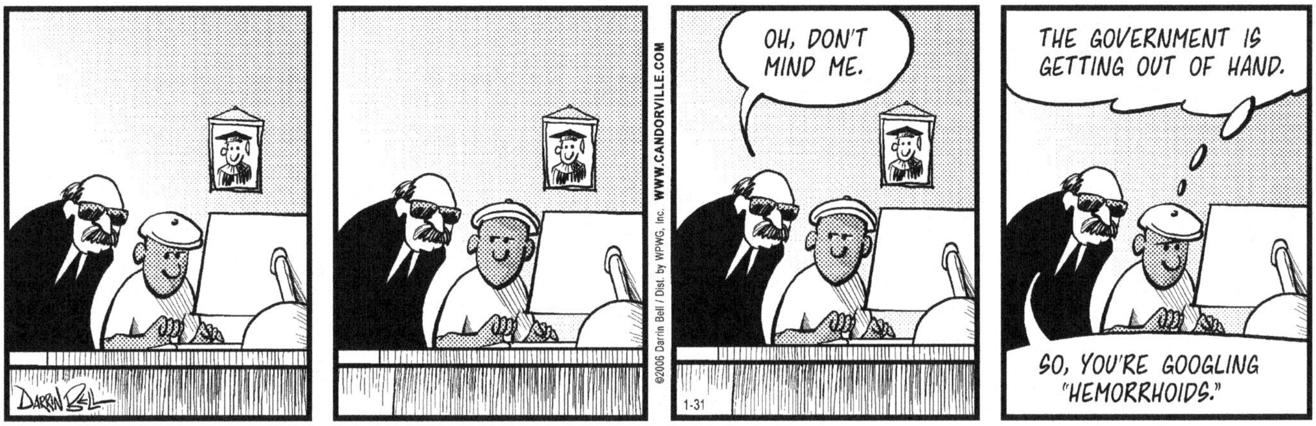
DARRIN BELL
©2006 Darrin Bell / Dist. by WPWG, Inc. WWW.CANDORVILLE.COM
OH, DON'T MIND ME.
1-31
THE GOVERNMENT IS GETTING OUT OF HAND.
SO, YOU'RE GOOGLING "HEMORRHOIDS."

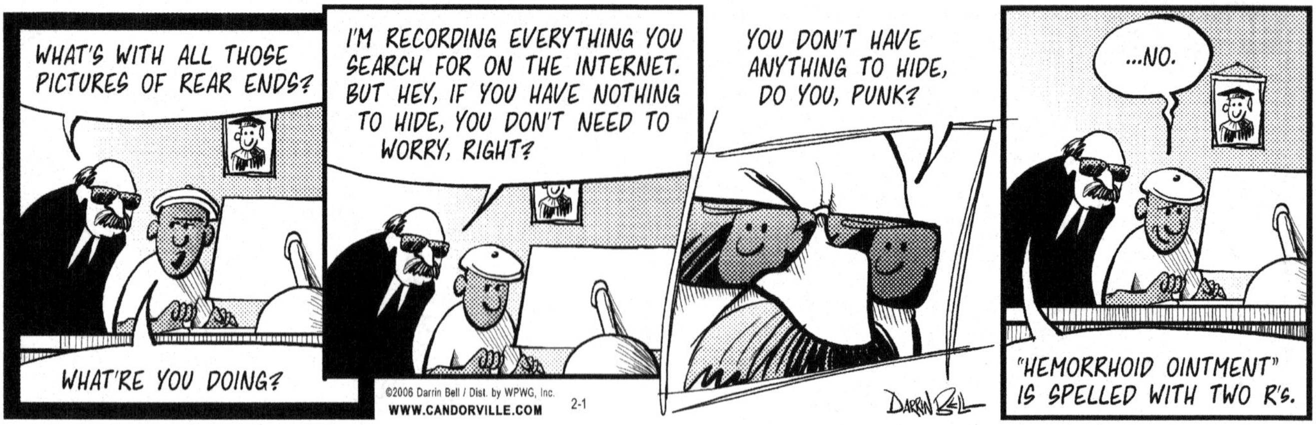
WHAT'S WITH ALL THOSE PICTURES OF REAR ENDS?
WHAT'RE YOU DOING?
I'M RECORDING EVERYTHING YOU SEARCH FOR ON THE INTERNET. BUT HEY, IF YOU HAVE NOTHING TO HIDE, YOU DON'T NEED TO WORRY, RIGHT?
©2006 Darrin Bell / Dist. by WPWG, Inc.
WWW.CANDORVILLE.COM
2-1
YOU DON'T HAVE ANYTHING TO HIDE, DO YOU, PUNK?
DARRIN BELL
...NO.
"HEMORRHOID OINTMENT" IS SPELLED WITH TWO R'S.

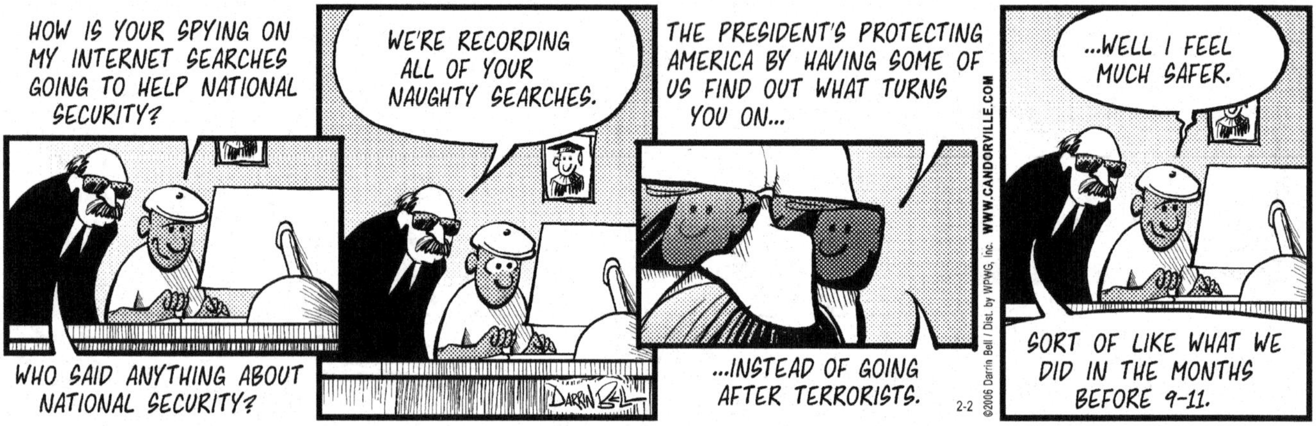
HOW IS YOUR SPYING ON MY INTERNET SEARCHES GOING TO HELP NATIONAL SECURITY?
WHO SAID ANYTHING ABOUT NATIONAL SECURITY?
WE'RE RECORDING ALL OF YOUR NAUGHTY SEARCHES.
DARRIN BELL
THE PRESIDENT'S PROTECTING AMERICA BY HAVING SOME OF US FIND OUT WHAT TURNS YOU ON...
...INSTEAD OF GOING AFTER TERRORISTS.
2-2
©2006 Darrin Bell / Dist. by WPWG, Inc. WWW.CANDORVILLE.COM
...WELL I FEEL MUCH SAFER.
SORT OF LIKE WHAT WE DID IN THE MONTHS BEFORE 9-11.

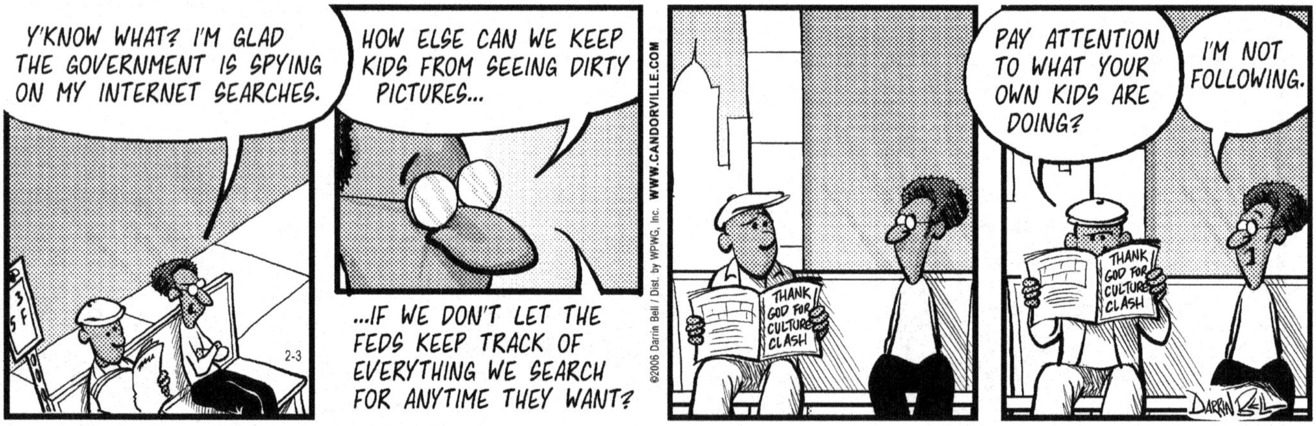
Y'KNOW WHAT? I'M GLAD THE GOVERNMENT IS SPYING ON MY INTERNET SEARCHES.
2-3
HOW ELSE CAN WE KEEP KIDS FROM SEEING DIRTY PICTURES...
...IF WE DON'T LET THE FEDS KEEP TRACK OF EVERYTHING WE SEARCH FOR ANYTIME THEY WANT?
©2006 Darrin Bell / Dist. by WPWG, Inc. WWW.CANDORVILLE.COM
THANK GOD FOR CULTURE CLASH
PAY ATTENTION TO WHAT YOUR OWN KIDS ARE DOING?
I'M NOT FOLLOWING.
DARRIN BELL

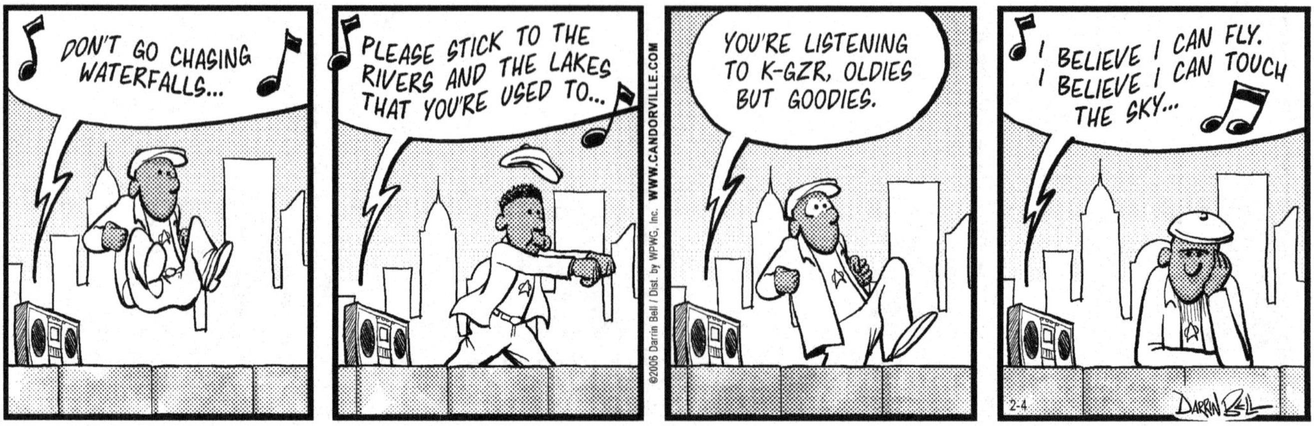
DON'T GO CHASING WATERFALLS...
PLEASE STICK TO THE RIVERS AND THE LAKES THAT YOU'RE USED TO...
©2006 Darrin Bell / Dist. by WPWG, Inc. WWW.CANDORVILLE.COM
YOU'RE LISTENING TO K-GZR, OLDIES BUT GOODIES.
I BELIEVE I CAN FLY. I BELIEVE I CAN TOUCH THE SKY...
2-4
DARRIN BELL

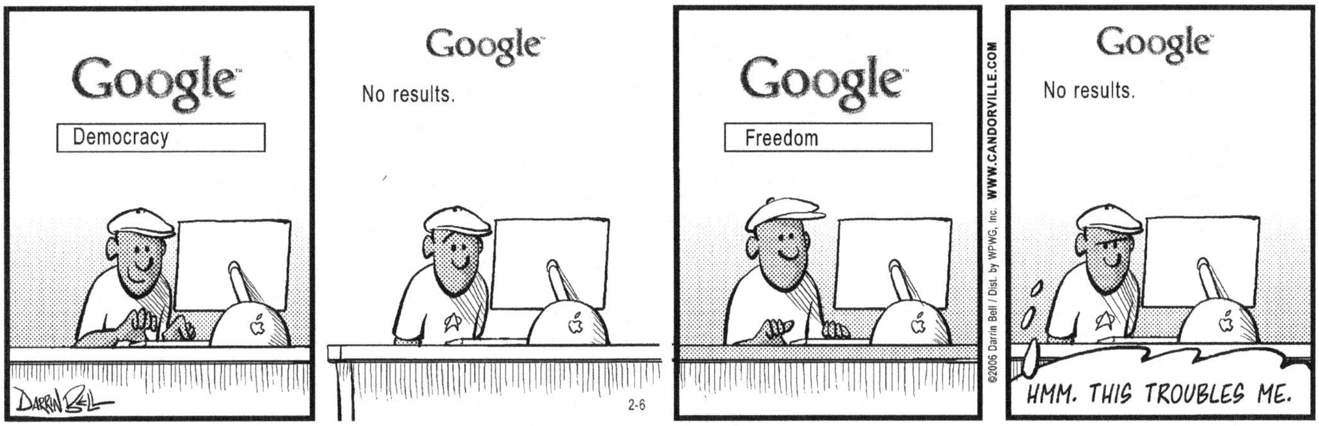
Google
Democracy
Google
No results.
Google
Freedom
Google
No results.
HMM. THIS TROUBLES ME.
DARRIN BELL
2-6
©2006 Darrin Bell / Dist. by WPWG, Inc. WWW.CANDORVILLE.COM

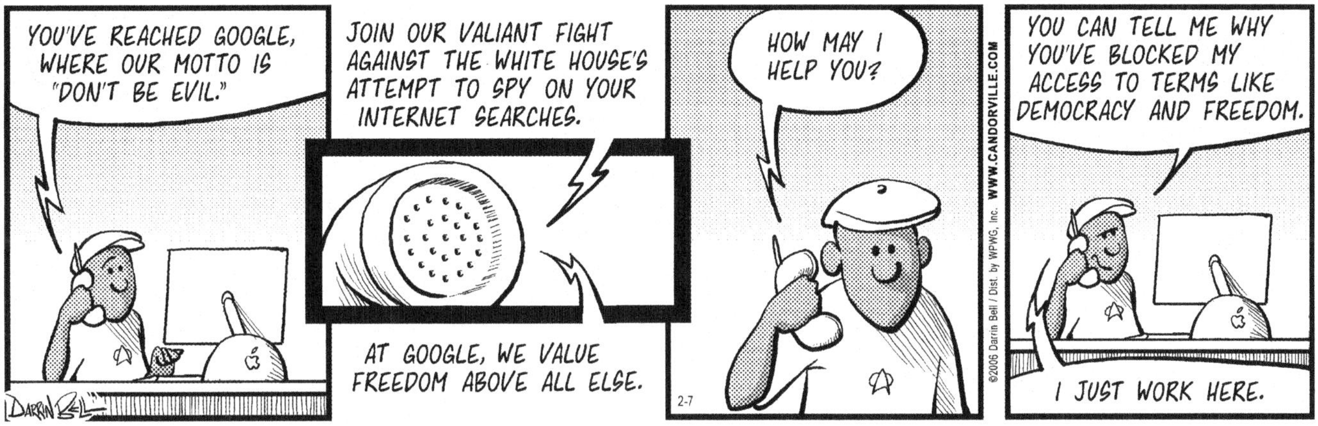
YOU'VE REACHED GOOGLE, WHERE OUR MOTTO IS "DON'T BE EVIL."
JOIN OUR VALIANT FIGHT AGAINST THE WHITE HOUSE'S ATTEMPT TO SPY ON YOUR INTERNET SEARCHES.
AT GOOGLE, WE VALUE FREEDOM ABOVE ALL ELSE.
HOW MAY I HELP YOU?
YOU CAN TELL ME WHY YOU'VE BLOCKED MY ACCESS TO TERMS LIKE DEMOCRACY AND FREEDOM.
I JUST WORK HERE.
DARRIN BELL
2-7
©2006 Darrin Bell / Dist. by WPWG, Inc. WWW.CANDORVILLE.COM

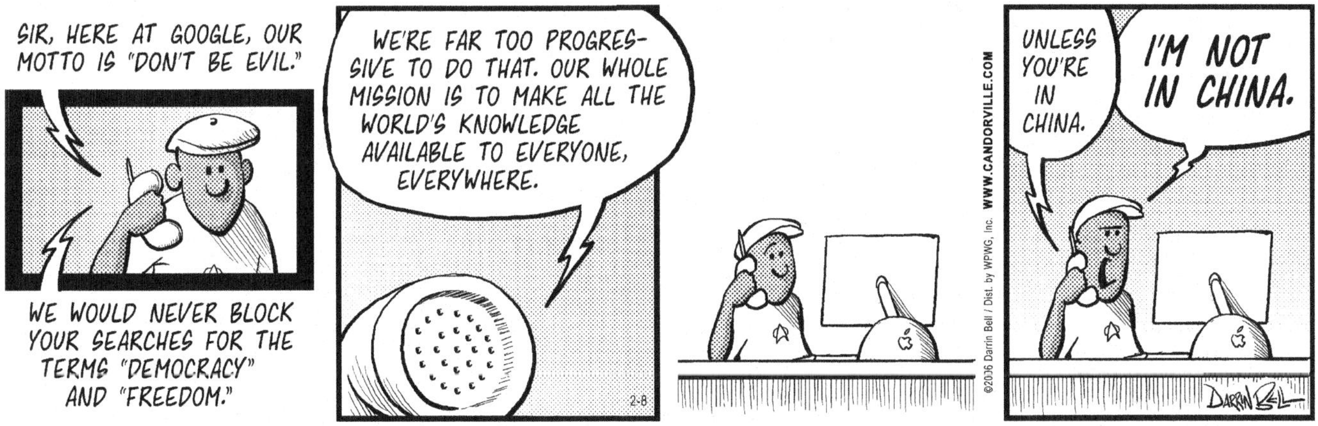
SIR, HERE AT GOOGLE, OUR MOTTO IS "DON'T BE EVIL."
WE WOULD NEVER BLOCK YOUR SEARCHES FOR THE TERMS "DEMOCRACY" AND "FREEDOM."
WE'RE FAR TOO PROGRES-SIVE TO DO THAT. OUR WHOLE MISSION IS TO MAKE ALL THE WORLD'S KNOWLEDGE AVAILABLE TO EVERYONE, EVERYWHERE.
UNLESS YOU'RE IN CHINA.
I'M NOT IN CHINA.
2-8
DARRIN BELL
©2006 Darrin Bell / Dist. by WPWG, Inc. WWW.CANDORVILLE.COM

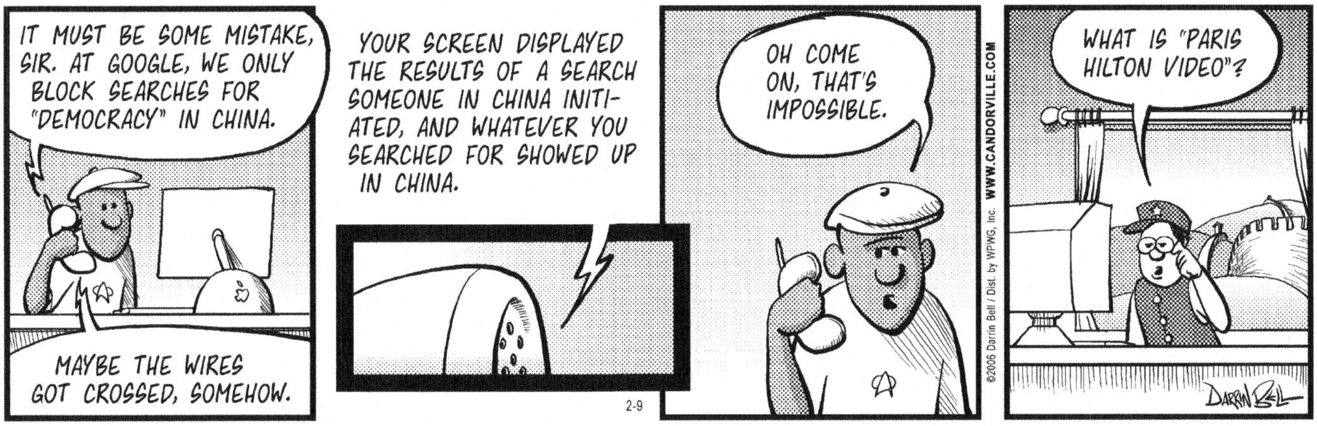
IT MUST BE SOME MISTAKE, SIR. AT GOOGLE, WE ONLY BLOCK SEARCHES FOR "DEMOCRACY" IN CHINA.
MAYBE THE WIRES GOT CROSSED, SOMEHOW.
YOUR SCREEN DISPLAYED THE RESULTS OF A SEARCH SOMEONE IN CHINA INITI-ATED, AND WHATEVER YOU SEARCHED FOR SHOWED UP IN CHINA.
OH COME ON, THAT'S IMPOSSIBLE.
WHAT IS "PARIS HILTON VIDEO"?
2-9
DARRIN BELL
©2006 Darrin Bell / Dist. by WPWG, Inc. WWW.CANDORVILLE.COM

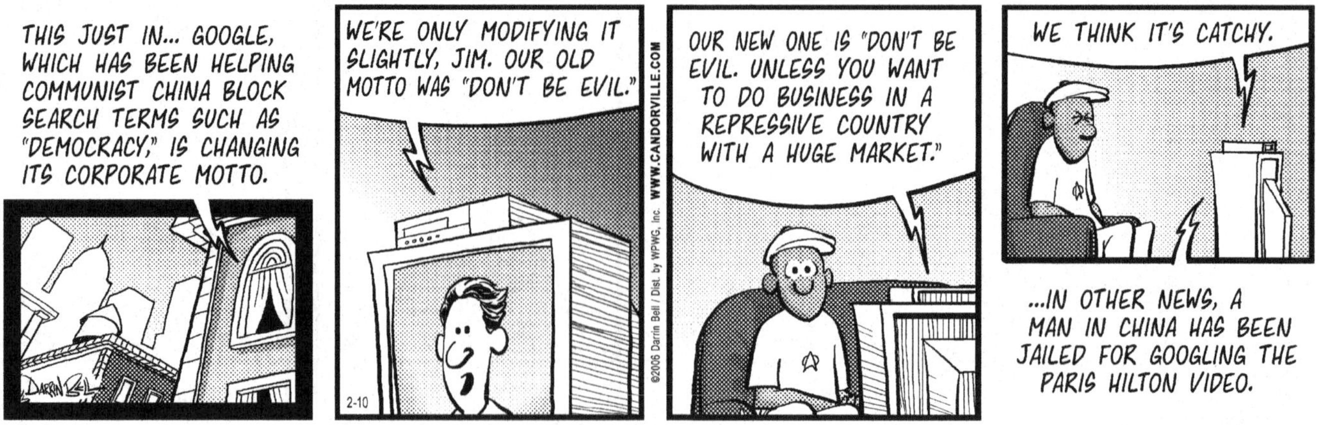
THIS JUST IN... GOOGLE, WHICH HAS BEEN HELPING COMMUNIST CHINA BLOCK SEARCH TERMS SUCH AS "DEMOCRACY," IS CHANGING ITS CORPORATE MOTTO.
DARRIN BELL
WE'RE ONLY MODIFYING IT SLIGHTLY, JIM. OUR OLD MOTTO WAS "DON'T BE EVIL."
2-10
©2006 Darrin Bell / Dist. by WPWG, Inc. WWW.CANDORVILLE.COM
OUR NEW ONE IS "DON'T BE EVIL. UNLESS YOU WANT TO DO BUSINESS IN A REPRESSIVE COUNTRY WITH A HUGE MARKET."
WE THINK IT'S CATCHY.
...IN OTHER NEWS, A MAN IN CHINA HAS BEEN JAILED FOR GOOGLING THE PARIS HILTON VIDEO.

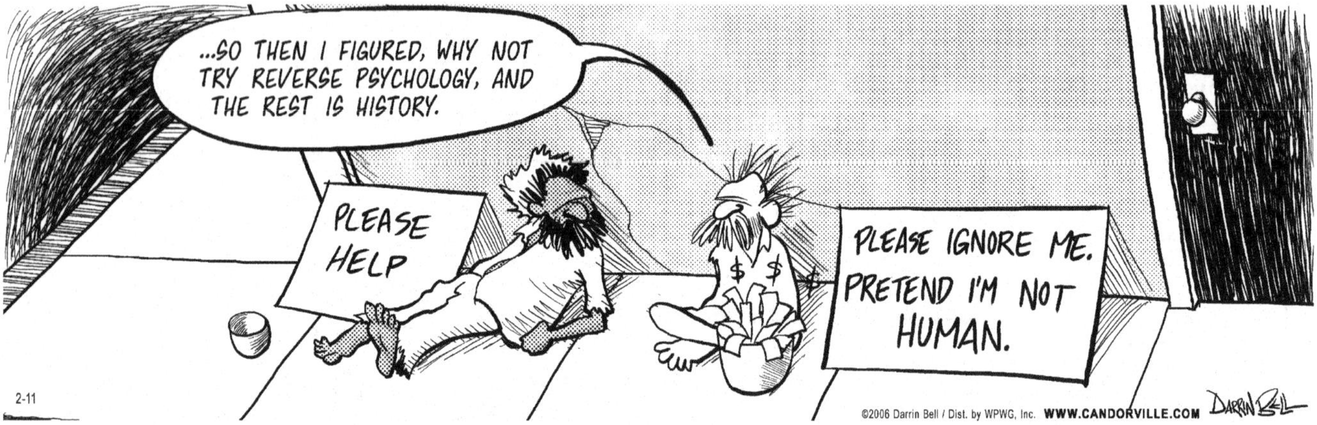
...SO THEN I FIGURED, WHY NOT TRY REVERSE PSYCHOLOGY, AND THE REST IS HISTORY.
PLEASE HELP
PLEASE IGNORE ME. PRETEND I'M NOT HUMAN.
2-11
©2006 Darrin Bell / Dist. by WPWG, Inc. WWW.CANDORVILLE.COM
DARRIN BELL

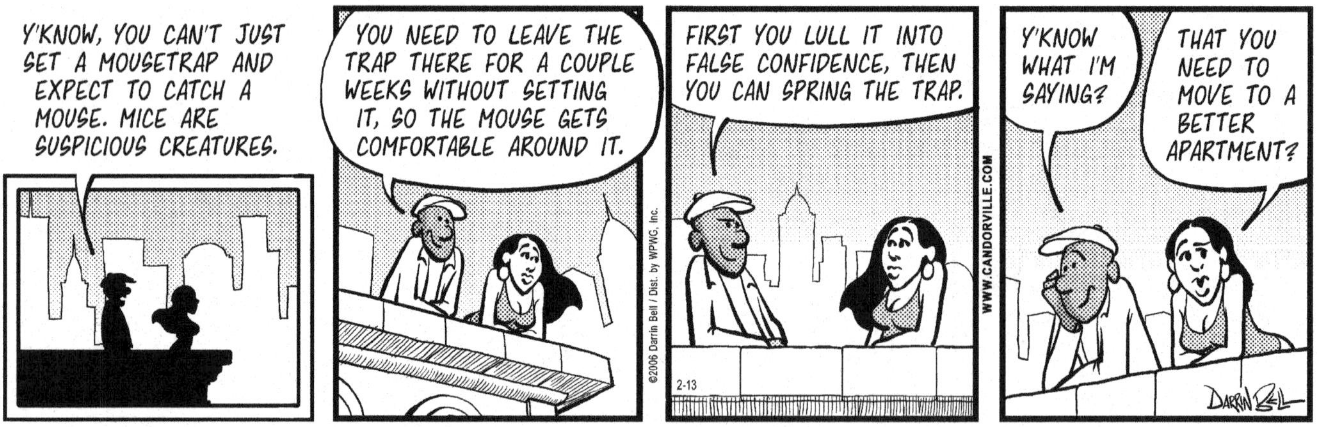
Y'KNOW, YOU CAN'T JUST SET A MOUSETRAP AND EXPECT TO CATCH A MOUSE. MICE ARE SUSPICIOUS CREATURES.
YOU NEED TO LEAVE THE TRAP THERE FOR A COUPLE WEEKS WITHOUT SETTING IT, SO THE MOUSE GETS COMFORTABLE AROUND IT.
©2006 Darrin Bell / Dist. by WPWG, Inc.
FIRST YOU LULL IT INTO FALSE CONFIDENCE, THEN YOU CAN SPRING THE TRAP.
2-13
WWW.CANDORVILLE.COM
Y'KNOW WHAT I'M SAYING?
THAT YOU NEED TO MOVE TO A BETTER APARTMENT?
DARRIN BELL

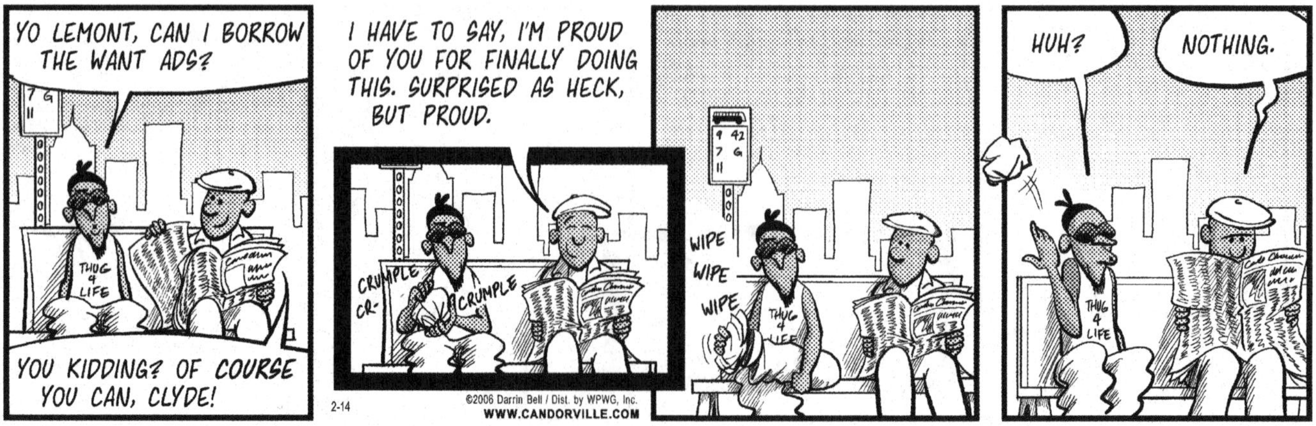
YO LEMONT, CAN I BORROW THE WANT ADS?
THUG 4 LIFE
YOU KIDDING? OF COURSE YOU CAN, CLYDE!
I HAVE TO SAY, I'M PROUD OF YOU FOR FINALLY DOING THIS. SURPRISED AS HECK, BUT PROUD.
CRUMPLE
CR-
CRUMPLE
2-14
©2006 Darrin Bell / Dist. by WPWG, Inc. WWW.CANDORVILLE.COM
WIPE
WIPE
WIPE
HUH?
NOTHING.

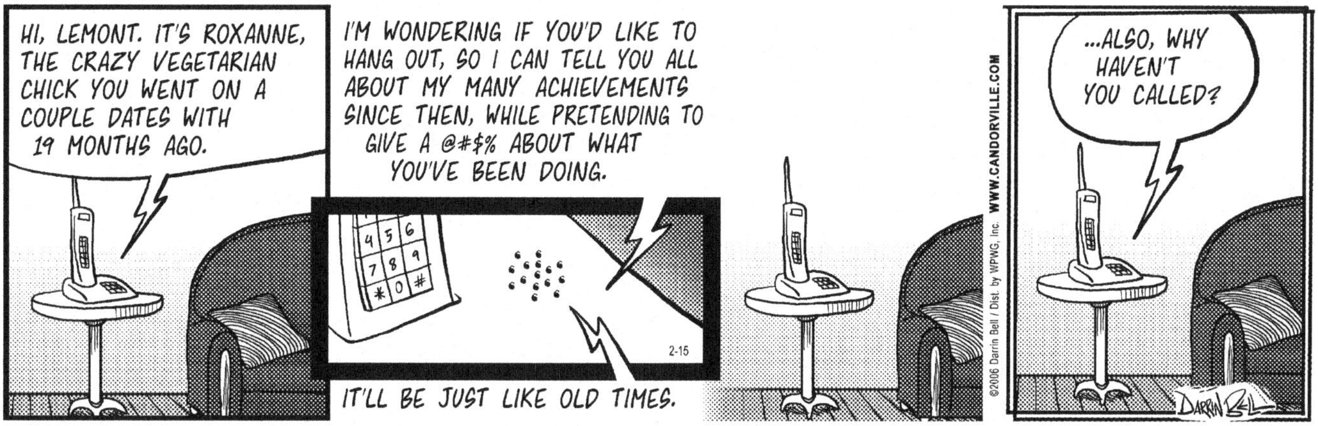
HI, LEMONT. IT'S ROXANNE, THE CRAZY VEGETARIAN CHICK YOU WENT ON A COUPLE DATES WITH 19 MONTHS AGO.
I'M WONDERING IF YOU'D LIKE TO HANG OUT, SO I CAN TELL YOU ALL ABOUT MY MANY ACHIEVEMENTS SINCE THEN, WHILE PRETENDING TO GIVE A @#$% ABOUT WHAT YOU'VE BEEN DOING.
IT'LL BE JUST LIKE OLD TIMES.
...ALSO, WHY HAVEN'T YOU CALLED?
2-15
©2006 Darrin Bell / Dist. by WPWG, Inc. WWW.CANDORVILLE.COM
DARRIN BELL

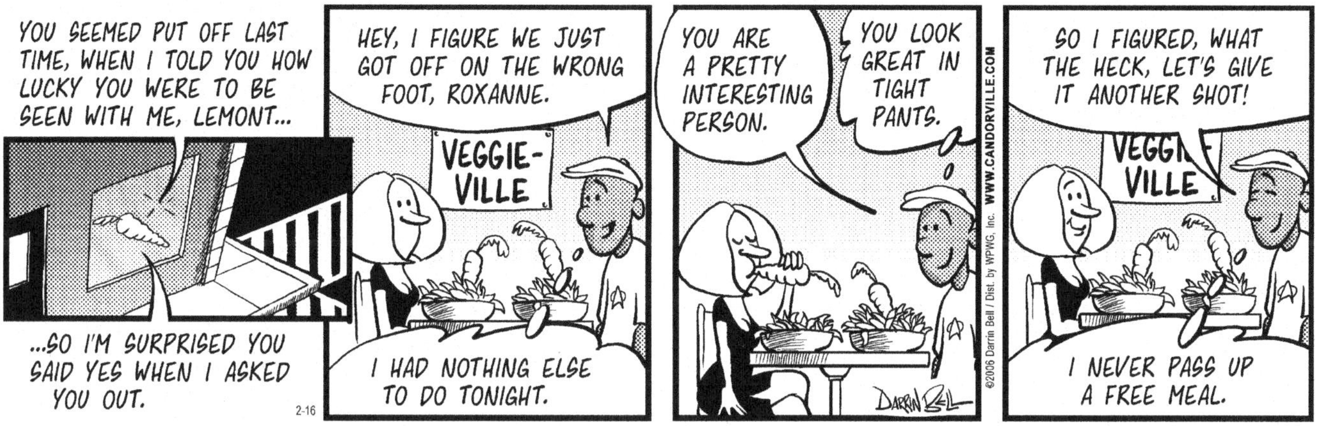
YOU SEEMED PUT OFF LAST TIME, WHEN I TOLD YOU HOW LUCKY YOU WERE TO BE SEEN WITH ME, LEMONT...
...SO I'M SURPRISED YOU SAID YES WHEN I ASKED YOU OUT.
2-16
HEY, I FIGURE WE JUST GOT OFF ON THE WRONG FOOT, ROXANNE.
VEGGIE-VILLE
I HAD NOTHING ELSE TO DO TONIGHT.
YOU ARE A PRETTY INTERESTING PERSON.
YOU LOOK GREAT IN TIGHT PANTS.
DARRIN BELL
©2006 Darrin Bell / Dist. by WPWG, Inc. WWW.CANDORVILLE.COM
SO I FIGURED, WHAT THE HECK, LET'S GIVE IT ANOTHER SHOT!
I NEVER PASS UP A FREE MEAL.

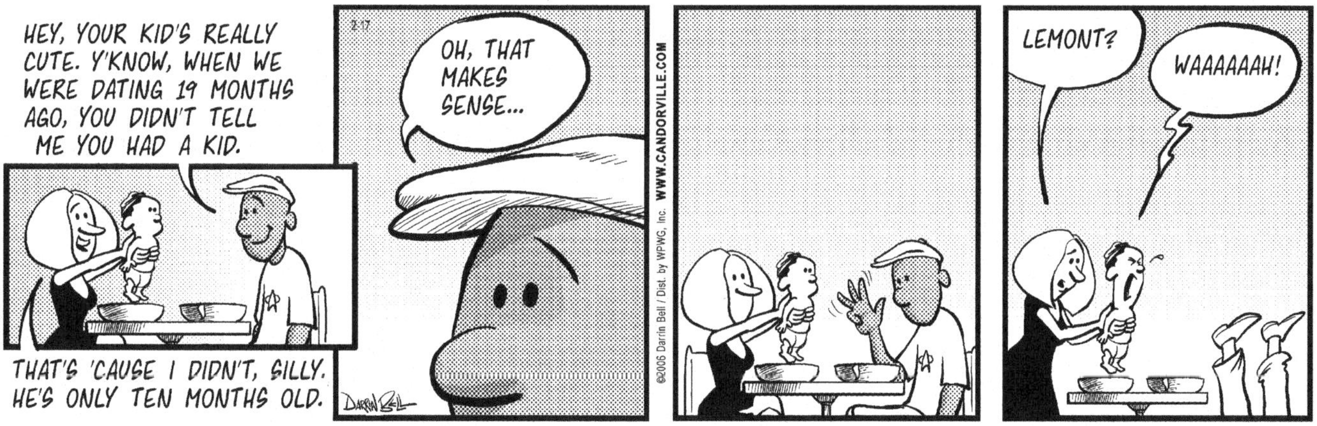
HEY, YOUR KID'S REALLY CUTE. Y'KNOW, WHEN WE WERE DATING 19 MONTHS AGO, YOU DIDN'T TELL ME YOU HAD A KID.
THAT'S 'CAUSE I DIDN'T, SILLY. HE'S ONLY TEN MONTHS OLD.
DARRIN BELL
2-17
OH, THAT MAKES SENSE...
©2006 Darrin Bell / Dist. by WPWG, Inc. WWW.CANDORVILLE.COM
LEMONT?
WAAAAAAH!

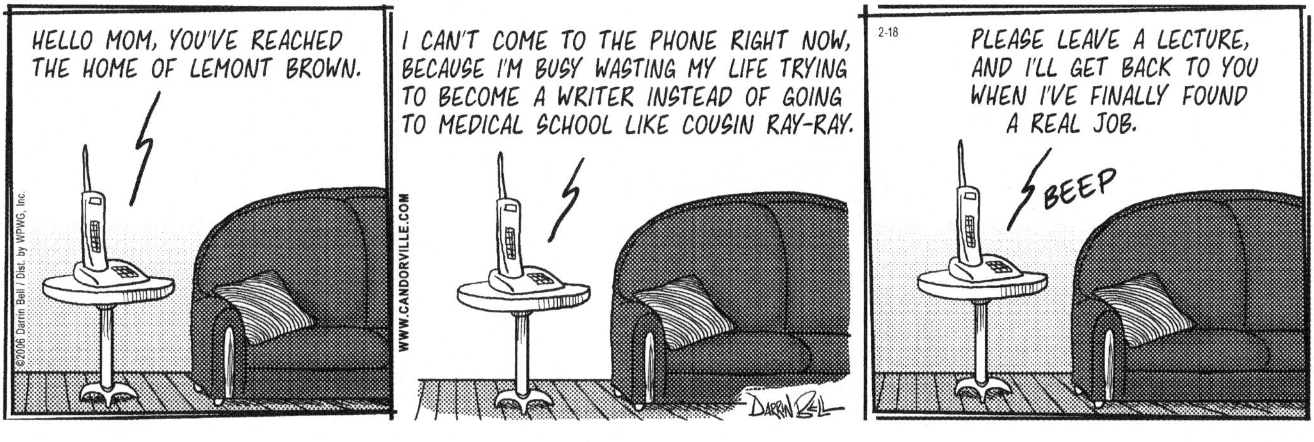
HELLO MOM, YOU'VE REACHED THE HOME OF LEMONT BROWN.
©2006 Darrin Bell / Dist. by WPWG, Inc.
I CAN'T COME TO THE PHONE RIGHT NOW, BECAUSE I'M BUSY WASTING MY LIFE TRYING TO BECOME A WRITER INSTEAD OF GOING TO MEDICAL SCHOOL LIKE COUSIN RAY-RAY.
WWW.CANDORVILLE.COM
DARRIN BELL
2-18
PLEASE LEAVE A LECTURE, AND I'LL GET BACK TO YOU WHEN I'VE FINALLY FOUND A REAL JOB.
BEEP

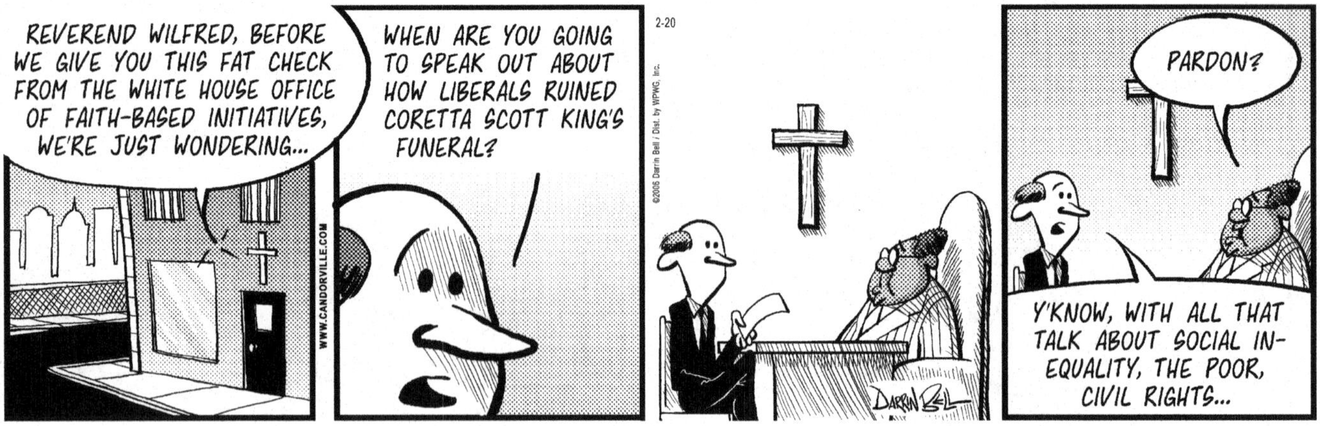
REVEREND WILFRED, BEFORE WE GIVE YOU THIS FAT CHECK FROM THE WHITE HOUSE OFFICE OF FAITH-BASED INITIATIVES, WE'RE JUST WONDERING...
WWW.CANDORVILLE.COM
WHEN ARE YOU GOING TO SPEAK OUT ABOUT HOW LIBERALS RUINED CORETTA SCOTT KING'S FUNERAL?
2-20
©2006 Darrin Bell / Dist. by WPWG, Inc.
DARRIN BELL
PARDON?
Y'KNOW, WITH ALL THAT TALK ABOUT SOCIAL IN-EQUALITY, THE POOR, CIVIL RIGHTS...

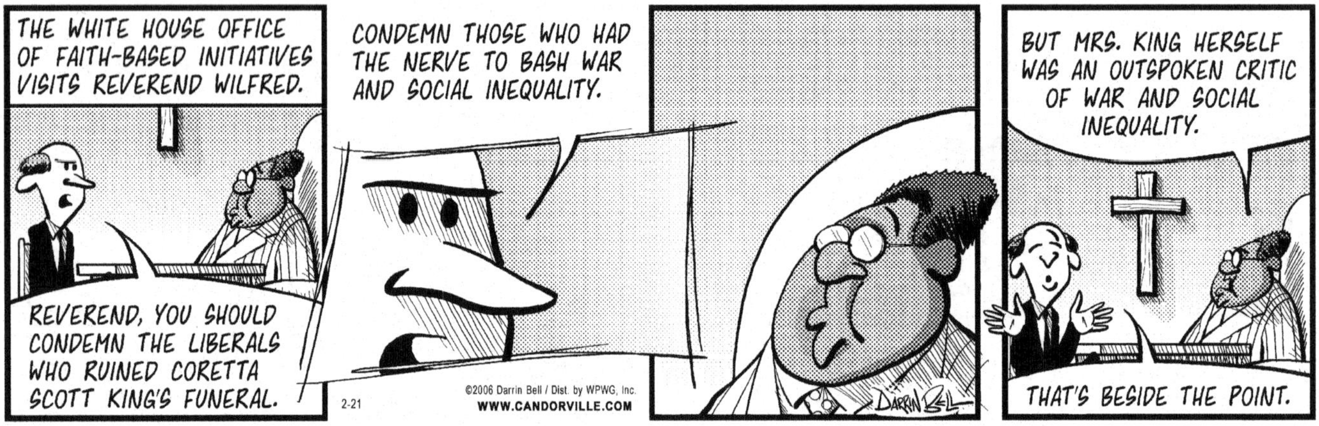
THE WHITE HOUSE OFFICE OF FAITH-BASED INITIATIVES VISITS REVEREND WILFRED.
REVEREND, YOU SHOULD CONDEMN THE LIBERALS WHO RUINED CORETTA SCOTT KING'S FUNERAL.
CONDEMN THOSE WHO HAD THE NERVE TO BASH WAR AND SOCIAL INEQUALITY.
2-21
©2006 Darrin Bell / Dist. by WPWG, Inc.
WWW.CANDORVILLE.COM
DARRIN BELL
BUT MRS. KING HERSELF WAS AN OUTSPOKEN CRITIC OF WAR AND SOCIAL INEQUALITY.
THAT'S BESIDE THE POINT.

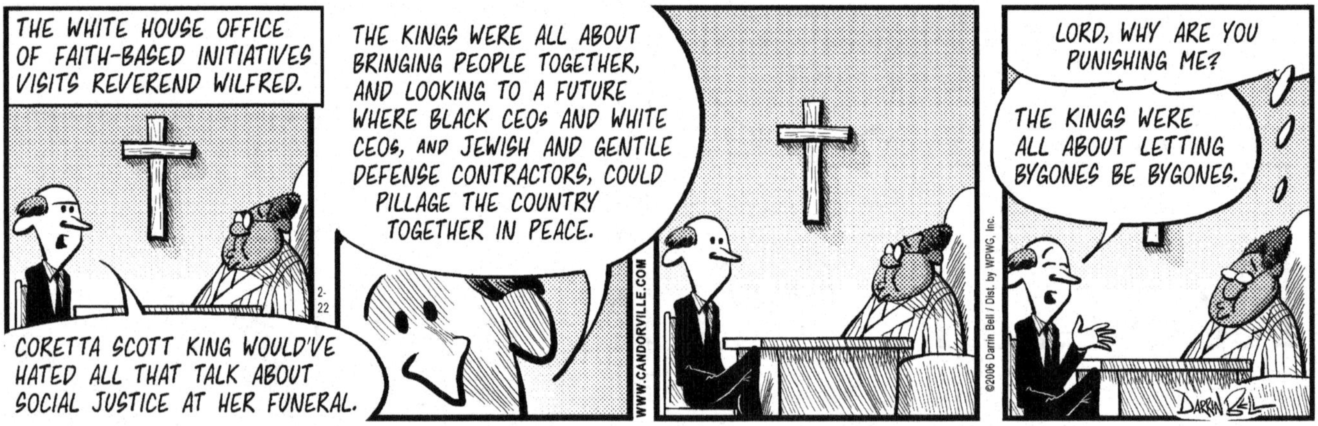
THE WHITE HOUSE OFFICE OF FAITH-BASED INITIATIVES VISITS REVEREND WILFRED.
CORETTA SCOTT KING WOULD'VE HATED ALL THAT TALK ABOUT SOCIAL JUSTICE AT HER FUNERAL.
2-22
THE KINGS WERE ALL ABOUT BRINGING PEOPLE TOGETHER, AND LOOKING TO A FUTURE WHERE BLACK CEOs AND WHITE CEOs, AND JEWISH AND GENTILE DEFENSE CONTRACTORS, COULD PILLAGE THE COUNTRY TOGETHER IN PEACE.
WWW.CANDORVILLE.COM
©2006 Darrin Bell / Dist. by WPWG, Inc.
LORD, WHY ARE YOU PUNISHING ME?
THE KINGS WERE ALL ABOUT LETTING BYGONES BE BYGONES.
DARRIN BELL

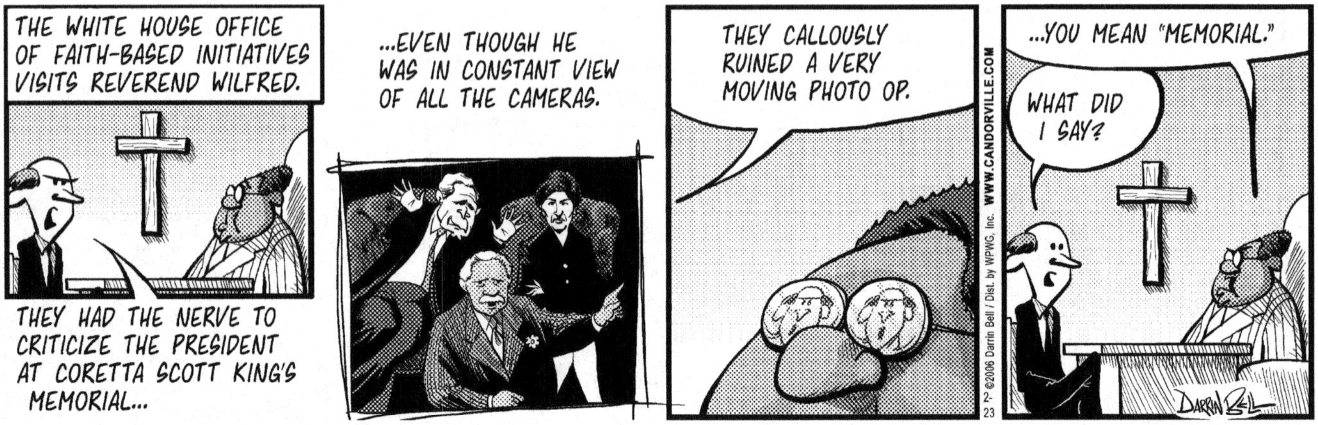
THE WHITE HOUSE OFFICE OF FAITH-BASED INITIATIVES VISITS REVEREND WILFRED.
THEY HAD THE NERVE TO CRITICIZE THE PRESIDENT AT CORETTA SCOTT KING'S MEMORIAL...
...EVEN THOUGH HE WAS IN CONSTANT VIEW OF ALL THE CAMERAS.
THEY CALLOUSLY RUINED A VERY MOVING PHOTO OP.
2-23
©2006 Darrin Bell / Dist. by WPWG, Inc.
WWW.CANDORVILLE.COM
...YOU MEAN "MEMORIAL."
WHAT DID I SAY?
DARRIN BELL

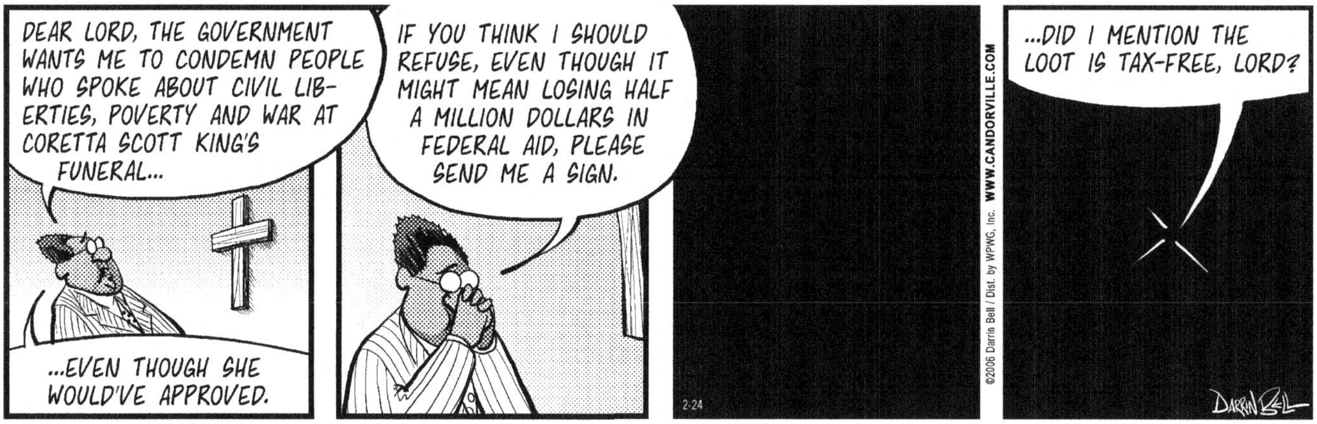

DEAR LORD, THE GOVERNMENT WANTS ME TO CONDEMN PEOPLE WHO SPOKE ABOUT CIVIL LIBERTIES, POVERTY AND WAR AT CORETTA SCOTT KING'S FUNERAL...
...EVEN THOUGH SHE WOULD'VE APPROVED.
IF YOU THINK I SHOULD REFUSE, EVEN THOUGH IT MIGHT MEAN LOSING HALF A MILLION DOLLARS IN FEDERAL AID, PLEASE SEND ME A SIGN.
2-24
©2006 Darrin Bell / Dist. by WPWG, Inc. WWW.CANDORVILLE.COM
...DID I MENTION THE LOOT IS TAX-FREE, LORD?
DARRIN BELL

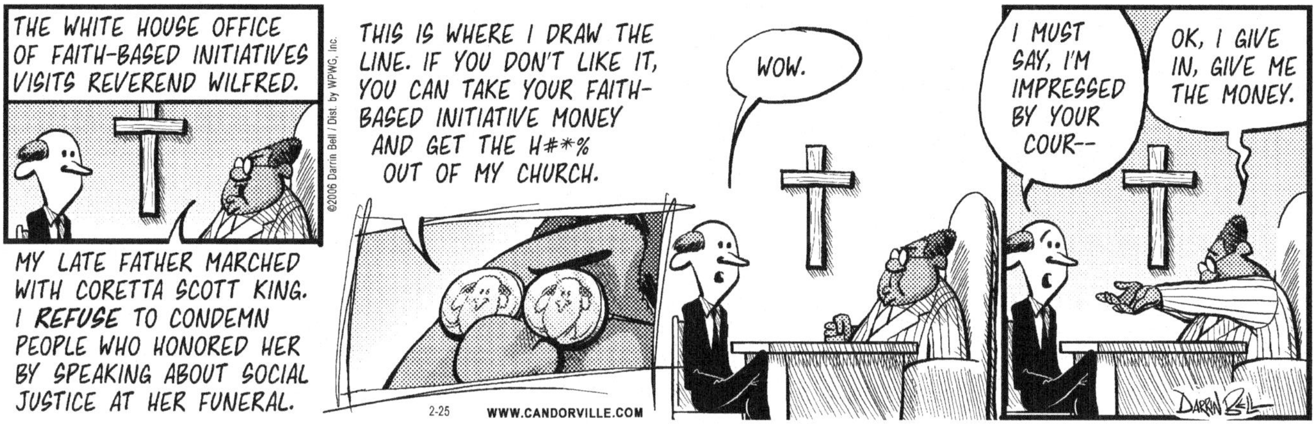

THE WHITE HOUSE OFFICE OF FAITH-BASED INITIATIVES VISITS REVEREND WILFRED.
©2006 Darrin Bell / Dist. by WPWG, Inc.
MY LATE FATHER MARCHED WITH CORETTA SCOTT KING. I **REFUSE** TO CONDEMN PEOPLE WHO HONORED HER BY SPEAKING ABOUT SOCIAL JUSTICE AT HER FUNERAL.
THIS IS WHERE I DRAW THE LINE. IF YOU DON'T LIKE IT, YOU CAN TAKE YOUR FAITH-BASED INITIATIVE MONEY AND GET THE H#*% OUT OF MY CHURCH.
2-25
WWW.CANDORVILLE.COM
WOW.
I MUST SAY, I'M IMPRESSED BY YOUR COUR--
OK, I GIVE IN, GIVE ME THE MONEY.
DARRIN BELL

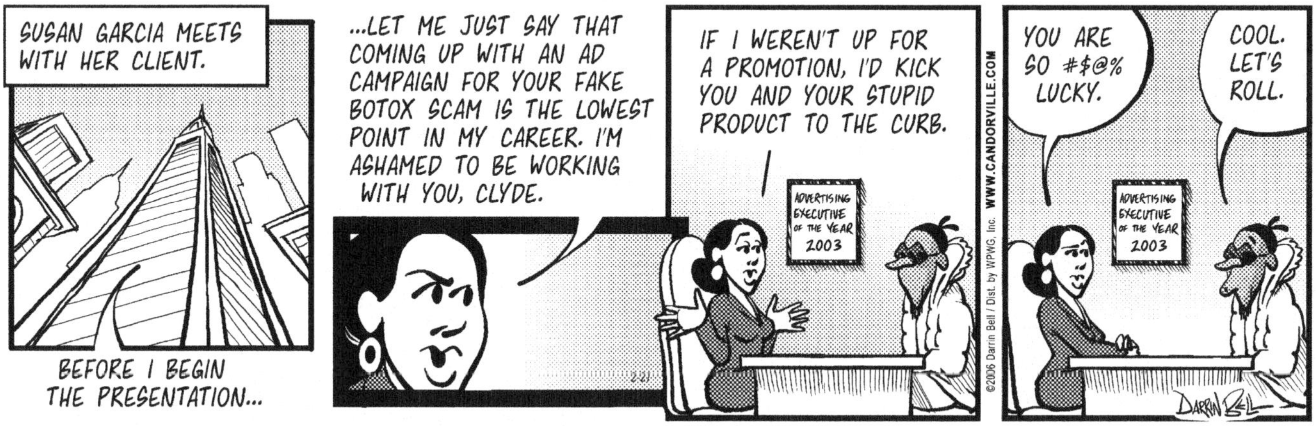

SUSAN GARCIA MEETS WITH HER CLIENT.
BEFORE I BEGIN THE PRESENTATION...
...LET ME JUST SAY THAT COMING UP WITH AN AD CAMPAIGN FOR YOUR FAKE BOTOX SCAM IS THE LOWEST POINT IN MY CAREER. I'M ASHAMED TO BE WORKING WITH YOU, CLYDE.
IF I WEREN'T UP FOR A PROMOTION, I'D KICK YOU AND YOUR STUPID PRODUCT TO THE CURB.
ADVERTISING EXECUTIVE OF THE YEAR 2003
©2006 Darrin Bell / Dist. by WPWG, Inc. WWW.CANDORVILLE.COM
YOU ARE SO #$@% LUCKY.
COOL. LET'S ROLL.
DARRIN BELL

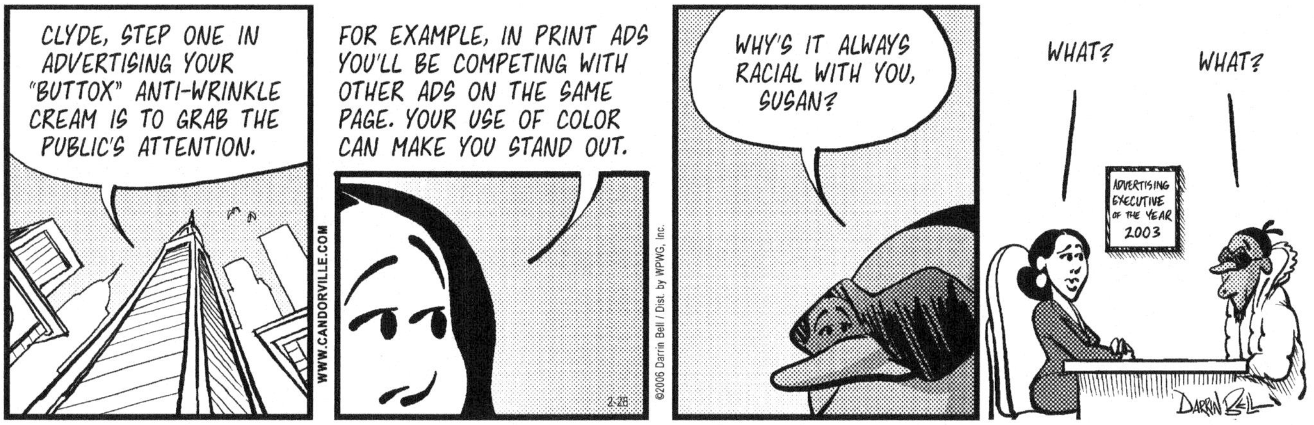

CLYDE, STEP ONE IN ADVERTISING YOUR "BUTTOX" ANTI-WRINKLE CREAM IS TO GRAB THE PUBLIC'S ATTENTION.
WWW.CANDORVILLE.COM
FOR EXAMPLE, IN PRINT ADS YOU'LL BE COMPETING WITH OTHER ADS ON THE SAME PAGE. YOUR USE OF COLOR CAN MAKE YOU STAND OUT.
2-28
©2006 Darrin Bell / Dist. by WPWG, Inc.
WHY'S IT ALWAYS RACIAL WITH YOU, SUSAN?
WHAT?
WHAT?
ADVERTISING EXECUTIVE OF THE YEAR 2003
DARRIN BELL

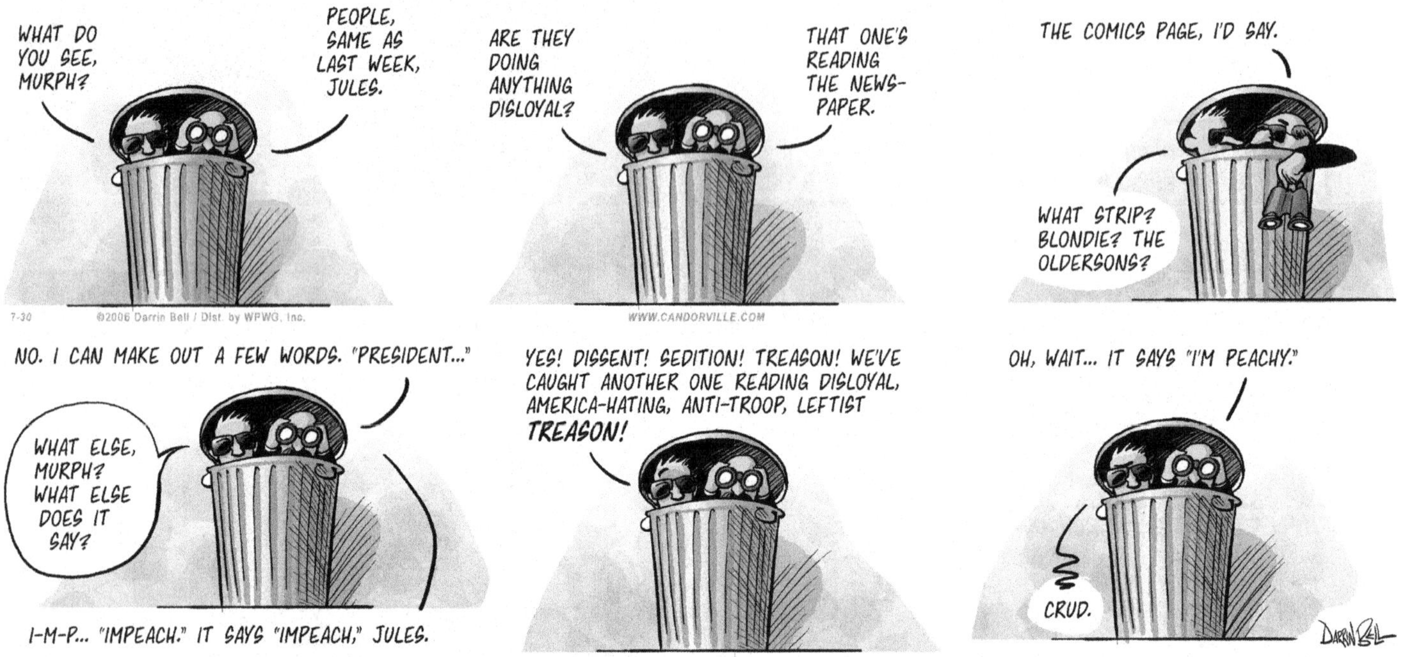
WHAT DO YOU SEE, MURPH?
PEOPLE, SAME AS LAST WEEK, JULES.
7-30
©2006 Darrin Bell / Dist. by WPWG, Inc.
ARE THEY DOING ANYTHING DISLOYAL?
THAT ONE'S READING THE NEWS-PAPER.
WWW.CANDORVILLE.COM
THE COMICS PAGE, I'D SAY.
WHAT STRIP? BLONDIE? THE OLDERSONS?
NO. I CAN MAKE OUT A FEW WORDS. "PRESIDENT..."
WHAT ELSE, MURPH? WHAT ELSE DOES IT SAY?
I-M-P... "IMPEACH." IT SAYS "IMPEACH," JULES.
YES! DISSENT! SEDITION! TREASON! WE'VE CAUGHT ANOTHER ONE READING DISLOYAL, AMERICA-HATING, ANTI-TROOP, LEFTIST TREASON!
OH, WAIT... IT SAYS "I'M PEACHY."
CRUD.
DARRIN BELL

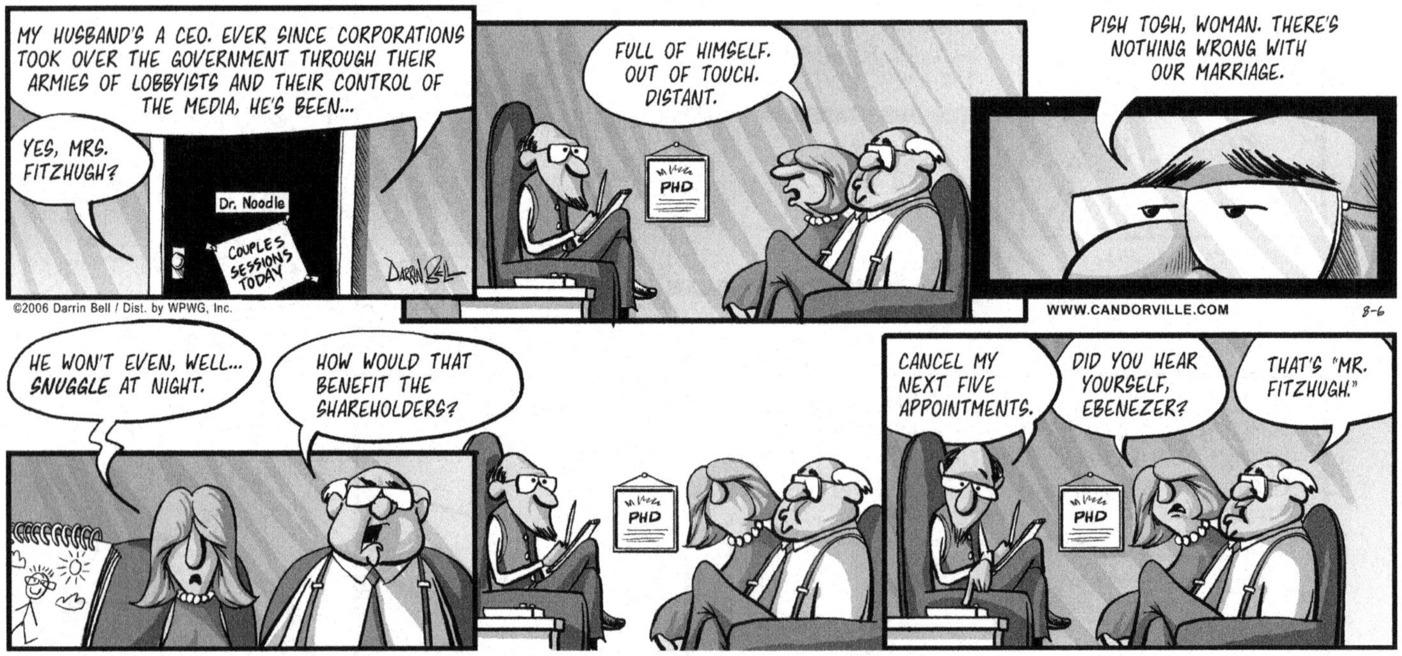
MY HUSBAND'S A CEO. EVER SINCE CORPORATIONS TOOK OVER THE GOVERNMENT THROUGH THEIR ARMIES OF LOBBYISTS AND THEIR CONTROL OF THE MEDIA, HE'S BEEN...
YES, MRS. FITZHUGH?
Dr. Noodle
COUPLES SESSIONS TODAY
DARRIN BELL
©2006 Darrin Bell / Dist. by WPWG, Inc.
FULL OF HIMSELF. OUT OF TOUCH. DISTANT.
PHD
PISH TOSH, WOMAN. THERE'S NOTHING WRONG WITH OUR MARRIAGE.
WWW.CANDORVILLE.COM
8-6
HE WON'T EVEN, WELL... SNUGGLE AT NIGHT.
HOW WOULD THAT BENEFIT THE SHAREHOLDERS?
PHD
CANCEL MY NEXT FIVE APPOINTMENTS.
DID YOU HEAR YOURSELF, EBENEZER?
THAT'S "MR. FITZHUGH."
PHD

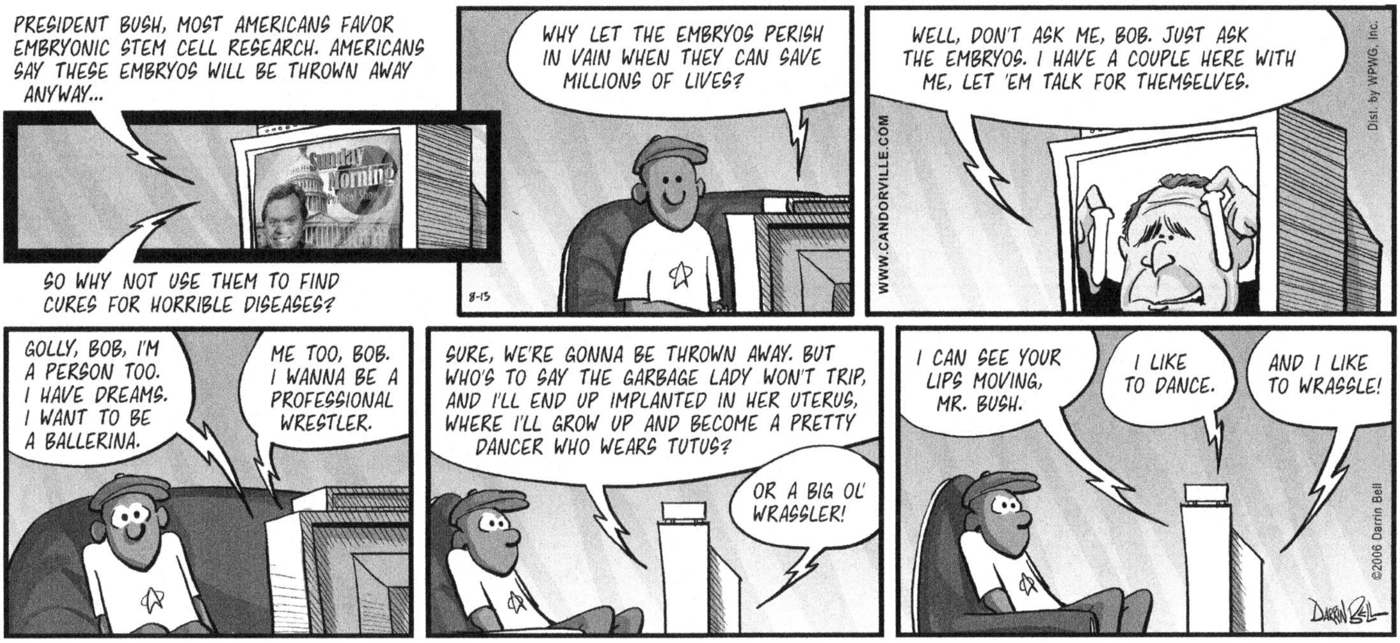
PRESIDENT BUSH, MOST AMERICANS FAVOR EMBRYONIC STEM CELL RESEARCH. AMERICANS SAY THESE EMBRYOS WILL BE THROWN AWAY ANYWAY...
SO WHY NOT USE THEM TO FIND CURES FOR HORRIBLE DISEASES?
WHY LET THE EMBRYOS PERISH IN VAIN WHEN THEY CAN SAVE MILLIONS OF LIVES?
8-13
WELL, DON'T ASK ME, BOB. JUST ASK THE EMBRYOS. I HAVE A COUPLE HERE WITH ME, LET 'EM TALK FOR THEMSELVES.
WWW.CANDORVILLE.COM
Dist. by WPWG, Inc.
GOLLY, BOB, I'M A PERSON TOO. I HAVE DREAMS. I WANT TO BE A BALLERINA.
ME TOO, BOB. I WANNA BE A PROFESSIONAL WRESTLER.
SURE, WE'RE GONNA BE THROWN AWAY. BUT WHO'S TO SAY THE GARBAGE LADY WON'T TRIP, AND I'LL END UP IMPLANTED IN HER UTERUS, WHERE I'LL GROW UP AND BECOME A PRETTY DANCER WHO WEARS TUTUS?
OR A BIG OL' WRASSLER!
I CAN SEE YOUR LIPS MOVING, MR. BUSH.
I LIKE TO DANCE.
AND I LIKE TO WRASSLE!
©2006 Darrin Bell
DARRIN BELL

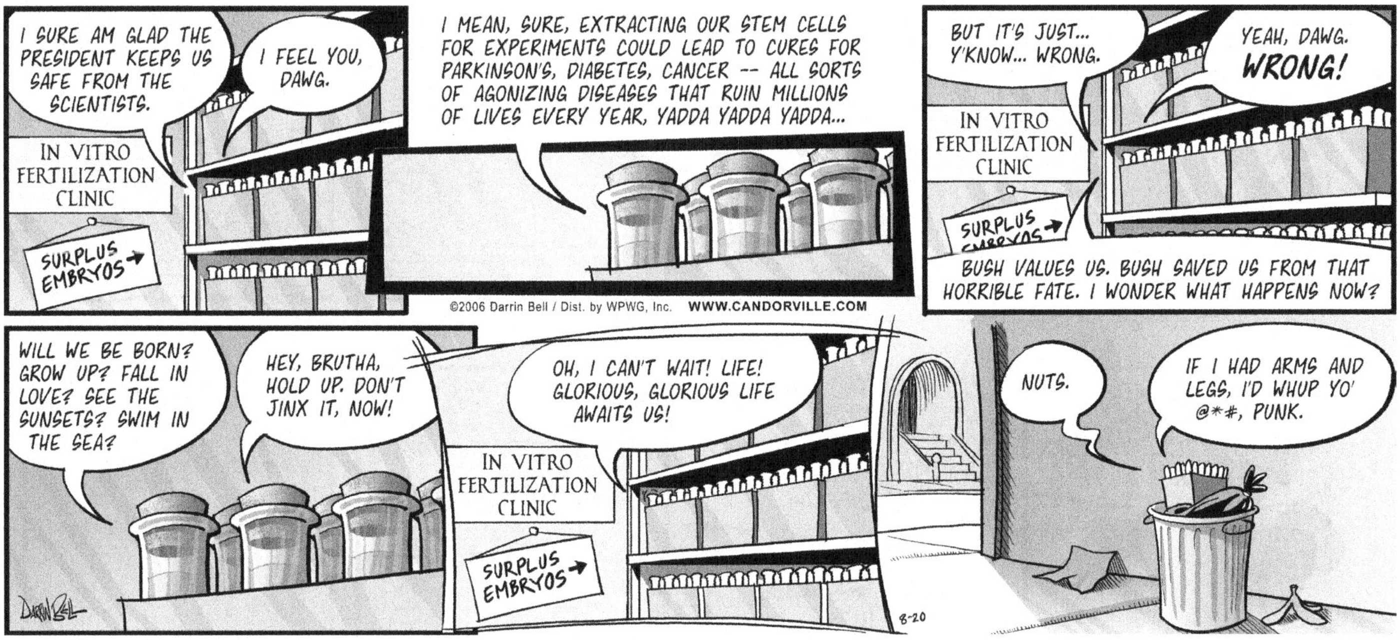
I SURE AM GLAD THE PRESIDENT KEEPS US SAFE FROM THE SCIENTISTS.
I FEEL YOU, DAWG.
IN VITRO FERTILIZATION CLINIC
SURPLUS EMBRYOS
I MEAN, SURE, EXTRACTING OUR STEM CELLS FOR EXPERIMENTS COULD LEAD TO CURES FOR PARKINSON'S, DIABETES, CANCER -- ALL SORTS OF AGONIZING DISEASES THAT RUIN MILLIONS OF LIVES EVERY YEAR, YADDA YADDA YADDA...
BUT IT'S JUST... Y'KNOW... WRONG.
YEAH, DAWG. **WRONG!**
IN VITRO FERTILIZATION CLINIC
BUSH VALUES US. BUSH SAVED US FROM THAT HORRIBLE FATE. I WONDER WHAT HAPPENS NOW?
©2006 Darrin Bell / Dist. by WPWG, Inc. WWW.CANDORVILLE.COM
WILL WE BE BORN? GROW UP? FALL IN LOVE? SEE THE SUNSETS? SWIM IN THE SEA?
HEY, BRUTHA, HOLD UP. DON'T JINX IT, NOW!
OH, I CAN'T WAIT! LIFE! GLORIOUS, GLORIOUS LIFE AWAITS US!
IN VITRO FERTILIZATION CLINIC
SURPLUS EMBRYOS
NUTS.
IF I HAD ARMS AND LEGS, I'D WHUP YO' @*#, PUNK.
DARRIN BELL
8-20

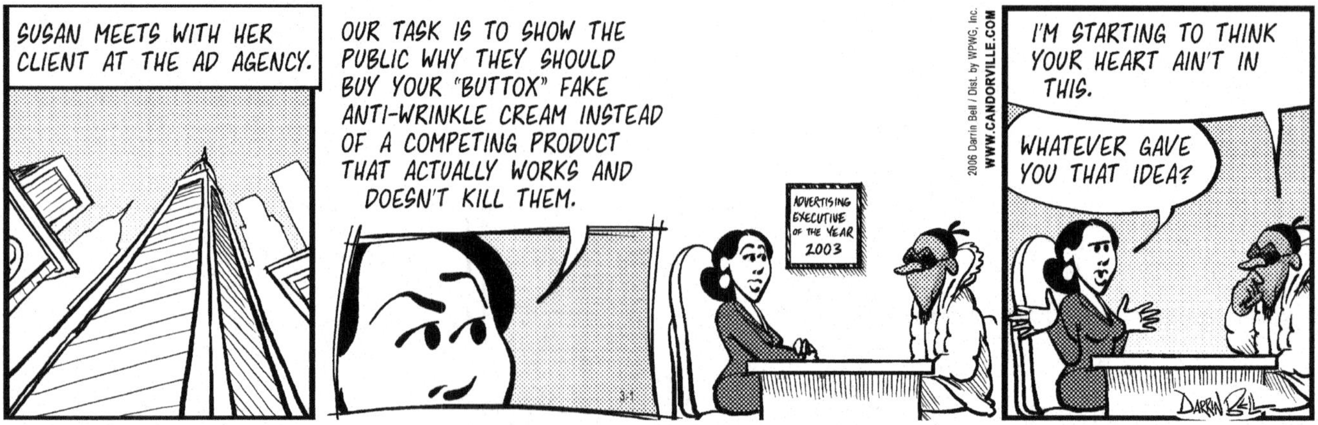
SUSAN MEETS WITH HER CLIENT AT THE AD AGENCY.
OUR TASK IS TO SHOW THE PUBLIC WHY THEY SHOULD BUY YOUR "BUTTOX" FAKE ANTI-WRINKLE CREAM INSTEAD OF A COMPETING PRODUCT THAT ACTUALLY WORKS AND DOESN'T KILL THEM.
3-1
ADVERTISING EXECUTIVE OF THE YEAR 2003
2006 Darrin Bell / Dist. by WPWG, Inc.
WWW.CANDORVILLE.COM
I'M STARTING TO THINK YOUR HEART AIN'T IN THIS.
WHATEVER GAVE YOU THAT IDEA?
DARRIN BELL

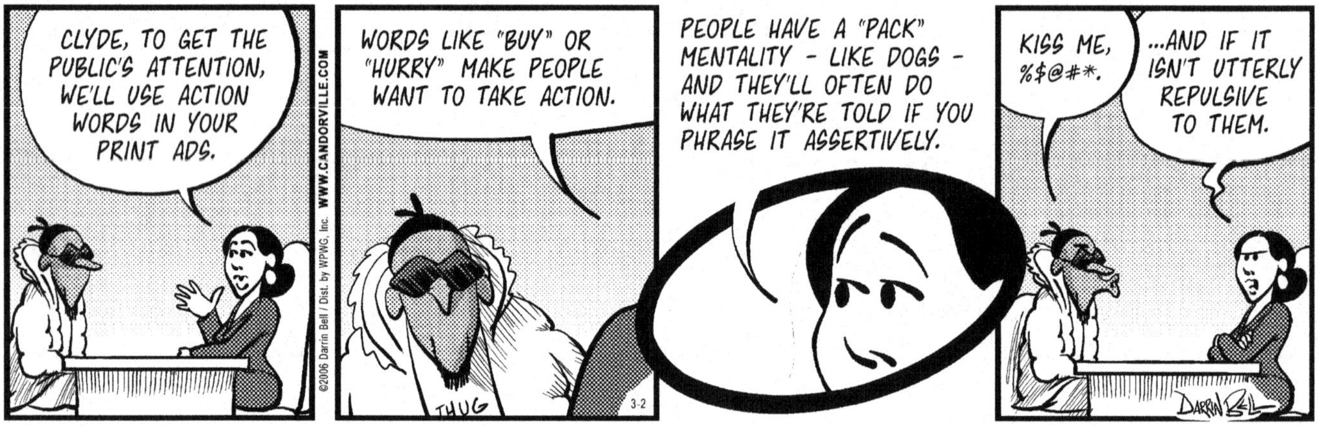
CLYDE, TO GET THE PUBLIC'S ATTENTION, WE'LL USE ACTION WORDS IN YOUR PRINT ADS.
©2006 Darrin Bell / Dist. by WPWG, Inc.
WWW.CANDORVILLE.COM
WORDS LIKE "BUY" OR "HURRY" MAKE PEOPLE WANT TO TAKE ACTION.
THUG
3-2
PEOPLE HAVE A "PACK" MENTALITY - LIKE DOGS - AND THEY'LL OFTEN DO WHAT THEY'RE TOLD IF YOU PHRASE IT ASSERTIVELY.
KISS ME, %$@#*.
...AND IF IT ISN'T UTTERLY REPULSIVE TO THEM.
DARRIN BELL

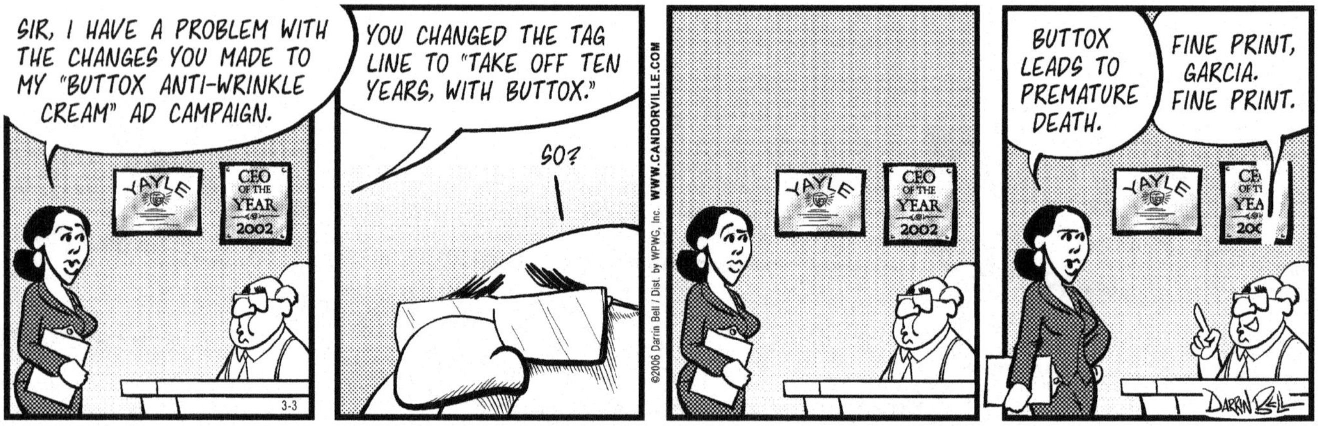
SIR, I HAVE A PROBLEM WITH THE CHANGES YOU MADE TO MY "BUTTOX ANTI-WRINKLE CREAM" AD CAMPAIGN.
YAYLE
CEO OF THE YEAR 2002
3-3
YOU CHANGED THE TAG LINE TO "TAKE OFF TEN YEARS, WITH BUTTOX."
SO?
©2006 Darrin Bell / Dist. by WPWG, Inc.
WWW.CANDORVILLE.COM
BUTTOX LEADS TO PREMATURE DEATH.
FINE PRINT, GARCIA. FINE PRINT.
DARRIN BELL

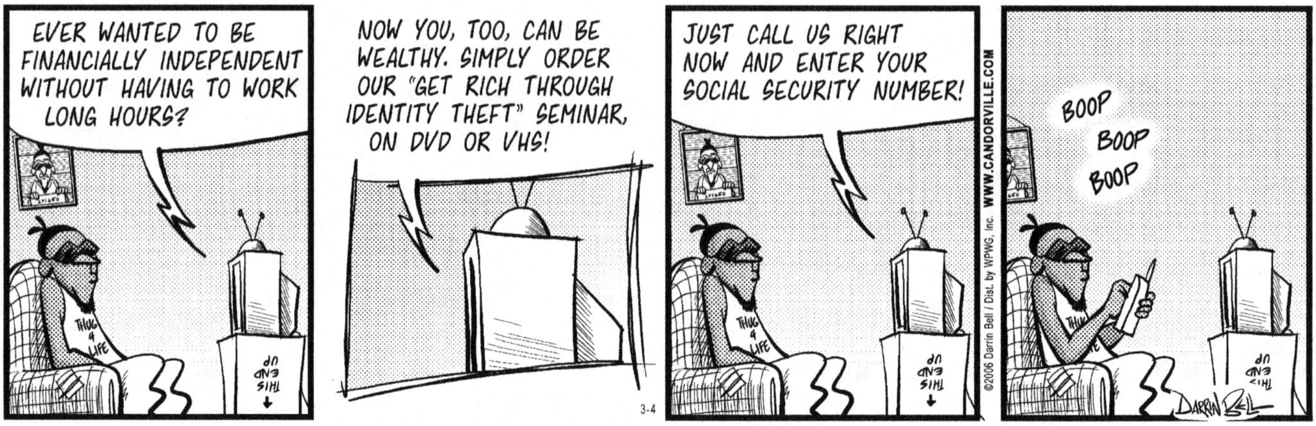
EVER WANTED TO BE FINANCIALLY INDEPENDENT WITHOUT HAVING TO WORK LONG HOURS?
THUG 4 LIFE
THIS END UP
NOW YOU, TOO, CAN BE WEALTHY. SIMPLY ORDER OUR "GET RICH THROUGH IDENTITY THEFT" SEMINAR, ON DVD OR VHS!
3-4
JUST CALL US RIGHT NOW AND ENTER YOUR SOCIAL SECURITY NUMBER!
©2006 Darrin Bell / Dist. by WPWG, Inc.
WWW.CANDORVILLE.COM
BOOP
BOOP
BOOP
DARRIN BELL

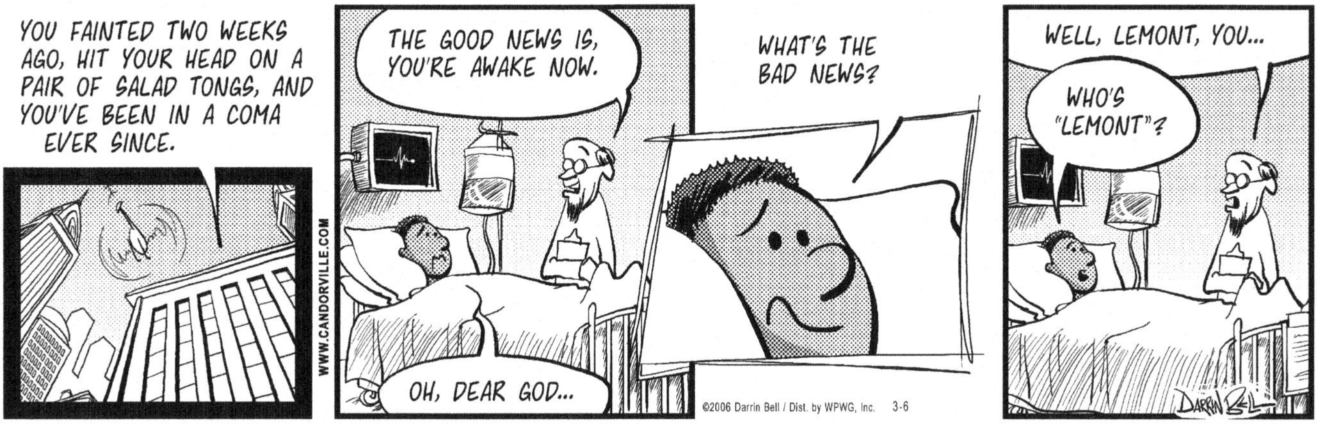
YOU FAINTED TWO WEEKS AGO, HIT YOUR HEAD ON A PAIR OF SALAD TONGS, AND YOU'VE BEEN IN A COMA EVER SINCE.
WWW.CANDORVILLE.COM
THE GOOD NEWS IS, YOU'RE AWAKE NOW.
OH, DEAR GOD...
WHAT'S THE BAD NEWS?
©2006 Darrin Bell / Dist. by WPWG, Inc. 3-6
WELL, LEMONT, YOU...
WHO'S "LEMONT"?
DARRIN BELL

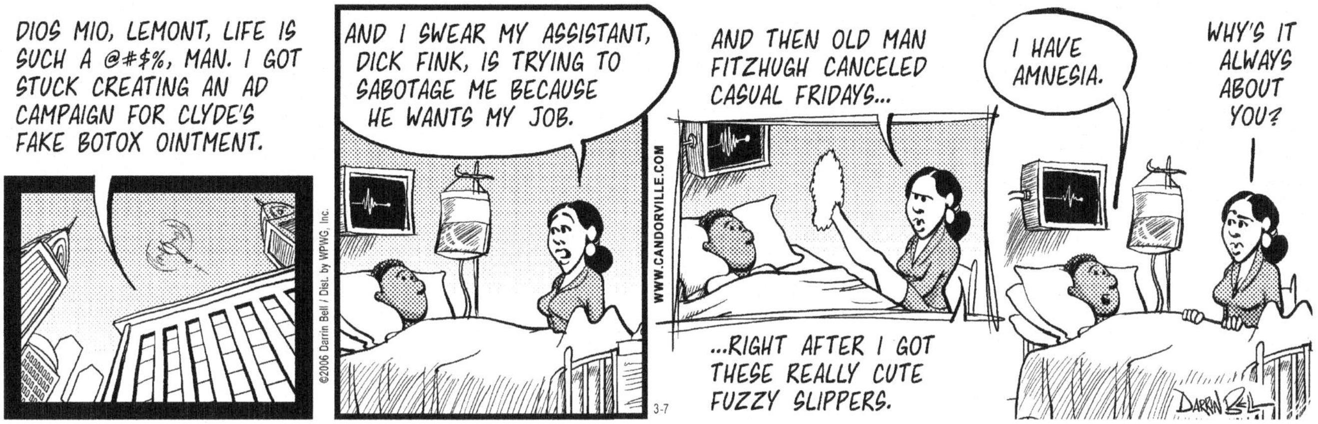
DIOS MIO, LEMONT, LIFE IS SUCH A @#$%, MAN. I GOT STUCK CREATING AN AD CAMPAIGN FOR CLYDE'S FAKE BOTOX OINTMENT.
©2006 Darrin Bell / Dist. by WPWG, Inc.
AND I SWEAR MY ASSISTANT, DICK FINK, IS TRYING TO SABOTAGE ME BECAUSE HE WANTS MY JOB.
3-7
WWW.CANDORVILLE.COM
AND THEN OLD MAN FITZHUGH CANCELED CASUAL FRIDAYS...
...RIGHT AFTER I GOT THESE REALLY CUTE FUZZY SLIPPERS.
I HAVE AMNESIA.
WHY'S IT ALWAYS ABOUT YOU?
DARRIN BELL

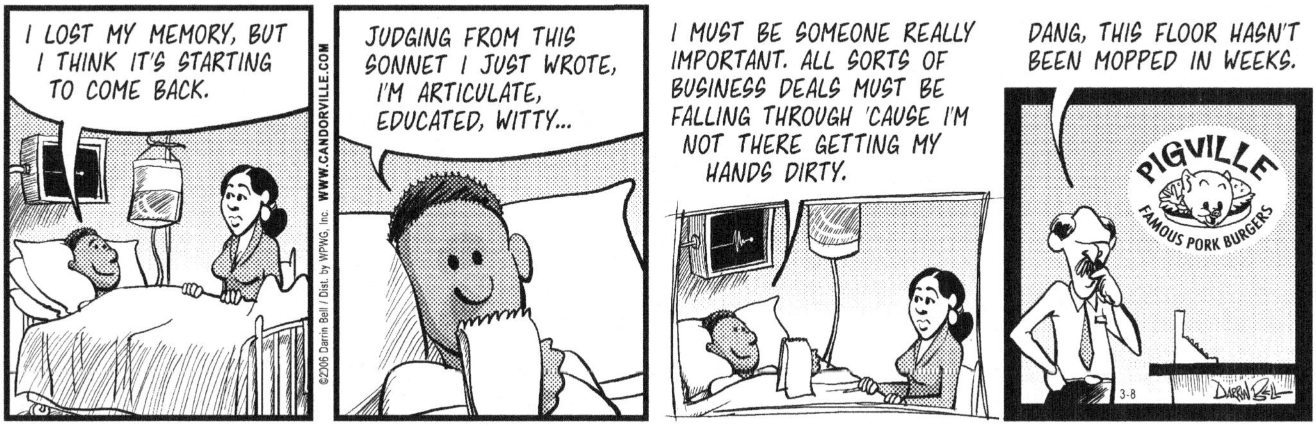
I LOST MY MEMORY, BUT I THINK IT'S STARTING TO COME BACK.
WWW.CANDORVILLE.COM
©2006 Darrin Bell / Dist. by WPWG, Inc.
JUDGING FROM THIS SONNET I JUST WROTE, I'M ARTICULATE, EDUCATED, WITTY...
I MUST BE SOMEONE REALLY IMPORTANT. ALL SORTS OF BUSINESS DEALS MUST BE FALLING THROUGH 'CAUSE I'M NOT THERE GETTING MY HANDS DIRTY.
DANG, THIS FLOOR HASN'T BEEN MOPPED IN WEEKS.
PIGVILLE
FAMOUS PORK BURGERS
3-8
DARRIN BELL

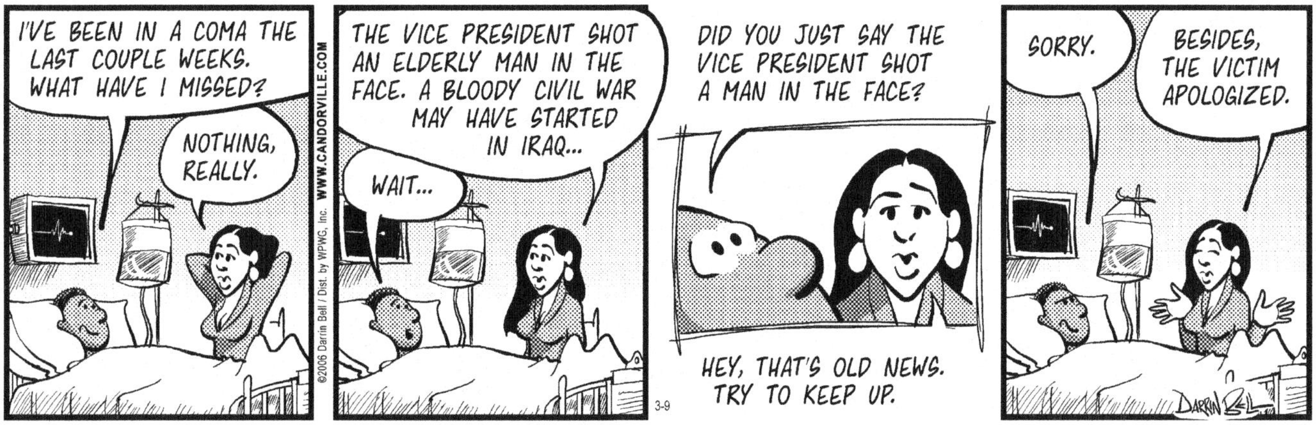
I'VE BEEN IN A COMA THE LAST COUPLE WEEKS. WHAT HAVE I MISSED?
NOTHING, REALLY.
WWW.CANDORVILLE.COM
©2006 Darrin Bell / Dist. by WPWG, Inc.
THE VICE PRESIDENT SHOT AN ELDERLY MAN IN THE FACE. A BLOODY CIVIL WAR MAY HAVE STARTED IN IRAQ...
WAIT...
3-9
DID YOU JUST SAY THE VICE PRESIDENT SHOT A MAN IN THE FACE?
HEY, THAT'S OLD NEWS. TRY TO KEEP UP.
SORRY.
BESIDES, THE VICTIM APOLOGIZED.
DARRIN BELL

Panel 1: ...IN OTHER NEWS, THE WHITE HOUSE HAS DECIDED TO SELL THE STATE OF DELAWARE TO THE UNITED ARAB EMIRATES.

Panel 2: CONGRESSIONAL LEADERS HAVE EXPRESSED CONCERN ABOUT THIS DEAL.

Panel 3: ...CONSIDERING THE DESPOTIC NATION HELPED FUND THE 9-11 TERRORISTS AND STILL HAS TIES TO AL QAEDA.

3-10

Panel 4: THE WHITE HOUSE SAYS DELAWARIANS HAVE NOTHING TO WORRY ABOUT...

©2006 Darrin Bell / Dist. by WPWG, Inc.

Panel 5: THE WHITE HOUSE HAS CONDEMNED CRITICS OF THEIR PROPOSED SALE OF DELAWARE TO THE UNITED ARAB EMIRATES.

3-11

Panel 6: DELAWARE WAS ONCE OWNED BY THE BRITISH, WHO ARE WHITE.

CRITICS ARE GOING TO HAVE TO EXPLAIN WHY IT'S OK FOR WHITE NATIONS TO OWN DELAWARE...

©2006 Darrin Bell / Dist. by WPWG, Inc.

Panel 7: ...BUT IT'S SUDDENLY NOT OK FOR A DESPOTIC NATION WITH TIES TO AL QAEDA TO OWN DELAWARE.

WWW.CANDORVILLE.COM

Panel 8: OBVIOUSLY, THE CRITICS ARE RACIST.

Panel 9: SUSAN, ARE WE MARRIED? HUH? WHAT?

Panel 10: WELL, EVER SINCE I WOKE UP FROM MY COMA WITH AMNESIA, YOU'VE BEEN VISITING ME.

3-13

Panel 11: YOU LOOKED SO WORRIED. YOU LOOK AT ME LIKE I'M THE MOST SPECIAL PERSON IN THE WORLD TO YOU. YOU LOOK AT ME LIKE YOU LOVE ME.

WWW.CANDORVILLE.COM
©2006 Darrin Bell / Dist. by WPWG, Inc

Panel 12: THAT WAS ACID REFLUX.

I WAS, YOU ARE, AND I DO.

Panel 13: NO, LEMONT, WE'RE NOT MARRIED. THAT'S TOO BAD, SUSAN.

3-14

Panel 14: I MEAN, YOU'RE THE KINDEST, SMARTEST, FUNNIEST, MOST BEAUTIFUL WOMAN I'VE EVER KNOWN.

©2006 Darrin Bell / Dist. by WPWG, Inc.
WWW.CANDORVILLE.COM

Panel 15:

Panel 16: OF COURSE, SINCE I HAVE AMNESIA, YOU'RE THE **ONLY** WOMAN I'VE EVER KNOWN.

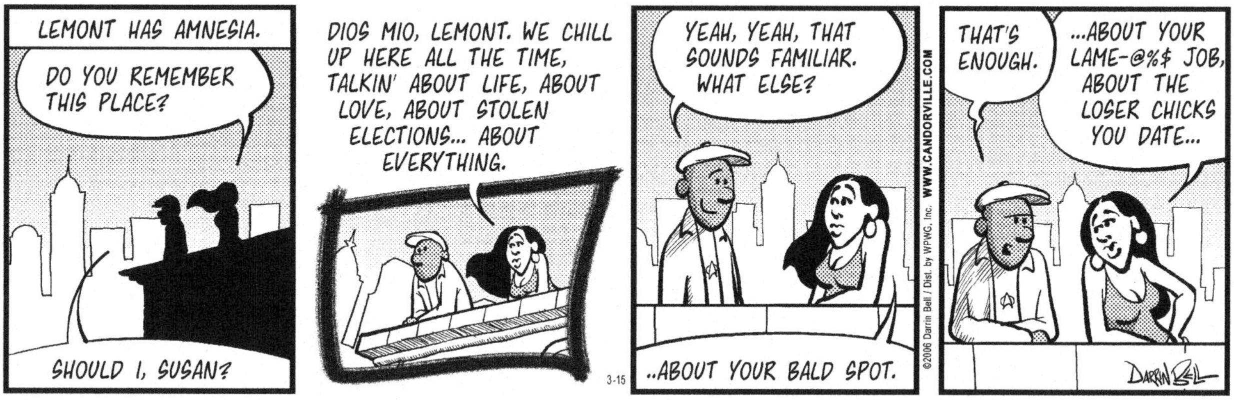
LEMONT HAS AMNESIA.
DO YOU REMEMBER THIS PLACE?
SHOULD I, SUSAN?
DIOS MIO, LEMONT. WE CHILL UP HERE ALL THE TIME, TALKIN' ABOUT LIFE, ABOUT LOVE, ABOUT STOLEN ELECTIONS... ABOUT EVERYTHING.
3-15
YEAH, YEAH, THAT SOUNDS FAMILIAR. WHAT ELSE?
..ABOUT YOUR BALD SPOT.
©2006 Darrin Bell / Dist. by WPWG, Inc. WWW.CANDORVILLE.COM
THAT'S ENOUGH.
...ABOUT YOUR LAME-@%$ JOB, ABOUT THE LOSER CHICKS YOU DATE...
DARRIN BELL

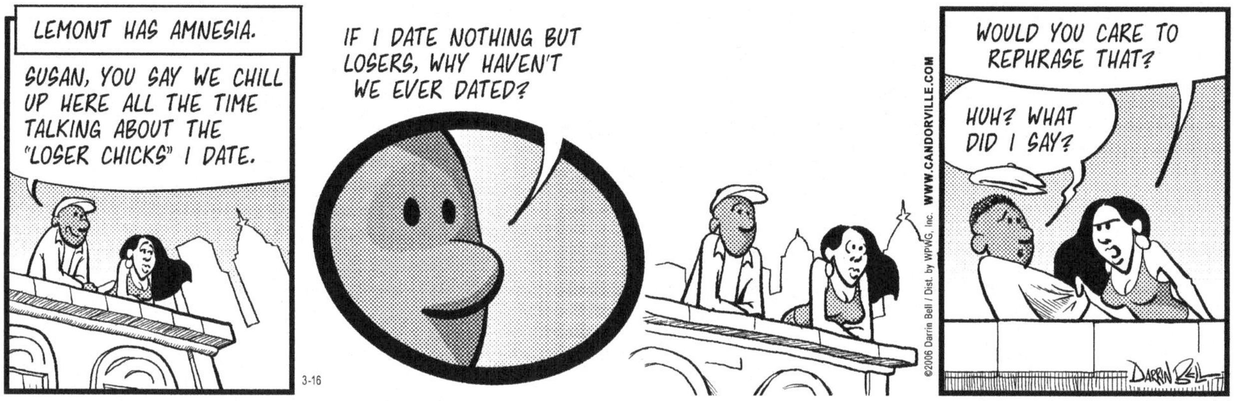
LEMONT HAS AMNESIA.
SUSAN, YOU SAY WE CHILL UP HERE ALL THE TIME TALKING ABOUT THE "LOSER CHICKS" I DATE.
3-16
IF I DATE NOTHING BUT LOSERS, WHY HAVEN'T WE EVER DATED?
©2006 Darrin Bell / Dist. by WPWG, Inc. WWW.CANDORVILLE.COM
WOULD YOU CARE TO REPHRASE THAT?
HUH? WHAT DID I SAY?
DARRIN BELL

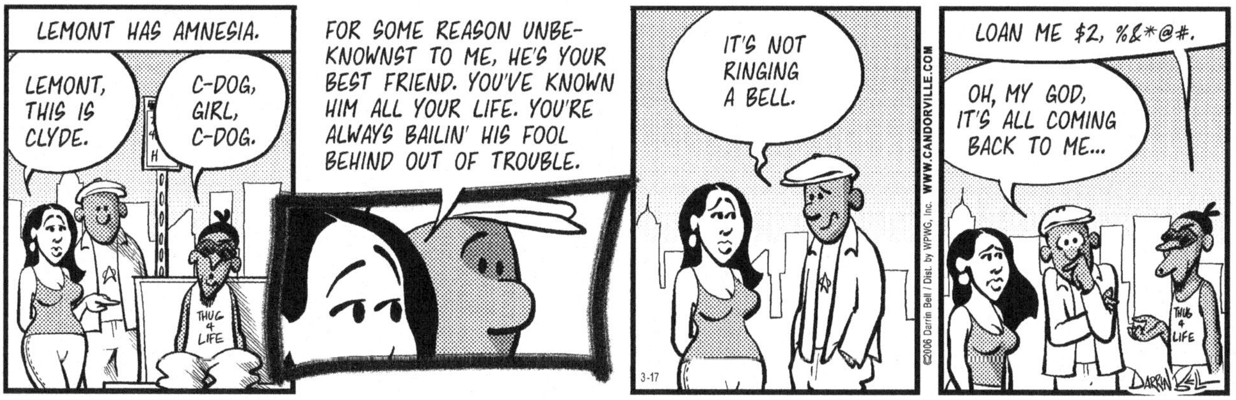
LEMONT HAS AMNESIA.
LEMONT, THIS IS CLYDE.
C-DOG, GIRL, C-DOG.
THUG 4 LIFE
FOR SOME REASON UNBE-KNOWNST TO ME, HE'S YOUR BEST FRIEND. YOU'VE KNOWN HIM ALL YOUR LIFE. YOU'RE ALWAYS BAILIN' HIS FOOL BEHIND OUT OF TROUBLE.
IT'S NOT RINGING A BELL.
3-17
©2006 Darrin Bell / Dist. by WPWG, Inc. WWW.CANDORVILLE.COM
LOAN ME $2, %&*@#.
OH, MY GOD, IT'S ALL COMING BACK TO ME...
THUG 4 LIFE
DARRIN BELL

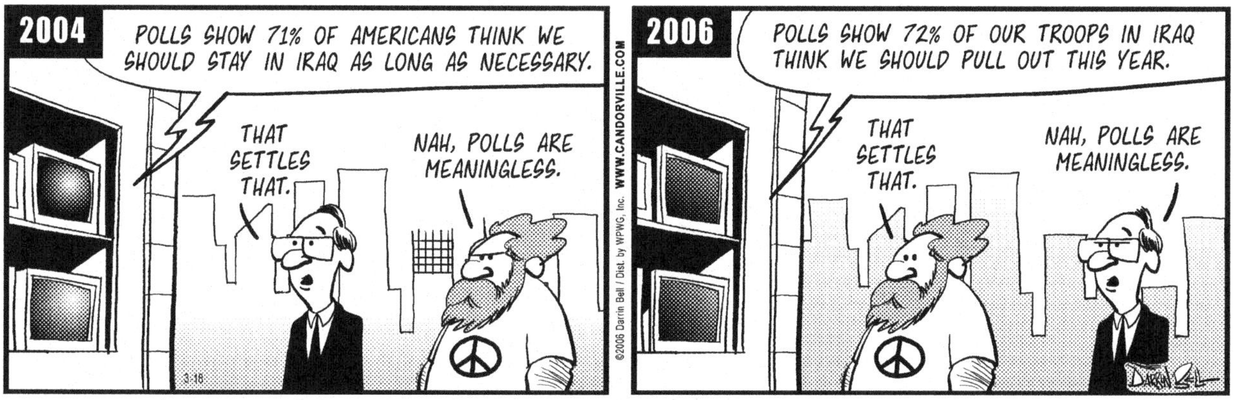
2004
POLLS SHOW 71% OF AMERICANS THINK WE SHOULD STAY IN IRAQ AS LONG AS NECESSARY.
THAT SETTLES THAT.
NAH, POLLS ARE MEANINGLESS.
3-18
©2006 Darrin Bell / Dist. by WPWG, Inc. WWW.CANDORVILLE.COM
2006
POLLS SHOW 72% OF OUR TROOPS IN IRAQ THINK WE SHOULD PULL OUT THIS YEAR.
THAT SETTLES THAT.
NAH, POLLS ARE MEANINGLESS.
DARRIN BELL

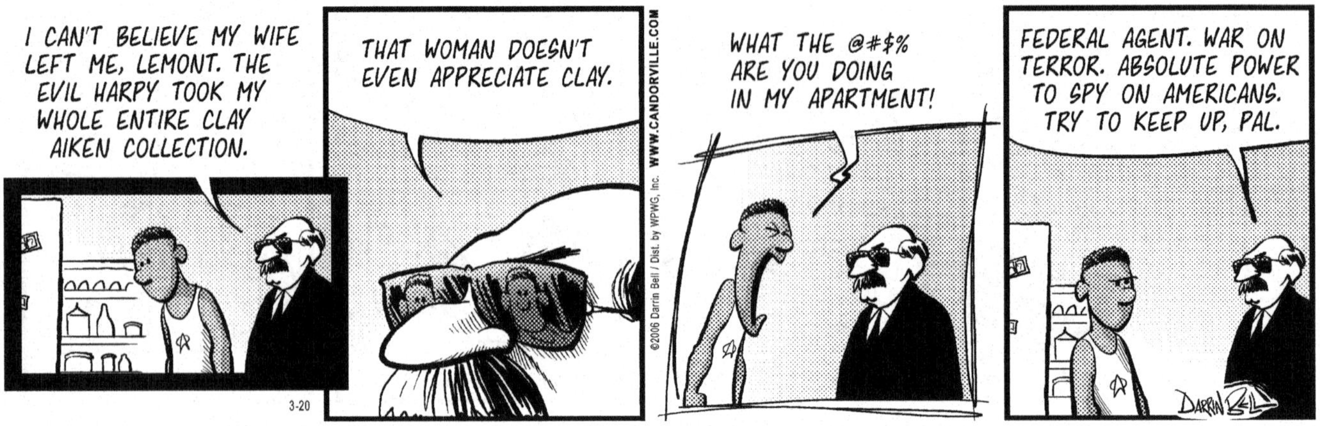
I CAN'T BELIEVE MY WIFE LEFT ME, LEMONT. THE EVIL HARPY TOOK MY WHOLE ENTIRE CLAY AIKEN COLLECTION.
3-20
THAT WOMAN DOESN'T EVEN APPRECIATE CLAY.
©2006 Darrin Bell / Dist. by WPWG, Inc. WWW.CANDORVILLE.COM
WHAT THE @#$% ARE YOU DOING IN MY APARTMENT!
FEDERAL AGENT. WAR ON TERROR. ABSOLUTE POWER TO SPY ON AMERICANS. TRY TO KEEP UP, PAL.
DARRIN BELL

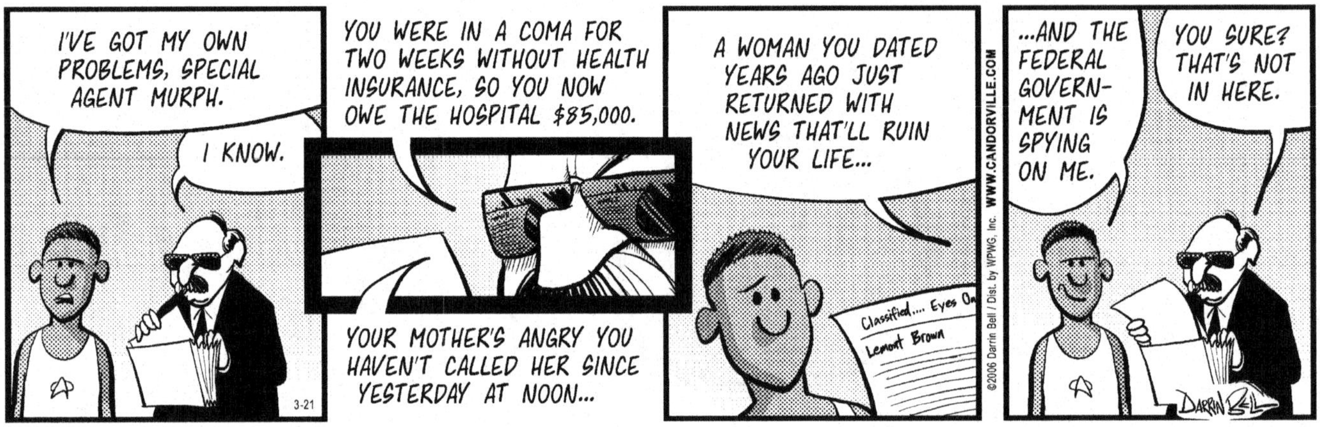
I'VE GOT MY OWN PROBLEMS, SPECIAL AGENT MURPH.
I KNOW.
3-21
YOU WERE IN A COMA FOR TWO WEEKS WITHOUT HEALTH INSURANCE, SO YOU NOW OWE THE HOSPITAL $85,000.
YOUR MOTHER'S ANGRY YOU HAVEN'T CALLED HER SINCE YESTERDAY AT NOON...
A WOMAN YOU DATED YEARS AGO JUST RETURNED WITH NEWS THAT'LL RUIN YOUR LIFE...
Classified.... Eyes On
Lemont Brown
©2006 Darrin Bell / Dist. by WPWG, Inc. WWW.CANDORVILLE.COM
...AND THE FEDERAL GOVERN-MENT IS SPYING ON ME.
YOU SURE? THAT'S NOT IN HERE.
DARRIN BELL

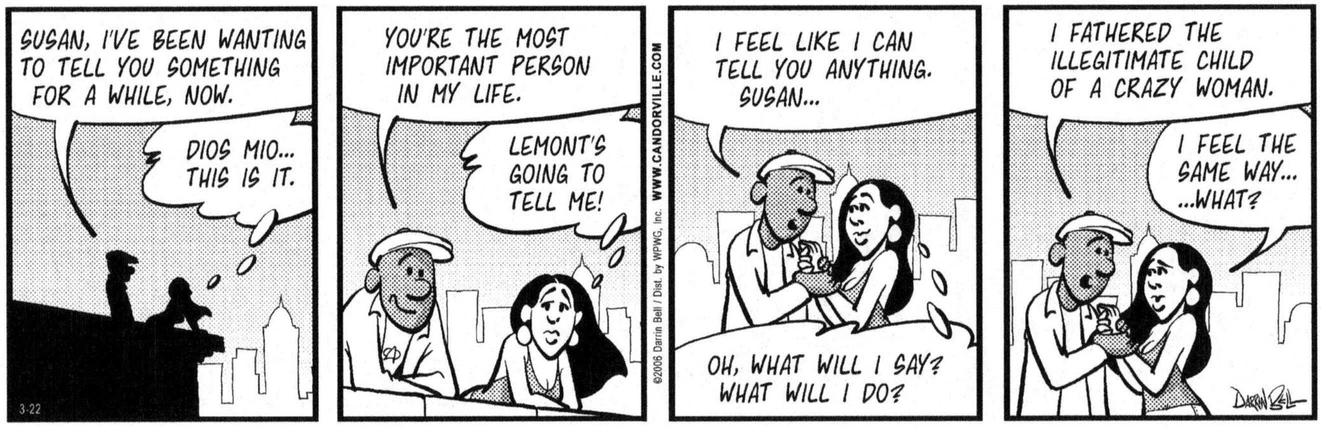
SUSAN, I'VE BEEN WANTING TO TELL YOU SOMETHING FOR A WHILE, NOW.
DIOS MIO... THIS IS IT.
3-22
YOU'RE THE MOST IMPORTANT PERSON IN MY LIFE.
LEMONT'S GOING TO TELL ME!
©2006 Darrin Bell / Dist. by WPWG, Inc. WWW.CANDORVILLE.COM
I FEEL LIKE I CAN TELL YOU ANYTHING. SUSAN...
OH, WHAT WILL I SAY? WHAT WILL I DO?
I FATHERED THE ILLEGITIMATE CHILD OF A CRAZY WOMAN.
I FEEL THE SAME WAY... ...WHAT?
DARRIN BELL

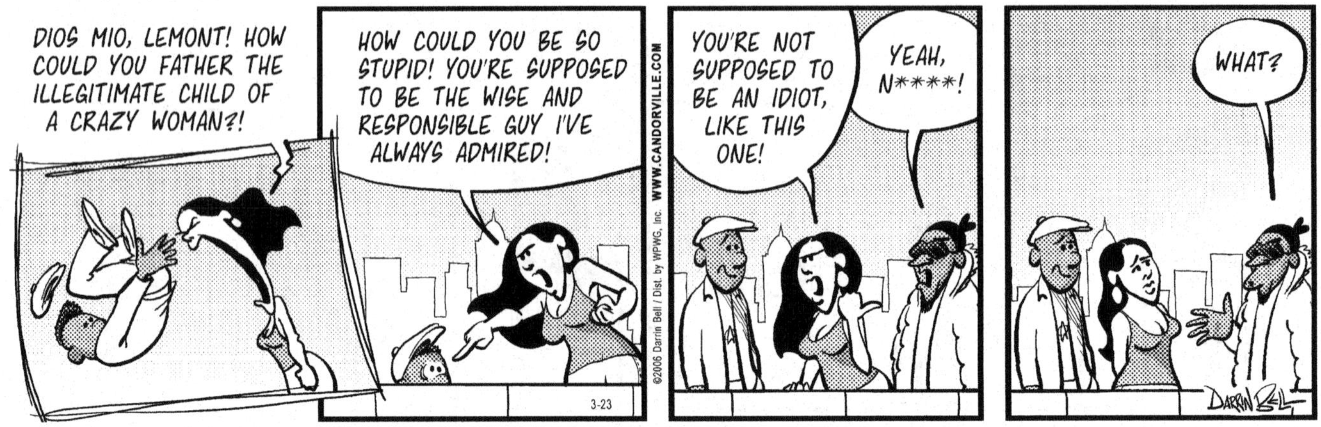
DIOS MIO, LEMONT! HOW COULD YOU FATHER THE ILLEGITIMATE CHILD OF A CRAZY WOMAN?!
HOW COULD YOU BE SO STUPID! YOU'RE SUPPOSED TO BE THE WISE AND RESPONSIBLE GUY I'VE ALWAYS ADMIRED!
3-23
©2006 Darrin Bell / Dist. by WPWG, Inc. WWW.CANDORVILLE.COM
YOU'RE NOT SUPPOSED TO BE AN IDIOT, LIKE THIS ONE!
YEAH, N****!
WHAT?
DARRIN BELL

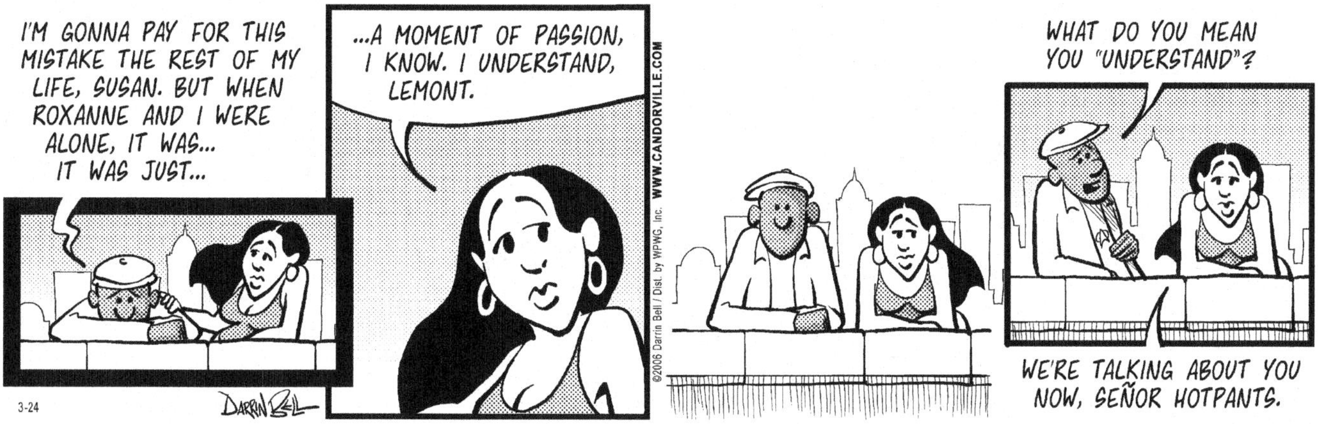
I'M GONNA PAY FOR THIS MISTAKE THE REST OF MY LIFE, SUSAN. BUT WHEN ROXANNE AND I WERE ALONE, IT WAS... IT WAS JUST...
...A MOMENT OF PASSION, I KNOW. I UNDERSTAND, LEMONT.
WHAT DO YOU MEAN YOU "UNDERSTAND"?
WE'RE TALKING ABOUT YOU NOW, SEÑOR HOTPANTS.
3-24
©2006 Darrin Bell / Dist. by WPWG, Inc. WWW.CANDORVILLE.COM

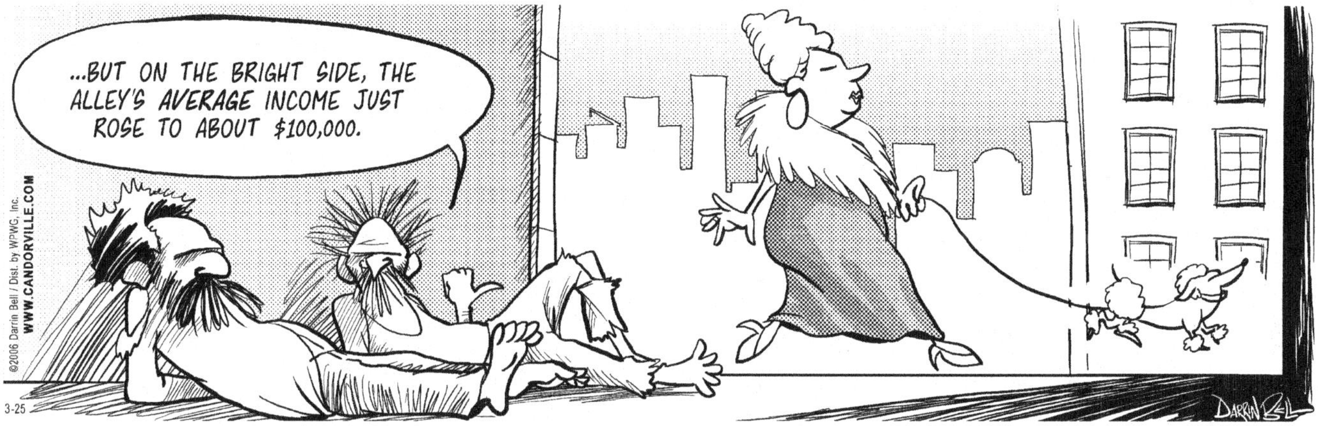
...BUT ON THE BRIGHT SIDE, THE ALLEY'S *AVERAGE* INCOME JUST ROSE TO ABOUT $100,000.
3-25
©2006 Darrin Bell / Dist. by WPWG, Inc. WWW.CANDORVILLE.COM

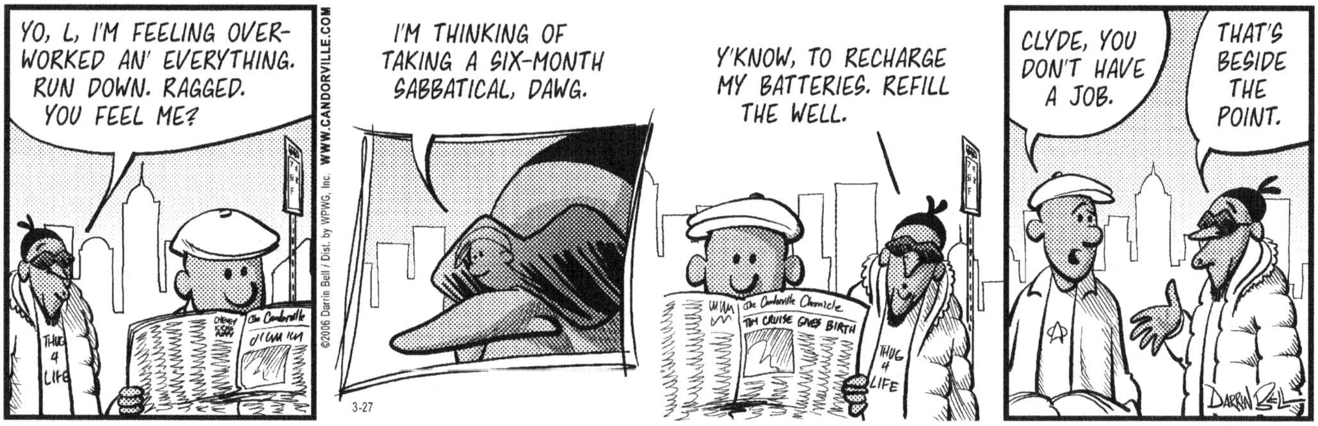
YO, L, I'M FEELING OVER-WORKED AN' EVERYTHING. RUN DOWN. RAGGED. YOU FEEL ME?
I'M THINKING OF TAKING A SIX-MONTH SABBATICAL, DAWG.
Y'KNOW, TO RECHARGE MY BATTERIES. REFILL THE WELL.
CLYDE, YOU DON'T HAVE A JOB.
THAT'S BESIDE THE POINT.
The Candorville Chronicle
TOM CRUISE GIVES BIRTH
THUG 4 LIFE
3-27
©2006 Darrin Bell / Dist. by WPWG, Inc. WWW.CANDORVILLE.COM

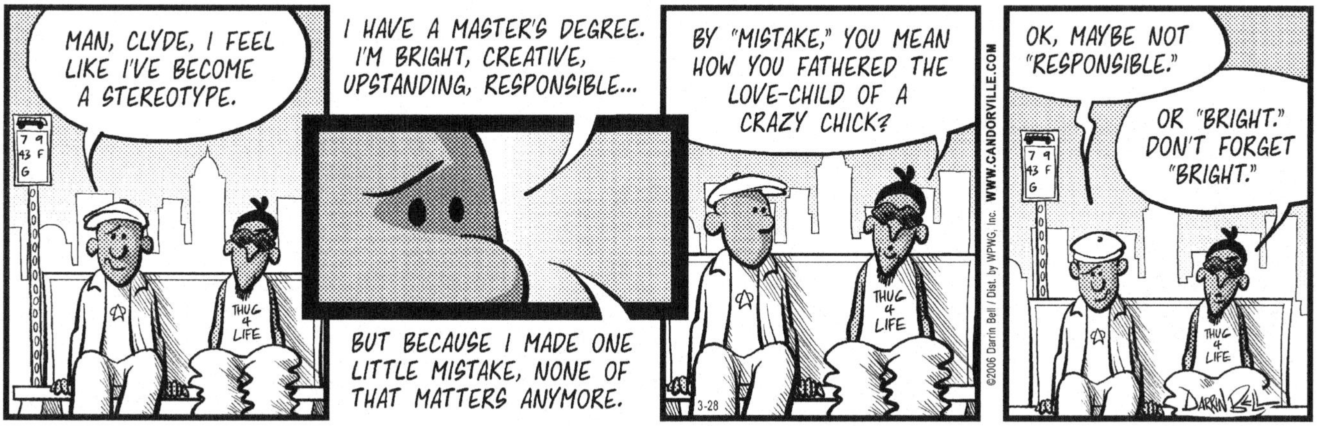
MAN, CLYDE, I FEEL LIKE I'VE BECOME A STEREOTYPE.
I HAVE A MASTER'S DEGREE. I'M BRIGHT, CREATIVE, UPSTANDING, RESPONSIBLE...
BUT BECAUSE I MADE ONE LITTLE MISTAKE, NONE OF THAT MATTERS ANYMORE.
BY "MISTAKE," YOU MEAN HOW YOU FATHERED THE LOVE-CHILD OF A CRAZY CHICK?
OK, MAYBE NOT "RESPONSIBLE."
OR "BRIGHT." DON'T FORGET "BRIGHT."
THUG 4 LIFE
3-28
©2006 Darrin Bell / Dist. by WPWG, Inc. WWW.CANDORVILLE.COM

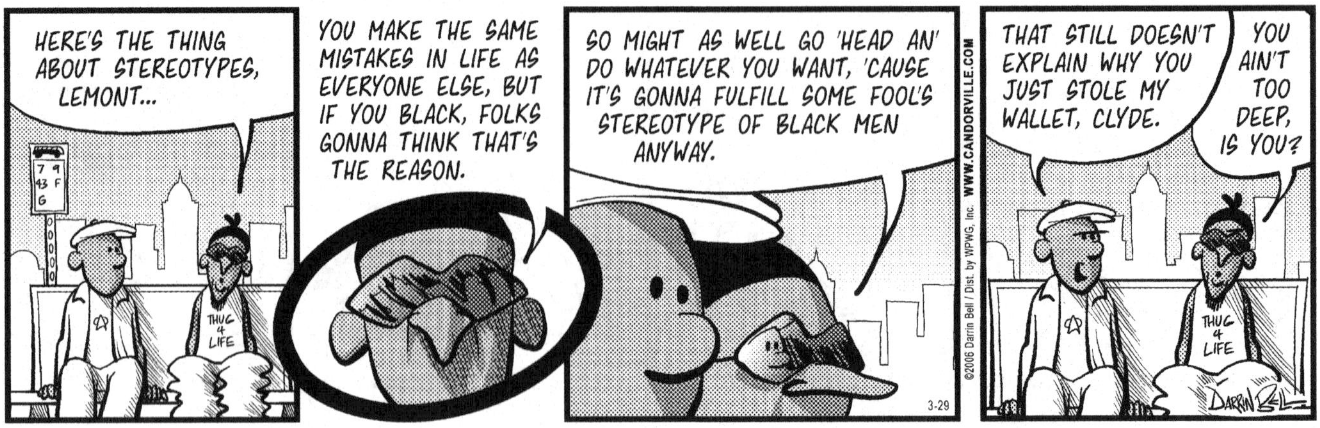
HERE'S THE THING ABOUT STEREOTYPES, LEMONT...
YOU MAKE THE SAME MISTAKES IN LIFE AS EVERYONE ELSE, BUT IF YOU BLACK, FOLKS GONNA THINK THAT'S THE REASON.
SO MIGHT AS WELL GO 'HEAD AN' DO WHATEVER YOU WANT, 'CAUSE IT'S GONNA FULFILL SOME FOOL'S STEREOTYPE OF BLACK MEN ANYWAY.
THAT STILL DOESN'T EXPLAIN WHY YOU JUST STOLE MY WALLET, CLYDE.
YOU AIN'T TOO DEEP, IS YOU?
THUG 4 LIFE
3-29
©2006 Darrin Bell / Dist. by WPWG, Inc. WWW.CANDORVILLE.COM

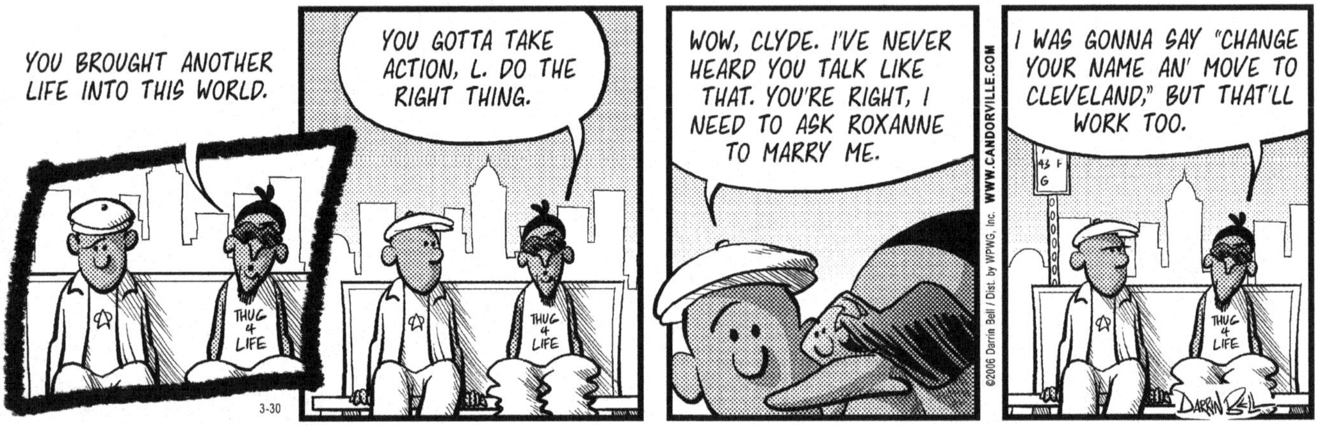
YOU BROUGHT ANOTHER LIFE INTO THIS WORLD.
YOU GOTTA TAKE ACTION, L. DO THE RIGHT THING.
WOW, CLYDE. I'VE NEVER HEARD YOU TALK LIKE THAT. YOU'RE RIGHT, I NEED TO ASK ROXANNE TO MARRY ME.
I WAS GONNA SAY "CHANGE YOUR NAME AN' MOVE TO CLEVELAND," BUT THAT'LL WORK TOO.
THUG 4 LIFE
3-30
©2006 Darrin Bell / Dist. by WPWG, Inc. WWW.CANDORVILLE.COM

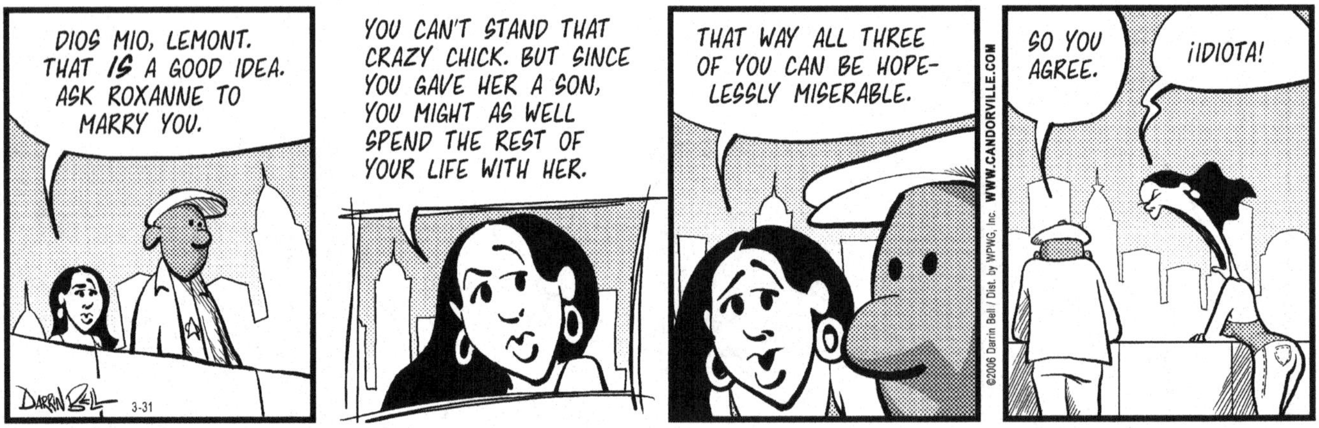
DIOS MIO, LEMONT. THAT IS A GOOD IDEA. ASK ROXANNE TO MARRY YOU.
YOU CAN'T STAND THAT CRAZY CHICK. BUT SINCE YOU GAVE HER A SON, YOU MIGHT AS WELL SPEND THE REST OF YOUR LIFE WITH HER.
THAT WAY ALL THREE OF YOU CAN BE HOPE-LESSLY MISERABLE.
SO YOU AGREE.
¡IDIOTA!
3-31
©2006 Darrin Bell / Dist. by WPWG, Inc. WWW.CANDORVILLE.COM

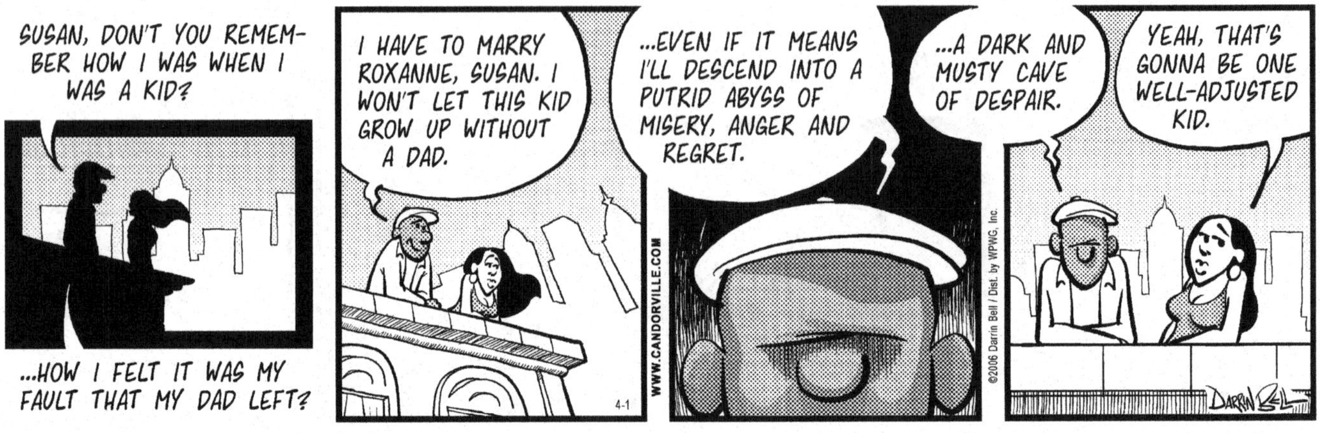
SUSAN, DON'T YOU REMEM-BER HOW I WAS WHEN I WAS A KID?
...HOW I FELT IT WAS MY FAULT THAT MY DAD LEFT?
I HAVE TO MARRY ROXANNE, SUSAN. I WON'T LET THIS KID GROW UP WITHOUT A DAD.
...EVEN IF IT MEANS I'LL DESCEND INTO A PUTRID ABYSS OF MISERY, ANGER AND REGRET.
...A DARK AND MUSTY CAVE OF DESPAIR.
YEAH, THAT'S GONNA BE ONE WELL-ADJUSTED KID.
4-1
WWW.CANDORVILLE.COM
©2006 Darrin Bell / Dist. by WPWG, Inc.

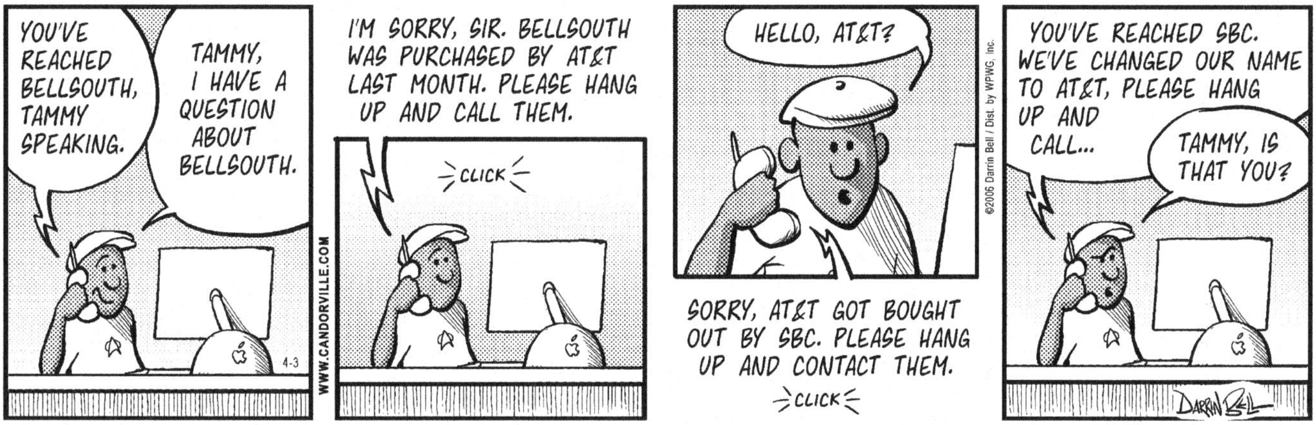
YOU'VE REACHED BELLSOUTH, TAMMY SPEAKING.
TAMMY, I HAVE A QUESTION ABOUT BELLSOUTH.
4-3
WWW.CANDORVILLE.COM
I'M SORRY, SIR. BELLSOUTH WAS PURCHASED BY AT&T LAST MONTH. PLEASE HANG UP AND CALL THEM.
CLICK
HELLO, AT&T?
SORRY, AT&T GOT BOUGHT OUT BY SBC. PLEASE HANG UP AND CONTACT THEM.
CLICK
©2006 Darrin Bell / Dist. by WPWG, Inc.
YOU'VE REACHED SBC. WE'VE CHANGED OUR NAME TO AT&T, PLEASE HANG UP AND CALL...
TAMMY, IS THAT YOU?
DARRIN BELL

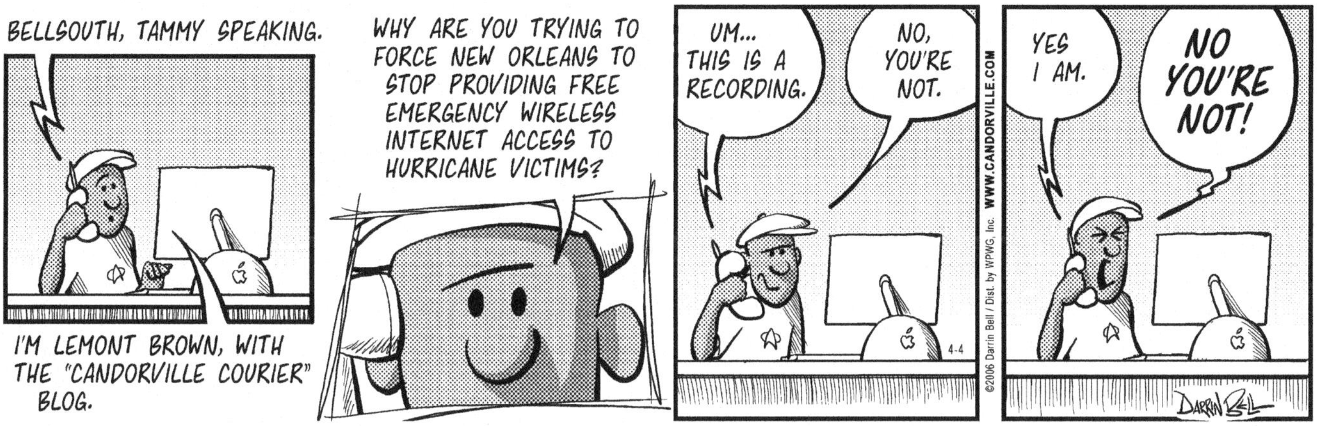
BELLSOUTH, TAMMY SPEAKING.
I'M LEMONT BROWN, WITH THE "CANDORVILLE COURIER" BLOG.
WHY ARE YOU TRYING TO FORCE NEW ORLEANS TO STOP PROVIDING FREE EMERGENCY WIRELESS INTERNET ACCESS TO HURRICANE VICTIMS?
UM... THIS IS A RECORDING.
NO, YOU'RE NOT.
4-4
©2006 Darrin Bell / Dist. by WPWG, Inc. WWW.CANDORVILLE.COM
YES I AM.
NO YOU'RE NOT!
DARRIN BELL

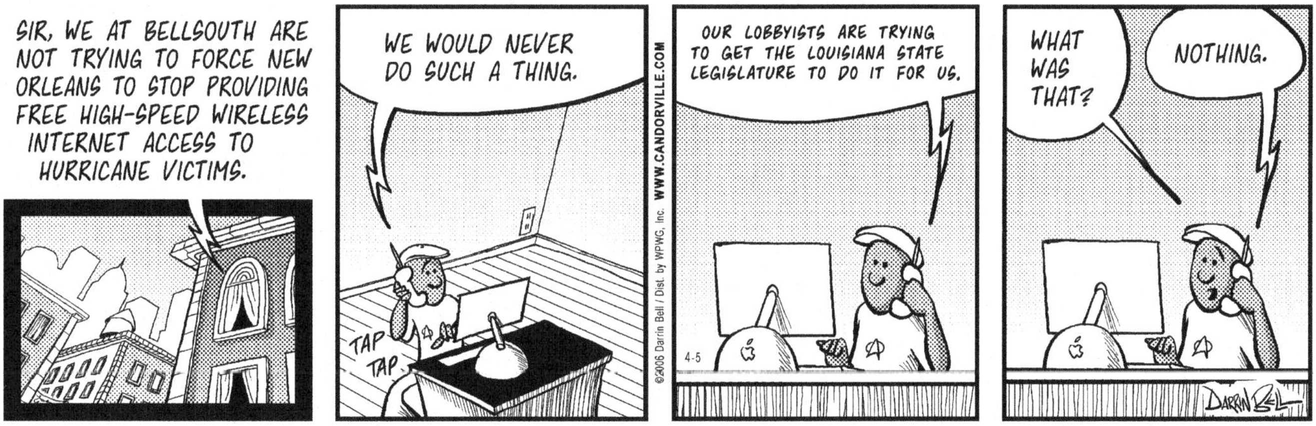
SIR, WE AT BELLSOUTH ARE NOT TRYING TO FORCE NEW ORLEANS TO STOP PROVIDING FREE HIGH-SPEED WIRELESS INTERNET ACCESS TO HURRICANE VICTIMS.
WE WOULD NEVER DO SUCH A THING.
TAP TAP
©2006 Darrin Bell / Dist. by WPWG, Inc. WWW.CANDORVILLE.COM
OUR LOBBYISTS ARE TRYING TO GET THE LOUISIANA STATE LEGISLATURE TO DO IT FOR US.
4-5
WHAT WAS THAT?
NOTHING.
DARRIN BELL

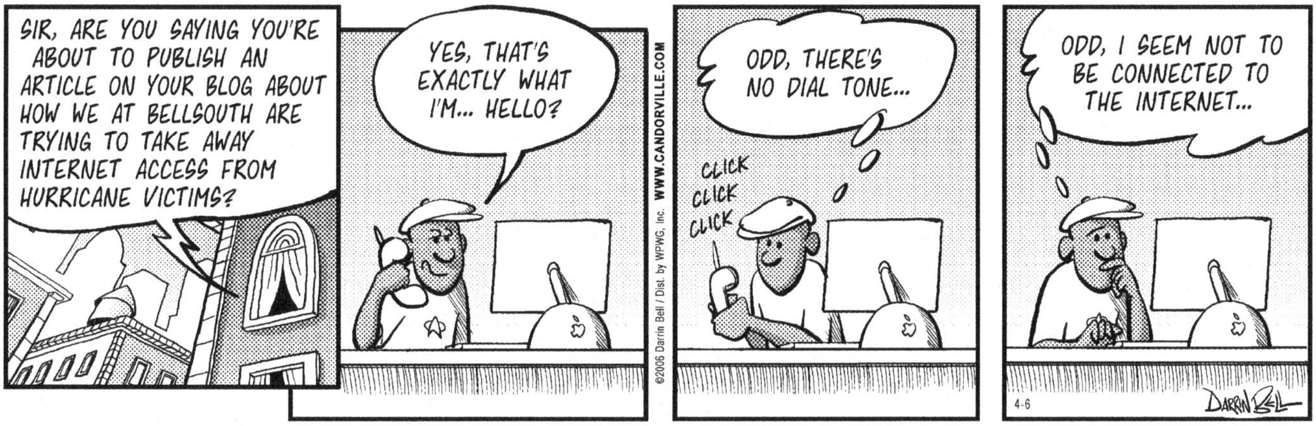
SIR, ARE YOU SAYING YOU'RE ABOUT TO PUBLISH AN ARTICLE ON YOUR BLOG ABOUT HOW WE AT BELLSOUTH ARE TRYING TO TAKE AWAY INTERNET ACCESS FROM HURRICANE VICTIMS?
YES, THAT'S EXACTLY WHAT I'M... HELLO?
©2006 Darrin Bell / Dist. by WPWG, Inc. WWW.CANDORVILLE.COM
ODD, THERE'S NO DIAL TONE...
CLICK CLICK CLICK
ODD, I SEEM NOT TO BE CONNECTED TO THE INTERNET...
4-6
DARRIN BELL

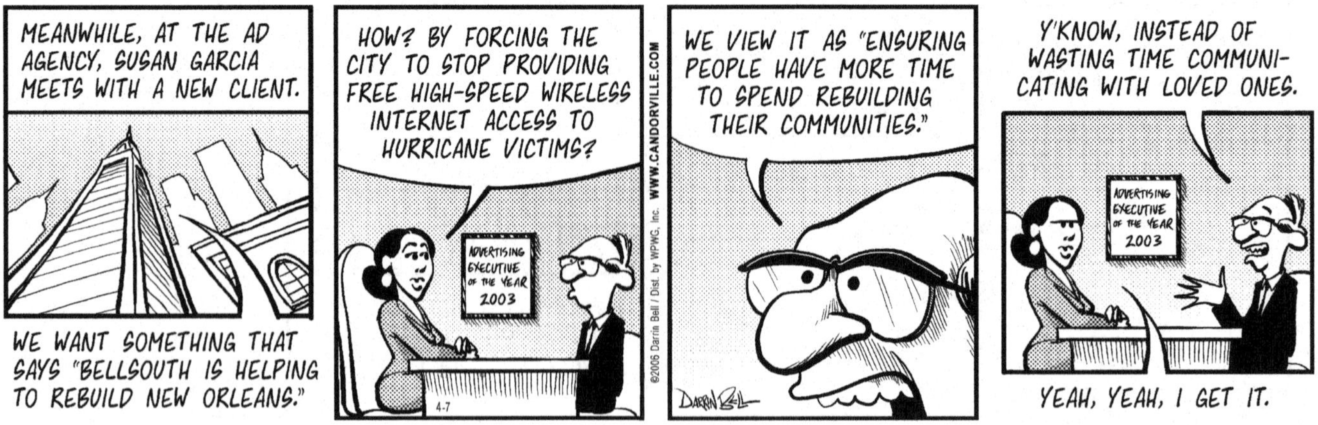
MEANWHILE, AT THE AD AGENCY, SUSAN GARCIA MEETS WITH A NEW CLIENT.
WE WANT SOMETHING THAT SAYS "BELLSOUTH IS HELPING TO REBUILD NEW ORLEANS."
HOW? BY FORCING THE CITY TO STOP PROVIDING FREE HIGH-SPEED WIRELESS INTERNET ACCESS TO HURRICANE VICTIMS?
ADVERTISING EXECUTIVE OF THE YEAR 2003
4-7
©2006 Darrin Bell / Dist. by WPWG, Inc. WWW.CANDORVILLE.COM
WE VIEW IT AS "ENSURING PEOPLE HAVE MORE TIME TO SPEND REBUILDING THEIR COMMUNITIES."
DARRIN BELL
Y'KNOW, INSTEAD OF WASTING TIME COMMUNICATING WITH LOVED ONES.
ADVERTISING EXECUTIVE OF THE YEAR 2003
YEAH, YEAH, I GET IT.

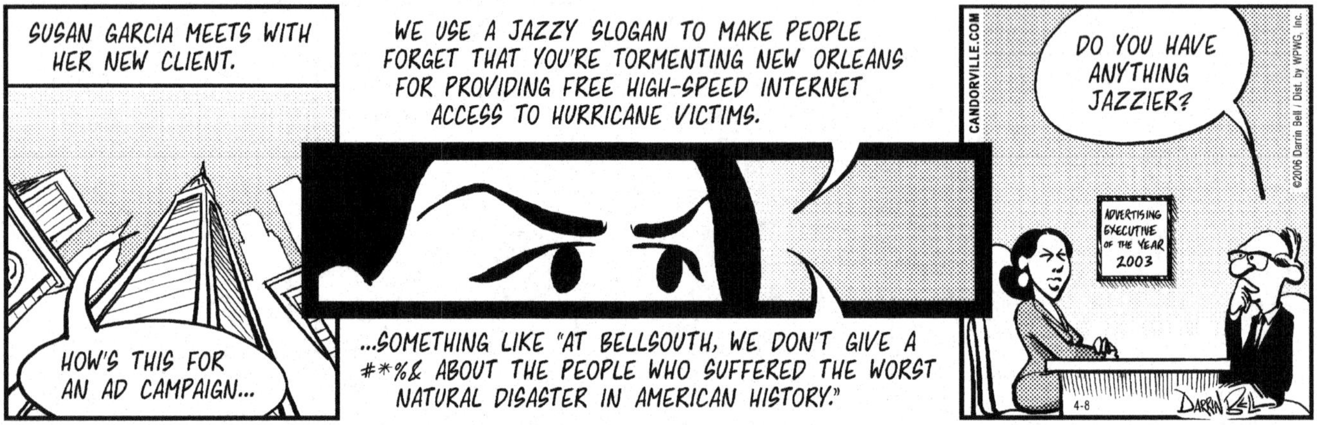
SUSAN GARCIA MEETS WITH HER NEW CLIENT.
HOW'S THIS FOR AN AD CAMPAIGN...
WE USE A JAZZY SLOGAN TO MAKE PEOPLE FORGET THAT YOU'RE TORMENTING NEW ORLEANS FOR PROVIDING FREE HIGH-SPEED INTERNET ACCESS TO HURRICANE VICTIMS.
...SOMETHING LIKE "AT BELLSOUTH, WE DON'T GIVE A #*%& ABOUT THE PEOPLE WHO SUFFERED THE WORST NATURAL DISASTER IN AMERICAN HISTORY."
CANDORVILLE.COM
©2006 Darrin Bell / Dist. by WPWG, Inc.
DO YOU HAVE ANYTHING JAZZIER?
ADVERTISING EXECUTIVE OF THE YEAR 2003
4-8
DARRIN BELL

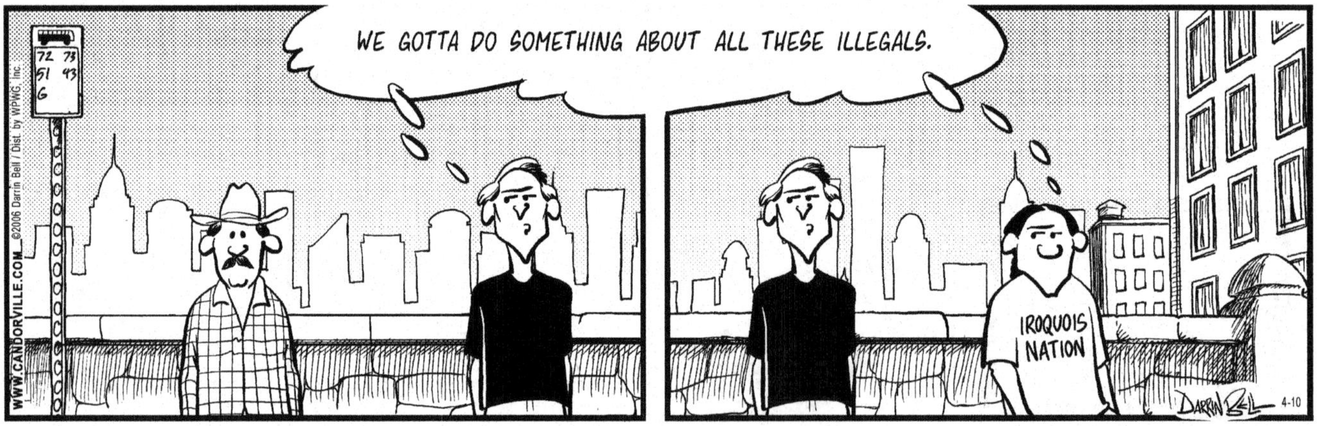
WWW.CANDORVILLE.COM ©2006 Darrin Bell / Dist. by WPWG, Inc.
72 73
51 93
G
WE GOTTA DO SOMETHING ABOUT ALL THESE ILLEGALS.
IROQUOIS NATION
DARRIN BELL
4-10

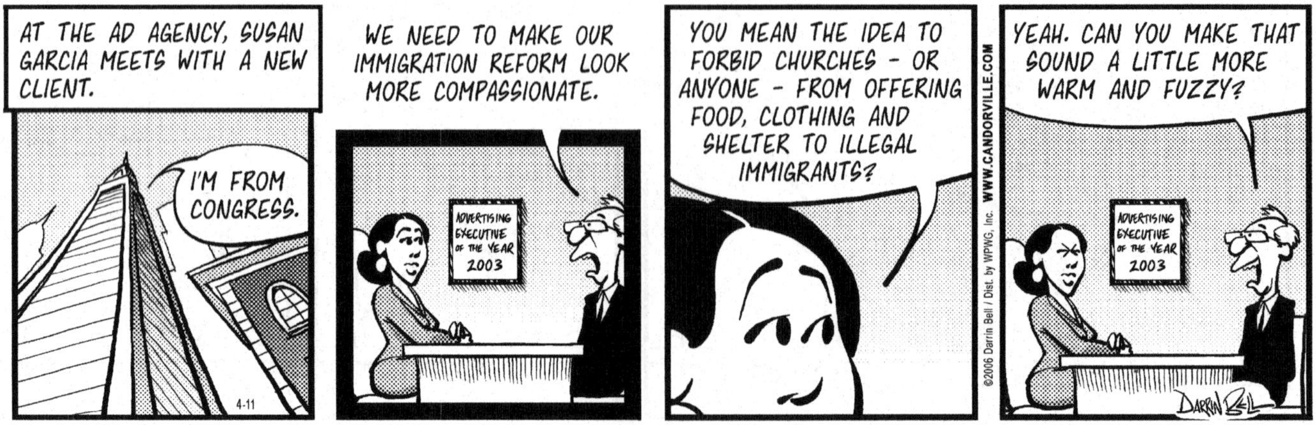
AT THE AD AGENCY, SUSAN GARCIA MEETS WITH A NEW CLIENT.
I'M FROM CONGRESS.
4-11
WE NEED TO MAKE OUR IMMIGRATION REFORM LOOK MORE COMPASSIONATE.
ADVERTISING EXECUTIVE OF THE YEAR 2003
YOU MEAN THE IDEA TO FORBID CHURCHES - OR ANYONE - FROM OFFERING FOOD, CLOTHING AND SHELTER TO ILLEGAL IMMIGRANTS?
©2006 Darrin Bell / Dist. by WPWG, Inc. WWW.CANDORVILLE.COM
YEAH. CAN YOU MAKE THAT SOUND A LITTLE MORE WARM AND FUZZY?
ADVERTISING EXECUTIVE OF THE YEAR 2003
DARRIN BELL

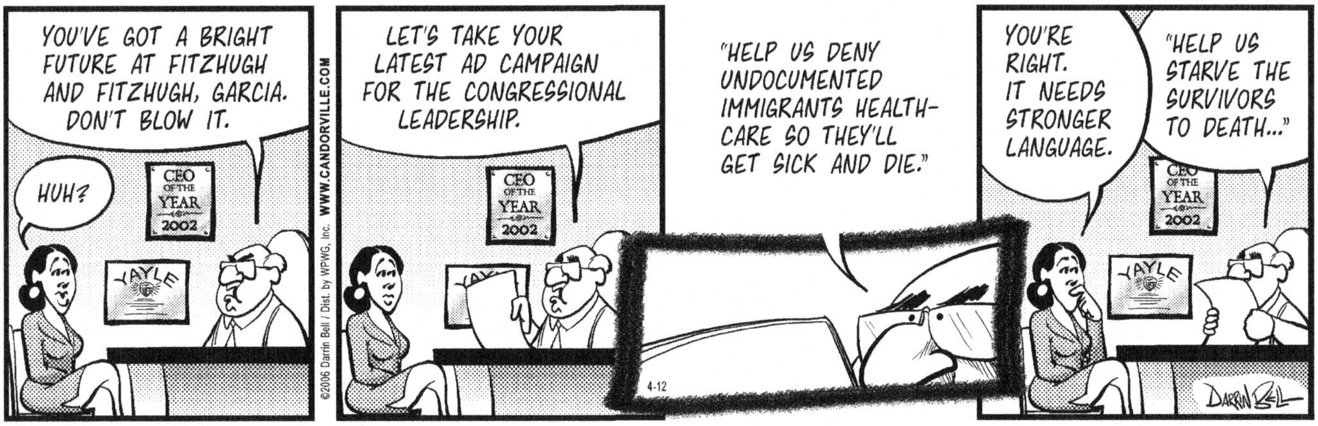
YOU'VE GOT A BRIGHT FUTURE AT FITZHUGH AND FITZHUGH, GARCIA. DON'T BLOW IT.
HUH?
CEO OF THE YEAR 2002
YAYLE
©2006 Darrin Bell / Dist. by WPWG, Inc. WWW.CANDORVILLE.COM
LET'S TAKE YOUR LATEST AD CAMPAIGN FOR THE CONGRESSIONAL LEADERSHIP.
"HELP US DENY UNDOCUMENTED IMMIGRANTS HEALTH-CARE SO THEY'LL GET SICK AND DIE."
4-12
YOU'RE RIGHT. IT NEEDS STRONGER LANGUAGE.
"HELP US STARVE THE SURVIVORS TO DEATH..."
DARRIN BELL

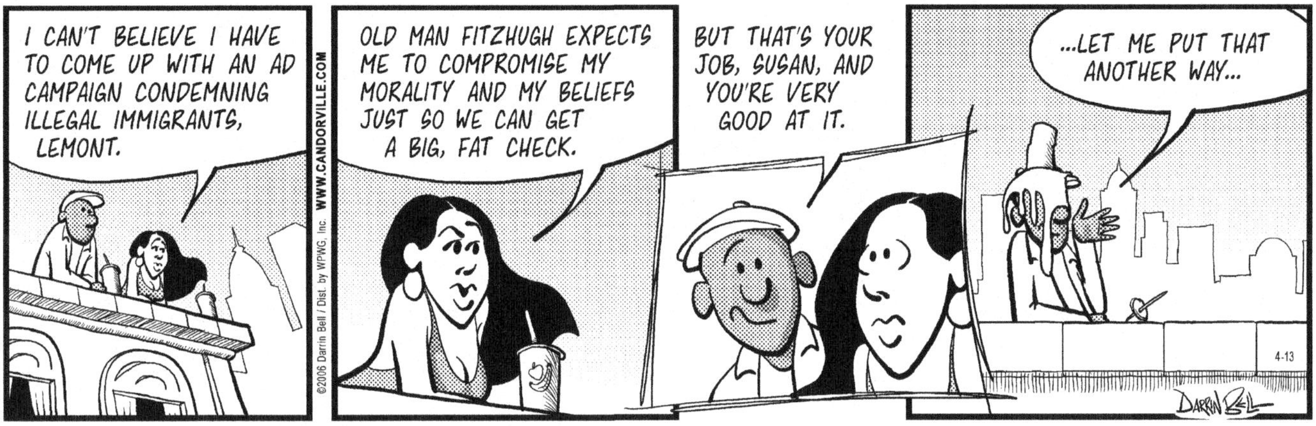
I CAN'T BELIEVE I HAVE TO COME UP WITH AN AD CAMPAIGN CONDEMNING ILLEGAL IMMIGRANTS, LEMONT.
©2006 Darrin Bell / Dist. by WPWG, Inc. WWW.CANDORVILLE.COM
OLD MAN FITZHUGH EXPECTS ME TO COMPROMISE MY MORALITY AND MY BELIEFS JUST SO WE CAN GET A BIG, FAT CHECK.
BUT THAT'S YOUR JOB, SUSAN, AND YOU'RE VERY GOOD AT IT.
...LET ME PUT THAT ANOTHER WAY...
4-13
DARRIN BELL

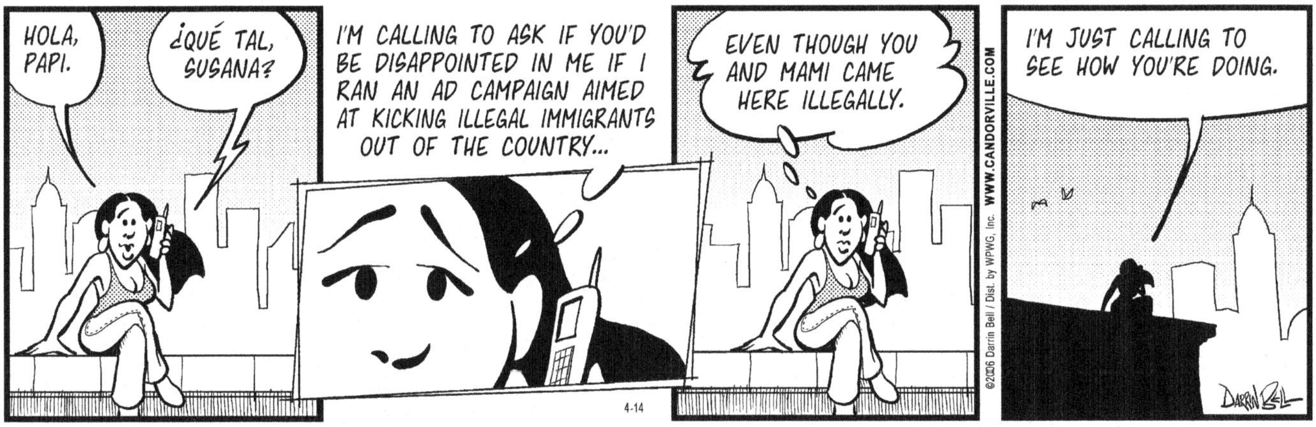
HOLA, PAPI.
¿QUÉ TAL, SUSANA?
I'M CALLING TO ASK IF YOU'D BE DISAPPOINTED IN ME IF I RAN AN AD CAMPAIGN AIMED AT KICKING ILLEGAL IMMIGRANTS OUT OF THE COUNTRY...
4-14
EVEN THOUGH YOU AND MAMI CAME HERE ILLEGALLY.
©2006 Darrin Bell / Dist. by WPWG, Inc. WWW.CANDORVILLE.COM
I'M JUST CALLING TO SEE HOW YOU'RE DOING.
DARRIN BELL

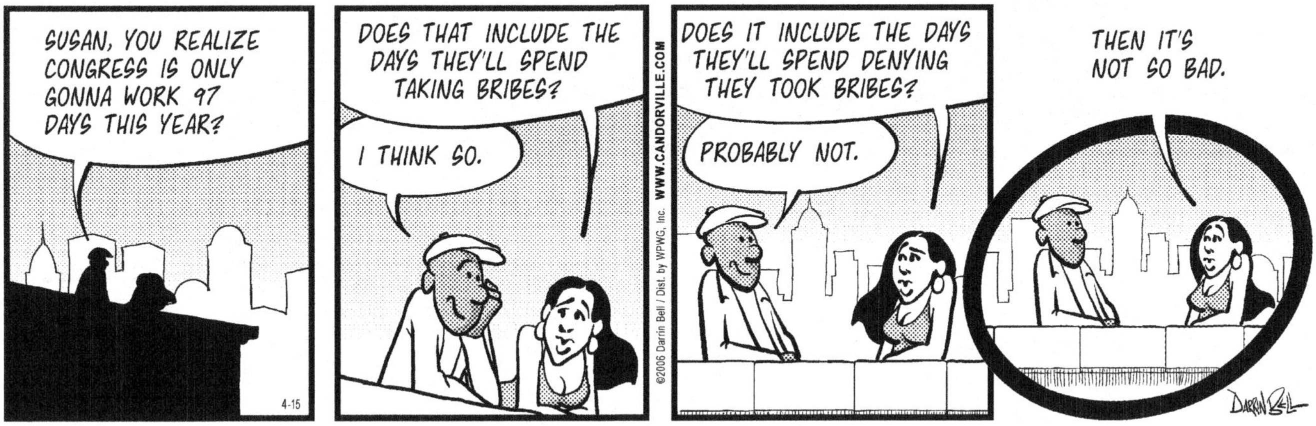
SUSAN, YOU REALIZE CONGRESS IS ONLY GONNA WORK 97 DAYS THIS YEAR?
4-15
DOES THAT INCLUDE THE DAYS THEY'LL SPEND TAKING BRIBES?
I THINK SO.
©2006 Darrin Bell / Dist. by WPWG, Inc. WWW.CANDORVILLE.COM
DOES IT INCLUDE THE DAYS THEY'LL SPEND DENYING THEY TOOK BRIBES?
PROBABLY NOT.
THEN IT'S NOT SO BAD.
DARRIN BELL

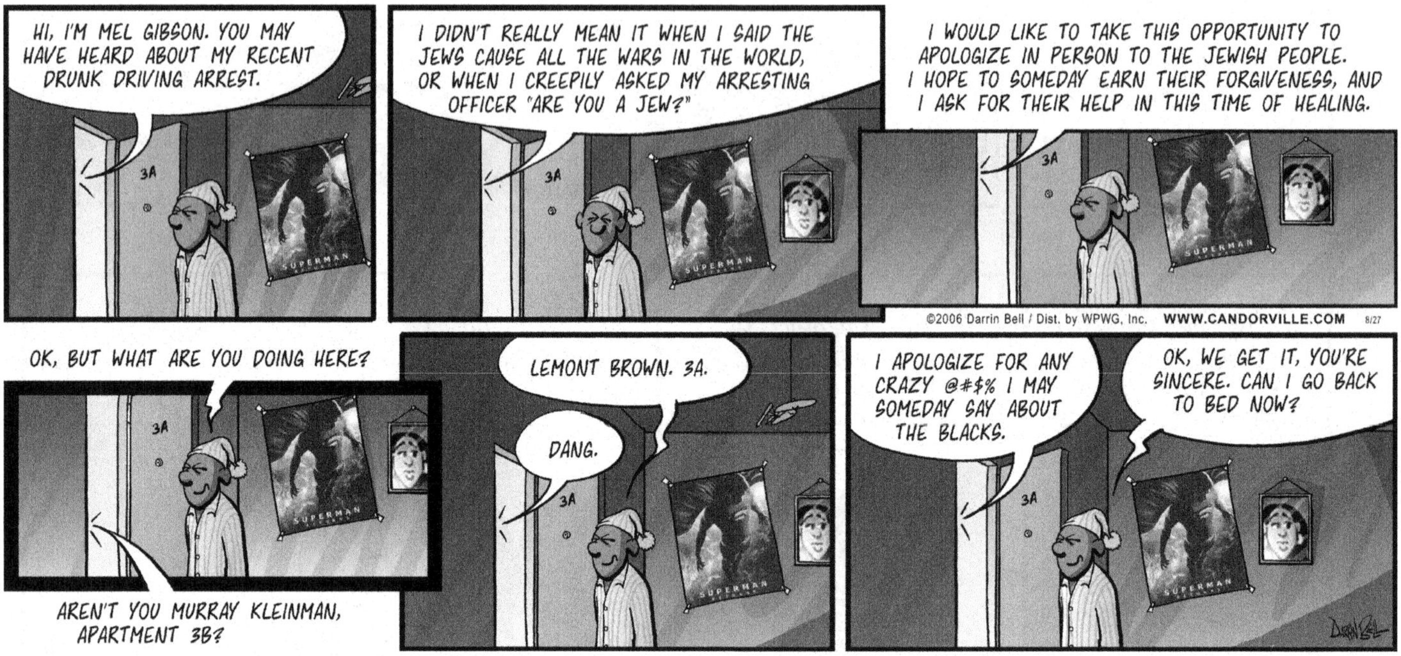
HI, I'M MEL GIBSON. YOU MAY HAVE HEARD ABOUT MY RECENT DRUNK DRIVING ARREST.
3A
SUPERMAN
I DIDN'T REALLY MEAN IT WHEN I SAID THE JEWS CAUSE ALL THE WARS IN THE WORLD, OR WHEN I CREEPILY ASKED MY ARRESTING OFFICER "ARE YOU A JEW?"
I WOULD LIKE TO TAKE THIS OPPORTUNITY TO APOLOGIZE IN PERSON TO THE JEWISH PEOPLE. I HOPE TO SOMEDAY EARN THEIR FORGIVENESS, AND I ASK FOR THEIR HELP IN THIS TIME OF HEALING.
©2006 Darrin Bell / Dist. by WPWG, Inc. WWW.CANDORVILLE.COM 8/27
OK, BUT WHAT ARE YOU DOING HERE?
AREN'T YOU MURRAY KLEINMAN, APARTMENT 3B?
LEMONT BROWN. 3A.
DANG.
I APOLOGIZE FOR ANY CRAZY @#$% I MAY SOMEDAY SAY ABOUT THE BLACKS.
OK, WE GET IT, YOU'RE SINCERE. CAN I GO BACK TO BED NOW?
DARRIN BELL

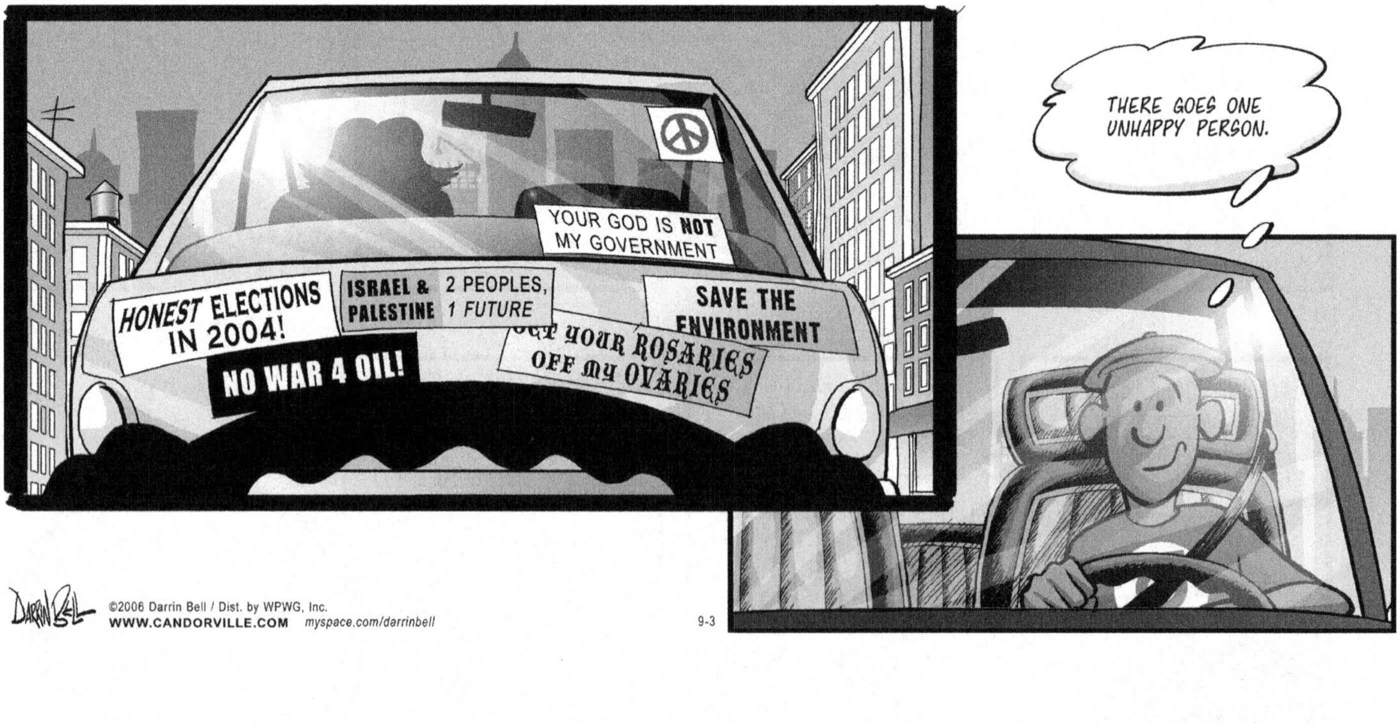
YOUR GOD IS NOT MY GOVERNMENT
HONEST ELECTIONS IN 2004!
ISRAEL & PALESTINE 2 PEOPLES, 1 FUTURE
SAVE THE ENVIRONMENT
NO WAR 4 OIL!
GET YOUR ROSARIES OFF MY OVARIES
THERE GOES ONE UNHAPPY PERSON.
DARRIN BELL
©2006 Darrin Bell / Dist. by WPWG, Inc.
WWW.CANDORVILLE.COM myspace.com/darrinbell
9-3

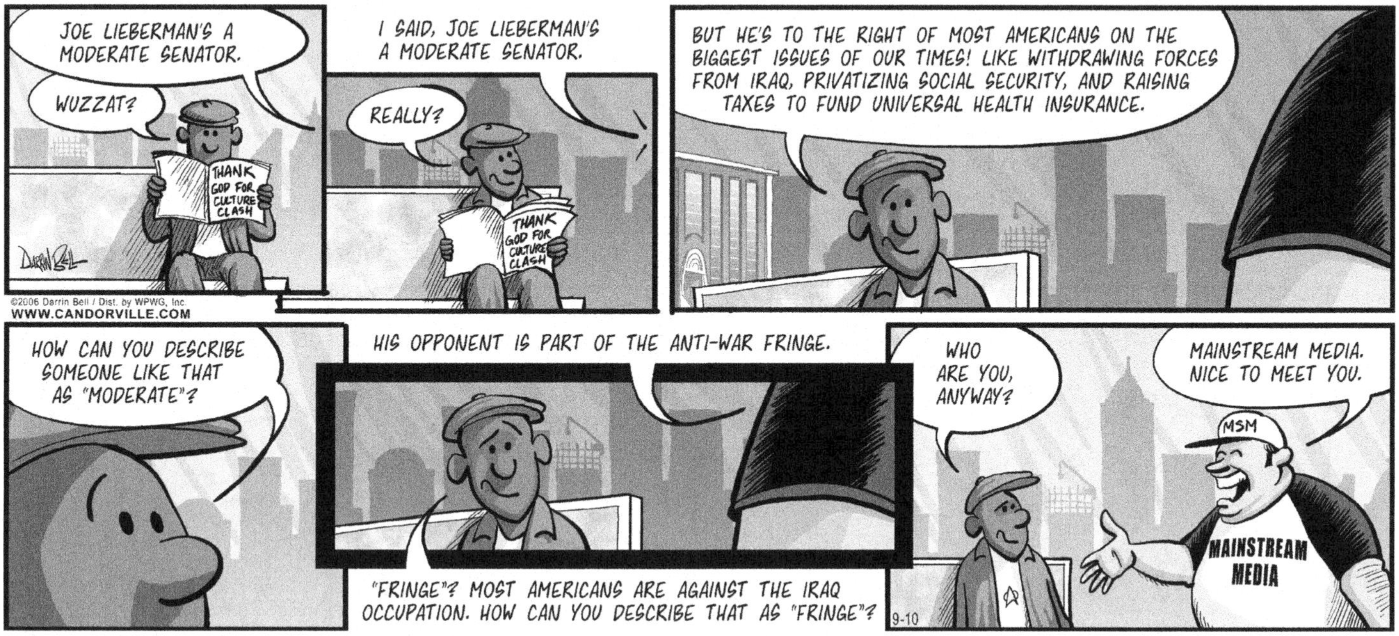
JOE LIEBERMAN'S A MODERATE SENATOR.
WUZZAT?
THANK GOD FOR CULTURE CLASH
©2006 Darrin Bell / Dist. by WPWG, Inc.
WWW.CANDORVILLE.COM
I SAID, JOE LIEBERMAN'S A MODERATE SENATOR.
REALLY?
THANK GOD FOR CULTURE CLASH
BUT HE'S TO THE RIGHT OF MOST AMERICANS ON THE BIGGEST ISSUES OF OUR TIMES! LIKE WITHDRAWING FORCES FROM IRAQ, PRIVATIZING SOCIAL SECURITY, AND RAISING TAXES TO FUND UNIVERSAL HEALTH INSURANCE.
HOW CAN YOU DESCRIBE SOMEONE LIKE THAT AS "MODERATE"?
HIS OPPONENT IS PART OF THE ANTI-WAR FRINGE.
"FRINGE"? MOST AMERICANS ARE AGAINST THE IRAQ OCCUPATION. HOW CAN YOU DESCRIBE THAT AS "FRINGE"?
WHO ARE YOU, ANYWAY?
MAINSTREAM MEDIA. NICE TO MEET YOU.
MSM
MAINSTREAM MEDIA
9-10

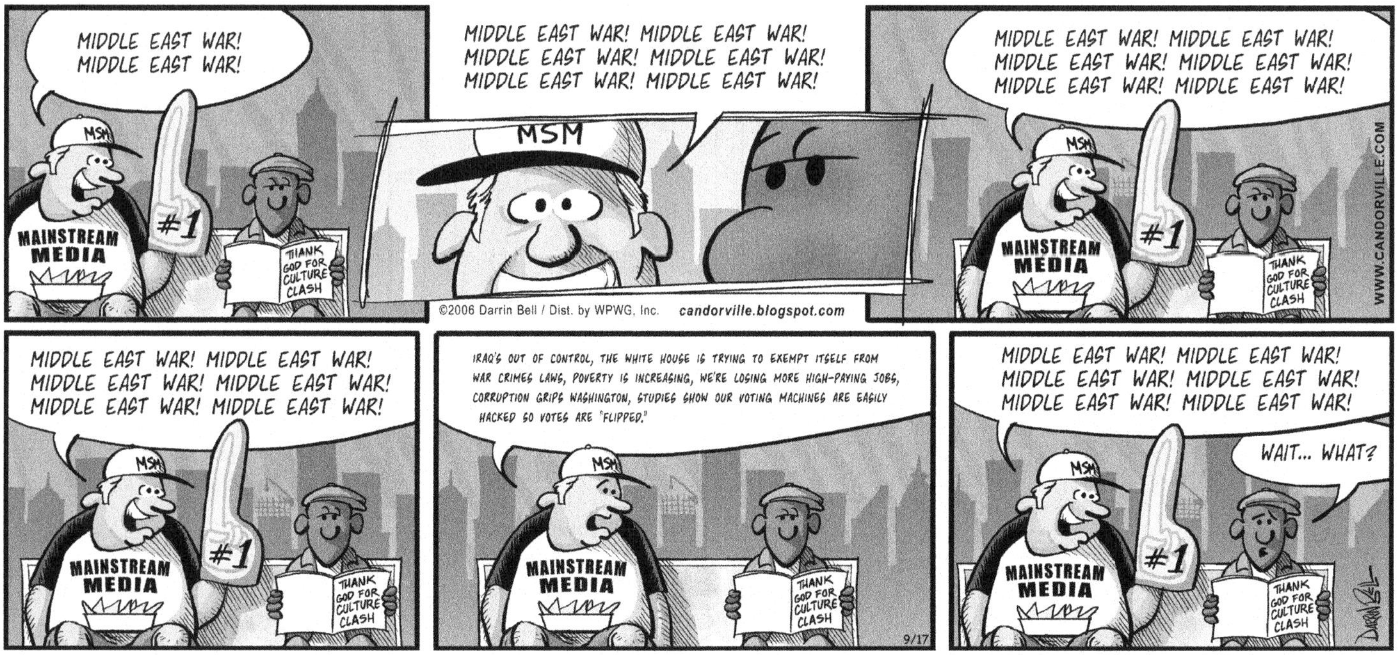
MIDDLE EAST WAR! MIDDLE EAST WAR!
MSM
MAINSTREAM MEDIA
#1
THANK GOD FOR CULTURE CLASH
MIDDLE EAST WAR! MIDDLE EAST WAR! MIDDLE EAST WAR! MIDDLE EAST WAR! MIDDLE EAST WAR! MIDDLE EAST WAR!
MSM
©2006 Darrin Bell / Dist. by WPWG, Inc. candorville.blogspot.com
MIDDLE EAST WAR! MIDDLE EAST WAR! MIDDLE EAST WAR! MIDDLE EAST WAR! MIDDLE EAST WAR! MIDDLE EAST WAR!
WWW.CANDORVILLE.COM
MIDDLE EAST WAR! MIDDLE EAST WAR! MIDDLE EAST WAR! MIDDLE EAST WAR! MIDDLE EAST WAR! MIDDLE EAST WAR!
IRAQ'S OUT OF CONTROL, THE WHITE HOUSE IS TRYING TO EXEMPT ITSELF FROM WAR CRIMES LAWS, POVERTY IS INCREASING, WE'RE LOSING MORE HIGH-PAYING JOBS, CORRUPTION GRIPS WASHINGTON, STUDIES SHOW OUR VOTING MACHINES ARE EASILY HACKED SO VOTES ARE "FLIPPED."
9/17
MIDDLE EAST WAR! MIDDLE EAST WAR! MIDDLE EAST WAR! MIDDLE EAST WAR! MIDDLE EAST WAR! MIDDLE EAST WAR!
WAIT... WHAT?

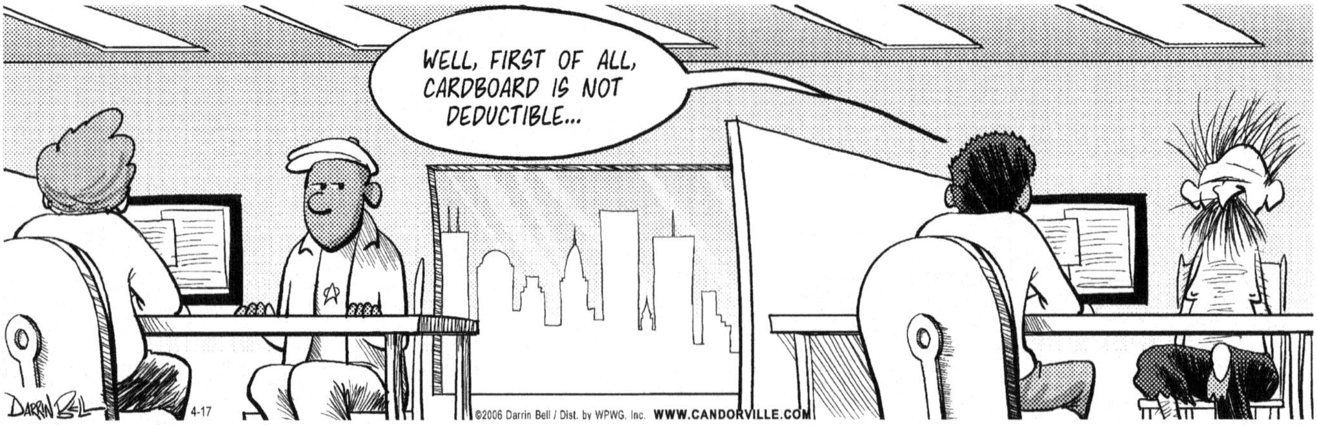
WELL, FIRST OF ALL, CARDBOARD IS NOT DEDUCTIBLE...
DARRIN BELL
4-17
©2006 Darrin Bell / Dist. by WPWG, Inc. WWW.CANDORVILLE.COM

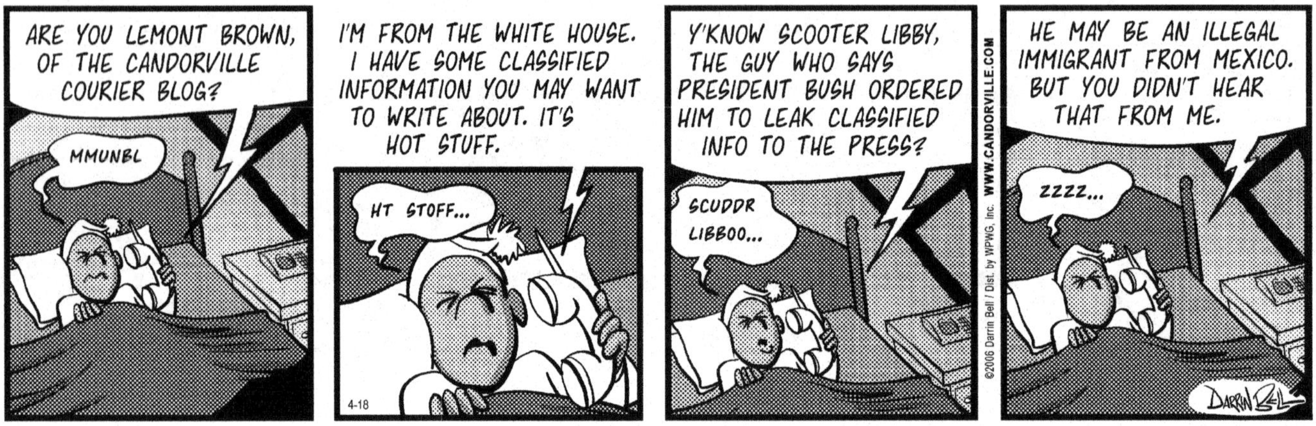
ARE YOU LEMONT BROWN, OF THE CANDORVILLE COURIER BLOG?
MMUNBL
I'M FROM THE WHITE HOUSE. I HAVE SOME CLASSIFIED INFORMATION YOU MAY WANT TO WRITE ABOUT. IT'S HOT STUFF.
HT STOFF...
4-18
Y'KNOW SCOOTER LIBBY, THE GUY WHO SAYS PRESIDENT BUSH ORDERED HIM TO LEAK CLASSIFIED INFO TO THE PRESS?
SCUDDR LIBBOO...
©2006 Darrin Bell / Dist. by WPWG, Inc. WWW.CANDORVILLE.COM
HE MAY BE AN ILLEGAL IMMIGRANT FROM MEXICO. BUT YOU DIDN'T HEAR THAT FROM ME.
ZZZZ...
DARRIN BELL

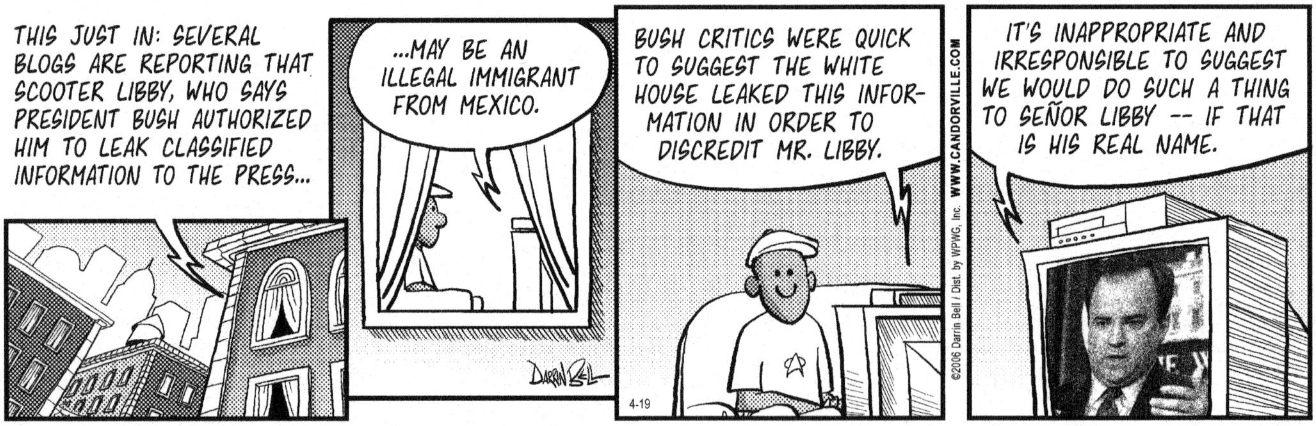
THIS JUST IN: SEVERAL BLOGS ARE REPORTING THAT SCOOTER LIBBY, WHO SAYS PRESIDENT BUSH AUTHORIZED HIM TO LEAK CLASSIFIED INFORMATION TO THE PRESS...
...MAY BE AN ILLEGAL IMMIGRANT FROM MEXICO.
DARRIN BELL
BUSH CRITICS WERE QUICK TO SUGGEST THE WHITE HOUSE LEAKED THIS INFORMATION IN ORDER TO DISCREDIT MR. LIBBY.
4-19
©2006 Darrin Bell / Dist. by WPWG, Inc. WWW.CANDORVILLE.COM
IT'S INAPPROPRIATE AND IRRESPONSIBLE TO SUGGEST WE WOULD DO SUCH A THING TO SEÑOR LIBBY -- IF THAT IS HIS REAL NAME.

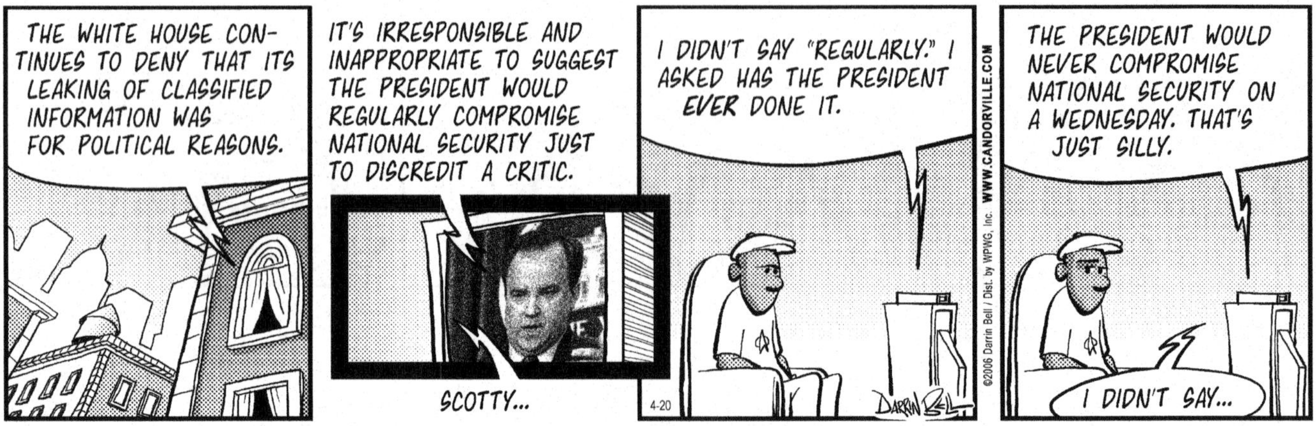
THE WHITE HOUSE CONTINUES TO DENY THAT ITS LEAKING OF CLASSIFIED INFORMATION WAS FOR POLITICAL REASONS.
IT'S IRRESPONSIBLE AND INAPPROPRIATE TO SUGGEST THE PRESIDENT WOULD REGULARLY COMPROMISE NATIONAL SECURITY JUST TO DISCREDIT A CRITIC.
SCOTTY...
I DIDN'T SAY "REGULARLY." I ASKED HAS THE PRESIDENT EVER DONE IT.
4-20
DARRIN BELL
©2006 Darrin Bell / Dist. by WPWG, Inc. WWW.CANDORVILLE.COM
THE PRESIDENT WOULD NEVER COMPROMISE NATIONAL SECURITY ON A WEDNESDAY. THAT'S JUST SILLY.
I DIDN'T SAY...

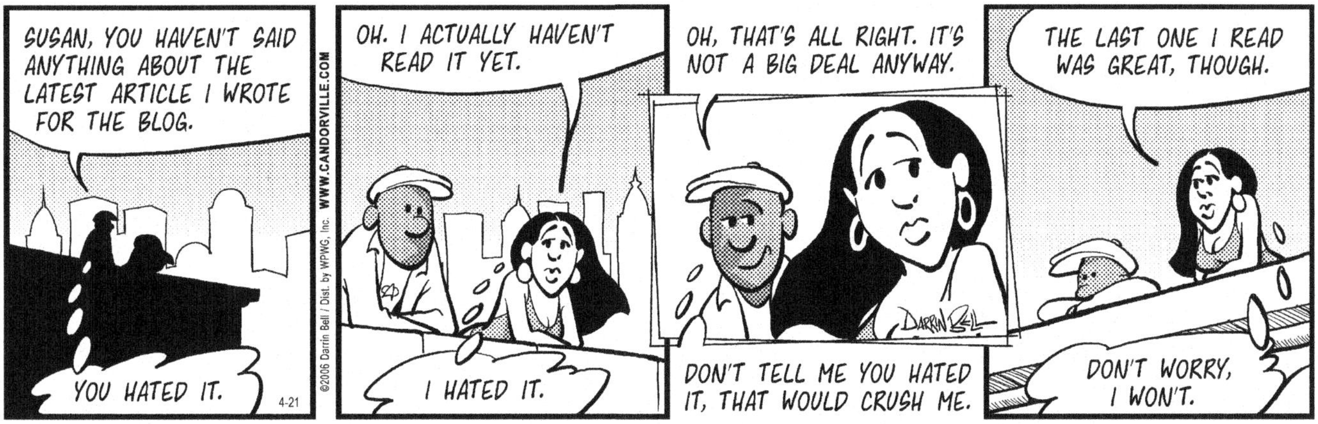
SUSAN, YOU HAVEN'T SAID ANYTHING ABOUT THE LATEST ARTICLE I WROTE FOR THE BLOG.
YOU HATED IT.
4-21
©2006 Darrin Bell / Dist. by WPWG, Inc. WWW.CANDORVILLE.COM
OH. I ACTUALLY HAVEN'T READ IT YET.
I HATED IT.
OH, THAT'S ALL RIGHT. IT'S NOT A BIG DEAL ANYWAY.
DON'T TELL ME YOU HATED IT, THAT WOULD CRUSH ME.
DARRIN BELL
THE LAST ONE I READ WAS GREAT, THOUGH.
DON'T WORRY, I WON'T.

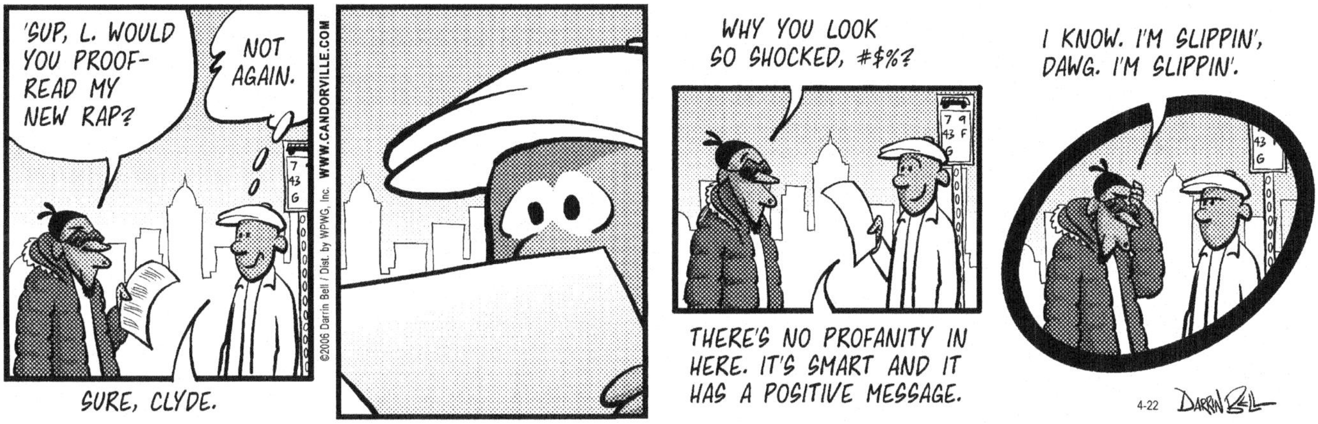
'SUP, L. WOULD YOU PROOF-READ MY NEW RAP?
NOT AGAIN.
SURE, CLYDE.
©2006 Darrin Bell / Dist. by WPWG, Inc. WWW.CANDORVILLE.COM
WHY YOU LOOK SO SHOCKED, #$%?
THERE'S NO PROFANITY IN HERE. IT'S SMART AND IT HAS A POSITIVE MESSAGE.
I KNOW. I'M SLIPPIN', DAWG. I'M SLIPPIN'.
4-22
DARRIN BELL

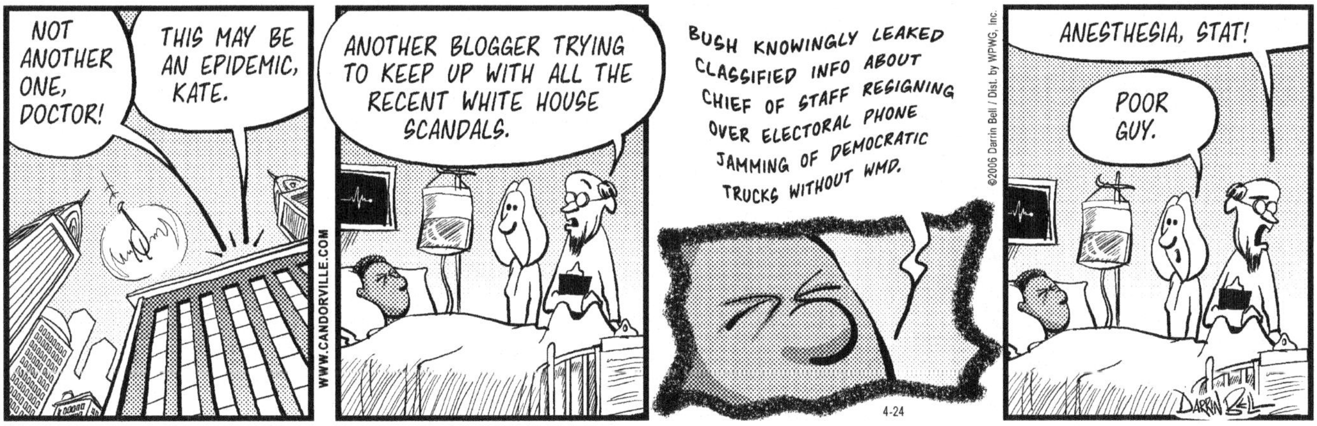
NOT ANOTHER ONE, DOCTOR!
THIS MAY BE AN EPIDEMIC, KATE.
WWW.CANDORVILLE.COM
ANOTHER BLOGGER TRYING TO KEEP UP WITH ALL THE RECENT WHITE HOUSE SCANDALS.
BUSH KNOWINGLY LEAKED CLASSIFIED INFO ABOUT CHIEF OF STAFF RESIGNING OVER ELECTORAL PHONE JAMMING OF DEMOCRATIC TRUCKS WITHOUT WMD.
4-24
©2006 Darrin Bell / Dist. by WPWG, Inc.
ANESTHESIA, STAT!
POOR GUY.
DARRIN BELL

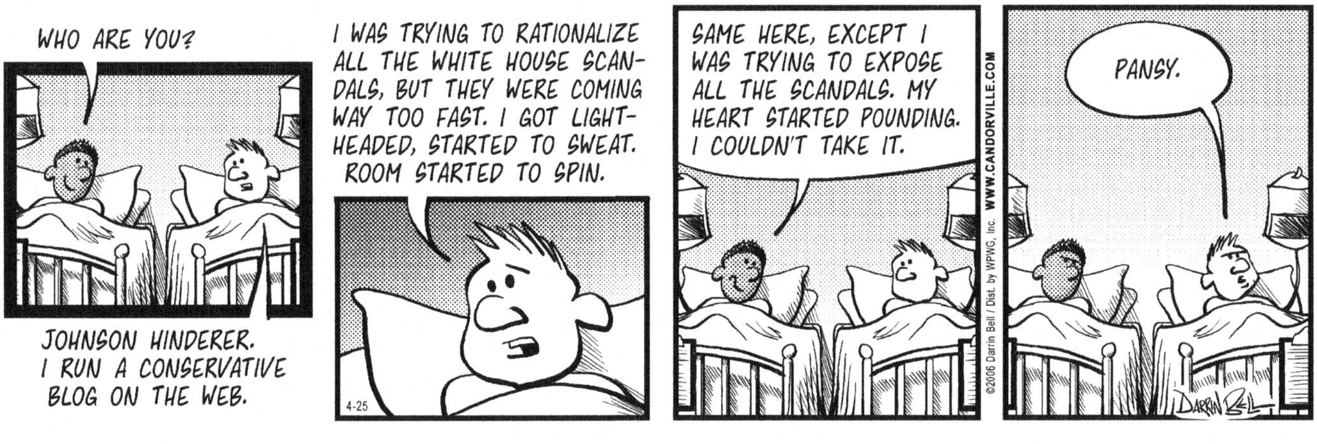
WHO ARE YOU?
JOHNSON HINDERER. I RUN A CONSERVATIVE BLOG ON THE WEB.
I WAS TRYING TO RATIONALIZE ALL THE WHITE HOUSE SCANDALS, BUT THEY WERE COMING WAY TOO FAST. I GOT LIGHT-HEADED, STARTED TO SWEAT. ROOM STARTED TO SPIN.
4-25
SAME HERE, EXCEPT I WAS TRYING TO EXPOSE ALL THE SCANDALS. MY HEART STARTED POUNDING. I COULDN'T TAKE IT.
©2006 Darrin Bell / Dist. by WPWG, Inc. WWW.CANDORVILLE.COM
PANSY.
DARRIN BELL

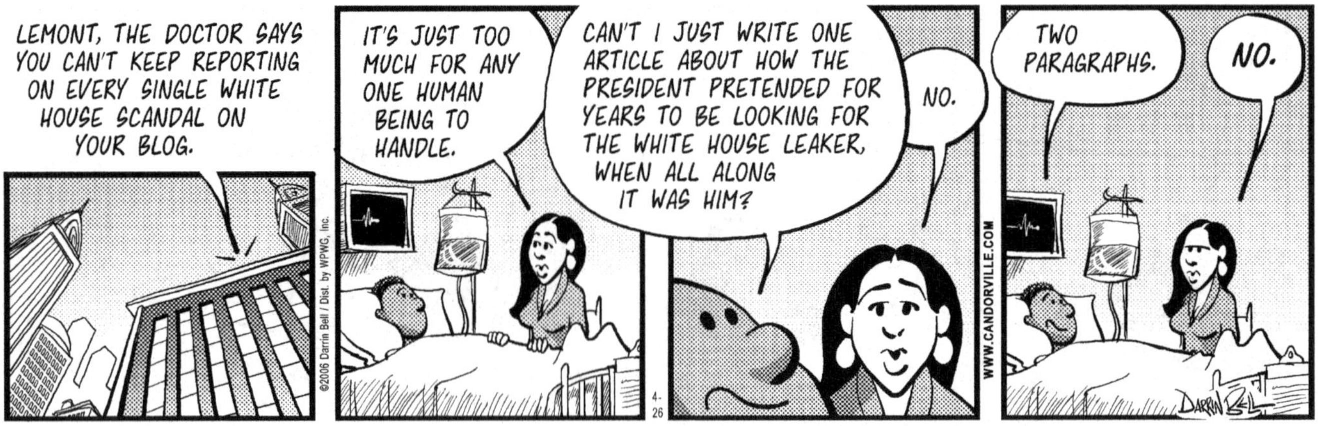
LEMONT, THE DOCTOR SAYS YOU CAN'T KEEP REPORTING ON EVERY SINGLE WHITE HOUSE SCANDAL ON YOUR BLOG.
©2006 Darrin Bell / Dist. by WPWG, Inc.
IT'S JUST TOO MUCH FOR ANY ONE HUMAN BEING TO HANDLE.
4-26
CAN'T I JUST WRITE ONE ARTICLE ABOUT HOW THE PRESIDENT PRETENDED FOR YEARS TO BE LOOKING FOR THE WHITE HOUSE LEAKER, WHEN ALL ALONG IT WAS HIM?
NO.
WWW.CANDORVILLE.COM
TWO PARAGRAPHS.
NO.
DARRIN BELL

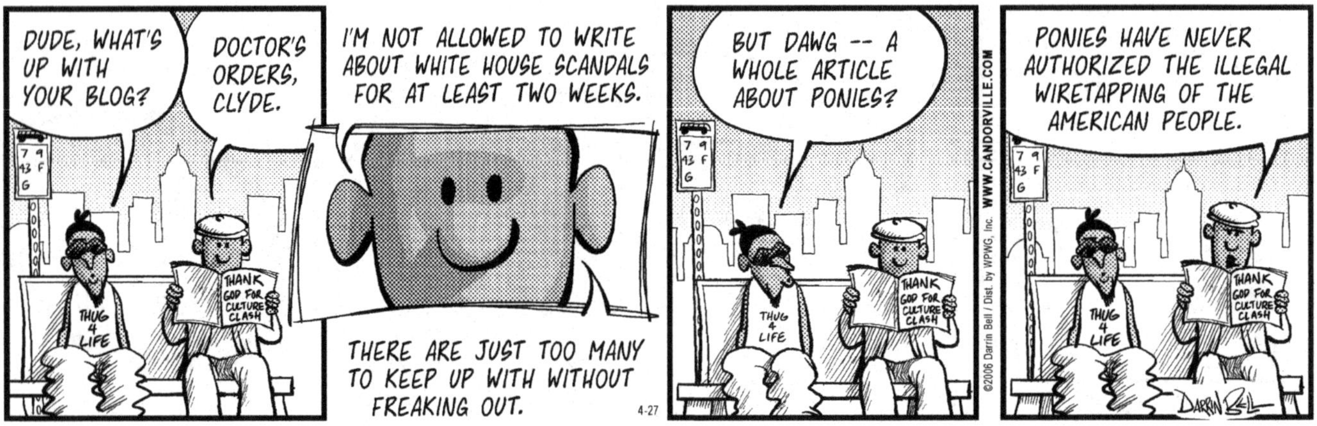
DUDE, WHAT'S UP WITH YOUR BLOG?
DOCTOR'S ORDERS, CLYDE.
THUG 4 LIFE
THANK GOD FOR CULTURE CLASH
I'M NOT ALLOWED TO WRITE ABOUT WHITE HOUSE SCANDALS FOR AT LEAST TWO WEEKS.
THERE ARE JUST TOO MANY TO KEEP UP WITH WITHOUT FREAKING OUT.
4-27
BUT DAWG -- A WHOLE ARTICLE ABOUT PONIES?
WWW.CANDORVILLE.COM
©2006 Darrin Bell / Dist. by WPWG, Inc.
PONIES HAVE NEVER AUTHORIZED THE ILLEGAL WIRETAPPING OF THE AMERICAN PEOPLE.
DARRIN BELL

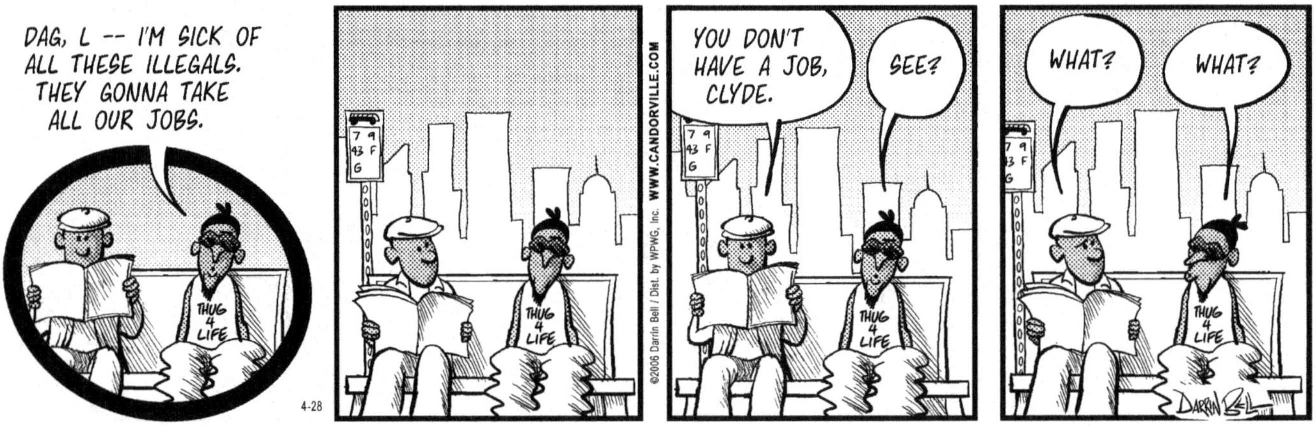
DAG, L -- I'M SICK OF ALL THESE ILLEGALS. THEY GONNA TAKE ALL OUR JOBS.
THUG 4 LIFE
4-28
©2006 Darrin Bell / Dist. by WPWG, Inc. WWW.CANDORVILLE.COM
YOU DON'T HAVE A JOB, CLYDE.
SEE?
WHAT?
WHAT?
DARRIN BELL

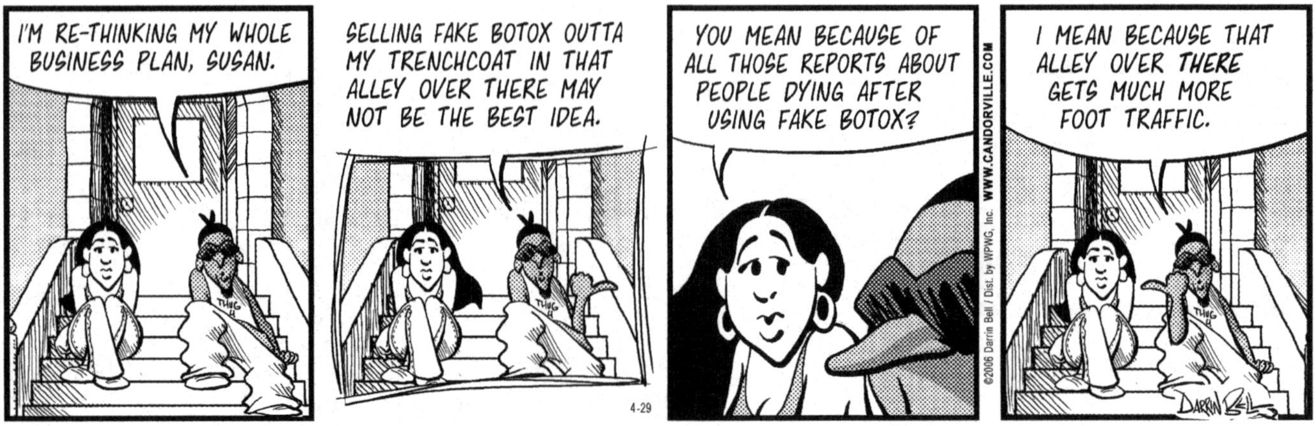
I'M RE-THINKING MY WHOLE BUSINESS PLAN, SUSAN.
SELLING FAKE BOTOX OUTTA MY TRENCHCOAT IN THAT ALLEY OVER THERE MAY NOT BE THE BEST IDEA.
4-29
YOU MEAN BECAUSE OF ALL THOSE REPORTS ABOUT PEOPLE DYING AFTER USING FAKE BOTOX?
©2006 Darrin Bell / Dist. by WPWG, Inc. WWW.CANDORVILLE.COM
I MEAN BECAUSE THAT ALLEY OVER THERE GETS MUCH MORE FOOT TRAFFIC.
DARRIN BELL

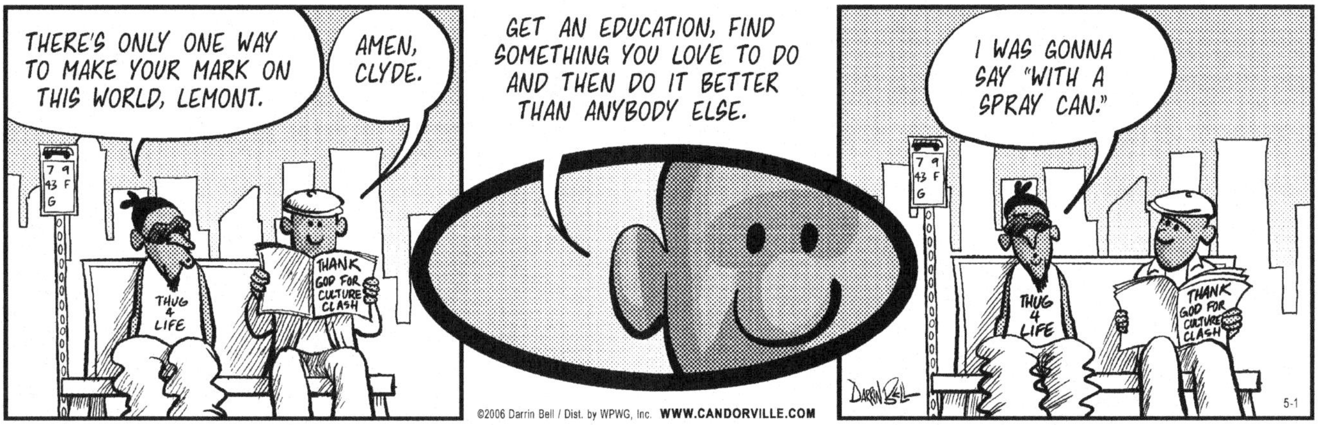
THERE'S ONLY ONE WAY TO MAKE YOUR MARK ON THIS WORLD, LEMONT.
AMEN, CLYDE.
THANK GOD FOR CULTURE CLASH
THUG 4 LIFE
GET AN EDUCATION, FIND SOMETHING YOU LOVE TO DO AND THEN DO IT BETTER THAN ANYBODY ELSE.
I WAS GONNA SAY "WITH A SPRAY CAN."
©2006 Darrin Bell / Dist. by WPWG, Inc. WWW.CANDORVILLE.COM
DARRIN BELL
5-1

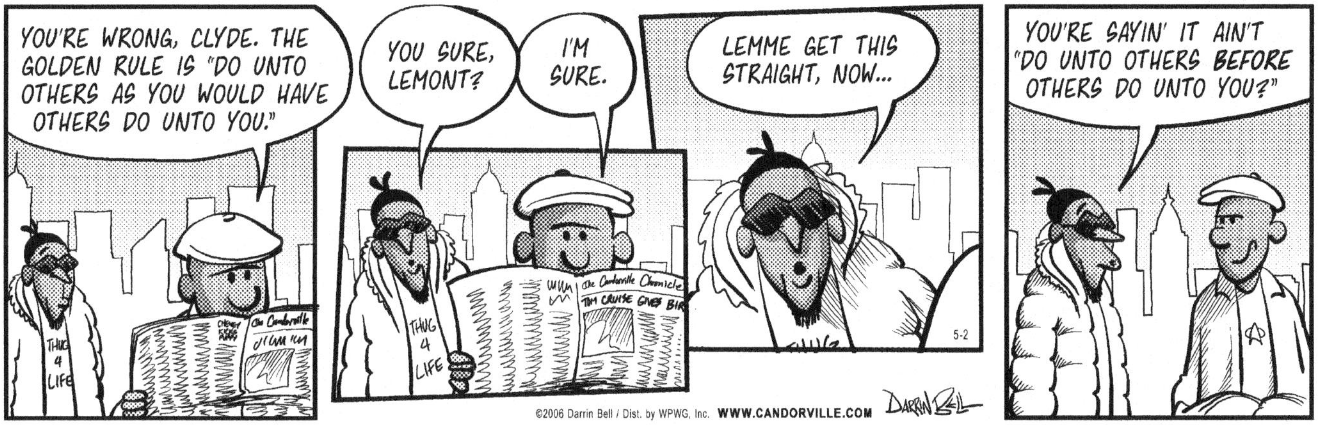
YOU'RE WRONG, CLYDE. THE GOLDEN RULE IS "DO UNTO OTHERS AS YOU WOULD HAVE OTHERS DO UNTO YOU."
YOU SURE, LEMONT?
I'M SURE.
LEMME GET THIS STRAIGHT, NOW...
YOU'RE SAYIN' IT AIN'T "DO UNTO OTHERS **BEFORE** OTHERS DO UNTO YOU?"
©2006 Darrin Bell / Dist. by WPWG, Inc. WWW.CANDORVILLE.COM
DARRIN BELL
5-2

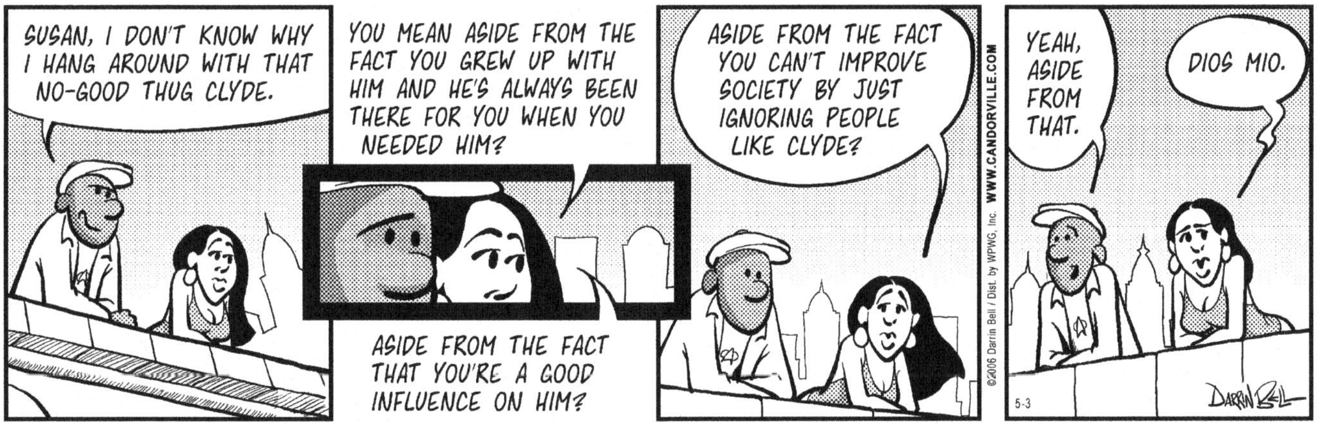
SUSAN, I DON'T KNOW WHY I HANG AROUND WITH THAT NO-GOOD THUG CLYDE.
YOU MEAN ASIDE FROM THE FACT YOU GREW UP WITH HIM AND HE'S ALWAYS BEEN THERE FOR YOU WHEN YOU NEEDED HIM?
ASIDE FROM THE FACT THAT YOU'RE A GOOD INFLUENCE ON HIM?
ASIDE FROM THE FACT YOU CAN'T IMPROVE SOCIETY BY JUST IGNORING PEOPLE LIKE CLYDE?
YEAH, ASIDE FROM THAT.
DIOS MIO.
©2006 Darrin Bell / Dist. by WPWG, Inc. WWW.CANDORVILLE.COM
DARRIN BELL
5-3

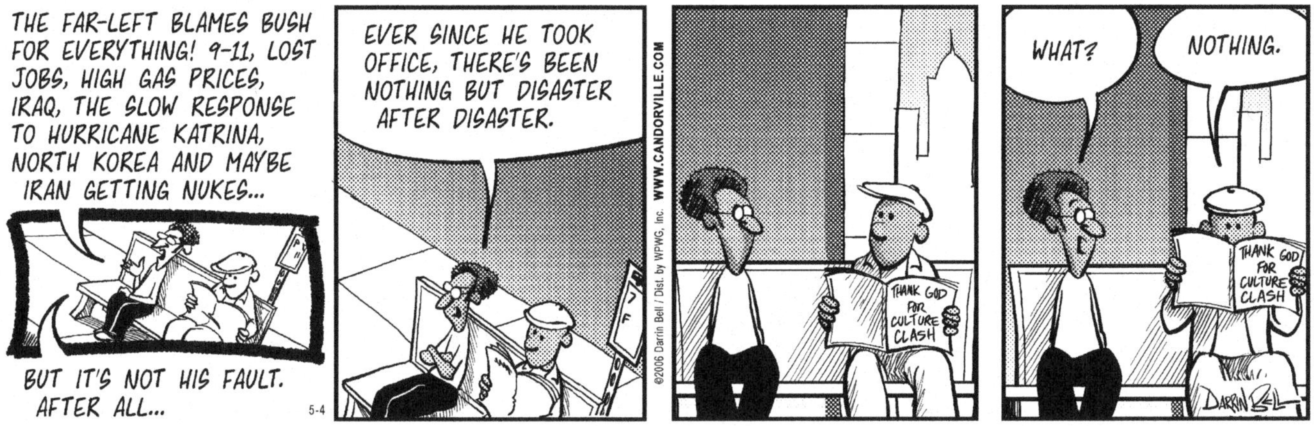
THE FAR-LEFT BLAMES BUSH FOR EVERYTHING! 9-11, LOST JOBS, HIGH GAS PRICES, IRAQ, THE SLOW RESPONSE TO HURRICANE KATRINA, NORTH KOREA AND MAYBE IRAN GETTING NUKES...
BUT IT'S NOT HIS FAULT. AFTER ALL...
5-4
EVER SINCE HE TOOK OFFICE, THERE'S BEEN NOTHING BUT DISASTER AFTER DISASTER.
©2006 Darrin Bell / Dist. by WPWG, Inc. WWW.CANDORVILLE.COM
THANK GOD FOR CULTURE CLASH
WHAT?
NOTHING.
THANK GOD FOR CULTURE CLASH
DARRIN BELL

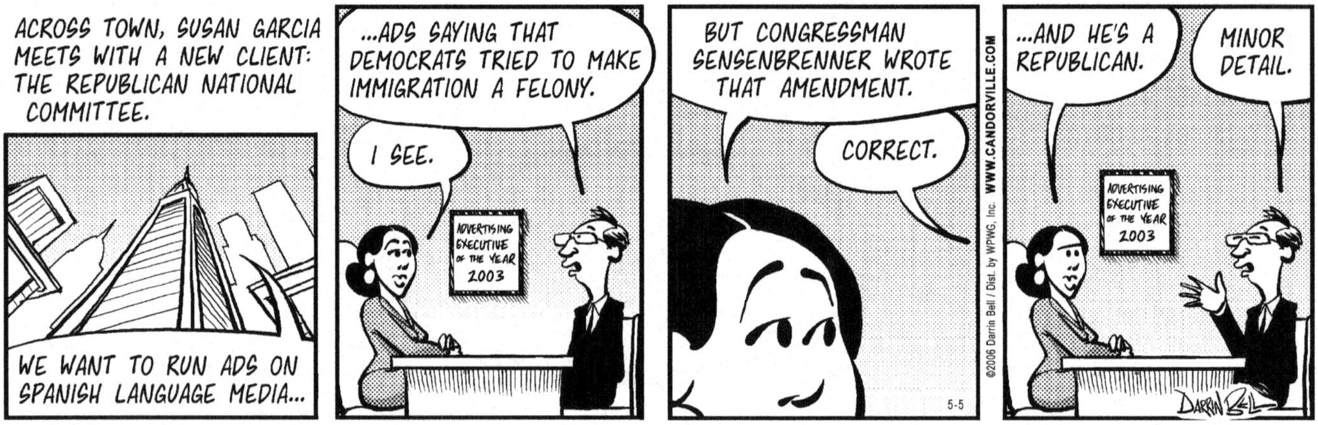
ACROSS TOWN, SUSAN GARCIA MEETS WITH A NEW CLIENT: THE REPUBLICAN NATIONAL COMMITTEE.
WE WANT TO RUN ADS ON SPANISH LANGUAGE MEDIA...
...ADS SAYING THAT DEMOCRATS TRIED TO MAKE IMMIGRATION A FELONY.
I SEE.
ADVERTISING EXECUTIVE OF THE YEAR 2003
BUT CONGRESSMAN SENSENBRENNER WROTE THAT AMENDMENT.
CORRECT.
5-5
©2006 Darrin Bell / Dist. by WPWG, Inc. WWW.CANDORVILLE.COM
...AND HE'S A REPUBLICAN.
MINOR DETAIL.
ADVERTISING EXECUTIVE OF THE YEAR 2003
DARRIN BELL

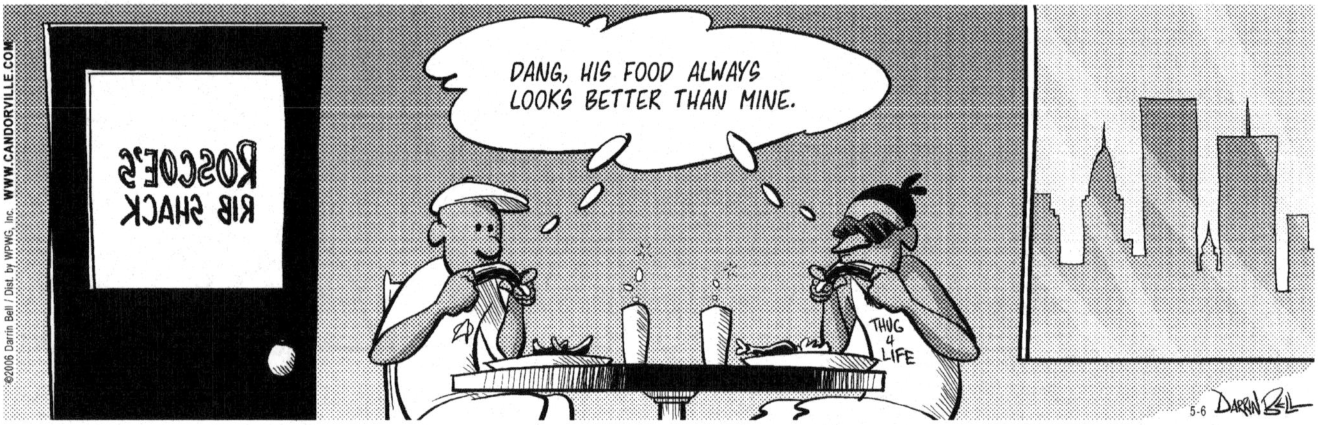
©2006 Darrin Bell / Dist. by WPWG, Inc. WWW.CANDORVILLE.COM
ROSCOE'S RIB SHACK
DANG, HIS FOOD ALWAYS LOOKS BETTER THAN MINE.
THUG 4 LIFE
5-6
DARRIN BELL

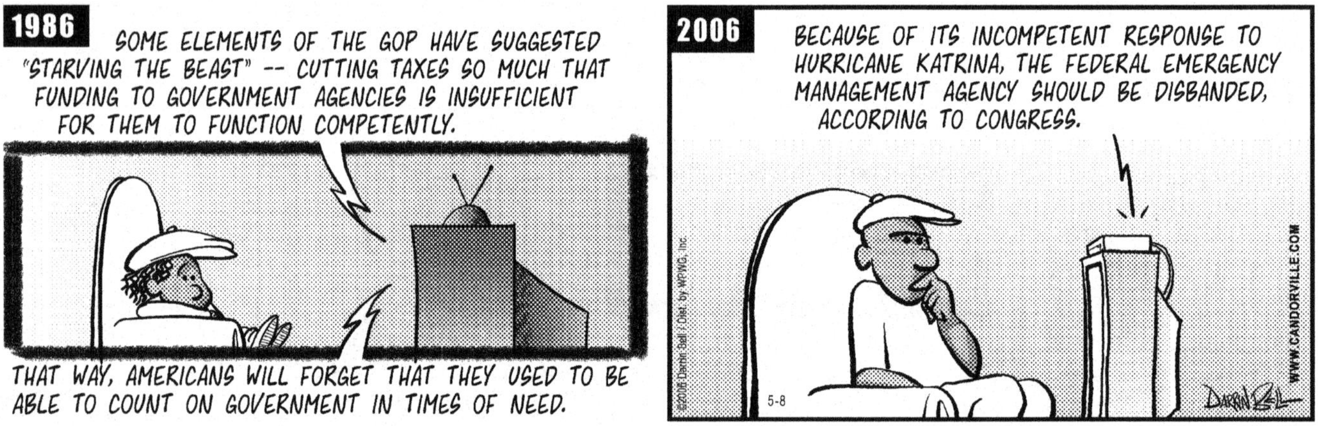
1986
SOME ELEMENTS OF THE GOP HAVE SUGGESTED "STARVING THE BEAST" -- CUTTING TAXES SO MUCH THAT FUNDING TO GOVERNMENT AGENCIES IS INSUFFICIENT FOR THEM TO FUNCTION COMPETENTLY.
THAT WAY, AMERICANS WILL FORGET THAT THEY USED TO BE ABLE TO COUNT ON GOVERNMENT IN TIMES OF NEED.
2006
BECAUSE OF ITS INCOMPETENT RESPONSE TO HURRICANE KATRINA, THE FEDERAL EMERGENCY MANAGEMENT AGENCY SHOULD BE DISBANDED, ACCORDING TO CONGRESS.
©2006 Darrin Bell / Dist. by WPWG, Inc.
WWW.CANDORVILLE.COM
5-8
DARRIN BELL

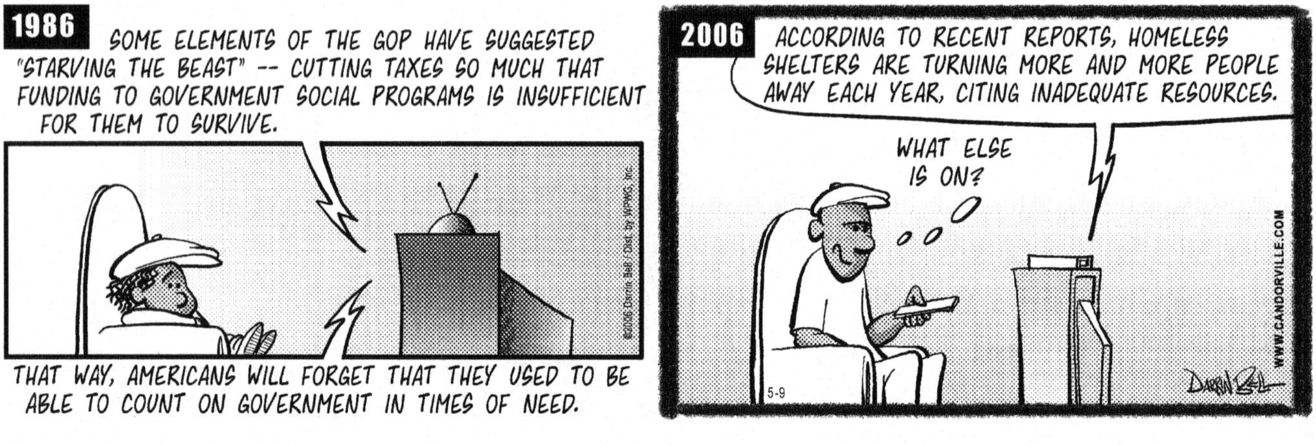
1986
SOME ELEMENTS OF THE GOP HAVE SUGGESTED "STARVING THE BEAST" -- CUTTING TAXES SO MUCH THAT FUNDING TO GOVERNMENT SOCIAL PROGRAMS IS INSUFFICIENT FOR THEM TO SURVIVE.
©2006 Darrin Bell / Dist. by WPWG, Inc.
THAT WAY, AMERICANS WILL FORGET THAT THEY USED TO BE ABLE TO COUNT ON GOVERNMENT IN TIMES OF NEED.
2006
ACCORDING TO RECENT REPORTS, HOMELESS SHELTERS ARE TURNING MORE AND MORE PEOPLE AWAY EACH YEAR, CITING INADEQUATE RESOURCES.
WHAT ELSE IS ON?
WWW.CANDORVILLE.COM
5-9
DARRIN BELL

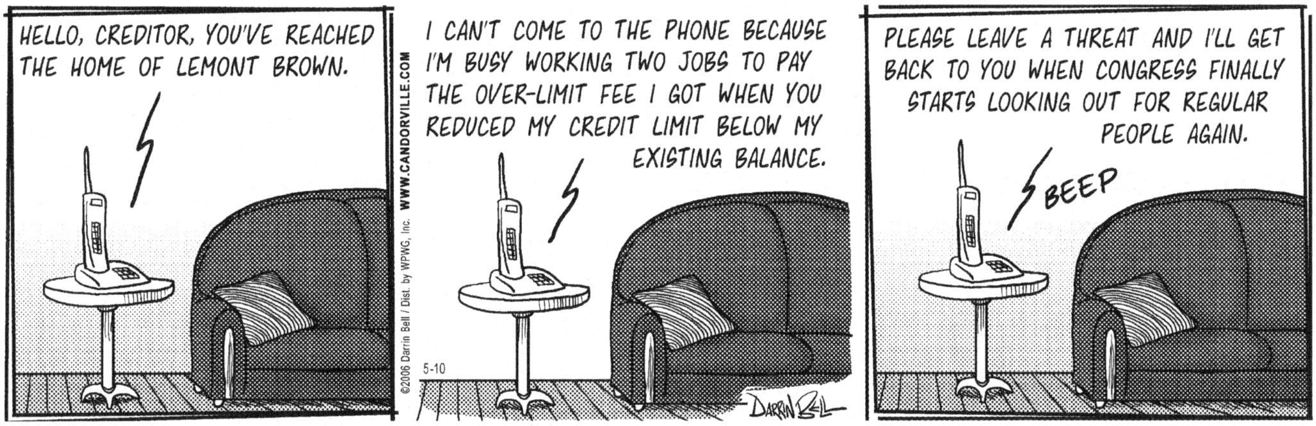
HELLO, CREDITOR, YOU'VE REACHED THE HOME OF LEMONT BROWN.
I CAN'T COME TO THE PHONE BECAUSE I'M BUSY WORKING TWO JOBS TO PAY THE OVER-LIMIT FEE I GOT WHEN YOU REDUCED MY CREDIT LIMIT BELOW MY EXISTING BALANCE.
PLEASE LEAVE A THREAT AND I'LL GET BACK TO YOU WHEN CONGRESS FINALLY STARTS LOOKING OUT FOR REGULAR PEOPLE AGAIN.
BEEP
©2006 Darrin Bell / Dist. by WPWG, Inc. WWW.CANDORVILLE.COM
5-10
DARRIN BELL

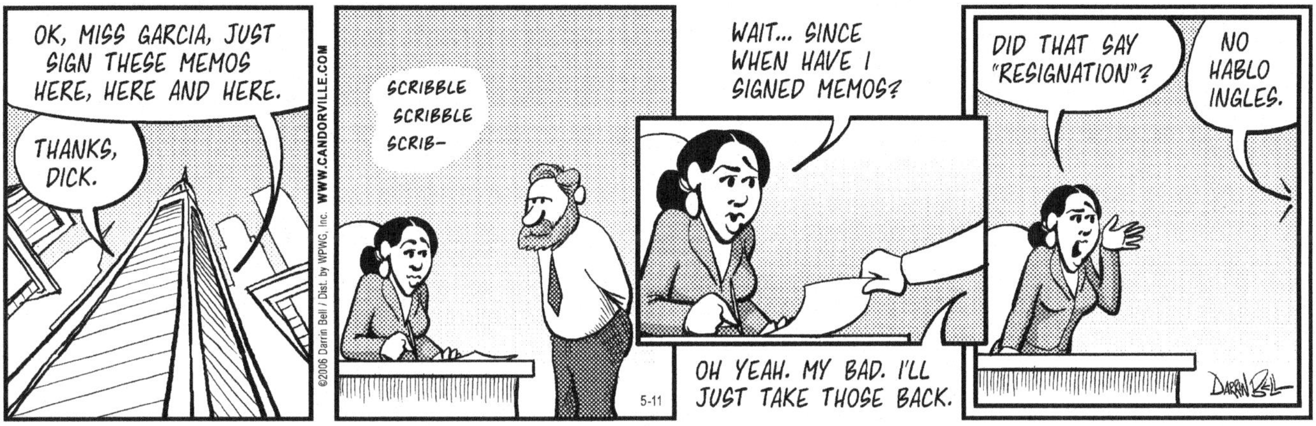
OK, MISS GARCIA, JUST SIGN THESE MEMOS HERE, HERE AND HERE.
THANKS, DICK.
SCRIBBLE SCRIBBLE SCRIB-
WAIT... SINCE WHEN HAVE I SIGNED MEMOS?
OH YEAH. MY BAD. I'LL JUST TAKE THOSE BACK.
DID THAT SAY "RESIGNATION"?
NO HABLO INGLES.
©2006 Darrin Bell / Dist. by WPWG, Inc. WWW.CANDORVILLE.COM
5-11
DARRIN BELL

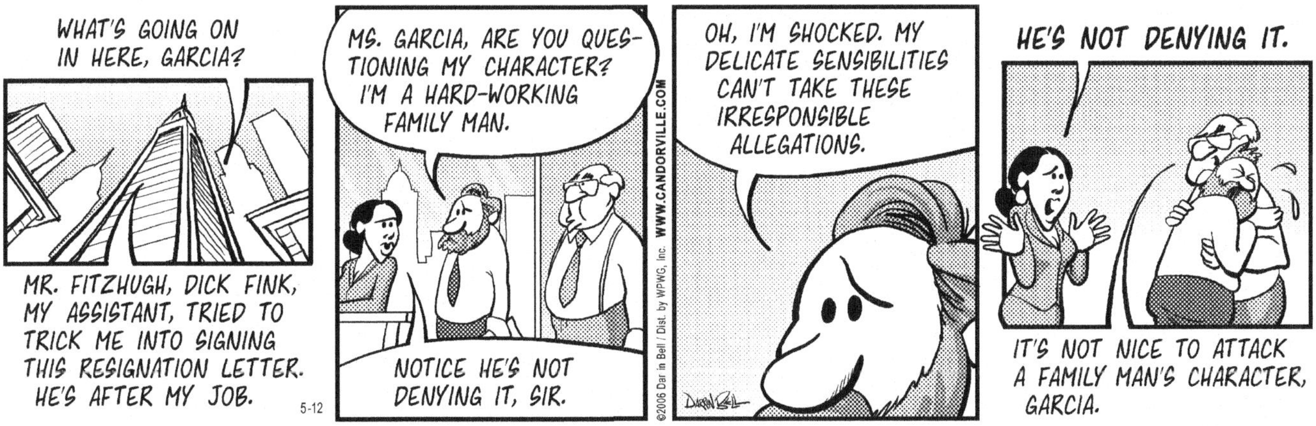
WHAT'S GOING ON IN HERE, GARCIA?
MR. FITZHUGH, DICK FINK, MY ASSISTANT, TRIED TO TRICK ME INTO SIGNING THIS RESIGNATION LETTER. HE'S AFTER MY JOB.
5-12
MS. GARCIA, ARE YOU QUESTIONING MY CHARACTER? I'M A HARD-WORKING FAMILY MAN.
NOTICE HE'S NOT DENYING IT, SIR.
©2006 Darrin Bell / Dist. by WPWG, Inc. WWW.CANDORVILLE.COM
OH, I'M SHOCKED. MY DELICATE SENSIBILITIES CAN'T TAKE THESE IRRESPONSIBLE ALLEGATIONS.
DARRIN BELL
HE'S NOT DENYING IT.
IT'S NOT NICE TO ATTACK A FAMILY MAN'S CHARACTER, GARCIA.

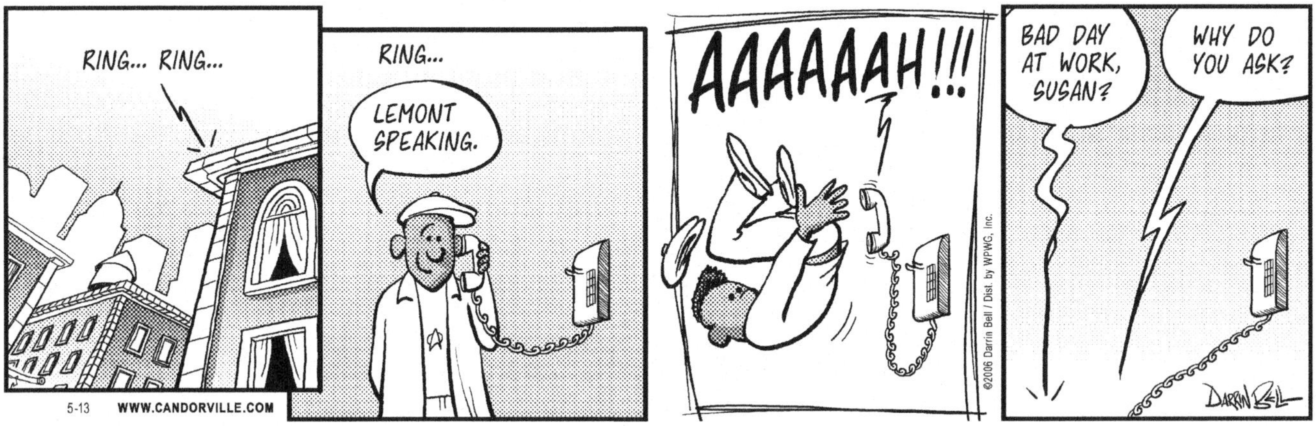
RING... RING...
5-13 WWW.CANDORVILLE.COM
RING...
LEMONT SPEAKING.
AAAAAAH!!!
©2006 Darrin Bell / Dist. by WPWG, Inc.
BAD DAY AT WORK, SUSAN?
WHY DO YOU ASK?
DARRIN BELL

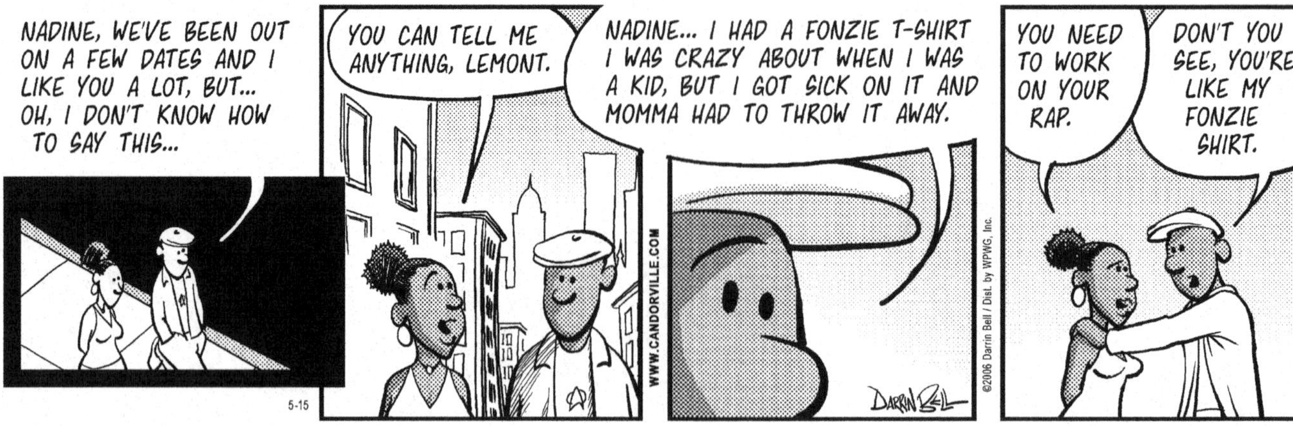
NADINE, WE'VE BEEN OUT ON A FEW DATES AND I LIKE YOU A LOT, BUT... OH, I DON'T KNOW HOW TO SAY THIS...
5-15
YOU CAN TELL ME ANYTHING, LEMONT.
WWW.CANDORVILLE.COM
NADINE... I HAD A FONZIE T-SHIRT I WAS CRAZY ABOUT WHEN I WAS A KID, BUT I GOT SICK ON IT AND MOMMA HAD TO THROW IT AWAY.
DARRIN BELL
©2006 Darrin Bell / Dist. by WPWG, Inc.
YOU NEED TO WORK ON YOUR RAP.
DON'T YOU SEE, YOU'RE LIKE MY FONZIE SHIRT.

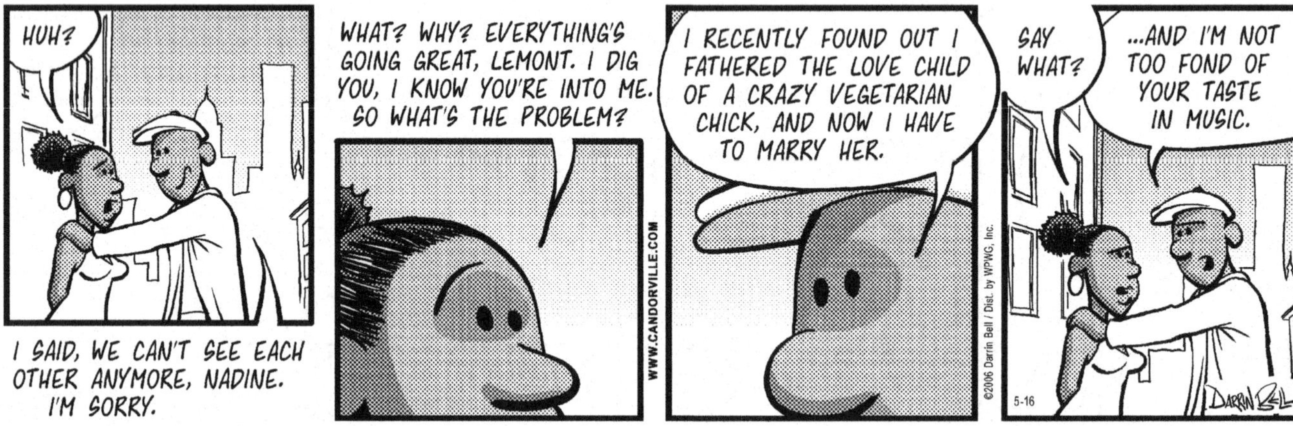
HUH?
I SAID, WE CAN'T SEE EACH OTHER ANYMORE, NADINE. I'M SORRY.
WHAT? WHY? EVERYTHING'S GOING GREAT, LEMONT. I DIG YOU, I KNOW YOU'RE INTO ME. SO WHAT'S THE PROBLEM?
WWW.CANDORVILLE.COM
I RECENTLY FOUND OUT I FATHERED THE LOVE CHILD OF A CRAZY VEGETARIAN CHICK, AND NOW I HAVE TO MARRY HER.
©2006 Darrin Bell / Dist. by WPWG, Inc.
SAY WHAT?
...AND I'M NOT TOO FOND OF YOUR TASTE IN MUSIC.
5-16
DARRIN BELL

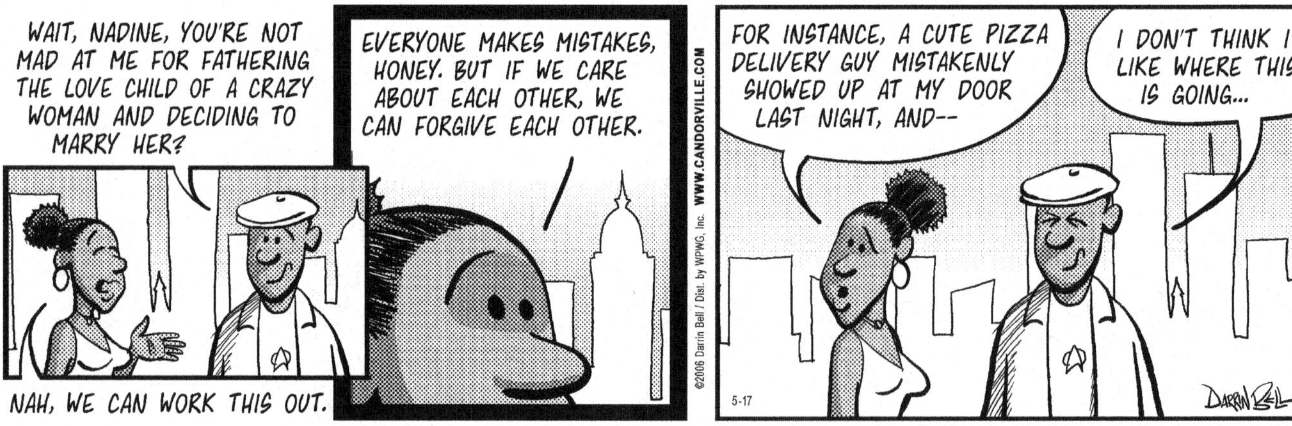
WAIT, NADINE, YOU'RE NOT MAD AT ME FOR FATHERING THE LOVE CHILD OF A CRAZY WOMAN AND DECIDING TO MARRY HER?
NAH, WE CAN WORK THIS OUT.
EVERYONE MAKES MISTAKES, HONEY. BUT IF WE CARE ABOUT EACH OTHER, WE CAN FORGIVE EACH OTHER.
©2006 Darrin Bell / Dist. by WPWG, Inc. WWW.CANDORVILLE.COM
FOR INSTANCE, A CUTE PIZZA DELIVERY GUY MISTAKENLY SHOWED UP AT MY DOOR LAST NIGHT, AND--
I DON'T THINK I LIKE WHERE THIS IS GOING...
5-17
DARRIN BELL

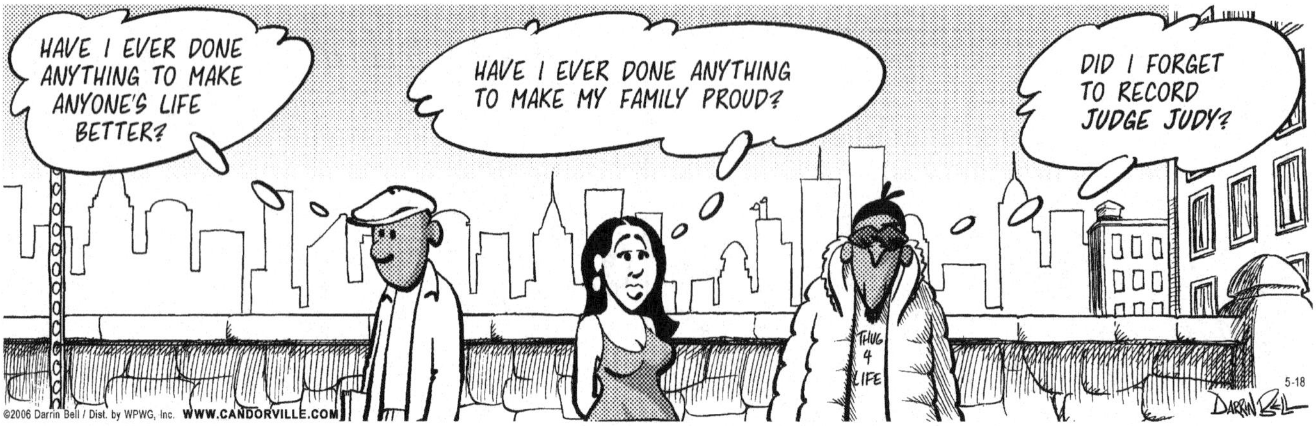
HAVE I EVER DONE ANYTHING TO MAKE ANYONE'S LIFE BETTER?
HAVE I EVER DONE ANYTHING TO MAKE MY FAMILY PROUD?
DID I FORGET TO RECORD JUDGE JUDY?
THUG 4 LIFE
5-18
DARRIN BELL
©2006 Darrin Bell / Dist. by WPWG, Inc. WWW.CANDORVILLE.COM

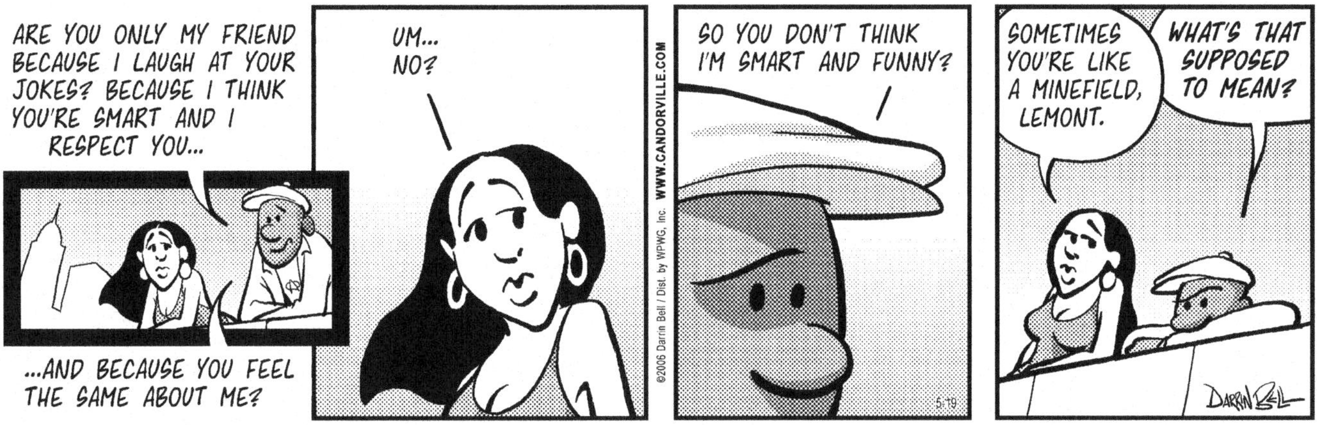
ARE YOU ONLY MY FRIEND BECAUSE I LAUGH AT YOUR JOKES? BECAUSE I THINK YOU'RE SMART AND I RESPECT YOU...
...AND BECAUSE YOU FEEL THE SAME ABOUT ME?
UM... NO?
©2006 Darrin Bell / Dist. by WPWG, Inc. WWW.CANDORVILLE.COM
SO YOU DON'T THINK I'M SMART AND FUNNY?
5-19
SOMETIMES YOU'RE LIKE A MINEFIELD, LEMONT.
WHAT'S THAT SUPPOSED TO MEAN?
DARRIN BELL

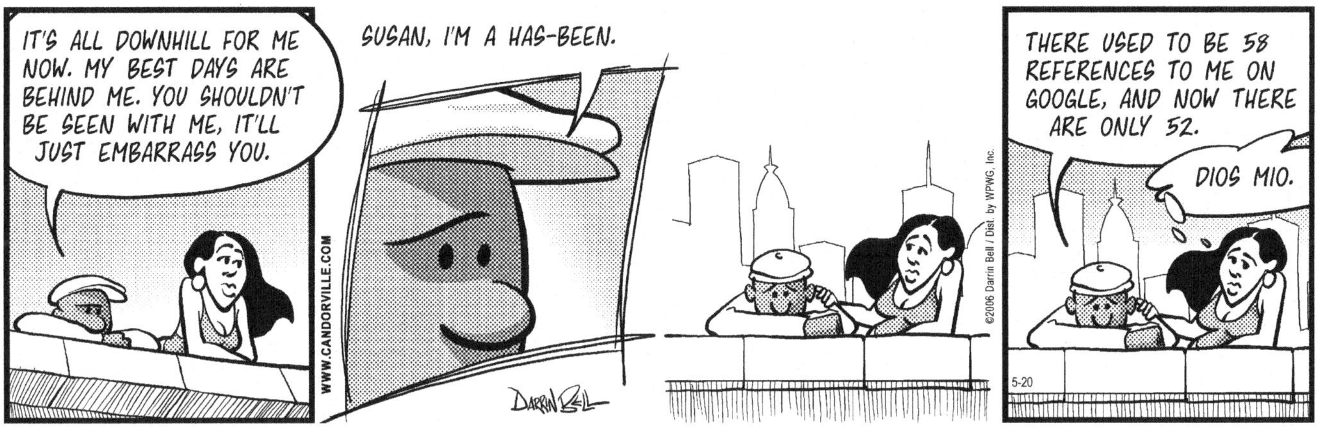
IT'S ALL DOWNHILL FOR ME NOW. MY BEST DAYS ARE BEHIND ME. YOU SHOULDN'T BE SEEN WITH ME, IT'LL JUST EMBARRASS YOU.
WWW.CANDORVILLE.COM
SUSAN, I'M A HAS-BEEN.
DARRIN BELL
©2006 Darrin Bell / Dist. by WPWG, Inc.
THERE USED TO BE 58 REFERENCES TO ME ON GOOGLE, AND NOW THERE ARE ONLY 52.
DIOS MIO.
5-20

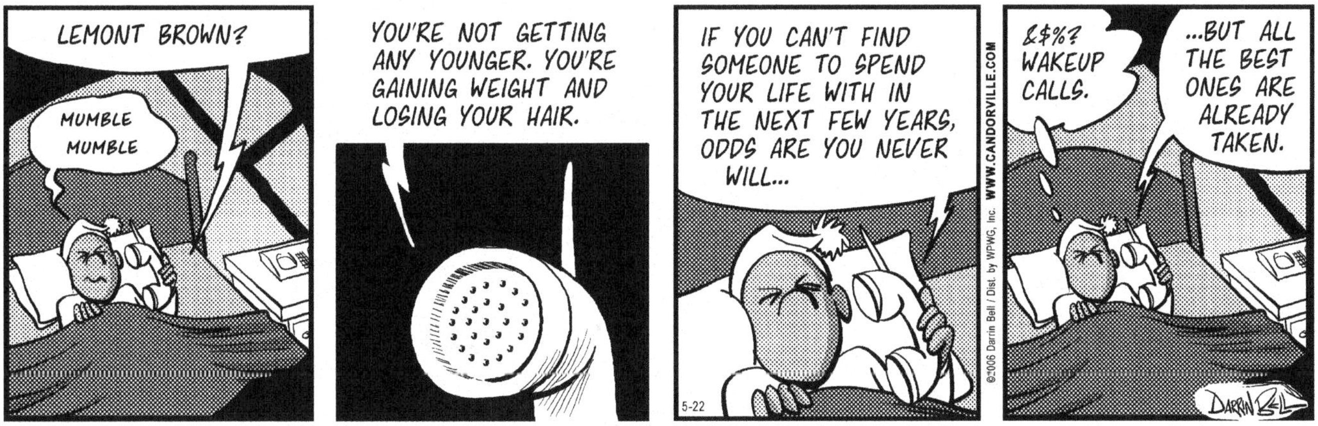
LEMONT BROWN?
MUMBLE MUMBLE
YOU'RE NOT GETTING ANY YOUNGER. YOU'RE GAINING WEIGHT AND LOSING YOUR HAIR.
IF YOU CAN'T FIND SOMEONE TO SPEND YOUR LIFE WITH IN THE NEXT FEW YEARS, ODDS ARE YOU NEVER WILL...
5-22
©2006 Darrin Bell / Dist. by WPWG, Inc. WWW.CANDORVILLE.COM
&$%? WAKEUP CALLS.
...BUT ALL THE BEST ONES ARE ALREADY TAKEN.
DARRIN BELL

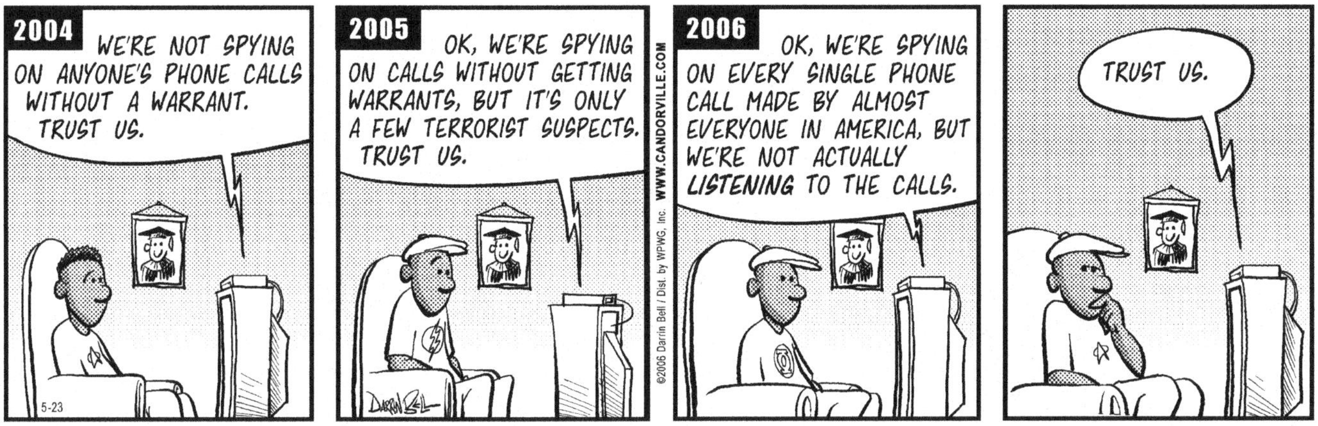
2004
WE'RE NOT SPYING ON ANYONE'S PHONE CALLS WITHOUT A WARRANT. TRUST US.
5-23
2005
OK, WE'RE SPYING ON CALLS WITHOUT GETTING WARRANTS, BUT IT'S ONLY A FEW TERRORIST SUSPECTS. TRUST US.
DARRIN BELL
©2006 Darrin Bell / Dist. by WPWG, Inc. WWW.CANDORVILLE.COM
2006
OK, WE'RE SPYING ON EVERY SINGLE PHONE CALL MADE BY ALMOST EVERYONE IN AMERICA, BUT WE'RE NOT ACTUALLY LISTENING TO THE CALLS.
TRUST US.

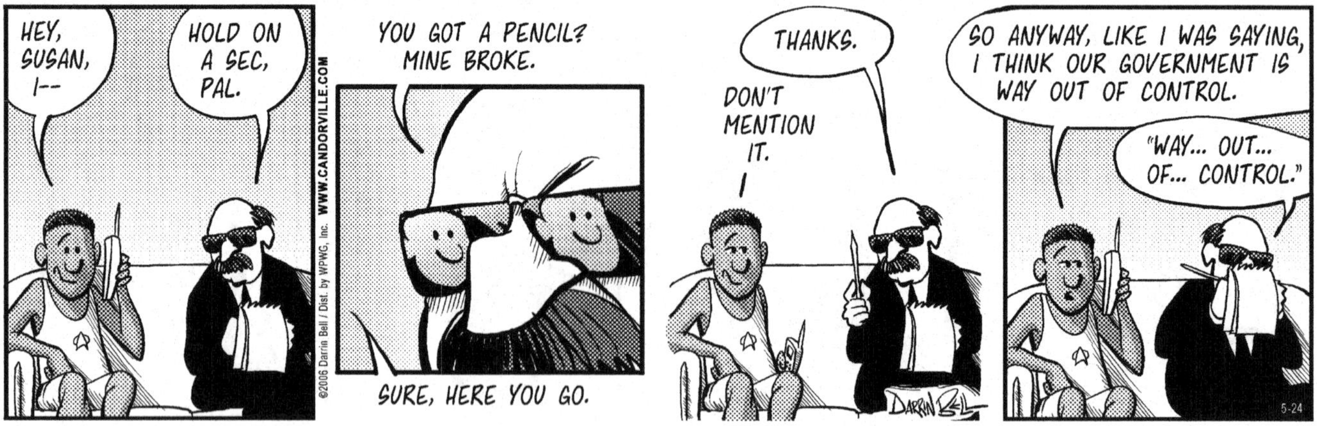
HEY, SUSAN, I--
HOLD ON A SEC, PAL.
©2006 Darrin Bell / Dist. by WPWG, Inc. WWW.CANDORVILLE.COM
YOU GOT A PENCIL? MINE BROKE.
SURE, HERE YOU GO.
THANKS.
DON'T MENTION IT.
SO ANYWAY, LIKE I WAS SAYING, I THINK OUR GOVERNMENT IS WAY OUT OF CONTROL.
"WAY... OUT... OF... CONTROL."
DARRIN BELL
5-24

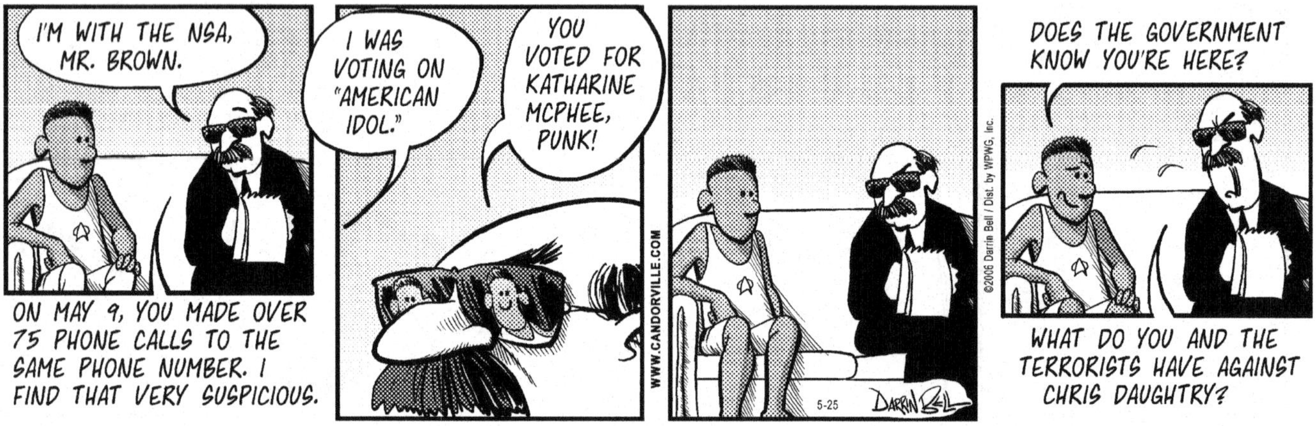
I'M WITH THE NSA, MR. BROWN.
ON MAY 9, YOU MADE OVER 75 PHONE CALLS TO THE SAME PHONE NUMBER. I FIND THAT VERY SUSPICIOUS.
I WAS VOTING ON "AMERICAN IDOL."
YOU VOTED FOR KATHARINE MCPHEE, PUNK!
WWW.CANDORVILLE.COM
5-25
DARRIN BELL
DOES THE GOVERNMENT KNOW YOU'RE HERE?
©2006 Darrin Bell / Dist. by WPWG, Inc.
WHAT DO YOU AND THE TERRORISTS HAVE AGAINST CHRIS DAUGHTRY?

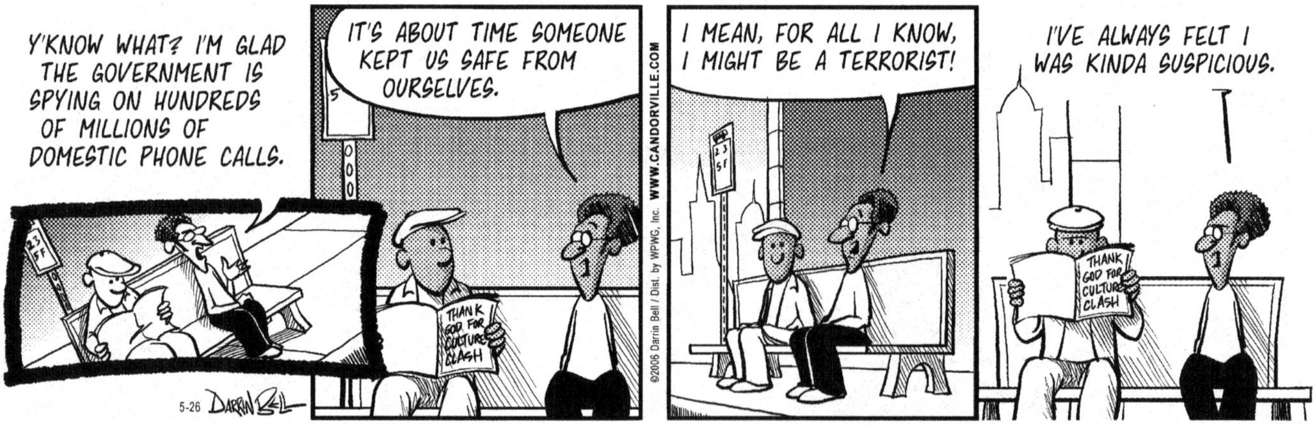
Y'KNOW WHAT? I'M GLAD THE GOVERNMENT IS SPYING ON HUNDREDS OF MILLIONS OF DOMESTIC PHONE CALLS.
5-26 DARRIN BELL
IT'S ABOUT TIME SOMEONE KEPT US SAFE FROM OURSELVES.
THANK GOD FOR CULTURE CLASH
©2006 Darrin Bell / Dist. by WPWG, Inc. WWW.CANDORVILLE.COM
I MEAN, FOR ALL I KNOW, I MIGHT BE A TERRORIST!
I'VE ALWAYS FELT I WAS KINDA SUSPICIOUS.
THANK GOD FOR CULTURE CLASH

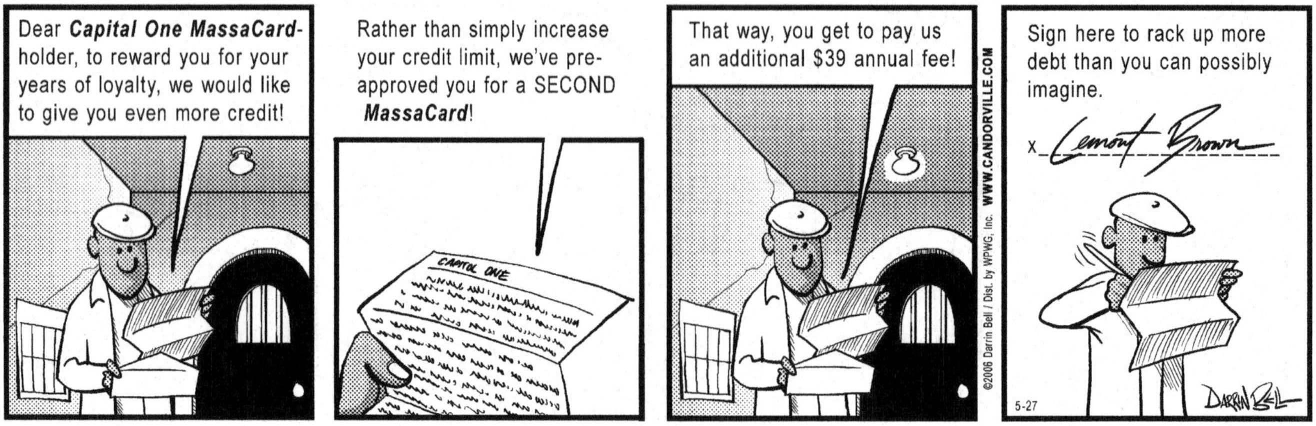
Dear **Capital One MassaCard**-holder, to reward you for your years of loyalty, we would like to give you even more credit!
Rather than simply increase your credit limit, we've pre-approved you for a SECOND ***MassaCard***!
CAPITOL ONE
That way, you get to pay us an additional $39 annual fee!
©2006 Darrin Bell / Dist. by WPWG, Inc. WWW.CANDORVILLE.COM
Sign here to rack up more debt than you can possibly imagine.
x Lemont Brown
5-27
DARRIN BELL

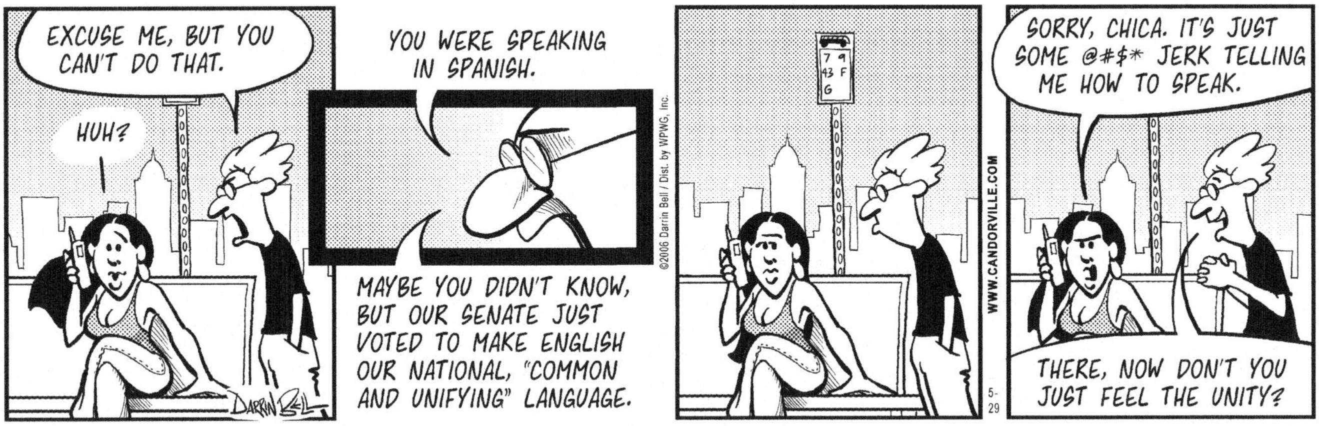
EXCUSE ME, BUT YOU CAN'T DO THAT.
HUH?
YOU WERE SPEAKING IN SPANISH.
MAYBE YOU DIDN'T KNOW, BUT OUR SENATE JUST VOTED TO MAKE ENGLISH OUR NATIONAL, "COMMON AND UNIFYING" LANGUAGE.
SORRY, CHICA. IT'S JUST SOME @#$* JERK TELLING ME HOW TO SPEAK.
THERE, NOW DON'T YOU JUST FEEL THE UNITY?
©2006 Darrin Bell / Dist. by WPWG, Inc.
WWW.CANDORVILLE.COM
5-29

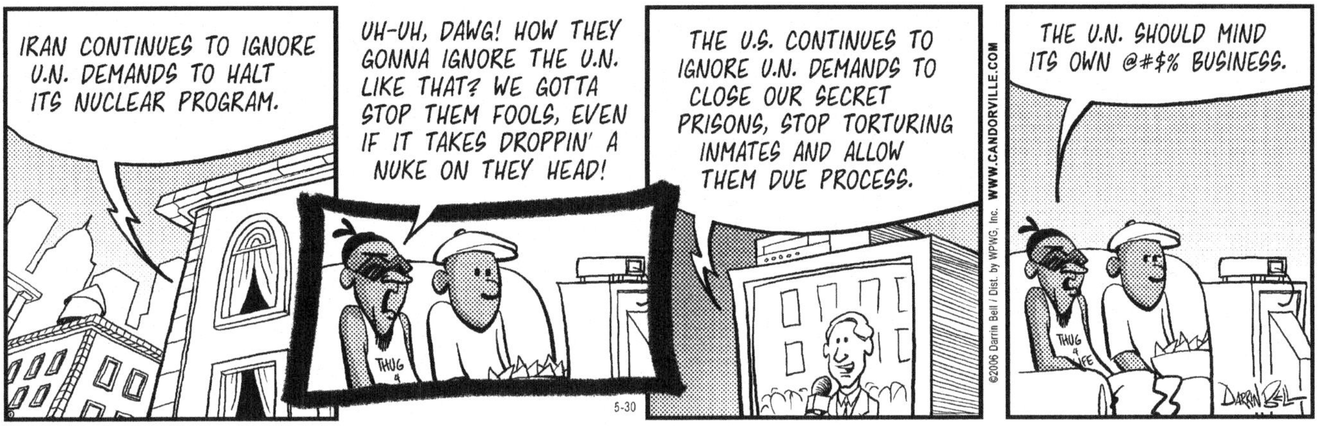
IRAN CONTINUES TO IGNORE U.N. DEMANDS TO HALT ITS NUCLEAR PROGRAM.
UH-UH, DAWG! HOW THEY GONNA IGNORE THE U.N. LIKE THAT? WE GOTTA STOP THEM FOOLS, EVEN IF IT TAKES DROPPIN' A NUKE ON THEY HEAD!
THE U.S. CONTINUES TO IGNORE U.N. DEMANDS TO CLOSE OUR SECRET PRISONS, STOP TORTURING INMATES AND ALLOW THEM DUE PROCESS.
THE U.N. SHOULD MIND ITS OWN @#$% BUSINESS.
5-30
©2006 Darrin Bell / Dist. by WPWG, Inc.
WWW.CANDORVILLE.COM

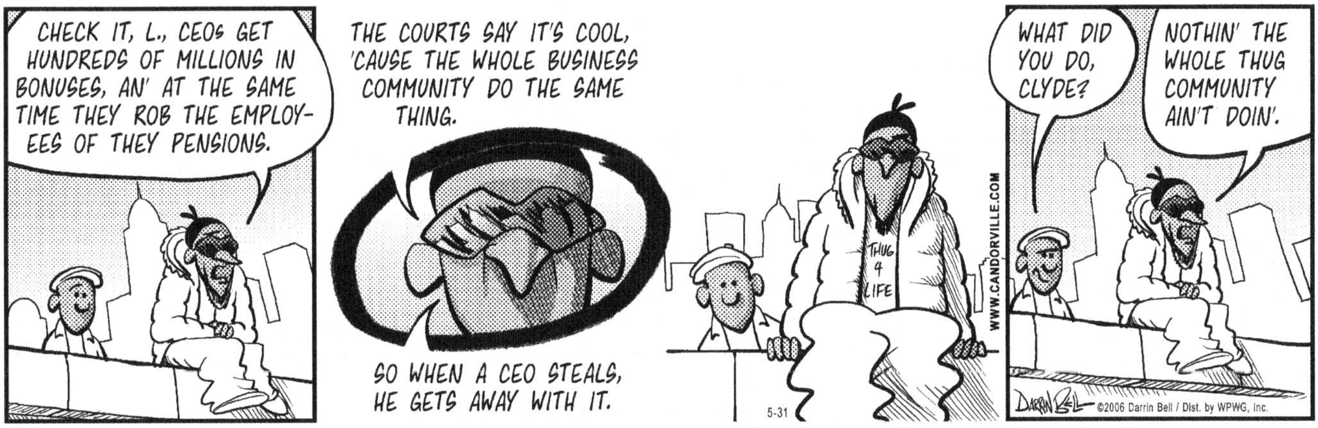
CHECK IT, L., CEOs GET HUNDREDS OF MILLIONS IN BONUSES, AN' AT THE SAME TIME THEY ROB THE EMPLOYEES OF THEY PENSIONS.
THE COURTS SAY IT'S COOL, 'CAUSE THE WHOLE BUSINESS COMMUNITY DO THE SAME THING.
SO WHEN A CEO STEALS, HE GETS AWAY WITH IT.
THUG 4 LIFE
WHAT DID YOU DO, CLYDE?
NOTHIN' THE WHOLE THUG COMMUNITY AIN'T DOIN'.
5-31
WWW.CANDORVILLE.COM
©2006 Darrin Bell / Dist. by WPWG, Inc.

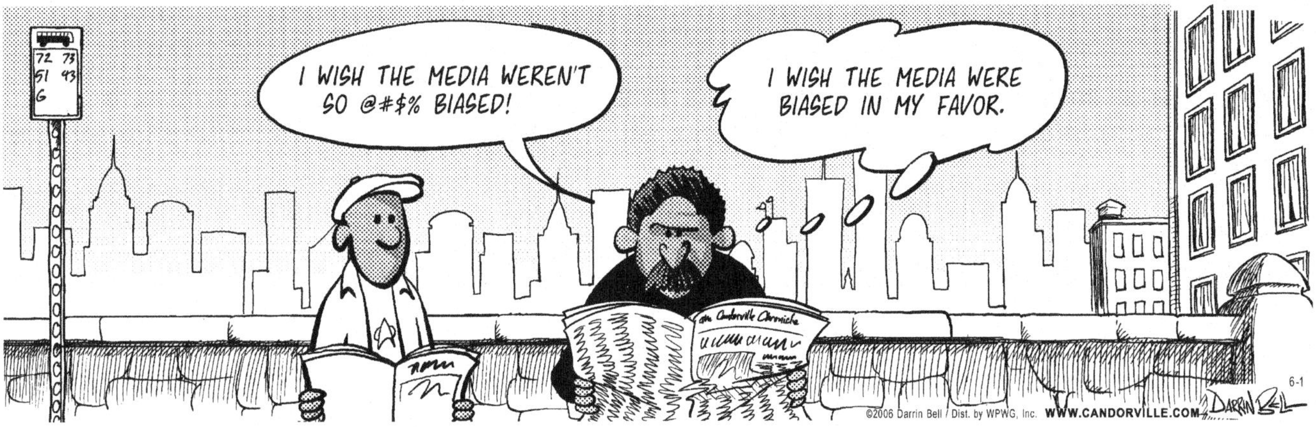
I WISH THE MEDIA WEREN'T SO @#$% BIASED!
I WISH THE MEDIA WERE BIASED IN MY FAVOR.
6-1
©2006 Darrin Bell / Dist. by WPWG, Inc. WWW.CANDORVILLE.COM

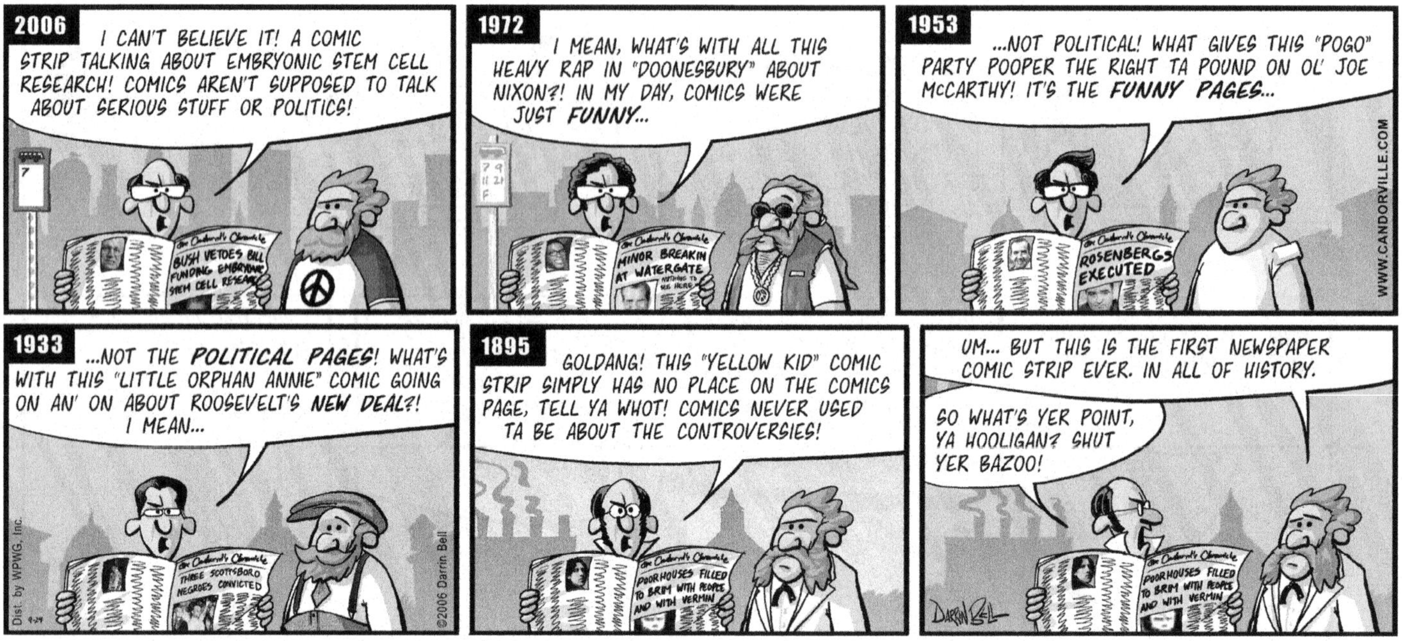
2006
I CAN'T BELIEVE IT! A COMIC STRIP TALKING ABOUT EMBRYONIC STEM CELL RESEARCH! COMICS AREN'T SUPPOSED TO TALK ABOUT SERIOUS STUFF OR POLITICS!
BUSH VETOES BILL FUNDING EMBRYONIC STEM CELL RESEARCH
1972
I MEAN, WHAT'S WITH ALL THIS HEAVY RAP IN "DOONESBURY" ABOUT NIXON?! IN MY DAY, COMICS WERE JUST FUNNY...
MINOR BREAKIN AT WATERGATE
1953
...NOT POLITICAL! WHAT GIVES THIS "POGO" PARTY POOPER THE RIGHT TA POUND ON OL' JOE McCARTHY! IT'S THE FUNNY PAGES...
ROSENBERGS EXECUTED
WWW.CANDORVILLE.COM
1933
...NOT THE POLITICAL PAGES! WHAT'S WITH THIS "LITTLE ORPHAN ANNIE" COMIC GOING ON AN' ON ABOUT ROOSEVELT'S NEW DEAL?! I MEAN...
THREE SCOTTSBORO NEGROES CONVICTED
Dist. by WPWG, Inc.
©2006 Darrin Bell
1895
GOLDANG! THIS "YELLOW KID" COMIC STRIP SIMPLY HAS NO PLACE ON THE COMICS PAGE, TELL YA WHOT! COMICS NEVER USED TA BE ABOUT THE CONTROVERSIES!
POORHOUSES FILLED TO BRIM WITH PEOPLE AND WITH VERMIN
UM... BUT THIS IS THE FIRST NEWSPAPER COMIC STRIP EVER. IN ALL OF HISTORY.
SO WHAT'S YER POINT, YA HOOLIGAN? SHUT YER BAZOO!
DARRIN BELL

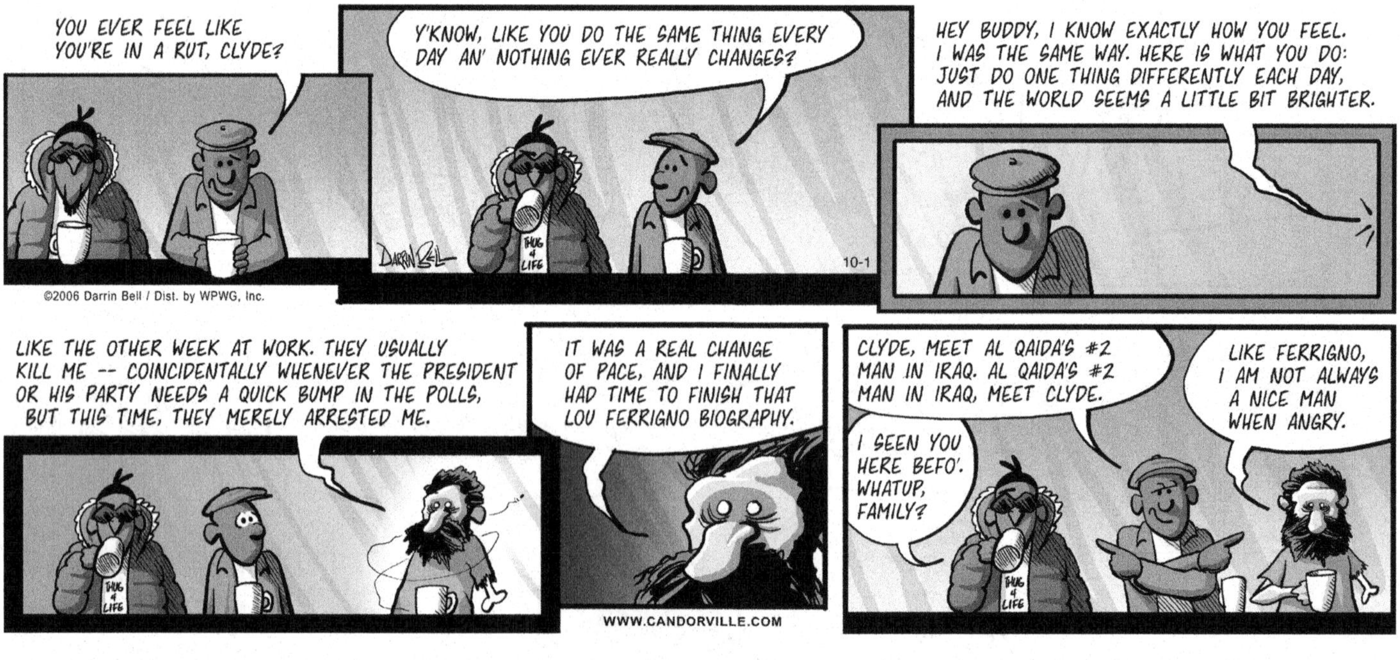
YOU EVER FEEL LIKE YOU'RE IN A RUT, CLYDE?
Y'KNOW, LIKE YOU DO THE SAME THING EVERY DAY AN' NOTHING EVER REALLY CHANGES?
HEY BUDDY, I KNOW EXACTLY HOW YOU FEEL. I WAS THE SAME WAY. HERE IS WHAT YOU DO: JUST DO ONE THING DIFFERENTLY EACH DAY, AND THE WORLD SEEMS A LITTLE BIT BRIGHTER.
DARRIN BELL
10-1
©2006 Darrin Bell / Dist. by WPWG, Inc.
LIKE THE OTHER WEEK AT WORK. THEY USUALLY KILL ME -- COINCIDENTALLY WHENEVER THE PRESIDENT OR HIS PARTY NEEDS A QUICK BUMP IN THE POLLS, BUT THIS TIME, THEY MERELY ARRESTED ME.
IT WAS A REAL CHANGE OF PACE, AND I FINALLY HAD TIME TO FINISH THAT LOU FERRIGNO BIOGRAPHY.
CLYDE, MEET AL QAIDA'S #2 MAN IN IRAQ. AL QAIDA'S #2 MAN IN IRAQ, MEET CLYDE.
LIKE FERRIGNO, I AM NOT ALWAYS A NICE MAN WHEN ANGRY.
I SEEN YOU HERE BEFO'. WHATUP, FAMILY?
WWW.CANDORVILLE.COM

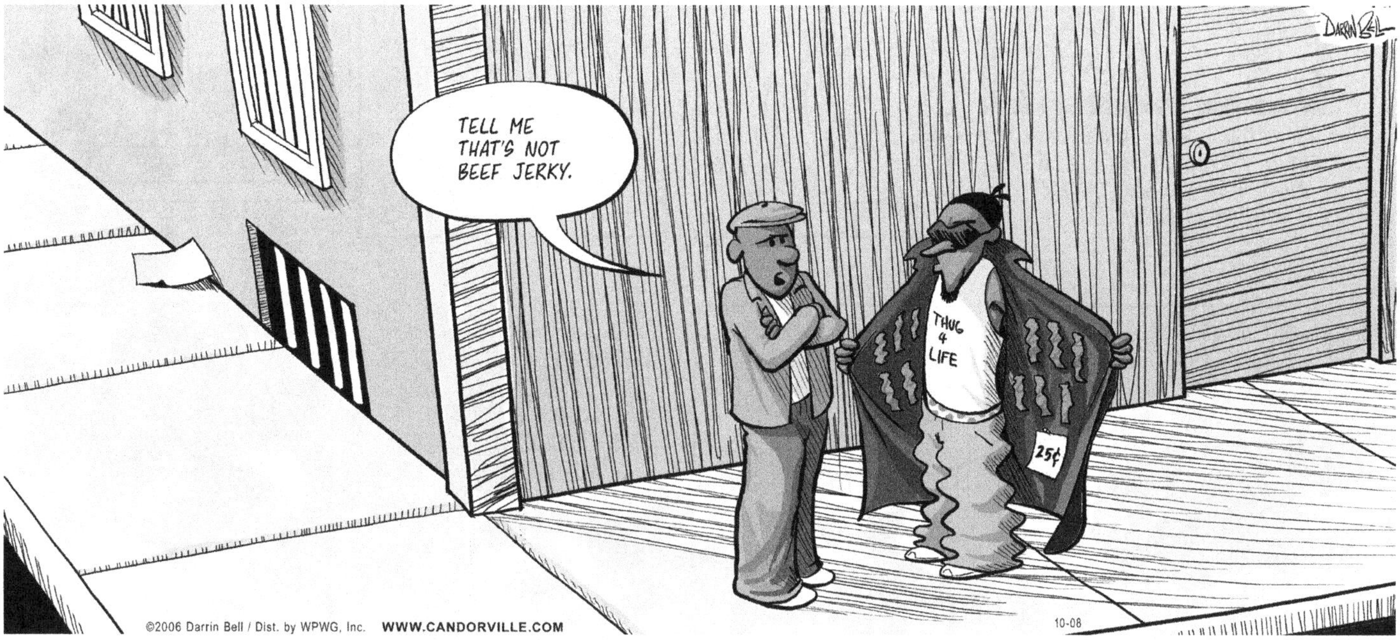
TELL ME THAT'S NOT BEEF JERKY.
THUG 4 LIFE
25¢
DARRIN BELL
©2006 Darrin Bell / Dist. by WPWG, Inc. WWW.CANDORVILLE.COM
10-08

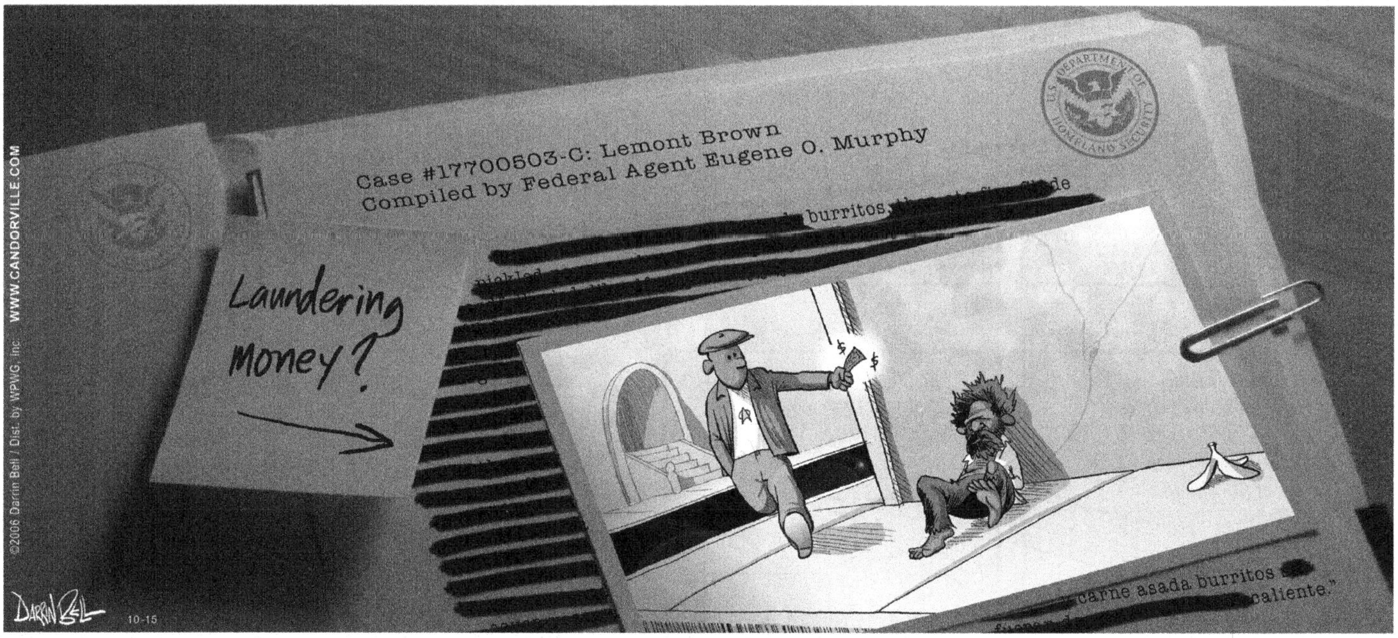
Case #17700503-C: Lemont Brown
Compiled by Federal Agent Eugene O. Murphy
[redacted] burritos [redacted]
Laundering money?
[redacted] carne asada burritos [redacted]
[redacted] caliente."
©2006 Darrin Bell / Dist. by WPWG, Inc. WWW.CANDORVILLE.COM
DARRIN BELL
10-15

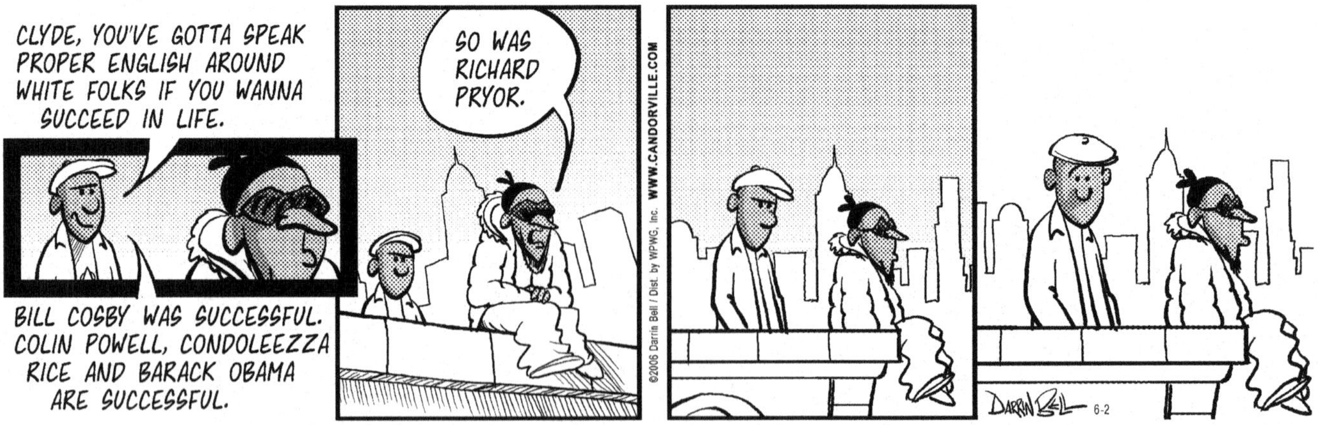
CLYDE, YOU'VE GOTTA SPEAK PROPER ENGLISH AROUND WHITE FOLKS IF YOU WANNA SUCCEED IN LIFE.
BILL COSBY WAS SUCCESSFUL. COLIN POWELL, CONDOLEEZZA RICE AND BARACK OBAMA ARE SUCCESSFUL.
SO WAS RICHARD PRYOR.
©2006 Darrin Bell / Dist. by WPWG, Inc. WWW.CANDORVILLE.COM
DARRIN BELL 6-2

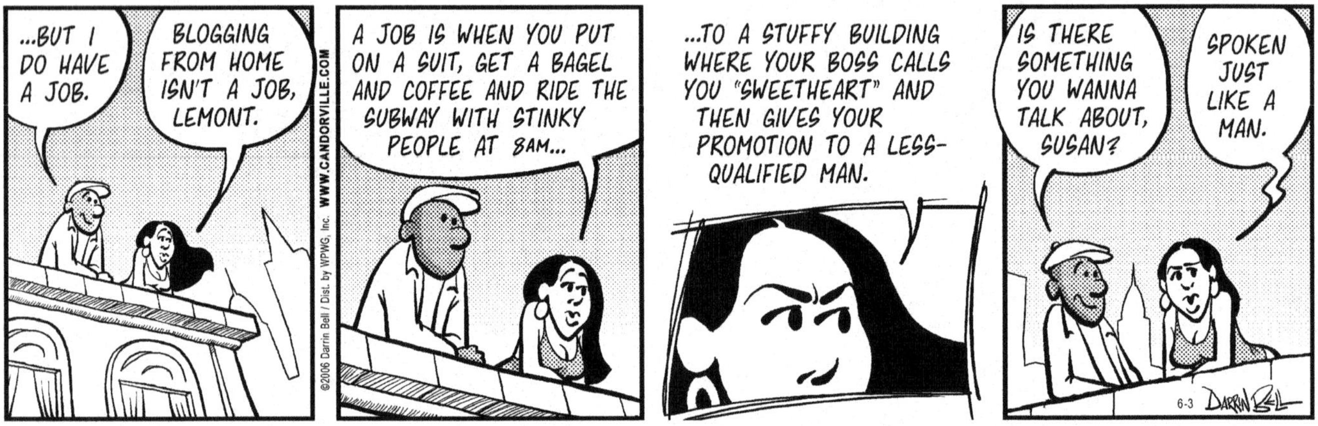
BLOGGING FROM HOME ISN'T A JOB, LEMONT.
...BUT I DO HAVE A JOB.
A JOB IS WHEN YOU PUT ON A SUIT, GET A BAGEL AND COFFEE AND RIDE THE SUBWAY WITH STINKY PEOPLE AT 8AM...
...TO A STUFFY BUILDING WHERE YOUR BOSS CALLS YOU "SWEETHEART" AND THEN GIVES YOUR PROMOTION TO A LESS-QUALIFIED MAN.
IS THERE SOMETHING YOU WANNA TALK ABOUT, SUSAN?
SPOKEN JUST LIKE A MAN.
©2006 Darrin Bell / Dist. by WPWG, Inc. WWW.CANDORVILLE.COM
6-3 DARRIN BELL

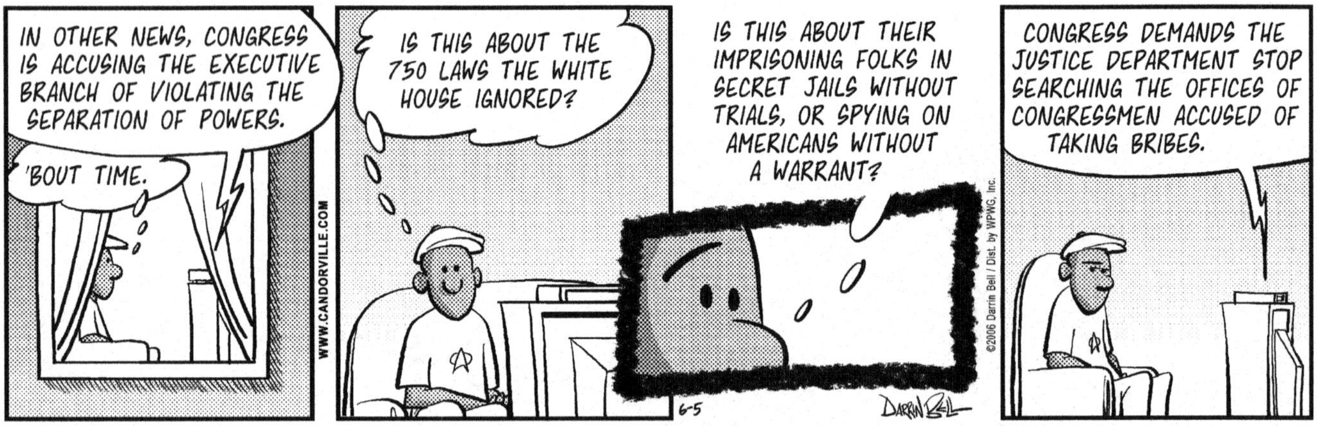
IN OTHER NEWS, CONGRESS IS ACCUSING THE EXECUTIVE BRANCH OF VIOLATING THE SEPARATION OF POWERS.
'BOUT TIME.
IS THIS ABOUT THE 750 LAWS THE WHITE HOUSE IGNORED?
IS THIS ABOUT THEIR IMPRISONING FOLKS IN SECRET JAILS WITHOUT TRIALS, OR SPYING ON AMERICANS WITHOUT A WARRANT?
CONGRESS DEMANDS THE JUSTICE DEPARTMENT STOP SEARCHING THE OFFICES OF CONGRESSMEN ACCUSED OF TAKING BRIBES.
©2006 Darrin Bell / Dist. by WPWG, Inc. WWW.CANDORVILLE.COM
6-5 DARRIN BELL

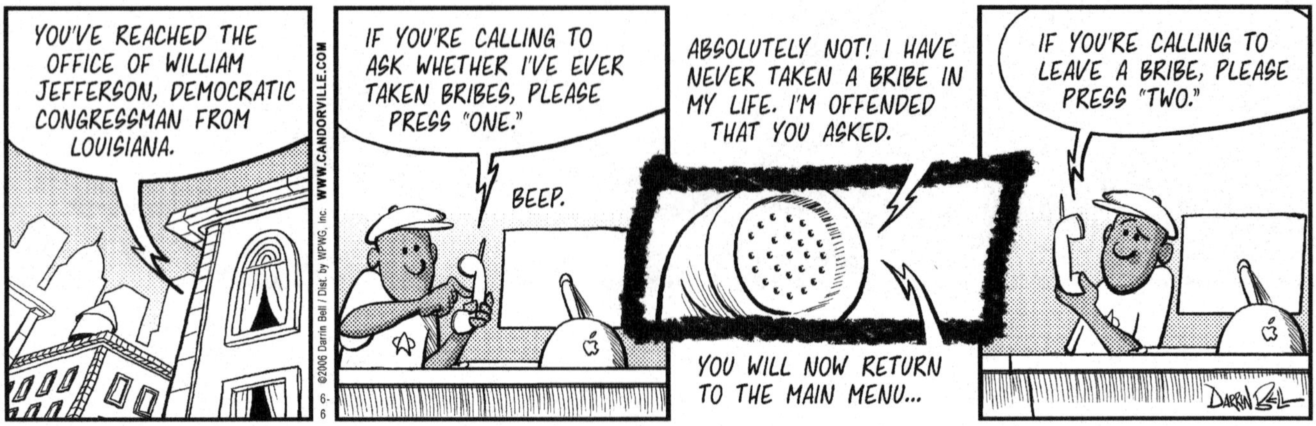
YOU'VE REACHED THE OFFICE OF WILLIAM JEFFERSON, DEMOCRATIC CONGRESSMAN FROM LOUISIANA.
IF YOU'RE CALLING TO ASK WHETHER I'VE EVER TAKEN BRIBES, PLEASE PRESS "ONE."
BEEP.
ABSOLUTELY NOT! I HAVE NEVER TAKEN A BRIBE IN MY LIFE. I'M OFFENDED THAT YOU ASKED.
YOU WILL NOW RETURN TO THE MAIN MENU...
IF YOU'RE CALLING TO LEAVE A BRIBE, PLEASE PRESS "TWO."
©2006 Darrin Bell / Dist. by WPWG, Inc. WWW.CANDORVILLE.COM
6-6
DARRIN BELL

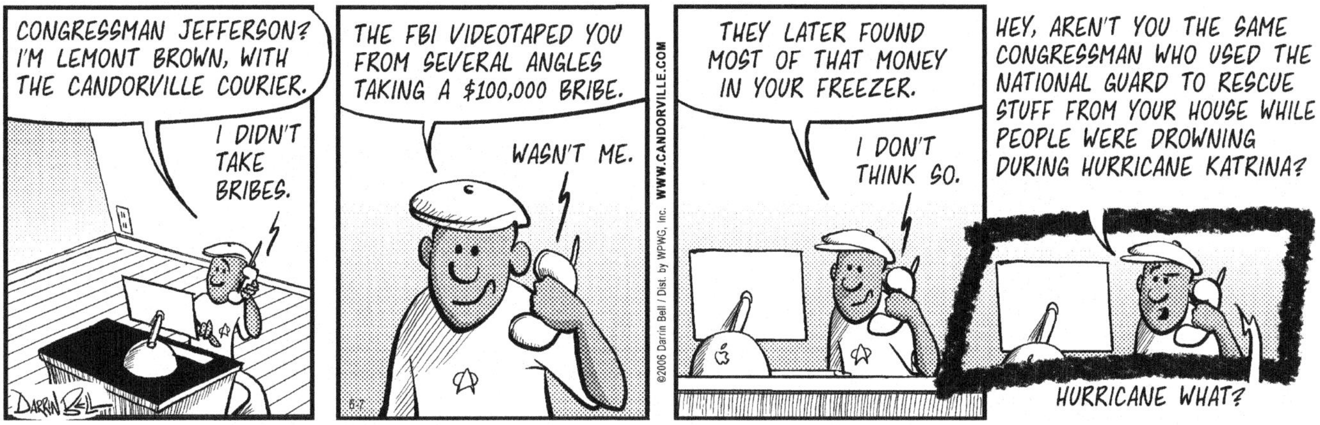
CONGRESSMAN JEFFERSON? I'M LEMONT BROWN, WITH THE CANDORVILLE COURIER.
I DIDN'T TAKE BRIBES.
DARRIN BELL
THE FBI VIDEOTAPED YOU FROM SEVERAL ANGLES TAKING A $100,000 BRIBE.
WASN'T ME.
6-7
©2006 Darrin Bell / Dist. by WPWG, Inc. WWW.CANDORVILLE.COM
THEY LATER FOUND MOST OF THAT MONEY IN YOUR FREEZER.
I DON'T THINK SO.
HEY, AREN'T YOU THE SAME CONGRESSMAN WHO USED THE NATIONAL GUARD TO RESCUE STUFF FROM YOUR HOUSE WHILE PEOPLE WERE DROWNING DURING HURRICANE KATRINA?
HURRICANE WHAT?

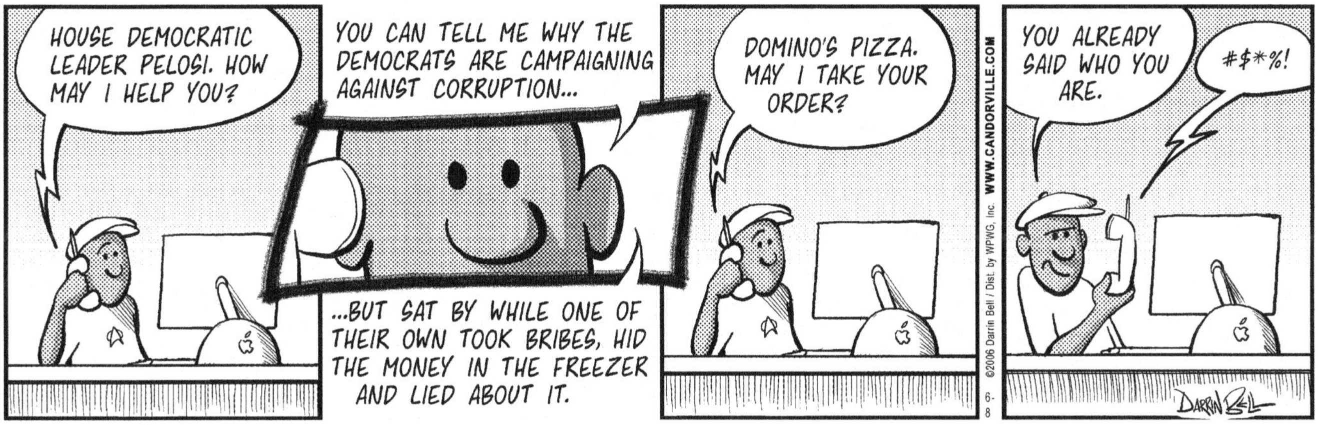
HOUSE DEMOCRATIC LEADER PELOSI. HOW MAY I HELP YOU?
YOU CAN TELL ME WHY THE DEMOCRATS ARE CAMPAIGNING AGAINST CORRUPTION...
...BUT SAT BY WHILE ONE OF THEIR OWN TOOK BRIBES, HID THE MONEY IN THE FREEZER AND LIED ABOUT IT.
DOMINO'S PIZZA. MAY I TAKE YOUR ORDER?
©2006 Darrin Bell / Dist. by WPWG, Inc. WWW.CANDORVILLE.COM
6-8
YOU ALREADY SAID WHO YOU ARE.
#$*%!
DARRIN BELL

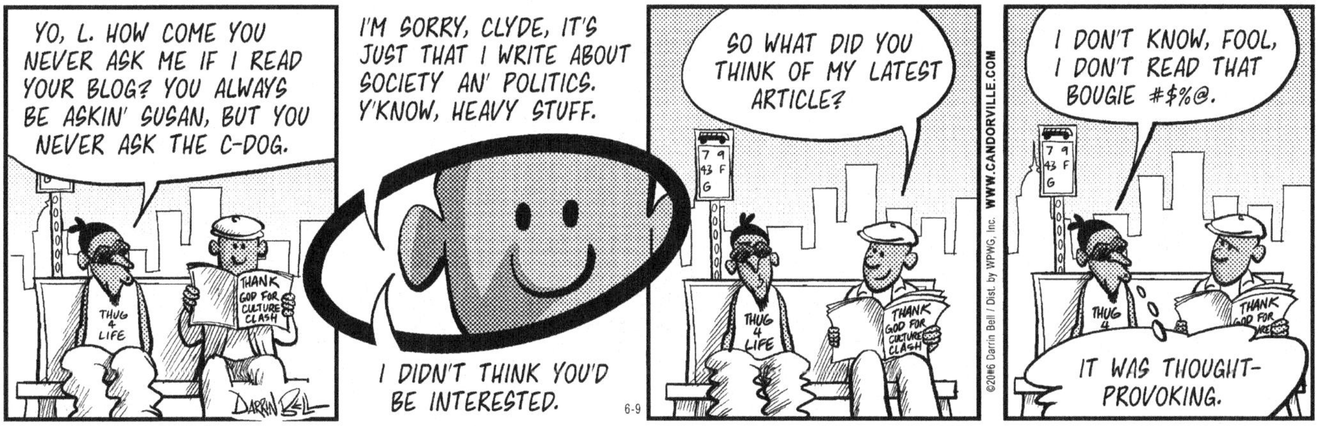
YO, L. HOW COME YOU NEVER ASK ME IF I READ YOUR BLOG? YOU ALWAYS BE ASKIN' SUSAN, BUT YOU NEVER ASK THE C-DOG.
THUG 4 LIFE
THANK GOD FOR CULTURE CLASH
DARRIN BELL
I'M SORRY, CLYDE, IT'S JUST THAT I WRITE ABOUT SOCIETY AN' POLITICS. Y'KNOW, HEAVY STUFF.
I DIDN'T THINK YOU'D BE INTERESTED.
6-9
SO WHAT DID YOU THINK OF MY LATEST ARTICLE?
©2006 Darrin Bell / Dist. by WPWG, Inc. WWW.CANDORVILLE.COM
I DON'T KNOW, FOOL, I DON'T READ THAT BOUGIE #$%@.
IT WAS THOUGHT-PROVOKING.

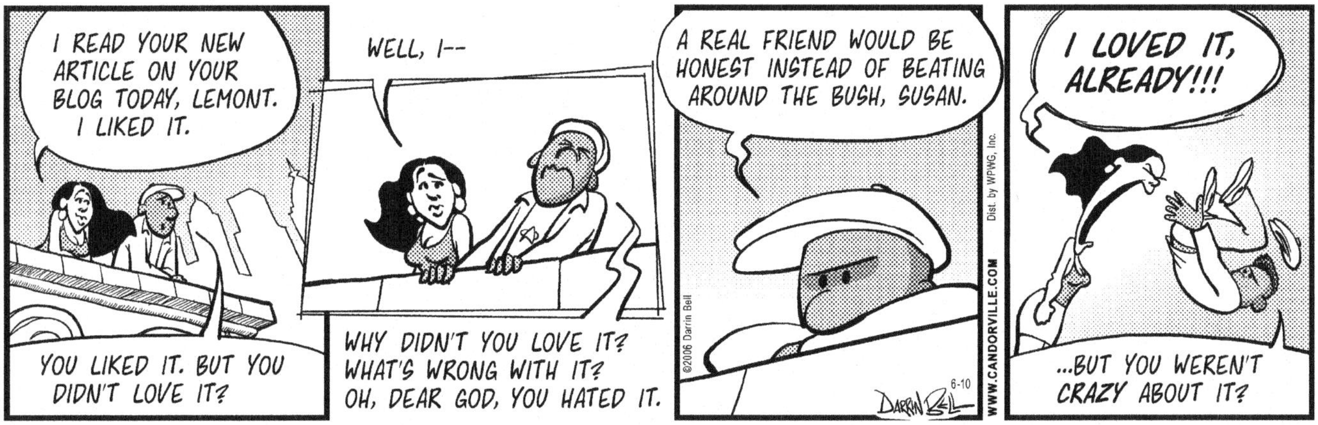
I READ YOUR NEW ARTICLE ON YOUR BLOG TODAY, LEMONT. I LIKED IT.
YOU LIKED IT. BUT YOU DIDN'T LOVE IT?
WELL, I--
WHY DIDN'T YOU LOVE IT? WHAT'S WRONG WITH IT? OH, DEAR GOD, YOU HATED IT.
©2006 Darrin Bell
A REAL FRIEND WOULD BE HONEST INSTEAD OF BEATING AROUND THE BUSH, SUSAN.
6-10
DARRIN BELL
WWW.CANDORVILLE.COM Dist. by WPWG, Inc.
I LOVED IT, ALREADY!!!
...BUT YOU WEREN'T CRAZY ABOUT IT?

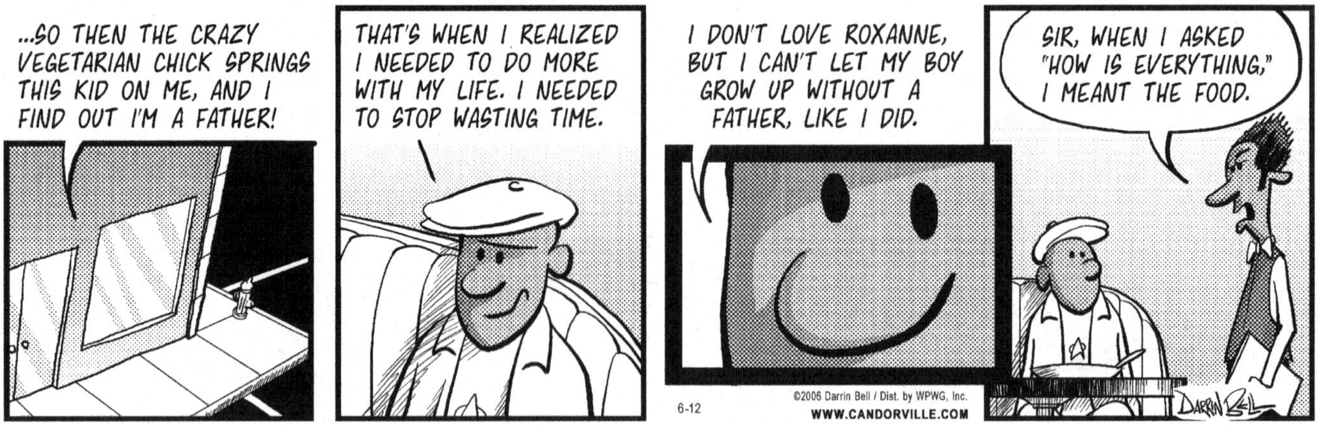
...SO THEN THE CRAZY VEGETARIAN CHICK SPRINGS THIS KID ON ME, AND I FIND OUT I'M A FATHER!
THAT'S WHEN I REALIZED I NEEDED TO DO MORE WITH MY LIFE. I NEEDED TO STOP WASTING TIME.
I DON'T LOVE ROXANNE, BUT I CAN'T LET MY BOY GROW UP WITHOUT A FATHER, LIKE I DID.
SIR, WHEN I ASKED "HOW IS EVERYTHING," I MEANT THE FOOD.
6-12
©2006 Darrin Bell / Dist. by WPWG, Inc.
WWW.CANDORVILLE.COM
DARRIN BELL

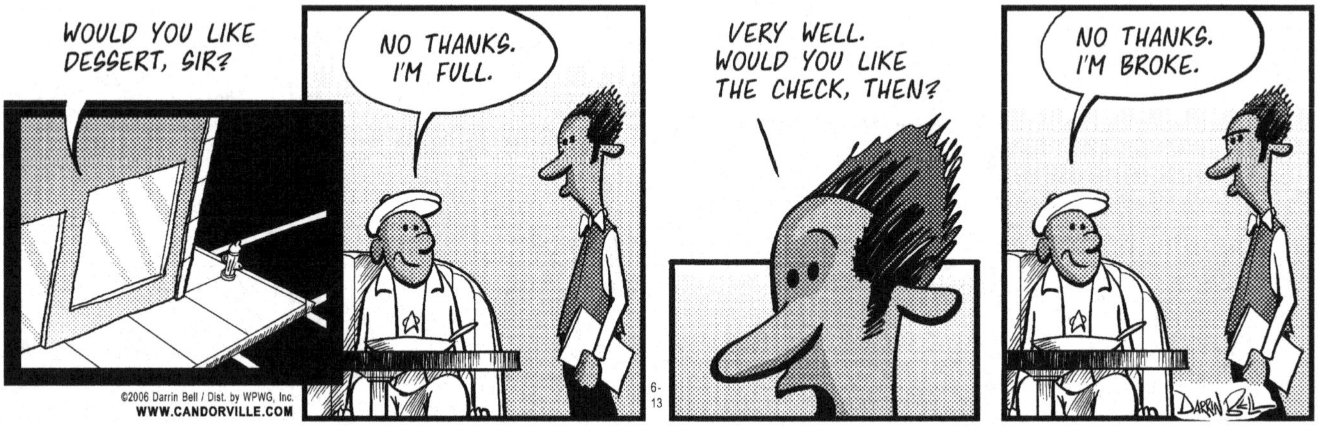
WOULD YOU LIKE DESSERT, SIR?
NO THANKS. I'M FULL.
VERY WELL. WOULD YOU LIKE THE CHECK, THEN?
NO THANKS. I'M BROKE.
©2006 Darrin Bell / Dist. by WPWG, Inc.
WWW.CANDORVILLE.COM
6-13
DARRIN BELL

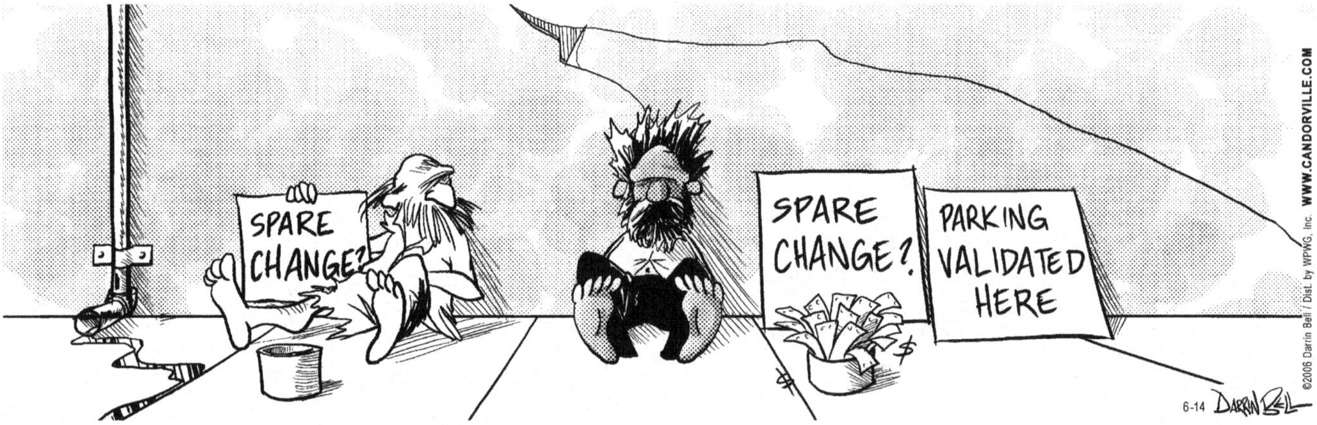
SPARE CHANGE?
SPARE CHANGE?
PARKING VALIDATED HERE
©2006 Darrin Bell / Dist. by WPWG, Inc. WWW.CANDORVILLE.COM
6-14
DARRIN BELL

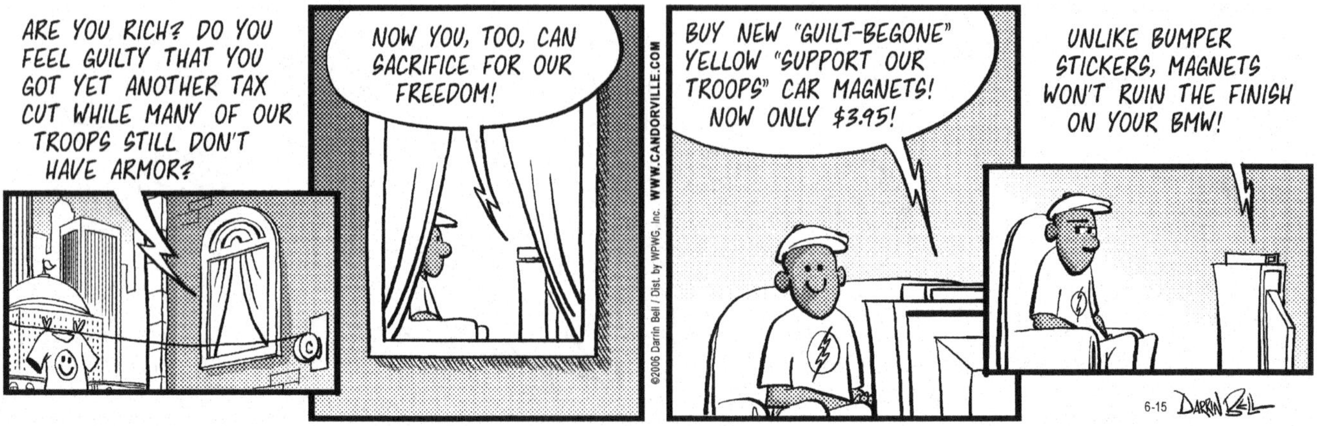
ARE YOU RICH? DO YOU FEEL GUILTY THAT YOU GOT YET ANOTHER TAX CUT WHILE MANY OF OUR TROOPS STILL DON'T HAVE ARMOR?
NOW YOU, TOO, CAN SACRIFICE FOR OUR FREEDOM!
BUY NEW "GUILT-BEGONE" YELLOW "SUPPORT OUR TROOPS" CAR MAGNETS! NOW ONLY $3.95!
UNLIKE BUMPER STICKERS, MAGNETS WON'T RUIN THE FINISH ON YOUR BMW!
©2006 Darrin Bell / Dist. by WPWG, Inc. WWW.CANDORVILLE.COM
6-15
DARRIN BELL

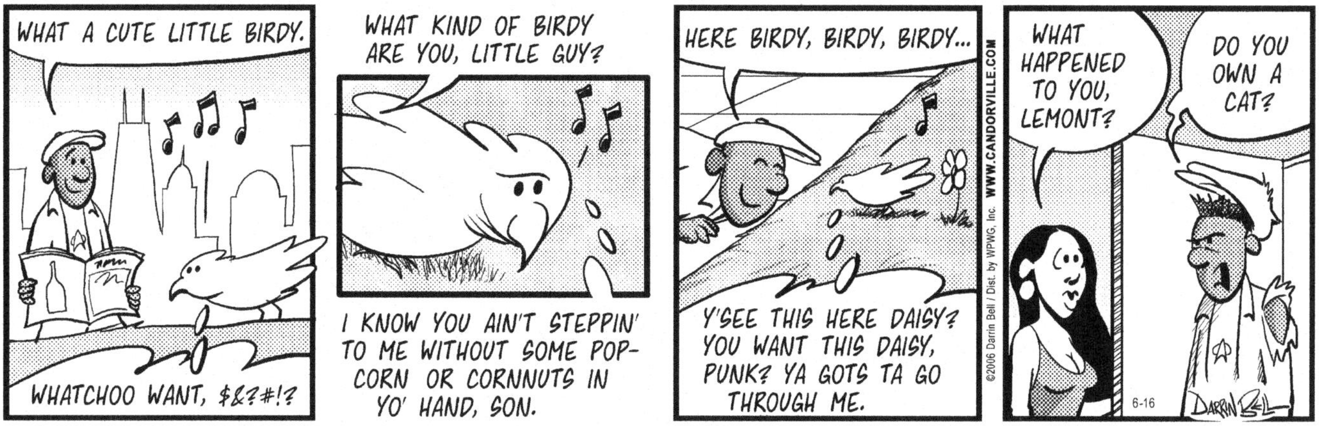
WHAT A CUTE LITTLE BIRDY.
WHATCHOO WANT, $&?#!?
WHAT KIND OF BIRDY ARE YOU, LITTLE GUY?
I KNOW YOU AIN'T STEPPIN' TO ME WITHOUT SOME POP-CORN OR CORNNUTS IN YO' HAND, SON.
HERE BIRDY, BIRDY, BIRDY...
Y'SEE THIS HERE DAISY? YOU WANT THIS DAISY, PUNK? YA GOTS TA GO THROUGH ME.
©2006 Darrin Bell / Dist. by WPWG, Inc. WWW.CANDORVILLE.COM
WHAT HAPPENED TO YOU, LEMONT?
DO YOU OWN A CAT?
6-16
DARRIN BELL

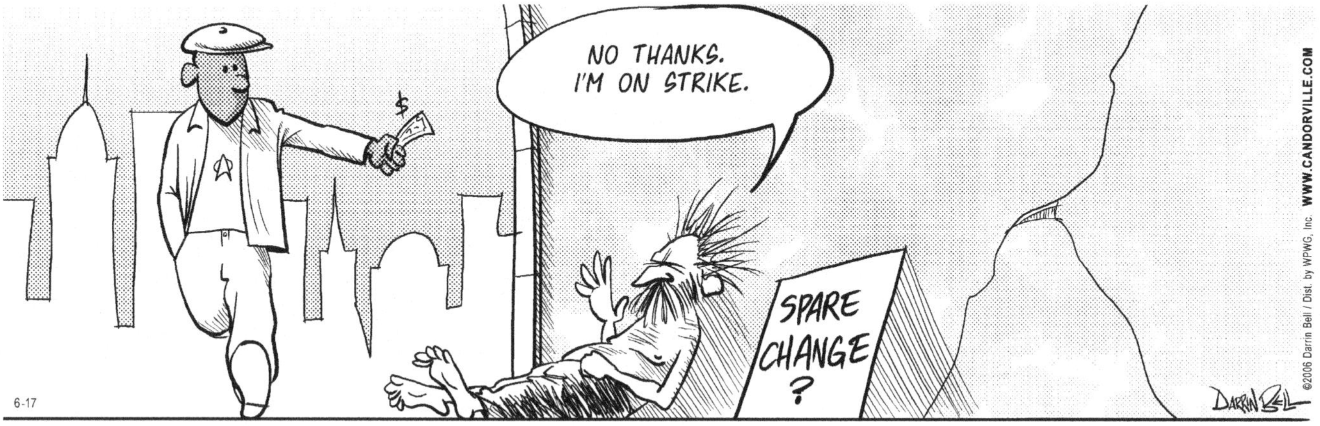
NO THANKS. I'M ON STRIKE.
$
SPARE CHANGE ?
6-17
©2006 Darrin Bell / Dist. by WPWG, Inc. WWW.CANDORVILLE.COM
DARRIN BELL

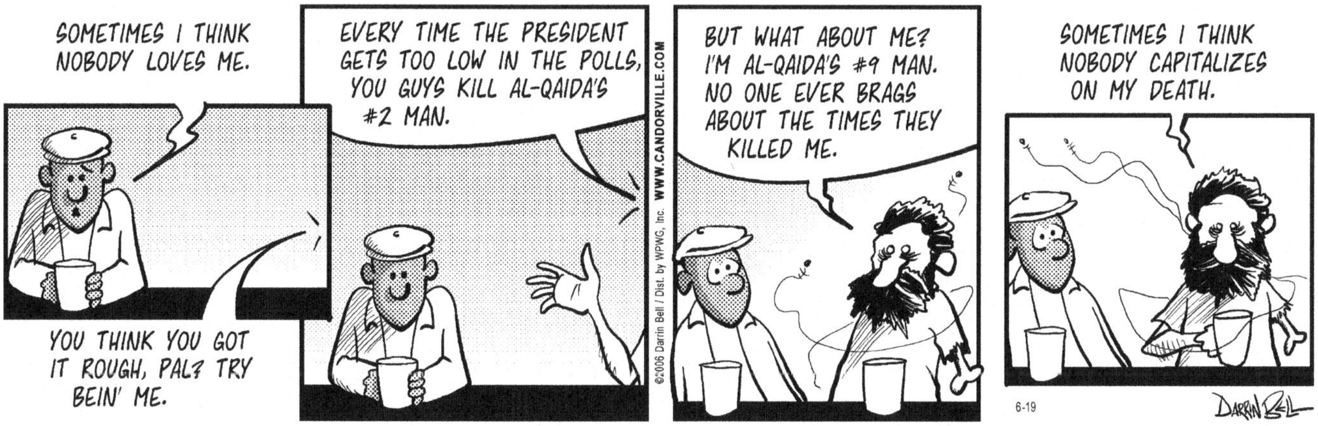
SOMETIMES I THINK NOBODY LOVES ME.
YOU THINK YOU GOT IT ROUGH, PAL? TRY BEIN' ME.
EVERY TIME THE PRESIDENT GETS TOO LOW IN THE POLLS, YOU GUYS KILL AL-QAIDA'S #2 MAN.
©2006 Darrin Bell / Dist. by WPWG, Inc. WWW.CANDORVILLE.COM
BUT WHAT ABOUT ME? I'M AL-QAIDA'S #9 MAN. NO ONE EVER BRAGS ABOUT THE TIMES THEY KILLED ME.
SOMETIMES I THINK NOBODY CAPITALIZES ON MY DEATH.
6-19
DARRIN BELL

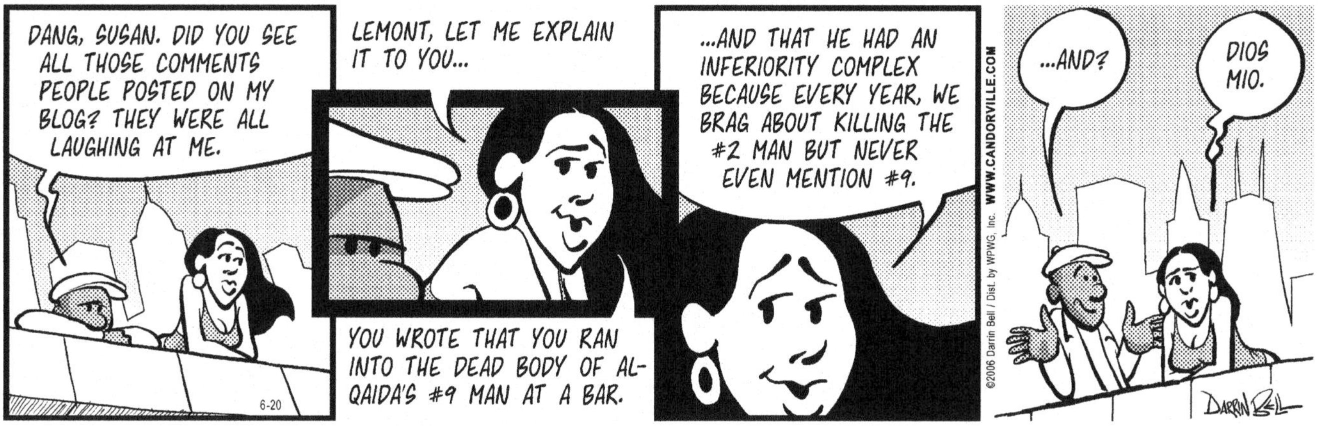
DANG, SUSAN. DID YOU SEE ALL THOSE COMMENTS PEOPLE POSTED ON MY BLOG? THEY WERE ALL LAUGHING AT ME.
6-20
LEMONT, LET ME EXPLAIN IT TO YOU...
YOU WROTE THAT YOU RAN INTO THE DEAD BODY OF AL-QAIDA'S #9 MAN AT A BAR.
...AND THAT HE HAD AN INFERIORITY COMPLEX BECAUSE EVERY YEAR, WE BRAG ABOUT KILLING THE #2 MAN BUT NEVER EVEN MENTION #9.
©2006 Darrin Bell / Dist. by WPWG, Inc. WWW.CANDORVILLE.COM
...AND?
DIOS MIO.
DARRIN BELL

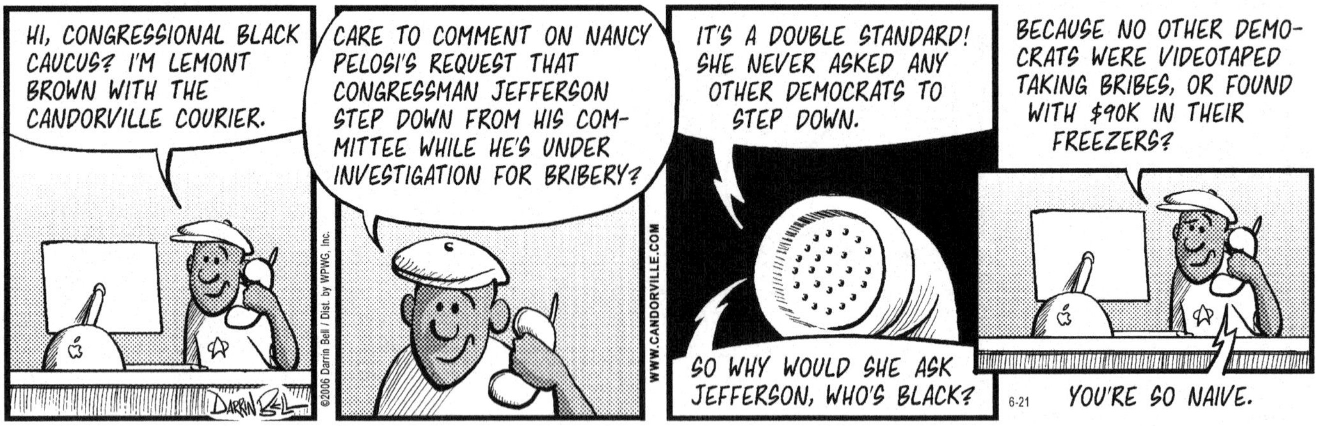
HI, CONGRESSIONAL BLACK CAUCUS? I'M LEMONT BROWN WITH THE CANDORVILLE COURIER.
CARE TO COMMENT ON NANCY PELOSI'S REQUEST THAT CONGRESSMAN JEFFERSON STEP DOWN FROM HIS COMMITTEE WHILE HE'S UNDER INVESTIGATION FOR BRIBERY?
IT'S A DOUBLE STANDARD! SHE NEVER ASKED ANY OTHER DEMOCRATS TO STEP DOWN.
SO WHY WOULD SHE ASK JEFFERSON, WHO'S BLACK?
BECAUSE NO OTHER DEMOCRATS WERE VIDEOTAPED TAKING BRIBES, OR FOUND WITH $90K IN THEIR FREEZERS?
YOU'RE SO NAIVE.
DARRIN BELL
©2006 Darrin Bell / Dist. by WPWG, Inc.
WWW.CANDORVILLE.COM
6-21

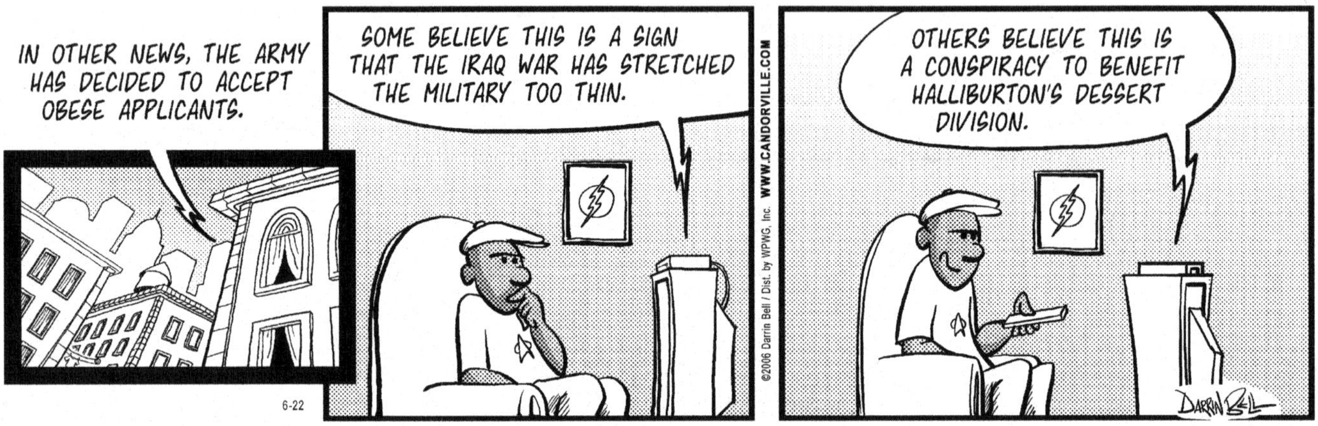
IN OTHER NEWS, THE ARMY HAS DECIDED TO ACCEPT OBESE APPLICANTS.
SOME BELIEVE THIS IS A SIGN THAT THE IRAQ WAR HAS STRETCHED THE MILITARY TOO THIN.
OTHERS BELIEVE THIS IS A CONSPIRACY TO BENEFIT HALLIBURTON'S DESSERT DIVISION.
6-22
©2006 Darrin Bell / Dist. by WPWG, Inc.
WWW.CANDORVILLE.COM
DARRIN BELL

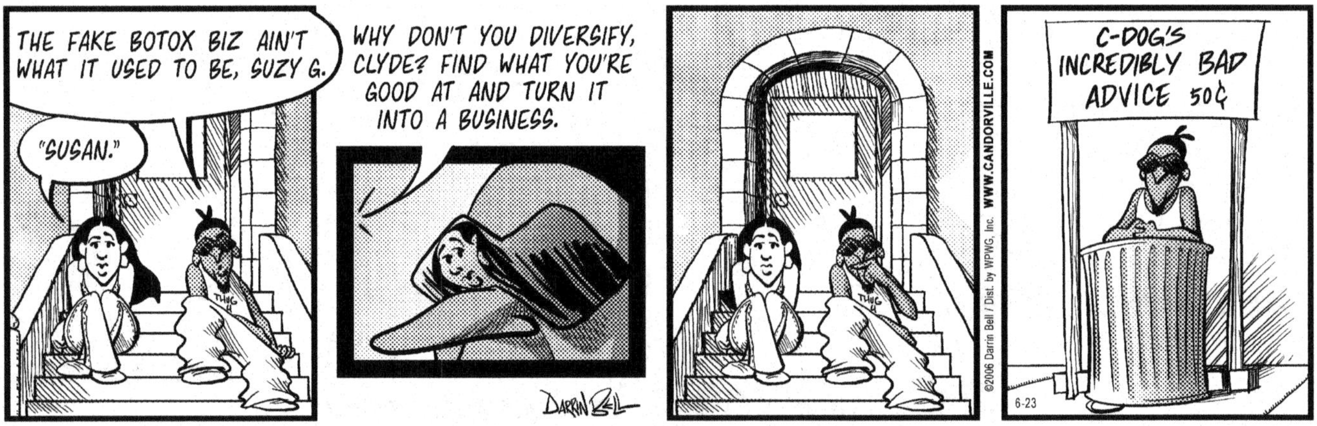
THE FAKE BOTOX BIZ AIN'T WHAT IT USED TO BE, SUZY G.
"SUSAN."
WHY DON'T YOU DIVERSIFY, CLYDE? FIND WHAT YOU'RE GOOD AT AND TURN IT INTO A BUSINESS.
DARRIN BELL
C-DOG'S INCREDIBLY BAD ADVICE 50¢
©2006 Darrin Bell / Dist. by WPWG, Inc.
WWW.CANDORVILLE.COM
6-23

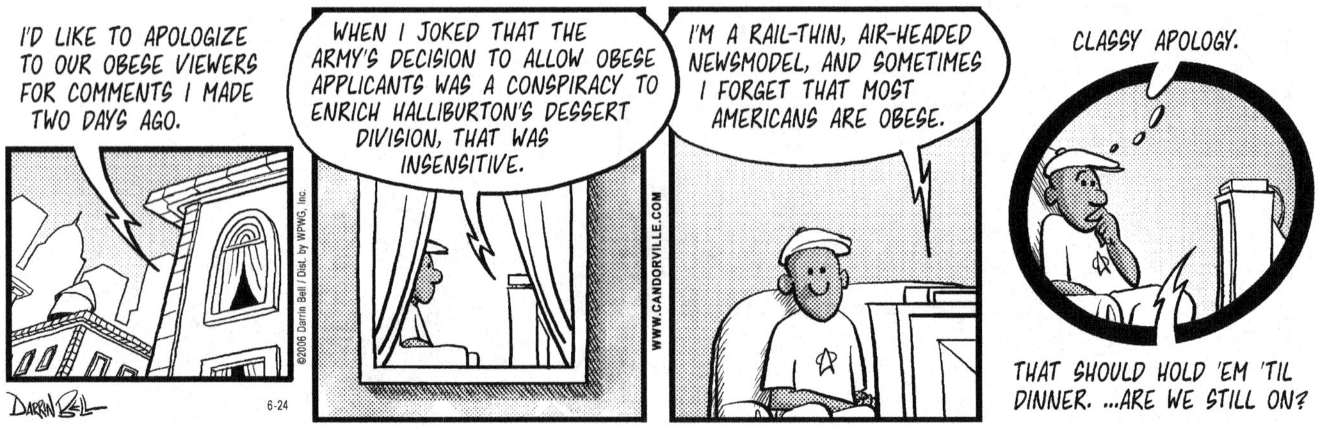
I'D LIKE TO APOLOGIZE TO OUR OBESE VIEWERS FOR COMMENTS I MADE TWO DAYS AGO.
WHEN I JOKED THAT THE ARMY'S DECISION TO ALLOW OBESE APPLICANTS WAS A CONSPIRACY TO ENRICH HALLIBURTON'S DESSERT DIVISION, THAT WAS INSENSITIVE.
I'M A RAIL-THIN, AIR-HEADED NEWSMODEL, AND SOMETIMES I FORGET THAT MOST AMERICANS ARE OBESE.
CLASSY APOLOGY.
THAT SHOULD HOLD 'EM 'TIL DINNER. ...ARE WE STILL ON?
DARRIN BELL
6-24
©2006 Darrin Bell / Dist. by WPWG, Inc.
WWW.CANDORVILLE.COM

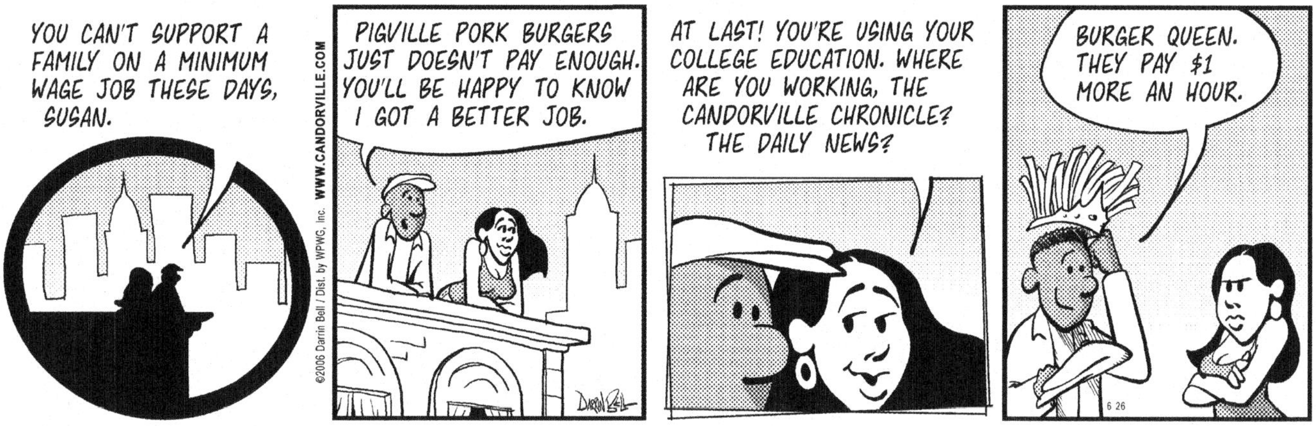
YOU CAN'T SUPPORT A FAMILY ON A MINIMUM WAGE JOB THESE DAYS, SUSAN.
©2006 Darrin Bell / Dist. by WPWG, Inc. WWW.CANDORVILLE.COM
PIGVILLE PORK BURGERS JUST DOESN'T PAY ENOUGH. YOU'LL BE HAPPY TO KNOW I GOT A BETTER JOB.
AT LAST! YOU'RE USING YOUR COLLEGE EDUCATION. WHERE ARE YOU WORKING, THE CANDORVILLE CHRONICLE? THE DAILY NEWS?
BURGER QUEEN. THEY PAY $1 MORE AN HOUR.
6-26

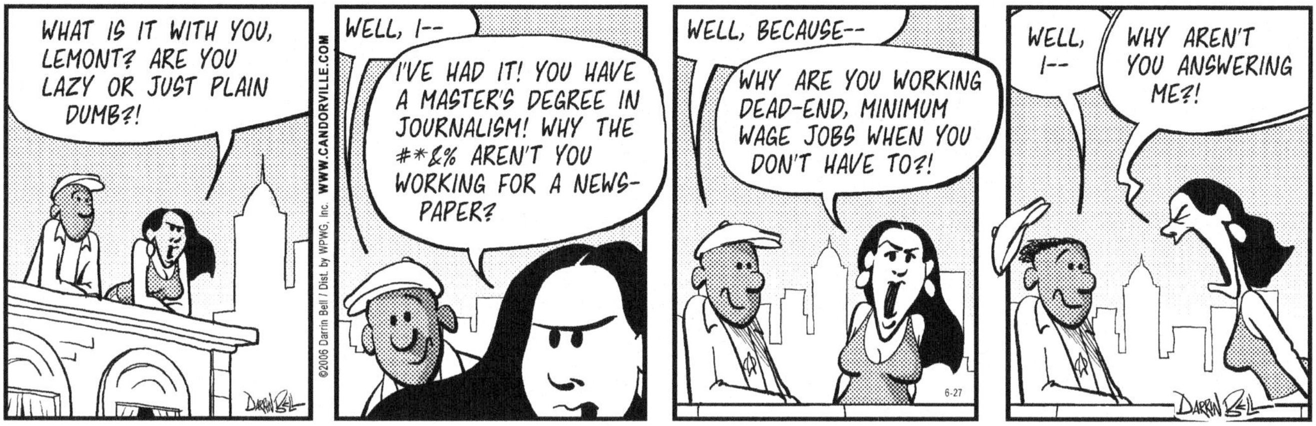
WHAT IS IT WITH YOU, LEMONT? ARE YOU LAZY OR JUST PLAIN DUMB?!
©2006 Darrin Bell / Dist. by WPWG, Inc. WWW.CANDORVILLE.COM
WELL, I--
I'VE HAD IT! YOU HAVE A MASTER'S DEGREE IN JOURNALISM! WHY THE #*&% AREN'T YOU WORKING FOR A NEWSPAPER?
WELL, BECAUSE--
WHY ARE YOU WORKING DEAD-END, MINIMUM WAGE JOBS WHEN YOU DON'T HAVE TO?!
6-27
WELL, I--
WHY AREN'T YOU ANSWERING ME?!

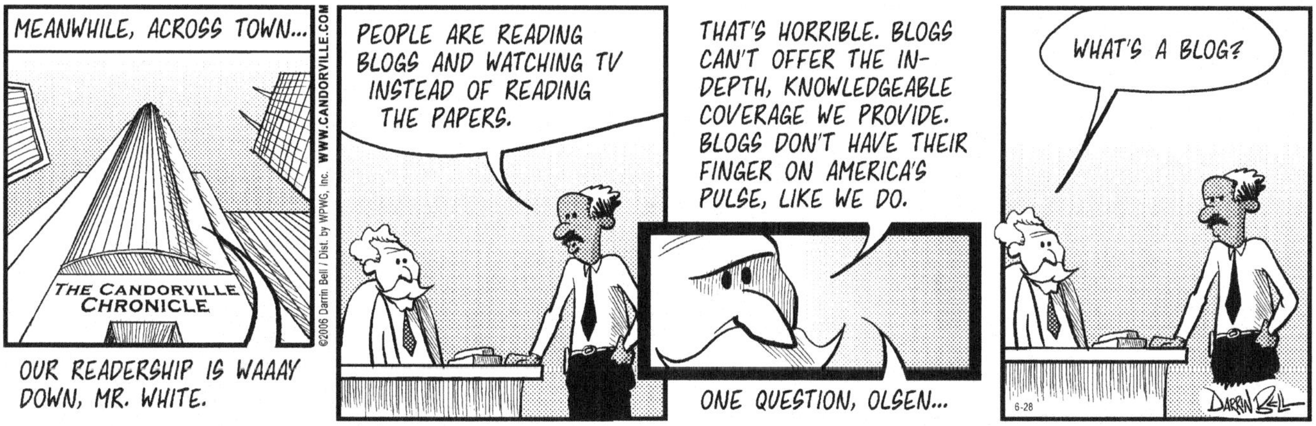
MEANWHILE, ACROSS TOWN...
THE CANDORVILLE CHRONICLE
OUR READERSHIP IS WAAAY DOWN, MR. WHITE.
©2006 Darrin Bell / Dist. by WPWG, Inc. WWW.CANDORVILLE.COM
PEOPLE ARE READING BLOGS AND WATCHING TV INSTEAD OF READING THE PAPERS.
THAT'S HORRIBLE. BLOGS CAN'T OFFER THE IN-DEPTH, KNOWLEDGEABLE COVERAGE WE PROVIDE. BLOGS DON'T HAVE THEIR FINGER ON AMERICA'S PULSE, LIKE WE DO.
ONE QUESTION, OLSEN...
WHAT'S A BLOG?
6-28

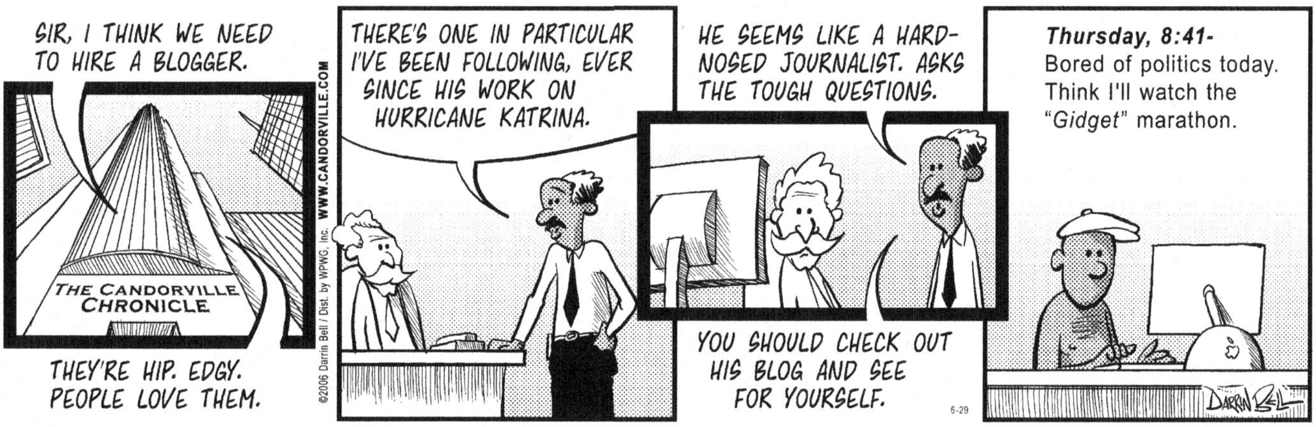
SIR, I THINK WE NEED TO HIRE A BLOGGER.
THE CANDORVILLE CHRONICLE
THEY'RE HIP. EDGY. PEOPLE LOVE THEM.
©2006 Darrin Bell / Dist. by WPWG, Inc. WWW.CANDORVILLE.COM
THERE'S ONE IN PARTICULAR I'VE BEEN FOLLOWING, EVER SINCE HIS WORK ON HURRICANE KATRINA.
HE SEEMS LIKE A HARD-NOSED JOURNALIST. ASKS THE TOUGH QUESTIONS.
YOU SHOULD CHECK OUT HIS BLOG AND SEE FOR YOURSELF.
6-29
Thursday, 8:41-
Bored of politics today. Think I'll watch the "Gidget" marathon.

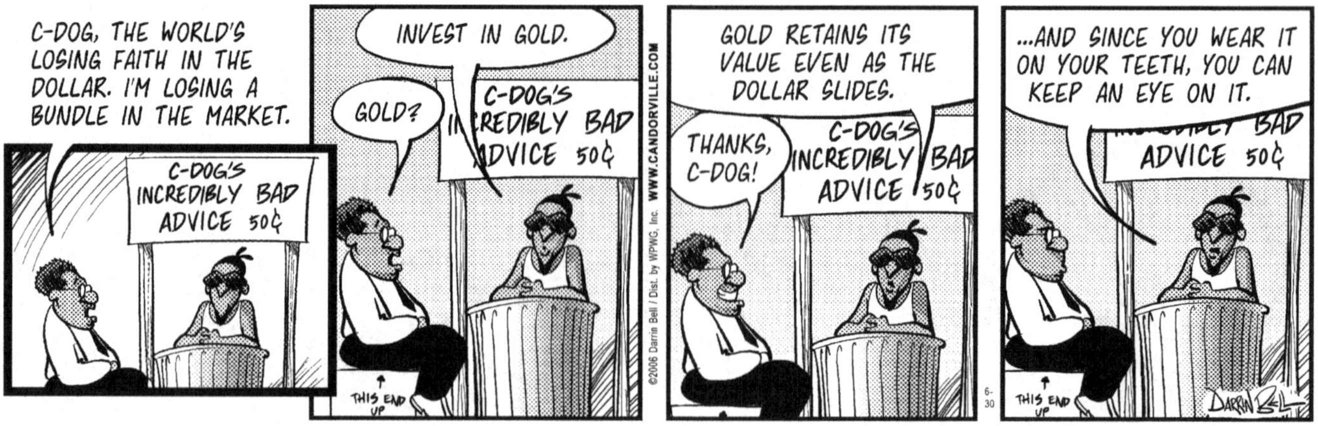
C-DOG, THE WORLD'S LOSING FAITH IN THE DOLLAR. I'M LOSING A BUNDLE IN THE MARKET.
C-DOG'S INCREDIBLY BAD ADVICE 50¢
INVEST IN GOLD.
GOLD?
THIS END UP
GOLD RETAINS ITS VALUE EVEN AS THE DOLLAR SLIDES.
THANKS, C-DOG!
...AND SINCE YOU WEAR IT ON YOUR TEETH, YOU CAN KEEP AN EYE ON IT.
©2006 Darrin Bell / Dist. by WPWG, Inc. WWW.CANDORVILLE.COM
6-30
DARRIN BELL

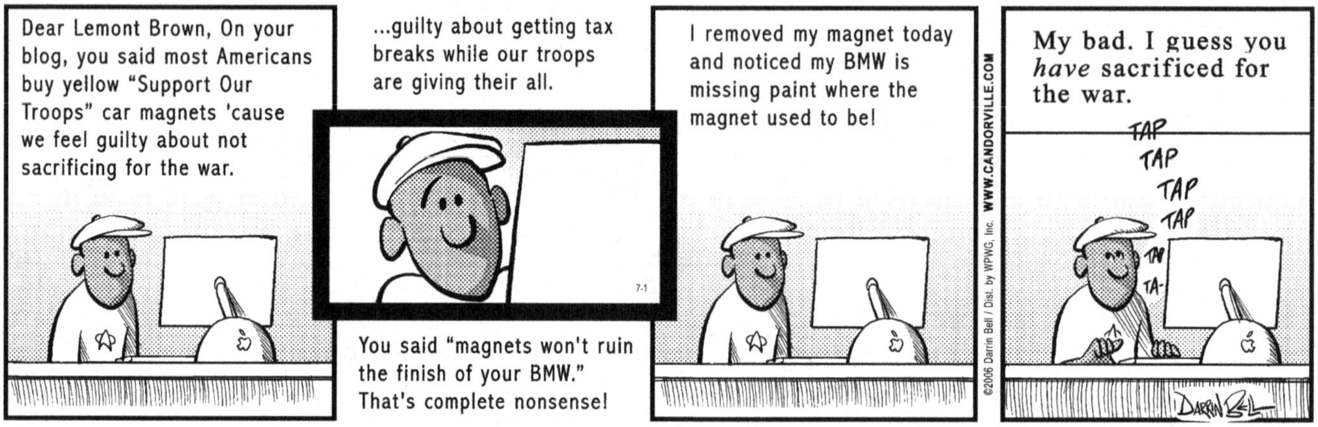
Dear Lemont Brown, On your blog, you said most Americans buy yellow "Support Our Troops" car magnets 'cause we feel guilty about not sacrificing for the war.
...guilty about getting tax breaks while our troops are giving their all.
You said "magnets won't ruin the finish of your BMW." That's complete nonsense!
I removed my magnet today and noticed my BMW is missing paint where the magnet used to be!
My bad. I guess you *have* sacrificed for the war.
TAP TAP TAP TAP TAP TA-
©2006 Darrin Bell / Dist. by WPWG, Inc. WWW.CANDORVILLE.COM
7-1
DARRIN BELL

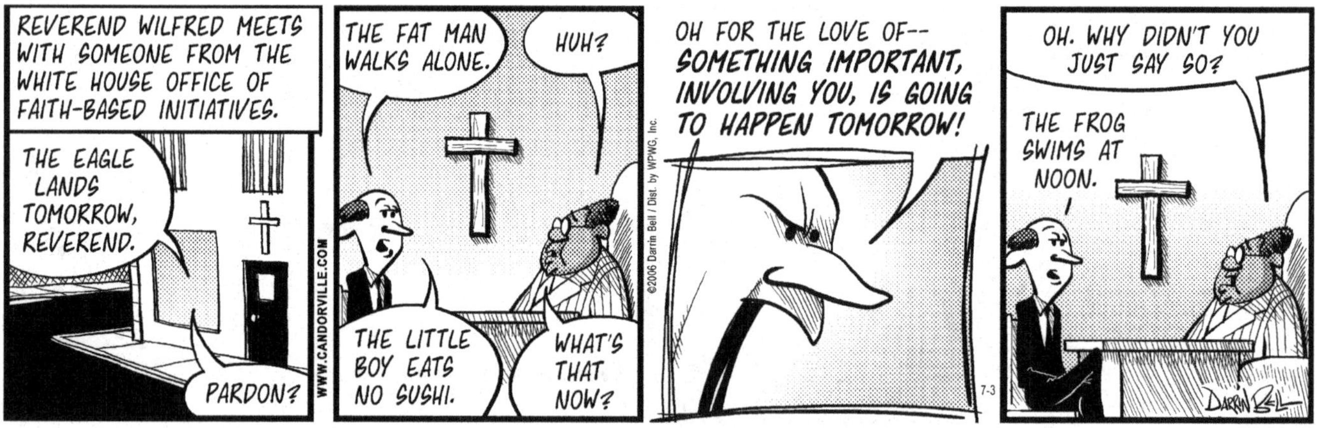
REVEREND WILFRED MEETS WITH SOMEONE FROM THE WHITE HOUSE OFFICE OF FAITH-BASED INITIATIVES.
THE EAGLE LANDS TOMORROW, REVEREND.
PARDON?
THE FAT MAN WALKS ALONE.
HUH?
THE LITTLE BOY EATS NO SUSHI.
WHAT'S THAT NOW?
OH FOR THE LOVE OF-- SOMETHING IMPORTANT, INVOLVING YOU, IS GOING TO HAPPEN TOMORROW!
OH. WHY DIDN'T YOU JUST SAY SO?
THE FROG SWIMS AT NOON.
WWW.CANDORVILLE.COM ©2006 Darrin Bell / Dist. by WPWG, Inc.
7-3
DARRIN BELL

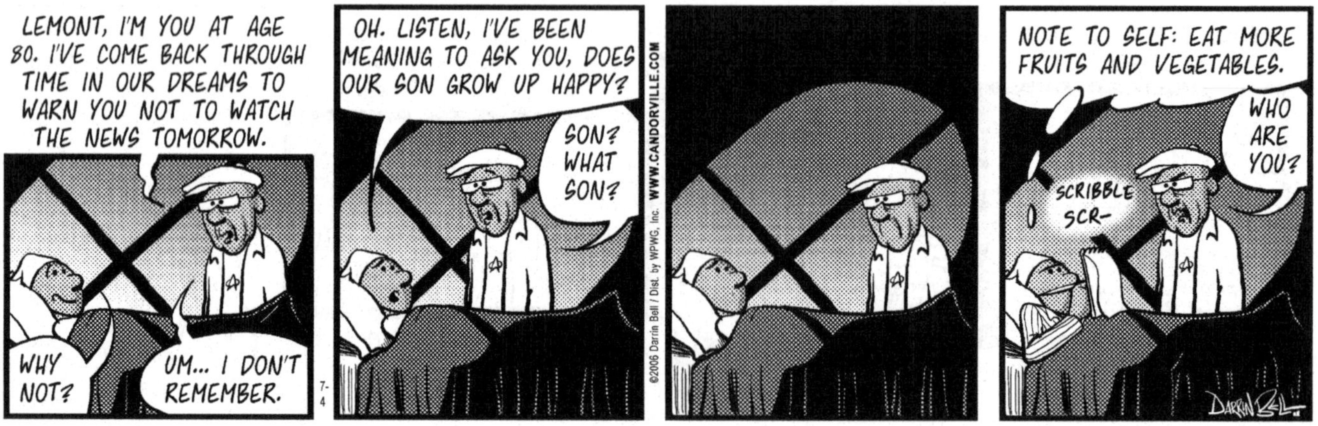
LEMONT, I'M YOU AT AGE 80. I'VE COME BACK THROUGH TIME IN OUR DREAMS TO WARN YOU NOT TO WATCH THE NEWS TOMORROW.
WHY NOT?
UM... I DON'T REMEMBER.
OH. LISTEN, I'VE BEEN MEANING TO ASK YOU, DOES OUR SON GROW UP HAPPY?
SON? WHAT SON?
NOTE TO SELF: EAT MORE FRUITS AND VEGETABLES.
WHO ARE YOU?
SCRIBBLE SCR-
©2006 Darrin Bell / Dist. by WPWG, Inc. WWW.CANDORVILLE.COM
7-4
DARRIN BELL

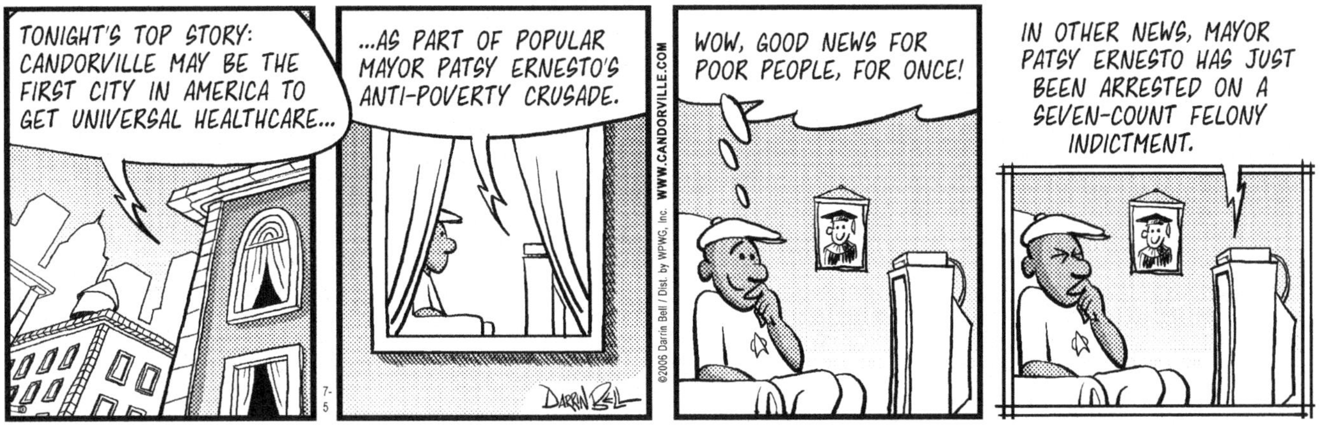
TONIGHT'S TOP STORY: CANDORVILLE MAY BE THE FIRST CITY IN AMERICA TO GET UNIVERSAL HEALTHCARE...
...AS PART OF POPULAR MAYOR PATSY ERNESTO'S ANTI-POVERTY CRUSADE.
WOW, GOOD NEWS FOR POOR PEOPLE, FOR ONCE!
IN OTHER NEWS, MAYOR PATSY ERNESTO HAS JUST BEEN ARRESTED ON A SEVEN-COUNT FELONY INDICTMENT.
7-5
©2006 Darrin Bell / Dist. by WPWG, Inc. WWW.CANDORVILLE.COM
DARRIN BELL

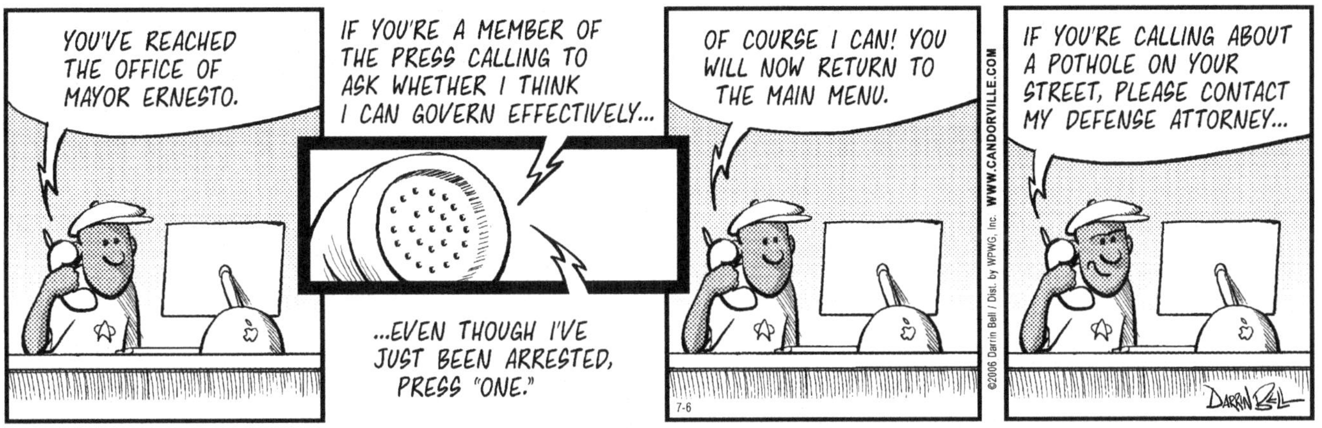
YOU'VE REACHED THE OFFICE OF MAYOR ERNESTO.
IF YOU'RE A MEMBER OF THE PRESS CALLING TO ASK WHETHER I THINK I CAN GOVERN EFFECTIVELY...
...EVEN THOUGH I'VE JUST BEEN ARRESTED, PRESS "ONE."
OF COURSE I CAN! YOU WILL NOW RETURN TO THE MAIN MENU.
IF YOU'RE CALLING ABOUT A POTHOLE ON YOUR STREET, PLEASE CONTACT MY DEFENSE ATTORNEY...
7-6
©2006 Darrin Bell / Dist. by WPWG, Inc. WWW.CANDORVILLE.COM
DARRIN BELL

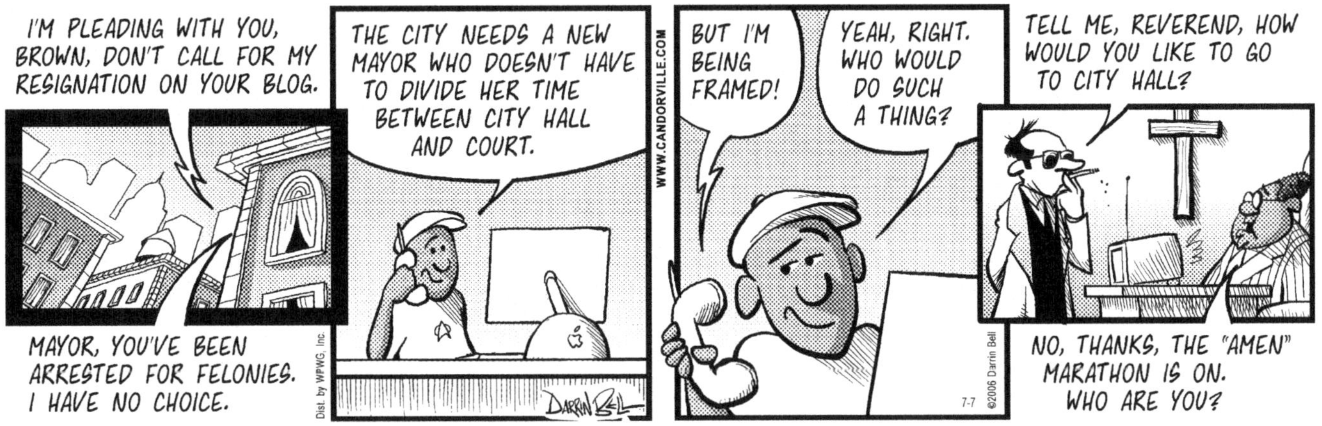
I'M PLEADING WITH YOU, BROWN, DON'T CALL FOR MY RESIGNATION ON YOUR BLOG.
MAYOR, YOU'VE BEEN ARRESTED FOR FELONIES. I HAVE NO CHOICE.
THE CITY NEEDS A NEW MAYOR WHO DOESN'T HAVE TO DIVIDE HER TIME BETWEEN CITY HALL AND COURT.
BUT I'M BEING FRAMED!
YEAH, RIGHT. WHO WOULD DO SUCH A THING?
TELL ME, REVEREND, HOW WOULD YOU LIKE TO GO TO CITY HALL?
NO, THANKS, THE "AMEN" MARATHON IS ON. WHO ARE YOU?
7-7
©2006 Darrin Bell / Dist. by WPWG, Inc. WWW.CANDORVILLE.COM
DARRIN BELL

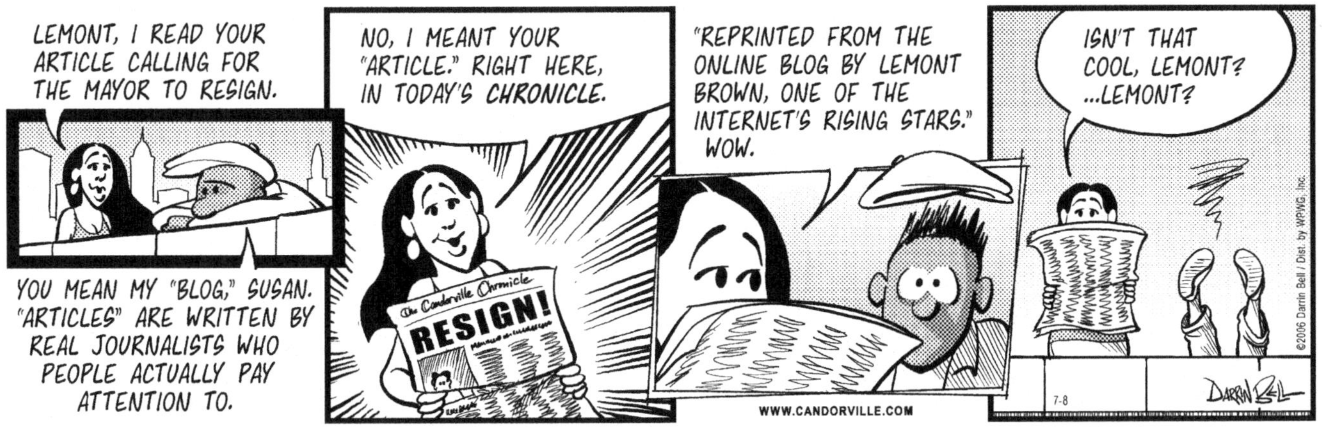
LEMONT, I READ YOUR ARTICLE CALLING FOR THE MAYOR TO RESIGN.
YOU MEAN MY "BLOG," SUSAN. "ARTICLES" ARE WRITTEN BY REAL JOURNALISTS WHO PEOPLE ACTUALLY PAY ATTENTION TO.
NO, I MEANT YOUR "ARTICLE." RIGHT HERE, IN TODAY'S CHRONICLE.
The Candorville Chronicle
RESIGN!
"REPRINTED FROM THE ONLINE BLOG BY LEMONT BROWN, ONE OF THE INTERNET'S RISING STARS." WOW.
ISN'T THAT COOL, LEMONT? ...LEMONT?
7-8
©2006 Darrin Bell / Dist. by WPWG, Inc.
WWW.CANDORVILLE.COM
DARRIN BELL

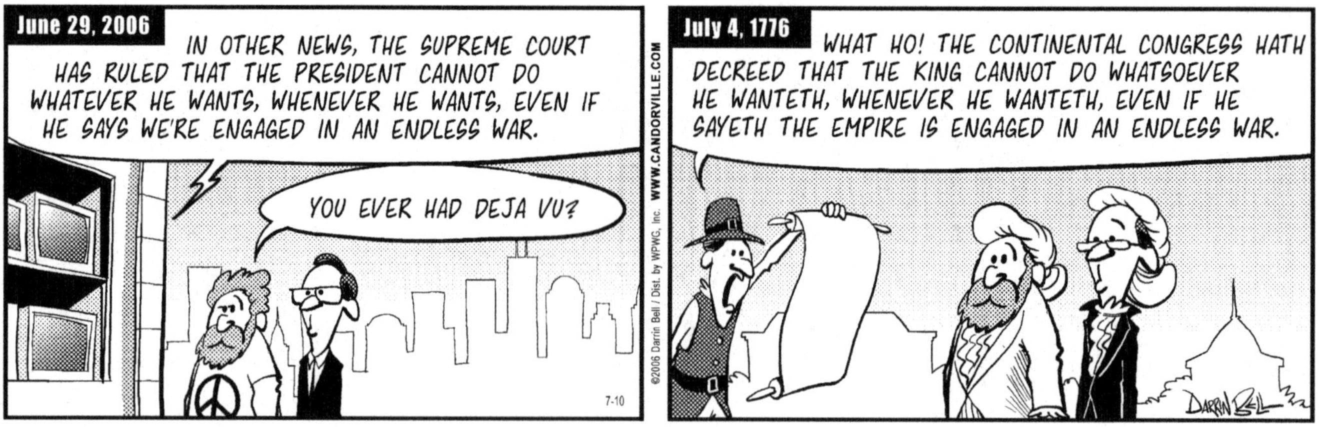
June 29, 2006
IN OTHER NEWS, THE SUPREME COURT HAS RULED THAT THE PRESIDENT CANNOT DO WHATEVER HE WANTS, WHENEVER HE WANTS, EVEN IF HE SAYS WE'RE ENGAGED IN AN ENDLESS WAR.
YOU EVER HAD DEJA VU?
7-10
©2006 Darrin Bell / Dist. by WPWG, Inc. WWW.CANDORVILLE.COM
July 4, 1776
WHAT HO! THE CONTINENTAL CONGRESS HATH DECREED THAT THE KING CANNOT DO WHATSOEVER HE WANTETH, WHENEVER HE WANTETH, EVEN IF HE SAYETH THE EMPIRE IS ENGAGED IN AN ENDLESS WAR.
DARRIN BELL

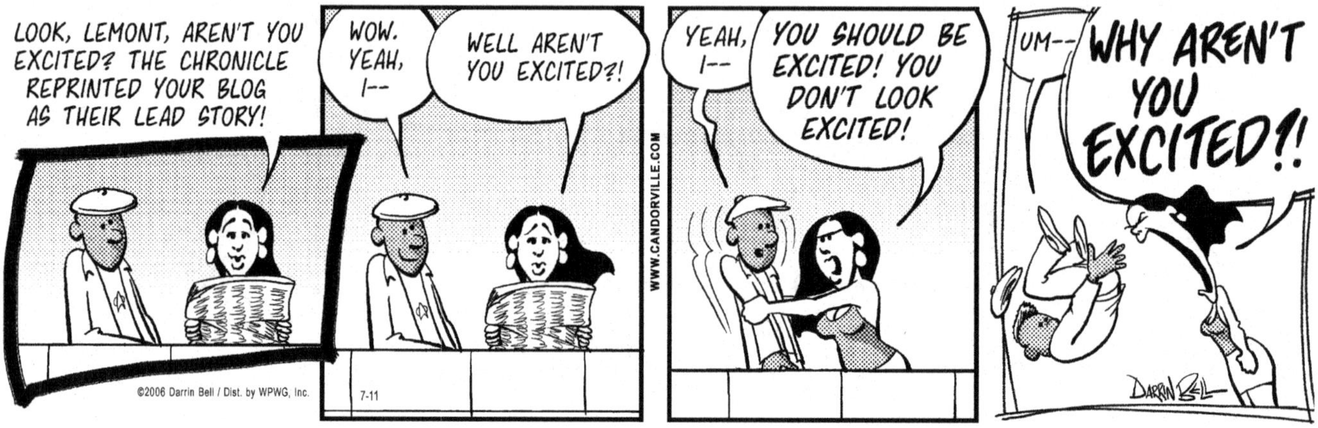
LOOK, LEMONT, AREN'T YOU EXCITED? THE CHRONICLE REPRINTED YOUR BLOG AS THEIR LEAD STORY!
©2006 Darrin Bell / Dist. by WPWG, Inc.
WOW. YEAH, I--
WELL AREN'T YOU EXCITED?!
7-11
WWW.CANDORVILLE.COM
YEAH, I--
YOU SHOULD BE EXCITED! YOU DON'T LOOK EXCITED!
UM--
WHY AREN'T YOU EXCITED?!
DARRIN BELL

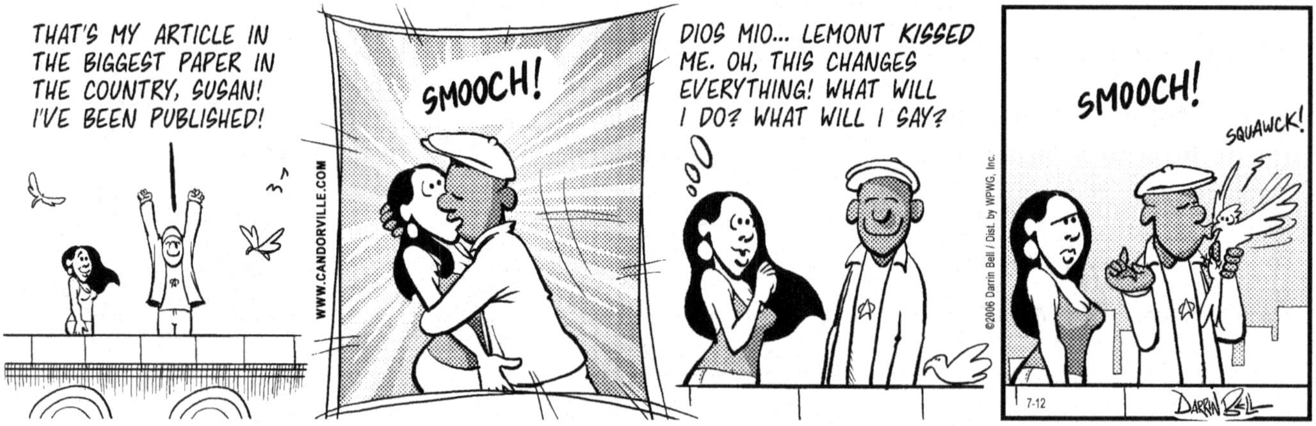
THAT'S MY ARTICLE IN THE BIGGEST PAPER IN THE COUNTRY, SUSAN! I'VE BEEN PUBLISHED!
WWW.CANDORVILLE.COM
SMOOCH!
DIOS MIO... LEMONT KISSED ME. OH, THIS CHANGES EVERYTHING! WHAT WILL I DO? WHAT WILL I SAY?
©2006 Darrin Bell / Dist. by WPWG, Inc.
SMOOCH!
SQUAWCK!
7-12
DARRIN BELL

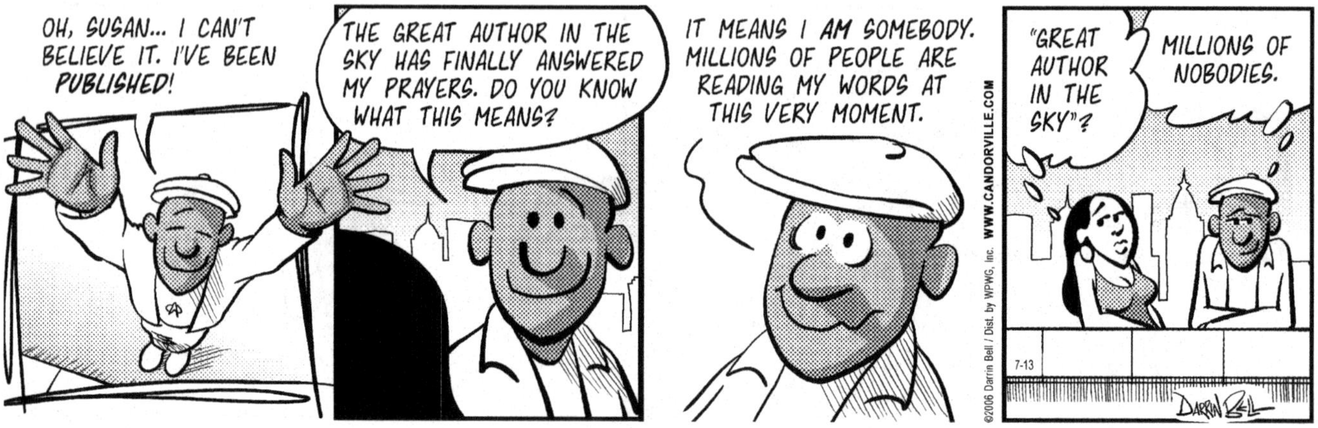
OH, SUSAN... I CAN'T BELIEVE IT. I'VE BEEN PUBLISHED!
THE GREAT AUTHOR IN THE SKY HAS FINALLY ANSWERED MY PRAYERS. DO YOU KNOW WHAT THIS MEANS?
IT MEANS I AM SOMEBODY. MILLIONS OF PEOPLE ARE READING MY WORDS AT THIS VERY MOMENT.
©2006 Darrin Bell / Dist. by WPWG, Inc. WWW.CANDORVILLE.COM
"GREAT AUTHOR IN THE SKY"?
MILLIONS OF NOBODIES.
7-13
DARRIN BELL

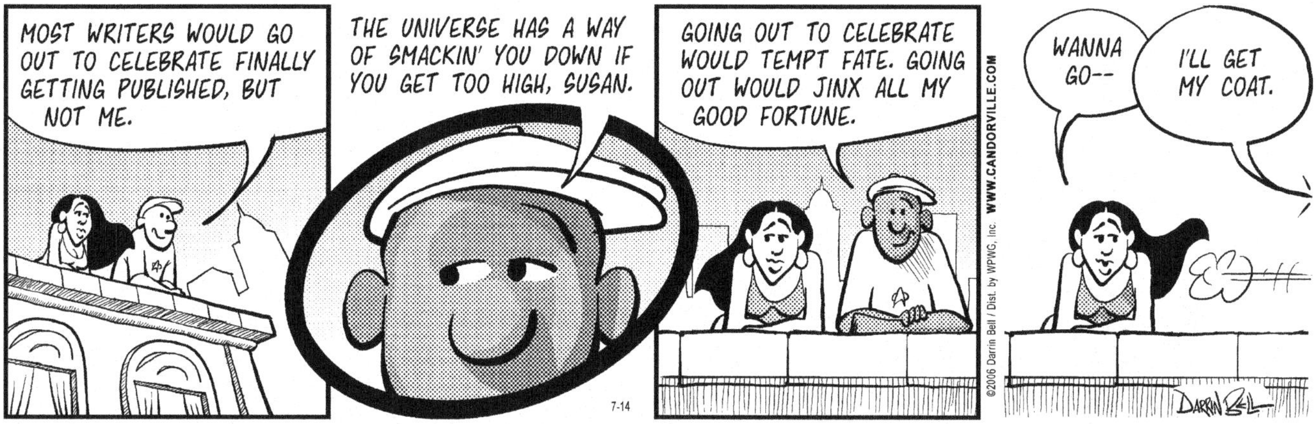
MOST WRITERS WOULD GO OUT TO CELEBRATE FINALLY GETTING PUBLISHED, BUT NOT ME.
THE UNIVERSE HAS A WAY OF SMACKIN' YOU DOWN IF YOU GET TOO HIGH, SUSAN.
7-14
GOING OUT TO CELEBRATE WOULD TEMPT FATE. GOING OUT WOULD JINX ALL MY GOOD FORTUNE.
©2006 Darrin Bell / Dist. by WPWG, Inc. WWW.CANDORVILLE.COM
WANNA GO--
I'LL GET MY COAT.
DARRIN BELL

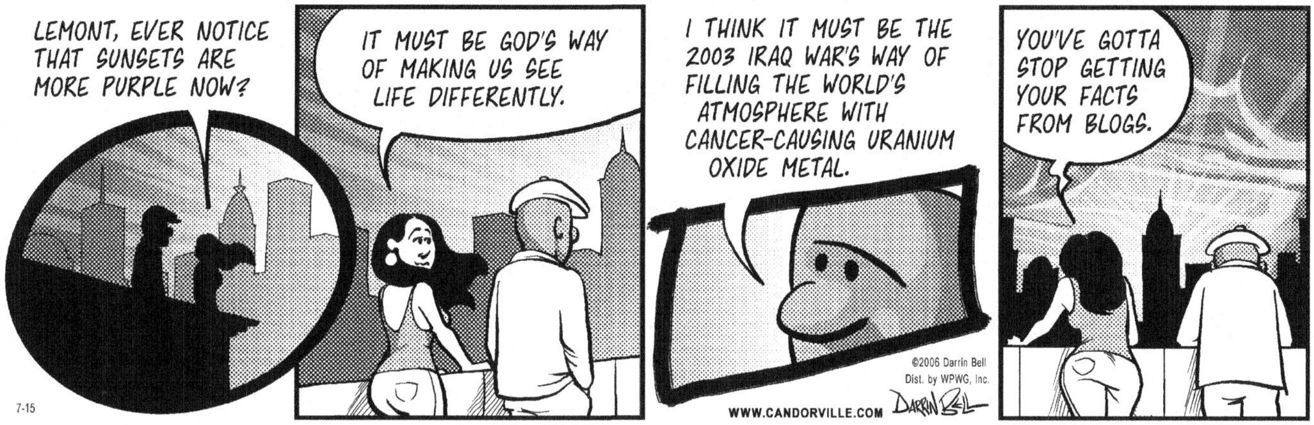
LEMONT, EVER NOTICE THAT SUNSETS ARE MORE PURPLE NOW?
7-15
IT MUST BE GOD'S WAY OF MAKING US SEE LIFE DIFFERENTLY.
I THINK IT MUST BE THE 2003 IRAQ WAR'S WAY OF FILLING THE WORLD'S ATMOSPHERE WITH CANCER-CAUSING URANIUM OXIDE METAL.
©2006 Darrin Bell Dist. by WPWG, Inc.
WWW.CANDORVILLE.COM
DARRIN BELL
YOU'VE GOTTA STOP GETTING YOUR FACTS FROM BLOGS.

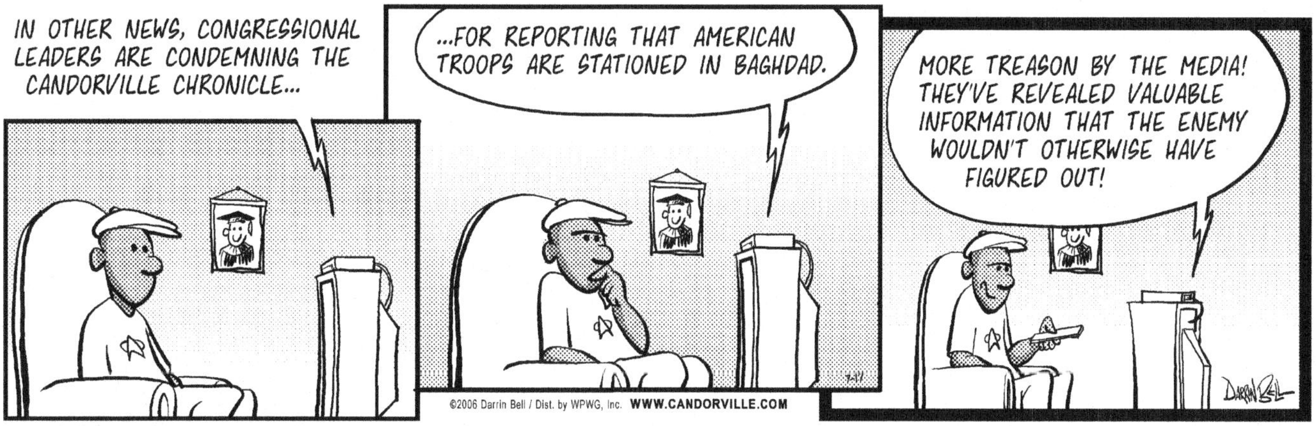
IN OTHER NEWS, CONGRESSIONAL LEADERS ARE CONDEMNING THE CANDORVILLE CHRONICLE...
...FOR REPORTING THAT AMERICAN TROOPS ARE STATIONED IN BAGHDAD.
©2006 Darrin Bell / Dist. by WPWG, Inc. WWW.CANDORVILLE.COM
MORE TREASON BY THE MEDIA! THEY'VE REVEALED VALUABLE INFORMATION THAT THE ENEMY WOULDN'T OTHERWISE HAVE FIGURED OUT!
DARRIN BELL

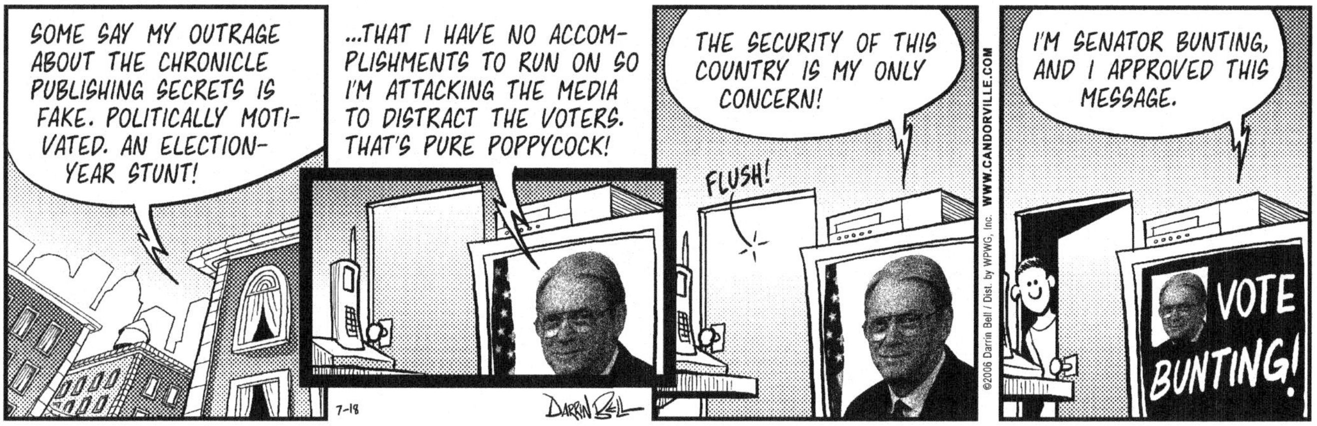
SOME SAY MY OUTRAGE ABOUT THE CHRONICLE PUBLISHING SECRETS IS FAKE. POLITICALLY MOTI-VATED. AN ELECTION-YEAR STUNT!
...THAT I HAVE NO ACCOM-PLISHMENTS TO RUN ON SO I'M ATTACKING THE MEDIA TO DISTRACT THE VOTERS. THAT'S PURE POPPYCOCK!
7-18
DARRIN BELL
THE SECURITY OF THIS COUNTRY IS MY ONLY CONCERN!
FLUSH!
©2006 Darrin Bell / Dist. by WPWG, Inc. WWW.CANDORVILLE.COM
I'M SENATOR BUNTING, AND I APPROVED THIS MESSAGE.
VOTE BUNTING!

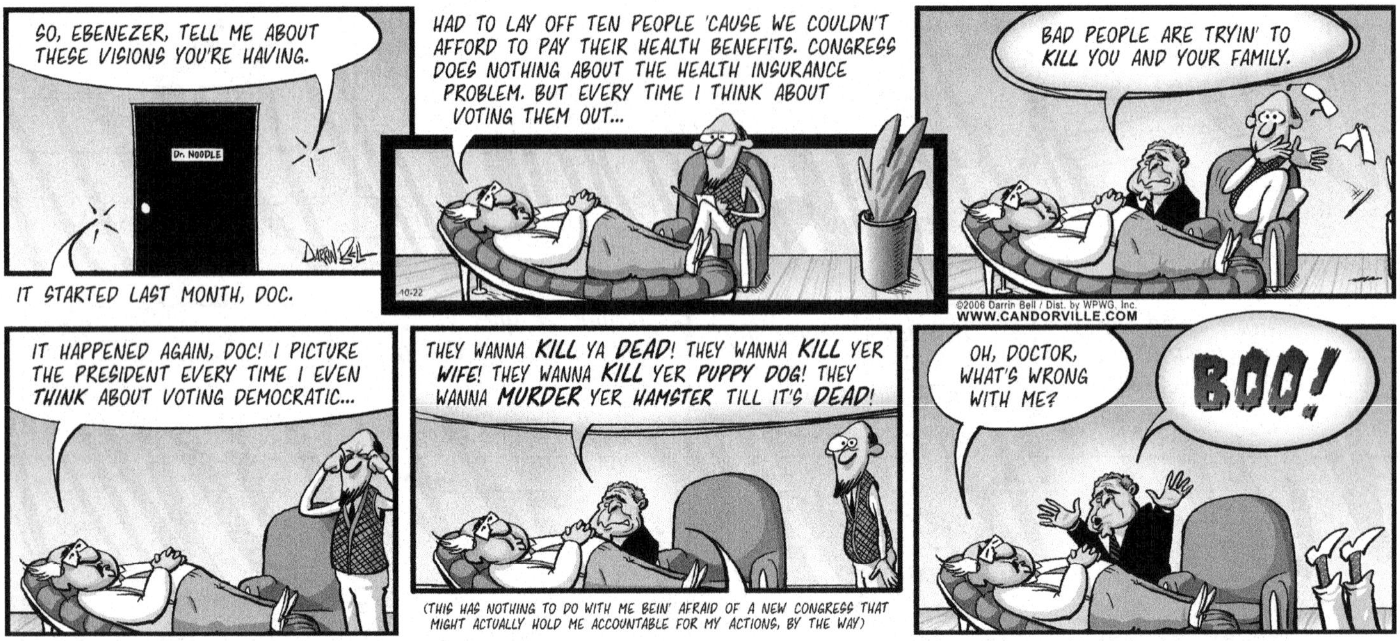
SO, EBENEZER, TELL ME ABOUT THESE VISIONS YOU'RE HAVING.
Dr. NOODLE
IT STARTED LAST MONTH, DOC.
HAD TO LAY OFF TEN PEOPLE 'CAUSE WE COULDN'T AFFORD TO PAY THEIR HEALTH BENEFITS. CONGRESS DOES NOTHING ABOUT THE HEALTH INSURANCE PROBLEM. BUT EVERY TIME I THINK ABOUT VOTING THEM OUT...
10-22
BAD PEOPLE ARE TRYIN' TO KILL YOU AND YOUR FAMILY.
©2006 Darrin Bell / Dist. by WPWG, Inc.
WWW.CANDORVILLE.COM
IT HAPPENED AGAIN, DOC! I PICTURE THE PRESIDENT EVERY TIME I EVEN THINK ABOUT VOTING DEMOCRATIC...
THEY WANNA KILL YA DEAD! THEY WANNA KILL YER WIFE! THEY WANNA KILL YER PUPPY DOG! THEY WANNA MURDER YER HAMSTER TILL IT'S DEAD!
(THIS HAS NOTHING TO DO WITH ME BEIN' AFRAID OF A NEW CONGRESS THAT MIGHT ACTUALLY HOLD ME ACCOUNTABLE FOR MY ACTIONS, BY THE WAY)
OH, DOCTOR, WHAT'S WRONG WITH ME?
BOO!

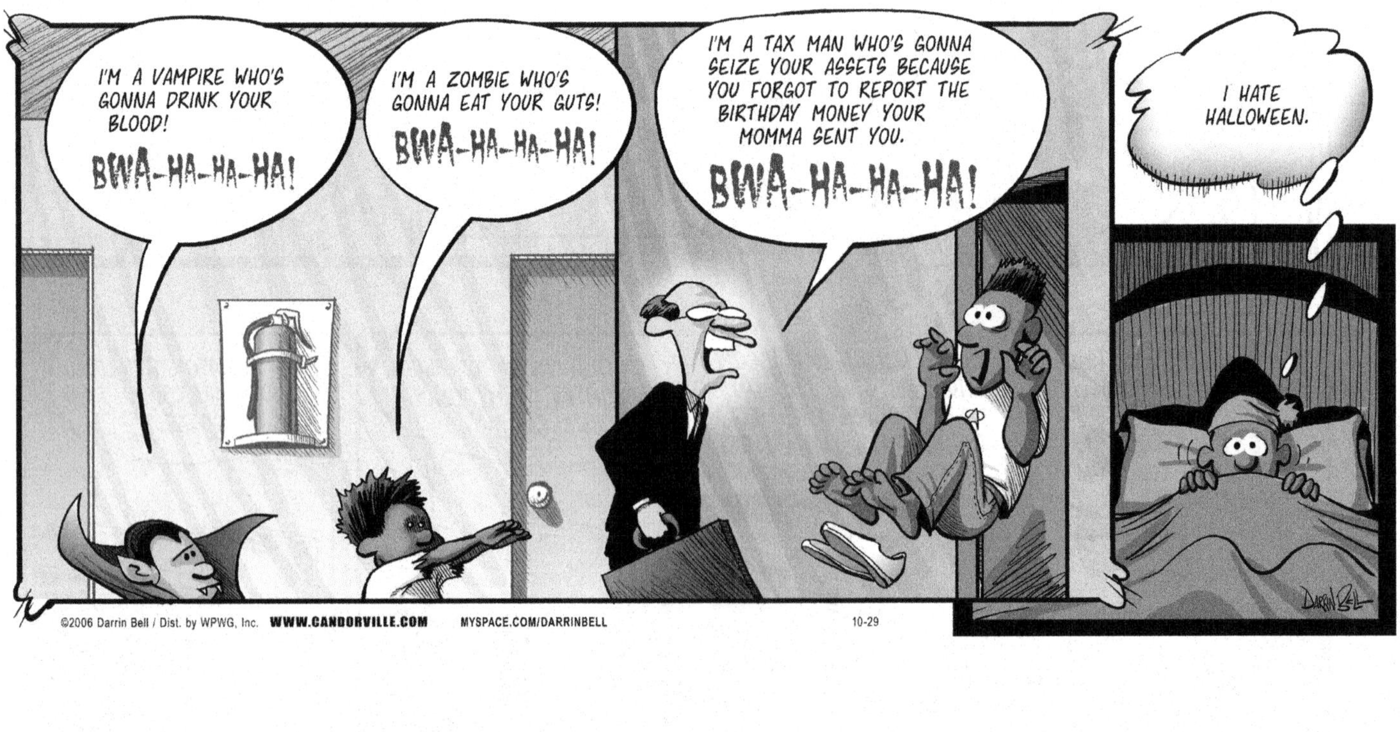
I'M A VAMPIRE WHO'S GONNA DRINK YOUR BLOOD!
BWA-HA-HA-HA!
I'M A ZOMBIE WHO'S GONNA EAT YOUR GUTS!
BWA-HA-HA-HA!
I'M A TAX MAN WHO'S GONNA SEIZE YOUR ASSETS BECAUSE YOU FORGOT TO REPORT THE BIRTHDAY MONEY YOUR MOMMA SENT YOU.
BWA-HA-HA-HA!
I HATE HALLOWEEN.
©2006 Darrin Bell / Dist. by WPWG, Inc. WWW.CANDORVILLE.COM MYSPACE.COM/DARRINBELL
10-29

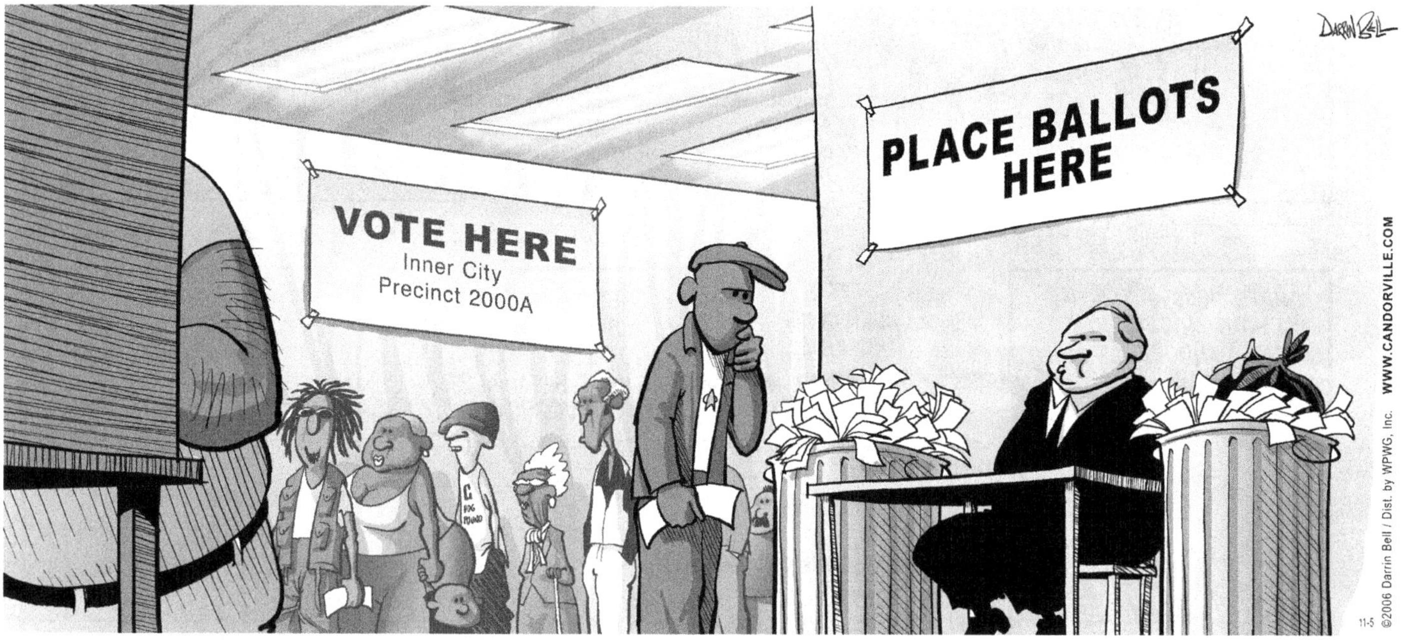

DARRIN BELL
VOTE HERE
Inner City
Precinct 2000A
PLACE BALLOTS HERE
11-5
©2006 Darrin Bell / Dist. by WPWG, Inc.
WWW.CANDORVILLE.COM

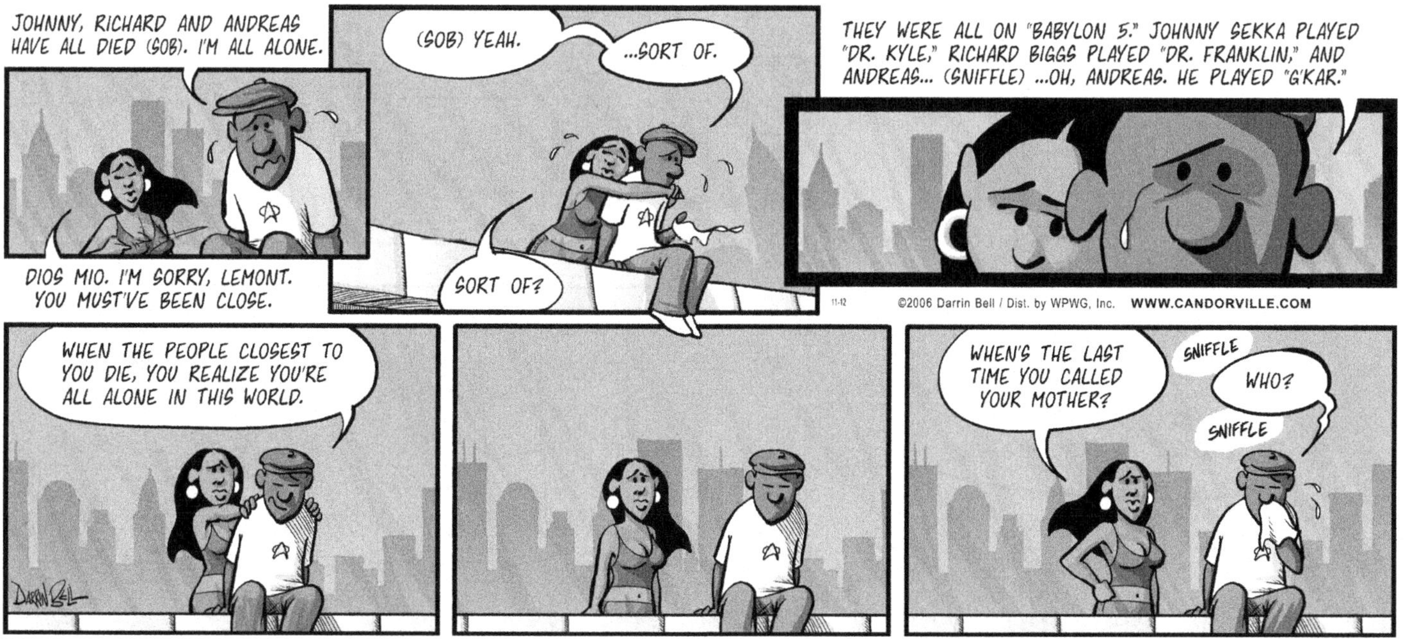

JOHNNY, RICHARD AND ANDREAS HAVE ALL DIED (SOB). I'M ALL ALONE.
DIOS MIO. I'M SORRY, LEMONT. YOU MUST'VE BEEN CLOSE.
(SOB) YEAH.
...SORT OF.
SORT OF?
THEY WERE ALL ON "BABYLON 5." JOHNNY SEKKA PLAYED "DR. KYLE," RICHARD BIGGS PLAYED "DR. FRANKLIN," AND ANDREAS... (SNIFFLE) ...OH, ANDREAS. HE PLAYED "G'KAR."
11-12
©2006 Darrin Bell / Dist. by WPWG, Inc.
WWW.CANDORVILLE.COM
WHEN THE PEOPLE CLOSEST TO YOU DIE, YOU REALIZE YOU'RE ALL ALONE IN THIS WORLD.
DARRIN BELL
WHEN'S THE LAST TIME YOU CALLED YOUR MOTHER?
SNIFFLE
WHO?
SNIFFLE

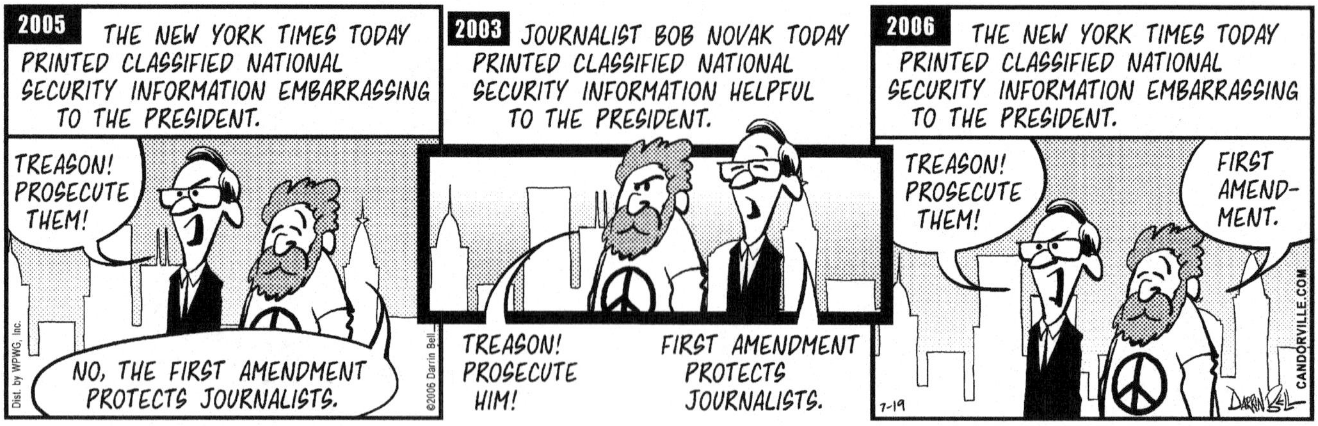
2005
THE NEW YORK TIMES TODAY PRINTED CLASSIFIED NATIONAL SECURITY INFORMATION EMBARRASSING TO THE PRESIDENT.
TREASON! PROSECUTE THEM!
NO, THE FIRST AMENDMENT PROTECTS JOURNALISTS.
Dist. by WPWG, Inc.
©2006 Darrin Bell
2003
JOURNALIST BOB NOVAK TODAY PRINTED CLASSIFIED NATIONAL SECURITY INFORMATION HELPFUL TO THE PRESIDENT.
TREASON! PROSECUTE HIM!
FIRST AMENDMENT PROTECTS JOURNALISTS.
2006
THE NEW YORK TIMES TODAY PRINTED CLASSIFIED NATIONAL SECURITY INFORMATION EMBARRASSING TO THE PRESIDENT.
TREASON! PROSECUTE THEM!
FIRST AMENDMENT.
7-19
DARRIN BELL
CANDORVILLE.COM

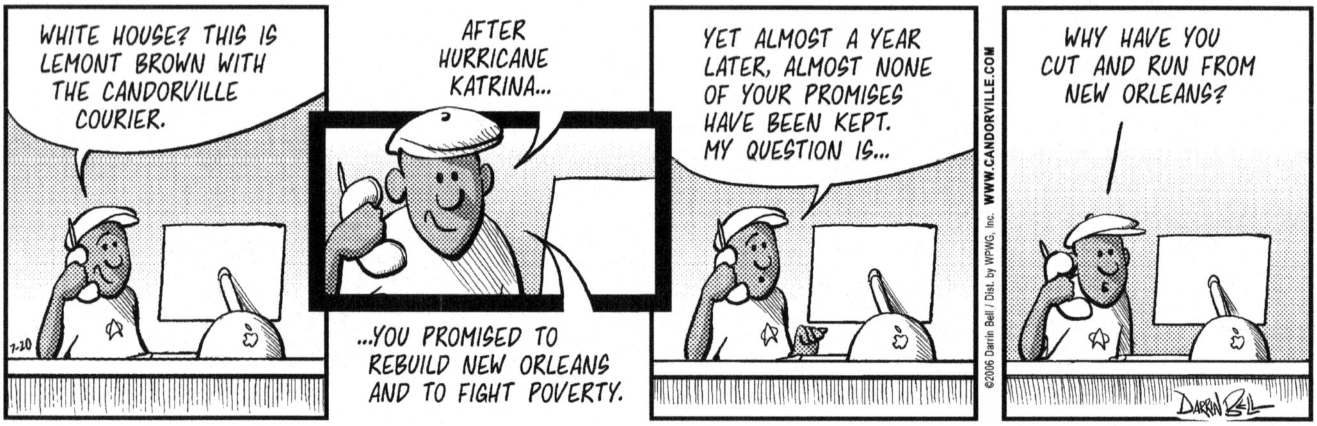
WHITE HOUSE? THIS IS LEMONT BROWN WITH THE CANDORVILLE COURIER.
7-20
AFTER HURRICANE KATRINA...
...YOU PROMISED TO REBUILD NEW ORLEANS AND TO FIGHT POVERTY.
YET ALMOST A YEAR LATER, ALMOST NONE OF YOUR PROMISES HAVE BEEN KEPT. MY QUESTION IS...
©2006 Darrin Bell / Dist. by WPWG, Inc. WWW.CANDORVILLE.COM
WHY HAVE YOU CUT AND RUN FROM NEW ORLEANS?
DARRIN BELL

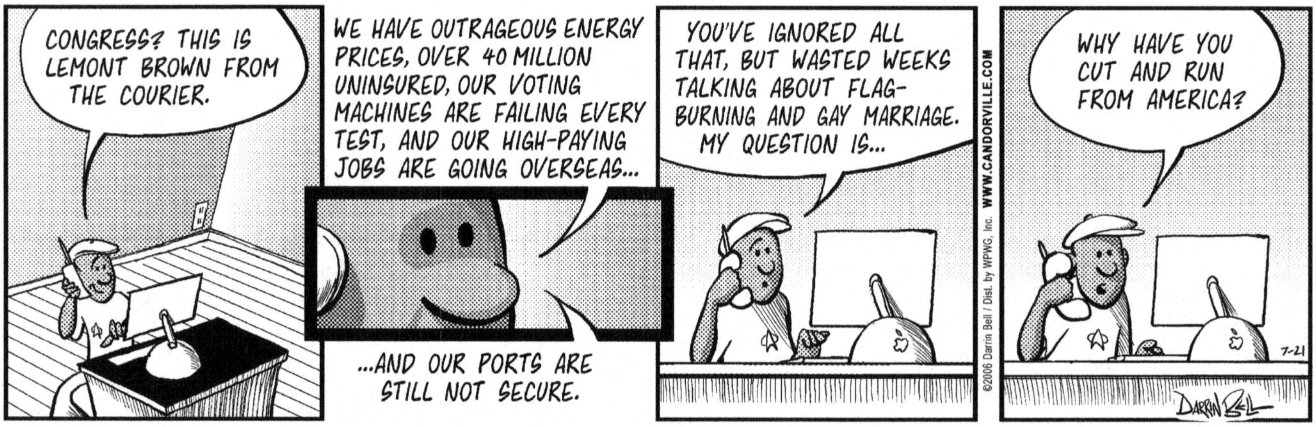
CONGRESS? THIS IS LEMONT BROWN FROM THE COURIER.
WE HAVE OUTRAGEOUS ENERGY PRICES, OVER 40 MILLION UNINSURED, OUR VOTING MACHINES ARE FAILING EVERY TEST, AND OUR HIGH-PAYING JOBS ARE GOING OVERSEAS...
...AND OUR PORTS ARE STILL NOT SECURE.
YOU'VE IGNORED ALL THAT, BUT WASTED WEEKS TALKING ABOUT FLAG-BURNING AND GAY MARRIAGE. MY QUESTION IS...
©2006 Darrin Bell / Dist. by WPWG, Inc. WWW.CANDORVILLE.COM
WHY HAVE YOU CUT AND RUN FROM AMERICA?
7-21
DARRIN BELL

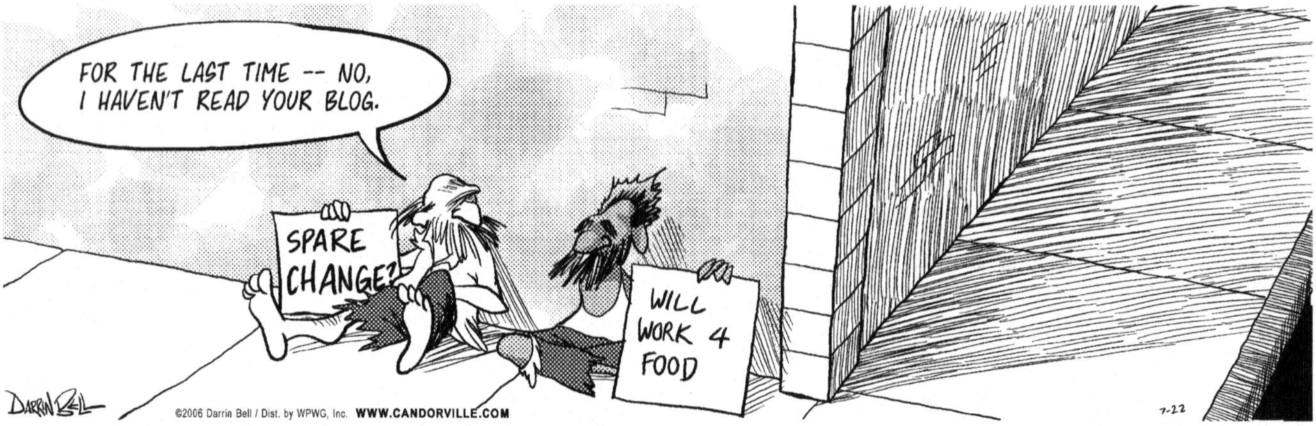
FOR THE LAST TIME -- NO, I HAVEN'T READ YOUR BLOG.
SPARE CHANGE?
WILL WORK 4 FOOD
DARRIN BELL
©2006 Darrin Bell / Dist. by WPWG, Inc. WWW.CANDORVILLE.COM
7-22

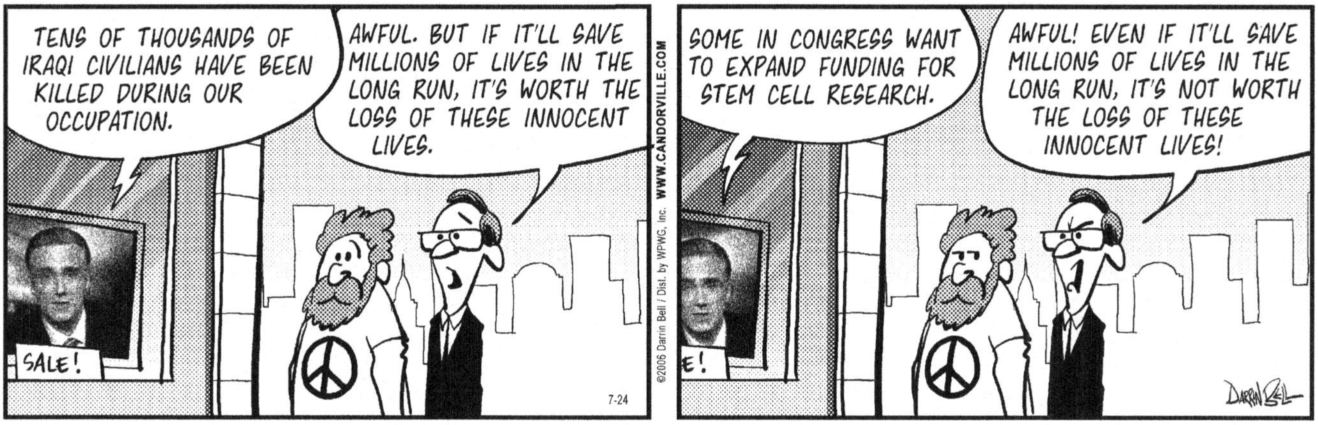
TENS OF THOUSANDS OF IRAQI CIVILIANS HAVE BEEN KILLED DURING OUR OCCUPATION.
AWFUL. BUT IF IT'LL SAVE MILLIONS OF LIVES IN THE LONG RUN, IT'S WORTH THE LOSS OF THESE INNOCENT LIVES.
SALE!
7-24
©2006 Darrin Bell / Dist. by WPWG, Inc. WWW.CANDORVILLE.COM
SOME IN CONGRESS WANT TO EXPAND FUNDING FOR STEM CELL RESEARCH.
AWFUL! EVEN IF IT'LL SAVE MILLIONS OF LIVES IN THE LONG RUN, IT'S NOT WORTH THE LOSS OF THESE INNOCENT LIVES!

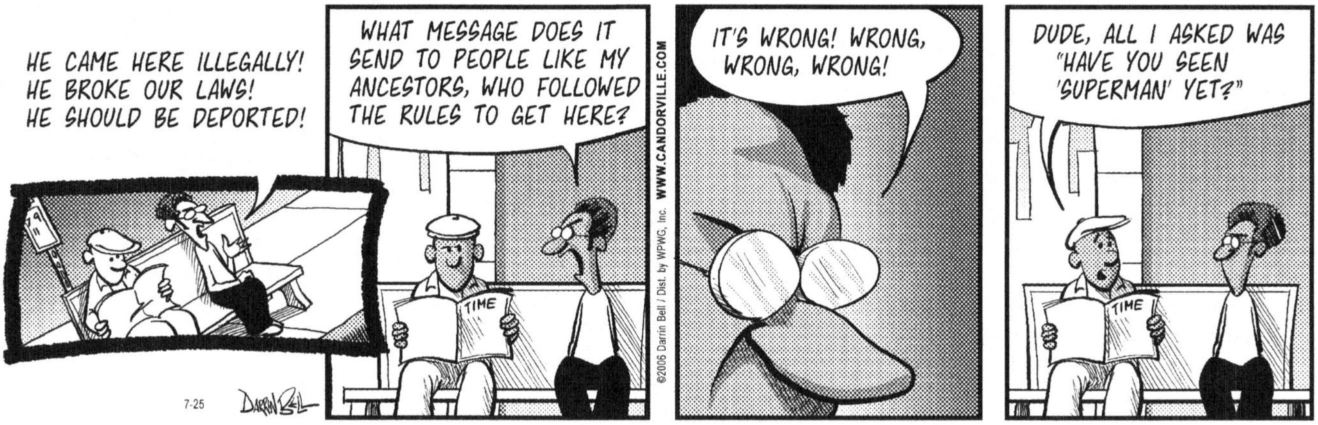
HE CAME HERE ILLEGALLY! HE BROKE OUR LAWS! HE SHOULD BE DEPORTED!
7-25
WHAT MESSAGE DOES IT SEND TO PEOPLE LIKE MY ANCESTORS, WHO FOLLOWED THE RULES TO GET HERE?
TIME
©2006 Darrin Bell / Dist. by WPWG, Inc. WWW.CANDORVILLE.COM
IT'S WRONG! WRONG, WRONG, WRONG!
DUDE, ALL I ASKED WAS "HAVE YOU SEEN 'SUPERMAN' YET?"
TIME

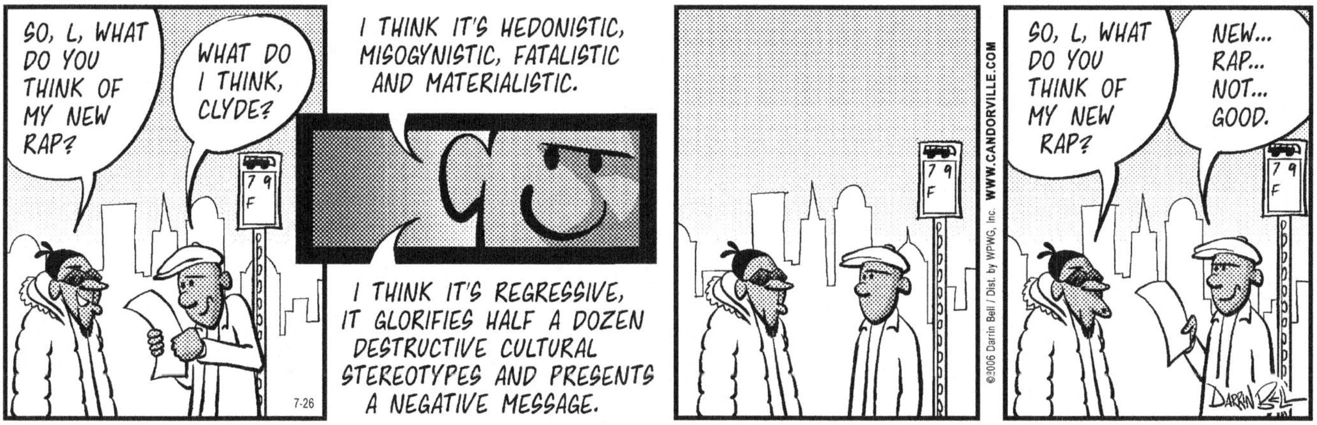
SO, L, WHAT DO YOU THINK OF MY NEW RAP?
WHAT DO I THINK, CLYDE?
7-26
I THINK IT'S HEDONISTIC, MISOGYNISTIC, FATALISTIC AND MATERIALISTIC.
I THINK IT'S REGRESSIVE, IT GLORIFIES HALF A DOZEN DESTRUCTIVE CULTURAL STEREOTYPES AND PRESENTS A NEGATIVE MESSAGE.
©2006 Darrin Bell / Dist. by WPWG, Inc. WWW.CANDORVILLE.COM
SO, L, WHAT DO YOU THINK OF MY NEW RAP?
NEW... RAP... NOT... GOOD.

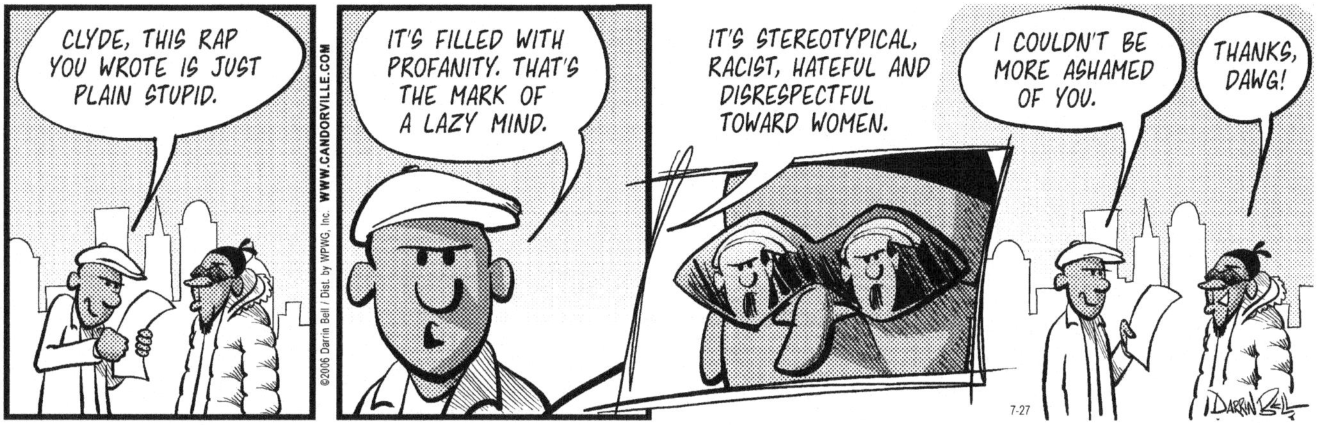
CLYDE, THIS RAP YOU WROTE IS JUST PLAIN STUPID.
©2006 Darrin Bell / Dist. by WPWG, Inc. WWW.CANDORVILLE.COM
IT'S FILLED WITH PROFANITY. THAT'S THE MARK OF A LAZY MIND.
IT'S STEREOTYPICAL, RACIST, HATEFUL AND DISRESPECTFUL TOWARD WOMEN.
I COULDN'T BE MORE ASHAMED OF YOU.
THANKS, DAWG!
7-27

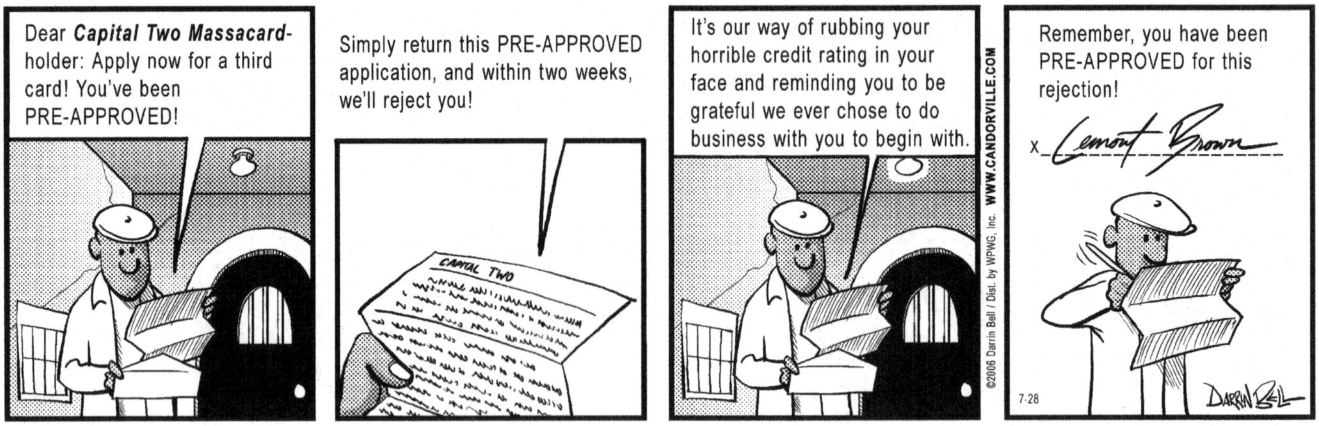

Dear **Capital Two Massacard**-holder: Apply now for a third card! You've been PRE-APPROVED!
Simply return this PRE-APPROVED application, and within two weeks, we'll reject you!
CAPITAL TWO
It's our way of rubbing your horrible credit rating in your face and reminding you to be grateful we ever chose to do business with you to begin with.
©2006 Darrin Bell / Dist. by WPWG, Inc. WWW.CANDORVILLE.COM
Remember, you have been PRE-APPROVED for this rejection!
x Lemont Brown
7-28
DARRIN BELL

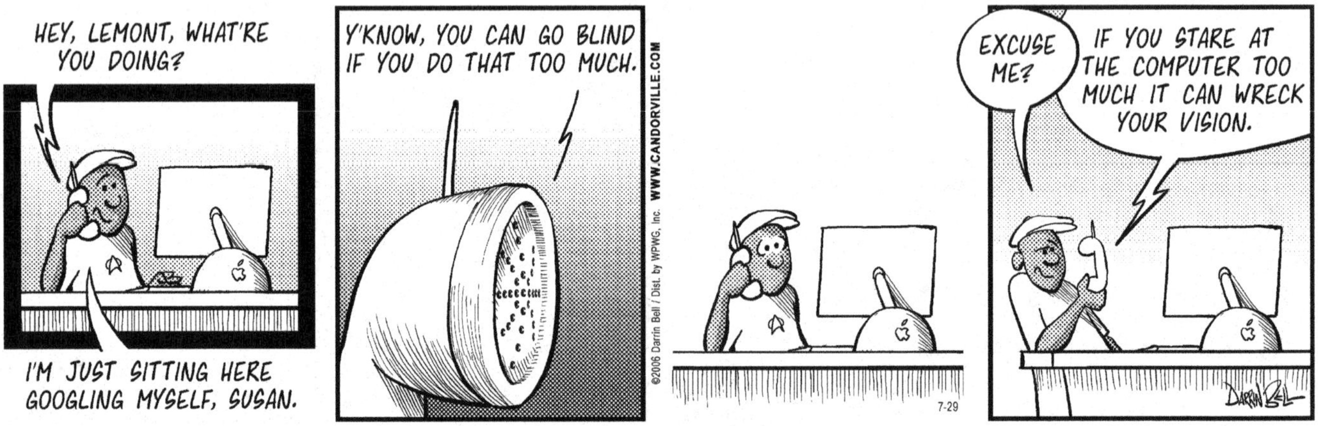

HEY, LEMONT, WHAT'RE YOU DOING?
I'M JUST SITTING HERE GOOGLING MYSELF, SUSAN.
Y'KNOW, YOU CAN GO BLIND IF YOU DO THAT TOO MUCH.
©2006 Darrin Bell / Dist. by WPWG, Inc. WWW.CANDORVILLE.COM
7-29
EXCUSE ME?
IF YOU STARE AT THE COMPUTER TOO MUCH IT CAN WRECK YOUR VISION.
DARRIN BELL

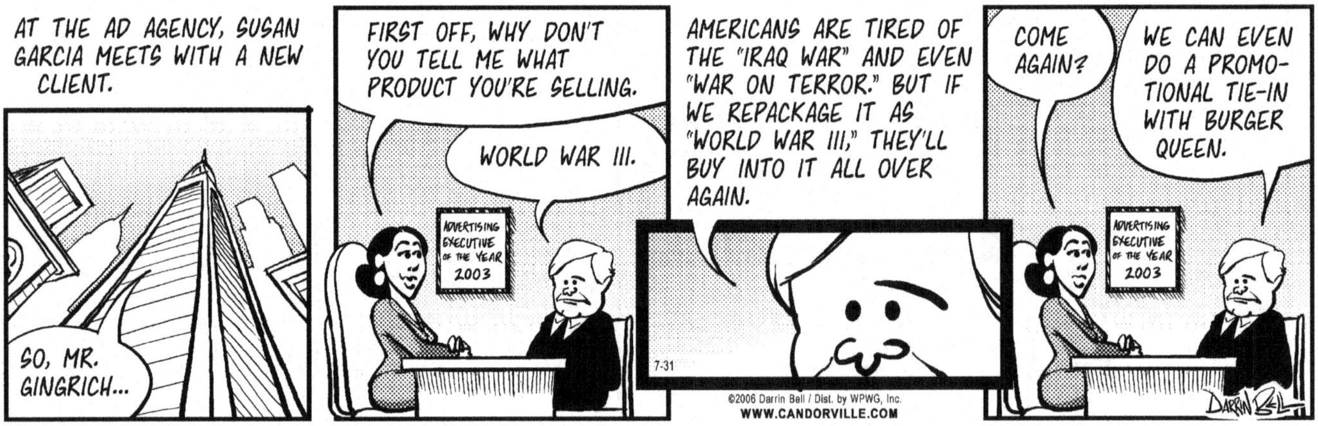

AT THE AD AGENCY, SUSAN GARCIA MEETS WITH A NEW CLIENT.
SO, MR. GINGRICH...
FIRST OFF, WHY DON'T YOU TELL ME WHAT PRODUCT YOU'RE SELLING.
WORLD WAR III.
ADVERTISING EXECUTIVE OF THE YEAR 2003
AMERICANS ARE TIRED OF THE "IRAQ WAR" AND EVEN "WAR ON TERROR." BUT IF WE REPACKAGE IT AS "WORLD WAR III," THEY'LL BUY INTO IT ALL OVER AGAIN.
7-31
©2006 Darrin Bell / Dist. by WPWG, Inc.
WWW.CANDORVILLE.COM
COME AGAIN?
WE CAN EVEN DO A PROMOTIONAL TIE-IN WITH BURGER QUEEN.
ADVERTISING EXECUTIVE OF THE YEAR 2003
DARRIN BELL

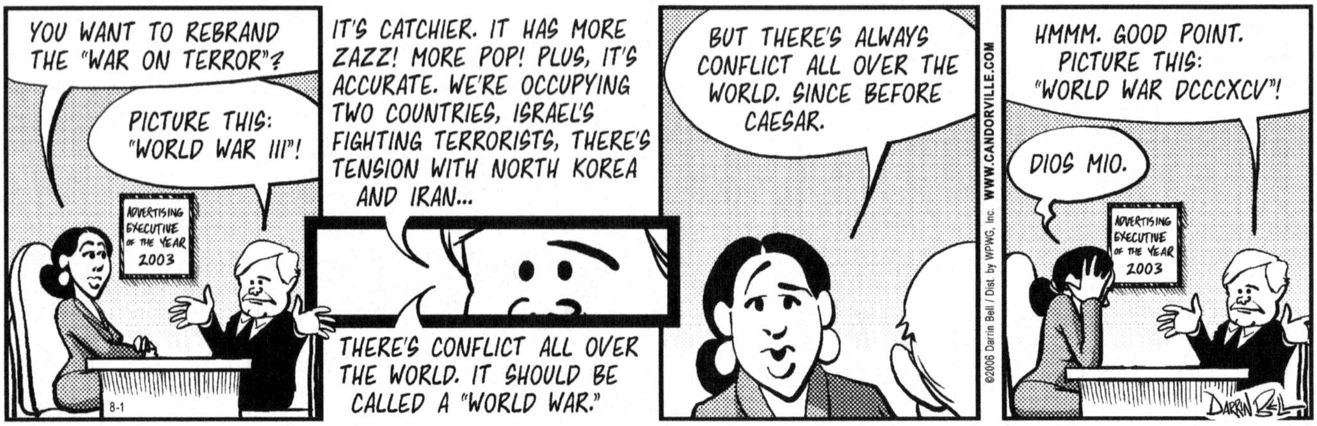

YOU WANT TO REBRAND THE "WAR ON TERROR"?
PICTURE THIS: "WORLD WAR III"!
ADVERTISING EXECUTIVE OF THE YEAR 2003
8-1
IT'S CATCHIER. IT HAS MORE ZAZZ! MORE POP! PLUS, IT'S ACCURATE. WE'RE OCCUPYING TWO COUNTRIES, ISRAEL'S FIGHTING TERRORISTS, THERE'S TENSION WITH NORTH KOREA AND IRAN...
THERE'S CONFLICT ALL OVER THE WORLD. IT SHOULD BE CALLED A "WORLD WAR."
BUT THERE'S ALWAYS CONFLICT ALL OVER THE WORLD. SINCE BEFORE CAESAR.
©2006 Darrin Bell / Dist. by WPWG, Inc. WWW.CANDORVILLE.COM
HMMM. GOOD POINT. PICTURE THIS: "WORLD WAR DCCCXCV"!
DIOS MIO.
ADVERTISING EXECUTIVE OF THE YEAR 2003
DARRIN BELL

Strip 1:

WHAT'S THE FIRST THING YOU THINK OF WHEN YOU HEAR THE PHRASE "WORLD WAR III"?

FOCUS GROUP #7

SOVIET UNION.

NUCLEAR BOMBS.

FLYING CARS!

ROBOTS SENT BACK IN TIME TO KILL LINDA HAMILTON.

MEL GIBSON IN TIGHT LEATHER PANTS.

FOCUS GROUP #7

I HEARD THERE'D BE DONUTS UP IN HERE, #$@%!

Strip 2:

...CLYDE, HOW'D YOU GET IN HERE?

THAT'S A DUMB QUESTION. THROUGH THE AIR DUCTS, OF COURSE.

I THINK OF MATTHEW BRODERICK.

FOCUS GROUP #7

8-2

Strip 3:

BAD NEWS, CALLING TODAY'S CONFLICTS "WORLD WAR III" TESTED POORLY WITH OUR FOCUS GROUP.

ADVERTISING EXECUTIVE OF THE YEAR 2003

THE CONSENSUS WAS THAT THE THIRD INSTALLMENT OF ANY TRILOGY IS JUST A LAME KNOCKOFF OF THE FIRST TWO.

RETURN OF THE JEDI, SUPERMAN 3, TERMINATOR 3...

IF YOU WANT TO REALLY INSPIRE PEOPLE...

ADVERTISING EXECUTIVE OF THE YEAR 2003

THE FOCUS GROUP PREFERRED "THE FIRST INTERGALACTIC WAR."

WORKS FOR ME.

ADVERTISING EXECUTIVE OF THE YEAR 2003

8-3

Strip 4:

MY GIRL CHEATS ALL THE TIME. WITH MAILMEN, CABLE GUYS... WITH ANYONE!

C-DOG'S INCREDIBLY BAD ADVICE $2

HERE'S WHAT YOU DO. YOU TELL HER... TELL HER...

C-DOG'S INCREDIBLY BAD ADVICE $2

THIS END UP

DAG, BRUH, IT'S WAY TOO COMPLICATED. TELL YOU WHAT...

C-DOG'S INCREDIBLY BAD ADVICE $2

THIS END UP

GIVE ME HER NUMBER, AND I'LL TELL HER FOR YOU.

WOW, THANKS, C-DOG!

C-DOG'S INCREDIBLY BAD ADVICE $2

8-4

Strip 5:

HELP THE HOMELESS

HAVE YOUR PICTURE TAKEN WITH AN AUTHENTIC HOMELESS GUY $5

8-5

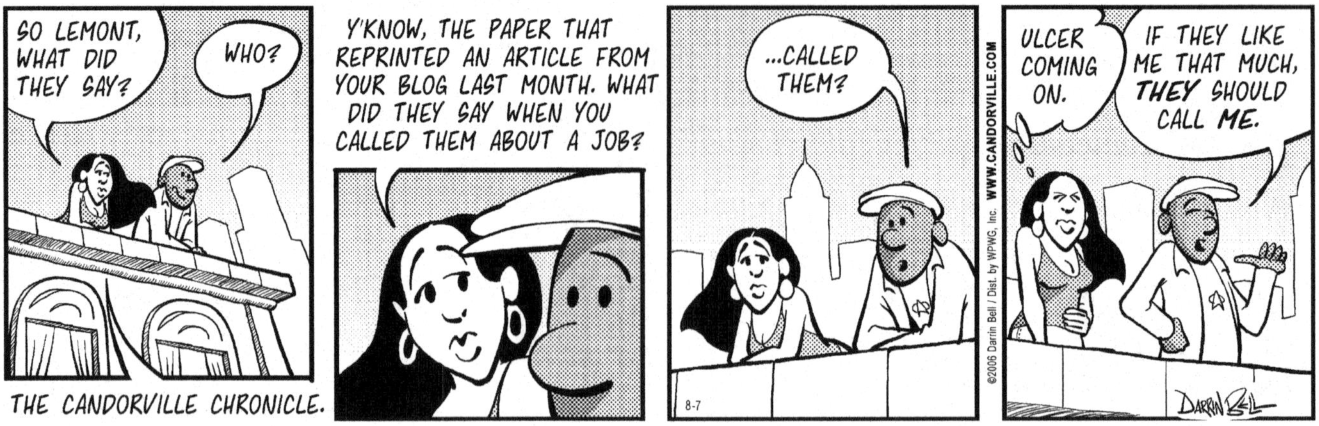
SO LEMONT, WHAT DID THEY SAY?
WHO?
THE CANDORVILLE CHRONICLE.
Y'KNOW, THE PAPER THAT REPRINTED AN ARTICLE FROM YOUR BLOG LAST MONTH. WHAT DID THEY SAY WHEN YOU CALLED THEM ABOUT A JOB?
...CALLED THEM?
8-7
©2006 Darrin Bell / Dist. by WPWG, Inc. WWW.CANDORVILLE.COM
ULCER COMING ON.
IF THEY LIKE ME THAT MUCH, THEY SHOULD CALL ME.
DARRIN BELL

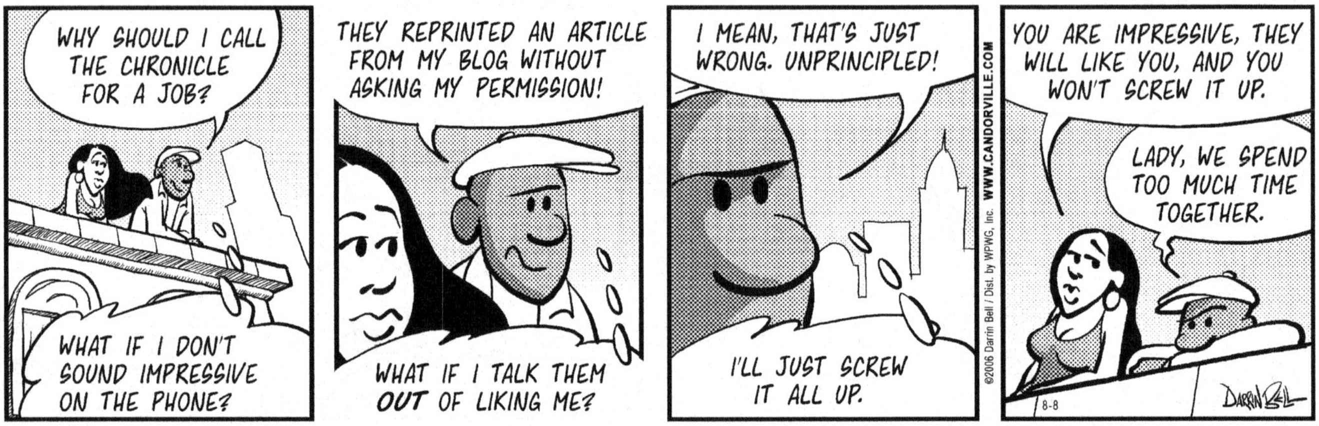
WHY SHOULD I CALL THE CHRONICLE FOR A JOB?
WHAT IF I DON'T SOUND IMPRESSIVE ON THE PHONE?
THEY REPRINTED AN ARTICLE FROM MY BLOG WITHOUT ASKING MY PERMISSION!
WHAT IF I TALK THEM OUT OF LIKING ME?
I MEAN, THAT'S JUST WRONG. UNPRINCIPLED!
I'LL JUST SCREW IT ALL UP.
©2006 Darrin Bell / Dist. by WPWG, Inc. WWW.CANDORVILLE.COM
YOU ARE IMPRESSIVE, THEY WILL LIKE YOU, AND YOU WON'T SCREW IT UP.
LADY, WE SPEND TOO MUCH TIME TOGETHER.
8-8
DARRIN BELL

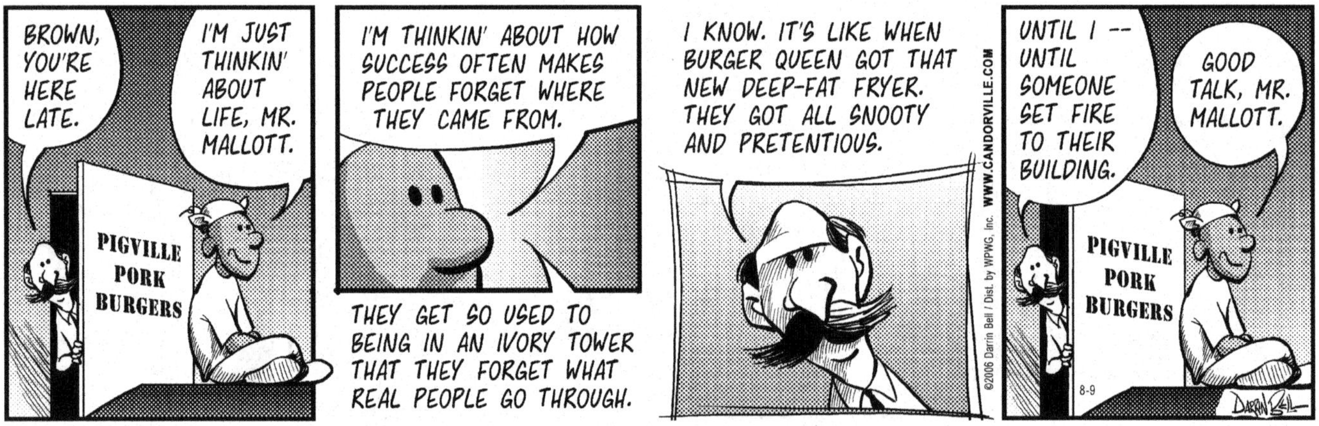
BROWN, YOU'RE HERE LATE.
I'M JUST THINKIN' ABOUT LIFE, MR. MALLOTT.
PIGVILLE PORK BURGERS
I'M THINKIN' ABOUT HOW SUCCESS OFTEN MAKES PEOPLE FORGET WHERE THEY CAME FROM.
THEY GET SO USED TO BEING IN AN IVORY TOWER THAT THEY FORGET WHAT REAL PEOPLE GO THROUGH.
I KNOW. IT'S LIKE WHEN BURGER QUEEN GOT THAT NEW DEEP-FAT FRYER. THEY GOT ALL SNOOTY AND PRETENTIOUS.
©2006 Darrin Bell / Dist. by WPWG, Inc. WWW.CANDORVILLE.COM
UNTIL I -- UNTIL SOMEONE SET FIRE TO THEIR BUILDING.
GOOD TALK, MR. MALLOTT.
PIGVILLE PORK BURGERS
8-9
DARRIN BELL

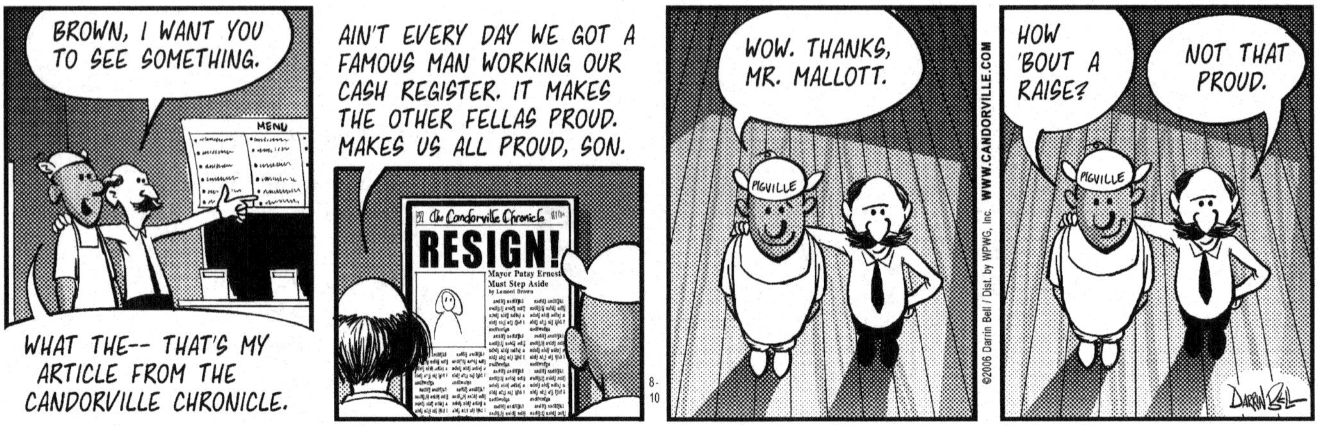
BROWN, I WANT YOU TO SEE SOMETHING.
MENU
WHAT THE-- THAT'S MY ARTICLE FROM THE CANDORVILLE CHRONICLE.
AIN'T EVERY DAY WE GOT A FAMOUS MAN WORKING OUR CASH REGISTER. IT MAKES THE OTHER FELLAS PROUD. MAKES US ALL PROUD, SON.
The Candorville Chronicle
RESIGN!
Mayor Patsy Ernest Must Step Aside
by Lemont Brown
8-10
WOW. THANKS, MR. MALLOTT.
PIGVILLE
©2006 Darrin Bell / Dist. by WPWG, Inc. WWW.CANDORVILLE.COM
HOW 'BOUT A RAISE?
NOT THAT PROUD.
PIGVILLE
DARRIN BELL

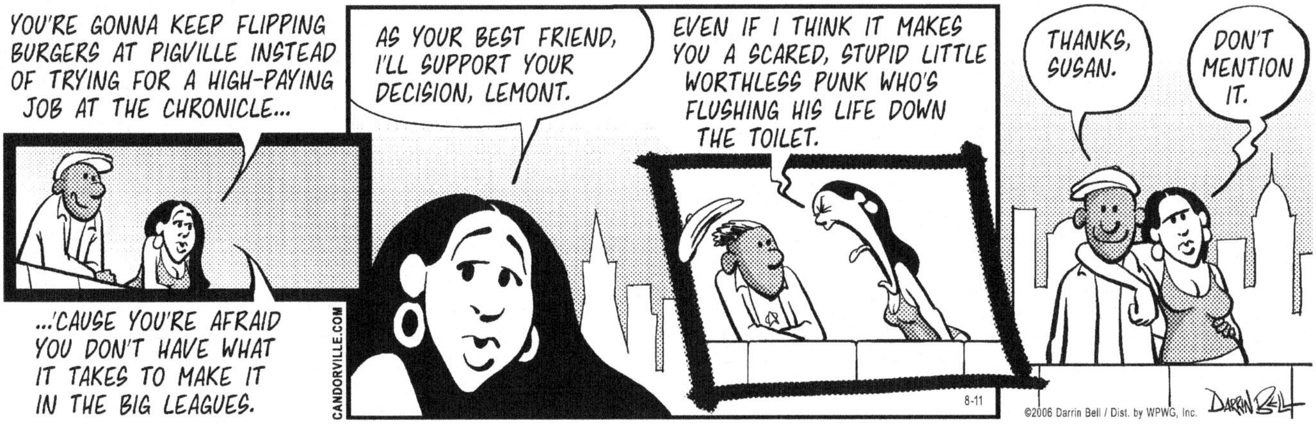
YOU'RE GONNA KEEP FLIPPING BURGERS AT PIGVILLE INSTEAD OF TRYING FOR A HIGH-PAYING JOB AT THE CHRONICLE...
...'CAUSE YOU'RE AFRAID YOU DON'T HAVE WHAT IT TAKES TO MAKE IT IN THE BIG LEAGUES.
CANDORVILLE.COM
AS YOUR BEST FRIEND, I'LL SUPPORT YOUR DECISION, LEMONT.
EVEN IF I THINK IT MAKES YOU A SCARED, STUPID LITTLE WORTHLESS PUNK WHO'S FLUSHING HIS LIFE DOWN THE TOILET.
8-11
THANKS, SUSAN.
DON'T MENTION IT.
©2006 Darrin Bell / Dist. by WPWG, Inc.
DARRIN BELL

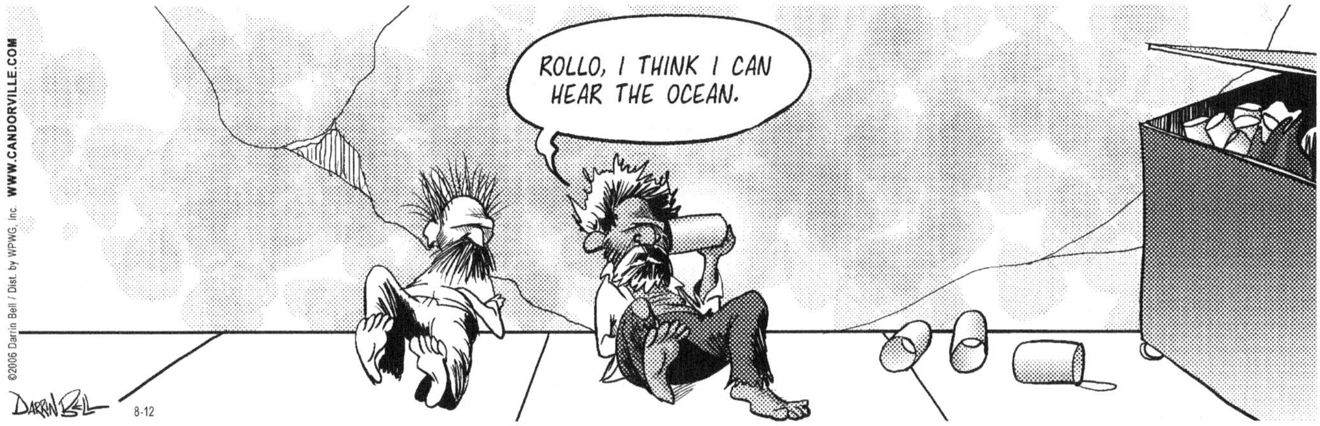
©2006 Darrin Bell / Dist. by WPWG, Inc. WWW.CANDORVILLE.COM
ROLLO, I THINK I CAN HEAR THE OCEAN.
DARRIN BELL
8-12

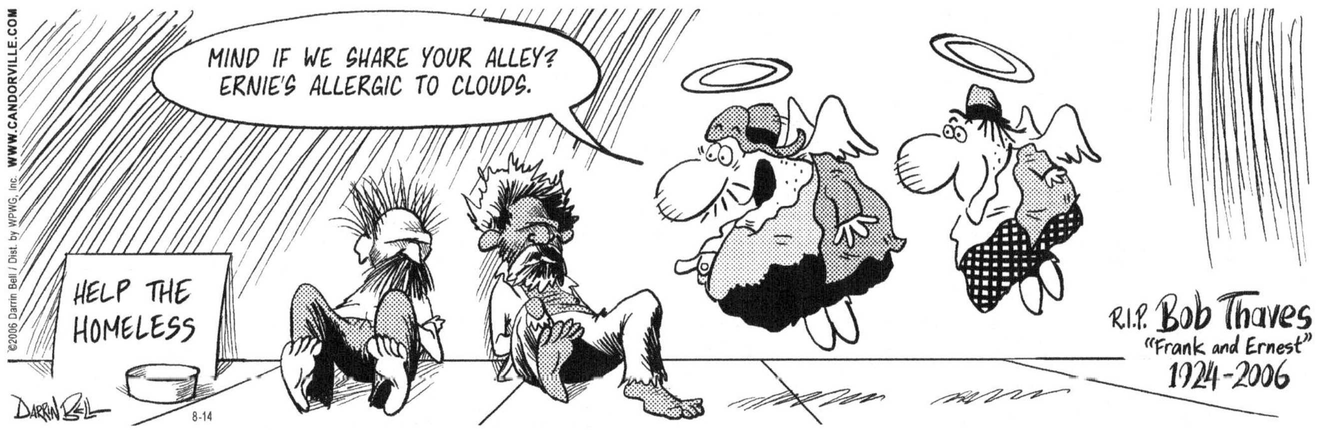
©2006 Darrin Bell / Dist. by WPWG, Inc. WWW.CANDORVILLE.COM
MIND IF WE SHARE YOUR ALLEY? ERNIE'S ALLERGIC TO CLOUDS.
HELP THE HOMELESS
R.I.P. Bob Thaves
"Frank and Ernest"
1924-2006
DARRIN BELL
8-14

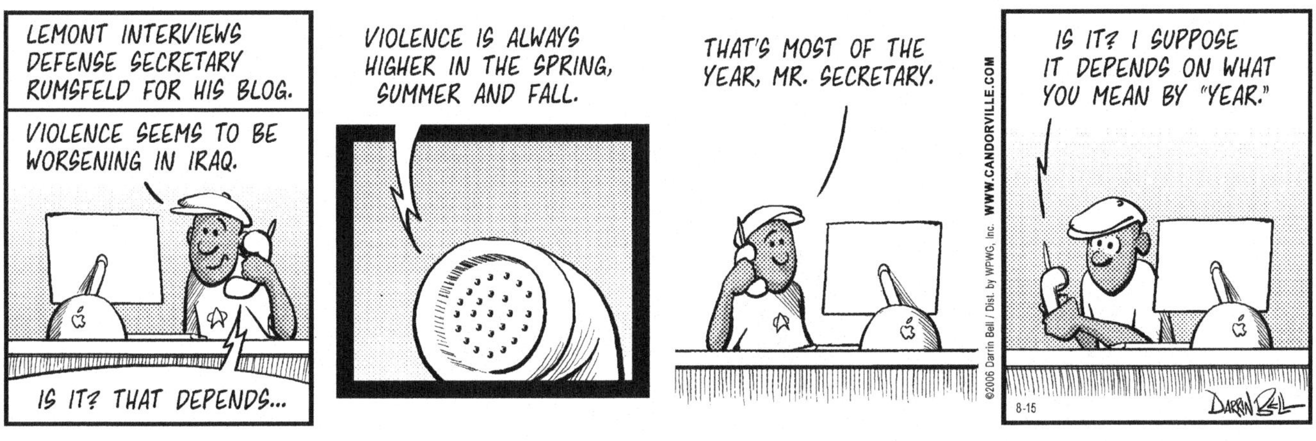
LEMONT INTERVIEWS DEFENSE SECRETARY RUMSFELD FOR HIS BLOG.
VIOLENCE SEEMS TO BE WORSENING IN IRAQ.
IS IT? THAT DEPENDS...
VIOLENCE IS ALWAYS HIGHER IN THE SPRING, SUMMER AND FALL.
THAT'S MOST OF THE YEAR, MR. SECRETARY.
©2006 Darrin Bell / Dist. by WPWG, Inc. WWW.CANDORVILLE.COM
IS IT? I SUPPOSE IT DEPENDS ON WHAT YOU MEAN BY "YEAR."
8-15
DARRIN BELL

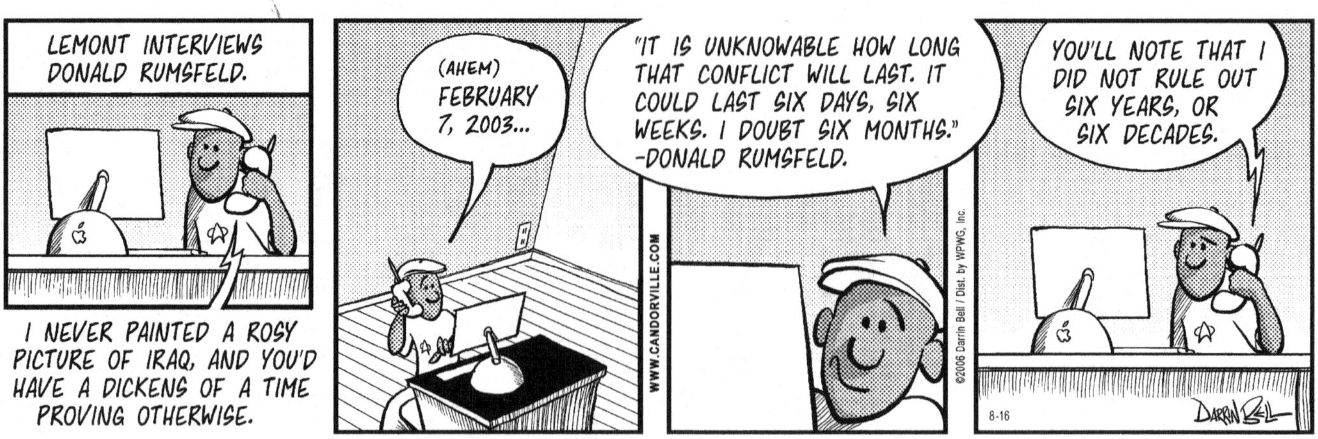
LEMONT INTERVIEWS DONALD RUMSFELD.
I NEVER PAINTED A ROSY PICTURE OF IRAQ, AND YOU'D HAVE A DICKENS OF A TIME PROVING OTHERWISE.
(AHEM) FEBRUARY 7, 2003...
"IT IS UNKNOWABLE HOW LONG THAT CONFLICT WILL LAST. IT COULD LAST SIX DAYS, SIX WEEKS. I DOUBT SIX MONTHS." -DONALD RUMSFELD.
YOU'LL NOTE THAT I DID NOT RULE OUT SIX YEARS, OR SIX DECADES.
WWW.CANDORVILLE.COM
©2006 Darrin Bell / Dist. by WPWG, Inc.
8-16
DARRIN BELL

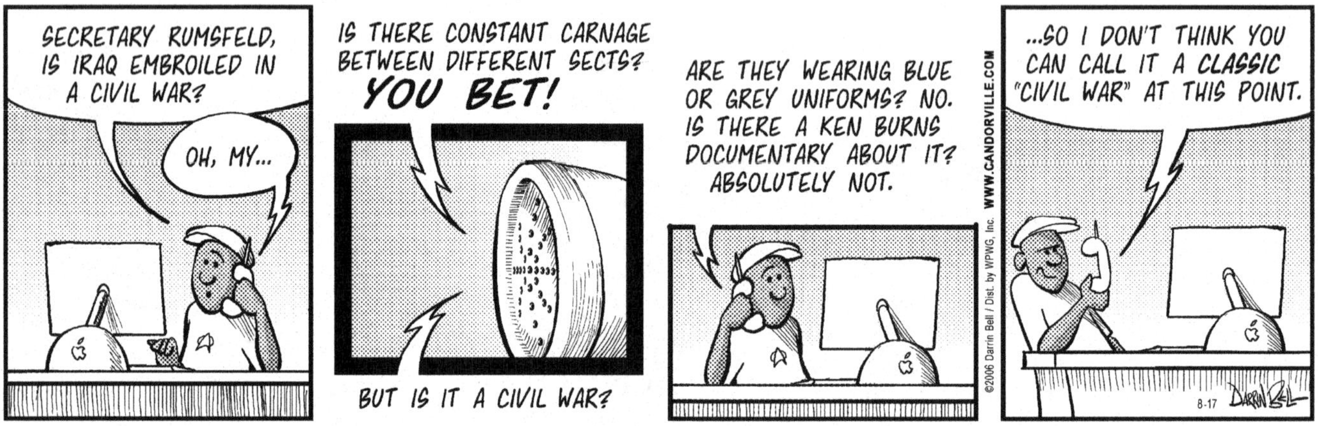
SECRETARY RUMSFELD, IS IRAQ EMBROILED IN A CIVIL WAR?
OH, MY...
IS THERE CONSTANT CARNAGE BETWEEN DIFFERENT SECTS? YOU BET!
BUT IS IT A CIVIL WAR?
ARE THEY WEARING BLUE OR GREY UNIFORMS? NO. IS THERE A KEN BURNS DOCUMENTARY ABOUT IT? ABSOLUTELY NOT.
...SO I DON'T THINK YOU CAN CALL IT A CLASSIC "CIVIL WAR" AT THIS POINT.
WWW.CANDORVILLE.COM
©2006 Darrin Bell / Dist. by WPWG, Inc.
8-17
DARRIN BELL

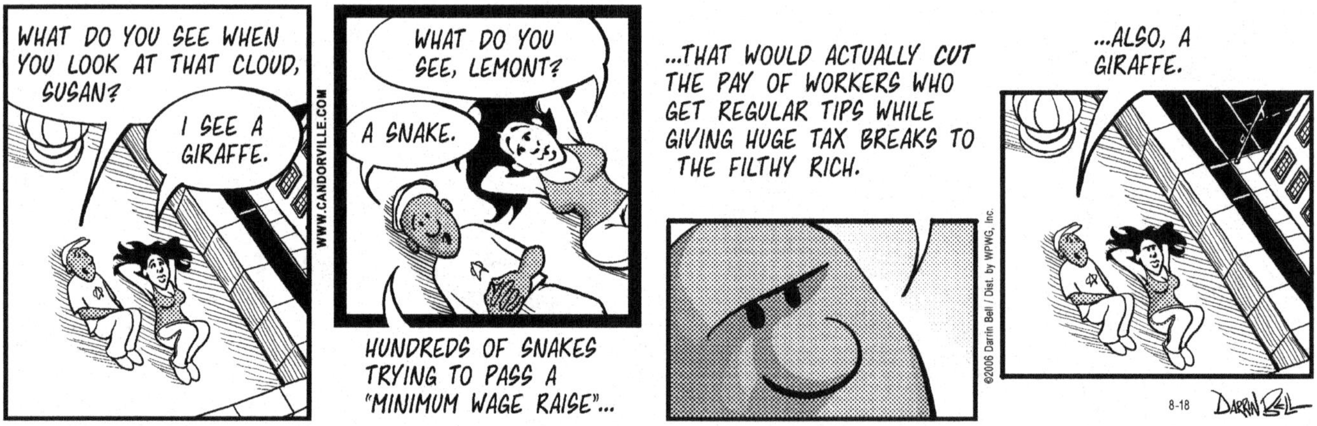
WHAT DO YOU SEE WHEN YOU LOOK AT THAT CLOUD, SUSAN?
I SEE A GIRAFFE.
WHAT DO YOU SEE, LEMONT?
A SNAKE.
HUNDREDS OF SNAKES TRYING TO PASS A "MINIMUM WAGE RAISE"...
...THAT WOULD ACTUALLY CUT THE PAY OF WORKERS WHO GET REGULAR TIPS WHILE GIVING HUGE TAX BREAKS TO THE FILTHY RICH.
...ALSO, A GIRAFFE.
WWW.CANDORVILLE.COM
©2006 Darrin Bell / Dist. by WPWG, Inc.
8-18
DARRIN BELL

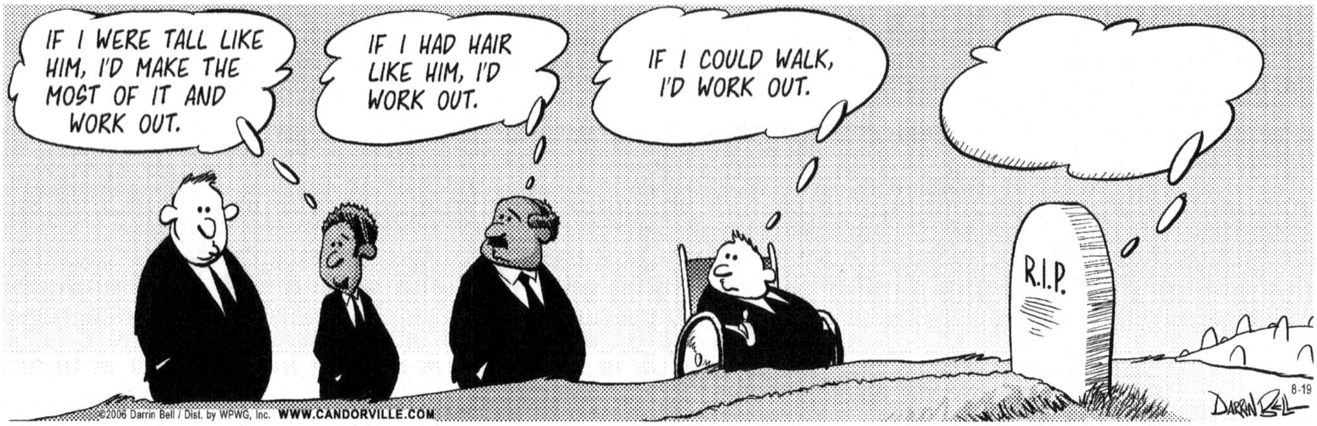
IF I WERE TALL LIKE HIM, I'D MAKE THE MOST OF IT AND WORK OUT.
IF I HAD HAIR LIKE HIM, I'D WORK OUT.
IF I COULD WALK, I'D WORK OUT.
R.I.P.
©2006 Darrin Bell / Dist. by WPWG, Inc. WWW.CANDORVILLE.COM
8-19
DARRIN BELL

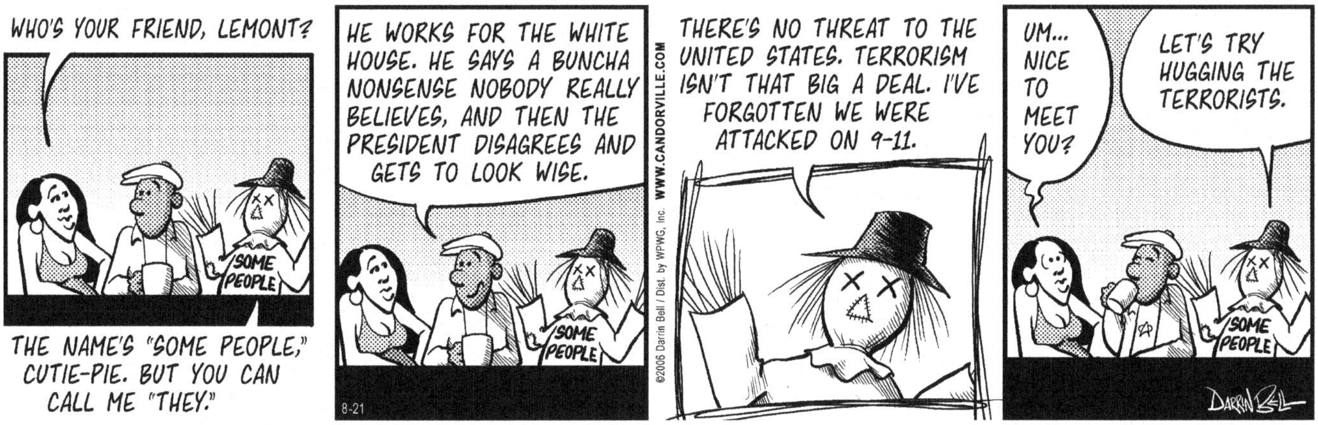
WHO'S YOUR FRIEND, LEMONT?
SOME PEOPLE
THE NAME'S "SOME PEOPLE," CUTIE-PIE. BUT YOU CAN CALL ME "THEY."
HE WORKS FOR THE WHITE HOUSE. HE SAYS A BUNCHA NONSENSE NOBODY REALLY BELIEVES, AND THEN THE PRESIDENT DISAGREES AND GETS TO LOOK WISE.
SOME PEOPLE
8-21
©2006 Darrin Bell / Dist. by WPWG, Inc. WWW.CANDORVILLE.COM
THERE'S NO THREAT TO THE UNITED STATES. TERRORISM ISN'T THAT BIG A DEAL. I'VE FORGOTTEN WE WERE ATTACKED ON 9-11.
UM... NICE TO MEET YOU?
LET'S TRY HUGGING THE TERRORISTS.
SOME PEOPLE
DARRIN BELL

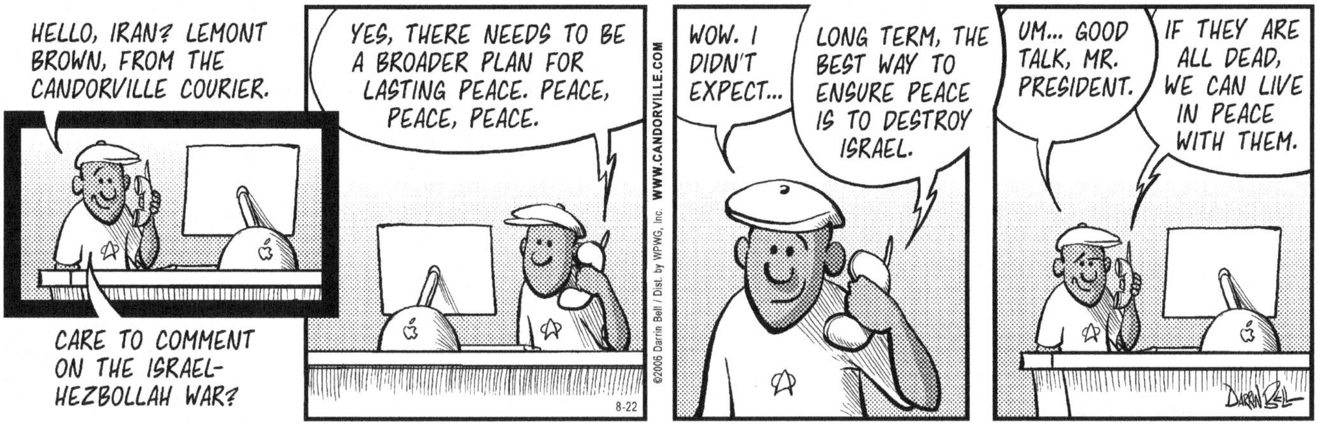
HELLO, IRAN? LEMONT BROWN, FROM THE CANDORVILLE COURIER.
CARE TO COMMENT ON THE ISRAEL-HEZBOLLAH WAR?
YES, THERE NEEDS TO BE A BROADER PLAN FOR LASTING PEACE. PEACE, PEACE, PEACE.
8-22
©2006 Darrin Bell / Dist. by WPWG, Inc. WWW.CANDORVILLE.COM
WOW. I DIDN'T EXPECT...
LONG TERM, THE BEST WAY TO ENSURE PEACE IS TO DESTROY ISRAEL.
UM... GOOD TALK, MR. PRESIDENT.
IF THEY ARE ALL DEAD, WE CAN LIVE IN PEACE WITH THEM.
DARRIN BELL

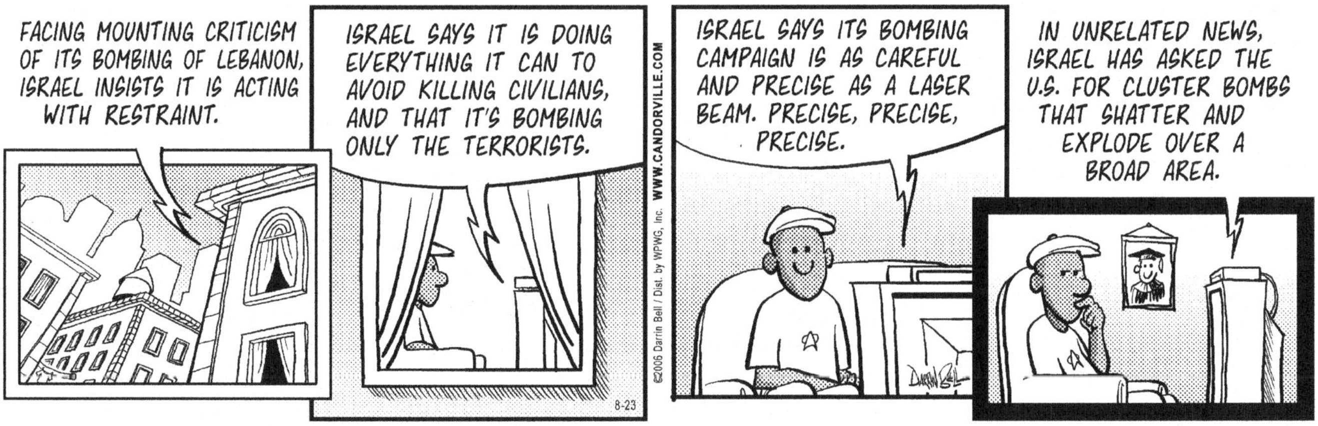
FACING MOUNTING CRITICISM OF ITS BOMBING OF LEBANON, ISRAEL INSISTS IT IS ACTING WITH RESTRAINT.
ISRAEL SAYS IT IS DOING EVERYTHING IT CAN TO AVOID KILLING CIVILIANS, AND THAT IT'S BOMBING ONLY THE TERRORISTS.
8-23
©2006 Darrin Bell / Dist. by WPWG, Inc. WWW.CANDORVILLE.COM
ISRAEL SAYS ITS BOMBING CAMPAIGN IS AS CAREFUL AND PRECISE AS A LASER BEAM. PRECISE, PRECISE, PRECISE.
DARRIN BELL
IN UNRELATED NEWS, ISRAEL HAS ASKED THE U.S. FOR CLUSTER BOMBS THAT SHATTER AND EXPLODE OVER A BROAD AREA.

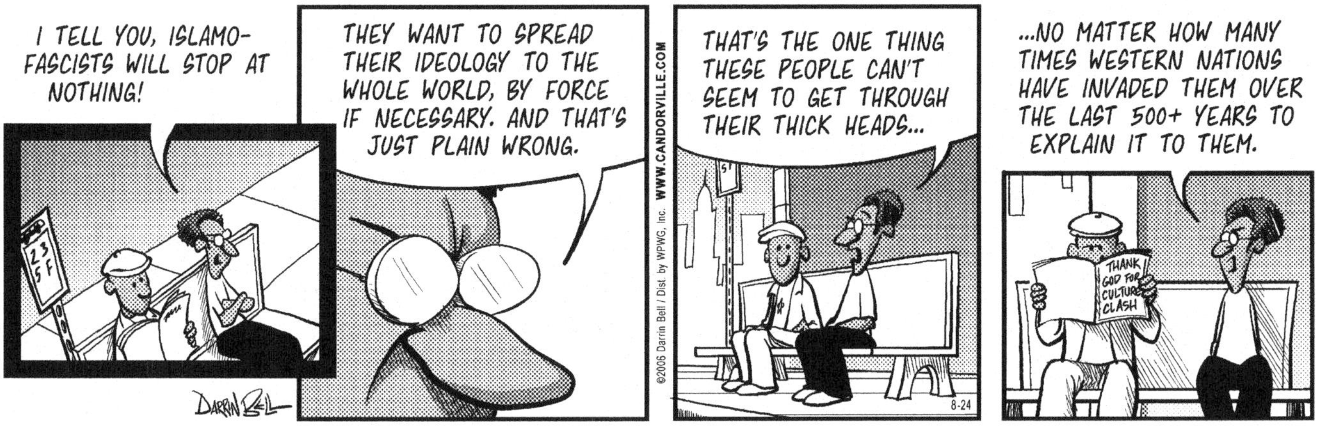
I TELL YOU, ISLAMO-FASCISTS WILL STOP AT NOTHING!
DARRIN BELL
THEY WANT TO SPREAD THEIR IDEOLOGY TO THE WHOLE WORLD, BY FORCE IF NECESSARY. AND THAT'S JUST PLAIN WRONG.
©2006 Darrin Bell / Dist. by WPWG, Inc. WWW.CANDORVILLE.COM
THAT'S THE ONE THING THESE PEOPLE CAN'T SEEM TO GET THROUGH THEIR THICK HEADS...
8-24
...NO MATTER HOW MANY TIMES WESTERN NATIONS HAVE INVADED THEM OVER THE LAST 500+ YEARS TO EXPLAIN IT TO THEM.
THANK GOD FOR CULTURE CLASH

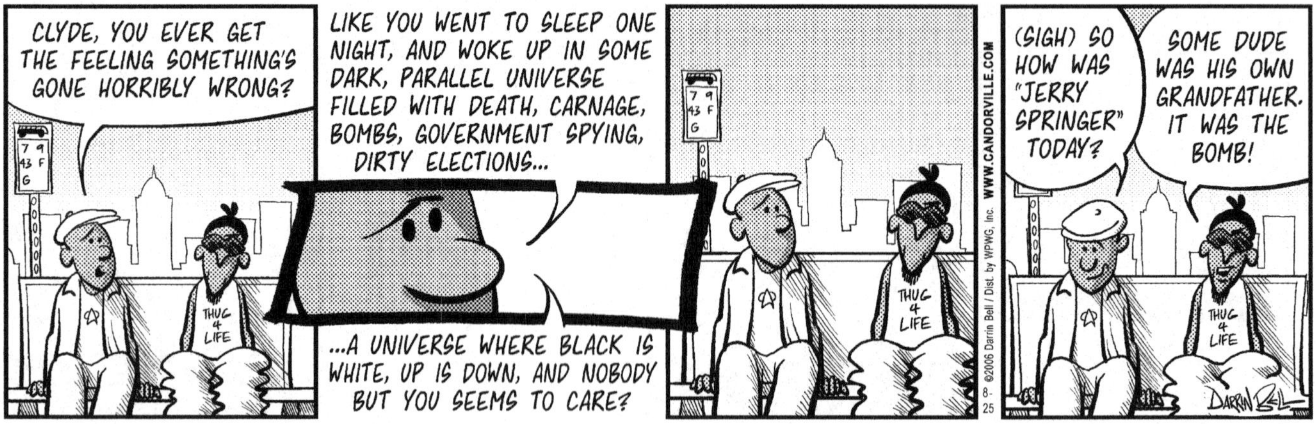
CLYDE, YOU EVER GET THE FEELING SOMETHING'S GONE HORRIBLY WRONG?
LIKE YOU WENT TO SLEEP ONE NIGHT, AND WOKE UP IN SOME DARK, PARALLEL UNIVERSE FILLED WITH DEATH, CARNAGE, BOMBS, GOVERNMENT SPYING, DIRTY ELECTIONS...
...A UNIVERSE WHERE BLACK IS WHITE, UP IS DOWN, AND NOBODY BUT YOU SEEMS TO CARE?
(SIGH) SO HOW WAS "JERRY SPRINGER" TODAY?
SOME DUDE WAS HIS OWN GRANDFATHER. IT WAS THE BOMB!
THUG 4 LIFE
©2006 Darrin Bell / Dist. by WPWG, Inc. WWW.CANDORVILLE.COM
8-25
DARRIN BELL

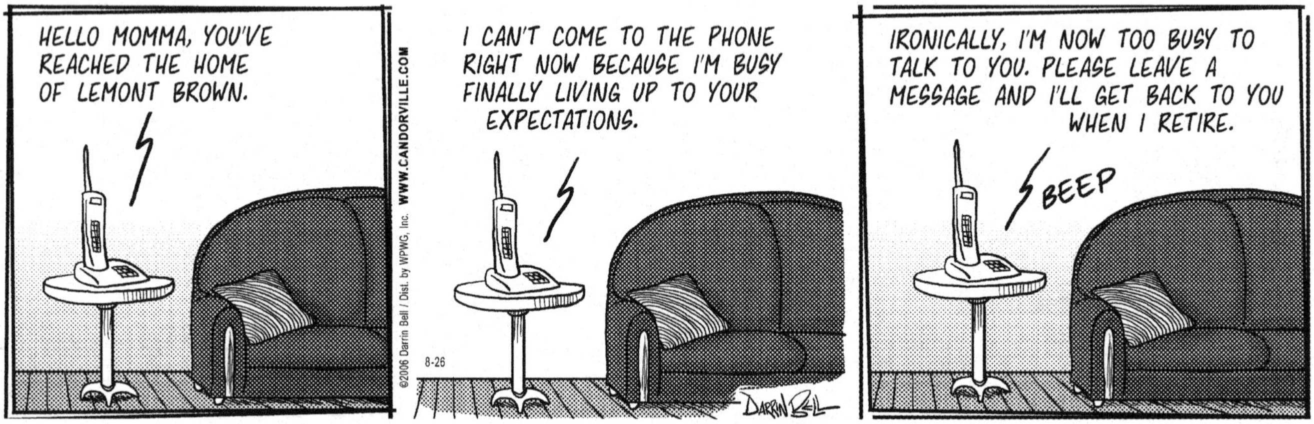
HELLO MOMMA, YOU'VE REACHED THE HOME OF LEMONT BROWN.
I CAN'T COME TO THE PHONE RIGHT NOW BECAUSE I'M BUSY FINALLY LIVING UP TO YOUR EXPECTATIONS.
IRONICALLY, I'M NOW TOO BUSY TO TALK TO YOU. PLEASE LEAVE A MESSAGE AND I'LL GET BACK TO YOU WHEN I RETIRE.
BEEP
©2006 Darrin Bell / Dist. by WPWG, Inc. WWW.CANDORVILLE.COM
8-26
DARRIN BELL

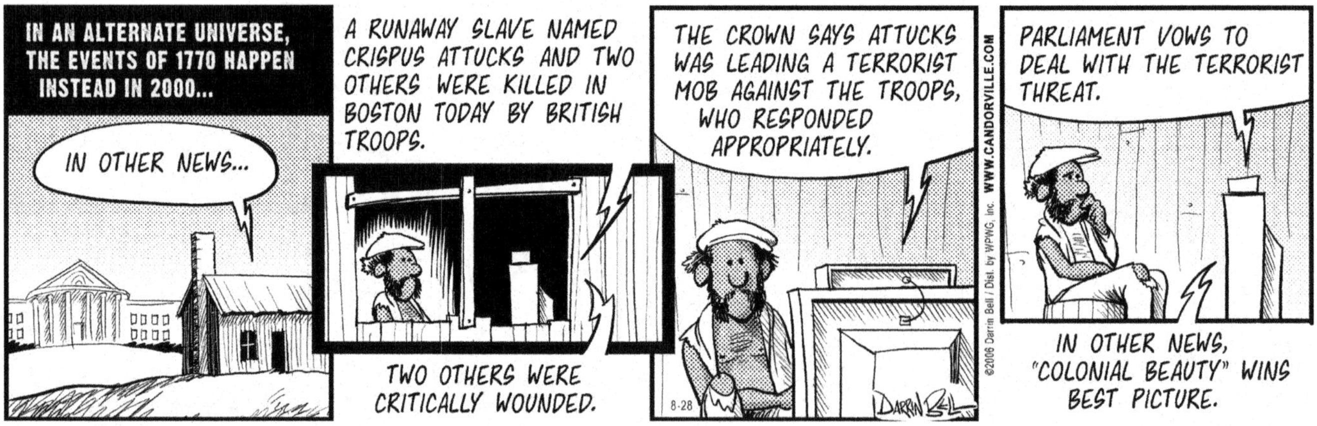
IN AN ALTERNATE UNIVERSE, THE EVENTS OF 1770 HAPPEN INSTEAD IN 2000...
IN OTHER NEWS...
A RUNAWAY SLAVE NAMED CRISPUS ATTUCKS AND TWO OTHERS WERE KILLED IN BOSTON TODAY BY BRITISH TROOPS.
TWO OTHERS WERE CRITICALLY WOUNDED.
THE CROWN SAYS ATTUCKS WAS LEADING A TERRORIST MOB AGAINST THE TROOPS, WHO RESPONDED APPROPRIATELY.
PARLIAMENT VOWS TO DEAL WITH THE TERRORIST THREAT.
IN OTHER NEWS, "COLONIAL BEAUTY" WINS BEST PICTURE.
©2006 Darrin Bell / Dist. by WPWG, Inc. WWW.CANDORVILLE.COM
8-28
DARRIN BELL

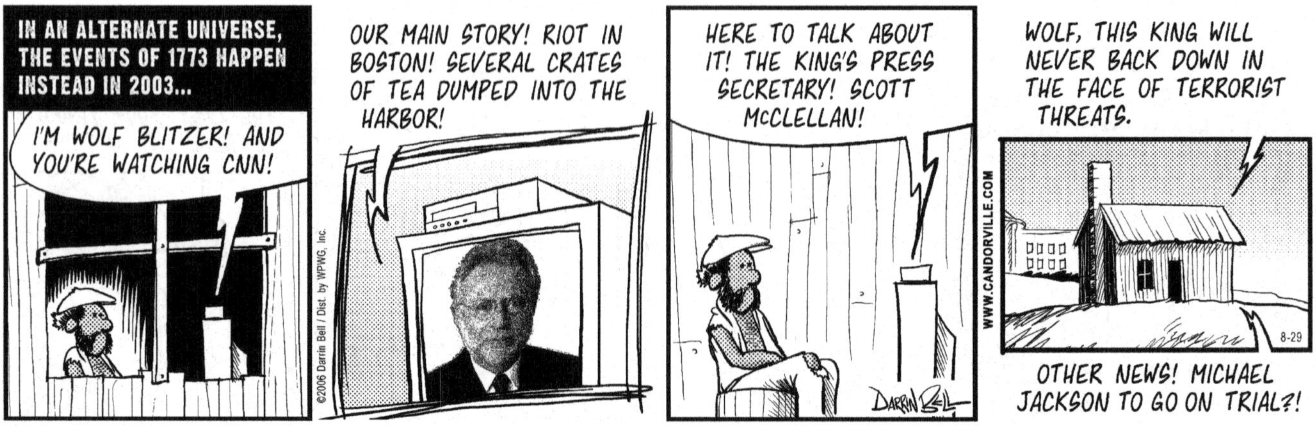
IN AN ALTERNATE UNIVERSE, THE EVENTS OF 1773 HAPPEN INSTEAD IN 2003...
I'M WOLF BLITZER! AND YOU'RE WATCHING CNN!
OUR MAIN STORY! RIOT IN BOSTON! SEVERAL CRATES OF TEA DUMPED INTO THE HARBOR!
HERE TO TALK ABOUT IT! THE KING'S PRESS SECRETARY! SCOTT McCLELLAN!
WOLF, THIS KING WILL NEVER BACK DOWN IN THE FACE OF TERRORIST THREATS.
OTHER NEWS! MICHAEL JACKSON TO GO ON TRIAL?!
©2006 Darrin Bell / Dist. by WPWG, Inc.
WWW.CANDORVILLE.COM
8-29
DARRIN BELL

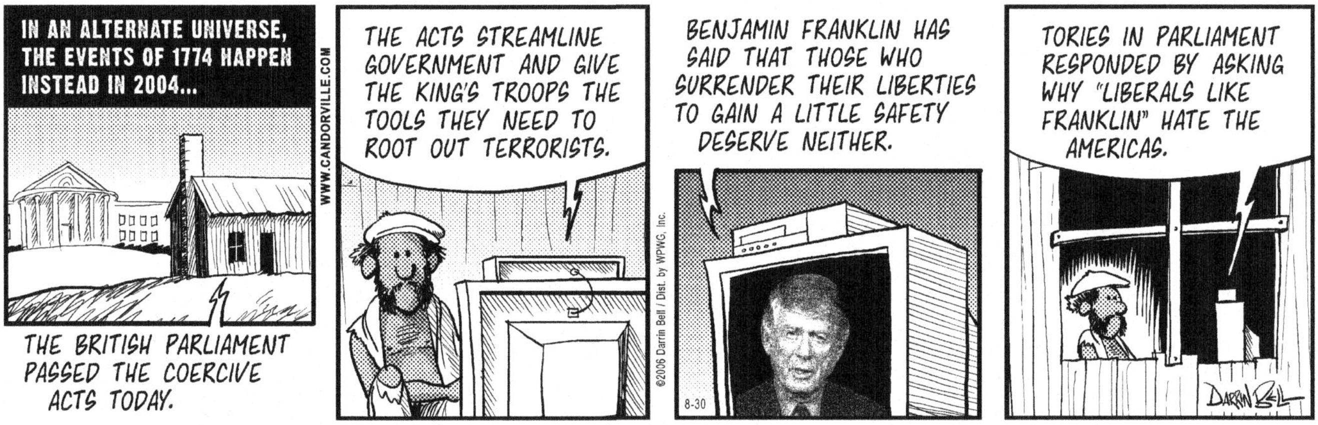
IN AN ALTERNATE UNIVERSE, THE EVENTS OF 1774 HAPPEN INSTEAD IN 2004...
THE BRITISH PARLIAMENT PASSED THE COERCIVE ACTS TODAY.
WWW.CANDORVILLE.COM
THE ACTS STREAMLINE GOVERNMENT AND GIVE THE KING'S TROOPS THE TOOLS THEY NEED TO ROOT OUT TERRORISTS.
©2006 Darrin Bell / Dist. by WPWG, Inc.
BENJAMIN FRANKLIN HAS SAID THAT THOSE WHO SURRENDER THEIR LIBERTIES TO GAIN A LITTLE SAFETY DESERVE NEITHER.
8-30
TORIES IN PARLIAMENT RESPONDED BY ASKING WHY "LIBERALS LIKE FRANKLIN" HATE THE AMERICAS.
DARRIN BELL

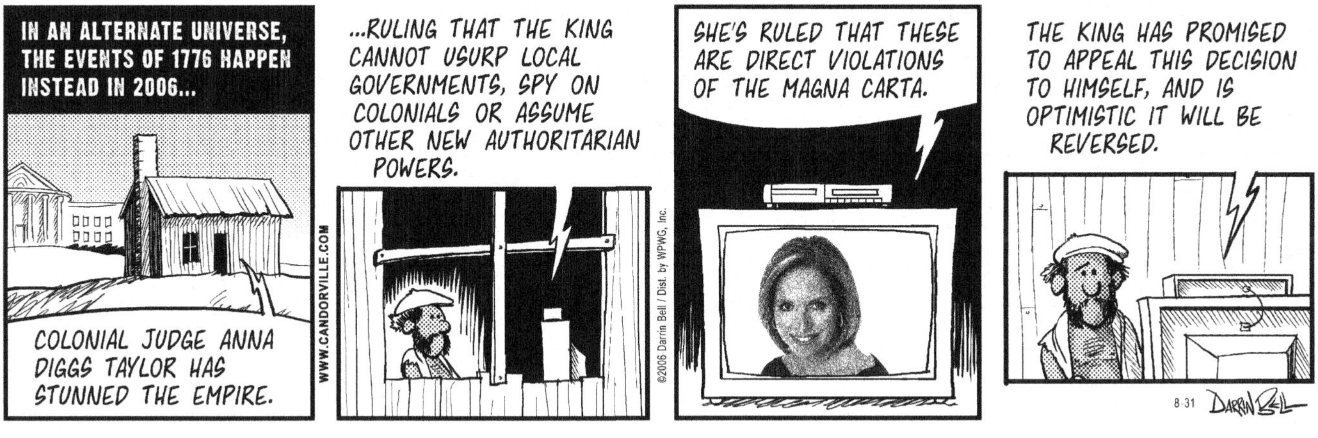
IN AN ALTERNATE UNIVERSE, THE EVENTS OF 1776 HAPPEN INSTEAD IN 2006...
COLONIAL JUDGE ANNA DIGGS TAYLOR HAS STUNNED THE EMPIRE.
WWW.CANDORVILLE.COM
...RULING THAT THE KING CANNOT USURP LOCAL GOVERNMENTS, SPY ON COLONIALS OR ASSUME OTHER NEW AUTHORITARIAN POWERS.
©2006 Darrin Bell / Dist. by WPWG, Inc.
SHE'S RULED THAT THESE ARE DIRECT VIOLATIONS OF THE MAGNA CARTA.
THE KING HAS PROMISED TO APPEAL THIS DECISION TO HIMSELF, AND IS OPTIMISTIC IT WILL BE REVERSED.
8-31
DARRIN BELL

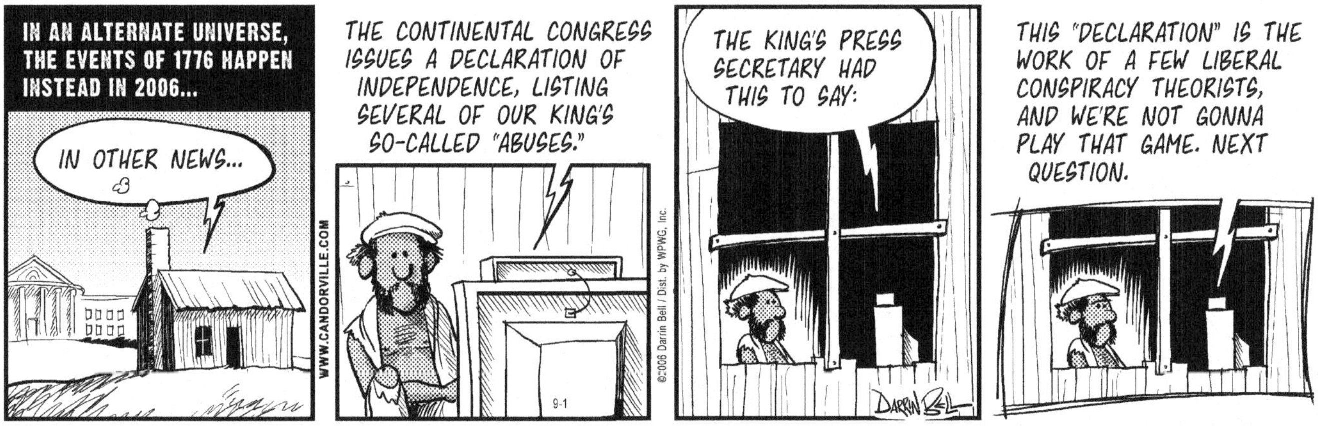
IN AN ALTERNATE UNIVERSE, THE EVENTS OF 1776 HAPPEN INSTEAD IN 2006...
IN OTHER NEWS...
WWW.CANDORVILLE.COM
THE CONTINENTAL CONGRESS ISSUES A DECLARATION OF INDEPENDENCE, LISTING SEVERAL OF OUR KING'S SO-CALLED "ABUSES."
9-1
©2006 Darrin Bell / Dist. by WPWG, Inc.
THE KING'S PRESS SECRETARY HAD THIS TO SAY:
DARRIN BELL
THIS "DECLARATION" IS THE WORK OF A FEW LIBERAL CONSPIRACY THEORISTS, AND WE'RE NOT GONNA PLAY THAT GAME. NEXT QUESTION.

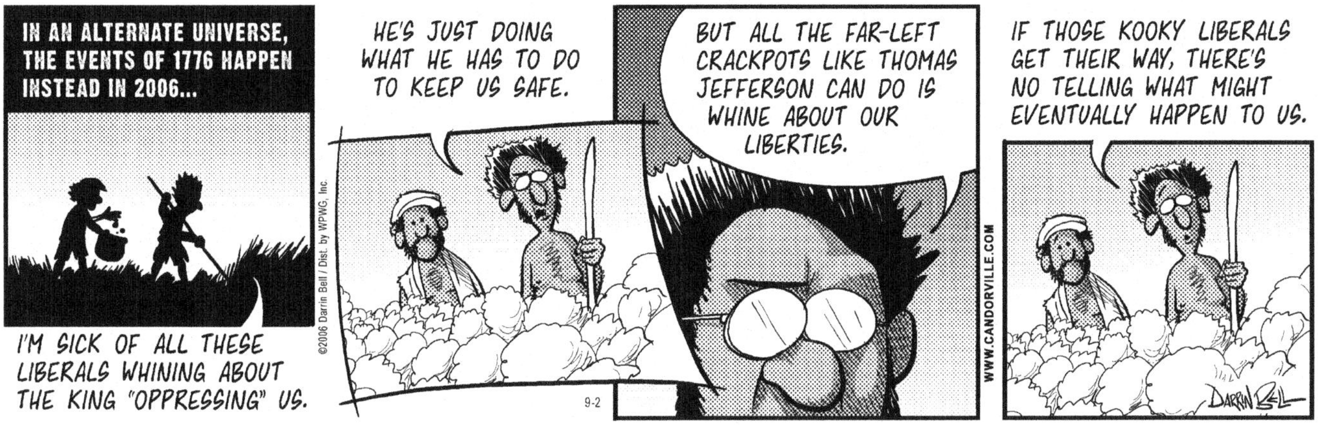
IN AN ALTERNATE UNIVERSE, THE EVENTS OF 1776 HAPPEN INSTEAD IN 2006...
I'M SICK OF ALL THESE LIBERALS WHINING ABOUT THE KING "OPPRESSING" US.
©2006 Darrin Bell / Dist. by WPWG, Inc.
HE'S JUST DOING WHAT HE HAS TO DO TO KEEP US SAFE.
9-2
BUT ALL THE FAR-LEFT CRACKPOTS LIKE THOMAS JEFFERSON CAN DO IS WHINE ABOUT OUR LIBERTIES.
WWW.CANDORVILLE.COM
IF THOSE KOOKY LIBERALS GET THEIR WAY, THERE'S NO TELLING WHAT MIGHT EVENTUALLY HAPPEN TO US.
DARRIN BELL

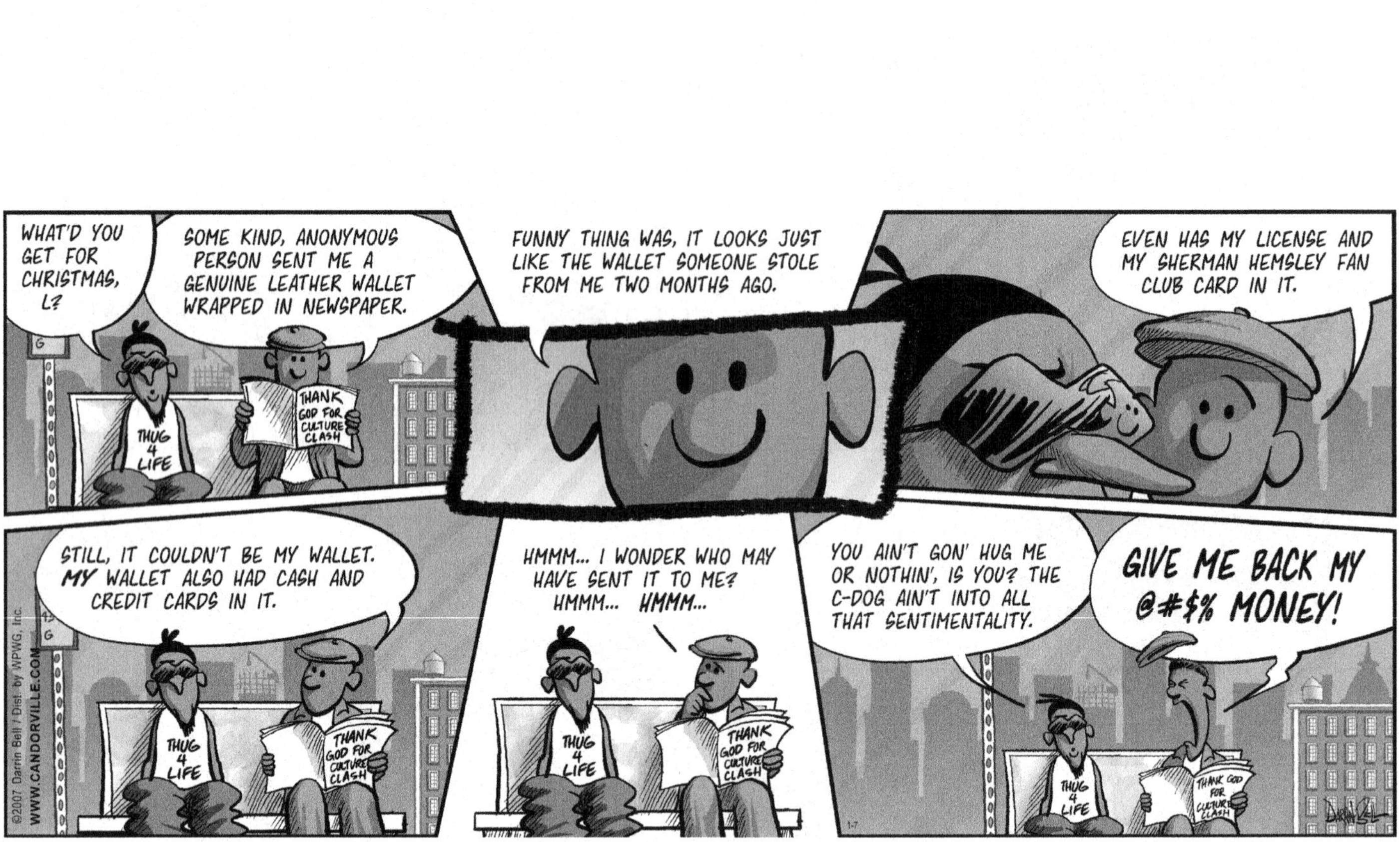
WHAT'D YOU GET FOR CHRISTMAS, L?
SOME KIND, ANONYMOUS PERSON SENT ME A GENUINE LEATHER WALLET WRAPPED IN NEWSPAPER.
THUG 4 LIFE
THANK GOD FOR CULTURE CLASH
FUNNY THING WAS, IT LOOKS JUST LIKE THE WALLET SOMEONE STOLE FROM ME TWO MONTHS AGO.
EVEN HAS MY LICENSE AND MY SHERMAN HEMSLEY FAN CLUB CARD IN IT.
STILL, IT COULDN'T BE MY WALLET. MY WALLET ALSO HAD CASH AND CREDIT CARDS IN IT.
HMMM... I WONDER WHO MAY HAVE SENT IT TO ME? HMMM... HMMM...
YOU AIN'T GON' HUG ME OR NOTHIN', IS YOU? THE C-DOG AIN'T INTO ALL THAT SENTIMENTALITY.
GIVE ME BACK MY @#$% MONEY!
©2007 Darrin Bell / Dist. by WPWG, Inc.
WWW.CANDORVILLE.COM
1-7
DARRIN BELL

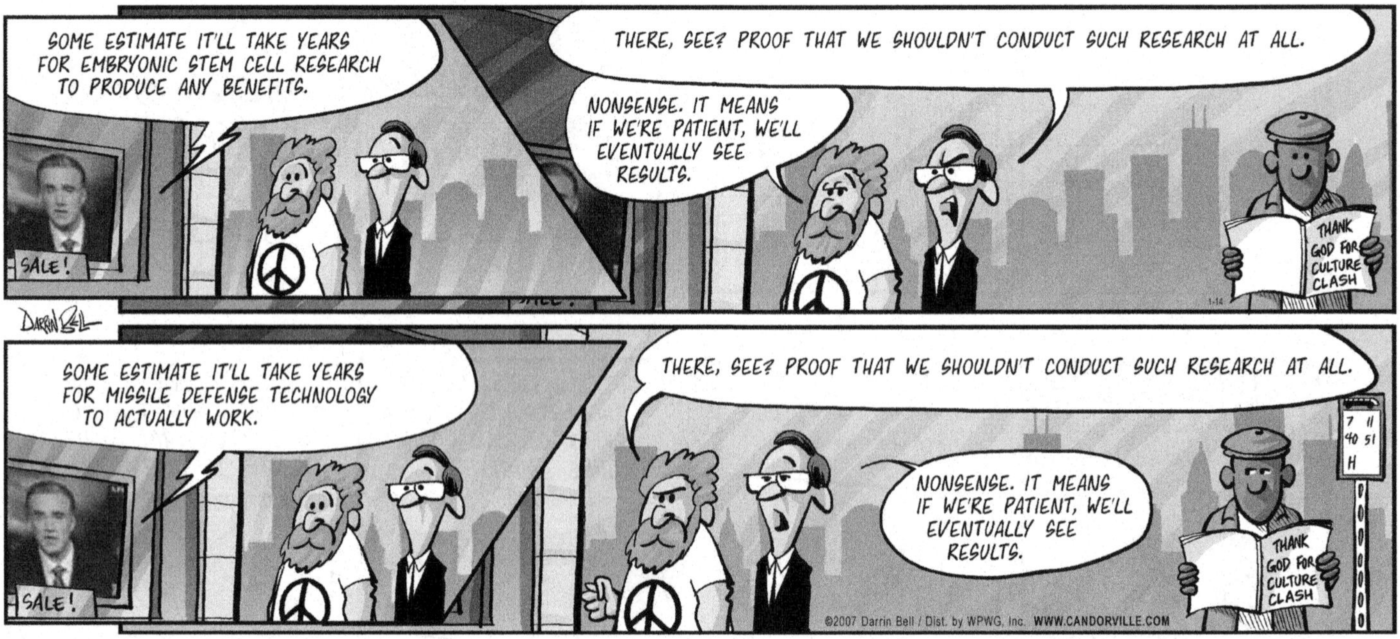
SOME ESTIMATE IT'LL TAKE YEARS FOR EMBRYONIC STEM CELL RESEARCH TO PRODUCE ANY BENEFITS.
SALE!
NONSENSE. IT MEANS IF WE'RE PATIENT, WE'LL EVENTUALLY SEE RESULTS.
THERE, SEE? PROOF THAT WE SHOULDN'T CONDUCT SUCH RESEARCH AT ALL.
THANK GOD FOR CULTURE CLASH
1-14
DARRIN BELL
SOME ESTIMATE IT'LL TAKE YEARS FOR MISSILE DEFENSE TECHNOLOGY TO ACTUALLY WORK.
SALE!
THERE, SEE? PROOF THAT WE SHOULDN'T CONDUCT SUCH RESEARCH AT ALL.
NONSENSE. IT MEANS IF WE'RE PATIENT, WE'LL EVENTUALLY SEE RESULTS.
THANK GOD FOR CULTURE CLASH
©2007 Darrin Bell / Dist. by WPWG, Inc. WWW.CANDORVILLE.COM

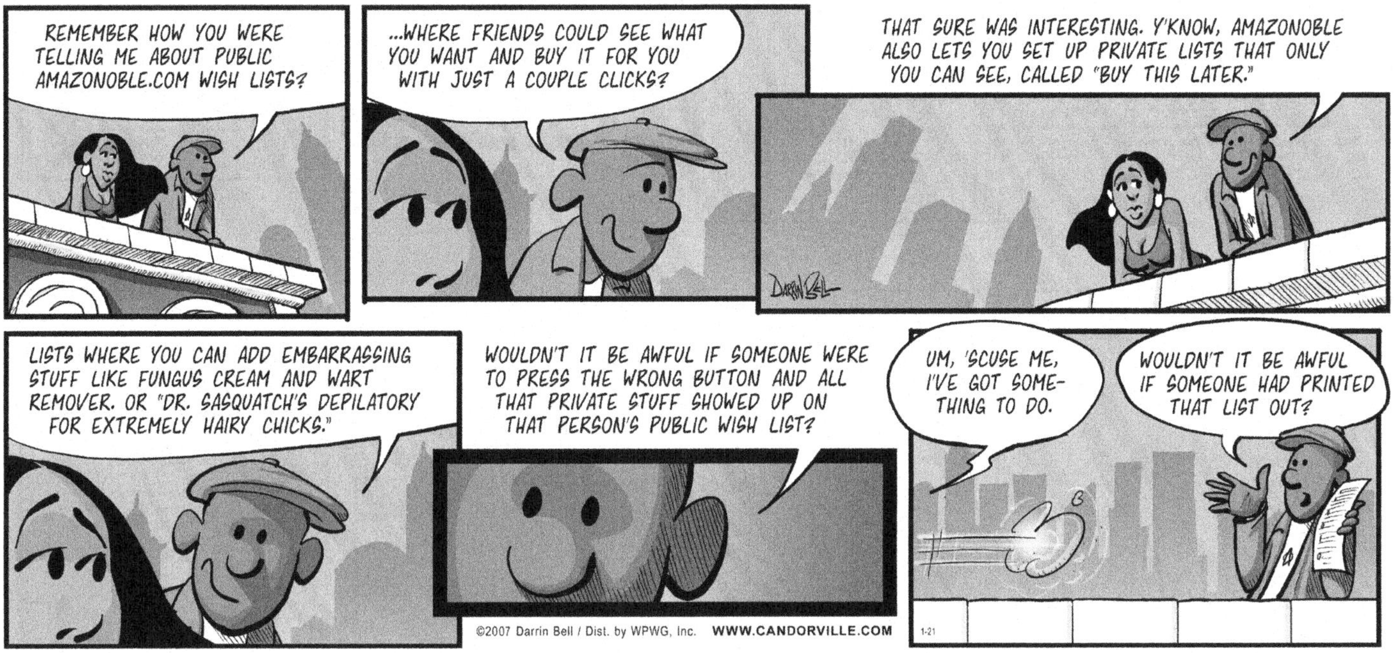
REMEMBER HOW YOU WERE TELLING ME ABOUT PUBLIC AMAZONOBLE.COM WISH LISTS?
...WHERE FRIENDS COULD SEE WHAT YOU WANT AND BUY IT FOR YOU WITH JUST A COUPLE CLICKS?
THAT SURE WAS INTERESTING. Y'KNOW, AMAZONOBLE ALSO LETS YOU SET UP PRIVATE LISTS THAT ONLY YOU CAN SEE, CALLED "BUY THIS LATER."
LISTS WHERE YOU CAN ADD EMBARRASSING STUFF LIKE FUNGUS CREAM AND WART REMOVER. OR "DR. SASQUATCH'S DEPILATORY FOR EXTREMELY HAIRY CHICKS."
WOULDN'T IT BE AWFUL IF SOMEONE WERE TO PRESS THE WRONG BUTTON AND ALL THAT PRIVATE STUFF SHOWED UP ON THAT PERSON'S PUBLIC WISH LIST?
UM, 'SCUSE ME, I'VE GOT SOMETHING TO DO.
WOULDN'T IT BE AWFUL IF SOMEONE HAD PRINTED THAT LIST OUT?
©2007 Darrin Bell / Dist. by WPWG, Inc. WWW.CANDORVILLE.COM
1-21

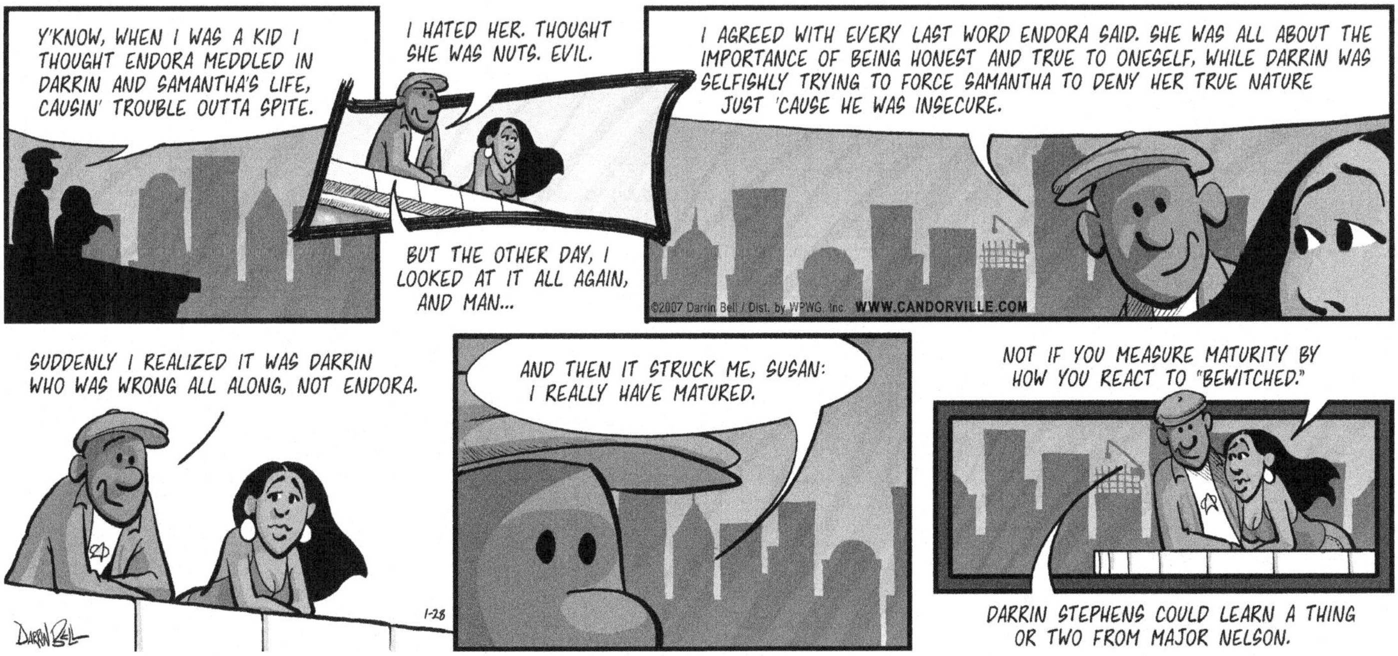
Y'KNOW, WHEN I WAS A KID I THOUGHT ENDORA MEDDLED IN DARRIN AND SAMANTHA'S LIFE, CAUSIN' TROUBLE OUTTA SPITE.
I HATED HER. THOUGHT SHE WAS NUTS. EVIL.
BUT THE OTHER DAY, I LOOKED AT IT ALL AGAIN, AND MAN...
I AGREED WITH EVERY LAST WORD ENDORA SAID. SHE WAS ALL ABOUT THE IMPORTANCE OF BEING HONEST AND TRUE TO ONESELF, WHILE DARRIN WAS SELFISHLY TRYING TO FORCE SAMANTHA TO DENY HER TRUE NATURE JUST 'CAUSE HE WAS INSECURE.
©2007 Darrin Bell / Dist. by WPWG, Inc. WWW.CANDORVILLE.COM
SUDDENLY I REALIZED IT WAS DARRIN WHO WAS WRONG ALL ALONG, NOT ENDORA.
1-28
AND THEN IT STRUCK ME, SUSAN: I REALLY HAVE MATURED.
NOT IF YOU MEASURE MATURITY BY HOW YOU REACT TO "BEWITCHED."
DARRIN STEPHENS COULD LEARN A THING OR TWO FROM MAJOR NELSON.

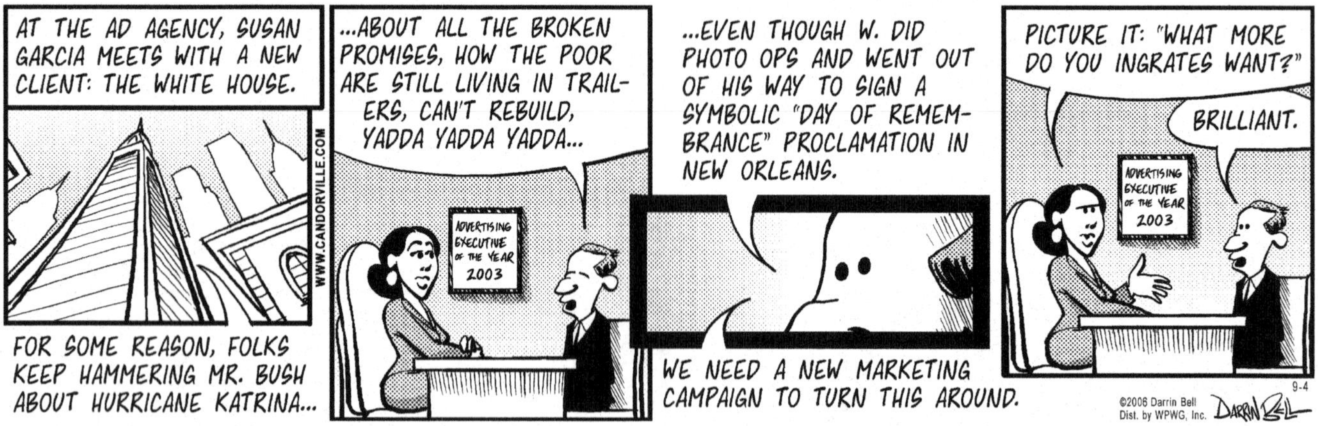
AT THE AD AGENCY, SUSAN GARCIA MEETS WITH A NEW CLIENT: THE WHITE HOUSE.
FOR SOME REASON, FOLKS KEEP HAMMERING MR. BUSH ABOUT HURRICANE KATRINA...
WWW.CANDORVILLE.COM
...ABOUT ALL THE BROKEN PROMISES, HOW THE POOR ARE STILL LIVING IN TRAILERS, CAN'T REBUILD, YADDA YADDA YADDA...
ADVERTISING EXECUTIVE OF THE YEAR 2003
...EVEN THOUGH W. DID PHOTO OPS AND WENT OUT OF HIS WAY TO SIGN A SYMBOLIC "DAY OF REMEMBRANCE" PROCLAMATION IN NEW ORLEANS.
WE NEED A NEW MARKETING CAMPAIGN TO TURN THIS AROUND.
PICTURE IT: "WHAT MORE DO YOU INGRATES WANT?"
BRILLIANT.
ADVERTISING EXECUTIVE OF THE YEAR 2003
9-4
©2006 Darrin Bell Dist. by WPWG, Inc.
DARRIN BELL

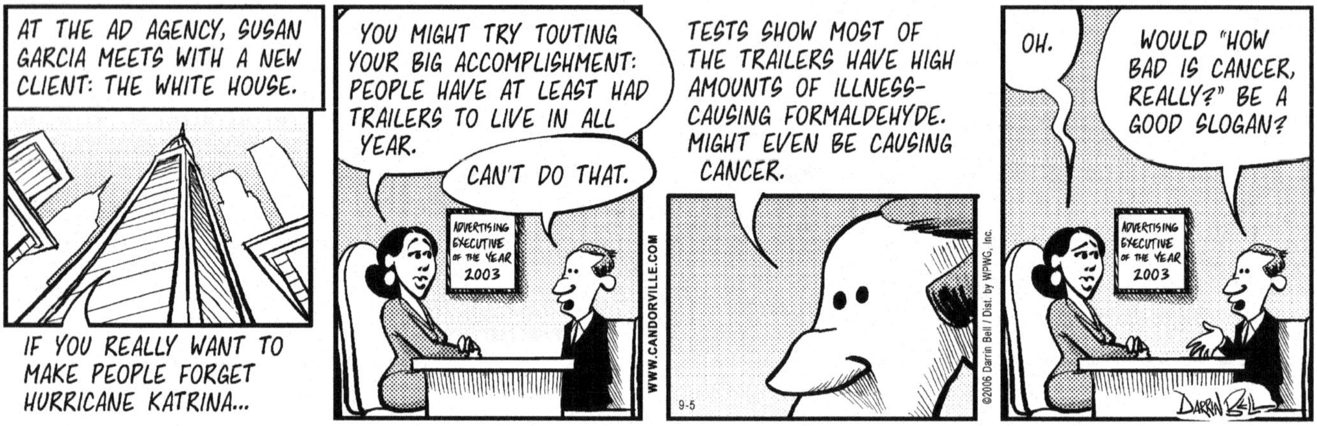
AT THE AD AGENCY, SUSAN GARCIA MEETS WITH A NEW CLIENT: THE WHITE HOUSE.
IF YOU REALLY WANT TO MAKE PEOPLE FORGET HURRICANE KATRINA...
YOU MIGHT TRY TOUTING YOUR BIG ACCOMPLISHMENT: PEOPLE HAVE AT LEAST HAD TRAILERS TO LIVE IN ALL YEAR.
CAN'T DO THAT.
ADVERTISING EXECUTIVE OF THE YEAR 2003
WWW.CANDORVILLE.COM
TESTS SHOW MOST OF THE TRAILERS HAVE HIGH AMOUNTS OF ILLNESS-CAUSING FORMALDEHYDE. MIGHT EVEN BE CAUSING CANCER.
9-5
©2006 Darrin Bell / Dist. by WPWG, Inc.
OH.
WOULD "HOW BAD IS CANCER, REALLY?" BE A GOOD SLOGAN?
ADVERTISING EXECUTIVE OF THE YEAR 2003
DARRIN BELL

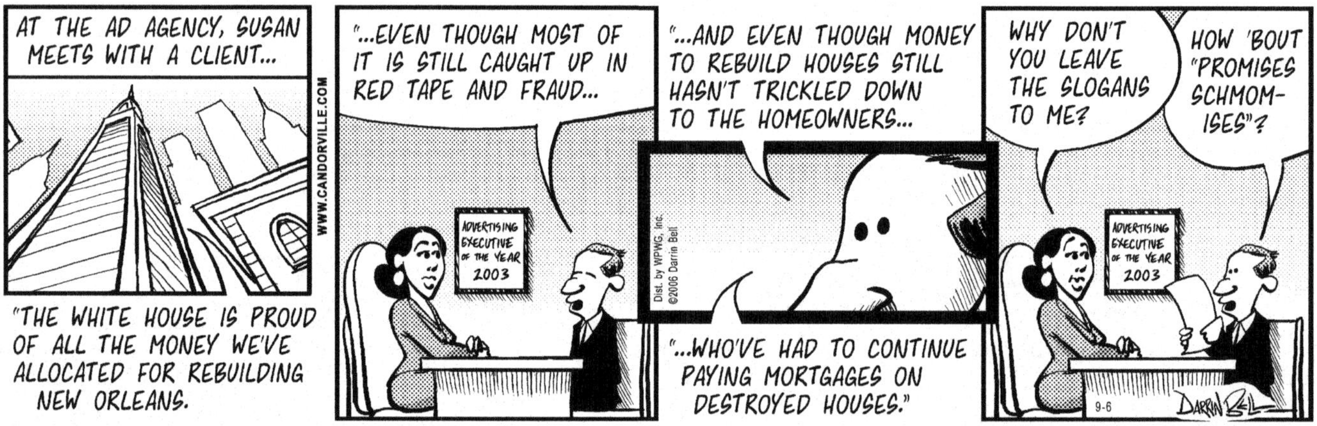
AT THE AD AGENCY, SUSAN MEETS WITH A CLIENT...
WWW.CANDORVILLE.COM
"THE WHITE HOUSE IS PROUD OF ALL THE MONEY WE'VE ALLOCATED FOR REBUILDING NEW ORLEANS.
"...EVEN THOUGH MOST OF IT IS STILL CAUGHT UP IN RED TAPE AND FRAUD...
ADVERTISING EXECUTIVE OF THE YEAR 2003
"...AND EVEN THOUGH MONEY TO REBUILD HOUSES STILL HASN'T TRICKLED DOWN TO THE HOMEOWNERS...
Dist. by WPWG, Inc. ©2006 Darrin Bell
"...WHO'VE HAD TO CONTINUE PAYING MORTGAGES ON DESTROYED HOUSES."
WHY DON'T YOU LEAVE THE SLOGANS TO ME?
HOW 'BOUT "PROMISES SCHMOMISES"?
ADVERTISING EXECUTIVE OF THE YEAR 2003
9-6
DARRIN BELL

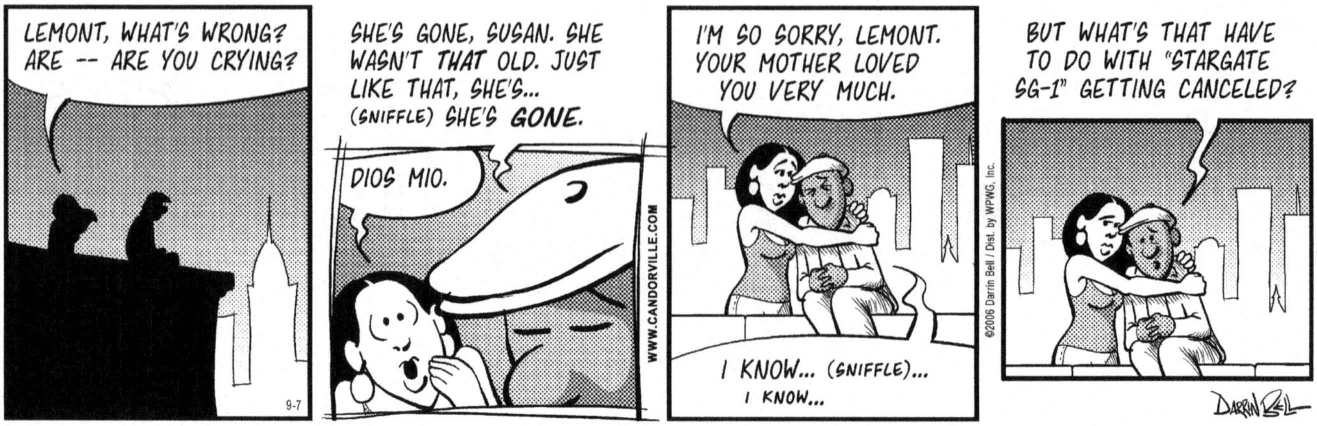
LEMONT, WHAT'S WRONG? ARE -- ARE YOU CRYING?
9-7
SHE'S GONE, SUSAN. SHE WASN'T THAT OLD. JUST LIKE THAT, SHE'S... (SNIFFLE) SHE'S GONE.
DIOS MIO.
WWW.CANDORVILLE.COM
I'M SO SORRY, LEMONT. YOUR MOTHER LOVED YOU VERY MUCH.
I KNOW... (SNIFFLE)... I KNOW...
©2006 Darrin Bell / Dist. by WPWG, Inc.
BUT WHAT'S THAT HAVE TO DO WITH "STARGATE SG-1" GETTING CANCELED?
DARRIN BELL

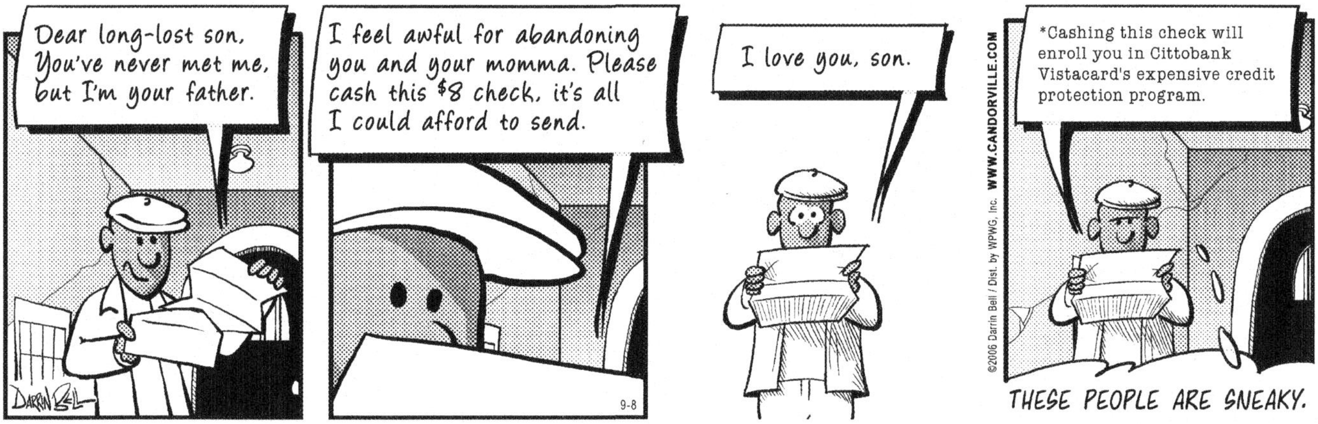
Dear long-lost son, You've never met me, but I'm your father.
I feel awful for abandoning you and your momma. Please cash this $8 check, it's all I could afford to send.
I love you, son.
*Cashing this check will enroll you in Cittobank Vistacard's expensive credit protection program.
THESE PEOPLE ARE SNEAKY.
9-8
©2006 Darrin Bell / Dist. by WPWG, Inc. WWW.CANDORVILLE.COM

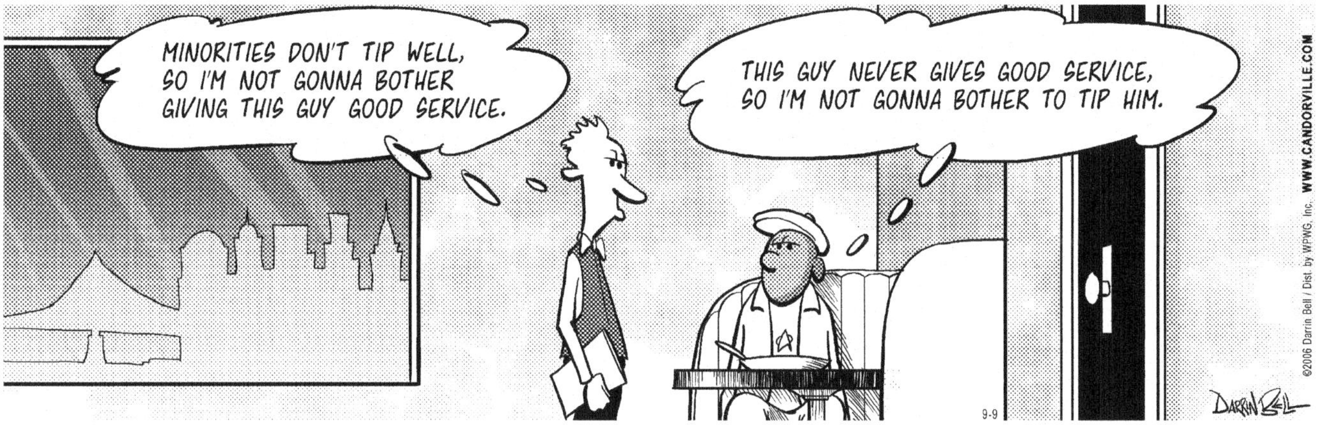
MINORITIES DON'T TIP WELL, SO I'M NOT GONNA BOTHER GIVING THIS GUY GOOD SERVICE.
THIS GUY NEVER GIVES GOOD SERVICE, SO I'M NOT GONNA BOTHER TO TIP HIM.
9-9
©2006 Darrin Bell / Dist. by WPWG, Inc. WWW.CANDORVILLE.COM

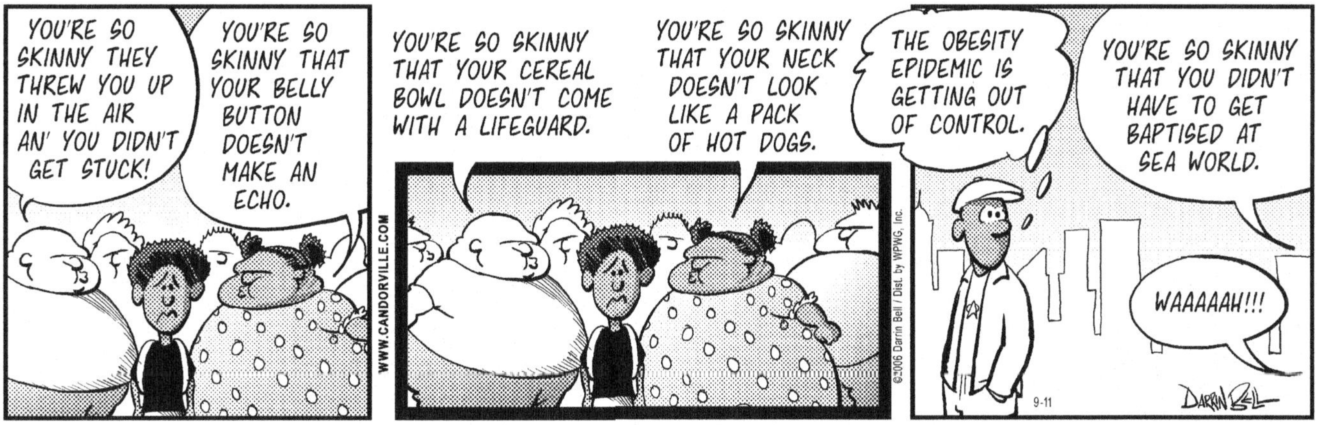
YOU'RE SO SKINNY THEY THREW YOU UP IN THE AIR AN' YOU DIDN'T GET STUCK!
YOU'RE SO SKINNY THAT YOUR BELLY BUTTON DOESN'T MAKE AN ECHO.
YOU'RE SO SKINNY THAT YOUR CEREAL BOWL DOESN'T COME WITH A LIFEGUARD.
YOU'RE SO SKINNY THAT YOUR NECK DOESN'T LOOK LIKE A PACK OF HOT DOGS.
THE OBESITY EPIDEMIC IS GETTING OUT OF CONTROL.
YOU'RE SO SKINNY THAT YOU DIDN'T HAVE TO GET BAPTISED AT SEA WORLD.
WAAAAAH!!!
9-11
©2006 Darrin Bell / Dist. by WPWG, Inc. WWW.CANDORVILLE.COM

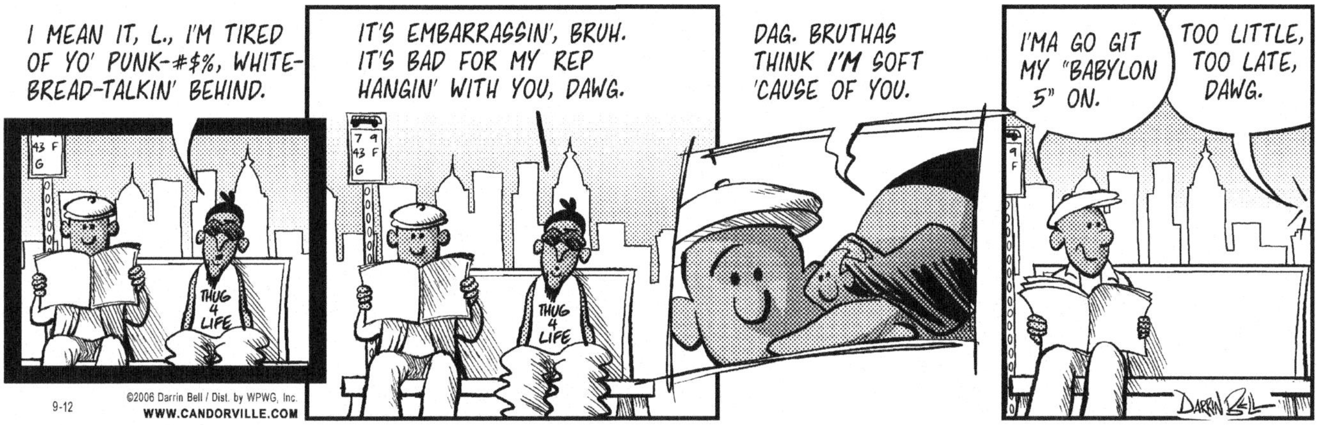
I MEAN IT, L., I'M TIRED OF YO' PUNK-#$%, WHITE-BREAD-TALKIN' BEHIND.
IT'S EMBARRASSIN', BRUH. IT'S BAD FOR MY REP HANGIN' WITH YOU, DAWG.
DAG. BRUTHAS THINK I'M SOFT 'CAUSE OF YOU.
I'MA GO GIT MY "BABYLON 5" ON.
TOO LITTLE, TOO LATE, DAWG.
THUG 4 LIFE
9-12
©2006 Darrin Bell / Dist. by WPWG, Inc. WWW.CANDORVILLE.COM

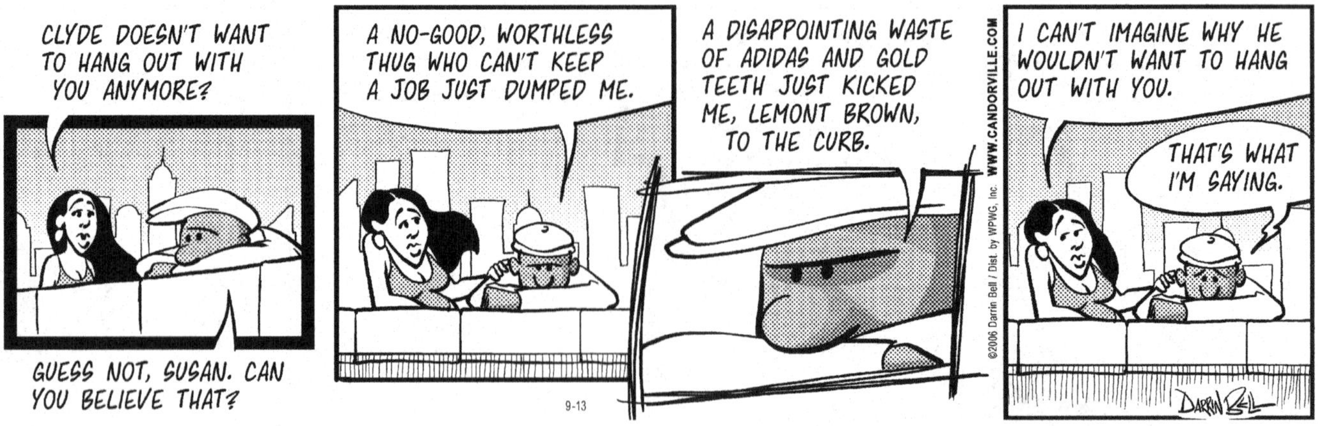
CLYDE DOESN'T WANT TO HANG OUT WITH YOU ANYMORE?
GUESS NOT, SUSAN. CAN YOU BELIEVE THAT?
A NO-GOOD, WORTHLESS THUG WHO CAN'T KEEP A JOB JUST DUMPED ME.
9-13
A DISAPPOINTING WASTE OF ADIDAS AND GOLD TEETH JUST KICKED ME, LEMONT BROWN, TO THE CURB.
©2006 Darrin Bell / Dist. by WPWG, Inc. WWW.CANDORVILLE.COM
I CAN'T IMAGINE WHY HE WOULDN'T WANT TO HANG OUT WITH YOU.
THAT'S WHAT I'M SAYING.
DARRIN BELL

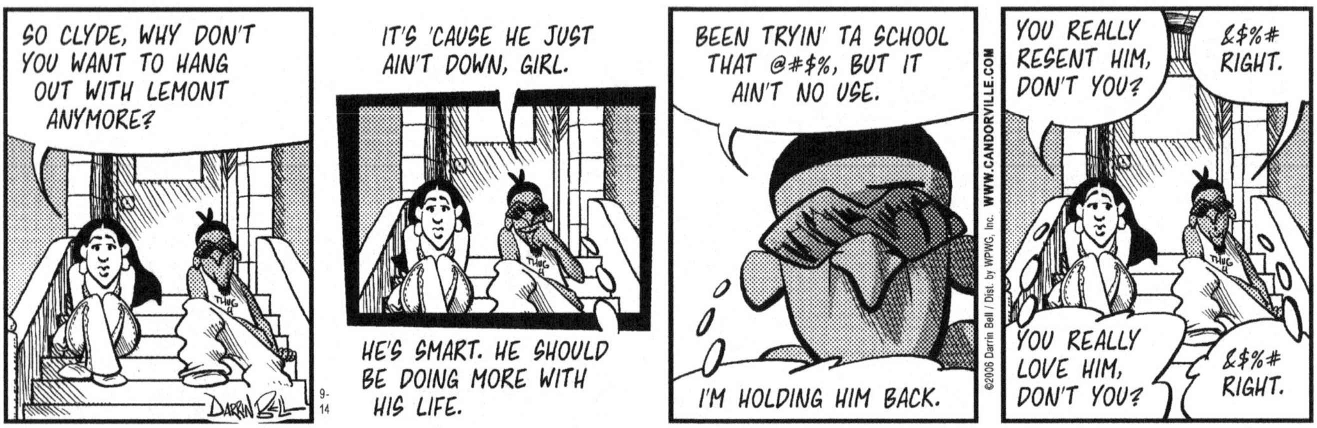
SO CLYDE, WHY DON'T YOU WANT TO HANG OUT WITH LEMONT ANYMORE?
DARRIN BELL
9-14
IT'S 'CAUSE HE JUST AIN'T DOWN, GIRL.
HE'S SMART. HE SHOULD BE DOING MORE WITH HIS LIFE.
BEEN TRYIN' TA SCHOOL THAT @#$%, BUT IT AIN'T NO USE.
I'M HOLDING HIM BACK.
©2006 Darrin Bell / Dist. by WPWG, Inc. WWW.CANDORVILLE.COM
YOU REALLY RESENT HIM, DON'T YOU?
&$%# RIGHT.
YOU REALLY LOVE HIM, DON'T YOU?
&$%# RIGHT.

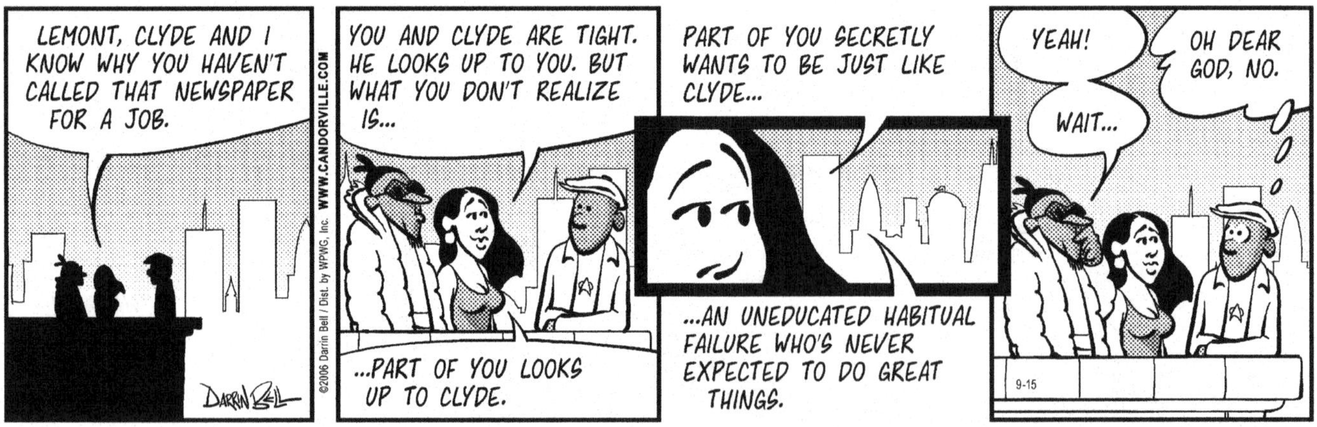
LEMONT, CLYDE AND I KNOW WHY YOU HAVEN'T CALLED THAT NEWSPAPER FOR A JOB.
DARRIN BELL
©2006 Darrin Bell / Dist. by WPWG, Inc. WWW.CANDORVILLE.COM
YOU AND CLYDE ARE TIGHT. HE LOOKS UP TO YOU. BUT WHAT YOU DON'T REALIZE IS...
...PART OF YOU LOOKS UP TO CLYDE.
PART OF YOU SECRETLY WANTS TO BE JUST LIKE CLYDE...
...AN UNEDUCATED HABITUAL FAILURE WHO'S NEVER EXPECTED TO DO GREAT THINGS.
YEAH!
OH DEAR GOD, NO.
WAIT...
9-15

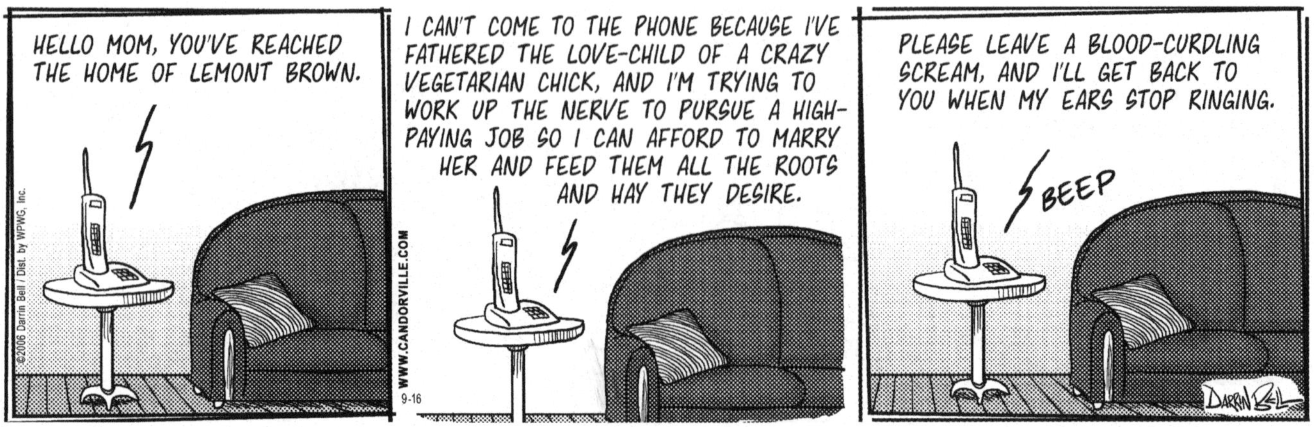
HELLO MOM, YOU'VE REACHED THE HOME OF LEMONT BROWN.
©2006 Darrin Bell / Dist. by WPWG, Inc.
I CAN'T COME TO THE PHONE BECAUSE I'VE FATHERED THE LOVE-CHILD OF A CRAZY VEGETARIAN CHICK, AND I'M TRYING TO WORK UP THE NERVE TO PURSUE A HIGH-PAYING JOB SO I CAN AFFORD TO MARRY HER AND FEED THEM ALL THE ROOTS AND HAY THEY DESIRE.
WWW.CANDORVILLE.COM
9-16
PLEASE LEAVE A BLOOD-CURDLING SCREAM, AND I'LL GET BACK TO YOU WHEN MY EARS STOP RINGING.
BEEP
DARRIN BELL

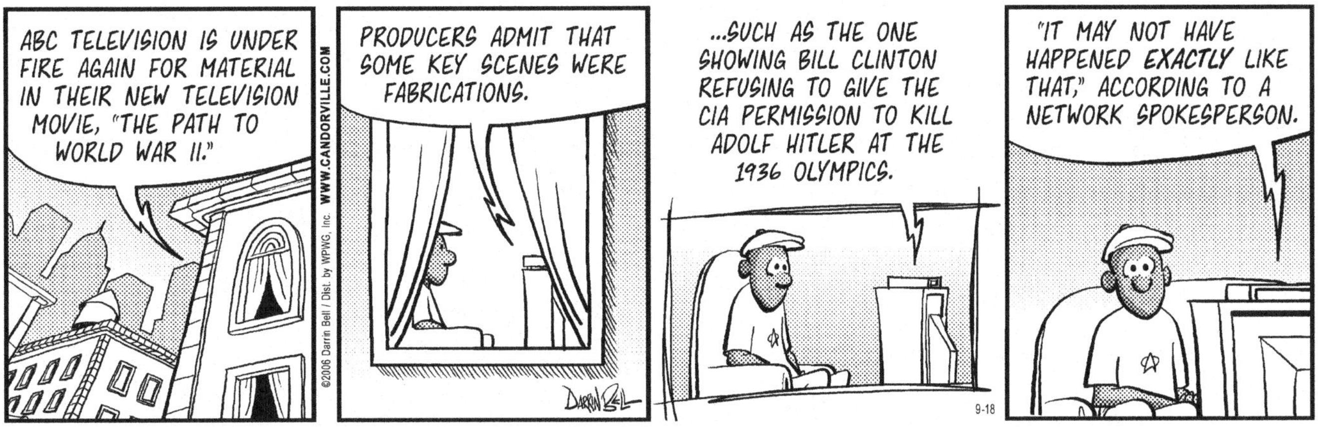
ABC TELEVISION IS UNDER FIRE AGAIN FOR MATERIAL IN THEIR NEW TELEVISION MOVIE, "THE PATH TO WORLD WAR II."
©2006 Darrin Bell / Dist. by WPWG, Inc. WWW.CANDORVILLE.COM
PRODUCERS ADMIT THAT SOME KEY SCENES WERE FABRICATIONS.
...SUCH AS THE ONE SHOWING BILL CLINTON REFUSING TO GIVE THE CIA PERMISSION TO KILL ADOLF HITLER AT THE 1936 OLYMPICS.
"IT MAY NOT HAVE HAPPENED EXACTLY LIKE THAT," ACCORDING TO A NETWORK SPOKESPERSON.
9-18

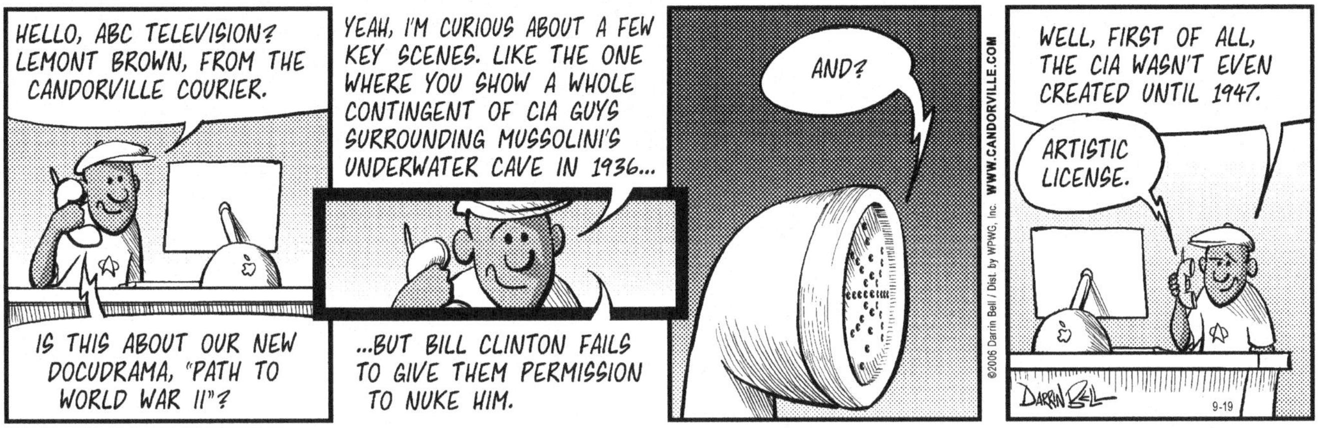
HELLO, ABC TELEVISION? LEMONT BROWN, FROM THE CANDORVILLE COURIER.
IS THIS ABOUT OUR NEW DOCUDRAMA, "PATH TO WORLD WAR II"?
YEAH, I'M CURIOUS ABOUT A FEW KEY SCENES. LIKE THE ONE WHERE YOU SHOW A WHOLE CONTINGENT OF CIA GUYS SURROUNDING MUSSOLINI'S UNDERWATER CAVE IN 1936...
...BUT BILL CLINTON FAILS TO GIVE THEM PERMISSION TO NUKE HIM.
AND?
©2006 Darrin Bell / Dist. by WPWG, Inc. WWW.CANDORVILLE.COM
WELL, FIRST OF ALL, THE CIA WASN'T EVEN CREATED UNTIL 1947.
ARTISTIC LICENSE.
9-19

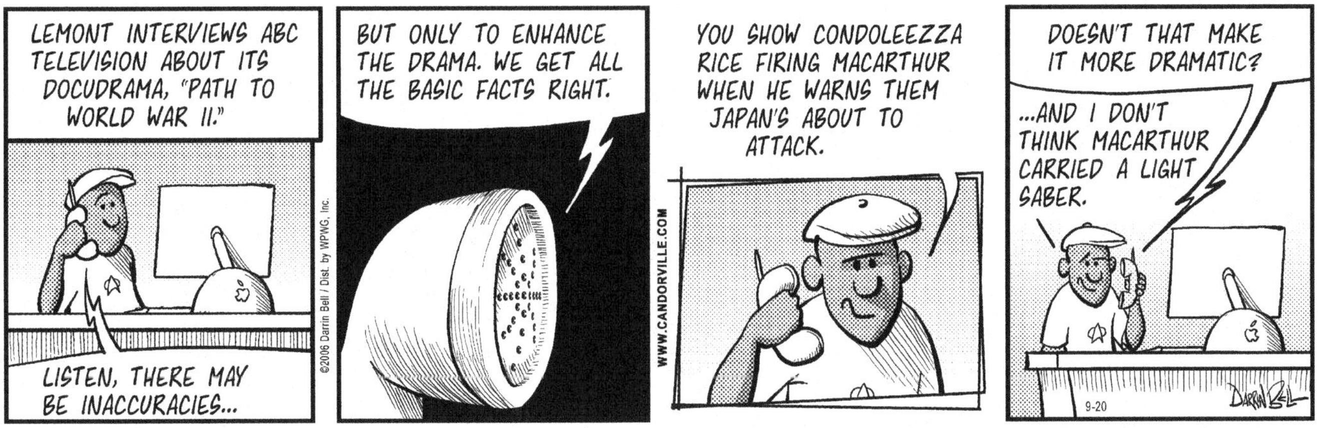
LEMONT INTERVIEWS ABC TELEVISION ABOUT ITS DOCUDRAMA, "PATH TO WORLD WAR II."
LISTEN, THERE MAY BE INACCURACIES...
©2006 Darrin Bell / Dist. by WPWG, Inc.
BUT ONLY TO ENHANCE THE DRAMA. WE GET ALL THE BASIC FACTS RIGHT.
WWW.CANDORVILLE.COM
YOU SHOW CONDOLEEZZA RICE FIRING MACARTHUR WHEN HE WARNS THEM JAPAN'S ABOUT TO ATTACK.
DOESN'T THAT MAKE IT MORE DRAMATIC?
...AND I DON'T THINK MACARTHUR CARRIED A LIGHT SABER.
9-20

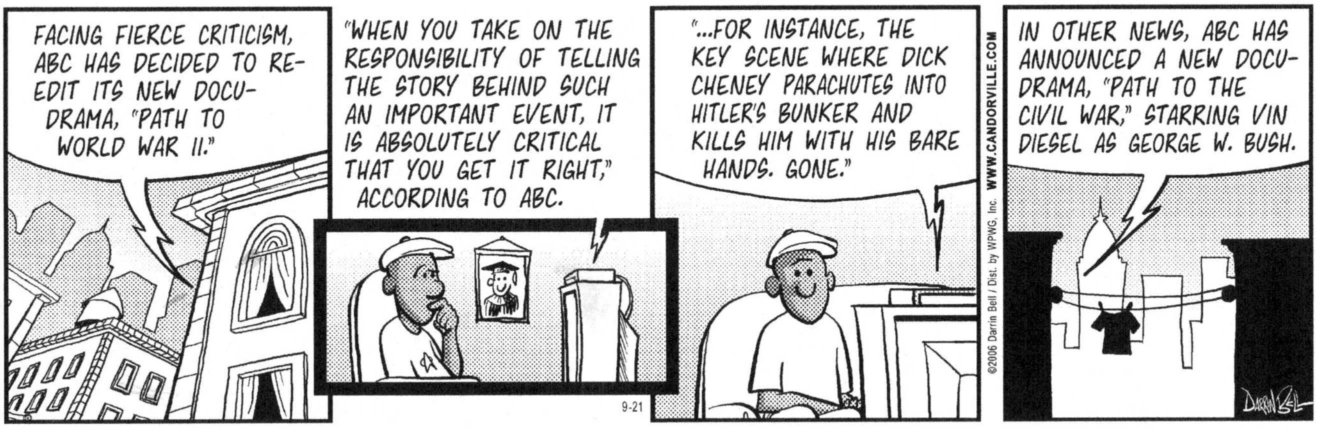
FACING FIERCE CRITICISM, ABC HAS DECIDED TO RE-EDIT ITS NEW DOCU-DRAMA, "PATH TO WORLD WAR II."
"WHEN YOU TAKE ON THE RESPONSIBILITY OF TELLING THE STORY BEHIND SUCH AN IMPORTANT EVENT, IT IS ABSOLUTELY CRITICAL THAT YOU GET IT RIGHT," ACCORDING TO ABC.
9-21
"...FOR INSTANCE, THE KEY SCENE WHERE DICK CHENEY PARACHUTES INTO HITLER'S BUNKER AND KILLS HIM WITH HIS BARE HANDS. GONE."
©2006 Darrin Bell / Dist. by WPWG, Inc. WWW.CANDORVILLE.COM
IN OTHER NEWS, ABC HAS ANNOUNCED A NEW DOCU-DRAMA, "PATH TO THE CIVIL WAR," STARRING VIN DIESEL AS GEORGE W. BUSH.

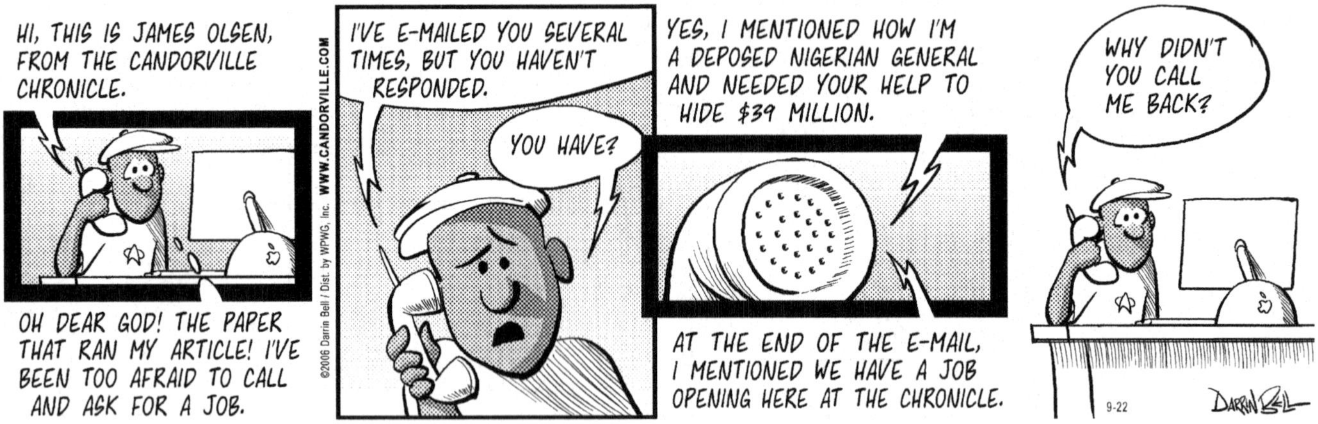
HI, THIS IS JAMES OLSEN, FROM THE CANDORVILLE CHRONICLE.
OH DEAR GOD! THE PAPER THAT RAN MY ARTICLE! I'VE BEEN TOO AFRAID TO CALL AND ASK FOR A JOB.
I'VE E-MAILED YOU SEVERAL TIMES, BUT YOU HAVEN'T RESPONDED.
YOU HAVE?
YES, I MENTIONED HOW I'M A DEPOSED NIGERIAN GENERAL AND NEEDED YOUR HELP TO HIDE $39 MILLION.
AT THE END OF THE E-MAIL, I MENTIONED WE HAVE A JOB OPENING HERE AT THE CHRONICLE.
WHY DIDN'T YOU CALL ME BACK?
©2006 Darrin Bell / Dist. by WPWG, Inc. WWW.CANDORVILLE.COM
9-22
DARRIN BELL

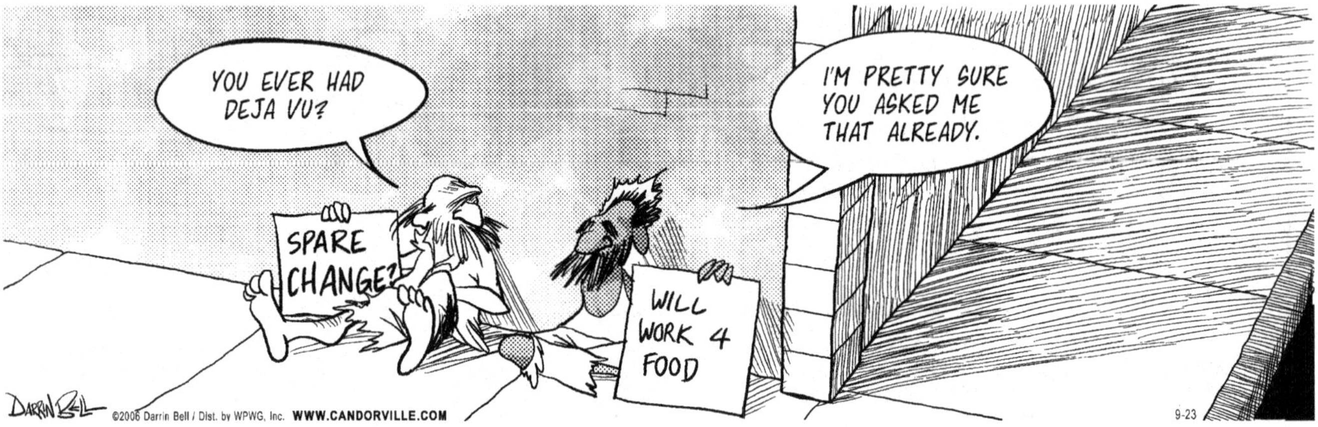
YOU EVER HAD DEJA VU?
I'M PRETTY SURE YOU ASKED ME THAT ALREADY.
SPARE CHANGE?
WILL WORK 4 FOOD
DARRIN BELL
©2006 Darrin Bell / Dist. by WPWG, Inc. WWW.CANDORVILLE.COM
9-23

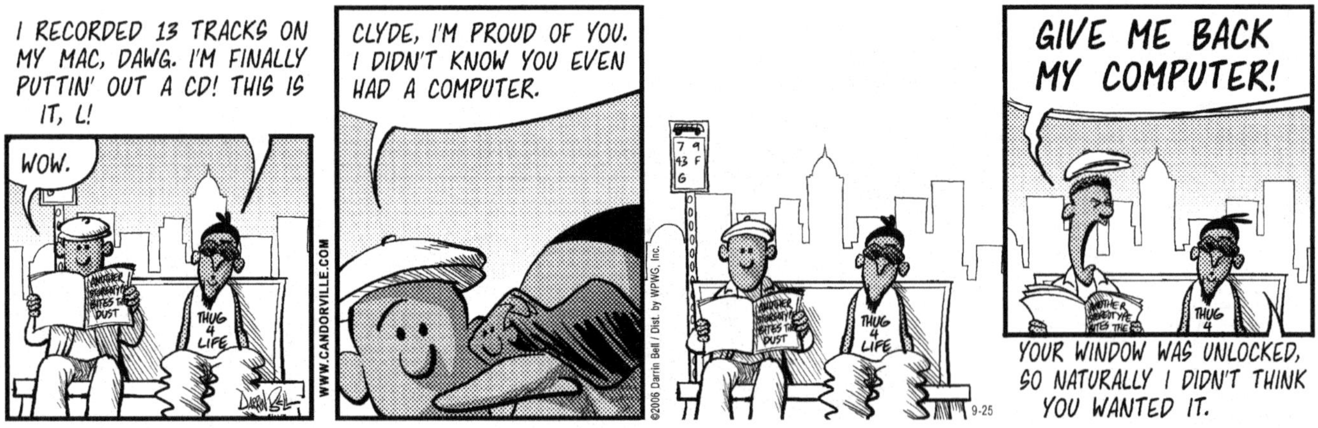
I RECORDED 13 TRACKS ON MY MAC, DAWG. I'M FINALLY PUTTIN' OUT A CD! THIS IS IT, L!
WOW.
THUG 4 LIFE
CLYDE, I'M PROUD OF YOU. I DIDN'T KNOW YOU EVEN HAD A COMPUTER.
GIVE ME BACK MY COMPUTER!
YOUR WINDOW WAS UNLOCKED, SO NATURALLY I DIDN'T THINK YOU WANTED IT.
©2006 Darrin Bell / Dist. by WPWG, Inc. WWW.CANDORVILLE.COM
9-25

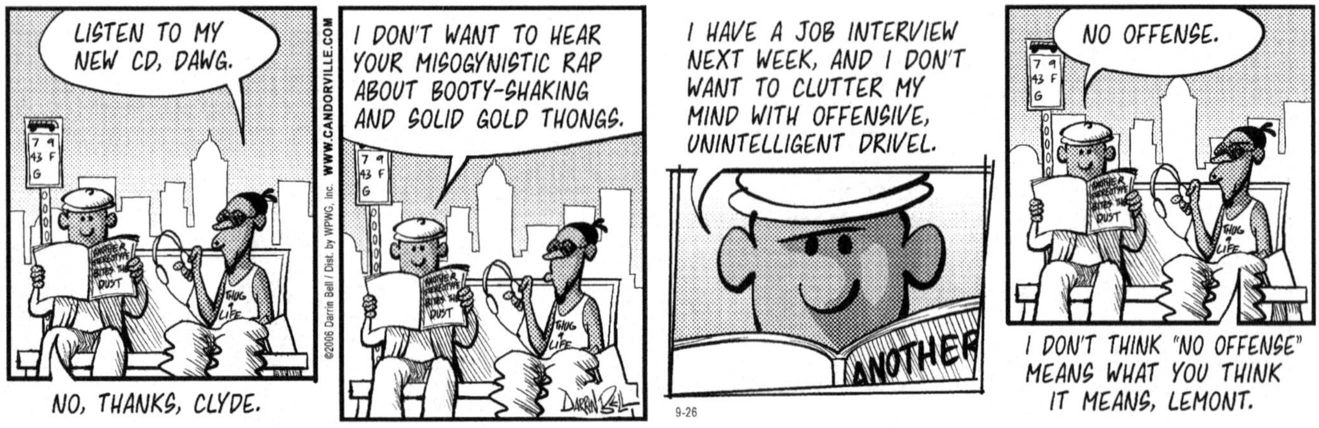
LISTEN TO MY NEW CD, DAWG.
NO, THANKS, CLYDE.
I DON'T WANT TO HEAR YOUR MISOGYNISTIC RAP ABOUT BOOTY-SHAKING AND SOLID GOLD THONGS.
I HAVE A JOB INTERVIEW NEXT WEEK, AND I DON'T WANT TO CLUTTER MY MIND WITH OFFENSIVE, UNINTELLIGENT DRIVEL.
ANOTHER
NO OFFENSE.
I DON'T THINK "NO OFFENSE" MEANS WHAT YOU THINK IT MEANS, LEMONT.
©2006 Darrin Bell / Dist. by WPWG, Inc. WWW.CANDORVILLE.COM
9-26

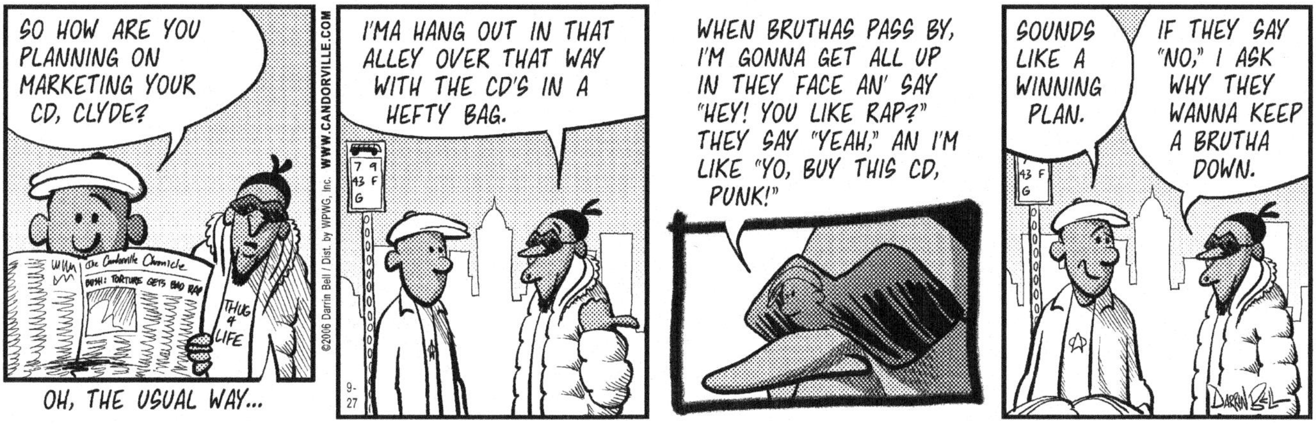
SO HOW ARE YOU PLANNING ON MARKETING YOUR CD, CLYDE?
The Candorville Chronicle
BUSH: TORTURE GETS BAD RAP
THUG 4 LIFE
OH, THE USUAL WAY...
I'MA HANG OUT IN THAT ALLEY OVER THAT WAY WITH THE CD'S IN A HEFTY BAG.
WHEN BRUTHAS PASS BY, I'M GONNA GET ALL UP IN THEY FACE AN' SAY "HEY! YOU LIKE RAP?" THEY SAY "YEAH," AN I'M LIKE "YO, BUY THIS CD, PUNK!"
SOUNDS LIKE A WINNING PLAN.
IF THEY SAY "NO," I ASK WHY THEY WANNA KEEP A BRUTHA DOWN.
©2006 Darrin Bell / Dist. by WPWG, Inc. WWW.CANDORVILLE.COM
9-27
DARRIN BELL

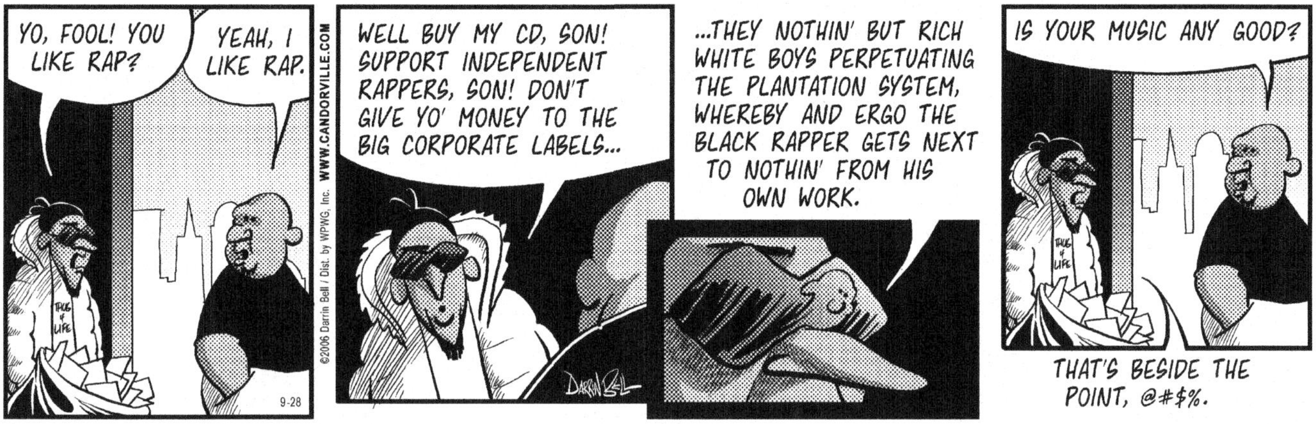
YO, FOOL! YOU LIKE RAP?
YEAH, I LIKE RAP.
WELL BUY MY CD, SON! SUPPORT INDEPENDENT RAPPERS, SON! DON'T GIVE YO' MONEY TO THE BIG CORPORATE LABELS...
...THEY NOTHIN' BUT RICH WHITE BOYS PERPETUATING THE PLANTATION SYSTEM, WHEREBY AND ERGO THE BLACK RAPPER GETS NEXT TO NOTHIN' FROM HIS OWN WORK.
IS YOUR MUSIC ANY GOOD?
THAT'S BESIDE THE POINT, @#$%.
©2006 Darrin Bell / Dist. by WPWG, Inc. WWW.CANDORVILLE.COM
9-28
DARRIN BELL

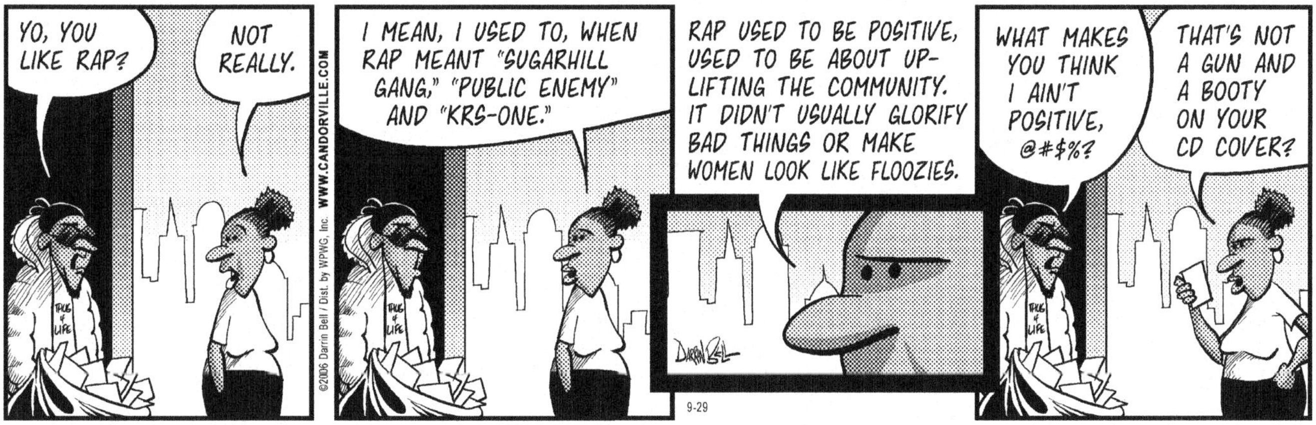
YO, YOU LIKE RAP?
NOT REALLY.
I MEAN, I USED TO, WHEN RAP MEANT "SUGARHILL GANG," "PUBLIC ENEMY" AND "KRS-ONE."
RAP USED TO BE POSITIVE, USED TO BE ABOUT UPLIFTING THE COMMUNITY. IT DIDN'T USUALLY GLORIFY BAD THINGS OR MAKE WOMEN LOOK LIKE FLOOZIES.
WHAT MAKES YOU THINK I AIN'T POSITIVE, @#$%?
THAT'S NOT A GUN AND A BOOTY ON YOUR CD COVER?
©2006 Darrin Bell / Dist. by WPWG, Inc. WWW.CANDORVILLE.COM
9-29
DARRIN BELL

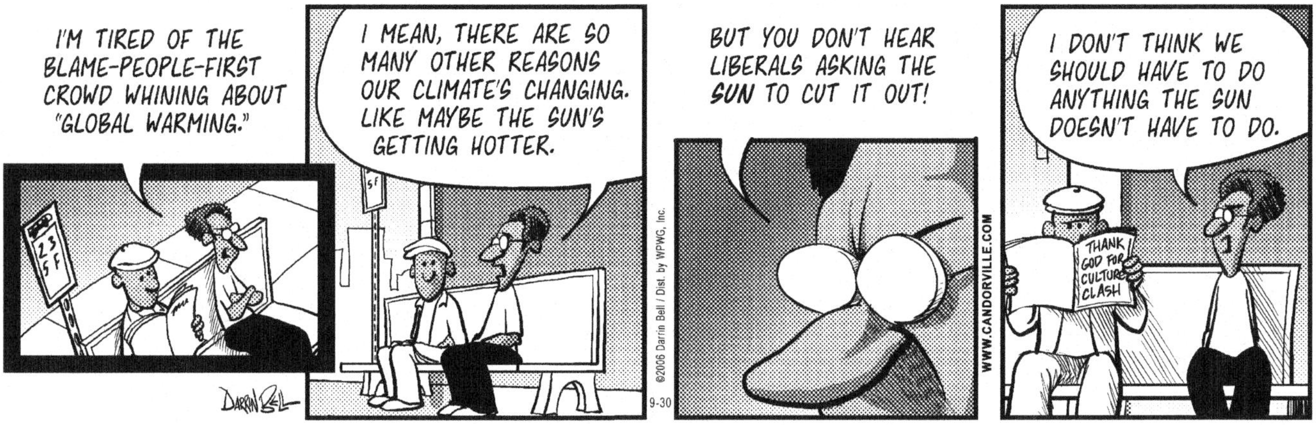
I'M TIRED OF THE BLAME-PEOPLE-FIRST CROWD WHINING ABOUT "GLOBAL WARMING."
I MEAN, THERE ARE SO MANY OTHER REASONS OUR CLIMATE'S CHANGING. LIKE MAYBE THE SUN'S GETTING HOTTER.
BUT YOU DON'T HEAR LIBERALS ASKING THE SUN TO CUT IT OUT!
I DON'T THINK WE SHOULD HAVE TO DO ANYTHING THE SUN DOESN'T HAVE TO DO.
THANK GOD FOR CULTURE CLASH
©2006 Darrin Bell / Dist. by WPWG, Inc. WWW.CANDORVILLE.COM
9-30
DARRIN BELL

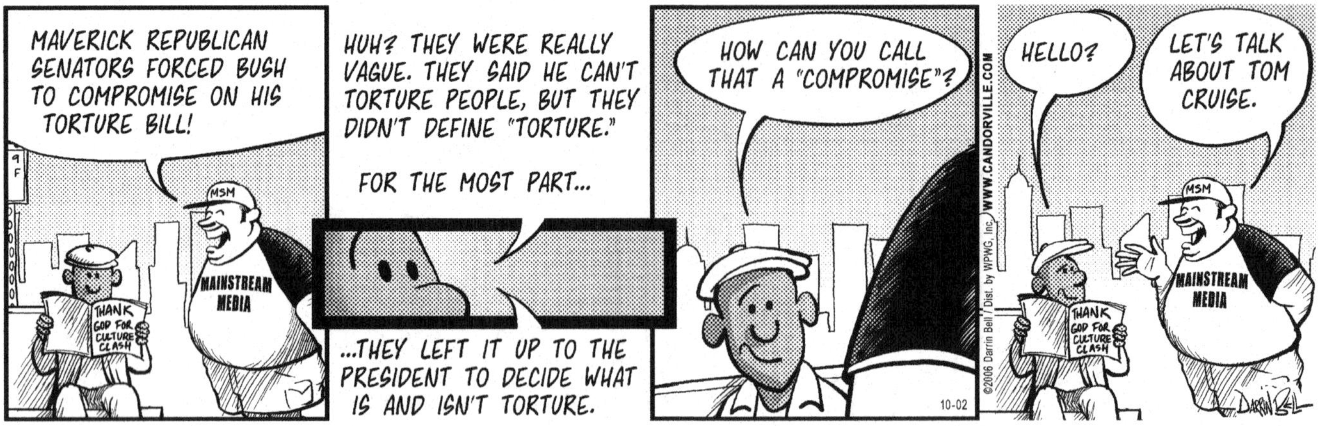
MAVERICK REPUBLICAN SENATORS FORCED BUSH TO COMPROMISE ON HIS TORTURE BILL!
HUH? THEY WERE REALLY VAGUE. THEY SAID HE CAN'T TORTURE PEOPLE, BUT THEY DIDN'T DEFINE "TORTURE."
FOR THE MOST PART...
...THEY LEFT IT UP TO THE PRESIDENT TO DECIDE WHAT IS AND ISN'T TORTURE.
HOW CAN YOU CALL THAT A "COMPROMISE"?
HELLO?
LET'S TALK ABOUT TOM CRUISE.
MSM
MAINSTREAM MEDIA
THANK GOD FOR CULTURE CLASH
©2006 Darrin Bell / Dist. by WPWG, Inc.
WWW.CANDORVILLE.COM
10-02

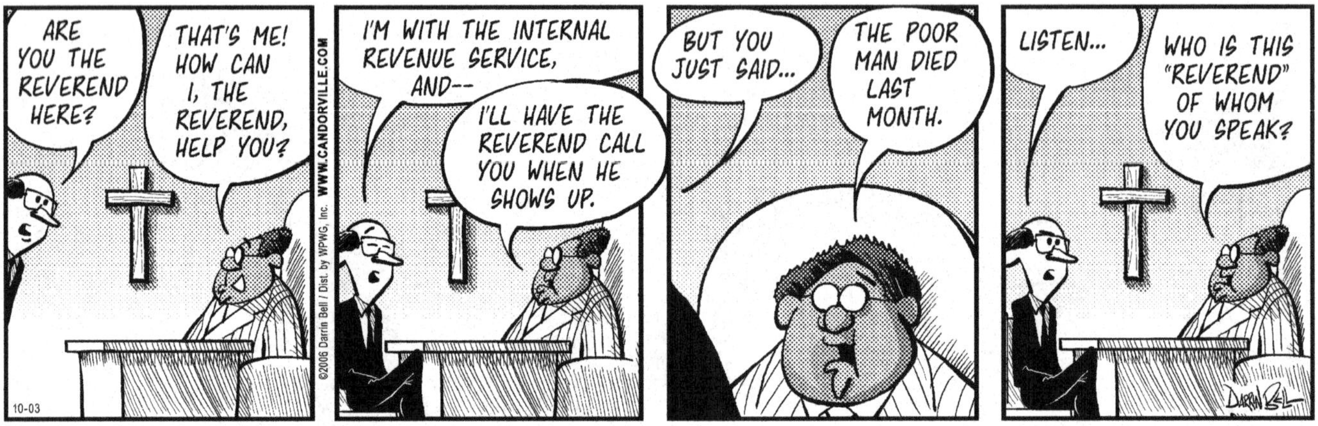
ARE YOU THE REVEREND HERE?
THAT'S ME! HOW CAN I, THE REVEREND, HELP YOU?
I'M WITH THE INTERNAL REVENUE SERVICE, AND--
I'LL HAVE THE REVEREND CALL YOU WHEN HE SHOWS UP.
BUT YOU JUST SAID...
THE POOR MAN DIED LAST MONTH.
LISTEN...
WHO IS THIS "REVEREND" OF WHOM YOU SPEAK?
©2006 Darrin Bell / Dist. by WPWG, Inc.
WWW.CANDORVILLE.COM
10-03

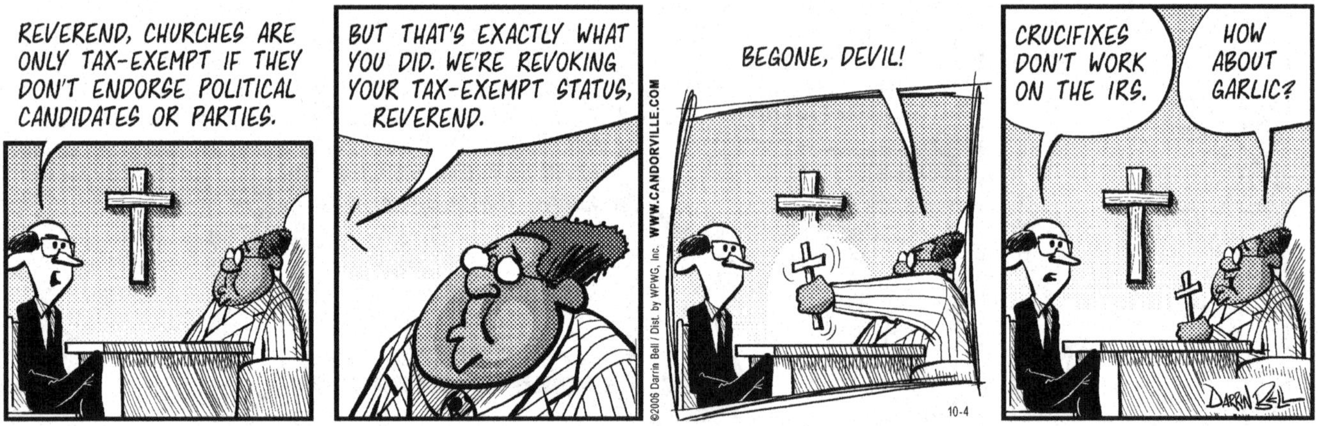
REVEREND, CHURCHES ARE ONLY TAX-EXEMPT IF THEY DON'T ENDORSE POLITICAL CANDIDATES OR PARTIES.
BUT THAT'S EXACTLY WHAT YOU DID. WE'RE REVOKING YOUR TAX-EXEMPT STATUS, REVEREND.
BEGONE, DEVIL!
CRUCIFIXES DON'T WORK ON THE IRS.
HOW ABOUT GARLIC?
©2006 Darrin Bell / Dist. by WPWG, Inc.
WWW.CANDORVILLE.COM
10-4

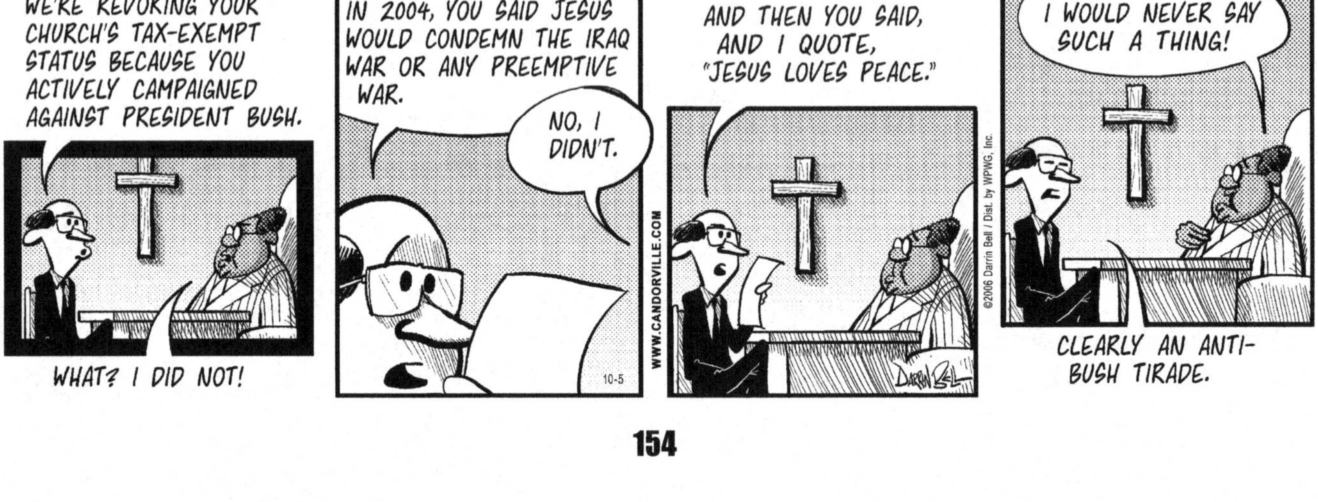
WE'RE REVOKING YOUR CHURCH'S TAX-EXEMPT STATUS BECAUSE YOU ACTIVELY CAMPAIGNED AGAINST PRESIDENT BUSH.
WHAT? I DID NOT!
IN 2004, YOU SAID JESUS WOULD CONDEMN THE IRAQ WAR OR ANY PREEMPTIVE WAR.
NO, I DIDN'T.
AND THEN YOU SAID, AND I QUOTE, "JESUS LOVES PEACE."
I WOULD NEVER SAY SUCH A THING!
CLEARLY AN ANTI-BUSH TIRADE.
©2006 Darrin Bell / Dist. by WPWG, Inc.
WWW.CANDORVILLE.COM
10-5

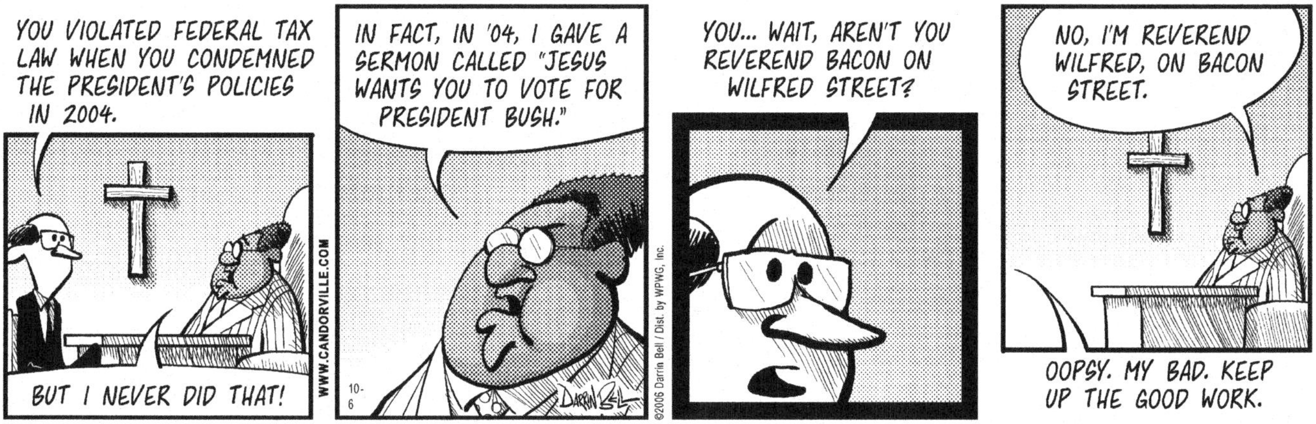
YOU VIOLATED FEDERAL TAX LAW WHEN YOU CONDEMNED THE PRESIDENT'S POLICIES IN 2004.
BUT I NEVER DID THAT!
IN FACT, IN '04, I GAVE A SERMON CALLED "JESUS WANTS YOU TO VOTE FOR PRESIDENT BUSH."
YOU... WAIT, AREN'T YOU REVEREND BACON ON WILFRED STREET?
NO, I'M REVEREND WILFRED, ON BACON STREET.
OOPSY. MY BAD. KEEP UP THE GOOD WORK.
WWW.CANDORVILLE.COM
10-6
DARRIN BELL
©2006 Darrin Bell / Dist. by WPWG, Inc.

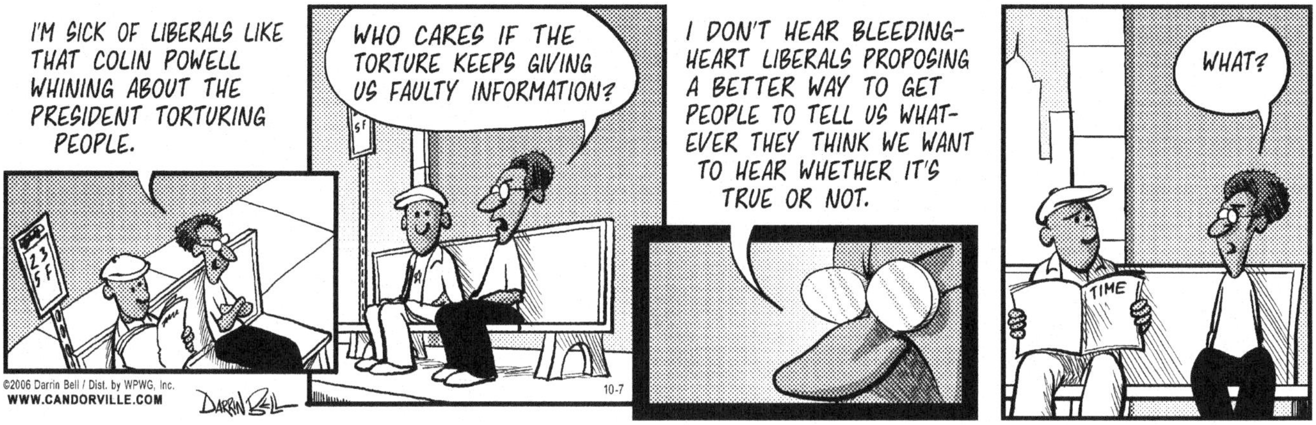
I'M SICK OF LIBERALS LIKE THAT COLIN POWELL WHINING ABOUT THE PRESIDENT TORTURING PEOPLE.
WHO CARES IF THE TORTURE KEEPS GIVING US FAULTY INFORMATION?
I DON'T HEAR BLEEDING-HEART LIBERALS PROPOSING A BETTER WAY TO GET PEOPLE TO TELL US WHAT-EVER THEY THINK WE WANT TO HEAR WHETHER IT'S TRUE OR NOT.
WHAT?
TIME
©2006 Darrin Bell / Dist. by WPWG, Inc.
WWW.CANDORVILLE.COM
DARRIN BELL
10-7

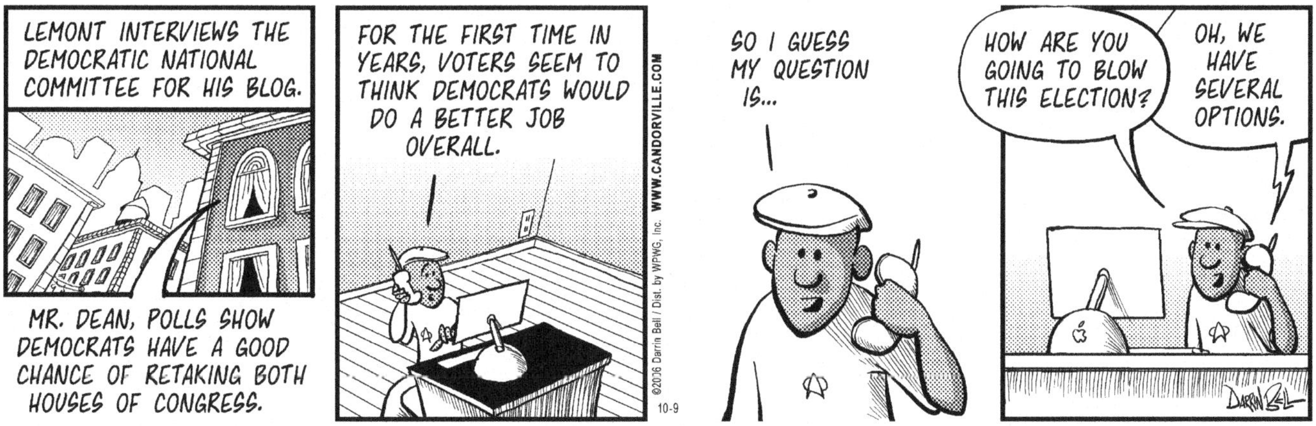
LEMONT INTERVIEWS THE DEMOCRATIC NATIONAL COMMITTEE FOR HIS BLOG.
MR. DEAN, POLLS SHOW DEMOCRATS HAVE A GOOD CHANCE OF RETAKING BOTH HOUSES OF CONGRESS.
FOR THE FIRST TIME IN YEARS, VOTERS SEEM TO THINK DEMOCRATS WOULD DO A BETTER JOB OVERALL.
WWW.CANDORVILLE.COM
©2006 Darrin Bell / Dist. by WPWG, Inc.
10-9
SO I GUESS MY QUESTION IS...
HOW ARE YOU GOING TO BLOW THIS ELECTION?
OH, WE HAVE SEVERAL OPTIONS.
DARRIN BELL

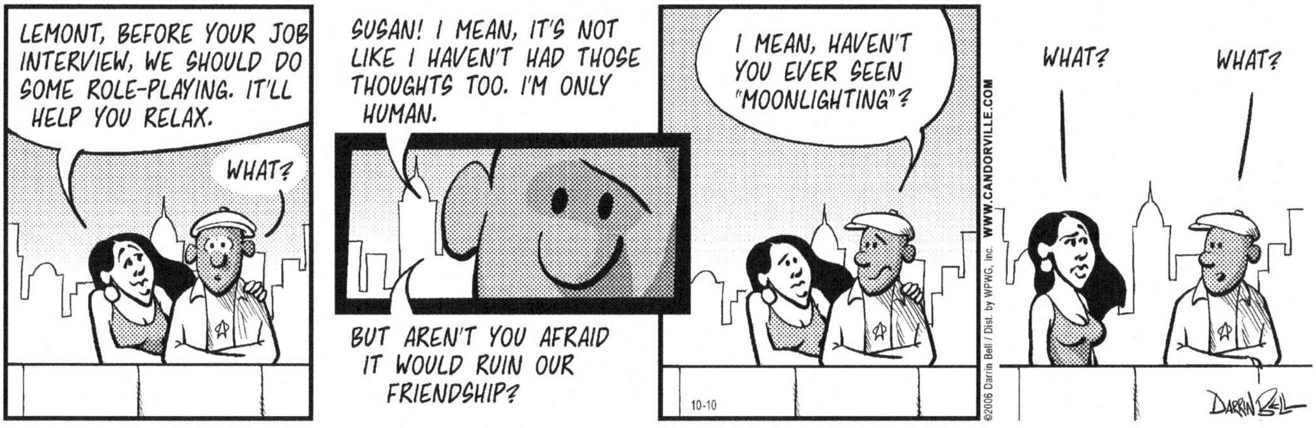
LEMONT, BEFORE YOUR JOB INTERVIEW, WE SHOULD DO SOME ROLE-PLAYING. IT'LL HELP YOU RELAX.
WHAT?
SUSAN! I MEAN, IT'S NOT LIKE I HAVEN'T HAD THOSE THOUGHTS TOO. I'M ONLY HUMAN.
BUT AREN'T YOU AFRAID IT WOULD RUIN OUR FRIENDSHIP?
I MEAN, HAVEN'T YOU EVER SEEN "MOONLIGHTING"?
10-10
WWW.CANDORVILLE.COM
©2006 Darrin Bell / Dist. by WPWG, Inc.
WHAT?
WHAT?
DARRIN BELL

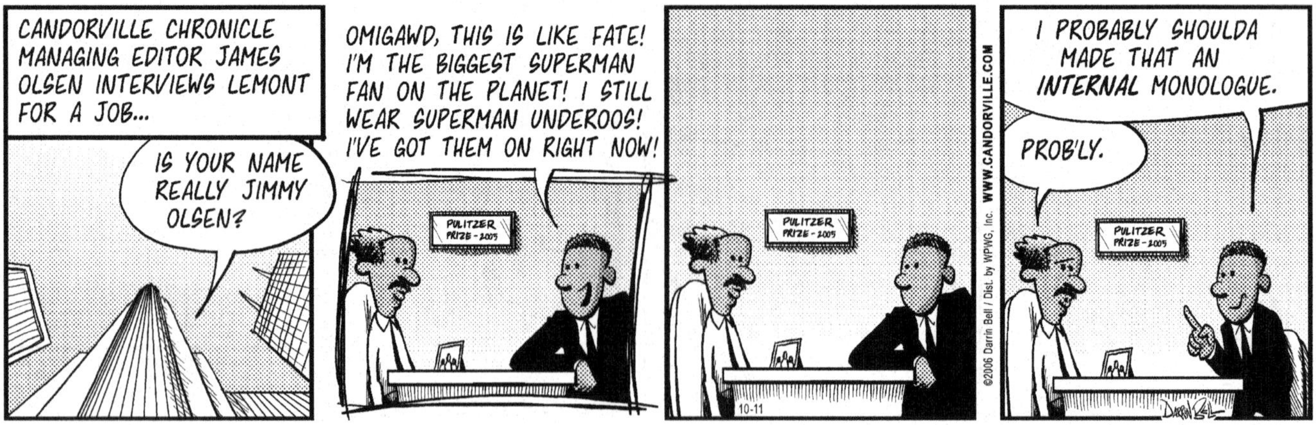
CANDORVILLE CHRONICLE MANAGING EDITOR JAMES OLSEN INTERVIEWS LEMONT FOR A JOB...
IS YOUR NAME REALLY JIMMY OLSEN?
OMIGAWD, THIS IS LIKE FATE! I'M THE BIGGEST SUPERMAN FAN ON THE PLANET! I STILL WEAR SUPERMAN UNDEROOS! I'VE GOT THEM ON RIGHT NOW!
PULITZER PRIZE - 2005
10-11
©2006 Darrin Bell / Dist. by WPWG, Inc. WWW.CANDORVILLE.COM
I PROBABLY SHOULDA MADE THAT AN *INTERNAL* MONOLOGUE.
PROB'LY.
DARRIN BELL

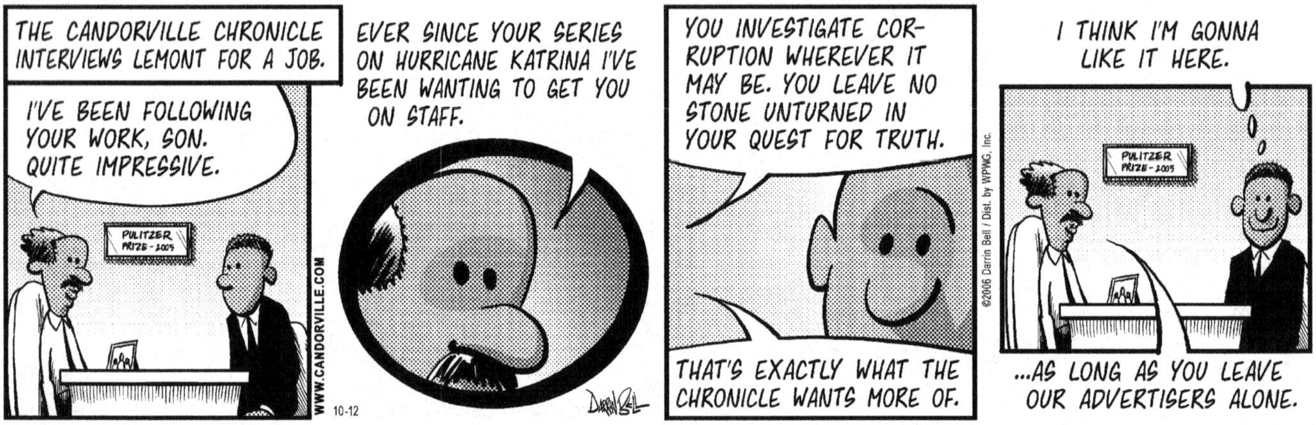
THE CANDORVILLE CHRONICLE INTERVIEWS LEMONT FOR A JOB.
I'VE BEEN FOLLOWING YOUR WORK, SON. QUITE IMPRESSIVE.
PULITZER PRIZE - 2005
WWW.CANDORVILLE.COM
10-12
EVER SINCE YOUR SERIES ON HURRICANE KATRINA I'VE BEEN WANTING TO GET YOU ON STAFF.
DARRIN BELL
YOU INVESTIGATE CORRUPTION WHEREVER IT MAY BE. YOU LEAVE NO STONE UNTURNED IN YOUR QUEST FOR TRUTH.
THAT'S EXACTLY WHAT THE CHRONICLE WANTS MORE OF.
©2006 Darrin Bell / Dist. by WPWG, Inc.
I THINK I'M GONNA LIKE IT HERE.
...AS LONG AS YOU LEAVE OUR ADVERTISERS ALONE.

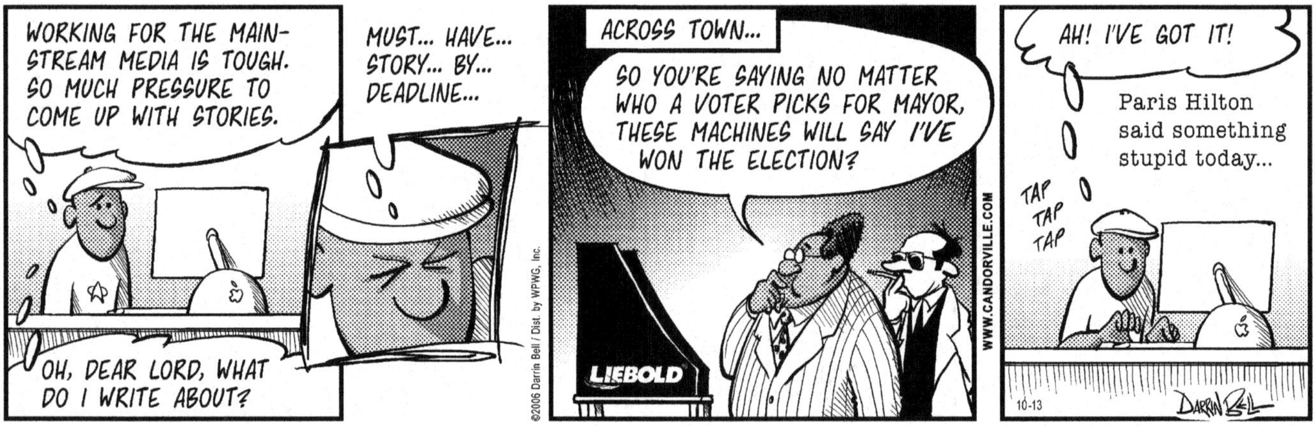
WORKING FOR THE MAINSTREAM MEDIA IS TOUGH. SO MUCH PRESSURE TO COME UP WITH STORIES.
OH, DEAR LORD, WHAT DO I WRITE ABOUT?
MUST... HAVE... STORY... BY... DEADLINE...
©2006 Darrin Bell / Dist. by WPWG, Inc.
ACROSS TOWN...
SO YOU'RE SAYING NO MATTER WHO A VOTER PICKS FOR MAYOR, THESE MACHINES WILL SAY *I'VE* WON THE ELECTION?
LIEBOLD
WWW.CANDORVILLE.COM
AH! I'VE GOT IT!
Paris Hilton said something stupid today...
TAP TAP TAP
10-13
DARRIN BELL

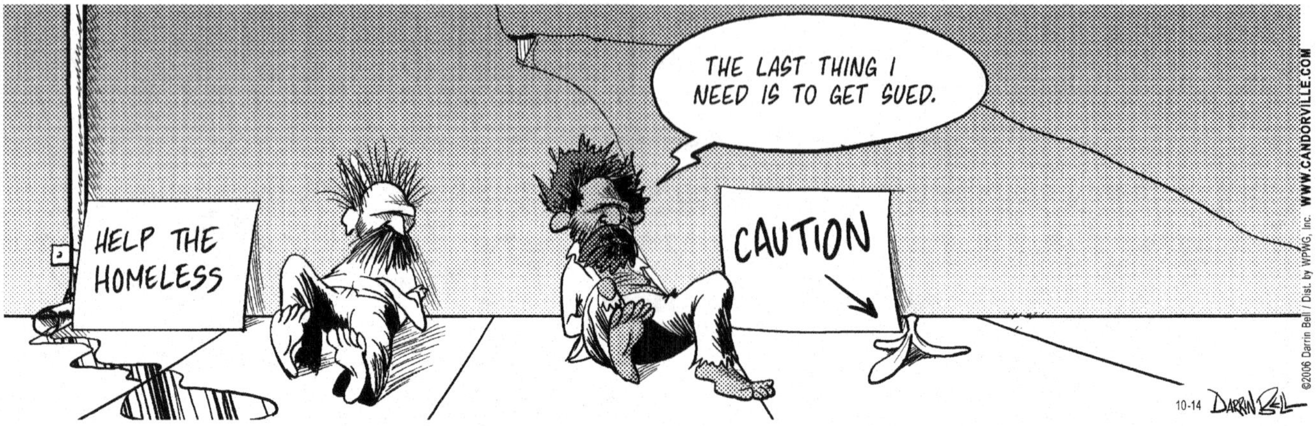
THE LAST THING I NEED IS TO GET SUED.
HELP THE HOMELESS
CAUTION
©2006 Darrin Bell / Dist. by WPWG, Inc. WWW.CANDORVILLE.COM
10-14
DARRIN BELL

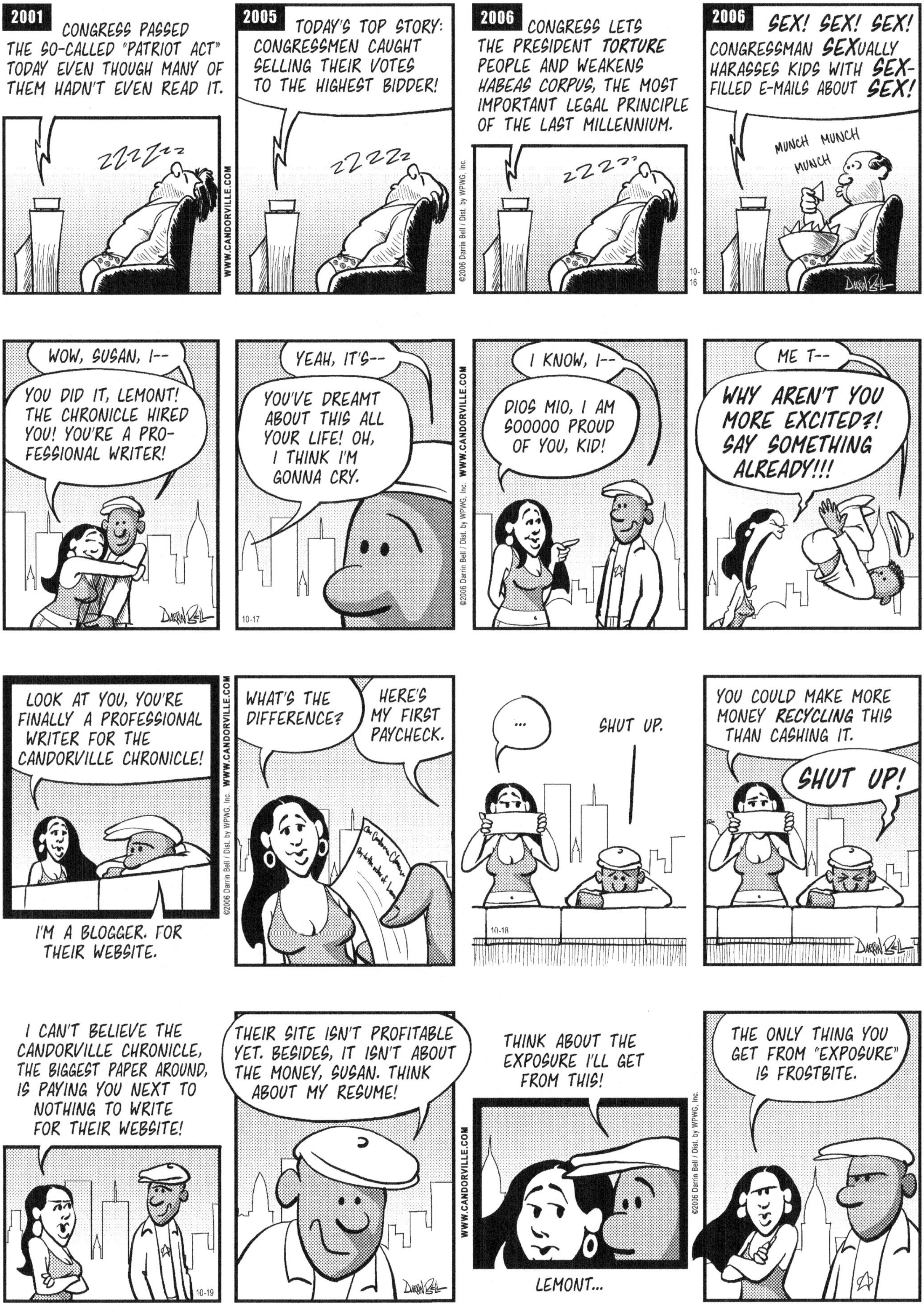
2001
CONGRESS PASSED THE SO-CALLED "PATRIOT ACT" TODAY EVEN THOUGH MANY OF THEM HADN'T EVEN READ IT.
ZZZZzz
WWW.CANDORVILLE.COM
2005
TODAY'S TOP STORY: CONGRESSMEN CAUGHT SELLING THEIR VOTES TO THE HIGHEST BIDDER!
ZZZZZz
©2006 Darrin Bell / Dist. by WPWG, Inc.
2006
CONGRESS LETS THE PRESIDENT TORTURE PEOPLE AND WEAKENS HABEAS CORPUS, THE MOST IMPORTANT LEGAL PRINCIPLE OF THE LAST MILLENNIUM.
ZZZZ
10-16
2006
SEX! SEX! SEX! CONGRESSMAN SEXUALLY HARASSES KIDS WITH SEX-FILLED E-MAILS ABOUT SEX!
MUNCH MUNCH
MUNCH
DARRIN BELL
WOW, SUSAN, I--
YOU DID IT, LEMONT! THE CHRONICLE HIRED YOU! YOU'RE A PROFESSIONAL WRITER!
DARRIN BELL
YEAH, IT'S--
YOU'VE DREAMT ABOUT THIS ALL YOUR LIFE! OH, I THINK I'M GONNA CRY.
10-17
WWW.CANDORVILLE.COM
©2006 Darrin Bell / Dist. by WPWG, Inc.
I KNOW, I--
DIOS MIO, I AM SOOOOO PROUD OF YOU, KID!
ME T--
WHY AREN'T YOU MORE EXCITED?! SAY SOMETHING ALREADY!!!
LOOK AT YOU, YOU'RE FINALLY A PROFESSIONAL WRITER FOR THE CANDORVILLE CHRONICLE!
I'M A BLOGGER. FOR THEIR WEBSITE.
WWW.CANDORVILLE.COM
©2006 Darrin Bell / Dist. by WPWG, Inc.
WHAT'S THE DIFFERENCE?
HERE'S MY FIRST PAYCHECK.
...
SHUT UP.
10-18
YOU COULD MAKE MORE MONEY RECYCLING THIS THAN CASHING IT.
SHUT UP!
DARRIN BELL
I CAN'T BELIEVE THE CANDORVILLE CHRONICLE, THE BIGGEST PAPER AROUND, IS PAYING YOU NEXT TO NOTHING TO WRITE FOR THEIR WEBSITE!
10-19
THEIR SITE ISN'T PROFITABLE YET. BESIDES, IT ISN'T ABOUT THE MONEY, SUSAN. THINK ABOUT MY RESUME!
DARRIN BELL
WWW.CANDORVILLE.COM
THINK ABOUT THE EXPOSURE I'LL GET FROM THIS!
LEMONT...
THE ONLY THING YOU GET FROM "EXPOSURE" IS FROSTBITE.
©2006 Darrin Bell / Dist. by WPWG, Inc.

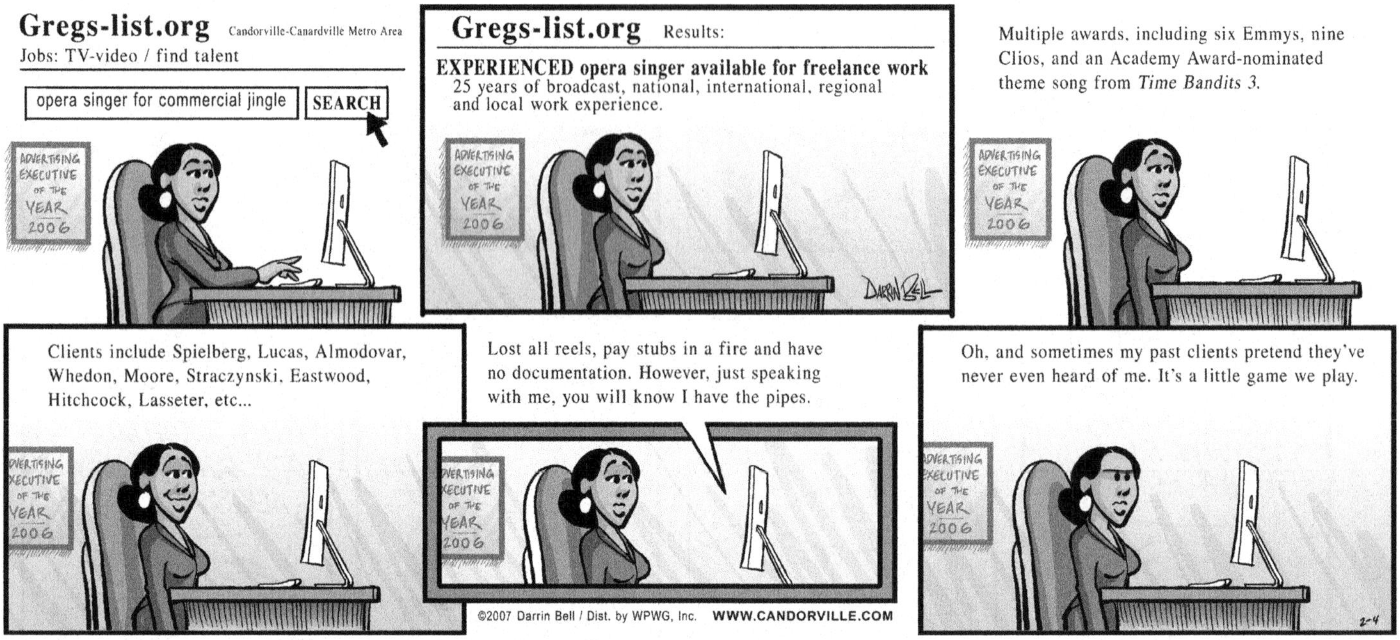
Gregs-list.org Candorville-Canardville Metro Area
Jobs: TV-video / find talent
opera singer for commercial jingle
SEARCH
ADVERTISING EXECUTIVE OF THE YEAR 2006
Gregs-list.org Results:
EXPERIENCED opera singer available for freelance work
25 years of broadcast, national, international, regional and local work experience.
Multiple awards, including six Emmys, nine Clios, and an Academy Award-nominated theme song from Time Bandits 3.
Clients include Spielberg, Lucas, Almodovar, Whedon, Moore, Straczynski, Eastwood, Hitchcock, Lasseter, etc...
Lost all reels, pay stubs in a fire and have no documentation. However, just speaking with me, you will know I have the pipes.
Oh, and sometimes my past clients pretend they've never even heard of me. It's a little game we play.
©2007 Darrin Bell / Dist. by WPWG, Inc. WWW.CANDORVILLE.COM

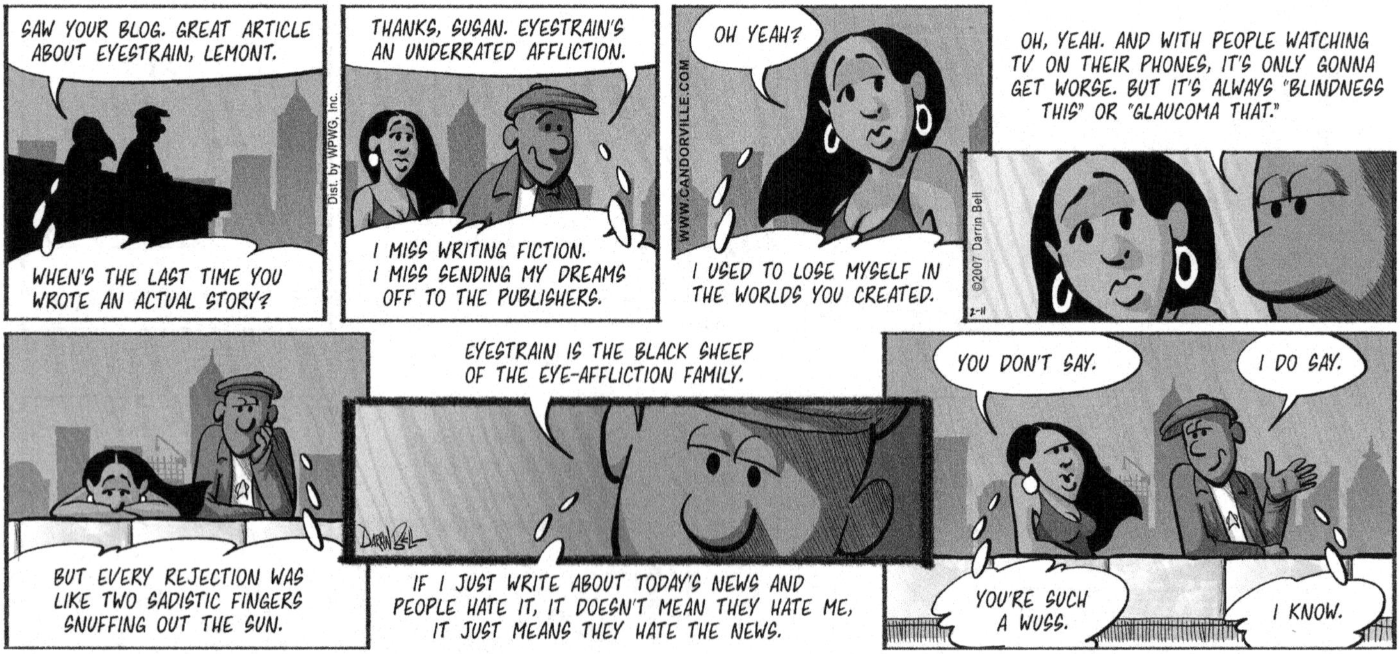
SAW YOUR BLOG. GREAT ARTICLE ABOUT EYESTRAIN, LEMONT.
WHEN'S THE LAST TIME YOU WROTE AN ACTUAL STORY?
THANKS, SUSAN. EYESTRAIN'S AN UNDERRATED AFFLICTION.
I MISS WRITING FICTION. I MISS SENDING MY DREAMS OFF TO THE PUBLISHERS.
OH YEAH?
I USED TO LOSE MYSELF IN THE WORLDS YOU CREATED.
OH, YEAH. AND WITH PEOPLE WATCHING TV ON THEIR PHONES, IT'S ONLY GONNA GET WORSE. BUT IT'S ALWAYS "BLINDNESS THIS" OR "GLAUCOMA THAT."
BUT EVERY REJECTION WAS LIKE TWO SADISTIC FINGERS SNUFFING OUT THE SUN.
EYESTRAIN IS THE BLACK SHEEP OF THE EYE-AFFLICTION FAMILY.
IF I JUST WRITE ABOUT TODAY'S NEWS AND PEOPLE HATE IT, IT DOESN'T MEAN THEY HATE ME, IT JUST MEANS THEY HATE THE NEWS.
YOU DON'T SAY.
I DO SAY.
YOU'RE SUCH A WUSS.
I KNOW.
Dist. by WPWG, Inc. WWW.CANDORVILLE.COM ©2007 Darrin Bell

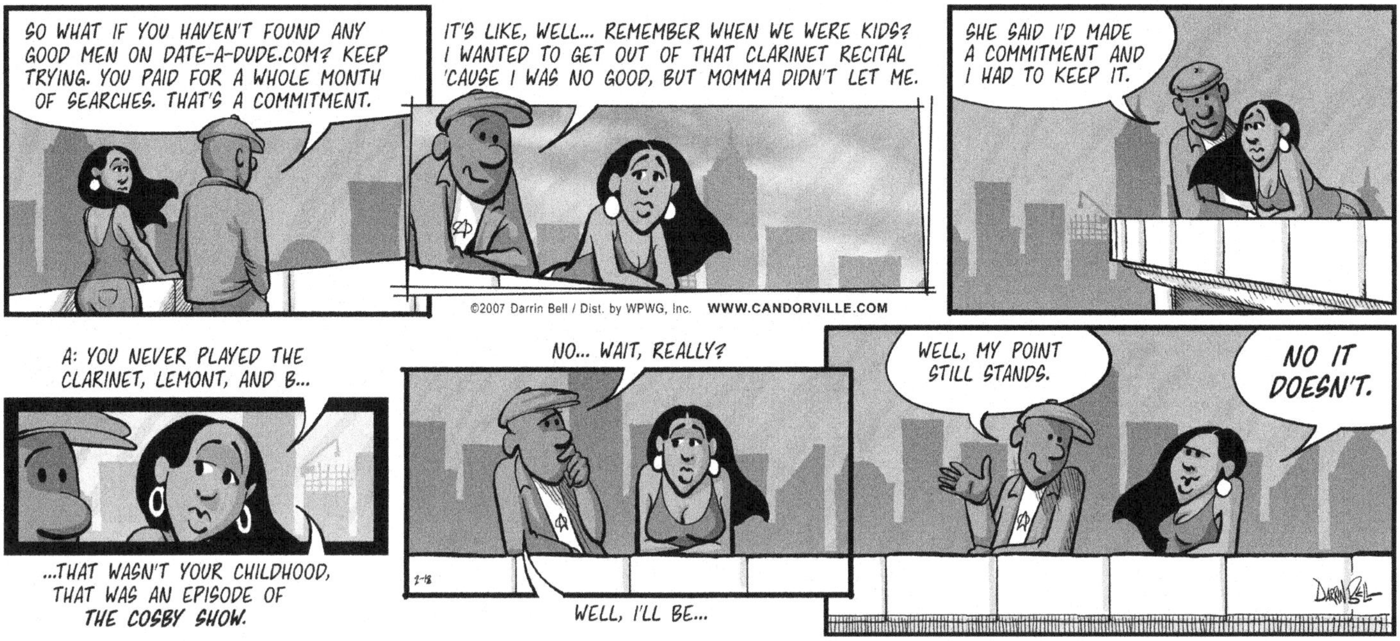
SO WHAT IF YOU HAVEN'T FOUND ANY GOOD MEN ON DATE-A-DUDE.COM? KEEP TRYING. YOU PAID FOR A WHOLE MONTH OF SEARCHES. THAT'S A COMMITMENT.
IT'S LIKE, WELL... REMEMBER WHEN WE WERE KIDS? I WANTED TO GET OUT OF THAT CLARINET RECITAL 'CAUSE I WAS NO GOOD, BUT MOMMA DIDN'T LET ME.
SHE SAID I'D MADE A COMMITMENT AND I HAD TO KEEP IT.
©2007 Darrin Bell / Dist. by WPWG, Inc. WWW.CANDORVILLE.COM
A: YOU NEVER PLAYED THE CLARINET, LEMONT, AND B...
...THAT WASN'T YOUR CHILDHOOD, THAT WAS AN EPISODE OF THE COSBY SHOW.
NO... WAIT, REALLY?
WELL, I'LL BE...
WELL, MY POINT STILL STANDS.
NO IT DOESN'T.
DARRIN BELL

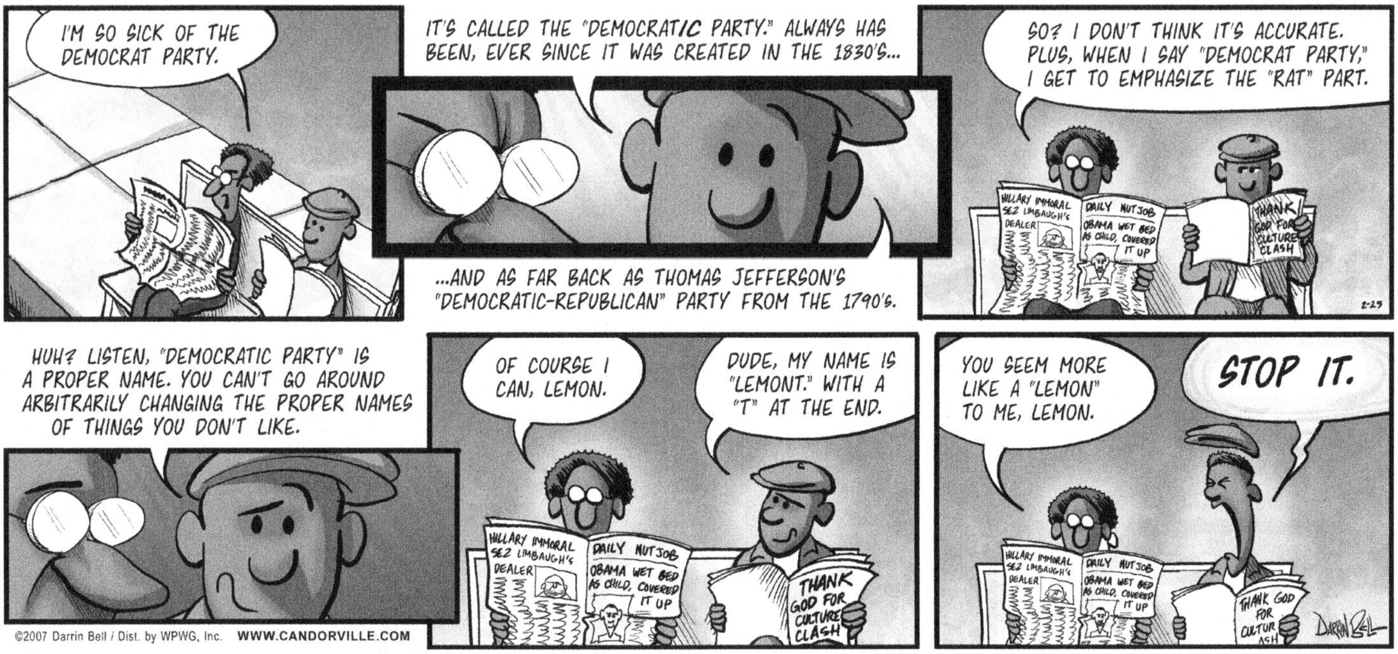
I'M SO SICK OF THE DEMOCRAT PARTY.
IT'S CALLED THE "DEMOCRATIC PARTY." ALWAYS HAS BEEN, EVER SINCE IT WAS CREATED IN THE 1830'S...
...AND AS FAR BACK AS THOMAS JEFFERSON'S "DEMOCRATIC-REPUBLICAN" PARTY FROM THE 1790'S.
SO? I DON'T THINK IT'S ACCURATE. PLUS, WHEN I SAY "DEMOCRAT PARTY," I GET TO EMPHASIZE THE "RAT" PART.
HILLARY IMMORAL SEZ LIMBAUGH'S DEALER
DAILY NUTJOB
OBAMA WET BED AS CHILD, COVERED IT UP
THANK GOD FOR CULTURE CLASH
HUH? LISTEN, "DEMOCRATIC PARTY" IS A PROPER NAME. YOU CAN'T GO AROUND ARBITRARILY CHANGING THE PROPER NAMES OF THINGS YOU DON'T LIKE.
©2007 Darrin Bell / Dist. by WPWG, Inc. WWW.CANDORVILLE.COM
OF COURSE I CAN, LEMON.
DUDE, MY NAME IS "LEMONT." WITH A "T" AT THE END.
YOU SEEM MORE LIKE A "LEMON" TO ME, LEMON.
STOP IT.
DARRIN BELL

CAN YOU BELIEVE IT'S BEEN EXACTLY THREE YEARS SINCE I BROUGHT YOU GUYS HERE? THREE YEARS.

THREE LONG YEARS FILLED WITH FUTILE WARS, STOLEN ELECTIONS, LOST CITIES, NEW JOBS, RECEDING HAIRLINES, BABIES BORN, ICONS DYING...

ROSCOE'S RIB SHACK

MENU

WWW.CANDORVILLE.COM

10-20

THREE WHOLE YEARS, YOU GUYS.

©2006 Darrin Bell / Dist. by WPWG, Inc.

LEMONT, I'M SURE THAT'S NOT THE SAME GUM YOU PUT UNDER THE TABLE.

DON'T Y'ALL EVER CLEAN UP IN HERE?

NOW I LAY ME DOWN TO SLEEP, I PRAY THE LORD MY SOUL TO KEEP.

IF I GET E-MAIL 'FORE I WAKE...

I PRAY THE LORD DON'T LET IT BE FROM A PERVERTED OLD CONGRESSMAN!

TOO MUCH CNN FOR THIS GUY...

©2006 Darrin Bell / Dist. by WPWG, Inc.

WWW.CANDORVILLE.COM

10-21

FOR THE LAST TIME, NO, I DON'T THINK THAT SIGN MAKES YOU LOOK FAT.

WILL WORK 4 FOOD

©2006 Darrin Bell / Dist. by WPWG, Inc.

WWW.CANDORVILLE.COM

10-23

IN OTHER NEWS, THE LOCAL PROFESSIONAL JOURNALISTS SOCIETY GAVE THEIR ANNUAL "COURAGE" AWARD TO LEMONT BROWN TODAY...

ZZZZ Z

LEMONT

...FOR HIS POWERFUL EXPOSÉ THAT LED TO THE RESIGNATION OF MAYOR PATSY ERNESTO.

WHAT THE?! I WON AN AWARD? OH DEAR LORD... I'VE GOTTA TELL SUSAN!

WWW.CANDORVILLE.COM

©2006 Darrin Bell / Dist. by WPWG, Inc.

I'VE GOTTA TELL--

BROWN, PICTURED HERE, ACCEPTED THE AWARD AT A BANQUET THIS MORNING.

LEMONT

--CLYDE?

YO, I WANNA THANK ALL MY &#*$&?%.

LEMONT

10-24

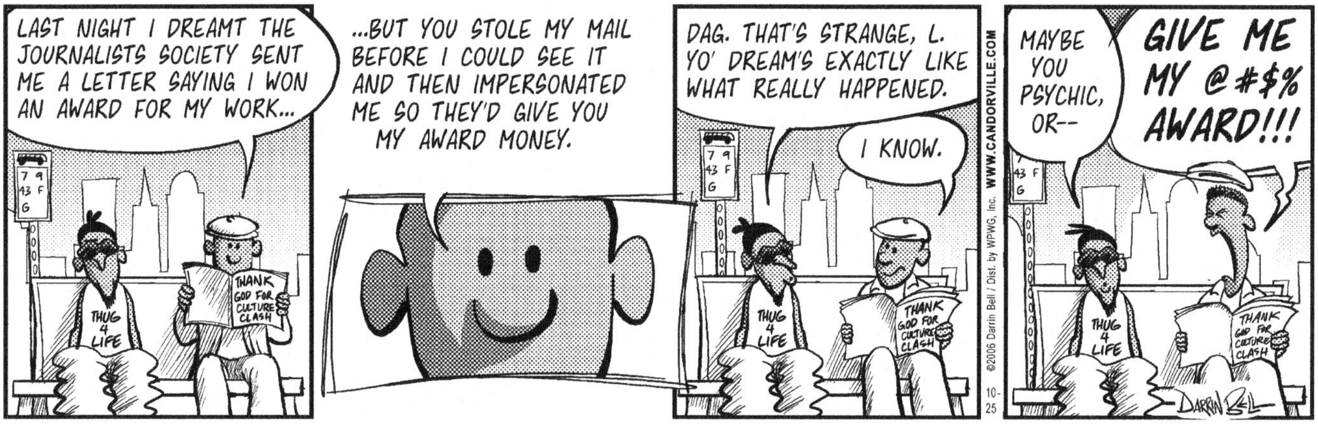
LAST NIGHT I DREAMT THE JOURNALISTS SOCIETY SENT ME A LETTER SAYING I WON AN AWARD FOR MY WORK...
...BUT YOU STOLE MY MAIL BEFORE I COULD SEE IT AND THEN IMPERSONATED ME SO THEY'D GIVE YOU MY AWARD MONEY.
DAG. THAT'S STRANGE, L. YO' DREAM'S EXACTLY LIKE WHAT REALLY HAPPENED.
I KNOW.
MAYBE YOU PSYCHIC, OR--
GIVE ME MY @#$% AWARD!!!
THUG 4 LIFE
THANK GOD FOR CULTURE CLASH
©2006 Darrin Bell / Dist. by WPWG, Inc. WWW.CANDORVILLE.COM
10-25
DARRIN BELL

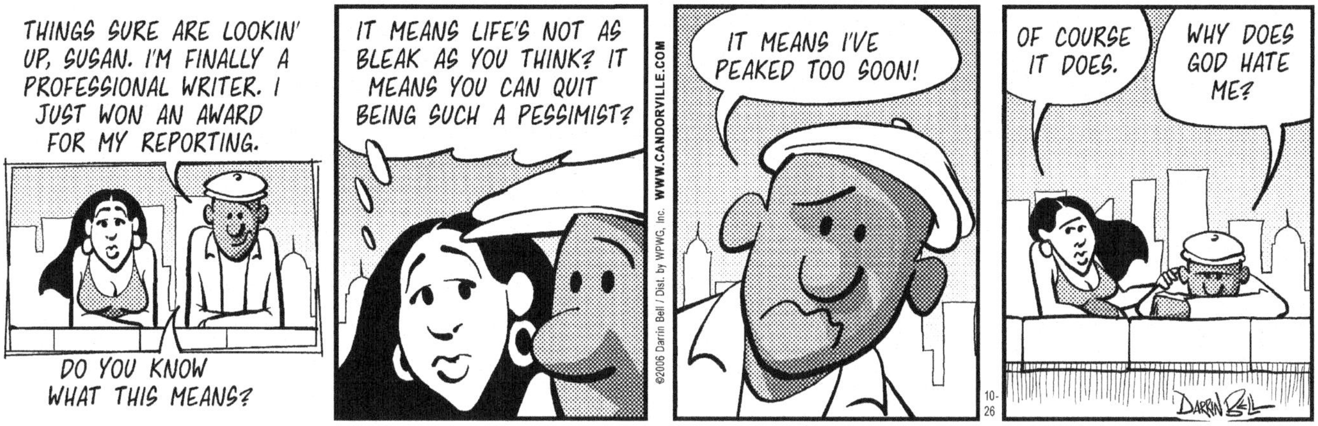
THINGS SURE ARE LOOKIN' UP, SUSAN. I'M FINALLY A PROFESSIONAL WRITER. I JUST WON AN AWARD FOR MY REPORTING.
DO YOU KNOW WHAT THIS MEANS?
IT MEANS LIFE'S NOT AS BLEAK AS YOU THINK? IT MEANS YOU CAN QUIT BEING SUCH A PESSIMIST?
IT MEANS I'VE PEAKED TOO SOON!
OF COURSE IT DOES.
WHY DOES GOD HATE ME?
©2006 Darrin Bell / Dist. by WPWG, Inc. WWW.CANDORVILLE.COM
10-26
DARRIN BELL

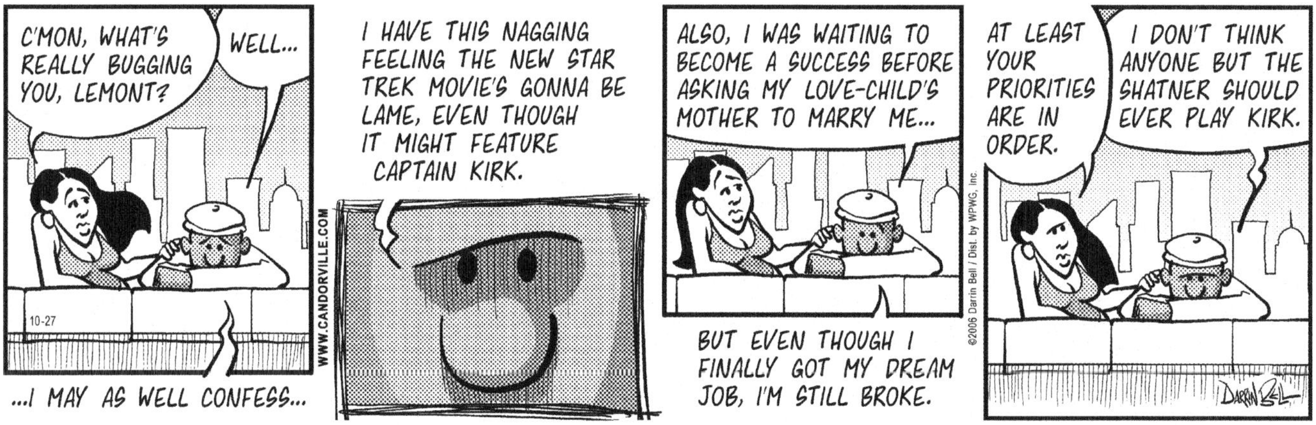
C'MON, WHAT'S REALLY BUGGING YOU, LEMONT?
WELL...
...I MAY AS WELL CONFESS...
I HAVE THIS NAGGING FEELING THE NEW STAR TREK MOVIE'S GONNA BE LAME, EVEN THOUGH IT MIGHT FEATURE CAPTAIN KIRK.
ALSO, I WAS WAITING TO BECOME A SUCCESS BEFORE ASKING MY LOVE-CHILD'S MOTHER TO MARRY ME...
BUT EVEN THOUGH I FINALLY GOT MY DREAM JOB, I'M STILL BROKE.
AT LEAST YOUR PRIORITIES ARE IN ORDER.
I DON'T THINK ANYONE BUT THE SHATNER SHOULD EVER PLAY KIRK.
10-27
WWW.CANDORVILLE.COM
©2006 Darrin Bell / Dist. by WPWG, Inc.
DARRIN BELL

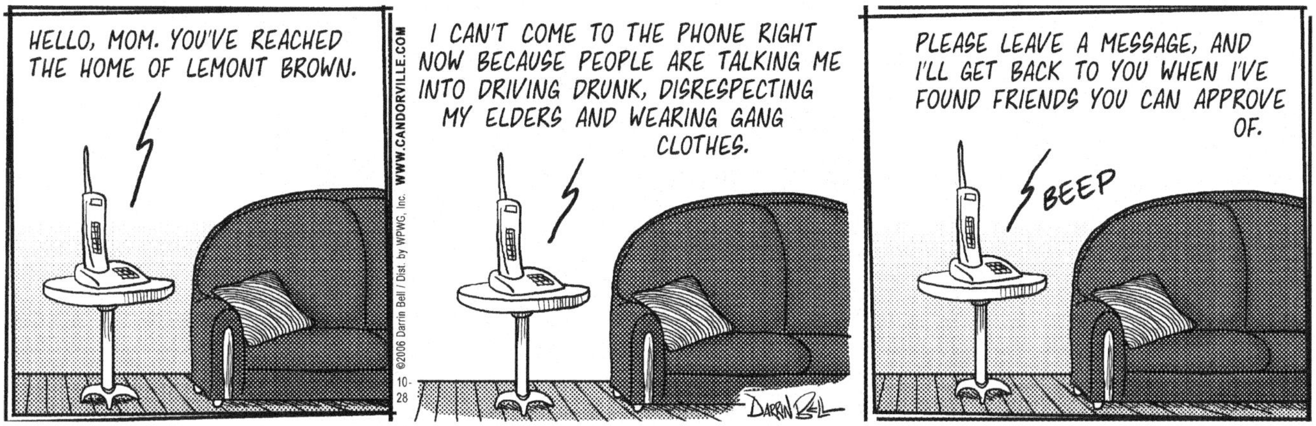
HELLO, MOM. YOU'VE REACHED THE HOME OF LEMONT BROWN.
I CAN'T COME TO THE PHONE RIGHT NOW BECAUSE PEOPLE ARE TALKING ME INTO DRIVING DRUNK, DISRESPECTING MY ELDERS AND WEARING GANG CLOTHES.
PLEASE LEAVE A MESSAGE, AND I'LL GET BACK TO YOU WHEN I'VE FOUND FRIENDS YOU CAN APPROVE OF.
BEEP
©2006 Darrin Bell / Dist. by WPWG, Inc. WWW.CANDORVILLE.COM
10-28
DARRIN BELL

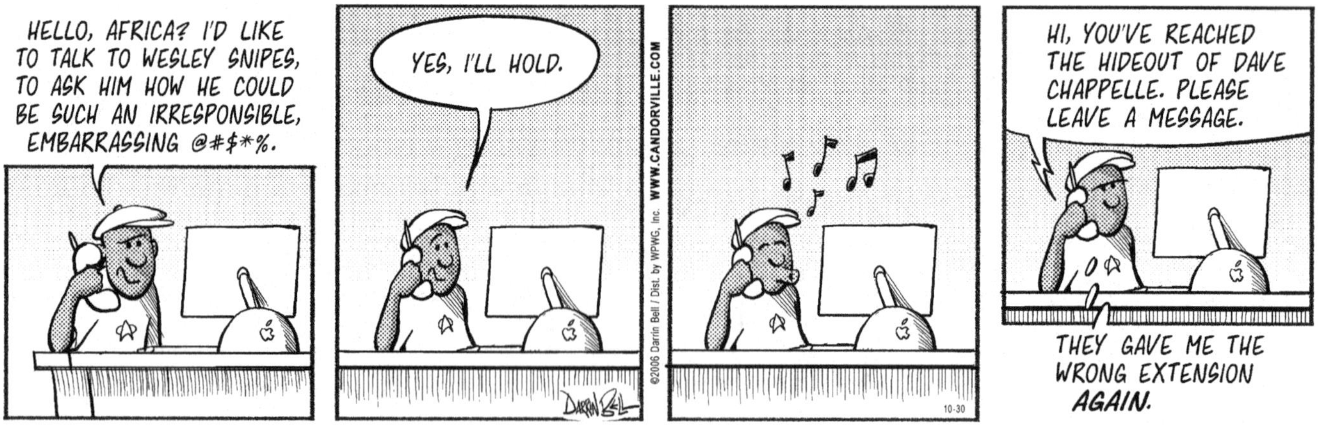
HELLO, AFRICA? I'D LIKE TO TALK TO WESLEY SNIPES, TO ASK HIM HOW HE COULD BE SUCH AN IRRESPONSIBLE, EMBARRASSING @#$*%.
YES, I'LL HOLD.
©2006 Darrin Bell / Dist. by WPWG, Inc. WWW.CANDORVILLE.COM
DARRIN BELL
10-30
HI, YOU'VE REACHED THE HIDEOUT OF DAVE CHAPPELLE. PLEASE LEAVE A MESSAGE.
THEY GAVE ME THE WRONG EXTENSION AGAIN.

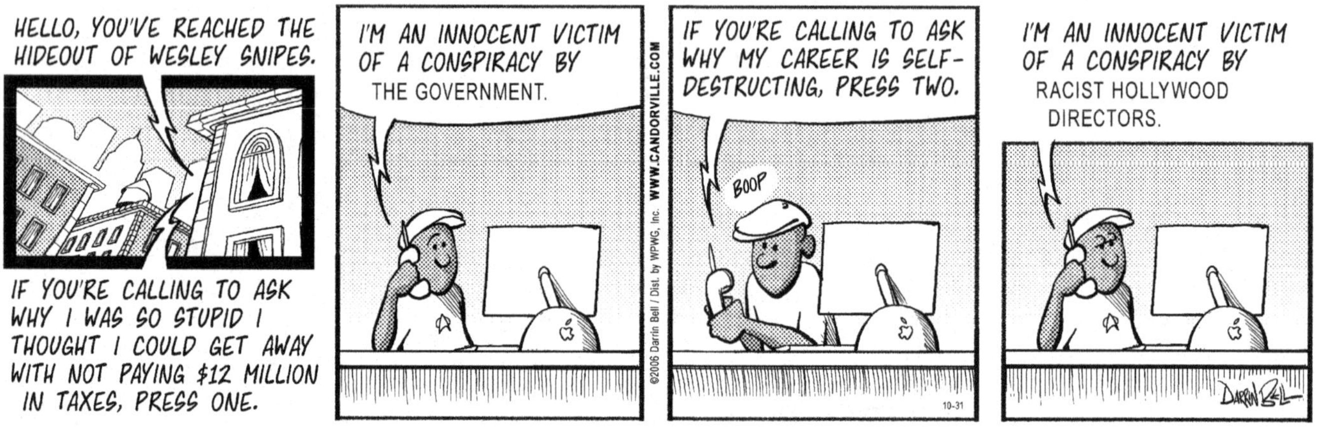
HELLO, YOU'VE REACHED THE HIDEOUT OF WESLEY SNIPES.
IF YOU'RE CALLING TO ASK WHY I WAS SO STUPID I THOUGHT I COULD GET AWAY WITH NOT PAYING $12 MILLION IN TAXES, PRESS ONE.
I'M AN INNOCENT VICTIM OF A CONSPIRACY BY THE GOVERNMENT.
©2006 Darrin Bell / Dist. by WPWG, Inc. WWW.CANDORVILLE.COM
IF YOU'RE CALLING TO ASK WHY MY CAREER IS SELF-DESTRUCTING, PRESS TWO.
BOOP
10-31
I'M AN INNOCENT VICTIM OF A CONSPIRACY BY RACIST HOLLYWOOD DIRECTORS.
DARRIN BELL

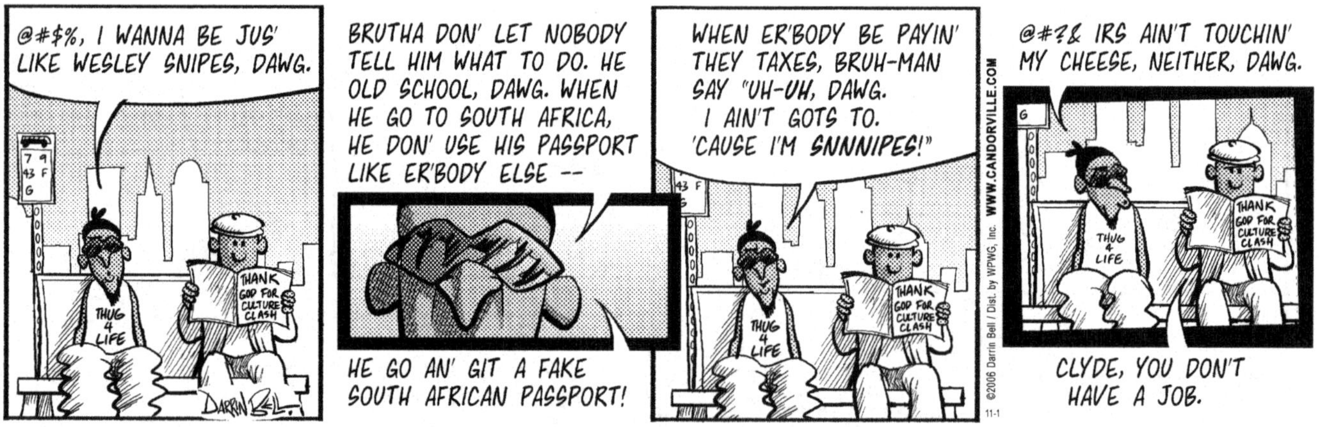
@#$%, I WANNA BE JUS' LIKE WESLEY SNIPES, DAWG.
THUG 4 LIFE
THANK GOD FOR CULTURE CLASH
DARRIN BELL
BRUTHA DON' LET NOBODY TELL HIM WHAT TO DO. HE OLD SCHOOL, DAWG. WHEN HE GO TO SOUTH AFRICA, HE DON' USE HIS PASSPORT LIKE ER'BODY ELSE --
HE GO AN' GIT A FAKE SOUTH AFRICAN PASSPORT!
WHEN ER'BODY BE PAYIN' THEY TAXES, BRUH-MAN SAY "UH-UH, DAWG. I AIN'T GOTS TO. 'CAUSE I'M SNNNIPES!"
©2006 Darrin Bell / Dist. by WPWG, Inc. WWW.CANDORVILLE.COM
11-1
@#?& IRS AIN'T TOUCHIN' MY CHEESE, NEITHER, DAWG.
CLYDE, YOU DON'T HAVE A JOB.

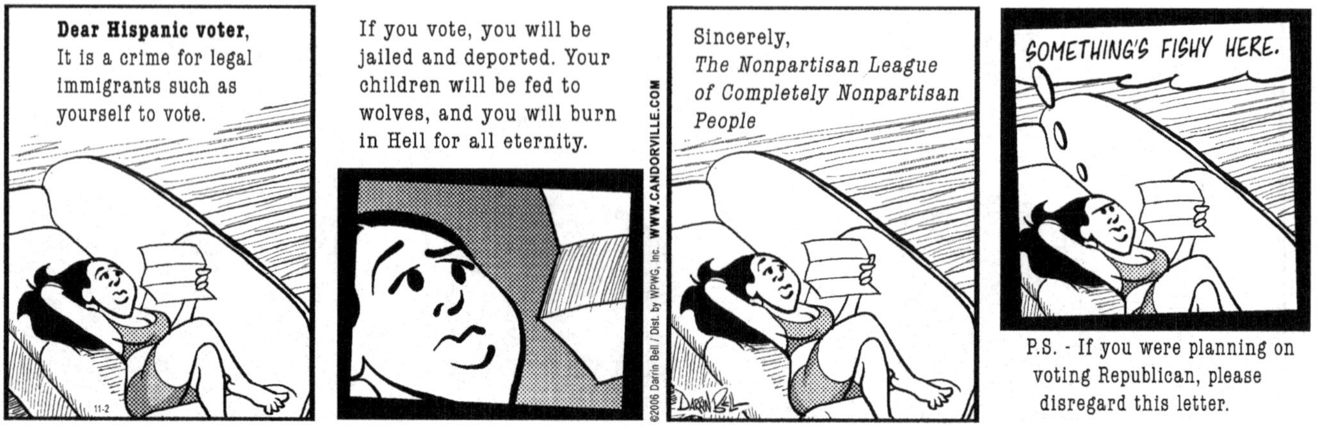
Dear Hispanic voter,
It is a crime for legal immigrants such as yourself to vote.
11-2
If you vote, you will be jailed and deported. Your children will be fed to wolves, and you will burn in Hell for all eternity.
©2006 Darrin Bell / Dist. by WPWG, Inc. WWW.CANDORVILLE.COM
Sincerely,
The Nonpartisan League of Completely Nonpartisan People
DARRIN BELL
SOMETHING'S FISHY HERE.
P.S. - If you were planning on voting Republican, please disregard this letter.

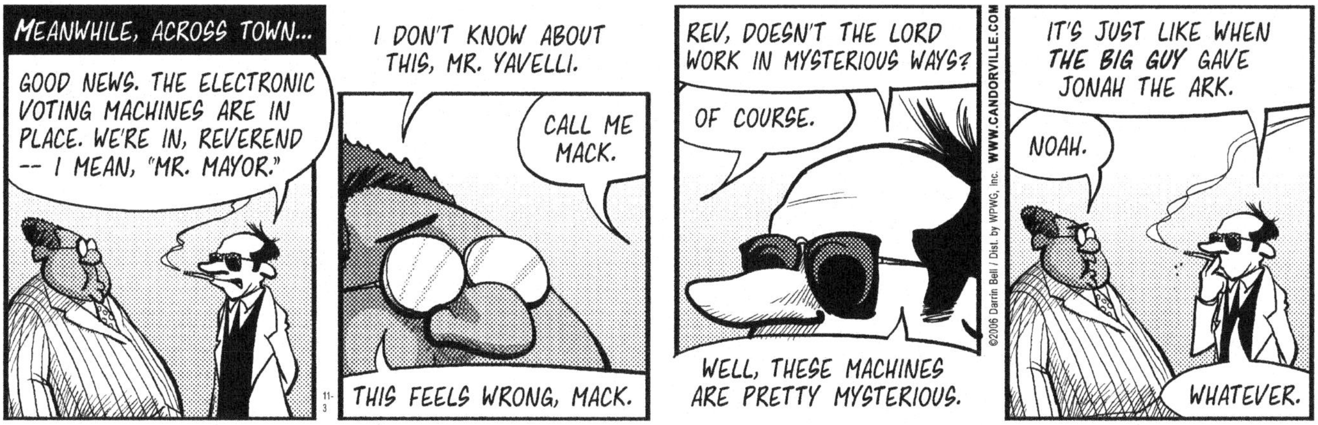
MEANWHILE, ACROSS TOWN...
GOOD NEWS. THE ELECTRONIC VOTING MACHINES ARE IN PLACE. WE'RE IN, REVEREND -- I MEAN, "MR. MAYOR."
11-3
I DON'T KNOW ABOUT THIS, MR. YAVELLI.
CALL ME MACK.
THIS FEELS WRONG, MACK.
REV, DOESN'T THE LORD WORK IN MYSTERIOUS WAYS?
OF COURSE.
WELL, THESE MACHINES ARE PRETTY MYSTERIOUS.
©2006 Darrin Bell / Dist. by WPWG, Inc. WWW.CANDORVILLE.COM
IT'S JUST LIKE WHEN **THE BIG GUY** GAVE JONAH THE ARK.
NOAH.
WHATEVER.

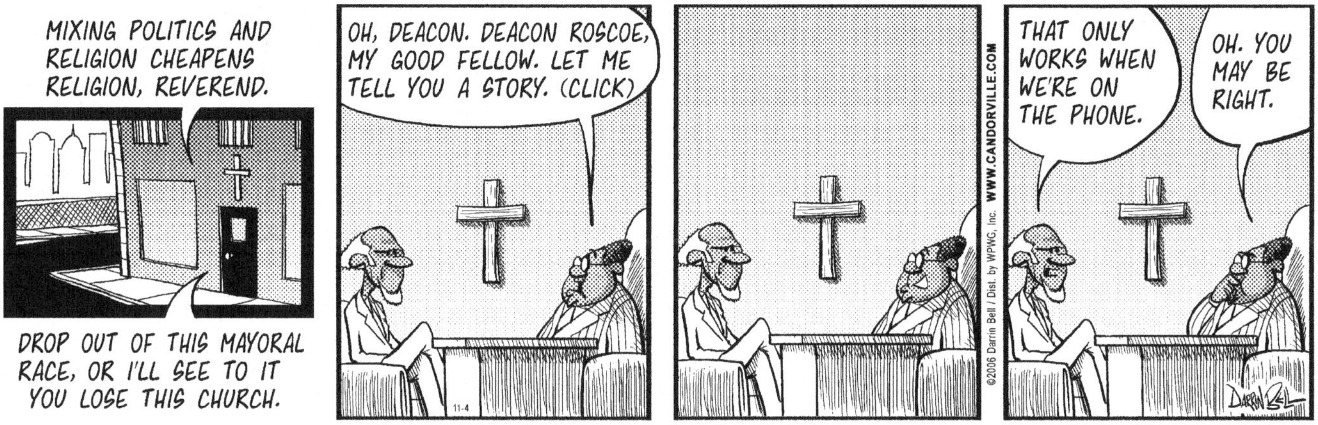
MIXING POLITICS AND RELIGION CHEAPENS RELIGION, REVEREND.
DROP OUT OF THIS MAYORAL RACE, OR I'LL SEE TO IT YOU LOSE THIS CHURCH.
OH, DEACON. DEACON ROSCOE, MY GOOD FELLOW. LET ME TELL YOU A STORY. (CLICK)
11-4
©2006 Darrin Bell / Dist. by WPWG, Inc. WWW.CANDORVILLE.COM
THAT ONLY WORKS WHEN WE'RE ON THE PHONE.
OH. YOU MAY BE RIGHT.

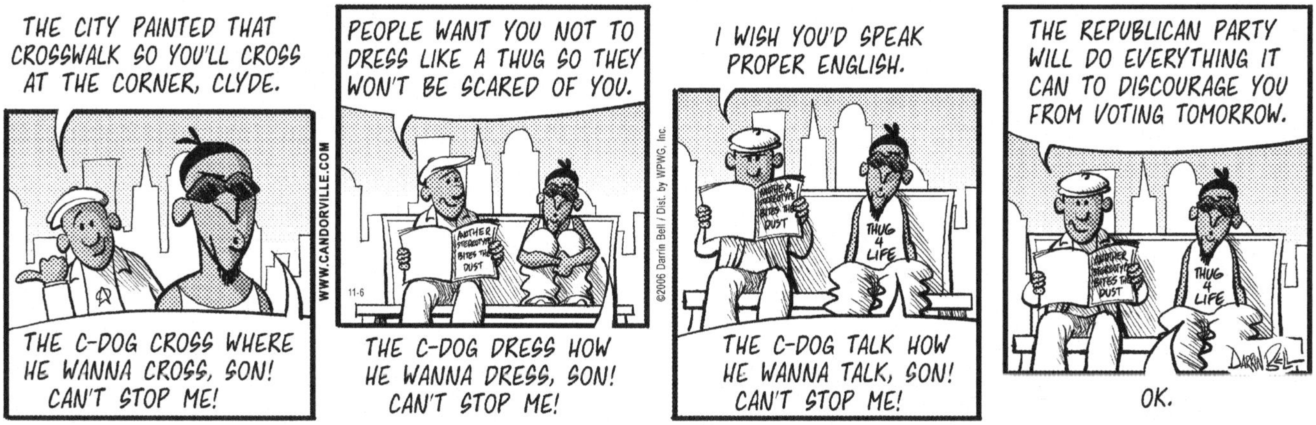
THE CITY PAINTED THAT CROSSWALK SO YOU'LL CROSS AT THE CORNER, CLYDE.
THE C-DOG CROSS WHERE HE WANNA CROSS, SON! CAN'T STOP ME!
WWW.CANDORVILLE.COM
PEOPLE WANT YOU NOT TO DRESS LIKE A THUG SO THEY WON'T BE SCARED OF YOU.
11-6
THE C-DOG DRESS HOW HE WANNA DRESS, SON! CAN'T STOP ME!
©2006 Darrin Bell / Dist. by WPWG, Inc.
I WISH YOU'D SPEAK PROPER ENGLISH.
THUG 4 LIFE
THE C-DOG TALK HOW HE WANNA TALK, SON! CAN'T STOP ME!
THE REPUBLICAN PARTY WILL DO EVERYTHING IT CAN TO DISCOURAGE YOU FROM VOTING TOMORROW.
OK.

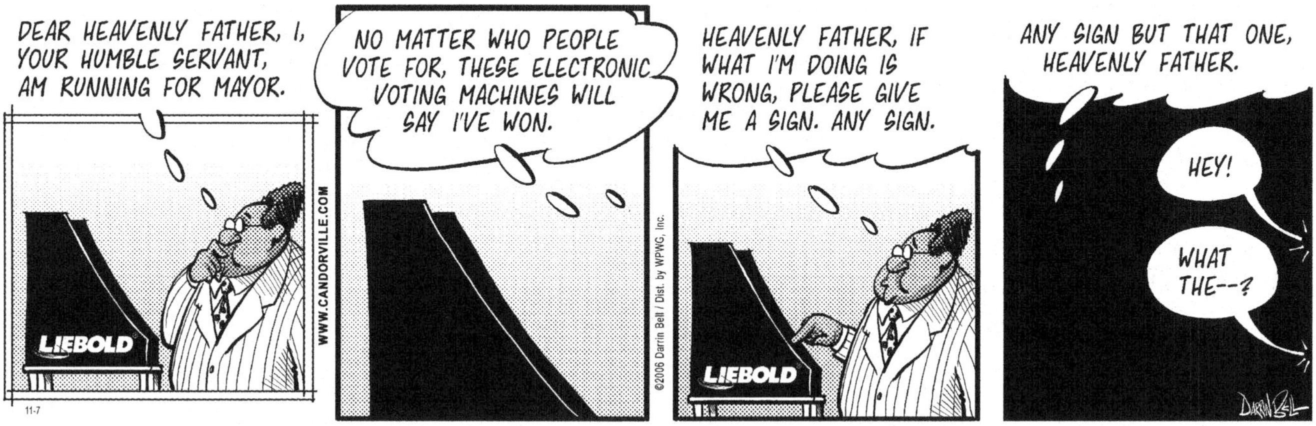
DEAR HEAVENLY FATHER, I, YOUR HUMBLE SERVANT, AM RUNNING FOR MAYOR.
LIEBOLD
WWW.CANDORVILLE.COM
11-7
NO MATTER WHO PEOPLE VOTE FOR, THESE ELECTRONIC VOTING MACHINES WILL SAY I'VE WON.
©2006 Darrin Bell / Dist. by WPWG, Inc.
HEAVENLY FATHER, IF WHAT I'M DOING IS WRONG, PLEASE GIVE ME A SIGN. ANY SIGN.
LIEBOLD
ANY SIGN BUT THAT ONE, HEAVENLY FATHER.
HEY!
WHAT THE--?

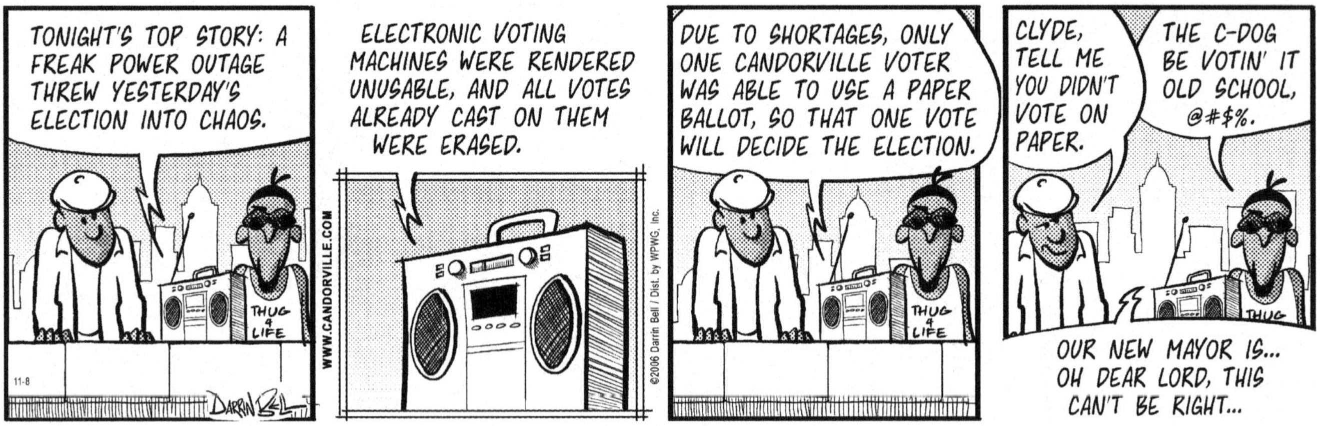
TONIGHT'S TOP STORY: A FREAK POWER OUTAGE THREW YESTERDAY'S ELECTION INTO CHAOS.
THUG 4 LIFE
11-8
DARRIN BELL
WWW.CANDORVILLE.COM
ELECTRONIC VOTING MACHINES WERE RENDERED UNUSABLE, AND ALL VOTES ALREADY CAST ON THEM WERE ERASED.
©2006 Darrin Bell / Dist. by WPWG, Inc.
DUE TO SHORTAGES, ONLY ONE CANDORVILLE VOTER WAS ABLE TO USE A PAPER BALLOT, SO THAT ONE VOTE WILL DECIDE THE ELECTION.
THUG 4 LIFE
CLYDE, TELL ME YOU DIDN'T VOTE ON PAPER.
THE C-DOG BE VOTIN' IT OLD SCHOOL, @#$%.
OUR NEW MAYOR IS... OH DEAR LORD, THIS CAN'T BE RIGHT...

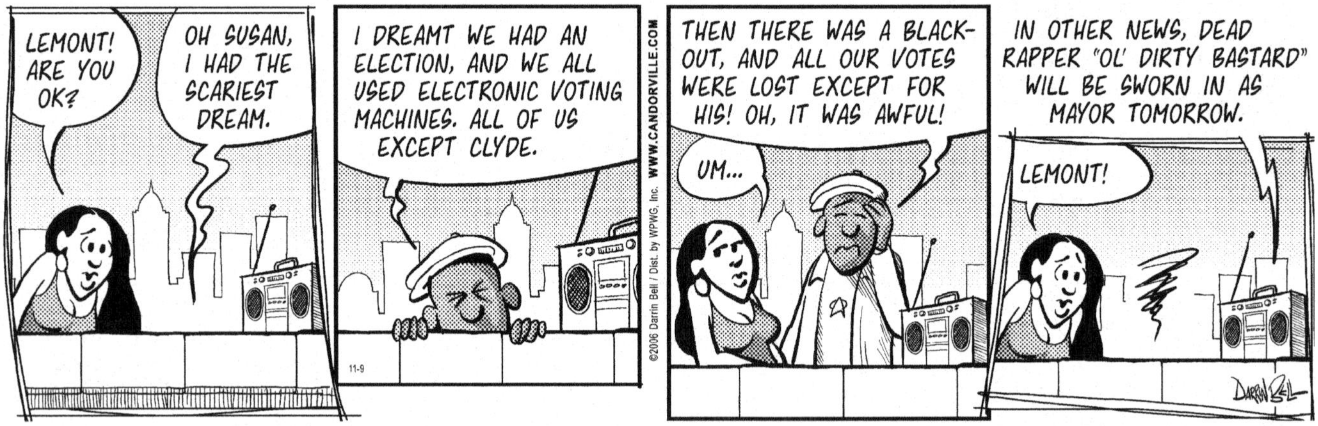
LEMONT! ARE YOU OK?
OH SUSAN, I HAD THE SCARIEST DREAM.
I DREAMT WE HAD AN ELECTION, AND WE ALL USED ELECTRONIC VOTING MACHINES. ALL OF US EXCEPT CLYDE.
11-9
©2006 Darrin Bell / Dist. by WPWG, Inc. WWW.CANDORVILLE.COM
THEN THERE WAS A BLACK-OUT, AND ALL OUR VOTES WERE LOST EXCEPT FOR HIS! OH, IT WAS AWFUL!
UM...
IN OTHER NEWS, DEAD RAPPER "OL' DIRTY BASTARD" WILL BE SWORN IN AS MAYOR TOMORROW.
LEMONT!
DARRIN BELL

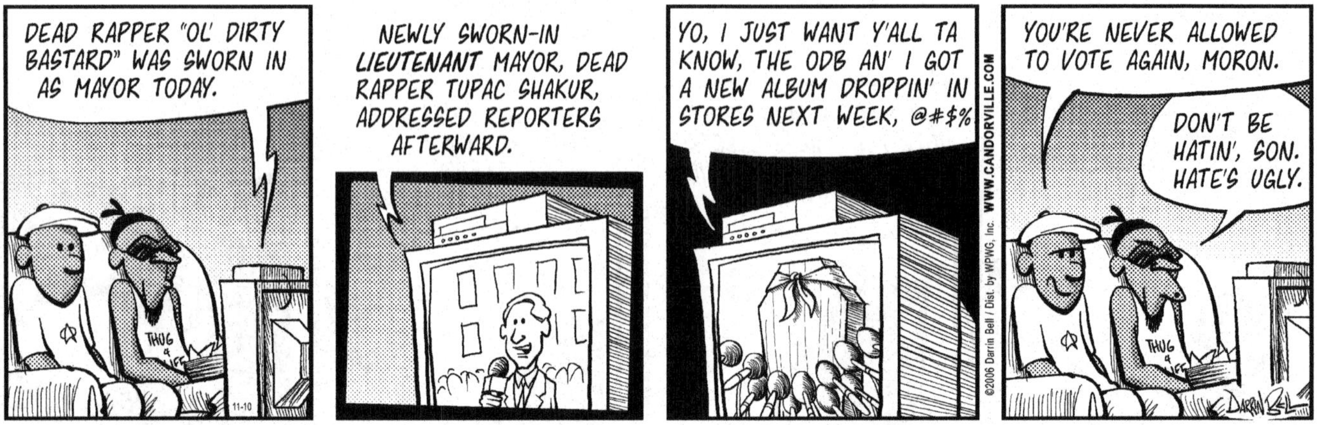
DEAD RAPPER "OL' DIRTY BASTARD" WAS SWORN IN AS MAYOR TODAY.
THUG 4 LIFE
11-10
NEWLY SWORN-IN LIEUTENANT MAYOR, DEAD RAPPER TUPAC SHAKUR, ADDRESSED REPORTERS AFTERWARD.
YO, I JUST WANT Y'ALL TA KNOW, THE ODB AN' I GOT A NEW ALBUM DROPPIN' IN STORES NEXT WEEK, @#$%.
©2006 Darrin Bell / Dist. by WPWG, Inc. WWW.CANDORVILLE.COM
YOU'RE NEVER ALLOWED TO VOTE AGAIN, MORON.
DON'T BE HATIN', SON. HATE'S UGLY.
THUG 4 LIFE
DARRIN BELL

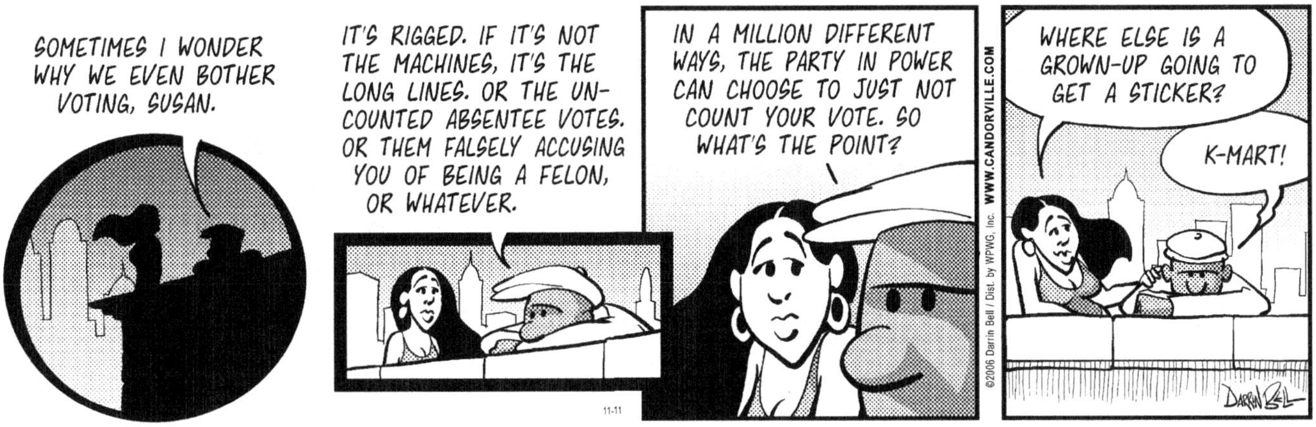
SOMETIMES I WONDER WHY WE EVEN BOTHER VOTING, SUSAN.
IT'S RIGGED. IF IT'S NOT THE MACHINES, IT'S THE LONG LINES. OR THE UN-COUNTED ABSENTEE VOTES. OR THEM FALSELY ACCUSING YOU OF BEING A FELON, OR WHATEVER.
11-11
IN A MILLION DIFFERENT WAYS, THE PARTY IN POWER CAN CHOOSE TO JUST NOT COUNT YOUR VOTE. SO WHAT'S THE POINT?
©2006 Darrin Bell / Dist. by WPWG, Inc. WWW.CANDORVILLE.COM
WHERE ELSE IS A GROWN-UP GOING TO GET A STICKER?
K-MART!
DARRIN BELL

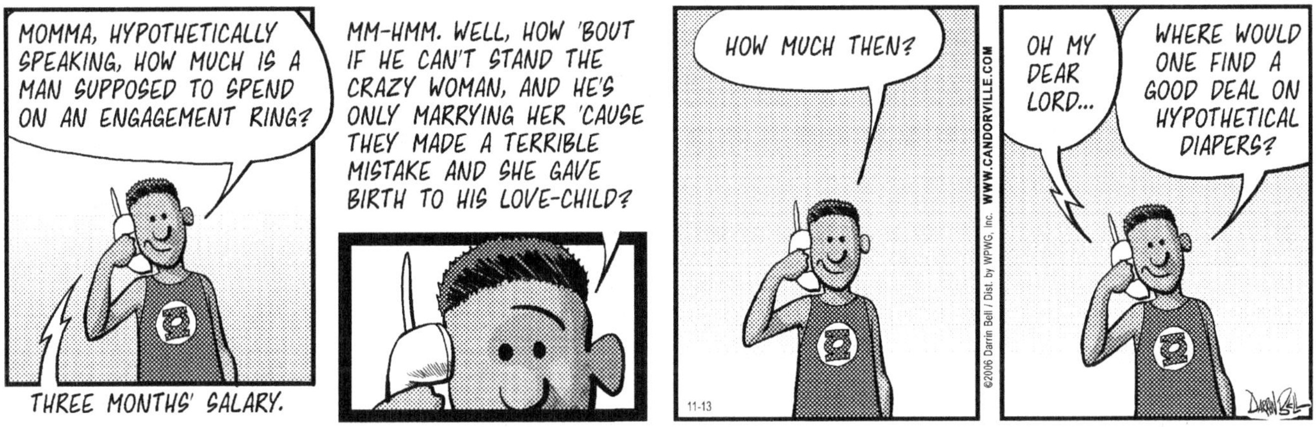
MOMMA, HYPOTHETICALLY SPEAKING, HOW MUCH IS A MAN SUPPOSED TO SPEND ON AN ENGAGEMENT RING?
THREE MONTHS' SALARY.
MM-HMM. WELL, HOW 'BOUT IF HE CAN'T STAND THE CRAZY WOMAN, AND HE'S ONLY MARRYING HER 'CAUSE THEY MADE A TERRIBLE MISTAKE AND SHE GAVE BIRTH TO HIS LOVE-CHILD?
HOW MUCH THEN?
11-13
©2006 Darrin Bell / Dist. by WPWG, Inc. WWW.CANDORVILLE.COM
OH MY DEAR LORD...
WHERE WOULD ONE FIND A GOOD DEAL ON HYPOTHETICAL DIAPERS?
DARRIN BELL

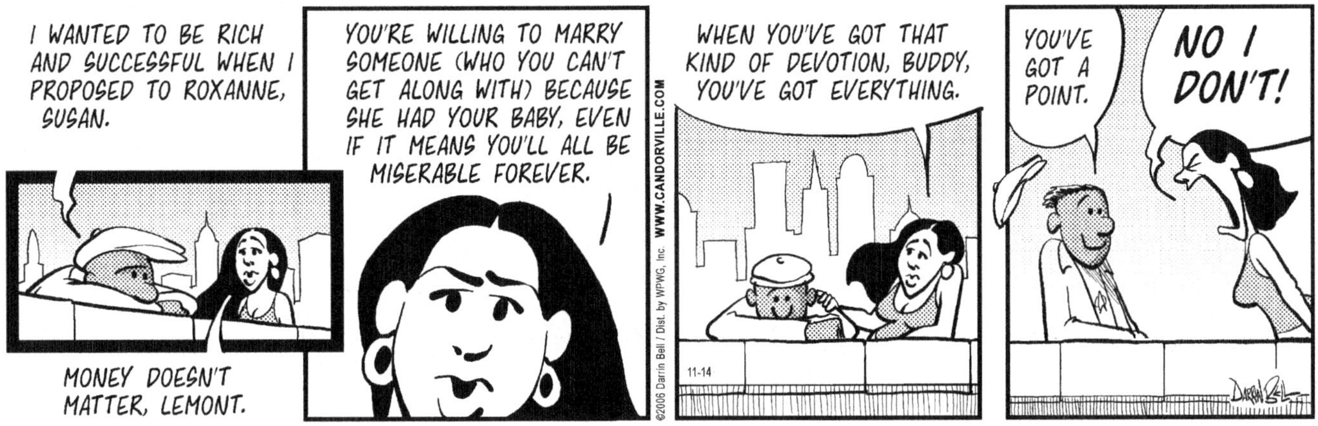
I WANTED TO BE RICH AND SUCCESSFUL WHEN I PROPOSED TO ROXANNE, SUSAN.
MONEY DOESN'T MATTER, LEMONT.
YOU'RE WILLING TO MARRY SOMEONE (WHO YOU CAN'T GET ALONG WITH) BECAUSE SHE HAD YOUR BABY, EVEN IF IT MEANS YOU'LL ALL BE MISERABLE FOREVER.
©2006 Darrin Bell / Dist. by WPWG, Inc. WWW.CANDORVILLE.COM
WHEN YOU'VE GOT THAT KIND OF DEVOTION, BUDDY, YOU'VE GOT EVERYTHING.
11-14
YOU'VE GOT A POINT.
NO I DON'T!
DARRIN BELL

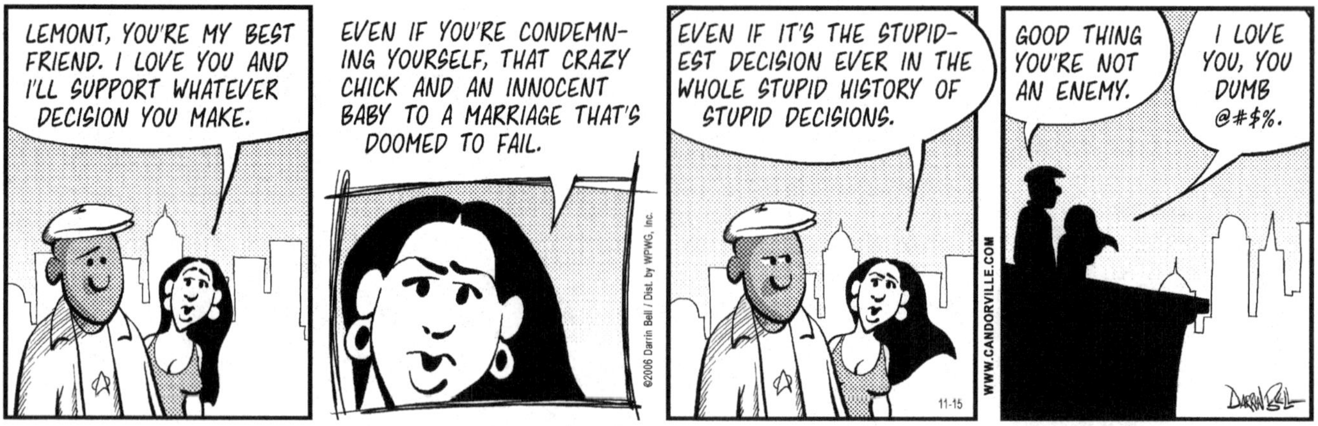
LEMONT, YOU'RE MY BEST FRIEND. I LOVE YOU AND I'LL SUPPORT WHATEVER DECISION YOU MAKE.
EVEN IF YOU'RE CONDEMNING YOURSELF, THAT CRAZY CHICK AND AN INNOCENT BABY TO A MARRIAGE THAT'S DOOMED TO FAIL.
EVEN IF IT'S THE STUPIDEST DECISION EVER IN THE WHOLE STUPID HISTORY OF STUPID DECISIONS.
GOOD THING YOU'RE NOT AN ENEMY.
I LOVE YOU, YOU DUMB @#$%.
©2006 Darrin Bell / Dist. by WPWG, Inc.
WWW.CANDORVILLE.COM
11-15

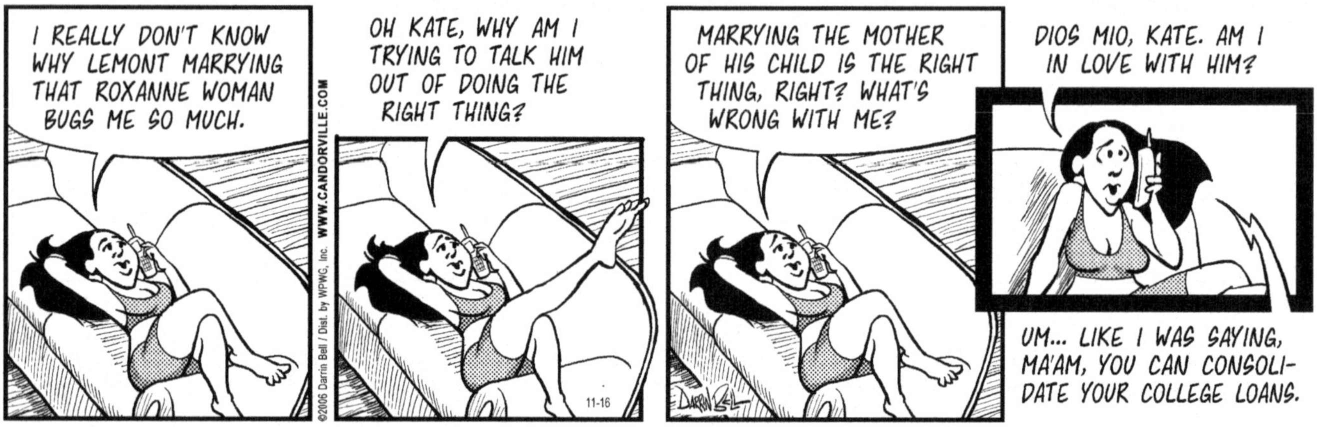
I REALLY DON'T KNOW WHY LEMONT MARRYING THAT ROXANNE WOMAN BUGS ME SO MUCH.
OH KATE, WHY AM I TRYING TO TALK HIM OUT OF DOING THE RIGHT THING?
MARRYING THE MOTHER OF HIS CHILD IS THE RIGHT THING, RIGHT? WHAT'S WRONG WITH ME?
DIOS MIO, KATE. AM I IN LOVE WITH HIM?
UM... LIKE I WAS SAYING, MA'AM, YOU CAN CONSOLIDATE YOUR COLLEGE LOANS.
©2006 Darrin Bell / Dist. by WPWG, Inc.
WWW.CANDORVILLE.COM
11-16

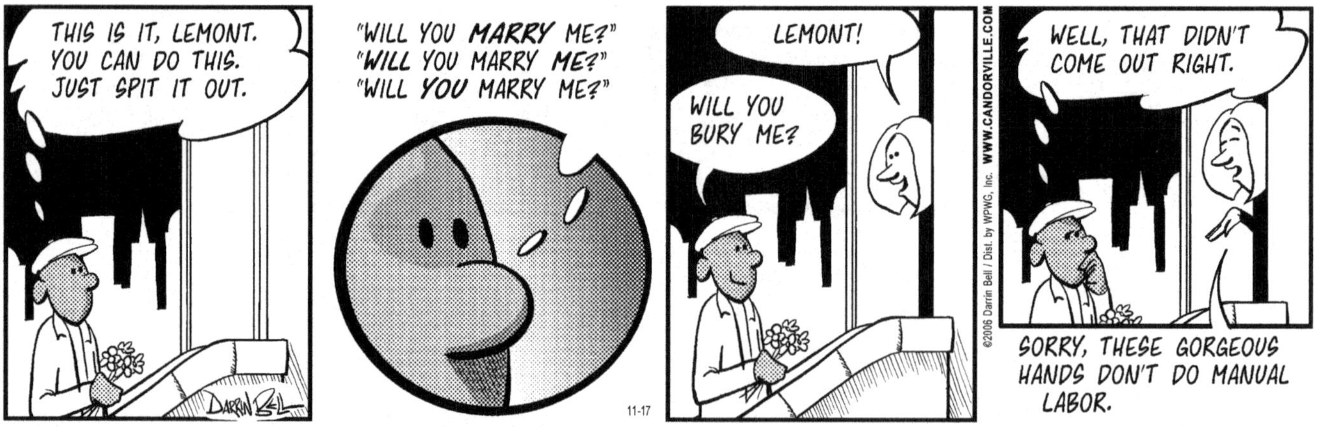
THIS IS IT, LEMONT. YOU CAN DO THIS. JUST SPIT IT OUT.
"WILL YOU MARRY ME?" "WILL YOU MARRY ME?" "WILL YOU MARRY ME?"
LEMONT!
WILL YOU BURY ME?
WELL, THAT DIDN'T COME OUT RIGHT.
SORRY, THESE GORGEOUS HANDS DON'T DO MANUAL LABOR.
©2006 Darrin Bell / Dist. by WPWG, Inc.
WWW.CANDORVILLE.COM
11-17

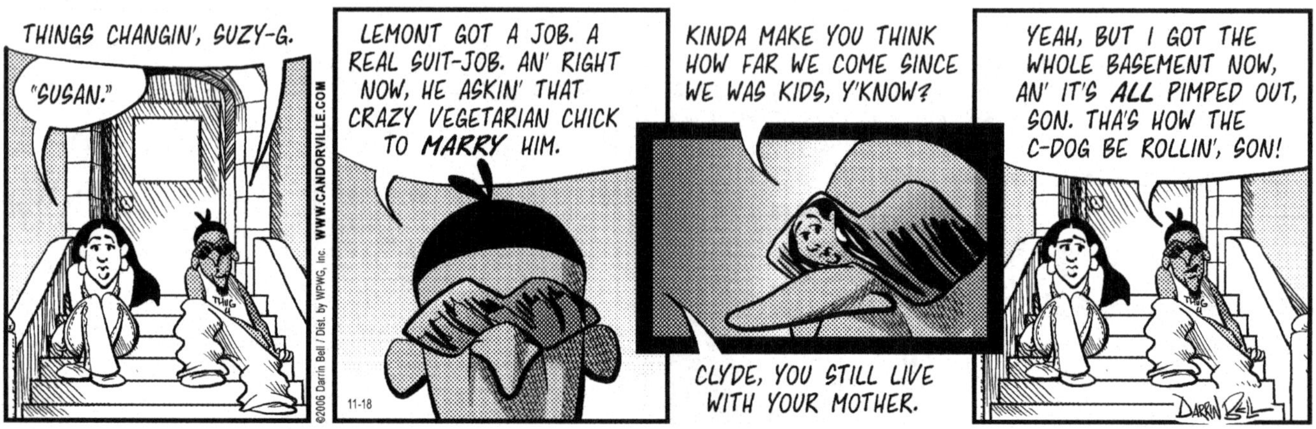
THINGS CHANGIN', SUZY-G.
"SUSAN."
LEMONT GOT A JOB. A REAL SUIT-JOB. AN' RIGHT NOW, HE ASKIN' THAT CRAZY VEGETARIAN CHICK TO MARRY HIM.
KINDA MAKE YOU THINK HOW FAR WE COME SINCE WE WAS KIDS, Y'KNOW?
CLYDE, YOU STILL LIVE WITH YOUR MOTHER.
YEAH, BUT I GOT THE WHOLE BASEMENT NOW, AN' IT'S ALL PIMPED OUT, SON. THA'S HOW THE C-DOG BE ROLLIN', SON!
©2006 Darrin Bell / Dist. by WPWG, Inc.
WWW.CANDORVILLE.COM
11-18

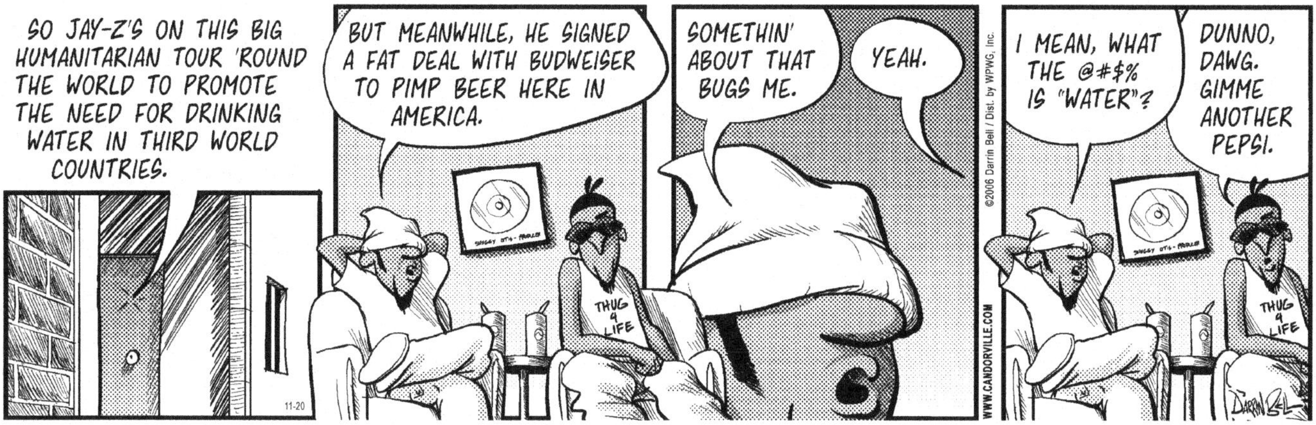
SO JAY-Z'S ON THIS BIG HUMANITARIAN TOUR 'ROUND THE WORLD TO PROMOTE THE NEED FOR DRINKING WATER IN THIRD WORLD COUNTRIES.
BUT MEANWHILE, HE SIGNED A FAT DEAL WITH BUDWEISER TO PIMP BEER HERE IN AMERICA.
THUG 4 LIFE
SOMETHIN' ABOUT THAT BUGS ME.
YEAH.
I MEAN, WHAT THE @#$% IS "WATER"?
DUNNO, DAWG. GIMME ANOTHER PEPSI.
©2006 Darrin Bell / Dist. by WPWG, Inc.
WWW.CANDORVILLE.COM
11-20
DARRIN BELL

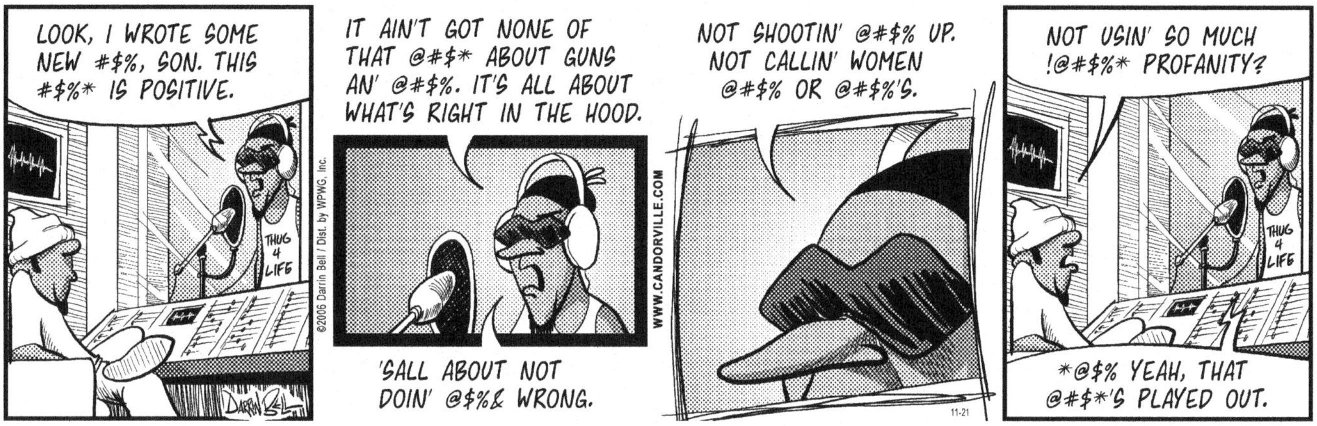
LOOK, I WROTE SOME NEW #$%, SON. THIS #$%* IS POSITIVE.
THUG 4 LIFE
IT AIN'T GOT NONE OF THAT @#$* ABOUT GUNS AN' @#$%. IT'S ALL ABOUT WHAT'S RIGHT IN THE HOOD.
'SALL ABOUT NOT DOIN' @$%& WRONG.
NOT SHOOTIN' @#$% UP. NOT CALLIN' WOMEN @#$% OR @#$%'S.
NOT USIN' SO MUCH !@#$%* PROFANITY?
@$% YEAH, THAT @#$'S PLAYED OUT.
©2006 Darrin Bell / Dist. by WPWG, Inc.
WWW.CANDORVILLE.COM
11-21
DARRIN BELL

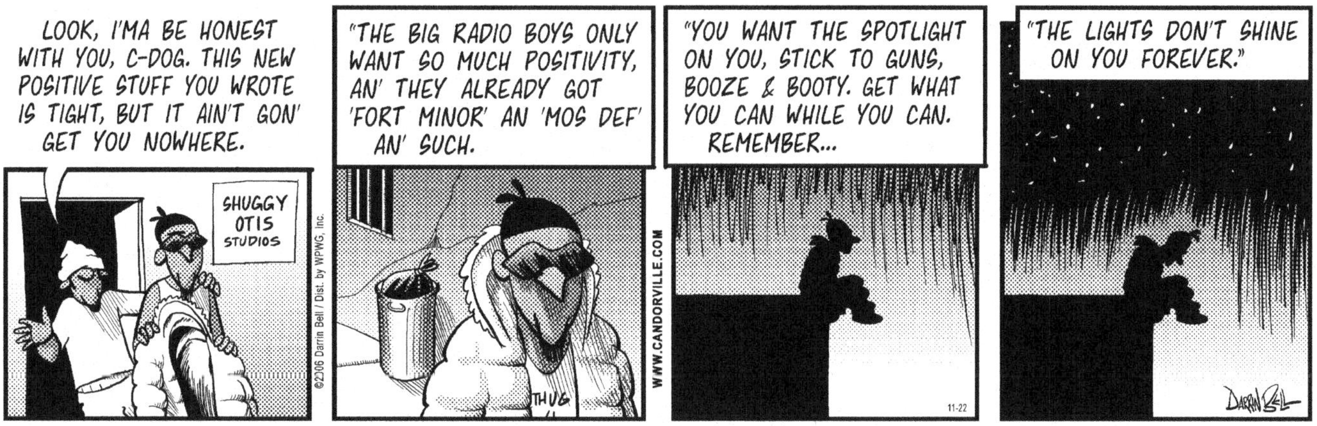
LOOK, I'MA BE HONEST WITH YOU, C-DOG. THIS NEW POSITIVE STUFF YOU WROTE IS TIGHT, BUT IT AIN'T GON' GET YOU NOWHERE.
SHUGGY OTIS STUDIOS
"THE BIG RADIO BOYS ONLY WANT SO MUCH POSITIVITY, AN' THEY ALREADY GOT 'FORT MINOR' AN 'MOS DEF' AN' SUCH.
"YOU WANT THE SPOTLIGHT ON YOU, STICK TO GUNS, BOOZE & BOOTY. GET WHAT YOU CAN WHILE YOU CAN. REMEMBER...
"THE LIGHTS DON'T SHINE ON YOU FOREVER."
©2006 Darrin Bell / Dist. by WPWG, Inc.
WWW.CANDORVILLE.COM
11-22
DARRIN BELL

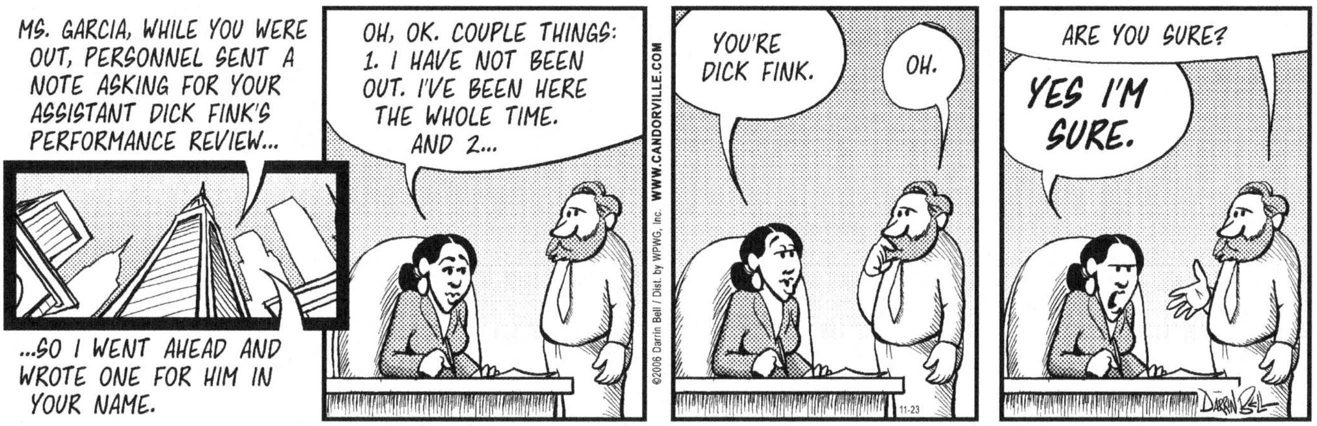
MS. GARCIA, WHILE YOU WERE OUT, PERSONNEL SENT A NOTE ASKING FOR YOUR ASSISTANT DICK FINK'S PERFORMANCE REVIEW...
...SO I WENT AHEAD AND WROTE ONE FOR HIM IN YOUR NAME.
OH, OK. COUPLE THINGS: 1. I HAVE NOT BEEN OUT. I'VE BEEN HERE THE WHOLE TIME. AND 2...
YOU'RE DICK FINK.
OH.
ARE YOU SURE?
YES I'M SURE.
©2006 Darrin Bell / Dist. by WPWG, Inc.
WWW.CANDORVILLE.COM
11-23
DARRIN BELL

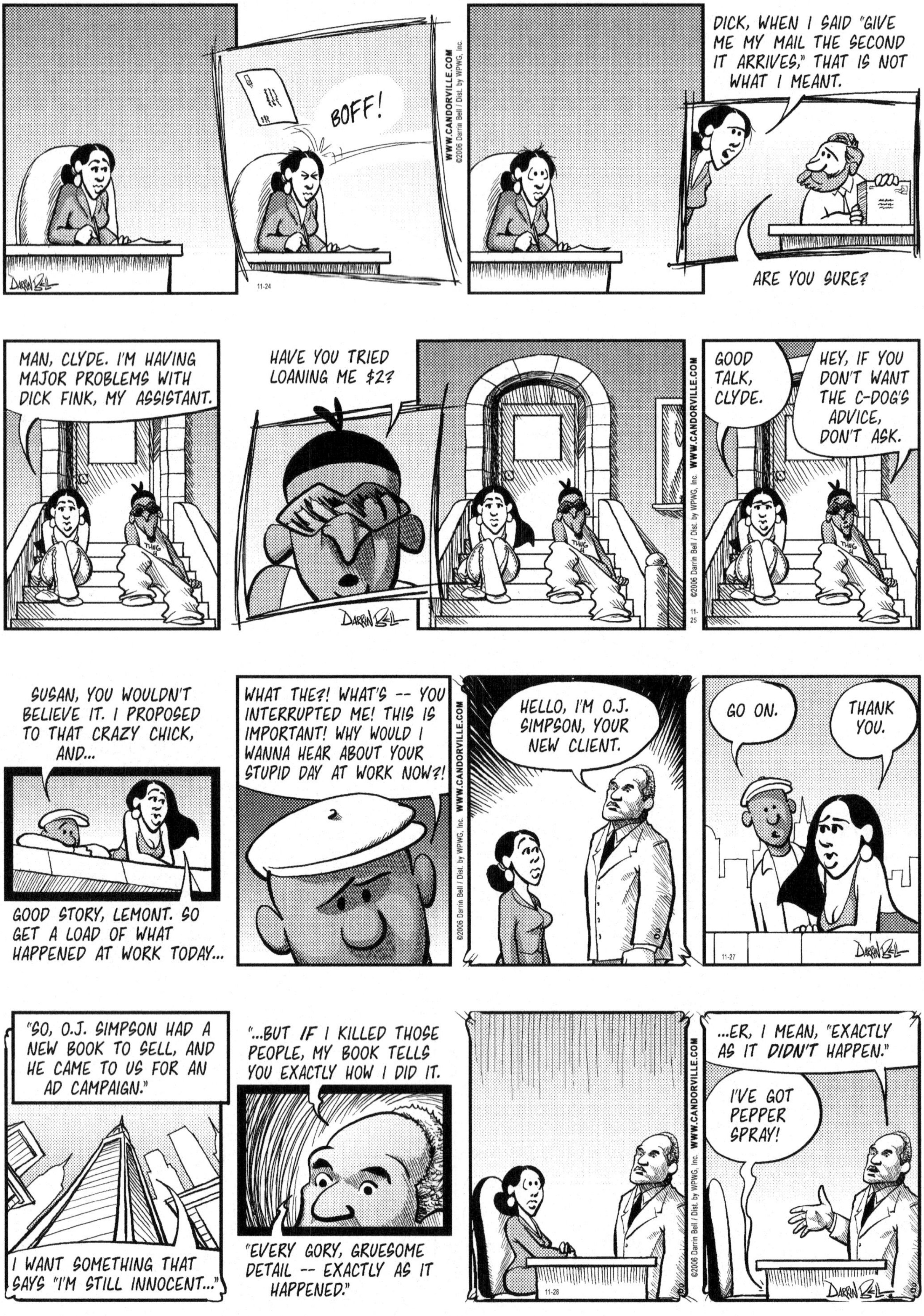
BOFF!
WWW.CANDORVILLE.COM
©2006 Darrin Bell / Dist. by WPWG, Inc.
DICK, WHEN I SAID "GIVE ME MY MAIL THE SECOND IT ARRIVES," THAT IS NOT WHAT I MEANT.
ARE YOU SURE?
MAN, CLYDE. I'M HAVING MAJOR PROBLEMS WITH DICK FINK, MY ASSISTANT.
HAVE YOU TRIED LOANING ME $2?
WWW.CANDORVILLE.COM
©2006 Darrin Bell / Dist. by WPWG, Inc.
GOOD TALK, CLYDE.
HEY, IF YOU DON'T WANT THE C-DOG'S ADVICE, DON'T ASK.
SUSAN, YOU WOULDN'T BELIEVE IT. I PROPOSED TO THAT CRAZY CHICK, AND...
GOOD STORY, LEMONT. SO GET A LOAD OF WHAT HAPPENED AT WORK TODAY...
WHAT THE?! WHAT'S -- YOU INTERRUPTED ME! THIS IS IMPORTANT! WHY WOULD I WANNA HEAR ABOUT YOUR STUPID DAY AT WORK NOW?!
WWW.CANDORVILLE.COM
©2006 Darrin Bell / Dist. by WPWG, Inc.
HELLO, I'M O.J. SIMPSON, YOUR NEW CLIENT.
GO ON.
THANK YOU.
"SO, O.J. SIMPSON HAD A NEW BOOK TO SELL, AND HE CAME TO US FOR AN AD CAMPAIGN."
I WANT SOMETHING THAT SAYS "I'M STILL INNOCENT..."
"...BUT IF I KILLED THOSE PEOPLE, MY BOOK TELLS YOU EXACTLY HOW I DID IT.
"EVERY GORY, GRUESOME DETAIL -- EXACTLY AS IT HAPPENED."
WWW.CANDORVILLE.COM
©2006 Darrin Bell / Dist. by WPWG, Inc.
...ER, I MEAN, "EXACTLY AS IT DIDN'T HAPPEN."
I'VE GOT PEPPER SPRAY!

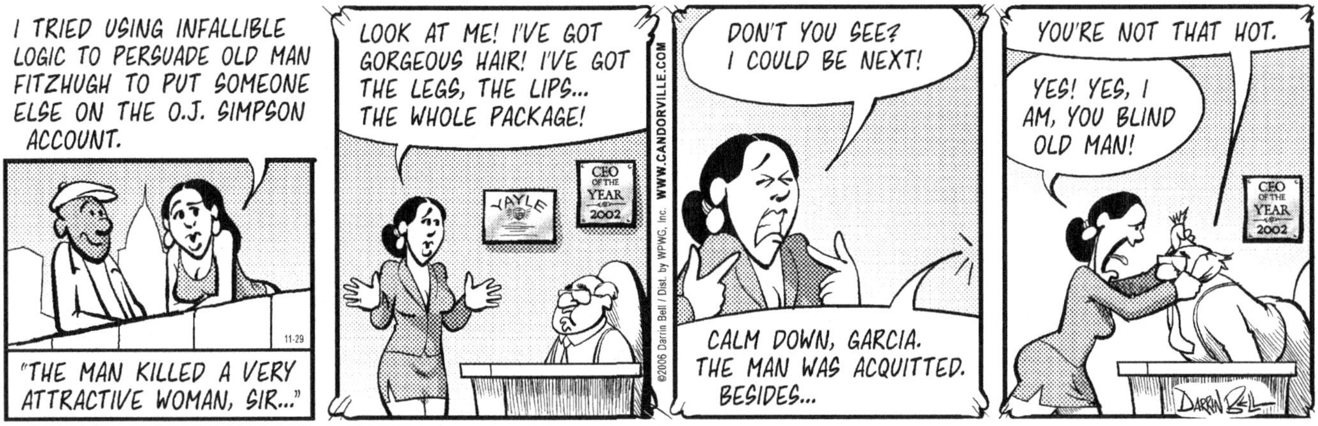
I TRIED USING INFALLIBLE LOGIC TO PERSUADE OLD MAN FITZHUGH TO PUT SOMEONE ELSE ON THE O.J. SIMPSON ACCOUNT.
"THE MAN KILLED A VERY ATTRACTIVE WOMAN, SIR..."
11-29
LOOK AT ME! I'VE GOT GORGEOUS HAIR! I'VE GOT THE LEGS, THE LIPS... THE WHOLE PACKAGE!
YAYLE
CEO OF THE YEAR 2002
©2006 Darrin Bell / Dist. by WPWG, Inc. WWW.CANDORVILLE.COM
DON'T YOU SEE? I COULD BE NEXT!
CALM DOWN, GARCIA. THE MAN WAS ACQUITTED. BESIDES...
YOU'RE NOT THAT HOT.
YES! YES, I AM, YOU BLIND OLD MAN!
CEO OF THE YEAR 2002
DARRIN BELL

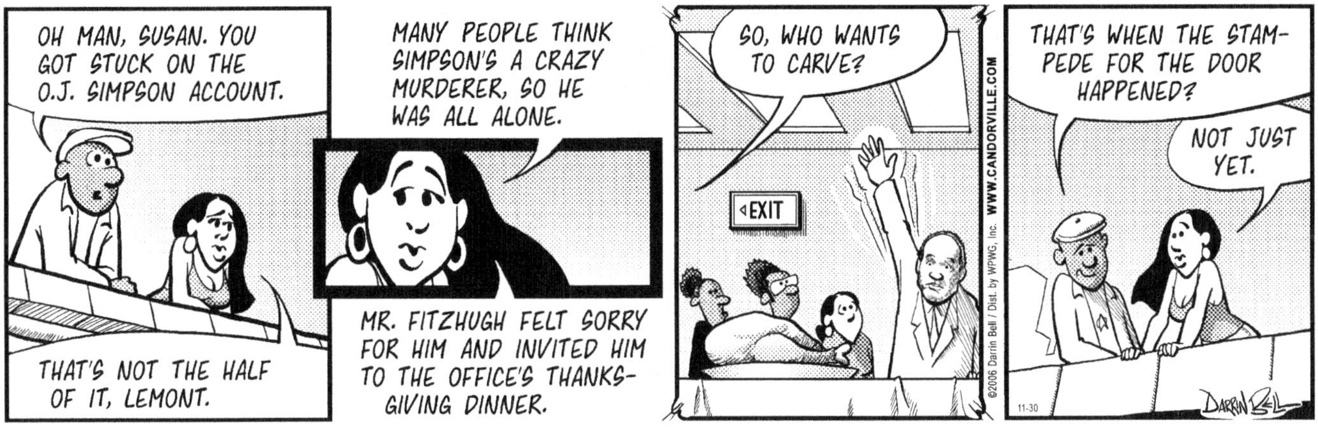
OH MAN, SUSAN. YOU GOT STUCK ON THE O.J. SIMPSON ACCOUNT.
THAT'S NOT THE HALF OF IT, LEMONT.
MANY PEOPLE THINK SIMPSON'S A CRAZY MURDERER, SO HE WAS ALL ALONE.
MR. FITZHUGH FELT SORRY FOR HIM AND INVITED HIM TO THE OFFICE'S THANKSGIVING DINNER.
SO, WHO WANTS TO CARVE?
EXIT
©2006 Darrin Bell / Dist. by WPWG, Inc. WWW.CANDORVILLE.COM
THAT'S WHEN THE STAMPEDE FOR THE DOOR HAPPENED?
NOT JUST YET.
11-30
DARRIN BELL

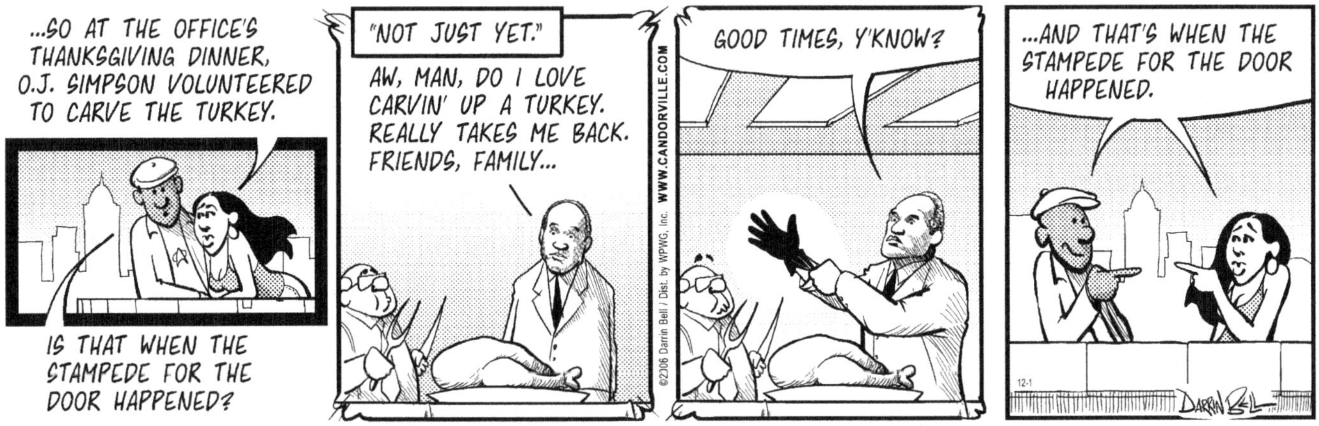
...SO AT THE OFFICE'S THANKSGIVING DINNER, O.J. SIMPSON VOLUNTEERED TO CARVE THE TURKEY.
IS THAT WHEN THE STAMPEDE FOR THE DOOR HAPPENED?
"NOT JUST YET."
AW, MAN, DO I LOVE CARVIN' UP A TURKEY. REALLY TAKES ME BACK. FRIENDS, FAMILY...
©2006 Darrin Bell / Dist. by WPWG, Inc. WWW.CANDORVILLE.COM
GOOD TIMES, Y'KNOW?
...AND THAT'S WHEN THE STAMPEDE FOR THE DOOR HAPPENED.
12-1
DARRIN BELL

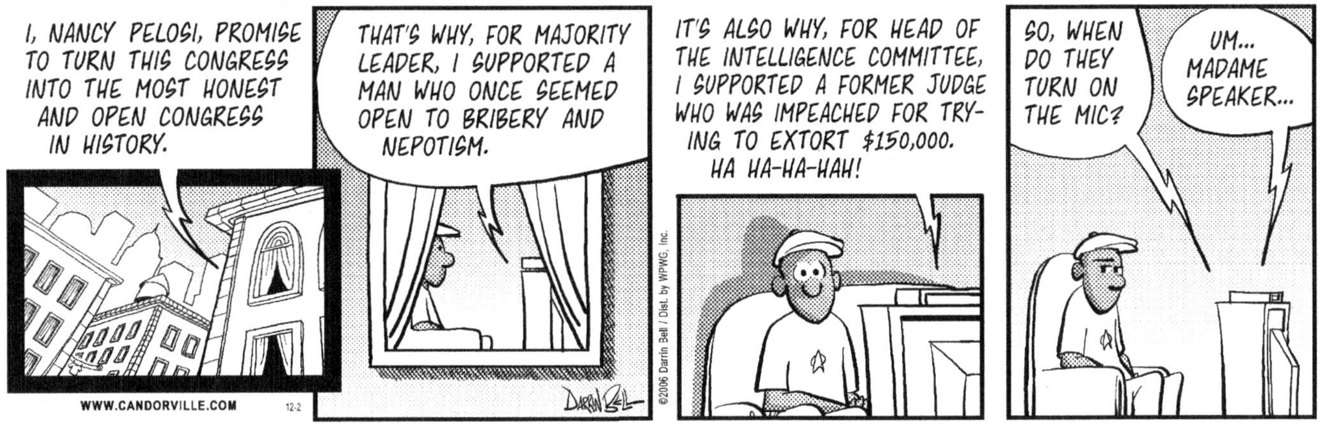
I, NANCY PELOSI, PROMISE TO TURN THIS CONGRESS INTO THE MOST HONEST AND OPEN CONGRESS IN HISTORY.
WWW.CANDORVILLE.COM
12-2
THAT'S WHY, FOR MAJORITY LEADER, I SUPPORTED A MAN WHO ONCE SEEMED OPEN TO BRIBERY AND NEPOTISM.
DARRIN BELL
©2006 Darrin Bell / Dist. by WPWG, Inc.
IT'S ALSO WHY, FOR HEAD OF THE INTELLIGENCE COMMITTEE, I SUPPORTED A FORMER JUDGE WHO WAS IMPEACHED FOR TRYING TO EXTORT $150,000. HA HA-HA-HAH!
SO, WHEN DO THEY TURN ON THE MIC?
UM... MADAME SPEAKER...

...WHAT?
CONGRATULATIONS SHERMAN!
Maricela's Decadent Cakes
Congrats on losing 50 pounds!
©2007 Darrin Bell / Dist. by WPWG
WWW.CANDORVILLE.COM
3-4
DARRIN BELL

©2007 Darrin Bell / Dist. by WPWG, Inc.
WWW.CANDORVILLE.COM
HOW TO BE MORE PRODUCTIVE
HOW TO BE MORE PRODUCTIVE
HOW TO BE MORE PRODUCTIVE
HOW TO BE MORE PRODUCTIVE
SCRATCH SCR—
HOW TO BE MORE PRODUCTIVE
DARRIN BELL
3-11

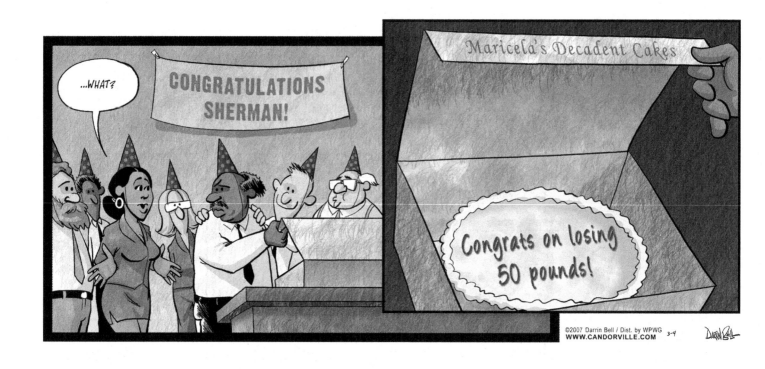

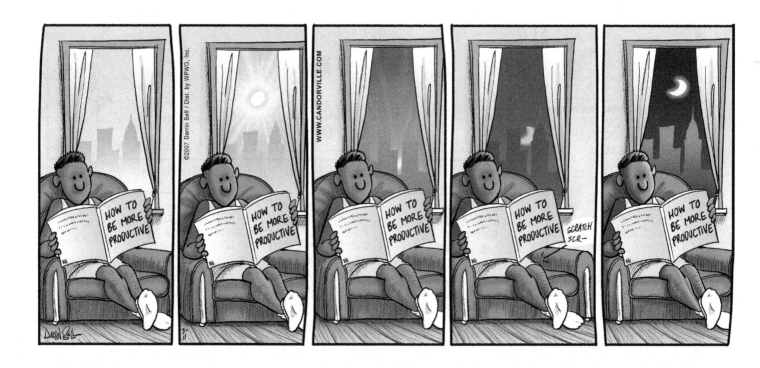

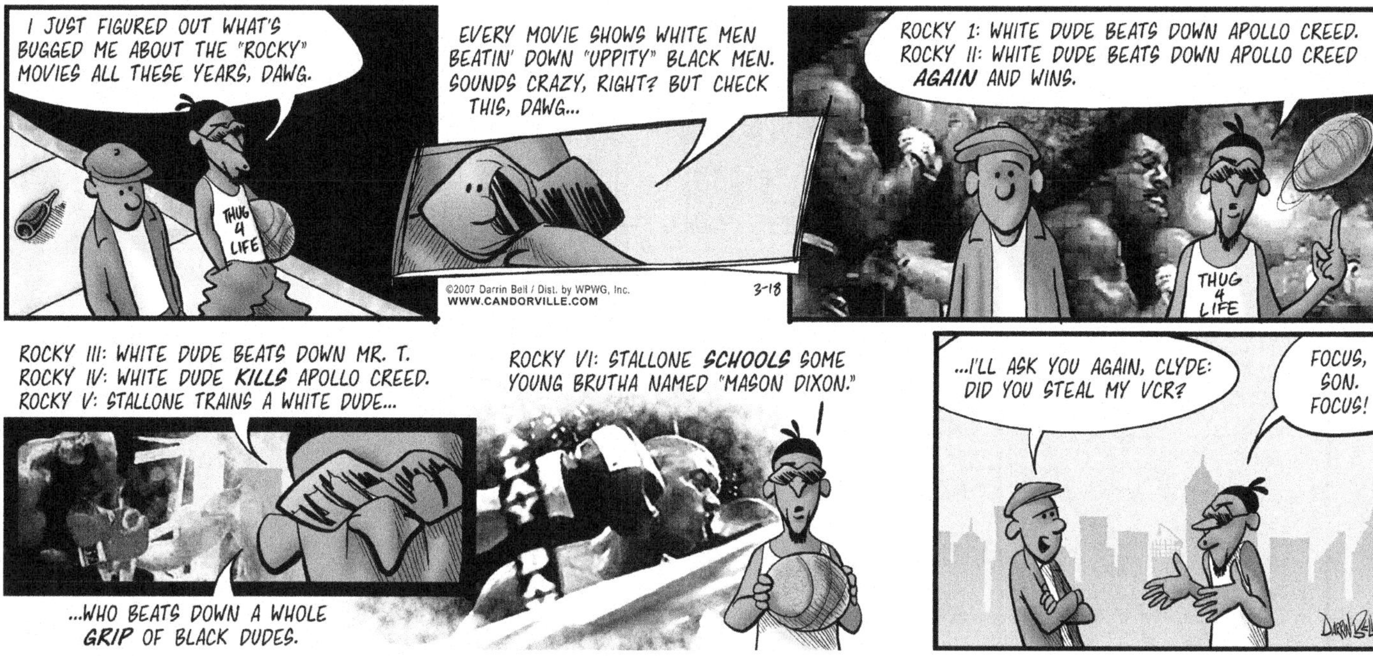
I JUST FIGURED OUT WHAT'S BUGGED ME ABOUT THE "ROCKY" MOVIES ALL THESE YEARS, DAWG.
THUG 4 LIFE
EVERY MOVIE SHOWS WHITE MEN BEATIN' DOWN "UPPITY" BLACK MEN. SOUNDS CRAZY, RIGHT? BUT CHECK THIS, DAWG...
©2007 Darrin Bell / Dist. by WPWG, Inc.
WWW.CANDORVILLE.COM
3-18
ROCKY 1: WHITE DUDE BEATS DOWN APOLLO CREED.
ROCKY II: WHITE DUDE BEATS DOWN APOLLO CREED AGAIN AND WINS.
THUG 4 LIFE
ROCKY III: WHITE DUDE BEATS DOWN MR. T.
ROCKY IV: WHITE DUDE KILLS APOLLO CREED.
ROCKY V: STALLONE TRAINS A WHITE DUDE...
...WHO BEATS DOWN A WHOLE GRIP OF BLACK DUDES.
ROCKY VI: STALLONE SCHOOLS SOME YOUNG BRUTHA NAMED "MASON DIXON."
!
...I'LL ASK YOU AGAIN, CLYDE: DID YOU STEAL MY VCR?
FOCUS, SON. FOCUS!
DARRIN BELL

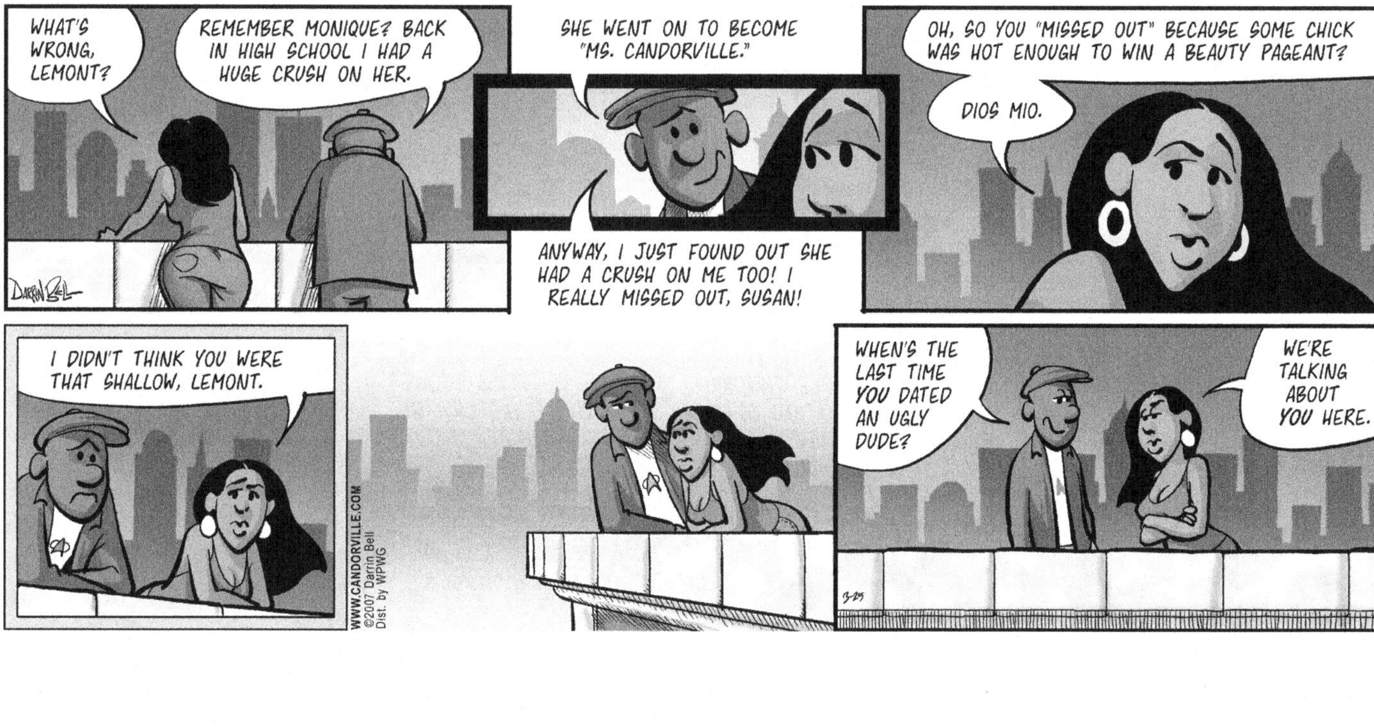
WHAT'S WRONG, LEMONT?
REMEMBER MONIQUE? BACK IN HIGH SCHOOL I HAD A HUGE CRUSH ON HER.
DARRIN BELL
SHE WENT ON TO BECOME "MS. CANDORVILLE."
ANYWAY, I JUST FOUND OUT SHE HAD A CRUSH ON ME TOO! I REALLY MISSED OUT, SUSAN!
OH, SO YOU "MISSED OUT" BECAUSE SOME CHICK WAS HOT ENOUGH TO WIN A BEAUTY PAGEANT?
DIOS MIO.
I DIDN'T THINK YOU WERE THAT SHALLOW, LEMONT.
WWW.CANDORVILLE.COM
©2007 Darrin Bell
Dist. by WPWG
WHEN'S THE LAST TIME YOU DATED AN UGLY DUDE?
WE'RE TALKING ABOUT YOU HERE.

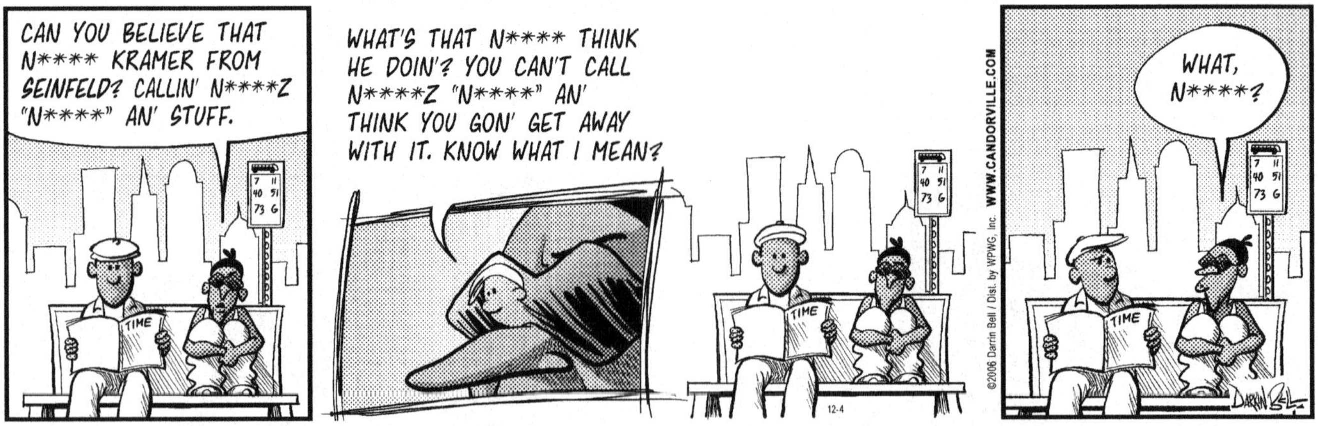
CAN YOU BELIEVE THAT N**** KRAMER FROM SEINFELD? CALLIN' N****Z "N****" AN' STUFF.
WHAT'S THAT N**** THINK HE DOIN'? YOU CAN'T CALL N****Z "N****" AN' THINK YOU GON' GET AWAY WITH IT. KNOW WHAT I MEAN?
WHAT, N****?
TIME
12-4
©2006 Darrin Bell / Dist. by WPWG, Inc. WWW.CANDORVILLE.COM

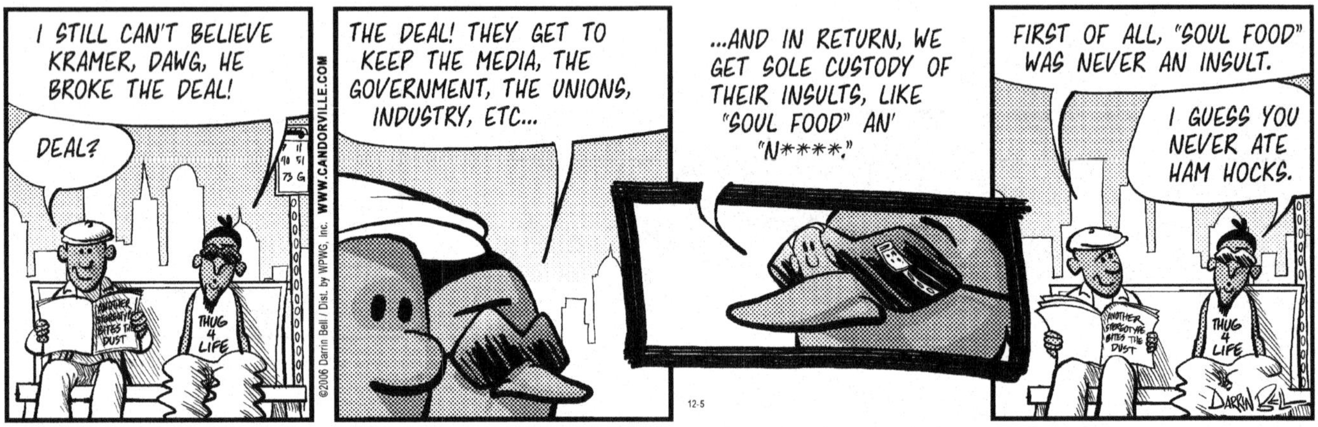
I STILL CAN'T BELIEVE KRAMER, DAWG, HE BROKE THE DEAL!
DEAL?
THE DEAL! THEY GET TO KEEP THE MEDIA, THE GOVERNMENT, THE UNIONS, INDUSTRY, ETC...
...AND IN RETURN, WE GET SOLE CUSTODY OF THEIR INSULTS, LIKE "SOUL FOOD" AN' "N****."
FIRST OF ALL, "SOUL FOOD" WAS NEVER AN INSULT.
I GUESS YOU NEVER ATE HAM HOCKS.
THUG 4 LIFE
12-5
©2006 Darrin Bell / Dist. by WPWG, Inc. WWW.CANDORVILLE.COM

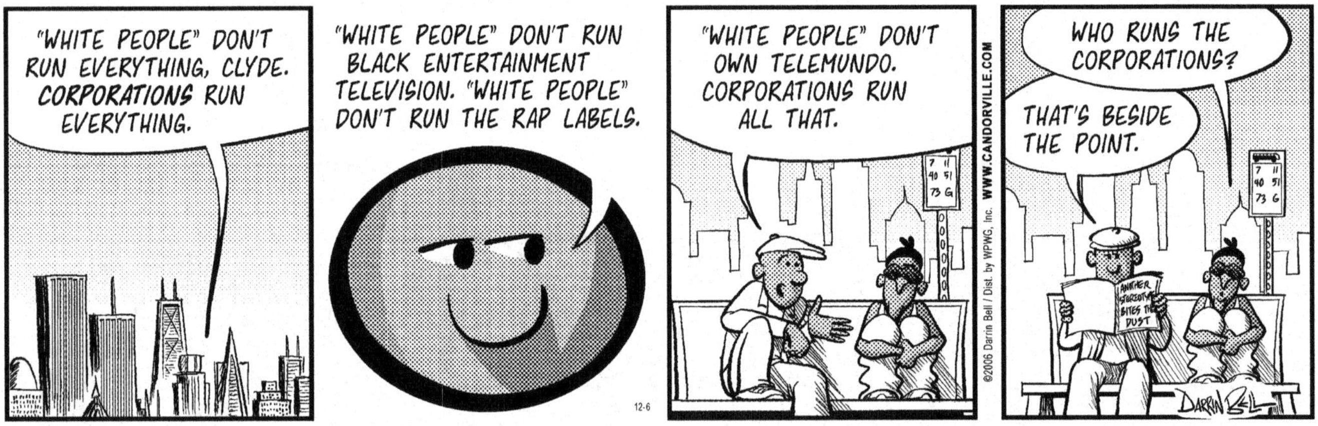
"WHITE PEOPLE" DON'T RUN EVERYTHING, CLYDE. CORPORATIONS RUN EVERYTHING.
"WHITE PEOPLE" DON'T RUN BLACK ENTERTAINMENT TELEVISION. "WHITE PEOPLE" DON'T RUN THE RAP LABELS.
"WHITE PEOPLE" DON'T OWN TELEMUNDO. CORPORATIONS RUN ALL THAT.
WHO RUNS THE CORPORATIONS?
THAT'S BESIDE THE POINT.
12-6
©2006 Darrin Bell / Dist. by WPWG, Inc. WWW.CANDORVILLE.COM

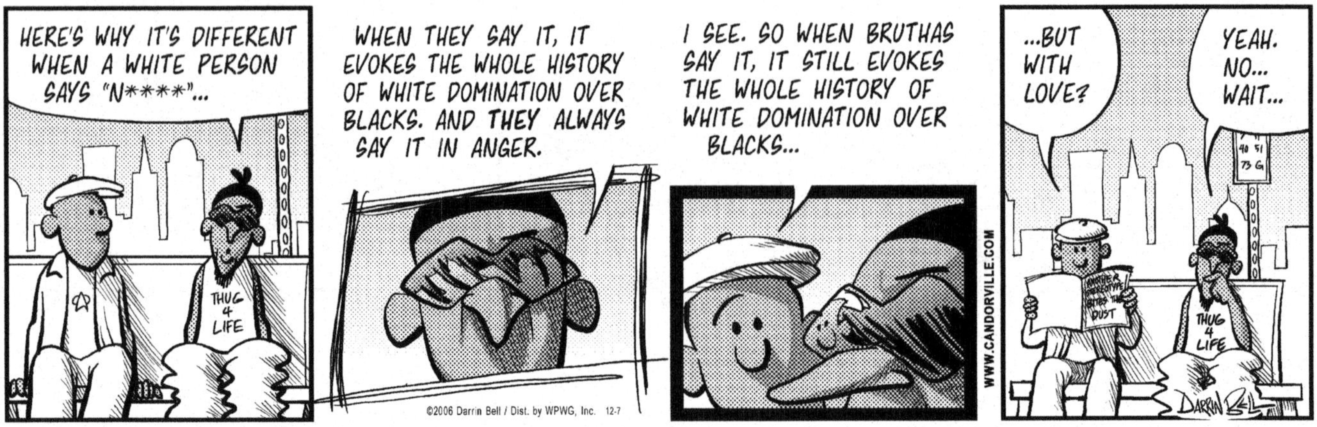
HERE'S WHY IT'S DIFFERENT WHEN A WHITE PERSON SAYS "N****"...
WHEN THEY SAY IT, IT EVOKES THE WHOLE HISTORY OF WHITE DOMINATION OVER BLACKS. AND THEY ALWAYS SAY IT IN ANGER.
I SEE. SO WHEN BRUTHAS SAY IT, IT STILL EVOKES THE WHOLE HISTORY OF WHITE DOMINATION OVER BLACKS...
...BUT WITH LOVE?
YEAH. NO... WAIT...
THUG 4 LIFE
©2006 Darrin Bell / Dist. by WPWG, Inc. 12-7
WWW.CANDORVILLE.COM

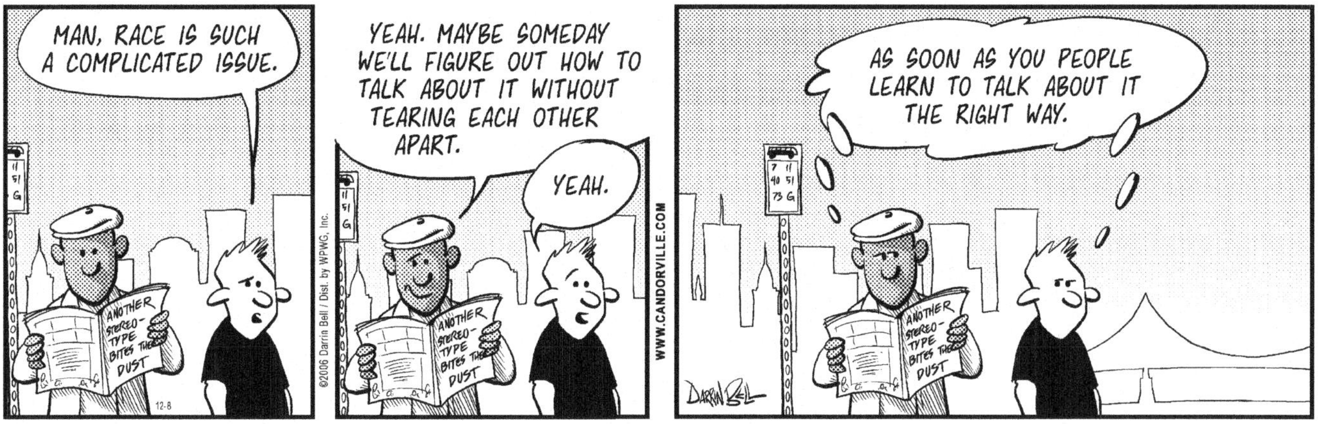
MAN, RACE IS SUCH A COMPLICATED ISSUE.
ANOTHER STEREO-TYPE BITES THE DUST
YEAH. MAYBE SOMEDAY WE'LL FIGURE OUT HOW TO TALK ABOUT IT WITHOUT TEARING EACH OTHER APART.
YEAH.
©2006 Darrin Bell / Dist. by WPWG, Inc.
WWW.CANDORVILLE.COM
AS SOON AS YOU PEOPLE LEARN TO TALK ABOUT IT THE RIGHT WAY.
DARRIN BELL
12-8

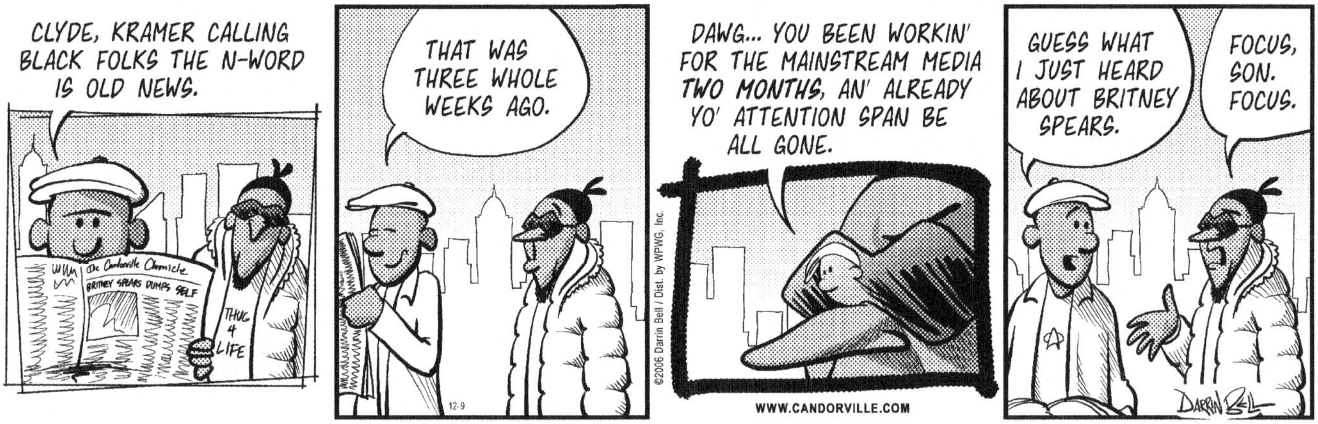
CLYDE, KRAMER CALLING BLACK FOLKS THE N-WORD IS OLD NEWS.
The Candorville Chronicle
BRITNEY SPEARS DUMPS SELF
THUG 4 LIFE
THAT WAS THREE WHOLE WEEKS AGO.
12-9
©2006 Darrin Bell / Dist. by WPWG, Inc.
DAWG... YOU BEEN WORKIN' FOR THE MAINSTREAM MEDIA **TWO MONTHS**, AN' ALREADY YO' ATTENTION SPAN BE ALL GONE.
WWW.CANDORVILLE.COM
GUESS WHAT I JUST HEARD ABOUT BRITNEY SPEARS.
FOCUS, SON. FOCUS.
DARRIN BELL

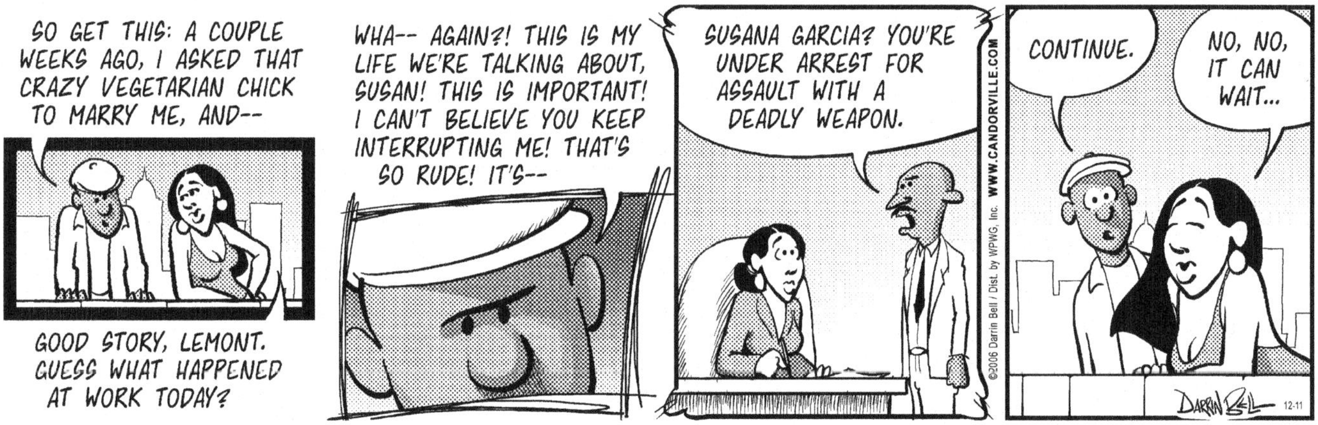
SO GET THIS: A COUPLE WEEKS AGO, I ASKED THAT CRAZY VEGETARIAN CHICK TO MARRY ME, AND--
GOOD STORY, LEMONT. GUESS WHAT HAPPENED AT WORK TODAY?
WHA-- AGAIN?! THIS IS MY LIFE WE'RE TALKING ABOUT, SUSAN! THIS IS IMPORTANT! I CAN'T BELIEVE YOU KEEP INTERRUPTING ME! THAT'S SO RUDE! IT'S--
SUSANA GARCIA? YOU'RE UNDER ARREST FOR ASSAULT WITH A DEADLY WEAPON.
WWW.CANDORVILLE.COM
©2006 Darrin Bell / Dist. by WPWG, Inc.
CONTINUE.
NO, NO, IT CAN WAIT...
DARRIN BELL
12-11

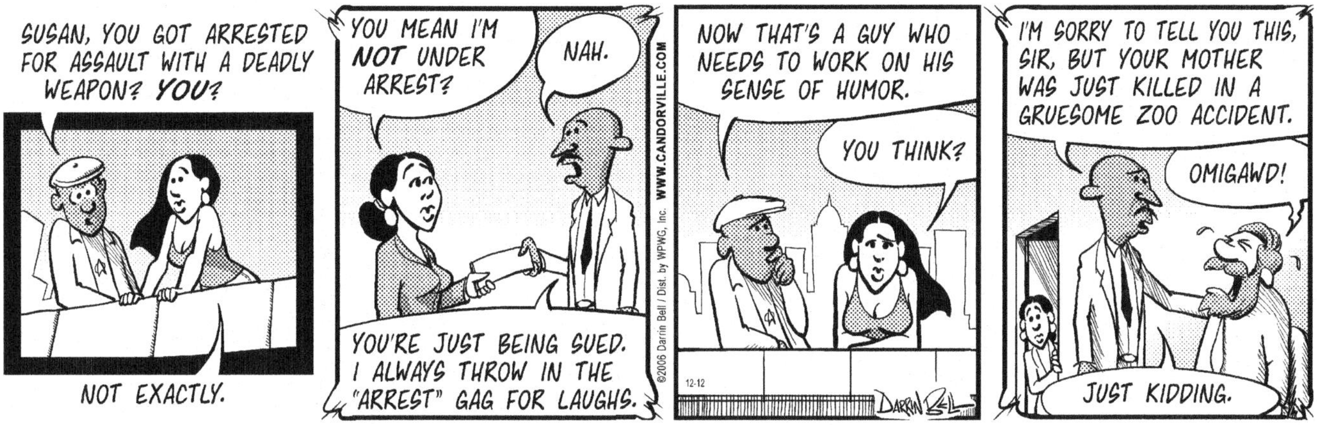
SUSAN, YOU GOT ARRESTED FOR ASSAULT WITH A DEADLY WEAPON? **YOU**?
NOT EXACTLY.
YOU MEAN I'M **NOT** UNDER ARREST?
NAH.
YOU'RE JUST BEING SUED. I ALWAYS THROW IN THE "ARREST" GAG FOR LAUGHS.
WWW.CANDORVILLE.COM
©2006 Darrin Bell / Dist. by WPWG, Inc.
NOW THAT'S A GUY WHO NEEDS TO WORK ON HIS SENSE OF HUMOR.
YOU THINK?
12-12
DARRIN BELL
I'M SORRY TO TELL YOU THIS, SIR, BUT YOUR MOTHER WAS JUST KILLED IN A GRUESOME ZOO ACCIDENT.
OMIGAWD!
JUST KIDDING.

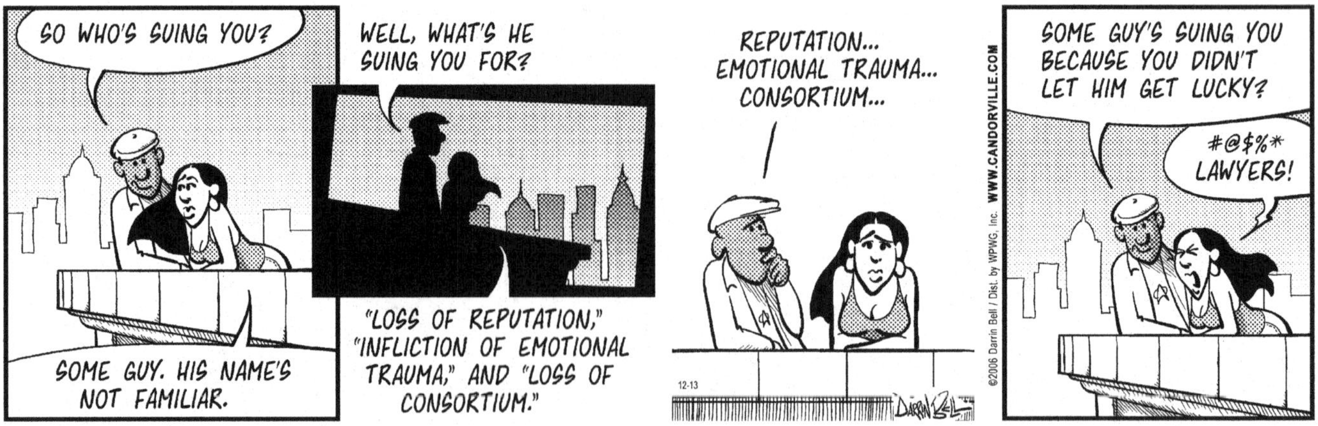
SO WHO'S SUING YOU?
SOME GUY. HIS NAME'S NOT FAMILIAR.
WELL, WHAT'S HE SUING YOU FOR?
"LOSS OF REPUTATION," "INFLICTION OF EMOTIONAL TRAUMA," AND "LOSS OF CONSORTIUM."
REPUTATION... EMOTIONAL TRAUMA... CONSORTIUM...
12-13
DARRIN BELL
©2006 Darrin Bell / Dist. by WPWG, Inc. WWW.CANDORVILLE.COM
SOME GUY'S SUING YOU BECAUSE YOU DIDN'T LET HIM GET LUCKY?
#@$%* LAWYERS!

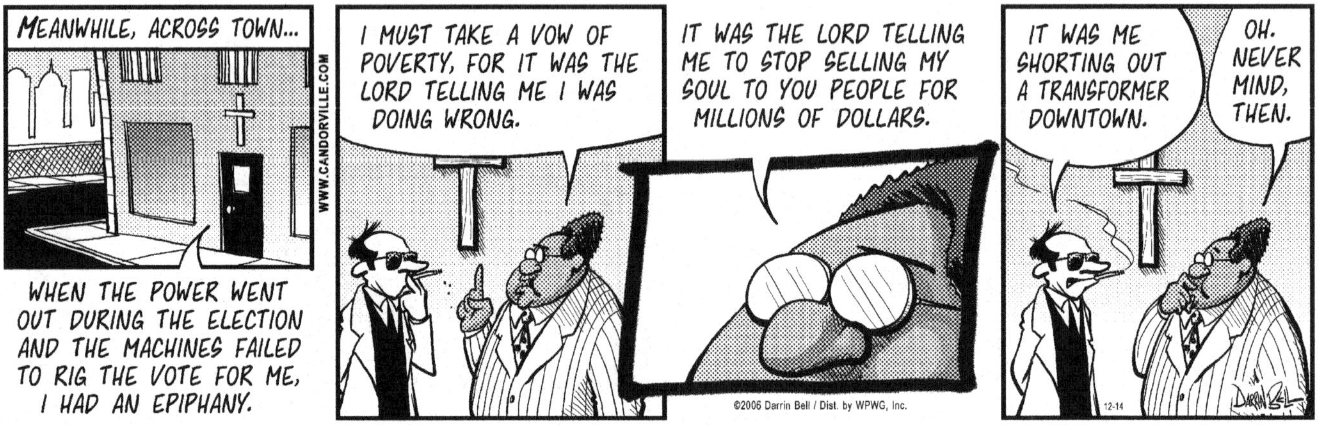
MEANWHILE, ACROSS TOWN...
WHEN THE POWER WENT OUT DURING THE ELECTION AND THE MACHINES FAILED TO RIG THE VOTE FOR ME, I HAD AN EPIPHANY.
WWW.CANDORVILLE.COM
I MUST TAKE A VOW OF POVERTY, FOR IT WAS THE LORD TELLING ME I WAS DOING WRONG.
IT WAS THE LORD TELLING ME TO STOP SELLING MY SOUL TO YOU PEOPLE FOR MILLIONS OF DOLLARS.
©2006 Darrin Bell / Dist. by WPWG, Inc.
IT WAS ME SHORTING OUT A TRANSFORMER DOWNTOWN.
OH. NEVER MIND, THEN.
12-14
DARRIN BELL

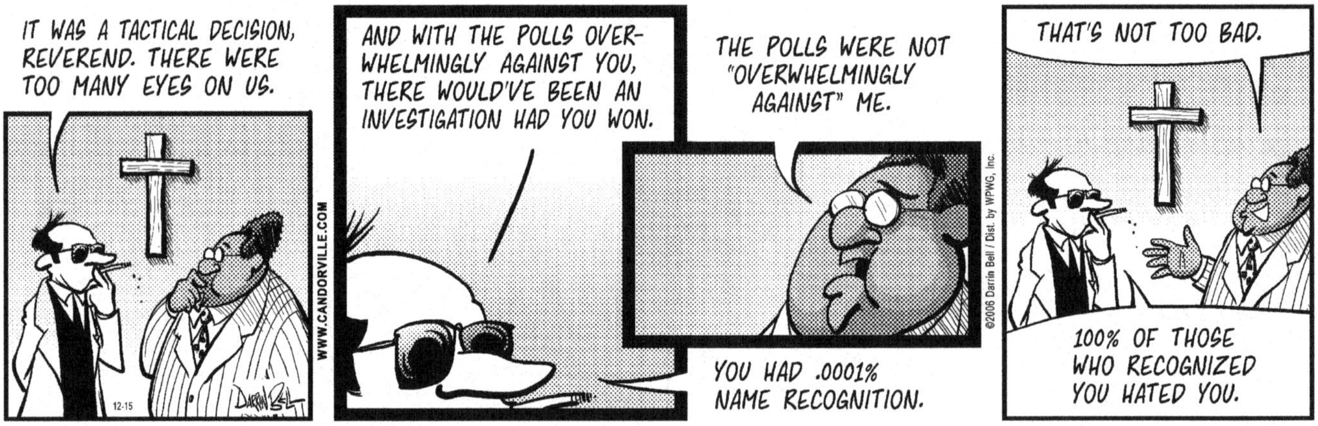
IT WAS A TACTICAL DECISION, REVEREND. THERE WERE TOO MANY EYES ON US.
12-15
DARRIN BELL
WWW.CANDORVILLE.COM
AND WITH THE POLLS OVER-WHELMINGLY AGAINST YOU, THERE WOULD'VE BEEN AN INVESTIGATION HAD YOU WON.
THE POLLS WERE NOT "OVERWHELMINGLY AGAINST" ME.
YOU HAD .0001% NAME RECOGNITION.
©2006 Darrin Bell / Dist. by WPWG, Inc.
THAT'S NOT TOO BAD.
100% OF THOSE WHO RECOGNIZED YOU HATED YOU.

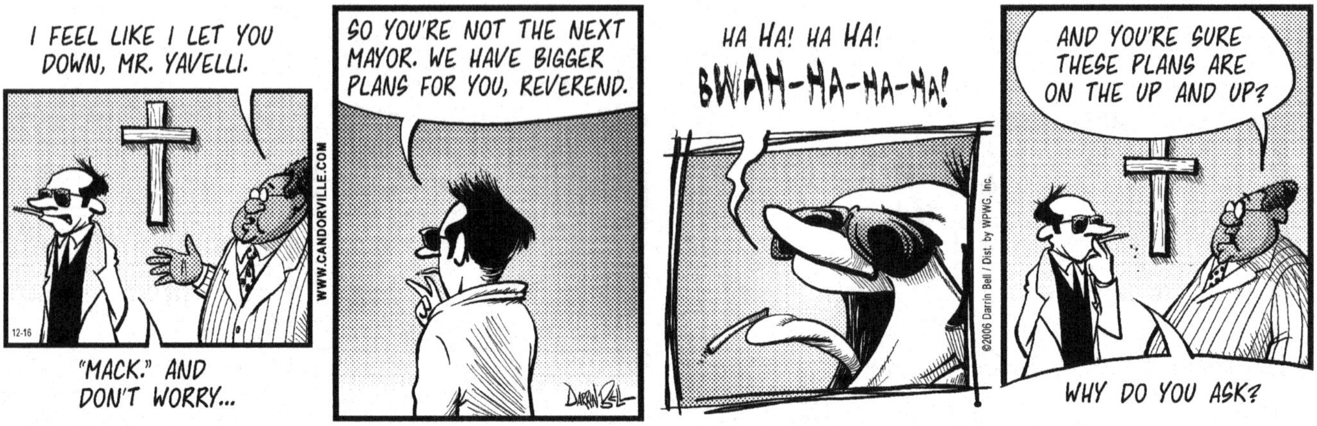
I FEEL LIKE I LET YOU DOWN, MR. YAVELLI.
"MACK." AND DON'T WORRY...
12-16
WWW.CANDORVILLE.COM
SO YOU'RE NOT THE NEXT MAYOR. WE HAVE BIGGER PLANS FOR YOU, REVEREND.
DARRIN BELL
HA HA! HA HA!
BWAH-HA-HA-HA!
©2006 Darrin Bell / Dist. by WPWG, Inc.
AND YOU'RE SURE THESE PLANS ARE ON THE UP AND UP?
WHY DO YOU ASK?

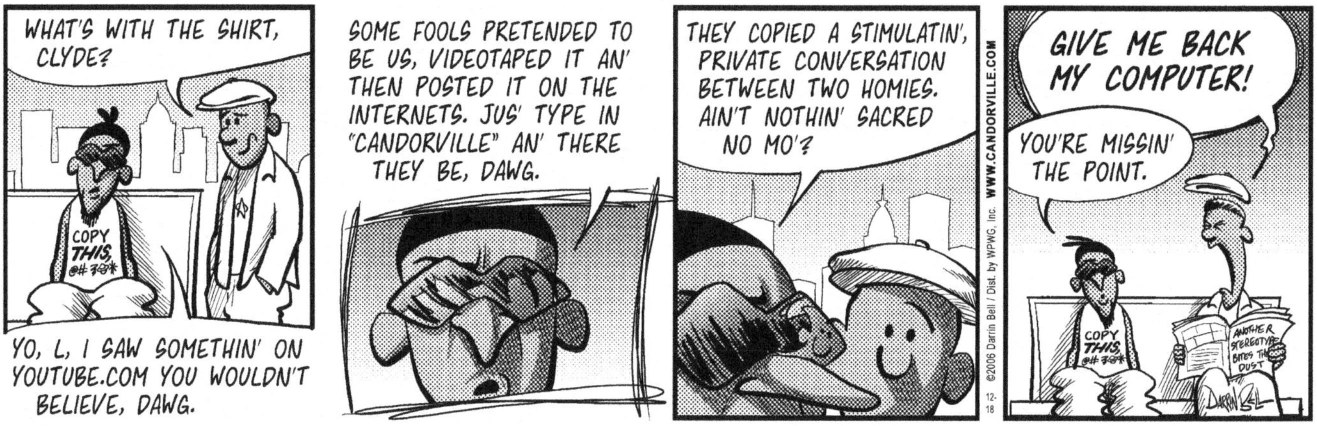
WHAT'S WITH THE SHIRT, CLYDE?
COPY THIS,
YO, L, I SAW SOMETHIN' ON YOUTUBE.COM YOU WOULDN'T BELIEVE, DAWG.
SOME FOOLS PRETENDED TO BE US, VIDEOTAPED IT AN' THEN POSTED IT ON THE INTERNETS. JUS' TYPE IN "CANDORVILLE" AN' THERE THEY BE, DAWG.
THEY COPIED A STIMULATIN', PRIVATE CONVERSATION BETWEEN TWO HOMIES. AIN'T NOTHIN' SACRED NO MO'?
©2006 Darrin Bell / Dist. by WPWG, Inc. WWW.CANDORVILLE.COM
12-18
GIVE ME BACK MY COMPUTER!
YOU'RE MISSIN' THE POINT.
COPY THIS,
ANOTHER STEREOTYPE BITES THE DUST

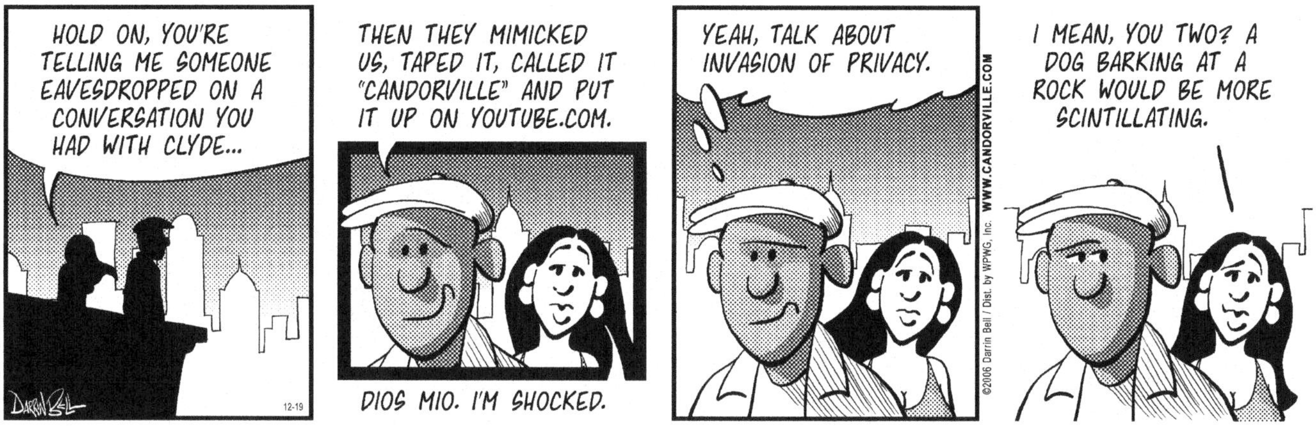
HOLD ON, YOU'RE TELLING ME SOMEONE EAVESDROPPED ON A CONVERSATION YOU HAD WITH CLYDE...
12-19
THEN THEY MIMICKED US, TAPED IT, CALLED IT "CANDORVILLE" AND PUT IT UP ON YOUTUBE.COM.
DIOS MIO. I'M SHOCKED.
YEAH, TALK ABOUT INVASION OF PRIVACY.
©2006 Darrin Bell / Dist. by WPWG, Inc. WWW.CANDORVILLE.COM
I MEAN, YOU TWO? A DOG BARKING AT A ROCK WOULD BE MORE SCINTILLATING.

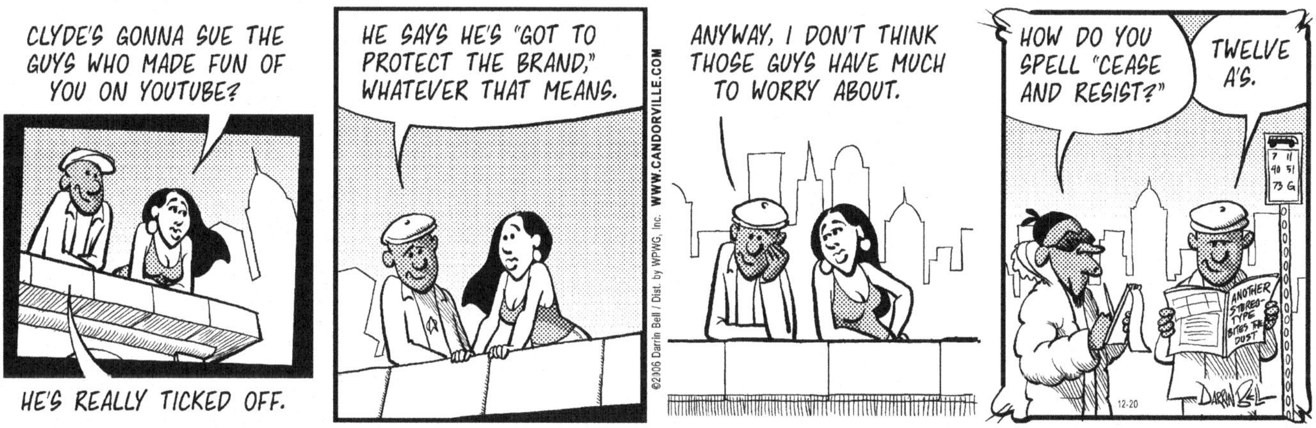
CLYDE'S GONNA SUE THE GUYS WHO MADE FUN OF YOU ON YOUTUBE?
HE'S REALLY TICKED OFF.
HE SAYS HE'S "GOT TO PROTECT THE BRAND," WHATEVER THAT MEANS.
©2006 Darrin Bell / Dist. by WPWG, Inc. WWW.CANDORVILLE.COM
ANYWAY, I DON'T THINK THOSE GUYS HAVE MUCH TO WORRY ABOUT.
HOW DO YOU SPELL "CEASE AND RESIST?"
TWELVE A'S.
ANOTHER STEREOTYPE BITES THE DUST
12-20

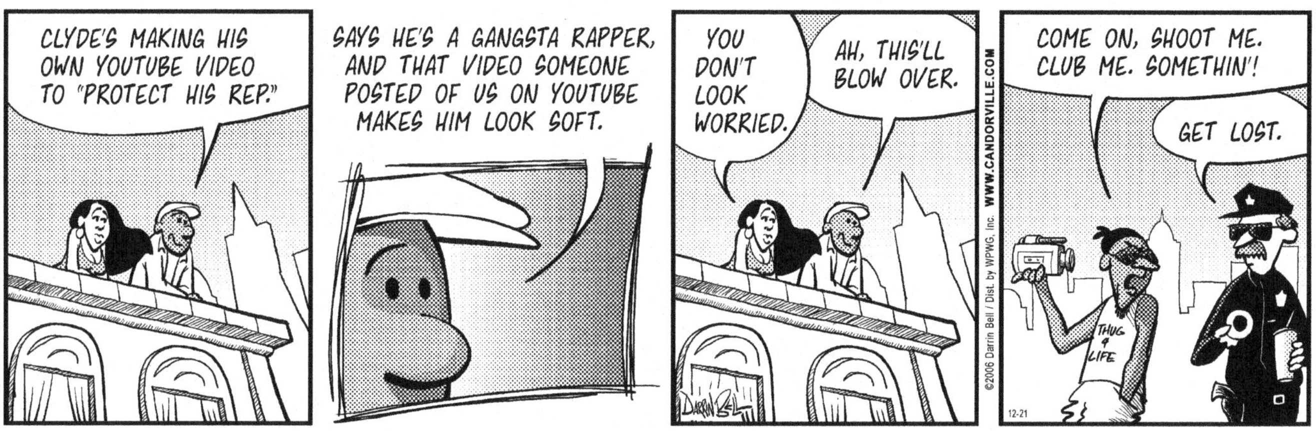
CLYDE'S MAKING HIS OWN YOUTUBE VIDEO TO "PROTECT HIS REP."
SAYS HE'S A GANGSTA RAPPER, AND THAT VIDEO SOMEONE POSTED OF US ON YOUTUBE MAKES HIM LOOK SOFT.
YOU DON'T LOOK WORRIED.
AH, THIS'LL BLOW OVER.
©2006 Darrin Bell / Dist. by WPWG, Inc. WWW.CANDORVILLE.COM
COME ON, SHOOT ME. CLUB ME. SOMETHIN'!
GET LOST.
THUG 4 LIFE
12-21

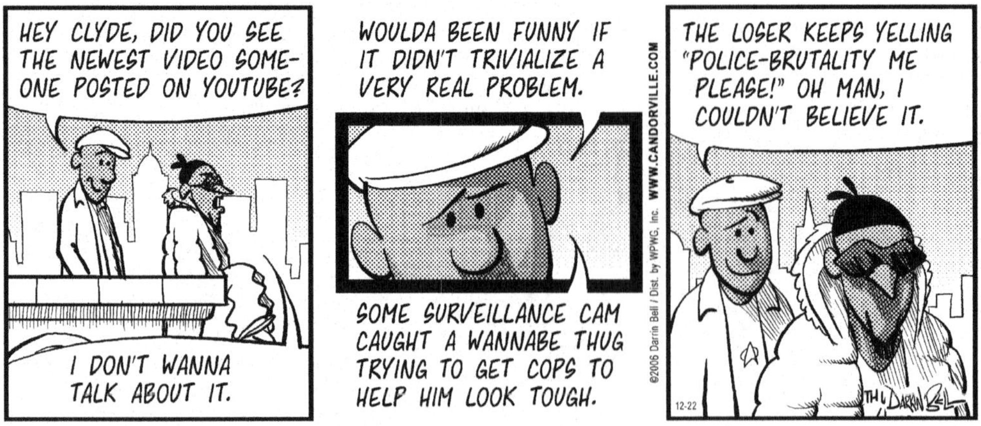
HEY CLYDE, DID YOU SEE THE NEWEST VIDEO SOMEONE POSTED ON YOUTUBE?
I DON'T WANNA TALK ABOUT IT.
WOULDA BEEN FUNNY IF IT DIDN'T TRIVIALIZE A VERY REAL PROBLEM.
SOME SURVEILLANCE CAM CAUGHT A WANNABE THUG TRYING TO GET COPS TO HELP HIM LOOK TOUGH.
©2006 Darrin Bell / Dist. by WPWG, Inc. WWW.CANDORVILLE.COM
THE LOSER KEEPS YELLING "POLICE-BRUTALITY ME PLEASE!" OH MAN, I COULDN'T BELIEVE IT.
12-22
SHUT UP. SHUT UP!
THEN HE STARTS CRYING WHEN THEY DRIVE AWAY.

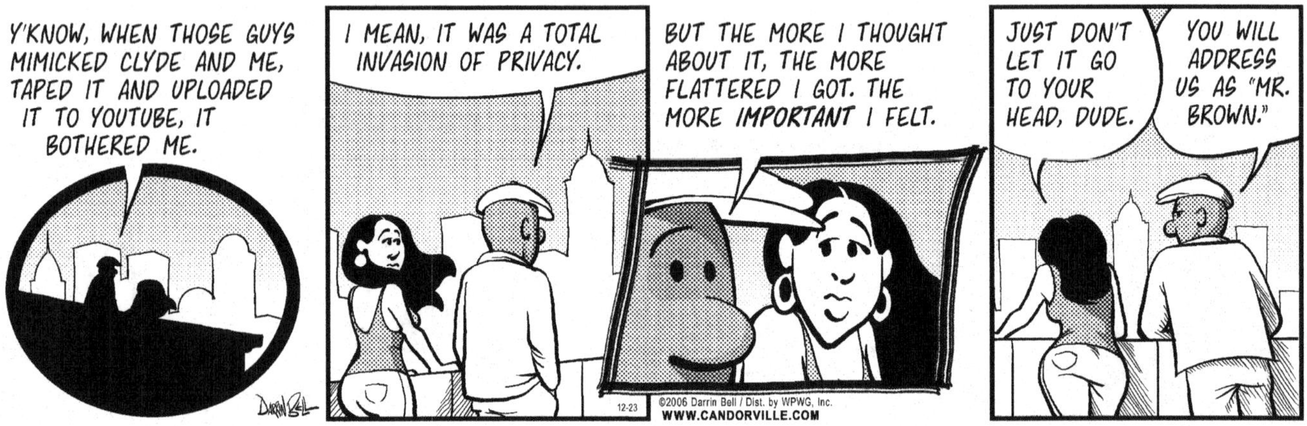
Y'KNOW, WHEN THOSE GUYS MIMICKED CLYDE AND ME, TAPED IT AND UPLOADED IT TO YOUTUBE, IT BOTHERED ME.
I MEAN, IT WAS A TOTAL INVASION OF PRIVACY.
12-23
BUT THE MORE I THOUGHT ABOUT IT, THE MORE FLATTERED I GOT. THE MORE IMPORTANT I FELT.
©2006 Darrin Bell / Dist. by WPWG, Inc.
WWW.CANDORVILLE.COM
JUST DON'T LET IT GO TO YOUR HEAD, DUDE.
YOU WILL ADDRESS US AS "MR. BROWN."

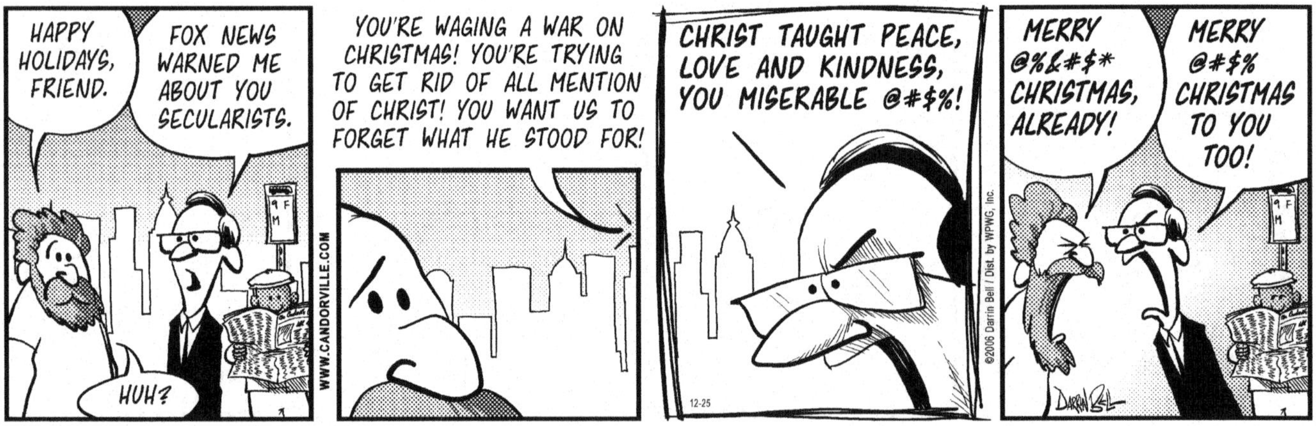
HAPPY HOLIDAYS, FRIEND.
FOX NEWS WARNED ME ABOUT YOU SECULARISTS.
HUH?
WWW.CANDORVILLE.COM
YOU'RE WAGING A WAR ON CHRISTMAS! YOU'RE TRYING TO GET RID OF ALL MENTION OF CHRIST! YOU WANT US TO FORGET WHAT HE STOOD FOR!
CHRIST TAUGHT PEACE, LOVE AND KINDNESS, YOU MISERABLE @#$%!
12-25
©2006 Darrin Bell / Dist. by WPWG, Inc.
MERRY @%&#$* CHRISTMAS, ALREADY!
MERRY @#$% CHRISTMAS TO YOU TOO!

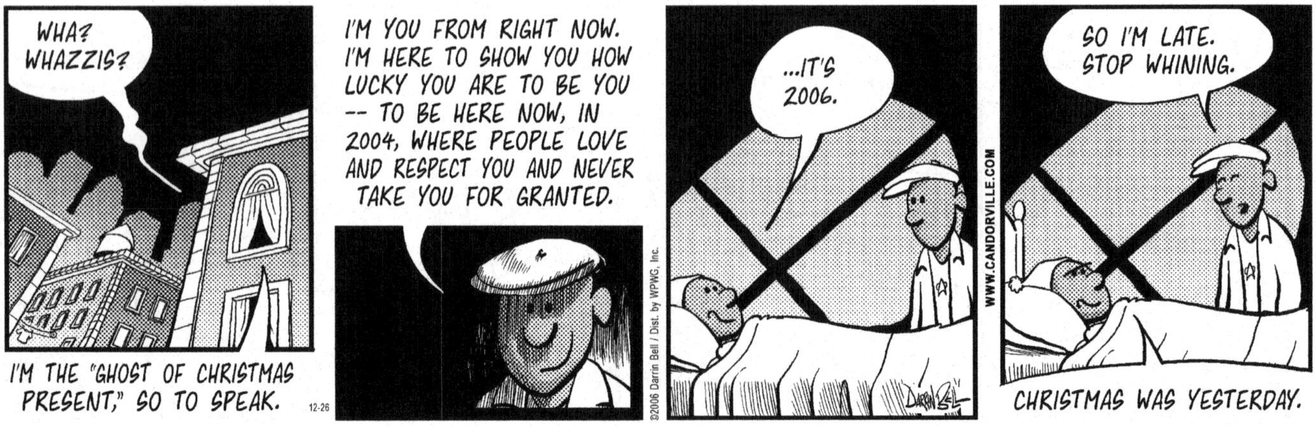
WHA? WHAZZIS?
I'M THE "GHOST OF CHRISTMAS PRESENT," SO TO SPEAK.
12-26
I'M YOU FROM RIGHT NOW. I'M HERE TO SHOW YOU HOW LUCKY YOU ARE TO BE YOU -- TO BE HERE NOW, IN 2004, WHERE PEOPLE LOVE AND RESPECT YOU AND NEVER TAKE YOU FOR GRANTED.
©2006 Darrin Bell / Dist. by WPWG, Inc.
...IT'S 2006.
WWW.CANDORVILLE.COM
SO I'M LATE. STOP WHINING.
CHRISTMAS WAS YESTERDAY.

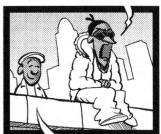

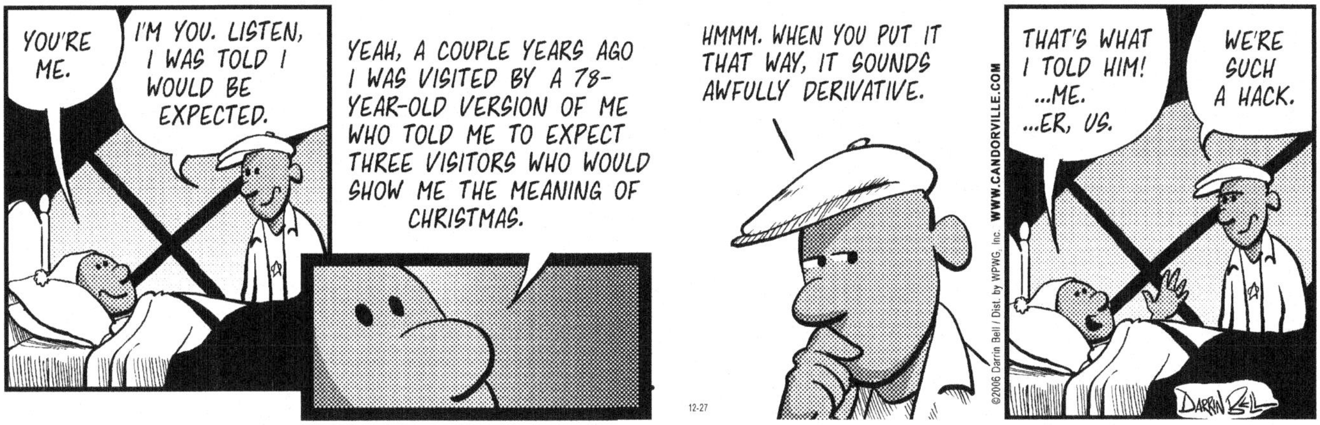
YOU'RE ME.
I'M YOU. LISTEN, I WAS TOLD I WOULD BE EXPECTED.
YEAH, A COUPLE YEARS AGO I WAS VISITED BY A 78-YEAR-OLD VERSION OF ME WHO TOLD ME TO EXPECT THREE VISITORS WHO WOULD SHOW ME THE MEANING OF CHRISTMAS.
HMMM. WHEN YOU PUT IT THAT WAY, IT SOUNDS AWFULLY DERIVATIVE.
THAT'S WHAT I TOLD HIM! ...ME. ...ER, US.
WE'RE SUCH A HACK.
12-27
©2006 Darrin Bell / Dist. by WPWG, Inc. WWW.CANDORVILLE.COM
DARRIN BELL

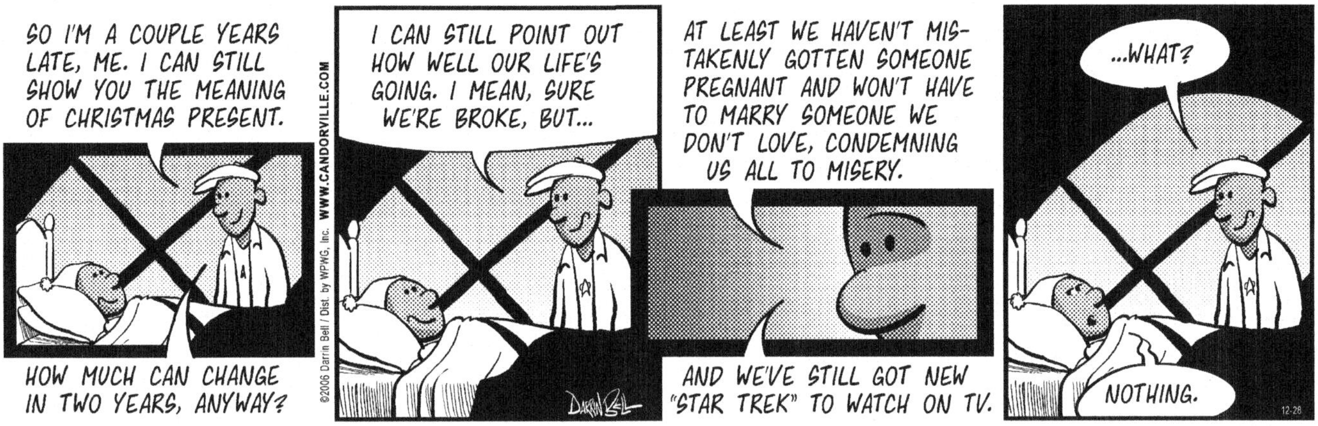
SO I'M A COUPLE YEARS LATE, ME. I CAN STILL SHOW YOU THE MEANING OF CHRISTMAS PRESENT.
HOW MUCH CAN CHANGE IN TWO YEARS, ANYWAY?
©2006 Darrin Bell / Dist. by WPWG, Inc. WWW.CANDORVILLE.COM
I CAN STILL POINT OUT HOW WELL OUR LIFE'S GOING. I MEAN, SURE WE'RE BROKE, BUT...
DARRIN BELL
AT LEAST WE HAVEN'T MISTAKENLY GOTTEN SOMEONE PREGNANT AND WON'T HAVE TO MARRY SOMEONE WE DON'T LOVE, CONDEMNING US ALL TO MISERY.
AND WE'VE STILL GOT NEW "STAR TREK" TO WATCH ON TV.
...WHAT?
NOTHING.
12-28

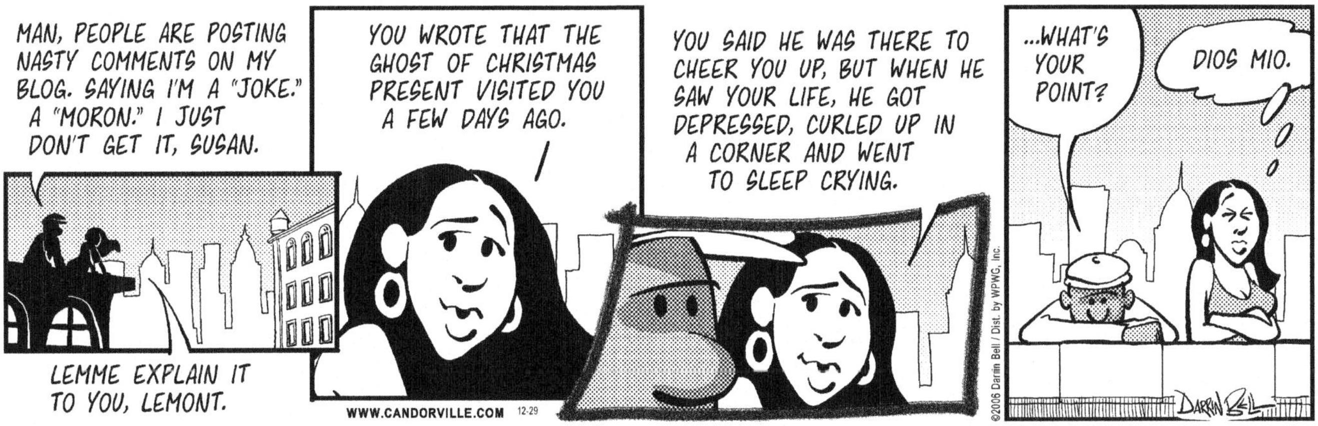
MAN, PEOPLE ARE POSTING NASTY COMMENTS ON MY BLOG. SAYING I'M A "JOKE." A "MORON." I JUST DON'T GET IT, SUSAN.
LEMME EXPLAIN IT TO YOU, LEMONT.
YOU WROTE THAT THE GHOST OF CHRISTMAS PRESENT VISITED YOU A FEW DAYS AGO.
WWW.CANDORVILLE.COM 12-29
YOU SAID HE WAS THERE TO CHEER YOU UP, BUT WHEN HE SAW YOUR LIFE, HE GOT DEPRESSED, CURLED UP IN A CORNER AND WENT TO SLEEP CRYING.
...WHAT'S YOUR POINT?
DIOS MIO.
©2006 Darrin Bell / Dist. by WPWG, Inc.
DARRIN BELL

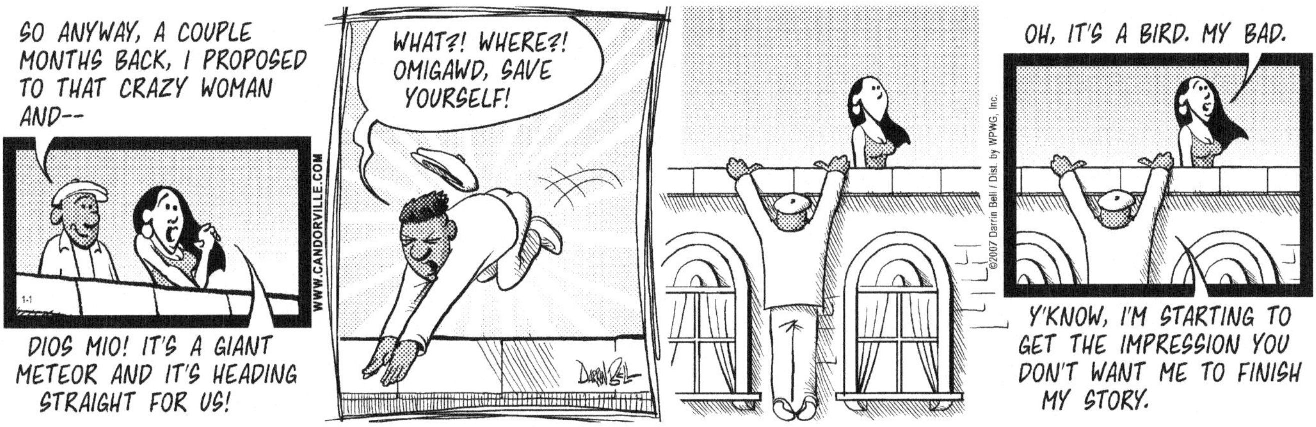
SO ANYWAY, A COUPLE MONTHS BACK, I PROPOSED TO THAT CRAZY WOMAN AND--
1-1
DIOS MIO! IT'S A GIANT METEOR AND IT'S HEADING STRAIGHT FOR US!
WWW.CANDORVILLE.COM
WHAT?! WHERE?! OMIGAWD, SAVE YOURSELF!
DARRIN BELL
©2007 Darrin Bell / Dist. by WPWG, Inc.
OH, IT'S A BIRD. MY BAD.
Y'KNOW, I'M STARTING TO GET THE IMPRESSION YOU DON'T WANT ME TO FINISH MY STORY.

Afterword

(Not by the Pope, the President or a Kennedy, but by *a typical Candorville reader!*)
xoxoxoxoxoxoxoxoxoxoxoxoxoxoxoxoxoxoxoxoxoxoxoxoxoxoxoxoxoxoxoxoxoxoxo

Darrin Bell has destroyed my childhood dreams.

Growing up on a diet of Peanuts and Doonesbury,[1] I knew that some day I would be a great cartoonist. I'd not only make people laugh each morning, but would also produce insightful political commentary to make them think. My characters would be well-rounded, with real personalities—actual people that my readers would care about. They'd have experiences that would shape those personalities, and grow in significant ways. Oh, and I'd toss in a lot of Star Trek and science fiction inside jokes, too.

But what's the point now? Why pick up a pen? Life has lost all meaning. Darrin Bell has already done everything I had planned, and far better than I could have.[2]

"Candorville" meets my criteria in all ways. It's funny without being sophomoric, political without being preachy, and real without being "Funky Winkerbean." I've come to care about the characters, and have a tendency to email Darrin Bell whenever they move in directions I want or don't want. ("Lemont needs to be with Susan! Get him away from that vampire! Susan needs to get a new job!") Bell has shown great restraint in refusing to comment upon my suggestions, and I have yet to see my suggestions used in his strip, but I am sure that he sits by his computer anxiously awaiting each one.

As a writer myself, I can spend days agonizing over the best words to use to help advance my character's development. I want my characters to not be clichés—to have their own biases and selfish behaviors and to sometimes do things that are not honorable or wise, just like real people.

I can't imagine having to do that with the limitations of three or four very small panels, which some papers often shrink to the size of a fortune cookie message (in bed) to make room for Junior Jumble and horoscopes (which, admittedly, are still funnier than "Wizard of Id"). To accomplish this requires a real talent: cutting down the dialogue to its bare essentials, debating over each word, and spending more time writing than doing the actual artwork.

Yet Bell does it. I actually care about what happens to Lemont and Susan and Clyde, because they aren't simply there to provide a quick laugh of the day. They are real people with goals and aspirations, and I generally am hoping that they can accomplish their dreams somewhere along the way. (I say "generally" because many of Clyde's dreams tend to involve Lemont's possessions, and I can't honestly say I am encouraging such behavior, even if it does produce laughs.)

At the same time, "Candorville" keeps itself firmly rooted in fantasy and satire. Because it is a comic strip, it can take great leaps into fantasy that would never be allowed in more traditional storytelling. Lemont can have arguments with his future and past selves, can become engaged to a vegetarian vampire, can meet ghosts, and become a god to mold spores.

Here's an important point, though: Even while doing these fantastic things, "Candorville" doesn't break the fourth wall. The characters are still believable. Other strips often give us a sly wink and a nod to acknowledge that they know they are merely comics ("Pearls Before Swine" and "Sherman's Lagoon" being wonderful examples where it works very well), but those strips are not trying to create real, actual, believable characters. (OK, admittedly, those two strips are about talking animals, but hey, you see the point. Shut up.)

"Candorville" meets the balance it has set for itself between humor and commentary, especially when dealing with social and political topics. It skewers both sides of the political spectrum when needed, as stupidity and hypocrisy knows no ideology. The conservative businessman and the bearded hippie who sometimes discuss the issues of the day share the punchlines fairly equally.

And sometimes "Candorville" just makes observations about our society that we might miss otherwise. One of my favorite bits recently found Clyde meeting a young Frederick Douglass who, upon finding one of Clyde's invitations to the Obama inauguration, can't understand why they have a picture of a slave of them. Another from a few years ago found a conservative waking up from years in a coma to discover that Republicans now controlled all three branches of government as well as most state houses. "This is amazing!" he said from his hospital bed. "Smaller government at last!" "Um, yeah... about that..." the doctor replies.

So curse you, Darrin Bell! You have accomplished my dreams before I could. And you're a better artist than I am.

-Michael Ventrella

Endnotes

(1) Delicious, by the way, especially if you add cream

(2) Mind you, Since I am much older than Mr. Bell, I don't really have much of an excuse. Maybe I didn't try all that hard. But it's the principle of the thing, dammit! In an alternate universe, I might have tried to be a cartoonist instead of a successful lawyer and writer whose web page is www.michaelaventrella.com

CPSIA information can be obtained
at www.ICGtesting.com
Printed in the USA
LVOW05s0157040118
561742LV00005B/114/P